Stance, Inter/Subjectivity and Identity in Discourse

Juana I. Marín-Arrese / Laura Hidalgo-Downing /
Juan Rafael Zamorano-Mansilla (eds.)

# Stance, Inter/Subjectivity and Identity in Discourse

PETER LANG

Bern · Berlin · Bruxelles · New York · Oxford

**Bibliographic Information published by the Deutsche Nationalbibliothek**
The Deutsche Nationalbibliothek lists this publication in the Deutsche Nationalbibliografie; detailed bibliographic data is available online at http://dnb.d-nb.de.

**Library of Congress Cataloging-in-Publication Data**
A CIP catalog record for this book has been applied for at the Library of Congress

We are grateful for the financial support for this volume from the research project Stance and Subjectivity in Discourse: Towards an Integrated Framework for the Analysis of Epistemicity, Effectivity, Evaluation and Inter/Subjectivity from a Critical Discourse Perspective. (STANCEDISC), Ref. PGC2018-095798-B-I00, funded by the Ministerio de Ciencia, Innovación y Universidades (Spanish Ministry of Science, Innovation and Universities).

ISBN 978-3-0343-4372-5 (Print)
E-ISBN 978-3-0343-4634-4 (E-PDF)
E-ISBN 978-3-0343-4635-1 (E-PUB)
DOI 10.3726/b20233



This publication has been peer reviewed.

# Table of Contents

## Section B. Stance, Evaluation, Metaphor



## Section C. Stance, Engagement, Evaluation and Emotion

# List of Contributors

Aoife Kathleen Ahern is Associate Professor at the Universidad Complutense de Madrid School of Education, where she works in the field of language teacher education. Her research interests are related to the interfaces of grammar and pragmatics, as well as to second language teaching, learning and acquisition, focused on English and Spanish, and to literacy education. She has published several books such as *Pragmática*, as co-author with V. Escandell-Vidal and J. Amenós Pons (Madrid: Akal 2020), *Comunicación y cognición en ELE: La perspectiva pragmática*, co-authored with J. Amenós Pons and V. Escandell-Vidal, *Procedural Meaning: Problems and Perspectives*, as co-author with V. Escandell-Vidal and M. Leonetti (Leiden: Brill, 2011). Her research, carried out through several projects funded by the Spanish Ministry for Education and Science and the Ministry for Economy and Competitivity of Spain, has also led to a range of articles in scientific journals and book chapters in collective volumes.

Jacqueline Aiello is an Assistant Professor at the University of Salerno, Italy. She earned her doctorate in Multilingual and Multicultural Studies from New York University. She is the recipient of a Fulbright ETA grant (2008) and two NYU Global Research Initiative Fellowships (2013, 2014). She is the author of *Negotiating Englishes and English-speaking Identities* (2018, Routledge), for which she was awarded the 2019 AIA Junior Book Prize, and *The Discursive Construction of the Modern Political Self* (2022, Routledge). Her research interests include language ownership and attitudes, and the relationship among language, identity and power.

José Amenós-Pons is a Senior Reader in Spanish Linguistics at the Universidad Complutense de Madrid. He specialises in cognitive pragmatics and foreign language acquisition processes and has published numerous articles on tense, aspect and mood, and more generally, on the relationships between grammar and pragmatics, and on how this relationship influences L2 learning. He has participated in different research projects funded by the Spanish national research authority, almost uninterruptedly from 2007 to the present day: Procedural Semantics and Explicit Content 1, 2 and 3 (2007–2015), The Semantics/Pragmatics Interface and the Resolution of Interpretive Mismatches (2015–2019), Evidentiality, Perspectivisation and Subjectivisation at the Interfaces of Language (2020–2023). He has taught Spanish as a second language for many years and been very actively involved in L2 teacher training. He has co-authored L2 Spanish textbooks and materials for teacher education.

Elena Domínguez Romero is Associate Professor of English Language and Linguistics at the Complutense University in Madrid. Her research interests include evidentiality and modality in media discourse. She has participated in the projects EUROEVIDMOD (FFI2011-23181), EVIDISPRAG, and STANCEDISC (PGC2018-095798-B-I00), all of them focusing on evidentiality, modality, stance, and subjectivity. She has coedited two volumes in the field *Evidentiality and Modality in European Languages* (Peter Lang 2017) and *Thinking Modally. English and Contrastive Studies on Modality* (Cambridge Scholars 2015), and has co-authored papers in international journals such as *Journal of Pragmatics* (2021) and *Intercultural Pragmatics* (2019).

Oana-Adriana Duţă is Senior Lecturer in Linguistics and Translation Studies at the University of Craiova. She holds a Ph.D. in Philology of the University of Bucharest and a Ph.D. in Finance of the University of Craiova and has published 12 literary and economic translations with prestigious publishing houses in Romania. She has authored two handbooks and numerous articles in international and national academic journals. She has a solid theoretical background in teaching methodology and has performed extensive research on foreign languages teaching in national and international projects. Her thorough acquaintance with linguistic policies is underpinned by her experience as an editorial secretary of the internationally peer-reviewed *Annals of the University of Craiova. Philology. Linguistics*, as well as by her active involvement in activities of internationalization at the faculty and university level.

Sergio Ferrer-Navas graduated in English Philology at Complutense University of Madrid, where he completed the teaching and research periods imparted within the post-graduate programme in *English Studies: Cognition, Communication and Interculturality*. At present, he is a PhD candidate in the doctoral programme in English Linguistics at Complutense University of Madrid. He spent a year in a doctoral stay at The University of Texas of the Permian Basin in 2016, where he contributed to several annual editions of a composition handbook for the students enrolled in the Composition course. He joined the Department of English Studies at Complutense University of Madrid as a lecturer in English Linguistics from 2017 to 2021. He has also participated in several international conferences. His main research areas are political discourse analysis, stancetaking and rhetoric.

Carolina Figueras is Associate Professor of Spanish Language and Linguistics at the University of Barcelona. She is the author of the book entitled *Pragmática de la puntuación* (Barcelona, Octaedro, 2001), and the editor, with Adrián Cabedo, of *Perspectives on Evidentiality in Spanish: Explorations across Genres* (Amsterdam, John Benjamins, 2018). She was the guest editor, together with Dorota Kotwica, of the special issue "Evidentiality, epistemicity and mitigation in Spanish", for *Corpus Pragmatics* (2020). Her research interests are focused on the topics of linguistic evidentiality, as related to mitigation in discourse, the construction of epistemic stance in non-solicited illness narratives, multimodal identities, and the dynamic expression of empathy in interaction. She has published her work in peer-reviewed journals such as *Qualitative Health Research, Pragmatics and Society, Rilce, Spanish in Context,* and *Journal of Pragmatics*, among others.

Laura Filardo-Llamas is Senior Lecturer in English Language and Linguistics at the Department of English Studies of the University of Valladolid, Spain. She was awarded her PhD in English Linguistics in 2007 and has been working at the University of Valladolid since then. She has been a visiting scholar at the University of Ulster-Jordanstown, the University of Lancaster, and the Vrije University of Amsterdam. Her research specialises on Critical Discourse Analysis, with a particular interest in political discourse analysis, an area in which she has published widely, both in prestigious journals and in edited collections. She was a co-editor of the volume published by Routledge *Space, Time and Evaluation in Ideological Discourse*. Her fields of academic interest are cognitive linguistics, gender studies, metaphor, multimodality, nationalist conflicts, political discourse, and politics and social media

Pedro Guijarro-Fuentes is a Professor in Spanish linguistics at the University of the Balearic Islands and has headed multiple projects on the acquisition of various phenomena on Spanish language including, but not limited to, the acquisition of ser/estar, tense and mood, differential object marking, all funded by the British Academy, Art and Humanities Research Council, the Deutsche Forschungsgemeinschaft, Spanish Ministry of Economy and Competitiveness and more recently by the European Union research foundation under the Horizon2020. He has authored and co-authored numerous journal articles, book chapters and books, published by various international publishers and in high impact journals. He has organized many professional meetings and has been a participant in many professional conferences.

Laura Hidalgo Downing is Full Professor at Universidad Autónoma, Madrid. She pursued an MA in Linguistics and Modern English Language, which was awarded with distinction, at the University of Nottingham, under a Fleming grant and obtained her PhD. at Universidad Complutense de Madrid (1997) Her research interests include discourse analysis at the cross-roads between functional linguistics and cognitive linguistics, stance and evaluation, multimodality and metaphor. She has co-edited, together with Blanca Kraljevic, the volume *Performing metaphoric creativity across modes and contexts* (John Benjamins, 2020) and the special issue 'Metaphorical creativity across modes' (*Metaphor in the Social World*, 2013). Together with Susan Cockroft, Robert Cokcroft and Craig Hamilton she is co-author of *Persuading People. An Introduction to Rhetoric* (third revised edition, Palgrave MacMillan, 2014). She is the coordinator of the Research group "Discourse, communication and creativity" (UAM, HUM-F060). She has been PI of six research projects since 2008, the last one in co-direction with Professor Marín-Arrese, on 'Stance, (inter)subjectivity and discourse' (PGC 2018-095798-B-100).

XIANG HUANG is PhD candidate in Applied Linguistics and Translation Studies at Pompeu Fabra University, Barcelona (Spain). She received her master's degree in Translation Studies from Guangdong University of Foreign Studies, Guangzhou, China. She is now working on her PhD project on discursive representation of obesity in the Chinese media. Her research interests include critical metaphor analysis, media discourse studies, discourse and social changes.

PASCALE LECLERCQ is a lecturer at Université Paul-Valéry Montpellier 3, where she is currently Head of the Teacher Training department. She teaches English linguistics, second language acquisition and research methodology to graduate and undergraduate students. Her research interests include SLA research methodology and epistemology, but also cross-linguistic influences in the L2 acquisition of discursive competence. She has recently published a variety of papers on the acquisition of nominal reference, TAM reference, and evidentiality. She is also interested in the study of L2 development in a study abroad context.

CARMEN MAÍZ-ARÉVALO obtained her PhD in English Linguistics in 2001. She has worked at the department of English Linguistics at the Complutense University of Madrid since 2006, where she currently holds a position of Associate Professor. She teaches Pragmatics, TEFL Methodology and Intercultural Studies, among other things. With regard to her research interests, her fields are pragmatics, intercultural pragmatics and computer-mediated communication, with a special focus on (im)politeness and humour. She has published many articles and given numerous talks in national and international conferences in these fields. Besides her research and teaching, Carmen Maíz-Arévalo has also worked for years as teacher trainer, giving a great amount of courses in different universities. She has also collaborated as an invited reviewer for different journals connected with pragmatics and EFL teaching such as the Journal of Pragmatics, Gist Journal of Education, Language Resources and Evaluation, Sage Open or the Journal of Politeness Research, among others. Currently, she is also the Academic Head of the Centre of Modern Languages at the University Complutense of Madrid.

Juana Isabel Marín-Arrese is Emeritus Professor of English Linguistics in the *Department of English Studies: Linguistics and Literature* at the UCM. She is a Fleming Award and Fulbright/Hays scholar. She holds an MA (University of Lancaster, UK, 1985), and a PhD with outstanding Doctoral Award (UCM, 1992). Her main research interests include the fields of discourse, semantics, and pragmatics, with special interest in cognitive linguistic studies, critical discourse studies, and cross-linguistic studies. Her recent research focuses on stance, epistemicity and the expression of inter/subjectivity in discourse. She has been PI in the research projects STANCEDISC (PGC2018-095798-B-I00), and EUROEVIDMOD (FFI2011-23181), and has participated as a research member in EVIDISPRAG (FFI2015-65474-P). She is co-editor of the collective volumes on evidentiality and modality: *Evidential Marking in European Languages. Toward a unitary comparative account* (De Gruyter, in press); *Evidentiality Revisited: Cognitive Grammar, Functional and Discourse-Pragmatic Perspectives* (John Benjamins, 2017), *Evidentiality and Modality in European Languages* (Peter Lang, 2017), *Evidentiality and the Semantics Pragmatics Interface* (*Belgian Journal of Linguistics* 29, Special issue, John Benjamins, 2015), and *English Modality: Core, Periphery and Evidentiality* (De Gruyter Mouton, 2013). Her recent publications on these topics include papers in peer-reviewed journals (*Journal of Pragmatics* 2021; *Cultura, Lenguaje y Representación* 2021; *Kalbotyra* 2017; *Belgian Journal of Linguistics* 2015; *Critical Discourse Studies* 2015; *Discourse Studies* 2015), and chapters in collective volumes (John Benjamins 2021, 2018, 2017; Routledge 2020, 2015; Peter Lang 2016; Vervuert 2016; De Gruyter Mouton 2013).

Victoria Martín de la Rosa is Associate Professor of English Language and Linguistics at Complutense University in Madrid. She has participated as a research member in a number of competitive projects on evidentiality/modality/stance: *Evidentiality and Modality in European Languages* (EUROEVIDMOD-FFI2011-23181), *Evidentiality: A Discourse-Pragmatic Study of English and Other European Languages* (EVIDISPRAG-FFI2015-65474-P), and *Stance and Subjectivity in Discourse: Towards an Integrated Framework for the Analysis of Epistemicity, Effectivity, Evaluation and Inter/Subjectivity* (STANCEDISC-PGC2018-095798-B-I00). She has co-edited the volumes *Evidentiality and Modality in European Languages* (Peter Lang, 2017) and *Thinking Modally: English and Contrastive Studies on Modality* (Cambridge Scholars, 2015). Related to the work conducted in those research projects, she has also co-authored papers in international journals on the role of modality in UN Security Council Resolutions such as Journal of *Pragmatics* (2021) and *Intercultural Pragmatics* (2019).

Vicent Montalt teaches medical, scientific and technical translation at the Universitat Jaume I, Spain and is director of the Master in Medical Translation, and of the research team Tradmed, both at the same University. He is author of *Manual de traduccio cientificotècnica* (2005), a book on scientific and technical translation published in Catalan, and *Medical Translation Step by Step* (2014), an approach to medical translation based on learner and learning-centred teaching tasks.

Natalia Mora-López holds a PhD in English Linguistics from the Complutense University of Madrid, where she also obtained her Master's in English Linguistics and Master's in Teacher training, as well as her BA degrees in English and Spanish studies. She has taught English-related subjects in several Spanish universities. Currently, she works at the Complutense University as an adjunct professor in the department of English Studies, and she teaches courses related to English for Specific Purposes. Her research interests include discourse analysis, evaluative language and the expression of opinion, on the one hand, and teaching innovation, on the other hand. Her research has been published by prestigious publishing houses, and she has participated in a number of international conferences.

Jennifer Moreno holds a degree in Translation and Interpreting (University of Murcia). She has also completed two master's degree, one in Foreign Language Teaching (UNED) and another one in Medical Translation (Universitat Jaume I). She is currently developing her doctoral research in the field of narrative medicine while working as a professor of EFL at the University of Zaragoza and as a freelance translator. In the professional field of translation, in 2019, she obtained a scholarship for a translation internship at the European Commission in Brussels. She also has extensive experience as a freelance translator and collaborates with companies from Italy, England and Germany, among others. In the field of research, she has completed a four-month research stay at the University of Modena and Reggio Emilia, co-funded by Ibercaja. Regarding conferences, she has also been part of the organising committee of several international congresses and has presented papers in different national and international conferences.

Celeste Moreno Palmero holds a Ph.D. in Linguistics from the Universidad Complutense de Madrid. Guided by a multidisciplinary approach, her research interests include Critical Discourse Analysis, Cognitive Linguistics, and Second Language Acquisition. Within the field of CDA, she has published and presented in numerous international conferences in issues related to Gender, Immigration, and the Cold War. With regards to her work in the field of SLA, she has carried out research and participated in numerous projects in areas such as hybrid methodologies, the use of online applications for independent learning, learning language through art, and the employment of real-based experiences in second language learning. After working for 10 years at Harvard University, where she taught Spanish Language in the Department of Romance Language and Literatures, in 2019 Celeste Moreno Palmero moved to Rome where she started her own company, Hyll School, which focuses on teaching languages using an innovative hybrid methodology that unites in-class instruction with online exploration and offers language courses, language coaching, and pedagogy consulting.

Ana Muñoz Miquel is an Associate Professor in the Translation and Communication Department at the Universitat Jaume I (UJI), where she teaches for the Degree in Translation and Interpreting and the master's degree in Medical and Health Translation. Her doctoral thesis, on the profile and competences of medical translators, won the Special Doctorate Award at the UJI and the Biennial Best Thesis Award granted by the Iberian Association for Translation and Interpreting Studies. She is currently a member of the GENTT research group (UJI) and a collaborator in the CiTrans group (Universitat de València). Her research interests include medical and health translation, translator training, doctor-patient communication and genres addressed to patients. She has published articles on these subjects in journals such as *Target, Interpreter and Translator Trainer, Linguistica Antverpiensia, Hermes, JoSTrans, Hermēneus* or *Panace@*, among others, and book chapters for Routledge, Peter Lang and Comares.

Begoña Núñez-Perucha is Senior Lecturer in the Department of English Studies: Linguistics and Literature at the Universidad Complutense de Madrid. Her research interests lie in the field of discourse analysis and, more specifically, along the lines of critical and functional approaches, areas in which she has published widely. From a critical perspective, her research has brought together the tools of Critical Discourse Analysis and Cognitive Linguistics for the analysis of the language of victimization, (counter) ideologies and identity construction in narrative, political and advertising discourses. From a functional perspective, drawing on appraisal and genre analysis theories, she has explored stance and (inter)subjectivity in journalistic discourse as well as (inter) textual features of lecture discourse and academic writing at university. She has also participated in numerous national and international research projects and served as an external reviewer for several scientific journals and monographic series (e.g. Discourse Context and Media, Lingua, EuroSLA Studies Series, Spanish Journal of Applied Linguistics, Review of Cognitive Linguistics or Humanities and Social Sciences Communications). Currently, she coordinates the "Master´s Programme in English Linguistics: New Applications and International Communication".

Paula Pérez-Sobrino is a lecturer at the Department of Modern Philologies at the University of La Rioja (Spain). Her publication record includes 24 publications (including 2 research monographs in John Benjamins and Cambridge UP, and 9 JCR articles), 20 invited talks and 43 conference talks. She edited a collective volume in John Benjamins in 2017 and is currently editing a special issue on research methods for Metaphor in the Social World. To date, she has been PI in 3 research projects (including a Marie Curie postdoctoral fellowship at the University of Birmingham) and has collaborated as a research member in other 4 research projects. She currently serves in 2 editorial boards for JCR indexed journals (Review of Cognitive Linguistics and Plos One). Between 2018 and 2019, she was consulted by the Joint Research Centre to lead a technical report European Commission.

Cecilia Mihaela Popescu is Full Professor in Applied Romance Linguistics, General Linguistics, and Pragmatics at the University of Craiova. She received her Ph.D. in 2006 with a thesis focused on a comparative study of the expression of the *potential* and the *irrealis* in Latin, French, and Romanian. She has been a visiting scholar at Charles de Gaulle University, Lille3 (2002), Denis Diderot University, Paris 7 (2009), and University of Rome 3 (2011). She co-organised many national and international conferences on historical linguistics and lexicology and has edited various joint volumes. In 2013, she published her post-doctoral thesis entitled *The Future and the Conditional in Romance Languages. A Morphosyntactic and Semantic Approach from a Diachronic Perspective*. She also published papers in *Revue de linguistique romane*, *Revue roumaine de linguistique*, and *Zeitschrift für französische Sprach und Literatur*, as well as in other international peer-reviewed volumes. Her research interests include historical linguistics (history of Latin language, history of Old French and Old Romanian, grammaticalization) and French borrowings into Romanian.

Mercedes Querol-Julián is an Associate Professor in the Department of English teaching at the Universidad Internacional de La Rioja (Spain). She leads the research group PRODIGI (Personal and Professional Development through Digital Genres). Her current research focuses mainly on the areas of interpersonal relationships and multimodality in academic spoken discourses, with particular interest in online teaching and English-medium education at university. She has published on these topics in journals such as English for Specific Purposes or System, and book chapters in Routledge or John Benjamins.

Boitshwarelo Rantsudu received her PhD in Language and Communication Research from Cardiff University, UK, and is currently a Lecturer at University of Botswana. Her research interests lie in the areas of Appraisal Theory and Critical Discourse Analysis. Within these areas she is interested in how language construes attitude, and how such attitude gets mitigated in order to assert objectivity in hard news reporting. She has explored this by investigating the appearance of evaluative language and strategic adherence to the principle of objectivity with specific reference to the representation of the 2011 public sector workers' strike in some Botswana newspapers.

María Paula Roverso is a Lecturer at the Department of Philology, University of Cantabria, Spain. She graduated at Universidad Nacional de Río Cuarto, Argentina, and holds a master's degree from the University of Cantabria, Spain, on "Second Language Learning and Teaching". She is currently enrolled in a doctoral programme at the University of Cantabria. Her research focuses on the field of English for Specific and Academic Purposes and follows a corpus-linguistics and text-analytic approach with a view to improving teaching and learning in this field.

Anna Ruskan is Associate Professor at the Department of English Philology at Vilnius University. Her research focuses on stance, evidentiality, epistemic modality, corpus linguistics, contrastive linguistics, academic discourse and media discourse. She has participated in national and international projects related to stance, modality and evidentiality (i.e. *Realizations of modality and evidentiality in Lithuanian*; *Evidentiality: A discourse-pragmatic study of English and other European languages*; *Stance and subjectivity in discourse*: *Towards an integrated framework for the analysis of epistemicity, effectivity, evaluation and inter/subjectivity from a critical discourse perspective*). Her publications include articles on epistemic qualifications, stance, and contrastive linguistics.

Alfonso Sánchez-Moya is currently a Postdoctoral Fellow at the Department of Government (FAS) at Harvard University. Embedded in the socio-cognitive approach to the understanding of discourse, his research explores linguistic mechanisms employed to represent social groups at risk (such as female survivors of partner violence in the UK or undocumented immigrants in the US), paying special attention to digital environments. His research is methodologically influenced by techniques and tools in corpus linguistics (such as sentiment analysis) and qualitative explorations of data. He participates in the research project Stance and Subjectivity in Discourse and collaborates as member and external advisor with the research groups Discourse and communication in English: functional and cognitive approaches (DISCOM-COGFUNC) (www.ucm.es/discom-cogfunc), GENTEXT: Gender, Language and Sexual (In)Equality Research Group (https://gentext.blogs.uv.es), and Language, Emotion and Identity (https://grupoleide.com/). Webpage: www.alfonsosanchezmoya.com.

Mario Serrano-Losada received his PhD in English Linguistics from the University of Santiago de Compostela in 2018 and is a Lecturer in the Department of English Studies at Complutense University of Madrid since 2019. His main research interests include language variation and change and grammaticalization, with a special focus on morphosyntactic and pragmatic change in English and Spanish. He has published his work on the diachronic development of evidential and mirative expressions in journals like *English Language and Linguistics* and the *Review of Cognitive Linguistics*.

Audronė Šolienė is Associate Professor at the Department of English Philology of the Faculty of Philology in Vilnius University since 2006. She also worked as a lecturer at the Department of English Philology of the Faculty of Foreign Languages at Vilnius Pedagogical University in 2002–2006. Her primary research interests lie in the fields of contrastive linguistics, corpus linguistics, epistemic modality, evidentiality, stance and subjectivity, discourse markers as well as translation. She is a member of the research teams of the two on-going projects: "Discourse markers in Lithuanian: a synchronic and diachronic study" (Ref. No. P-MIP-17-308, funded by the Research Council of Lithuania) and "Evidentiality: a discourse-pragmatic study of English and other European languages (EVIDISPRAG)" (Ref. No. FFI2015-65474-P, funded by MINECO, Spanish Ministry of Economy and Competitiveness).

JULIA T. WILLIAMS CAMUS is a lecturer at the Department of Philology, University of Cantabria (Spain), where she teaches English phonetics and phonology at undergraduate level and Discourse Analysis, Speaking and Listening Skills and English for Specific Purposes at postgraduate level. She also teaches a number of courses on English for Publication Purposes for lecturers and PhD students. Her research interests centre on (critical) discourse analysis, corpus-based analysis, metaphor studies, English for Specific and Academic Purposes, and translation studies. She has published extensively and attended numerous conferences in these areas. She has been a visiting scholar at the University of Lancaster and at the University of Birmingham. She has participated in four competitive research projects (FFI2014-57313-P, FFI2011-25755, FFI2008-00070/FISO, PGC2018-095798-B-I00).

JUAN RAFAEL ZAMORANO-MANSILLA obtained his PhD in English Literature and Linguistics in 2006 from the Complutense University of Madrid. His thesis, titled *The generation of tense and aspect in English and Spanish*, is a contrastive analysis taking a systemic-functional approach to language. He has been teaching as full-time untenured lecturer in the department of English Studies at the Complutense University of Madrid since 2010. His publications revolve around corpus linguistics, contrastive analysis English-Spanish, and tense, modality and evidentiality. He has participated in various projects on modality and corpus annotation, and is currently a member of the FUNCAP research group. His teaching covers different subjects in the areas of English as a foreign language and linguistics applied to the English language.

Juana I. Marín-Arrese, Laura Hidalgo-Downing &
Juan Rafael Zamorano-Mansilla

# Introduction

This volume addresses a variety of issues and perspectives on Stance and Inter/Subjectivity, and the ways in which Identity is reflected in the discourse. From a theoretical standpoint, the volume brings together different perspectives on the multifaceted nature of stance (Biber and Finegan 1989; Englebretson 2007). Most studies in the literature focus on one of the main dimensions of stance, such as epistemicity (Biber et al. 1999), evaluation (Thompson and Hunston 2000; Thompson and Alba-Juez 2014), appraisal (Martin & White 2005), affect and emotion (Ochs and Schieffelin 1989; DuBois and Kärkkäinen 2012), as well as stancetaking and dialogicality (DuBois 2007), or identity and the sociolinguistics of stance (Jaffe 2009).

This volume adopts a broad scope of the phenomenon of stance in discourse, and brings together studies on various dimensions related to stance as a broad field of study. The volume includes studies on the use of resources of epistemic modality and evidentiality, of deonticity and directivity, of evaluation and metaphor, as well as other areas of study within the domain of stance, such as mirativity, emotion, attribution, and the expression of inter/subjectivity and identity in discourse. In this way it provides a more in-depth and a wider perspective into the nature of stance. From a methodological point of view, the volume provides a variety of studies, corpus studies and contrastive studies as well as specific case studies on discursive tasks. The chapters also address the use of stance resources in a variety of discourse domains and genres: oral discourse, political discourse, news reports, editorials, opinion columns and scientific articles in newspapers, online fora on social issues, online mental health and peer support platforms, patient narratives, medical research articles and university lectures.

The volume is divided into three sections. Section A focuses on epistemicity and stance, as well as on effective stance in several languages (English, Catalan, French, Lithuanian, Romanian and Spanish). The seven chapters in the section present corpus studies in these languages and well as studies involving the acquisition of evidentiality and bilingualism. The chapter by Juana I. Marín-Arrese explores the use of stance resources as legitimation strategies and as the expression of inter/subjectivity (Nuyts 2012; Marín-Arrese 2011, 2015). The paper focuses on two macro categories of stance, the epistemic and the effective, and on the joint deployment of stance markers in these categories, which serve the strategic purposes of legitimation of knowledge and of action goals, and the indexing of inter/subjectivity. The paper presents a contrastive corpus study on the use of stance expressions in political and journalistic discourse, in the genres of political speeches and opinion columns. The chapter by Natalia Mora-López and Sergio Ferrer-Navas aims to determine the similarities and differences in the effective stance realisations found in newspaper and political discourse from an English-Spanish contrastive perspective. Additionally, the study investigates the extent to which these linguistic realisations may also reflect discourse strategies specific of these discourse domains and genres. The chapter by Elena Domínguez Romero and Victoria Martín de la Rosa aims to determine the similarities and differences in the distribution and use of epistemic stance resources found in newspaper and political discourse from an English-Spanish contrastive perspective. Additionally, the study looks into the extent to which these linguistic realisations may reflect similarities and differences in the expression of ideology in these discourse domains and genres. The chapter by Anna Ruskan and Audronė Šolienė explores the expression of epistemicity and effectivity in Lithuanian political discourse by comparing the distribution of epistemic and effective stance markers in the speeches of right-wing and left-wing Lithuanian politicians. Aoife Ahern, José Amenós-Pons and Pedro Guijarro-Fuentes present a study on the use of the future tense (FUT) for expressing conjectural evidential meaning by Majorcan Catalan-Spanish bilinguals. The study aims to analyse the impact of factors such as language dominance, mode of bilingualism (early simultaneous vs. sequential) and of the varying degrees of proficiency in each language on the expression and interpretation of conjectural FUT tense uses. Adopting a functional and developmental perspective, Pascale Leclercq explores the marking of inference in the stages of L2 acquisition and aims to determine how advanced French learners of English develop the means of expression of this conceptual domain, which is relatively rare in the L1 and L2 input. Cecilia Mihaela Popescu and Oana Adriana Duță study the existence of pragmaticalization processes developed by evidential markers in time, through a comparative analysis of two lexical particles, Romanian *cică* and Spanish *dizque*.

Section B contains six chapters on the relation between stance, evaluation and metaphor. Each of the chapters presents corpus studies which explore the expression of evaluation in different text types, namely, newspaper editorial and opinion articles, forums on social issues, political discourse, scientific texts in the press and twitter posts. The first four chapters apply the scheme for the annotation of evaluative stance developed by Hidalgo-Downing et al. (forthcoming) within a research project on Stance and Intersubjectivity (Marín-Arrese et al. 2020) to the analysis of different discursive genres. The chapter by Hidalgo-Downing and PÉREZ-SOBRINO studies the construal of negative evaluative stance in opinion articles on Brexit from a Critical Discourse Analysis perspective. The study presents the scheme for the annotation of evaluative stance which consists of four levels of analysis (part of speech, function, metaphoricity, value) and applies it to the analysis of the frequency and role of markers of evaluative stance in two samples of British opinion articles from the newspapers *The Times* and *The Guardian*. The chapter by NÚÑEZ-PERUCHA and FILARDO-LLAMAS studies the expression of evaluation in a sample of speeches by British Conservative and Labour politicians. The study investigates the frequency and distribution of evaluative strategies in the samples, their value-connotation, and their connection with the specific features of representation and ideological positioning that characterize Political Discourse. The chapter by SÁNCHEZ-MOYA and MAÍZ-ARÉVALO sets out to analyse the expression of evaluative stance in a 100,000-word dataset of publicly available forum posts dealing with a plethora of social issues. The study explores the frequency of evaluative stance categories in the corpus and discusses the extent to which the expression of negative evaluation is favoured in this corpus. The chapter by WILLIAMS CAMUS explores evaluative stance and metaphor in a corpus of popularisation articles on scientific advances drawn from *The Guardian* and *The Times*. The study examines the most frequent evaluative categories, it discusses the role of metaphorical language and the preference for the expression of positive value in this genre. The chapter by MORENO-PALMERO analyses the role of war metaphors as a resource for the expression of evaluation in political tweets posted by Trump, Johnson, Sánchez, and Conte on the Covid-19 crisis during March 2020. The study situates the analysis of metaphor within the broader framework of the study of evaluation in discourse and explores to what extent war metaphors are pervasive in the tweets used to talk about the pandemic. The chapter by HUANG examines how metaphor is used as a stance strategy and as a positioning resource in health communication around obesity in 98 obesity-related editorials from the *People's Daily*, China's major official newspaper. The chapter discusses how metaphors help the editorials position themselves both at the epistemic level (knowledge-related) and the affective level (emotion-related) around obesity and are used as a resource to express both self-positioning and other-positioning regarding obesity.

Section C contains seven chapters that offer insight into human communication and identity construction in English. The studies apply the categories of Stance, Engagement, Evaluation, and Emotion in a wide variety of settings and text types, ranging from social media, academic writing and lecturing, and news media. The first three chapters focus on language in the field of medicine: FIGUERAS explores how empathy is dealt with in two health online communities, revealing interesting differences in the strategies used; MORENO, MONTALT and MUÑOZ-MIQUEL analyse how patients use metaphors in communicating their disease experiences in a corpus of over 100 narratives; in ROVERSO and WILLIAMS CAMUS, we find an analysis of how medical researchers create writer identity through the use of first-person pronouns in a collection of 60 articles. The next chapter, by AIELLO, shifts the focus to politics and social media: by studying the stancetaking moves and discursive strategies by American Congresswoman Alexandria Ocasio-Cortez, the author offers some insights into how political identities and discourse are created in contemporary politics. Stancetaking is also the object of study in the next chapter by RANTSUDU, but this time in the field of journalistic writing. The author examines hard news reporting from two newspapers in order to understand how journalists include their position and evaluation in headlines and lead sentences. QUEROL-JULIÁN looks at the use of pronouns and modal verbs in educational contexts where English is the language of instruction, but not the first language of the participants. This allows the author to draw conclusions about the most common strategies to express evaluation and the relationship with interlocutors. Finally, SERRANO-LOSADA is a study of the expression *spoiler alert* in the COCA and NOW, which shows a shift in function from a warning expression to mirativity and assumed evidentiality.

We would like to acknowledge the financial support for this volume from the research project *Stance and Subjectivity in Discourse: Towards an Integrated Framework for the Analysis of Epistemicity, Effectivity, Evaluation and Inter/Subjectivity from a Critical Discourse Perspective.* (STANCEDISC), Ref. PGC2018-095798-B-I00, funded by the Ministerio de Ciencia, Innovación y Universidades (Spanish Ministry of Science, Innovation and Universities).

We thank all the contributors to this volume, and the colleagues who contributed by reviewing the drafts of the chapters. We would also like to thank Ms. Ulrike Döring for her invaluable help in the edition of this volume. Naturally, the usual disclaimers apply.

## References

Biber, D. and Finegan, E. (1989). 'Styles of stance in English: Lexical and grammatical marking of evidentiality and affect'. *Text* 1, 93–124.

Biber, D.; Johansson, S.; Leech, G.; Conrad, S. and Finnegan, E. (1999). *Longman Grammar of Spoken and Written English*. London: Longman.

DuBois, J. W. (2007). 'The stance triangle'. In Englebretson, Robert (ed) *Stancetaking in Discourse*, pp. 139–182. Amsterdam, John Benjamins.

DuBois, J.W. and Kärkkäinen, E. (2012). 'Taking a stance on emotion: affect, sequence, and intersubjectivity in dialogic interaction'. *Text & Talk, 32 (4)*, 433–451.

Englebretson, R. (2007). 'Introduction'. In R. Englebretson (ed.), *Stancetaking in Discourse*, pp. 1–26. Amsterdam, John Benjamins.

Hidalgo Downing, L., Pérez-Sobrino, P., Filardo-Llamas, L., Maíz-Arévalo, C., Núñez-Perucha, B., Sánchez-Moya, A. and Williams Camus, J.T. (forthcoming) 'A protocol for the annotation of evaluative stance and metaphor across four discourse genres'. *Revista Española de Lingüística Aplicada*.

Jaffe, A. (ed.) (2009). *Stance: Sociolinguistic Perspectives*. Oxford: Oxford University Press.

Marín-Arrese, J.I. (2011). 'Effective vs. epistemic stance and subjectivity in political discourse: Legitimising strategies and mystification of responsibility'. In C. Hart (ed.) *Critical Discourse Studies in Context and Cognition*, pp. 193–223. Amsterdam: John Benjamins.

Marín-Arrese, J.I. (2015). 'Epistemic legitimisation and inter/subjectivity in the discourse of parliamentary and public inquiries: A contrastive case study'. *Critical Discourse Studies, 12 (3)*, 261–278.

Marín-Arrese, J.I., Hidalgo Downing, L.; Carretero, M.; Domínguez Romero, E.; Ferrer Navas, S.; Filardo Llamas, L.; Maíz Arévalo, C.; Martín de la Rosa, V.; Mora López, N.; Núñez Perucha, B.; Pérez Sobrino, P.; Sánchez Moya, A.; Williams Camus, J. (2020). 'Stancetaking in discourses: epistemicity, effectivity, evaluation'. In L. López Ropero, S., Prieto García-Cañedo, and J.A. Sánchez Fajardo (eds.) *Actas del 43 Congreso de AEDEAN. Thresholds and Ways Forward in English Studies*, pp. 269–274. Servicio de Publicaciones de la Universidad de Alicante.

Martin, J. R. and White, P. R.R., (2005). *The Language of Evaluation. Appraisal in English*. Basingstoke/New York, Palgrave Macmillan.

Nuyts, J. (2012). 'Notions of (inter)subjectivity'. *English Text Construction, 5 (1)*, 53–76.

Ochs, E. and Schieffelin, B. (1989). 'Language has a heart'. In E. Ochs (ed.) *The Pragmatics of Affect*, special issue of *Text* 9, 7–25.

Thompson, G. and Hunston, S. (2000). 'Evaluation: An Introduction'. In S. Hunston and G. Thompson (eds.) *Evaluation in Text: Authorial Stance and the Construction of Discourse*, pp. 1–27. Oxford, Oxford University Press.

Thompson, G. and Alba-Juez, L. (eds.) (2014). *Evaluation in Context*. Amsterdam, John Benjamins.

# Section A. Stance, Epistemicity and Effectivity

Juana I. Marín-Arrese

# Epistemic and Effective Stance: Legitimation Strategies and the Expression of Inter/Subjectivity in Discourse[1]

**Abstract:** This paper aims to explore the use of stance resources as legitimation strategies and the indexing inter/subjectivity in political and journalistic discourse. The paper focuses on two macro categories of stance, the epistemic and the effective, and on the joint deployment of these stance markers, which serve the strategic purposes of legitimation of knowledge and of action plans and goals. The paper presents a corpus study on the use of stance expressions in the genre of political speeches by Conservative vs. Labour party members, as representatives of centre-right and centre-left ideologies, and in the genre of opinion columns in newspapers of both right-wing and left-wing leanings, *The Guardian* and *The Times*. The study addresses the following research issues: (i) variation in the deployment of epistemic and effective stance markers in the domains of newspaper vs political discourse; (ii) variation due to ideological slant in each genre and domain; (iii) encoding or indexing features of (inter)subjectivity in epistemic and effective stance markers. It is hypothesized that there will be variation in the expression of epistemicity and effectivity in the two discourse domains. Variation is also expected within each discourse domain and genre, as a result of ideological differences which may permeate the styles of persuasion. Variation in writers' overt/covert expression of (inter)subjectivity is expected due to differences in the felt need for the presence of the authorial voice in these genres and discourse domains and their different styles of persuasion.

**Keywords:** *epistemic, effective, stance strategies, inter/subjectivity, discourse domains*

## 1 Introduction

This paper aims to explore the use of stance resources as legitimation strategies and the indexing of inter/subjectivity in political and journalistic discourse. The paper brings together work on stance (Biber & Finegan 1989; DuBois 2007; Englebretson 2007; Simaki, Paradis & Kerren 2019, *inter alia*), and on the

1 This research has received support from the research project *Stance and Subjectivity in Discourse: Towards an Integrated Framework for the Analysis of Epistemicity, Effectivity, Evaluation and Inter/Subjectivity from a Critical Discourse Perspective.* (STANCEDISC), Ref. PGC2018-095798-B-I00, funded by the Ministerio de Ciencia, Innovación y Universidades (Spanish Ministry of Science, Innovation and Universities).

expression of epistemicity and effectivity in discourse (Langacker 2009; Marín-Arrese 2011). The paper draws on a model for the analysis of stance strategies which posits two macro categories of stance, the epistemic and the effective (Marín-Arrese 2011, 2021), and on the indexing of inter/subjectivity through these stance markers in discourse (Nuyts 2012; Marín-Arrese 2011, 2013, 2015).

The paper focuses on the epistemic and effective macro categories of stance, and on the joint deployment of these stance markers, which serve the strategic purposes of legitimation of knowledge and of coercive persuasion for action. Epistemic stance pertains to speaker/writer's striving for control of conceptions of reality (Langacker 2009, 2013), which involves the expression of their estimation of the veracity of the event designated and the likelihood of its realization, and/or their specification of the sources whereby they feel entitled to make an assertion, thus exerting an indirect persuasive function by providing justificatory support for a proposition (Boye 2012; Marín-Arrese 2011, 2015, 2021). Effective stance strategies are aimed at controlling hearers/readers' acceptance of action plans and of potential events, and exert a direct persuasive function by claiming the obligation, desirability, normativity or requirement of carrying out those actions, or by proclaiming intention or commitment to the actions or events, or their feasibility (Marín-Arrese 2011, 2021). From a critical discourse perspective (Chilton 2004; Hart 2011), it may be argued that the interplay of epistemic and effective expressions of dialogical positioning serve the joint strategic purposes of legitimation of knowledge and of action plans and goals.

The study addresses the following research issues: (i) the degree to which there is variation in the deployment of epistemic and effective stance markers in the domains of newspaper vs political discourse; (ii) whether variation may be due to ideological slant in each discourse domain and genre; (iii) how (inter) subjectivity is indexed or realized in epistemic and effective stance markers.

It is hypothesized that there will be variation in the expression of epistemicity and effectivity in the two discourse domains, as a result of differences in genre and text type, and in communicative goals. Variation is also expected within each discourse domain and genre, as a result of ideological differences which may permeate the styles of persuasion. Variation in speaker/writers' overt/covert expression of (inter)subjectivity is expected due to differences in the felt need for the presence of the authorial voice in these discourse domains and genres and their different styles of persuasion.

The chapter presents results of a corpus study on the use of stance strategies in the genre of political speeches by Conservative vs. Labour party members, as representatives of centre-right and centre-left ideologies, and in the genre of opinion columns in newspapers of both right-wing and left-wing leanings, *The Guardian* and *The Times*.

This chapter is organized as follows: Section 2 discusses the main features and functions of the categories of epistemic and effective stance strategies. Section 3 provides a description of methodological decisions and research procedures. In Section 4, the results and discussion of the study is presented. The conclusions are found in Section 5.

## 2 Stance and Inter/Subjectivity

### 2.1 Stance Strategies

The multifaceted nature of stance has been addressed from diverse and often overlapping perspectives. Current research on stance in discourse arises at the crossroads of various frameworks and research endeavours, such as the work on *stance* (Biber & Finegan 1989), *affect* and *emotion* (Ochs and Schieffelin 1989; Kärkkäinen and DuBois 2012), *evaluation* (Hunston and Thompson 2000; Thompson and Alba-Juez 2014), or *stancetaking* and *dialogicality* (DuBois 2007; Englebretson 2007), and stance identity (Jaffe 2009).

This paper focuses on stance as the way we construct subject positions in two key conceptual domains: epistemicity and the expression of justificatory support for the communicated proposition (Boye 2012), and effectivity as the expression of social or psychological force regarding the realization of events. The paper draws on a model for the analysis of stancetaking in discourse which focuses on two macro categories of stance, the epistemic and the effective (Marín-Arrese 2011, 2021). These categories reflect the systematic opposition in discourse between striving for control of conceptions of reality and striving for control of relations at the level of reality (Langacker 2009, 2013). From a critical discourse perspective, it has been argued that stance resources serve the strategic functions of legitimation and coercion (Chilton 2004; Marín-Arrese 2011, 2013). As Chilton (2004: 117) observes, one type of legitimation strategy is deontic, where "the speaker claims, explicitly or implicitly, to be not only 'right' in a cognitive sense, but 'right' in a moral sense".

Epistemic stance strategies involve speakers/writers' control of conceptions of reality in the discourse, through the expression of their estimation of the veracity of the event designated and the likelihood of its realization, and/or their specification of the sources whereby they feel entitled to make an assertion. Epistemic stance resources include a variety of lexico-grammatical elements, which may be grouped in the following categories: epistemic modal expressions

(EM), cognitive attitude predicates (CGA), indirect-inferential evidentials (IIE), personal cognitive factives (PFV) and impersonal factive predicates (IFV). All these expressions represent different modes of assessment of the epistemic status of the proposition and varying degrees of commitment of the speaker/writer towards the communicated information (cf., Marín-Arrese 2011, 2013).

Effective stance strategies are aimed at controlling hearers/readers' acceptance of relations at the level of reality and have a direct persuasive function. They are a means of exerting social and/or psychological force on the hearer/reader, by claiming the obligation or the compelling circumstances for the realization of actions, or by arguing in favour of the desirability, normativity or requirement for an event to take place, as well as the expression of speaker/writer's inclination, intention or commitment to carry out an action. Effective stance resources include a variety of lexico-grammatical elements, which may be grouped in the following categories: deontic modal expressions (DM), expressions of directivity (DIR), expressions of intentionality (INT), expressions of normativity or social desirability (NRM), and expressions of potentiality (POT) (Marín-Arrese, 2011, 2021).

## 2.2 Inter/Subjectivity: Epistemic vs. Effective Stance

The notion of *subjectivity* as the capacity of the speaking self to view him/herself as subject of enunciation (*sujet d'ènonciation*) is found in the seminal work by Benveniste (1966 [1958]), who also drew attention to the relationship of *intersubjectivity* between the speaker/writer and hearer/reader as a basic condition for linguistic communication. As Finegan (1995:1–2) defines the notion, subjectivity involves "the expression of self and the representation of a speaker's (or, more generally, a locutionary agent's) perspective or point of view in discourse – what has been called a speaker's imprint". The subjectivity of discourse is a crucial factor or facet of language, since it concerns "language as an expression –an incarnation, even– of perceiving, feeling, *speaking subjects*".

Subjectivity in language is associated with various ways in which the speaker/writer is present in the discourse, that is, the salience or overtness of the speaker/writer in the role of conceptualizer and the degree to which there is foregrounding of speaker/writer's consciousness (Langacker 1991). Traugott and Dasher (2002: 11) note that an epistemic modal like *may* "contributes to the contentful structure of the utterance, possibility on a scale between high probability (*must*) and low probability (*might*), but it also indexes subjective attitude (*I think it is possible …*)". Epistemic stance expressions index speakers/writers' positioning (subjectivity), both explicitly and implicitly, with regard to the validity of their assertions, and whether they align/disalign with potential addressees or text external voices (intersubjectivity).

An additional dimension of subjectivity vs. intersubjectivity concerns the degree to which the speaker/writer assumes personal responsibility for the evaluation of the evidence (subjectivity) or whether the assessment is potentially shared by others (intersubjectivity) (Nuyts 2012). Nuyts (2012: 58) defines the distinction between "subjectivity" and "intersubjectivity" in the following terms: "A modal evaluation is 'subjective' if it is presented as being strictly the assessor's sole responsibility. A modal evaluation is 'intersubjective' if it is presented as being shared between the assessor and a wider group of people, possibly (but not necessarily) including the hearer".

As regards the distinction between subjectivity and intersubjectivity in relation to epistemic vs. effective stance, Langacker (2008: 473) notes a number of features which distinguish the 'statement scenario' and the 'order scenario' (cf., Langacker, 2008: 474. Figure 13.5). In a usage event in which the speaker/writer produces a statement, s/he assumes the role of the conceptualizer (C) and subscribes to the proposition by adopting "an epistemic stance (e) toward the profiled occurrence (primarily by the presence or absence of a modal)". The speaker/writer's intended outcome is that "the hearer will momentarily join the speaker in attending to the proposition", and the "potential result of the usage event is that the hearer also identifies with C and subscribes to the proposition" (Langacker 2008: 473).

In the 'order scenario', as Langacker (2008: 474) observes, "the content expressed (e.g. *Leave!*) is not a proposition but simply a process". The prototypical clause in the order scenario, the imperative, "does not contain a separate grounding element: its verb cannot be inflected for tense (**Left!*) or take a modal (**Will leave!*)". As with root modals, the element that counts as grounding is the act of ordering, since "it relates the profiled process to the interlocutors" (Langacker 2008: 474). In the order scenario, effective stance involves the speaker/writer's intention of bringing about the occurrence of the profiled process. The speaker/writer realizes this intent by subjecting "the hearer to social and psychological force", with the projected outcome "that the hearer will share this intent and act accordingly" (Langacker 2008: 474).

We may sum up the main features of epistemic and effective stance in the following terms:

(a) Epistemic stance:
- Communicated content: proposition.
- Source of epistemic stance: The speaker/writer as conceptualizer (C) subscribes to the proposition by assessing the epistemic status (location vis-à-vis reality) of the profiled occurrence.
- Target: The hearer, who identifies with C and subscribes to the proposition.

- Potential result: speaker/writer's control of conceptions of reality (cf., Langacker 2009), that is, the legitimisation of the beliefs, knowledge or evidence that support or justify their claims. The hearer "identifies with C and subscribes to the proposition" (Langacker 2008: 473).

(b) Effective stance:
- Communicated content: process.
- Source of effective stance; The speaker/writer as conceptualizer (C), or by proxy some "deontic controller" (Chilton 2020), exerts social and/ or psychological force on the hearer in regard to the realization of some action or event.
- Target: The hearer, who shares intent with the speaker and acts accordingly.
- Potential result: speaker/writer's control of relations at the level of reality (cf., Langacker 2009), and the legitimisation of the realization of some action or event. The "hearer will share this intent and act accordingly" (Langacker 2008: 474).

## 2.3 Categories of Inter/Subjectivity in Epistemic Stance

Expressions of cognitive attitude (CGA) designating the speaker/writer explicitly (*I think*) indicate that s/he is solely responsible for the epistemic assessment of the proposition (p), whereas those expressions that refer to a collectivity (*We all know*) explicitly indicate that the information content of the utterance is known to, or accessible to a group of people, and thus invoke shared responsibility. Epistemic modals (*may*), which implicitly invoke the subject of conception, also index speaker/writer's personal responsibility for the assessment. Inferential evidential expressions (*It seems*), which do not designate the speaker/writer explicitly, are opaque in that they evoke a virtual or generalized conceptualizer, which by default is interpreted as the speaker/writer, but they also leave open the possibility of potentially sharing the evaluation with other voices in the discourse, so they may be interpreted as involving shared responsibility.

In this paper we focus on two parameters of subjectivity/intersubjectivity: (i) *Degree of salience or overtness of the role of conceptualizer*, which refers to the degree of explicitness, implicitness or opaqueness of the presence of the speaker/ writer as conceptualizer, and (ii) *Responsibility*, that is, personal vs. shared responsibility for the communicated information.

The following set of categories of subjectivity and intersubjectivity is proposed resulting from the interaction of the two parameters (cf. Marín-Arrese 2013, 2017b):

(i) **Salience:** We may posit a continuum in the degree of salience that the speaker/writer has as subject of conception in a particular predication (Langacker 1991, 2009), as in Figure 1.

(a) Explicit: These are expressions explicitly designating the speaker/writer in the expression of stance as the source of knowledge or assessment (*I know, I think*). The high degree of salience of the conceptualizer in these expressions has an effect on the construal of the conceptualization, such that the information communicated is maximally subjective.

(b) Implicit: These expressions invoke the speaker/conceptualizer as the implicit point of reference (modals: *may, …*). The speaker/writer is implicit and non-salient, and the role of conceptualizer is less prominent and more subjective, but these expressions with modal auxiliaries create subjectivity by foregrounding the speaker's attitudes or estimations of certainty (cf., Sanders 1999: 473).

| Explicit | Implicit | Virtual/Generalized |
|---|---|---|
| *I think* p<br>*We know* p | *may* p | *It seems* p<br>*It is possible* p |

**Figure 1.** Degree of salience of the conceptualizer

(c) Virtual/Generalized: These stance expressions evoke an implicit conceptualizer, which may be construed as a generalized or virtual entity, and which by default is interpreted as the speaker/writer/conceptualizer *(it seems*). As Langacker (2009: 286) notes, these impersonal predicates "defocus the mental activity of any particular conceptualizer" by evoking the conceptualizer in generalized fashion. He further makes the point that "evoking the conceptualizer in generalized fashion, abstracting away from any particular individual, gives C the status of a virtual entity". With impersonal modal predicates (*it is possible, …*), according to Langacker (2009), the conceptualizer is further backgrounded, and a more objective stance towards the communicated information is evoked.

(ii) **Personal vs. shared responsibility:** The degree to which the speaker assumes 'personal' responsibility for the information or presents the information as 'intersubjectively shared' (Nuyts 2012), as in Figure 2.

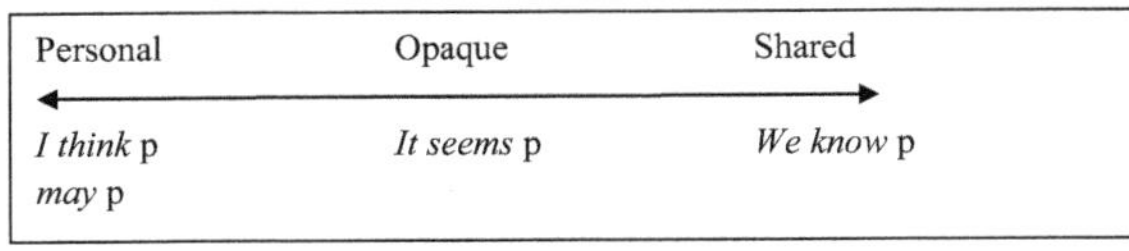


**Figure 2.** Degree of Speaker/Writer Responsibility

(a) Subjective, Explicit, Personal (SE): Expressions designating the speaker/writer explicitly (*I think*) indicate that s/he is 'personally' responsible for subscribing to the proposition, that the communicated information is part of their conception of reality.

(1) ***I believe*** *<EP, CGA, SE> that seeking the common ground and being prepared to make compromises in order to make progress does not entail a rejection of our values and convictions by one iota, rather …* (EPC)

(b) Intersubjective, Explicit, Shared (IE): Expressions explicitly designating the speech act participants, or a collectivity which typically includes the speaker/writer and others (*we all know*), present the information as 'shared' and thus the responsibility for the factive claim is potentially collective.

(2) *But* ***we all know*** *<EP, PFV, IE> our NHS is under existential threat. The predators are circling and the privatisation we've already seen is nothing in comparison to the threat posed by a Johnson-Trump trade deal.* (EPL)

(c) Subjective, Implicit, Personal (SI): With expressions which merely invoke an implicit, non-salient, speaker/conceptualizer (modals: *may*, modal adverbs: *certainly*), there is obfuscation of 'personal' responsibility for the epistemic assessment.

(3) *Conviction leavers seem to have understood that brute point, shifting their support from the Conservatives – who are reduced to single figures in the latest YouGov poll – to Nigel Farage's Brexit party, which* ***may*** *<EP, EM, SI> well grab first place next week.* (EOG)

(d) Subjective/Intersubjective, Virtual/Generalized, Opaque (IO): With expressions invoking an implicit conceptualizer which may construed as virtual or generalized (*it seems*), there is obfuscation of responsibility for the epistemic warrant and opacity with respect to whether responsibility is personal or shared (though by default the source is interpreted as the speaker/conceptualizer). These expressions present the communicated information as part of the epistemic dominion of some virtual or generalized conceptualizer, and as potentially accessible to the interlocutor or audience, so that the responsibility for the assessment is tacitly shared with others.

(4) *The reality is that the pace and scale of change overseas is phenomenal. Unfortunately, however, one measure that* ***appears*** *<EP, IIE, IO> to be accurate is the amount of debt globally.* (EOT)

In some cases, we find mystification of the role of experiencer, as in agentless passives (*It is believed*) or in impersonal or "vague" uses of pronouns (*You would think*) (cf., Kitagawa and Lehrer 1990), where the speaker/writer's voice and responsibility for the epistemic stance act is diffuse. In other cases, with impersonal factive predicates (*It is true, It is a fact*), the source of the epistemic assessment is not invoked in any way, and the information is presented as objective and potentially shared.

(5) *As for whether character is the crucial factor in "social mobility" – well* ***it's true*** *<EP, IFV, IO> that a handful of exceptional individuals do sometimes succeed in unimaginably difficult circumstances. But it's striking how many people of dreadful character and deplorable imagination remain immobile in the upper ranks of the Tory party, so clearly the reverse hypothesis doesn't hold.* (EOG)

## 2.4 Categories of Inter/Subjectivity in Effective Stance

Within effective stance, we similarly find that the two parameters of subjectivity/intersubjectivity may be applied: (i) *Degree of salience or overtness of the role of conceptualizer,* as source of the social and/or psychological force on the hearer in regard to the realization of the process, and (ii) *Responsibility* for striving for control over the realization of the process.

(a) Subjective, Explicit, Personal (SEF): Expressions designating the speaker/writer explicitly as the source of force, or "effective warrant" (Chilton, 2020), and thus responsible for the directive act.

(6) *So whether you voted leave or remain in 2016,* ***I urge*** *<EF, DIR, SEF> you to vote Labour, the party that is determined to bring the many together and take on the entrenched power of the few.* (EPL)

(b) Intersubjective, Explicit, Shared (IEF): Expressions explicitly designating a collectivity, in some cases the speech act participants, as the source of force involve shared responsibility for the directive act and the potential effect on the evolution of reality. Speakers/writers may also participate as both source and target of the realization of the proposed action.

(7) *The Lords have passed Labour's amendment and* ***we urge*** *<EF, DIR, IEF> the government to immediately bring forward a guarantee to protect the rights of all EU nationals resident here.* (EPL)

(8) *So,* ***let's*** *<EF, DIR, IEF> rise above the abuse. Let's <EF, DIR, IEF> make a positive case for our values that will cut through the bitterness and bile that is poisoning our politics.* (EPC)

The source of force may also express shared responsibility for the potentiality or the intention of carrying out the projected action.

(9) *So we have developed our Long Term Economic Plan for the Midlands. And it is already delivering. But* ***we can*** *<EF, POT, IEF>, and* ***will*** *<EF, INT, IEF>, do more.* (EPC)

(c) Subjective, Implicit, Personal (SIF): These are mostly deontic modal expressions, which invoke an implicit, non-salient, speaker/writer as the source of force, so that there is obfuscation of 'personal' responsibility for the intended control over the realization of the process.

(10) *To secure Brexit, candidates for the Tory leadership will need the hypocrisy of a Disraeli or a (peacetime) Churchill. They* ***must*** *<EF, DM, SIF> be ready to rat on their principles, turn against friends, deceive the media, and do so with populist panache.* (EOG)

(d) Subjective/Intersubjective, Virtual/Generalized, Opaque (IOF): We also find some impersonal expressions designating judgements of normativity or social advisability of the realization of actions, where there is obfuscation of the implicit source of force (virtual/generalized, by default the speaker) and of the virtual/generalized target.

(11) ***It's time*** *<EF, NRM, IOF> to stop obsessing about Oxbridge. Getting our children there consumes startling amounts of money, time and emotion— but is it really worth the trouble?* (EOT)

# 3 Methodology

## 3.1 Hypotheses

The paper posits the following hypotheses in relation to the research issues mentioned above.

(i) With regard to the degree to which there is variation in the deployment of epistemic and effective stance markers (dependent variable) in the domains of journalistic vs political discourse (independent variable), the following null hypotheses are posited:

$H_{01}$: There will be no significant variation in the use of epistemic and effective stance expressions in relation to discourse domains: no significant difference in the frequency of stance tokens and overuse in the political vs. the journalistic texts.

The null hypothesis is expressed as $H_{01}$: $\pi 1 = \pi 2$

(ii) With respect to whether there is variation in the use of epistemic or effective stance expressions (dependent variable) in relation to ideological position of political parties, Conservative vs. Labour parties (independent variable), or due to the ideological slant of the press, *The Times* vs. *The Guardian* (independent variable), the following null hypotheses are posited:

$H_{02}$: There will be no significant variation in the use of epistemic stance expressions in relation to ideological position of political parties, Conservative vs. Labour parties, or in relation to ideological slant of the press, *The Times* vs. *The Guardian*..
The null hypothesis is expressed as $H_{02}$: $\pi 1 = \pi 2$

$H_{03}$: There will be no significant variation in the use of effective stance expressions in relation to ideological position of political parties, Conservative vs. Labour parties, or in relation to ideological slant of the press, *The Times* vs. *The Guardian*.
The null hypothesis is expressed as $H_{03}$: $\pi 1 = \pi 2$

(iii) With respect to how (inter)subjectivity is realized or indexed by epistemic and effective stance markers in the domains of newspaper vs political discourse.

$H_{04}$: There will be no variation in the indexing of inter/subjectivity by epistemic stance expressions in relation to discourse domains: no significant difference in the frequency of tokens in the various categories of political vs. journalistic texts.
The null hypothesis is expressed as $H_{04}$: $\pi 1 = \pi 2$

$H_{05}$: There will be no variation in the indexing inter/subjectivity by effective stance expressions in relation to discourse domains: no significant difference in the frequency of tokens in the various categories of political vs. journalistic texts.
The null hypothesis is expressed as $H_{05}$: $\pi 1 = \pi 2$

## 3.2 Corpus

The tokens for epistemic and effective stance expressions were collected from the following two sections in our STANCEDISC corpus:

(i) STANCEDISC-English-Political: Political speeches by key politicians in the Conservative and Labour parties, 2016–2019.
- Labour party: 50,229 words (20 texts)
- Conservative party: 50,803 words (13 texts)
- Total: 101,032 words

(ii) STANCEDISC-English-Press: Opinion columns from two quality newspapers, 2016–2019.
- *The Guardian*: 51,455 words (53 texts)
- *The Times*: 51,090 words (60 texts)
- Total: 102,545 words

## 3.3 Research Objectives

The following research objectives were set in relation to the above hypotheses:

(i) Identification of expressions of Epistemic and Effective stance in our corpora.
(ii) Classification according to the framework of epistemic and effective stance categories and for inter/subjectivity described above, and annotation of tokens in the corpus.
(iii) Frequency comparison of use of stance expressions across discourse domains, and in relation to ideological positioning.

## 3.4 Epistemic and Effective Stance Categories and Resources

Epistemic stance resources were annotated and grouped into the following categories:

(a) Epistemic modality (EM): Speaker's/writer's expression of degree of certainty concerning the reality of the event designated, its actual occurrence or the likelihood of its realization (cf., 'epistemic support' for the proposition, Boye 2012). Epistemic modal auxiliaries, adverbs and predicative adjectives: *must, should, will, could, may, might, …, perhaps, maybe, possibly, probably, certainly, surely, …, possible, likely, bound to, …*
(b) Cognitive attitude (CGA): Expression of subjective beliefs and epistemic evaluations regarding the reality of the event designated ('epistemic support'). Epistemic complement-taking predicates and adverbs of cognitive attitude (cf., Cappelli 2007): *I/we think, believe, suppose, suspect, assume, imagine, expect, guess, doubt, …, I am sure/certain, I have no doubt, …, It seems to me, …, supposedly, presumably, no doubt, undoubtedly, doubtless, …*
(c) Indirect-inferential evidential expressions (IIE): Reference to sources of evidence or information, and modes of knowing (indirectly through perception-based, conception-based and communication-based inferences, cf. Marín-Arrese 2017a), whereby the speaker/writer feels entitled to make

a statement or claim (cf., Anderson 1986) (cf., 'epistemic justification' for the proposition, Boye 2012). Verbs, predicates and adverbs: *It seems, appears, looks (like), …, It is clear, evident, obvious, …, apparently, seemingly, clearly, obviously, …*

(d) Interpretation or reformulation of information (IIR): Expressions indicating inferences or deductions based on some kind of 'proof' or interpretation of information previously referred to by the speaker/writer. This category is akin to inferential evidentiality, since it involves inferential work that Bednarek (2006: 650) describes as some form of "backings for the speaker's knowledge", typically derived from contextual knowledge. Linguistic resources include lexical verbs, typically with a deictic subject element: *That suggests, that means, it indicates, it tells, it shows, …*

(e) Personal cognitive factives (PFV): Personal expressions of assignment of knowledge and factual status to the complement proposition (cf., Kiparsky & Kiparsky 1970; 'strong epistemic support', Boye 2012). Complement-taking predicates: *I/we know, realize, …, I am aware, …*

(f) Impersonal factive predicates (IFV): Impersonal expressions of assignment of knowledge and factual status to the proposition ('strong epistemic support', Boye 2012). Complement-taking predicates and adverbials: *The truth/fact/reality is, …, It is true, it is a fact, …, in truth, in fact, in reality, …*

Effective stance resources were annotated and grouped into the following categories:

(a) Deontic modality (DM): Expression of deontic necessity regarding the realization of the event. Deontic modal auxiliaries and semi-modals or quasi-modals: *must, should, ought to, cannot, can't, has/have to, need/s to, …*

(b) Directivity (DIR): Expression of directive illocutionary force regarding the realization of the event. Imperatives and hortatives, direct and indirect directive speech acts: *Do not/don't, Let us/Let's, …, Look, Remember, …, I/we urge, I (would) suggest, …*

(c) Intentionality (INT): Expression of intention, commitment or determination regarding the realization of the event designated. The speaker/writer participates as both source and target of the intent re the realization of the event. Complement-taking predicates: *I/We intend to, mean to, want to, …, I am/We are determined to, resolved to, …, I/we shall/will/'ll/won't, I am/we are going to, …*

(d) Inclination (INC): Expression of inclination or volition regarding the realization of the event designated. This category is related to intentionality

(INT), the distinction being that the target of the intent is not the speaker/writer. Personal predicates and modals of volition: *I/We want, hope, wish, would like, …*

(e) Normativity or social desirability (NRM): Expression of judgements of social desirability, instrumentality, appropriateness or fit to social norms regarding the event designated and its realization. Personal and impersonal complement-taking predicates and adverbials: *It is important, essential, crucial, vital, …, It is time to, …, It is right, best, …, quite rightly, …*

(f) Potentiality (POT): Expression of judgements of possibility or feasibility regarding the realization of the event designated. Modal auxiliaries and semi-modals of 'participant-external possibility', and 'non-prototypical generalized possibility' (cf., van der Auwera & Plungian 1998; Traugott and Dasher 2002): *I/We can, you can, cannot, …, It is possible, impossible, …*

### 3.5 Categories of Inter/Subjectivity

Inter/subjectivity in epistemic stance resources: tokens were annotated and grouped into the following categories:

(a) Subjective, Explicit, Personal (SE): *I know, I think, It seems to me, I am aware, …*
(b) Intersubjective, Explicit, Shared (IE): *We know, We are sure, We are clear, …*
(c) Subjective, Implicit, Personal (SI): *must, will, may, …, perhaps, possibly, probably, certainly, …*
(d) Subjective/Intersubjective, Virtual/Generalized, Opaque (IO): *It seems, It is possible, It is true, …, You would think, …, it is believed, …, that means, …*

Inter/subjectivity in effective stance resources: tokens were annotated and grouped into the following categories:

(a) Subjective, Explicit, Personal (SEF): *I urge you, I ask you, I want, I intend, I won't, …*
(b) Intersubjective, Explicit, Shared (IEF): *We urge, Let us, We want, We can, …*
(c) Subjective, Implicit, Personal (SIF): *must, should, ought to, …, can, cannot,* …, Imperatives, *don't, …*
(d) Subjective/Intersubjective, Virtual/Generalized, Opaque (IOF): *It is crucial, It is time to, It is right, …, It is possible, you can, you cannot, …*

## 3.6 Procedure and Statistical Analysis

### *3.6.1 Analysis and Annotation*

The analysis and annotation procedure were carried out as follows:

(i) An initial search, using Monoconc, was carried out for those expressions of epistemic and effective stance judged to be more prototypical (introspective, top-down process).
(ii) The texts were then examined closely and the tokens of effective and epistemic expressions present were tagged manually (text-driven, bottom-up process).
(iii) Annotation procedure: The texts were independently annotated by two annotators, who swapped texts and carried out a first revision. The second revision of the annotation in all the texts was carried out by a third annotator.
(iv) Quantification of data, and comparison of the quantitative results across discourse domains (Political vs. Journalistic), and ideological positioning (Labour vs. Conservative; *The Guardian* vs. *The Times*).

### *3.6.2 Statistical Analysis*

For analysis of the quantitative results, a set of statistical tests were used:

(i) SIGIL's Corpus Frequency Test Wizard:
<http://sigil.collocations.de/wizard.html>
This was used to measure the relative frequencies of tokens for each category (per thousand words), and to test whether the two subcorpora of the discourse domains (Political vs. Journalistic) were significantly different with respect to a particular category, measuring the chi-squared distribution with one degree of freedom (df = 1), in relation to the size of the sample or subcorpora
(ii) Log-likelihood (LL) and Log Ratio (LR) tests: UCREL's Log likelihood wizard <http://ucrel.lancs.ac.uk/llwizard.html>
The LL test measures the relative overuse or underuse of the observed frequency for each category in one of the corpora in comparison to the observed frequency for the same category in another corpus (O1: observed frequency in corpus 1; O2: observed frequency in corpus 2). The LR is an 'effect size' statistic, which measures the size of the difference between two corpora for one particular category.

(iii) Chi-square test (Chi^2): Social Sciences Statistics
<Chi Square Calculator - Up To 5x5, With Steps (socscistatistics.com)>
The Chi-square test provides a method for testing the degree to which there is association between the variables in a contingency table, by measuring the divergence of the observed values from the expected values under the null hypothesis of no association. If the p-value is significant, it indicates that there is some association between the variables, so that the observed values are not due to random variation.

# 4 Results and Discussion

## 4.1 Results for Epistemic and Effective Stance in Political and Journalistic Discourse

The results in Table 1 show the figures for Epistemic and Effective stance expressions in Political vs. Journalistic discourse, and the results for the Chi-square test (Chi^2), the chi-square distribution[2] re sample size and the Log likelihood test[3].

(i) $H_{01}$: Variation in the deployment of epistemic and effective stance markers (dependent variable) in the domains of journalistic vs political discourse (independent variable). The results of the chi-square test of independence (Chi^2= 302.8805; p-value < 0.00001) disprove the null hypothesis, and the alternative hypothesis is adopted: Discourse domains and genres do have a significant effect on the use and preferred stance type.

2 The value of significance was established at $p<0.05$. The following values were observed and coded by using asterisks: *** Difference significant at $p < .001$; ** significant at $p < .01$; * significant at $p < .05$.

3 A plus sign (+) indicates overuse in O1 (results in column 1) relative to O2 (results in column 2); a minus sign (-) indicates underuse in O1 relative to O2.

**Table 1.** Epistemic and Effective Stance: Political vs. Journalistic (N and ratio per thousand words) (Chi^2= 302.8805; p-value < 0.00001)

| STANCE | POLITICAL (101,032 w) | | JOURNAL. (102,545 w) | | POL. vs. JOURNAL. |
|---|---|---|---|---|---|
| EP vs. EF | N | R‰ | N | R‰ | X2 & LL |
| EPISTEMIC | 733 | **7.255** | 1007 | **9.820** | X2= 39.20822***<br>LL= -39.35/LR= -0.44 |
| EFFECTIVE | 1670 | **16.529** | 745 | **7.265** | X2 = 371.82955***<br>LL= +377.39/LR= +1.19 |
| TOTAL | **2403** | **23.785** | 1752 | **17.085** | X2 = 113.90692***<br>LL= +112.33/LR= +0.48 |

For each of the categories, the figures in Table 1 show marked differences (significant at p < .001) in the use of stance resources and clear correlations between discourse domain (political vs. journalistic) and type of stance expressions (epistemic vs. effective).

Effective stance is markedly preferred in political discourse (16.529 ‰), in comparison to journalistic discourse (7.265 ‰), indicating a significant relation between this dependent variable and the subcorpora variables (X2 = 371.82955; significant at p < .001). In contrast, the category of epistemic stance is found with a higher frequency in journalistic discourse (9.820 ‰).

The Log-likelihood test shows the relative frequencies of stance expressions, indicating either overuse or underuse of tokens for each category in relation to the discourse domain. There is a marked overuse of effective expressions (LL= + 377.39/LR= +1.19) in O1 (political) relative to O2 (journalistic), and, in contrast, there is considerable underuse of epistemic expressions (LL= -39.35/LR= -0.44) in O1 (political) relative to O2 (journalistic).

(ii) $H_{02}$: Variation in the use of epistemic stance expressions (dependent variable) in relation to ideological position of political parties, Conservative vs. Labour parties (independent variable), and in relation to the ideological slant of the press, *The Times* vs. *The Guardian* (independent variable).

Table 2 shows a significant difference in the distribution of the categories of epistemic stance in political discourse and journalistic discourse (Chi^2 = 153.1195; p-value < 0.00001).

**Table 2.** Categories of Epistemic Stance in Political and Journalistic discourse: Ideology.

| EPISTEMIC | POLITICAL (101,032 w) | | | JOURNALISTIC (102,545 w) | | |
|---|---|---|---|---|---|---|
| | Labour (50,229) | Cons. (50,803) | TOTAL | Guard. (51,455) | Times (51,090) | TOTAL |
| PFV | 66 | 50 | **116** | 11 | 12 | **23** |
| IFV | 19 | 18 | **37** | 39 | 23 | **62** |
| CGA | 39 | 87 | **126** | 39 | 44 | **83** |
| EM | 139 | 206 | **345** | 286 | 366 | **652** |
| IIE/IIR | 56 | 53 | **109** | 96 | 91 | **187** |
| TOTAL | **319** | **414** | **733** | **471** | **536** | **1007** |

There is a preference in both discourse domains for the use of markers of epistemic modality (EM), with a marked overuse of this category in journalistic discourse (LL= -91.58/LR= -0.90), as well as a substantial use of inferential evidentials or expressions of interpretation or reformulation of information (IIE/IIR) (LL= -20.57/LR= -0.77). In political discourse, apart from the preference for epistemic modality (EM), there is a marked overuse of personal cognitive factives (PFV) (LL= +69.37/LR= 2.36).

With respect to $H_{02}$ in political discourse, there is a significant dependency relation between the ideological variable of the two political parties and the variable of the distribution of the categories of epistemic stance (Chi^2 = 21.6653; p-value .000234, significant at $p < .05$). Labour politicians seem to favour epistemic modals (EM) and personal cognitive factives (PFV). Conservative politicians primarily favour epistemic modals (EM), followed by expressions of cognitive attitude (CGA).

Within journalistic discourse, the relation between the ideological variable of the two newspapers and the distribution of epistemic categories is also significant (Chi^2 = 10.2705; p-value: .036109; significant at $p < .05$). Journalists in both *The Guardian* and *The Times* share a marked preference for expressions of epistemic modality (EM), and also a preference for expressions of indirect inferential evidentiality (IIE). We can thus reject the null hypothesis, $H_{02}$, for results of the relation between epistemic categories and the ideological variables in both discourse domains, and adopt the alternative hypothesis.

(iii) $H_{03}$: Variation in the use of effective stance expressions (dependent variable) in relation to ideological position of political parties, Conservative vs. Labour parties (independent variable), and in relation to the ideological slant of the press, *The Times* vs. *The Guardian* (independent variable).

**Table 3.** Categories of Effective Stance in Political and Journalistic discourse: Ideology.

| EFFECTIVE | POLITICAL (101,032 w) | | | JOURNALISTIC (102,545 w) | | |
|---|---|---|---|---|---|---|
| | Labour (50,229) | Cons. (50,803) | TOTAL | Guard. (51,455) | Times (51,090) | TOTAL |
| DM | 214 | 256 | **470** | 134 | 156 | **290** |
| DIR | 79 | 58 | **137** | 62 | 31 | **93** |
| INT/INC | 348 | 280 | **628** | 12 | 8 | **20** |
| NRM | 34 | 40 | **74** | 27 | 41 | **68** |
| POT | 165 | 196 | **361** | 140 | 134 | **274** |
| TOTAL | **840** | **830** | **1670** | **375** | **370** | **745** |

Table 3 shows a significant difference in the distribution of the categories of effective stance in political discourse and in journalistic discourse (Chi^2 = 327.4316; p-value < 0.00001). There is overuse in political discourse in relation to journalistic discourse in all the categories, with a marked preference in the case of markers of intentionality (INT) (LL= +728.89/LR= 4.99), and with substantially higher markers of deontic modality (DM) (LL= +45.76/LR= 0.72).

With respect to $H_{03}$ in political discourse, there is significant variation in relation to the ideological position of political parties (Chi^2 = 17.4245; p-value: .001598, significant at p < .05.). The preferred effective stance strategy in the discourse of Labour is the use of expressions of intentionality or commitment (INT), and, to a lesser extent, deontic modality (DM) and potentiality (POT). The same categories are preferred by the Conservatives, with higher figures for deontic modality (DM), and for expressions of potentiality and capacity (POT).

In journalistic discourse, there is significant variation in relation to the ideological slant of the newspapers, albeit to a lesser degree (Chi^2 = 15.7832; p-value: .003324, significant at p < .05.). Both newspapers favour the categories of deontic modality (DM) and potentiality (POT), in an inverse relation. Some differences in frequencies are also found between *The Guardian* and *The Times* for the other categories: journalists in *The Guardian* seem to favour the use of expressions of directivity (DIR), whereas *The Times* seems to rely on expressions of normativity and social advisability (NRM) to a greater extent.

## 4.2 Results for Inter/Subjectivity in Political and Journalistic Discourse

Tables 4 and 5 present results for (inter)subjectivity, realized or indexed by epistemic and effective stance markers, respectively in the domains of political vs. journalistic discourse.

(iv) $H_{04}$: Variation in the indexing of inter/subjectivity by epistemic stance expressions (dependent variable) in relation to discourse domains (independent variable).

There is a significant relation between discourse domains and the expression of inter/subjectivity in epistemic stance expressions (Chi^2 = 163.5819; p-value: < 0.00001). The results disprove the null hypothesis, and thus the alternative hypothesis must be adopted.

Within political discourse, the preferred categories are subjective implicit (SI: 3.454 ‰), followed by both intersubjective opaque (IO) and subjective explicit (SE) stance expressions. Journalistic discourse also shows a marked preference for the subjective implicit (SI: 6.495 ‰) category, and for intersubjective opaque (IO) expressions. The inter/subjectivity clines for epistemic stance in these discourse domains are parallel and would be the following:

INTER/SUBJECTIVITY CLINE: EPISTEMIC
Political: SI (*may, might, perhaps, …*) > IO (*it seems, it is possible, …*) > SE (*I think, know, it seems to me, …*) > IE (*we all know, …*)
Journalistic: SI (*may, might, perhaps,…*) > IO (*it seems, it is possible, …*) > SE (*I think, I know, it seems to me, …*) > IE (*we all know, …*)

The chi-square results for the differences in the frequency of tokens between political and journalistic discourse are highly significant for all the various categories, and more specifically for the preferred category in both domains, subjective implicit (SI: X2 = 94.21420, significant at p < .001), and also for intersubjective explicit expressions (IE: X2 = 43.20644, significant at p < .001).

**Table 4.** Epistemic Stance and Inter/Subjectivity: Political vs. Journalistic (N and ratio per thousand words)

| **EPISTEMIC** | **POLITICAL (101,032 w)** | | **JOURNALISTIC (102,545 w)** | | **POL vs. JOURNAL** |
|---|---|---|---|---|---|
| **SUB/INT** | **N** | **R‰** | **N** | **R‰** | **X2& LL** |
| **SE** | 149 | **1.475** | 65 | **0.634** | X2 = 33.47417***<br>LL= +35.14 |
| **SI** | 349 | **3.454** | 666 | **6.495** | X2 = 94.21420***<br>LL= -96.02 |
| **IE** | 81 | **0.802** | 16 | **0.156** | X2 = 43.20644***<br>LL= +48.57 |
| **IO** | 154 | **1.524** | 260 | **2.535** | X2 = 25.14509***<br>LL= -25.89 |
| **TOTAL** | **733** | **7.255** | **1007** | **9.820** | X2= 39.20822***<br>LL= -39.35 |

The log-likelihood (LL) measures of comparison for overuse or underuse across the discourse domains shows that in political discourse there is substantial overuse of intersubjective explicit (IE = +48.57) expressions, and to a lesser extent also of subjective explicit (SE = +41.38) expressions. As expected, politicians choose to make themselves visible in their role of speakers/conceptualizers, and thus form part of the object of conceptualization (cf., Langacker 1991) to a greater extent than journalists. In contrast, in journalistic discourse there is a marked overuse of subjective implicit (SI = -96.02) and also of intersubjective opaque (IO = -25.89) expressions, merely invoking an implicit conceptualizer which may construed as virtual or generalized. In their role as speakers/conceptualizers, journalists opt for implicitness and obfuscation of responsibility for stance with regard to the communicated proposition.

(v) $H_{05}$: Variation in the indexing of inter/subjectivity by effective stance expressions (dependent variable) in relation to discourse domains (independent variable). There is a significant relation between discourse domains and the expression of inter/subjectivity in effective stance expressions (Chi^2 = 245.0022; p-value: < 0.00001). The results disprove the null hypothesis, and thus the alternative hypothesis must be adopted.

**Table 5.** Effective Stance and Inter/Subjectivity: Political vs. Journalistic (N and ratio per thousand words)

| **EFFECTIVE** | **POLITICAL (101,032 w)** | | **JOURNALISTIC (102,545 w)** | | **POL vs. JOURNAL** |
|---|---|---|---|---|---|
| **SUB/INT** | **N** | **R‰** | **N** | **R‰** | **LL & X2** |
| **SEF** | 105 | **1.039** | 21 | **0.205** | X2 = 55.95301*** LL= +62.39 |
| **SIF** | 796 | **7.879** | 585 | **5.705** | X2 = 35.37303*** LL= +35.58 |
| **IEF** | 526 | **5.206** | 42 | **0.409** | X2 = 419.12331*** LL= +495.05 |
| **IOF** | 243 | **2.405** | 97 | **0.946** | X2 = 64.12295*** LL= +66.97 |
| **TOTAL** | **1670** | **16.529** | **745** | **7.265** | X2 = 371.82955*** LL= +377.39 |

In political discourse, there is a very marked preference for subjective implicit (SIF: 7.879 ‰) and intersubjective explicit (IEF: 5.206 ‰) expressions. In journalistic discourse, the preferred category is subjective implicit (SIF: 5.705 ‰), and to a lesser degree intersubjective opaque (IOF: 0.946 ‰). The inter/subjectivity clines for effective stance in these discourse domains would thus be the following:

INTER/SUBJECTIVITY CLINE: EFFECTIVE STANCE
Political: SIF (*must, should, …*) > IEF (*We urge, Let us, …*) > IOF (*It is crucial, It is time to, …*) > SEF (*I urge, I ask you, …*)
Journalistic: SIF (*must, should, …*) > IOF (*It is crucial, It is time to, …*) > IEF (*We urge, Let us, …*) > SEF (*I urge, I ask you, …*)

The total figures for effective stance expressions are significantly higher in political discourse (X2 = 371.82955, significant at $p < .001$). The differences in the frequency of tokens between political and journalistic discourse are very significant for the following categories: intersubjective explicit (IEF: X2 = 419.12331, significant at $p < .001$), intersubjective opaque (IOF: X2 = 64.12295, significant at $p < .001$), and subjective explicit (SEF: X2 = 55.95301, significant at $p < .001$).

The log-likelihood (LL) measures of comparison for overuse or underuse across the discourse domains shows a pronounced overuse in political discourse in all the categories, with the highest overuse in intersubjective explicit (IEF= +495.05) expressions. In the expression of effective stance, again politicians choose to make themselves visible in their role of speakers/conceptualizers to a greater extent than journalists. They also favour the expression of intersubjective responsibility in their calls for action.

## 4.3 Discussion: Comparison of Results in Political and Journalistic Discourse

The results of the corpus study serve to characterize the configuration of the deployment of epistemic and effective stance expressions and the expression of inter/subjectivity in political discourse and in journalistic discourse. In the case of epistemic stance, which crucially involves the speaker/writer's striving for control of conceptions of reality (cf., Langacker 2009, 2013), the dimensions of inter/subjectivity, *Degree of salience or overtness of the role of conceptualizer* and *Responsibility* for the communicated proposition, reveal the ways in which the speaker/writer as conceptualizer (C) subscribes to the proposition. They may do so explicitly or implicitly and take personal or shared responsibility for their beliefs or knowledge, or for the evidence that supports or justifies their claims.

The presence of epistemic stance expressions is comparatively low in political discourse, when compared to the presence of effective stance. Epistemic stance is found mostly in the categories of epistemic modality (EM), cognitive attitude predicates (CGA), with smaller figures for personal factive verbs (PFV) and inferential evidentials or expressions of interpretation or reformulation of information (IIE/IIR). In terms of inter/subjectivity, we find a preference for implicit personal responsibility (SI: *may, perhaps, …*) and for intersubjective opaque expressions (IO: *it seems, that suggests*) in the expression of epistemic support for their claims, and for explicit personal responsibility (SE: *I think, I know, …*) in their expression of beliefs or knowledge.

In the case of effective stance, which involves speaker/writer's striving for control of relations at the level of reality (Langacker 2009, 2013), those dimensions of inter/subjectivity similarly reveal the ways in which the speaker/writer as conceptualizer (C) relates to the realization of the process. They may explicitly or implicitly exert social and/or psychological force on the hearer/reader, and take either personal or shared responsibility in striving for the realization of their action plans and goals.

As mentioned above, political discourse (see Figure 3) is characterised by an overwhelming use of effective stance, in particular expressions of intentionality (INT) and deontic modality (DM), and also potentiality (POT). As regards inter/subjectivity, politicians show a tendency either to use expressions of personal implicit responsibility (SIF: *must, should, …,* Imperatives) for their acts of exerting social and/or psychological force on the hearer, or to make explicit their roles as speakers/conceptualizers and to take shared responsibility (IEF: *we are determined, we will, we can, …*) in their expression of commitments and promises, as well as in the expression of potentiality. There is also a relatively substantial use of expressions involving a virtual/generalized conceptualizer (IOF: *It is crucial, It is time to, …*), where the responsibility is shared and opaque. Explicit expressions of personal responsibility (SEF: *I urge, …*) are rare in politicians.

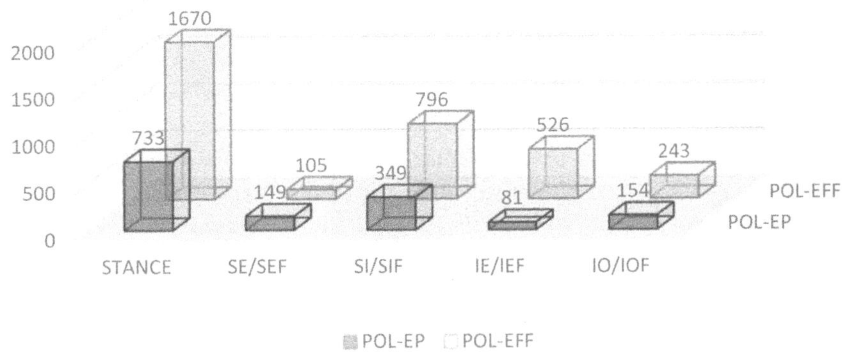


**Figure 3.** Epistemic and Effective Stance in Political Discourse: Inter/Subjectivity

There is thus a contrast in the degree to which politicians wish to make themselves visible and the extent to which they choose to take personal responsibility for their discourse acts. When those acts involve the epistemic status of the communicated information and serve to legitimise their beliefs, or the knowledge or evidence that support or justify their claims, politicians prefer to take personal responsibility, whether explicitly (SE) or implicitly (SI).

However, when those acts involve an effective force, exerting social and/or psychological force, whose aim is to lead to the realization of some action plan or goal and affect relations at the level of reality (cf., Langacker 2009), politicians prefer to keep a low profile by using expressions of implicit personal responsibility (SIF) for the expression of force, or else choose markers involving explicit shared responsibility (IEF), which partly obfuscate their responsibility.

Journalistic discourse (see Figure 4) is characterised by a greater balance between epistemic and effective stance acts. Within epistemic stance, there is a marked preference for epistemic modality (EM: *may, perhaps, …*) and to a lesser extent for inferential evidential expressions (IIE: *it seems, it appears, …*). Journalists favour expressions of implicit personal subjectivity (SI), or the evocation of a virtual/generalized conceptualizer (IO), in the expression of their assessments of the epistemic status of the proposition.

As regards effective stance, the preferred categories are deontic modality (DM: *must, should, …* Imperatives) and potentiality (POT: *we can, you can't, …*), and to a lesser extent directivity (DIR: *let us, …*). There is again a preference for implicitness (SIF) in the personal expression of force, and also a preference for intersubjective expressions (IEF).

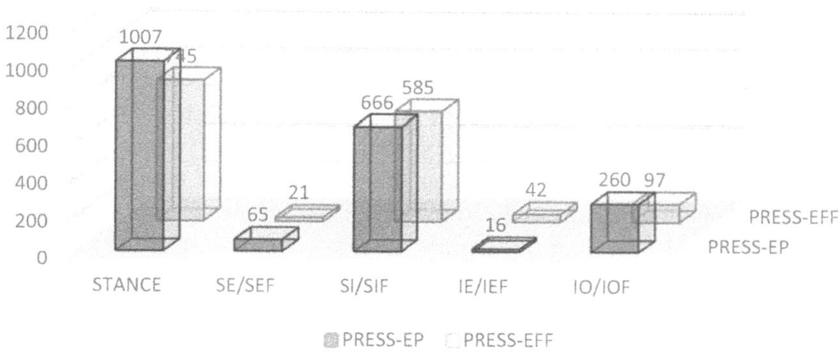


**Figure 4.** Epistemic and Effective Stance in Journalistic Discourse: Inter/Subjectivity

In both epistemic and effective stance, personal implicit subjectivity (SI/SIF) is the preferred choice, which is congruent with the social role of journalists as actors with a responsibility to provide visibility to any form of social shortcoming or injustice, and at the same time downplay their personal position and stake in the social issues they denounce. As White (2012: 57–58) has observed, in the discourse of the press there is a "regime of strategic impersonalisation by which the journalist's evaluative role is backgrounded".

## 5 Conclusions

This paper has focused on two macro categories of stance, the epistemic and the effective, and on the joint deployment of these stance markers, which serve the strategic purposes of legitimation of knowledge of events and of action plans and goals. The paper has also explored the ways in which these stance expressions index speaker/writer's inter/subjectivity. The paper has presented a corpus-based study on the use of stance expressions in political discourse and media discourse, and more specifically, in the genres of political speeches and opinion columns in quality newspapers.

Results indicate significant differences between discourse domains and genres. Stance strategies in political discourse show an extremely high presence of effective expressions, which points to striving for control of potential effects on the evolution of reality. There are also very high figures for both intersubjectivity, which involves shared responsibility, and for implicit subjectivity, whereby there is obfuscation of personal responsibility. In exerting social or psychological force over their audience, politicians tend to downtone their visibility by recourse to those two strategies.

In contrast, there is a balance between epistemic and effective expressions in the discourse of the press. In opinion columns, journalists are equally concerned with striving for control of readers' subscribing to their communicated propositions, and for control of the potential effect on the evolution of reality, through the social or psychological force they exert over their readers. Similarly, we find very high figures for subjective implicit expressions, and for expressions of intersubjectivity. There is thus a very low degree of salience of the journalist as conceptualizer, as the epistemic or effective source, and obfuscation of responsibility of the authorial voice.

As we have discussed above, it would seem that there are different motivations in the preference for the two strategies of downtoning of visibility and backgrounding of responsibility in politicians and in journalists. We may surmise that in the case of politicians obfuscation of personal responsibility in striving for epistemic and effective control in discourse is primarily motivated by their concern about accountability regarding truthfulness and their political commitments, whereas journalists are motivated by their purportedly neutral and impersonal stance in their conception and assessment of reality, and their concern for social desirability and normativity in relations at the level of reality.

## References

Anderson, L. B. (1986). 'Evidentials, paths of change, and mental maps: Typologically regular asymmetries'. In W. Chafe and J. Nichols (eds.), *Evidentiality: The linguistic coding of epistemology*, pp. 273–312. Norwood, NJ: Ablex.

Bednarek, M. (2006). Epistemological positioning and evidentiality in English news discourse: A text-driven approach. *Text & Talk*, 26 (6), 35–60.

Benveniste, É. (1966[1958]). De la subjectivité dans le langage. *Problems de Linguistique Générale*, pp. 258–266. Paris: Gallimard. (Orig. publ. in *Journal de psychologie* 55: 267f., 1958).

Biber, D. and Finegan, E. (1989). Styles of stance in English: Lexical and grammatical marking of evidentiality and affect. *Text, 1*, 93–124.

Boye, K. (2012). *Epistemic Meaning: A Crosslinguistic and Functional-Cognitive Study*. Berlin: Mouton de Gruyter.

Cappelli, G. (2007). "*I reckon I know how Leonardo da Vinci must have felt* …" *Epistemicity, evidentiality and English verbs of cognitive attitude*. Pari: Pari Publishing.

Chilton, P. (2004). *Analysing Political Discourse*. London: Routledge.

Chilton, P. (2020). 'Stance, Truth and Lies in a Post-Truth Discourse Environment'. Plenary paper at the *International Conference on Stance, Inter/Subjectivity and Identity in Discourse* (STANCEDISC'20), 9–11 September 2020, Madrid, Universidad Complutense de Madrid.

DuBois, J.W. (2007). 'The stance triangle'. In Englebretson, R. (ed.) *Stancetaking in Discourse*, pp. 139–182. Amsterdam: John Benjamins.

Englebretson, R. (2007). 'Introduction'. In R. Englebretson (ed.), *Stancetaking in Discourse*, pp. 1–26. Amsterdam: John Benjamins.

Finegan, E. (1995) 'Subjectivity and subjectivisation: an introduction'. In D. Stein and S. Wright (eds.) *Subjectivity and Subjectivisation: Linguistic Perspectives*, pp. 1–15. Cambridge: Cambridge University Press.

Hart, C. (2011). 'Legitimising assertions and the logico-rhetorical module: Evidence and epistemic vigilance in media discourse on immigration'. *Discourse Studies, 13 (6)*, 751–769.

Jaffe, A. (ed.) (2009). *Stance: Sociolinguistic Perspectives*. Oxford: Oxford University Press.

Kärkkäinen, E., and DuBois, J.W. (eds.) (2012). *Stance, Affect, and Intersubjectivity in Interaction: Sequential and Dialogic Perspectives*. Special Issue. *Text & Talk, 32(4)*.

Kiparsky, P. and Kiparsky, C. (1970). 'Fact'. In M. Bierwisch and K.E. Heidolph (eds.) *Progress in Linguistics*, pp. 143–73.The Hague: Mouton.

Kitagawa, C. and Lehrer, A. (1990). 'Impersonal uses of personal pronouns'. *Journal of Pragmatics*, 14, 739–759.

Langacker, R.W. (1991). *Foundations of Cognitive Grammar*, vol. II. Stanford, CA: Stanford University Press.

Langacker, R.W. (2008). *Cognitive Grammar. A Basic Introduction*. Oxford: Oxford University Press.

Langacker, R.W. (2009). *Investigations in Cognitive Grammar*. Berlin: Mouton de Gruyter.

Langacker, R.W. (2013). 'Modals: Striving for control'. In J.I. Marín-Arrese, M. Carretero, J. Arús, and J. van der Auwera (eds.) *English Modality: Core, Periphery and Evidentiality*, pp. 3–55. Berlin: Mouton de Gruyter.

Marín-Arrese, J.I. (2011). 'Effective vs. epistemic stance and subjectivity in political discourse: Legitimising strategies and mystification of responsibility'. In C. Hart (ed.) *Critical Discourse Studies in Context and Cognition*, pp. 193–223. Amsterdam: John Benjamins.

Marín-Arrese, J.I. (2013) 'Stancetaking and Inter/Subjectivity in the Iraq Inquiry: Blair vs. Brown'. In J.I. Marín-Arrese, M. Carretero, J. Arús and J. van der Auwera (eds.) *English Modality: Core, Periphery and Evidentiality*, pp. 411–445.Berlin: Mouton de Gruyter.

Marín-Arrese, J.I. (2015). 'Epistemic legitimisation and inter/subjectivity in the discourse of parliamentary and public inquiries: A contrastive case study'. *Critical Discourse Studies, 12 (3)*, 261–278.

Marín-Arrese, J.I. (2017a). 'Multifunctionality of evidential expressions in discourse domains and genres: Evidence from cross-linguistic case studies'. In J.I. Marín-Arrese, G. Hassler and M. Carretero (eds.), *Evidentiality revisited: Cognitive Grammar, functional and discourse-pragmatic perspectives*, pp. 195–223. Amsterdam/Philadelphia: Benjamins.

Marín-Arrese, J.I. (2017b). 'Stancetaking and inter/subjectivity in journalistic discourse: The Engagement system revisited'. In R. Breeze and I. Olza (eds.) *Evaluation in Media Discourse: European perspectives*, pp. 21–48. Bern: Peter Lang.

Marín-Arrese, J.I. (2021). 'Stance, Emotion and Persuasion: Terrorism and the Press'. *Journal of Pragmatics*, 177, 135–148.

Nuyts, J. (2012). 'Notions of (inter)subjectivity'. *English Text Construction, 5 (1)*, 53–76.

Sanders, J. (1999) 'Degree of subjectivity in epistemic modals and perspective representation'. In L.G. De Stadler and C. Eyrich (eds.) *Issues in Cognitive Linguistics*, pp. 471–489. Berlin: Mouton de Gruyter.

Simaki, V., Paradis, C., and Kerren, A. (2019). 'A two-step procedure to identify lexical elements of stance constructions in discourse from political blogs'. *Corpora, 14(3)*, 379–405.

Traugott, E.C. and Dasher, R.B. (2002). *Regularity in Semantic Change*. Cambridge: Cambridge University Press.

van der Auwera, J. and Plungian, V.A. (1998). 'Modality's semantic map'. *Linguistic Typology*, 2, 79–124.

White, Peter R.R. (2012). 'Exploring the axiological workings of 'reporter voice' news stories-Attribution and attitudinal positioning'. *Discourse, Context & Media*, 1, 57–67.

Natalia Mora-López & Sergio Ferrer-Navas

# An English-Spanish Contrastive Analysis of Effective Stance in Newspaper and Political Discourse

**Abstract:** This chapter shows some similarities and differences in the effective stance realizations found in newspaper and political discourse from an English-Spanish contrastive perspective. Additionally, it also looks into the extent to which these linguistic realizations may reflect discourse strategies specific of these discourse domains and genres. The corpus collected, which adds up to about 400,000 words, consists of political speeches of politicians from the Conservative party and Partido Popular (PP), on the one hand, and the Labour party and Partido Socialista Obrero Español (PSOE), on the other hand; and opinion columns from newspapers of both centre-left (*The Guardian* and *El País*) and centre-right (*The Times* and *ABC*). The corpus was annotated manually and classified into several categories inside Effective Stance, namely Deonticity, Directivity, Intentionality, Normativity and Potentiality (cf. Marín-Arrese 2011), which cover the different ways in which speakers position themselves with respect to the realization of events and try to determine or influence the course of reality itself (Langacker 2013). The analysis shows a marked overuse of effective stance expressions in political discourse in comparison to the discourse of the press. In addition, an overuse of the categories of Deonticity and Potentiality is identified in English, particularly in press discourse.

**Keywords:** *editorials, effectivity, English, ideological positioning, newspaper discourse, opinion articles, political discourse, political speeches, Spanish, stance.*

## 1 Introduction

This chapter explores the similarities and differences in the use of effective stance markers across genres, particularly in newspaper and political discourses, both in English and Spanish. Effective stance refers to how speakers or writers position themselves respect to the events and try to influence the course of reality (Langacker 2009). The use of such a positioning and intention is especially relevant in these two very influential communication means: mass media and politics. The study of Effectivity in opinion columns from newspapers and in political speeches may provide interesting results on how information and events are shaped to increase their potential compelling and persuasive effect and eventually have an influence on readers and listeners.

The purpose of this chapter is to take a deep look into the use of effective stance in English and Spanish political and newspaper discourse in order to point out the differences and similarities between that use across languages and genres. Thus, it will answer the following research questions.

- RQ1: Is there any difference in the frequency of the use of effective stance expressions in relation to discourse domain and genre: press vs. political texts?
- RQ2: Is there any difference in the frequency of use of effective stance expressions in relation to ideological slant in the press: *The Guardian* vs. *The Times* and *El País* vs. *ABC* (centre-left and centre-right, respectively in each language)?
- RQ3: Is there any difference in the frequency of use of effective stance expressions in relation to ideological position of political parties: The Conservative vs. The Labour parties, and PP (Spanish conservative party) vs. PSOE (Spanish labour party)?
- RQ4: Is there any difference in the frequency of use of effective stance expressions in relation to language: English vs. Spanish?

Some variation is expected to be found across discourse domains and ideologies because of their particularities associated with their linguistic nature and individual rhetorical styles. In addition, it is expected that the analysis of the collected corpora both in English and Spanish for this study will point out some differences in relation to the predominant effective stance markers in each language. However, it seems to be difficult to anticipate which categories might reveal a significant difference in their frequency of occurrence across the corpora.

The remainder of the chapter is organised as follows: first, a theoretical framework including Stance and Effectivity is given. Then, the corpus collected and the analysis procedure are explained. Finally, the results of the analysis and some discussion are provided, followed by some final conclusions.

## 2 Stance and Effectivity

During the last decades, there has been a growing interest in the notion of stance, which has been studied from different subdisciplines within the field of linguistics (Englebretson 2007:1). Defining this term is a complex endeavour because of its heterogeneous and multifaceted nature. As a matter of fact, a wide number of authors have further explained the phenomenon of stance using different but related terminology, such as affect (Ochs 1989), evaluation (Hunston and Thompson 2000), hedging (Hyland 1998), stancetaking (Englebretson 2007; DuBois 2007) or engagement (Martin and White 2005).

Biber and Finegan have defined *stance* as "the lexical and grammatical expression of attitudes, feelings, judgments, or commitment concerning the propositional content of a message" (1989: 92), and distinguish between three major semantic categories such as the epistemic domain, "speaker comments on the status of information in a proposition"; the attitudinal domain, the expression of "personal attitudes or feelings"; and the style of speaking domain, where the speaker "comments on the communication itself" (Biber et al. 1999: 972–5). However, Hunston and Thompson (2000: 5) prefer to use the term *evaluation* to refer to the "expression of the speaker or writer's attitude or stance towards, viewpoint on, or feelings about the entities or propositions that he or she is talking about" because of its flexibility in syntactic and morphological terms, and find an equivalence between a more restrictive use of the term *evaluation* in the literature and Biber's attitudinal stance. They point out that the speaker or writer's attitude "may relate to certainty, or obligation or desirability or any of a number of others sets of values".

On the other hand, Langacker (2013: 9–10) understands linguistic interaction as "a means of striving for control", which serves its users as an instrument to construct their mental world and to influence upon social reality. This author establishes a distinction between epistemic control, which relates to the conception of the world; and effective control, which attempts to influence the current state of affairs. Based on that distinction, Marín-Arrese (2011: 193) distinguishes between the macro categories of effective stance, related to the speaker's attempt to influence reality "through stancetaking acts"; and epistemic stance, which encodes the speaker's knowledge concerning the realization of a particular event.

The author notes that "Effective stance pertains to speaker/writer's evaluative positioning towards the realization of the event, in the expression of their attitudes and assessments regarding the designated event" (Marín-Arrese 2011: 201). Such positioning is conveyed through lexico-grammatical markers expressing norms or obligations and the speaker's intention to follow a particular course of action. She has put forward five sub-categories expressing effective stance. The persuasive function of Effectivity may be achieved by claiming the "deontic necessity of the realization of the event", Deonticity; by using direct or indirect expressions of the conventional illocutionary directive force, Directives; by expressing the speaker's "volition, intention, inclination, or determination regarding the realization of the event", Intentionality; by expressing the "judgements of social desirability" or appropriateness to social norms in relation to the realization of the event, Normativity; and by referring to participant-external possibility for the realization of the event designated, Potentiality (Marín-Arrese 2011, 2021).

Among the different definitions and conceptions related to this phenomenon, the present paper has approached the analysis of stance in newspaper and political discourse based on the epistemic and effective categories as described by Marín-Arrese (*ibid.*). Although they are closely interrelated, this chapter focuses on the realizations of effective stance.

# 3 Corpus and Methodology

## 3.1 Corpus Description

This paper is part of the work carried out in the funded research project "Stance and subjectivity in discourse: towards an integrated model of the analysis of epistemicity, effectivity, evaluation and intersubjectivity from a critical discourse perspective" (PGC2018-095798-B-I00), whose aim is to design and develop an integrated framework for stance and subjectivity through the compilation and analysis of a set of subcorpora for English, Spanish and Lithuanian from a variety of discourse domains, such as scientific, political, journalistic, advertising and fora. They were annotated and analysed following the framework and the annotation schema developed for each of the specific linguistic items studied. This chapter will focus on the analysis of Effectivity in the English and Spanish political and press subcorpora.

The corpus collected for this research is made up of eight collections of political speeches and opinion articles, each of them containing about 50,000 words. In total, the number of words amounts to about 400,000 words, whose distribution is shown in Table 1.

**Table 1.** Subcorpora collected and number of words.

| **Domain** | **English** | | **Spanish** | |
|---|---|---|---|---|
| **Political** | Labour Party (EPL): 50,229 words | Conservative Party (EPC): 50,756 words | Labour Party (SPL): 51,408 words | Conservative Party (SPC): 50,634 words |
| **Press** | *The Guardian* (EOG): 50,062 words | *The Times* (EOT): 50,607 words | *El País (SOP)*: 50,573 words | *ABC* (SOA): 50,227 words |

The four political corpora consist of a set of political speeches delivered by key representatives of the Labour (EPL) and Conservative (EPC) parties in the case of the English political corpus, and the PSOE (SPL), a left-wing party, and Partido Popular (SPC), a right-wing party, in the Spanish political corpus. Regarding the press corpora, a collection of recent opinion columns has been gathered from four quality newspapers with different ideology, that is, *The Guardian* (EOG) vs. *The Times* (EOT) on the one hand, and *El País* (SOP) vs. *ABC* (SOA) on the other.

### 3.2 Methodology

Taking as a point of departure Marín-Arrese's (2011, 2021) taxonomy on Effective stance, the different categories and tagsets were profusely discussed in workshops which aim at identifying the core expressions of Effective stance in our corpora. The data provided in this chapter was manually analysed and annotated. Two annotators worked independently on two different corpora to be later exchanged by those annotators for a second revision, which were finally revised by a third one. After having completed the process of annotation, the data was quantified in order to carry out the statistical analysis focusing on the log-likelihood and frequency of the results across discourse domains, Press vs. Political; and languages, English vs. Spanish.

## 4 Results and Discussion

### 4.1 General Usage and Realisations of Effectivity

This section describes the most common realisations used in the corpus analysed to convey effective meanings (EF). In general, the strategies found for English and Spanish were very similar, since they almost always included direct equivalents between the terms in those two languages. A specific exemplification for the realisations of each category in English and Spanish is presented below.

Deonticity (DM) was used to refer to important figures, institutions and citizens' duties and obligations. It was found to be based on the use of modal verbs. Some of the most common expressions to show Deonticity were *need to*, *should*, *have to* and *must* in the case of English, and *deber* [must], *haber de/que* [must], *tener que* [have to], *poder* [can], *necesitar* [need] for Spanish. Examples 1–8 illustrate these items in the English and Spanish, political and press corpora:

(1) *To transform our country and tackle injustice, inequality and the climate crisis we* ***need to*** *<EF, DM> unite the overwhelming majority of people and take on the privileged and powerful.* (EPL)
(2) *We all know that we* ***have to*** *<EF, DM> do more to restrict diesel use, to protect urban centres from pollution…* (EPC)

(3) ***Hemos de*** *<EF, DM> recargar el PSOE con la energía de las mujeres, con la fuerza de la paridad.* (SPL)
[We **must** <EF, DM> recharge PSOE with women's energy, with equity's strength.][1]

(4) *Votar es gratis, sí, pero puede salir carísimo y por eso* ***tenemos que*** *<EF, DM> pensar el voto con la cabeza.* (SPC)
[Voting is free, yes, but it may turn out very expensive and that's why we **have to** <EF, DM> think with our heads]

(5) *But it's not just Brexit, for we* ***must*** *<EF, DM> judge a prime minister by her own promises.* (EOG)

(6) *There are times when hatred* ***needs to*** *<EF, DM> be confronted but a permanent sense of victimhood is corrosive for any group.* (EOT)

(7) *La UE de hoy, como proyecto político en grado de madurez,* ***debe*** *<EF, DM> responder a las preguntas del para quién, para qué y con qué instrumentos se construye.* (SOP)
[The current EU, as a political and mature project, **must** <EF, DM> answer the questions for whom, for what and with which instruments it is built]

(8) *Las instituciones de la sociedad civil van a* ***tener que*** *<EF, DM> crear foros de pensamiento multidisciplinar que desentrañen la complejidad de cada uno de los temas y propongan vías de solución.* (SOA)
[Institutions in civil society will have to create multidisciplinary thought fora that unravel the complicity of each of the topics and propose ways to solve them]

Directivity (DIR), on the other hand, was used to urge the listeners to support the candidates and their policies by taking action and voting. Interestingly, a relevant number of Directivity realizations were concerned with policies that the candidate encouraged the electorate to put into place even though the electorate was not in the position of making such decisions. The directive illocutionary force was typically expressed through the use of hortatives, imperative forms both in English and Spanish, and verbs such as *urge* and *ask* followed by a *to*-infinitive clause or a *that*-clause in the case of English, and *pedir* [*ask*] and *sugerir* [suggest] in Spanish (Examples 9–12).

(9) *I* ***urge*** *<EF, DIR> you to vote Labour the party that is determined to bring the many together and take on the entrenched power of the few.* (EPL)

(10) *Together,* ***let's*** *<EF, DIR> build a better Britain.* (EPC)

(11) ***Combatamos*** *<EF, DIR> el miedo construyendo un futuro de esperanza.* (SPL)
[**Let's fight** <EF, DIR> fear by building a hopeful future]

(12) *Os* ***pido*** *<EF, DIR> que seamos leales entre nosotros…* (SPC)
[I **ask** <EF, DIR> you to be loyal among us]

Regarding Intentionality (INT), it commonly occurred in political speeches in order to explain the candidate's stand on a plethora of policies and express their

1 All translations are our own unless otherwise noted.

commitment to follow some future course of action if elected. This category is realized by means of verbs such as *will*, *want to*, *going to*, *intend*, *be determined*, along with similar noun phrases (Examples 13 and 14). In Spanish, however, that category was mainly realized through the corresponding inflectional forms to express future tense and the verbal periphrasis *ir a* [*going to*], as illustrated in Examples 15 and 16.

(13) ***Our priority is*** *<EF, INT> to get the best deal for people's jobs, living standards and the economy.* (EPL)

(14) *We are* ***going to*** *<EF, INT> crack global warming, with British clean technology and British green finance – in which we lead the world.* (EPC)

(15) ***Trabajaremos*** *<EF, INT> por recuperar la pluralidad de los medios de comunicación públicos.* (SPL)
[**We will work** <EF, INT> to recover plurality in public communication media]

(16) ***Vamos a*** *<EF, INT> poner freno al populismo bolivariano instalado también aquí en España.* (SPC)
[**We are going to** <EF, INT> put a stop to Bolivarian populism established here in Spain too]

Likewise, the political corpora provide examples in which the speaker claims the desirability and appropriateness of a particular position according to social norms. These examples illustrate the category of Normativity (NRM), which is typically expressed through phrases such as *it is essential*, *it's wrong*, *it's time*, *it's worth*, and *it's my duty* in the English corpus (Examples 17 and 18), and phrases like, *nuestro deber es* [*it's our duty*], *es el momento de* [*it's time to*], *es vital* [*it's vital*], and *es importante* [*it's important*] in the Spanish one (Examples 19 and 20).

(17) *We are the largest socialist party in Europe.* ***It is our duty*** *<EF, NRM> to lead.* (EPL)

(18) ***It is time*** *<EF, NRM> to stop treating the referendum result as though it were a plague of boils or a murrain on our cattle or an inexplicable aberration by 17.4 m people.* (EPC)

(19) ***Nuestro deber es*** *<EF, NRM> liderar un proyecto de democracia radical, basado en la ejemplaridad, ante el descrédito político e institucional del Gobierno.* (SPL)
[**It's our duty** <EF, NRM> to lead a Project or radical democracy, based on exemplarity, before the Government's political and institutional discredit]

(20) ***Es el momento de*** *<EF, NRM> rechazar lo que vaya contra la igualdad de los españoles y ante los que buscan mercadear con sus derechos.* (SPC)
[**It's time to** <EF, NRM> reject what goes against Spaniards' equality and before those who look for trading with their rights]

Finally, Potentiality (POT) was identified to express the participant-external possibility for the realization of events which, in the case of political speeches, mainly focuses on the changes that the implementation of the candidate's policies would imply for the electorate. The most common expressions to express

Potentiality in English are *can*, *could*, *be able to* and *would* (Examples 21 and 22), and the different inflectional forms of the verb *poder* [*can*] and the expression *ser capaz de* [*be able to*] in Spanish (Examples 23 and 24).

(21) *We have five weeks to win the General Election so we* ***can*** *<EF, POT> fundamentally transform Britain for the many not the few.* (EPL)

(22) *With control of our money, we* ***can*** *<EF, POT> spend more on our NHS.* (EPC)

(23) *El Partido Popular no cuenta con mayoría absoluta, por lo que con diálogo,* ***podremos*** *<EF, POT> revertir juntos ya muchas de las leyes retrógradas aprobadas por la derecha.* (SPL)
[The Partido Popular does not count with absolute majority, so through dialogue, **we will be able to** <EF, POT> revert together now many old-fashioned laws passed by the conservatives]

(24) ***Podemos*** *<EF, POT> tener también la confianza de que lo haremos de nuevo.* (SPC)
[**We can** <EF, POT> also have the confidence that we will do it again]

## 4.2 Press Discourse

This section discusses the results obtained from the newspaper subcorpora. The corpus collected to analyse effectivity in press discourse included opinion columns from four newspapers: *The Guardian* (EOG), *The Times* (EOT), *El País* (SOP) and *ABC* (SOA). The results for the occurrences of effectivity found in the first two, that is, in the English corpus, can be seen in Table 2.

The most frequent effectivity marker is Deonticity (i.e. 'someone must/needs to do something') in both English newspapers, with 123 and 148 occurrences (38.2 % and 48.1 % of the total number of occurrences in their respective subcorpora) in *The Guardian* and *The Times*, followed by Potentiality (i.e. 'I/we can do something'), also in both sources, with 110 and 86 occurrences (34.2 % and 27.9 %). However, despite them appearing more frequently in both newspapers, their frequency is not similar in the liberal and conservative texts: Deonticity is more preferred in conservative discourse (with a representation of 2.9245 ‰ regarding the total number of words in its subcorpus) than in the liberal one (2.4570 ‰), while Potentiality appears more frequently in the liberal (2.1973 ‰) than in the conservative texts (1.6994 ‰).

**Table 2.** Effectivity results in English press discourse.

| EFFECTIVITY: PRESS | *The Guardian* 50,062 words | | | *The Times* 50,067 words | | | TOTAL |
|---|---|---|---|---|---|---|---|
| ENGLISH | N | % | R/‰ | N | % | R/‰ | N |
| Deonticity | 123 | 38.2 | 2.4570 | 148 | 48.1 | 2.9245 | 271 |
| Directivity | 56 | 17.4 | 1.1186 | 28 | 9.1 | 0.5533 | 84 |
| Intentionality | 20 | 6.2 | 0.3995 | 14 | 4.5 | 0.2766 | 34 |
| Normativity | 13 | 4.0 | 0.2597 | 32 | 10.4 | 0.6323 | 45 |
| Potentiality | 110 | 34.2 | 2.1973 | 86 | 27.9 | 1.6994 | 196 |
| TOTAL | 322 | 100 | 6.4320 | 308 | 100 | 6.0861 | 630 |

There is some discrepancy in the least used marker, namely Intentionality (i.e., 'I/we want to do something') in *The Times*, with only 14 occurrences (4.5 %), but Normativity (i.e. 'it's essential/wrong to do something') in *The Guardian*, with 13 (4.0 %). However, if all occurrences in both sources are taken into account, Intentionality is still the least used resource in general, with only a 5.3 % of the total number of effectivity occurrences in these texts versus a 7.1 % of total Normativity cases.

The fact that both sources make a higher use of Deonticity and Potentiality markers indicates that, regarding the use of effective stance, English authors in this genre, and conservative authors in particular, have an interest in pointing out what must be done and who must do it, as well as what they alone or together the community (conveyed by the use of the first-person plural) can do, specially liberal authors. However, it is interesting to note that the difference in the use of Directivity markers (17.4 % in *The Guardian* and 9.1 % in *The Times*) and Normativity markers (4.0 % in *The Guardian* and 10.4 % in *The Times*) indicates that liberal authors have a higher tendency to give direct orders to readers while conservative authors prefer to appeal to social norms when calling to action.

With respect to Spanish, the results for the occurrences in *El País* and *ABC* can be found in Table 3. The most frequent effectivity marker is Deonticity in both newspapers (185 cases or 76.4 % and 141cases or 68.8 %, respectively), followed by Normativity (28 cases or 11.6 % and 29 cases or 14.1 %), also in both. Although both newspapers share the most common categories, there is a difference in the frequency of appearance of Deonticity. This has some additional occurrences in *El País*, the liberal newspaper, in contrast to what was found in the English corpus. However, Normativity, which presented a higher frequency in the English conservative newspaper, shows no difference in use between the Spanish ones.

**Table 3.** Effectivity results in Spanish press discourse.

| **EFFECTIVITY: PRESS** | ***El País* 50,573 words** | | | ***ABC* 50,227 words** | | | **TOTAL** |
|---|---|---|---|---|---|---|---|
| **SPANISH** | **N** | % | **R/‰** | **N** | % | **R/‰** | **N** |
| **Deonticity** | 185 | 76.4 | 3.6833 | 141 | 68.8 | 2.7880 | 326 |
| **Directivity** | 13 | 5.4 | 0.2588 | 15 | 7.3 | 0.2966 | 28 |
| **Intentionality** | 6 | 2.5 | 0.1195 | 10 | 4.9 | 0.1977 | 16 |
| **Normativity** | 28 | 11.6 | 0.5575 | 29 | 14.1 | 0.5734 | 57 |
| **Potentiality** | 10 | 4.1 | 0.1991 | 10 | 4.9 | 0.1977 | 20 |
| **TOTAL** | 242 | 100 | 4.8181 | 205 | 100 | 4.0535 | 447 |

The least used effectivity marker is Intentionality in *El País*, with only 6 occurrences (2.5 %), while not only Intentionality but also Potentiality (4.9 %) with 10 occurrences each in *ABC*. However, Intentionality is still the least used resource in general, as it was in the English corpus. The difference between the Spanish liberal and the conservative newspapers regarding this category is lower than it was in the English texts.

These results seem to indicate that Spanish authors in this genre, and liberal authors in particular, when conveying effectivity, mostly turn to mentions about the obligation and necessity of doing something, either focusing on the action itself or the agents in charge of carrying it out. Less frequently, but also commonly in both newspapers, authors make use of references to social expectations or norms about what is to be done. In general, the two Spanish newspapers showed more similarities than the two English ones in the distribution of effectivity categories.

A comparison between the English and Spanish corpora is shown in Table 4. This table does not include a division in terms of ideological slant, but it is only based on language.

**Table 4.** Effectivity results in English and Spanish press discourse.

| **EFFECTIVITY: PRESS** | **English 100,669 words** | | **Spanish 100,800 words** | | **EN vs. ES** |
|---|---|---|---|---|---|
| **EN & ES** | **N** | **R/‰** | **N** | **R/‰** | **Log L. & Freq Comp** |
| **Deonticity** | 271 | 2.6920 | 326 | 3.2341 | -5.00<br>X2 = 5.067<br>p < .0244 |
| **Directivity** | 84 | 0.8344 | 28 | 0.2778 | -29.37<br>X2 = 28.000<br>p < .0001 |
| **Intentionality** | 34 | 0.3377 | 16 | 0.1587 | -6.65<br>X2 = 6.480<br>p < .0109 |
| **Normativity** | 45 | 0.4470 | 57 | 0.5655 | -1.40<br>X2 = 1.412<br>p < .2348 |
| **Potentiality** | 196 | 1.9470 | 20 | 0.1984 | -166.40<br>X2 = 143.407<br>p < .0001 |
| **TOTAL** | 630 | 6.2581 | 447 | 4.4345 | -31.48<br>X2 = 31,095<br>p < .0001 |

While Spanish press shows a more frequent use of Deonticity and Normativity elements than English, Directivity, Intentionality and Potentiality are more commonly found in English instead. Therefore, English authors have a higher preference for direct commands on the one hand, and for the author's expression of what they want and can do, on the other, than Spanish authors. These focus their use of effective markers, whose frequency is also higher than in the English texts, on expressing obligation and necessity as well as social desirability or requirement about the events.

It is particularly remarkable that Normativity is not only more frequent in Spanish than in English, but it is also the second most common Effectivity category used. Conversely, Potentiality is not only far more frequent in English than in Spanish, but it is the second most used effective resource in that language. Therefore, English Effectivity elements would be used following this preference: Deonticity > Potentiality > Directivity > Normativity > Intentionality; while the Spanish Effectivity elements would be used in this order: Deonticity >

Normativity > Directivity > Potentiality > Intentionality. As can be seen, there is a swap in the positions of Normativity and Potentiality.

As has been seen, English and Spanish press corpora have some similarities but also some differences. For example, they both share a high use of Deonticity markers, this being the most used category in both of them, although this use is higher in Spanish (72.93 %) than in English (43.01 %). Therefore, all authors, and Spanish authors in particular, focus on introducing explicit mentions to people's obligations. English and Spanish authors also share a common disregard for the use of Intentionality markers, which points to a possible disinterest in talking about themselves but focusing on society, politicians and other agents and entities referred to in their articles.

Finally, it must also be noted that the English corpus shows a much higher use of effective markers, in general (630 English tokens vs. 205 Spanish tokens).

## 4.3 Political Discourse

This section will discuss the results of the analysis on Effective stance in the political corpora, which consist of collections of political speeches delivered by the Labour Party (EPL) and the Conservative Party (EPC) in the English corpora, and the Partido Socialista Obrero Español (SPL) and the Partido Popular (SPC) in the Spanish ones.

**Table 5.** Effectivity results in English political discourse.

| EFFECTIVITY: POLITICAL | Labour Party 50,229 words | | | Conservative Party 50,756 words | | | TOTAL |
|---|---|---|---|---|---|---|---|
| ENGLISH | N | % | R/‰ | N | % | R/‰ | N |
| Deonticity | 216 | 29.4 | 4.3003 | 252 | 34.8 | 4.9649 | 468 |
| Directivity | 61 | 8.3 | 1.2144 | 58 | 8.0 | 1.1427 | 119 |
| Intentionality | 351 | 47.8 | 6.9880 | 228 | 31.4 | 4.4921 | 579 |
| Normativity | 29 | 4.0 | 0.5774 | 38 | 5.2 | 0.7487 | 67 |
| Potentiality | 77 | 10.5 | 1.5330 | 149 | 20.6 | 2.9356 | 226 |
| TOTAL | 734 | 100 | 14.6131 | 725 | 100 | 14.2840 | 1,459 |

The most striking result to emerge from the data is the higher occurrence of the category of Intentionality in the case of the Labour Party with 351 tokens (47.8 %), as opposed to the Conservative party with 228 tokens (31.4 %), as observed in Table 5. It is also remarkable that the number of examples of Potentiality used by the Conservative Party, 149 tokens (20.1 %), almost doubles the 77 tokens (10.5 %) identified under the same category in the case of the Labour Party. On the other hand, the least frequent effectivity marker in English political corpora is Normativity, for which 29 tokens (3.6 %) and 38 tokens (5.2 %) have been identified respectively.

From an ideological viewpoint, there are no significant differences in occurrence when it comes to the categories of Deonticity, Directivity and Normativity. However, while the Labour Party seems to prefer the use of the Effective category of Intentionality (47.8 %), the Conservative Party relies more frequently on Deonticity (34.8 %).

With regard to the Spanish political corpora, the most common effective markers are Deonticity with 255 (37.7 %) in the PSOE and 281 (43.0 %) in the PP, followed by the category of Intentionality with 276 (40.8 %) and 232 (35.4 %) tokens respectively. As shown in Table 6, the predominant category occurring in PSOE is Intentionality whereas the PP prefers the use of Deonticity.

**Table 6.** Effectivity results in Spanish political discourse.

| **EFFECTIVITY: POLITICAL** | **PSOE 51,408 words** | | | **PP 50,634 words** | | | TOTAL |
|---|---|---|---|---|---|---|---|
| **SPANISH** | **N** | % | **R/‰** | **N** | % | **R/‰** | **N** |
| **Deonticity** | 255 | 37.7 | 4.9603 | 281 | 43.0 | 5.5496 | 536 |
| **Directivity** | 89 | 13.1 | 1.7312 | 82 | 12.5 | 1.6195 | 171 |
| **Intentionality** | 276 | 40.8 | 5.3688 | 232 | 35.4 | 4.5819 | 508 |
| **Normativity** | 32 | 4.7 | 0.6225 | 24 | 3.7 | 0.4740 | 56 |
| **Potentiality** | 25 | 3.7 | 0.4863 | 35 | 5.4 | 0.691 | 60 |
| TOTAL | 677 | 100 | 13.1692 | 654 | 100 | 12.9162 | 1331 |

However, Normativity and Potentiality seem to be the residual categories used in both corpora. While PSOE uses more frequently Normativity with 32 tokens (4.7 %), as opposed to Potentiality with 25 tokens (3.7 %), there are 24 tokens (3.7 %) and 35 tokens (5.4 %) under the categories of Normativity and Potentiality respectively in the case of PP. Therefore, both categories only represent the 8.4 % in the case of PSOE, and 9.3 % in the case of PP of the total number of effective markers in each corpus.

Ideologically speaking, it seems to be remarkable the clear preference for Intentionality in both languages in the left-wing parties under analysis in our data, while the conservative parties rely more frequently on deontic stance markers. This data may reveal a major focus during their speeches on the description of the future policies that left-wing candidates intend to implement if they are elected, in contrast with a greater emphasis on the need for the implementation of the policies that have been proposed by right-wing candidates during their political speeches. Further research needs to be carried out in the future to confirm this possible trend.

Regarding the differences between the occurrence of the five effective categories across English and Spanish, the data shows that, while Intentionality is the preferred category in English political corpora, Deonticity is the predominant category in Spanish, immediately followed by Intentionality.

**Table 7.** Effectivity results in English and Spanish political discourse

| **EFFECTIVITY: PRESS** | **English 100,669 words** | | **Spanish 100,800 words** | | **EN vs. ES** |
|---|---|---|---|---|---|
| **EN & ES** | **N** | **R/‰** | **N** | **R/‰** | **Log L. & Freq Comp** |
| Deonticity | 468 | 4.6344 | 536 | 5.2527 | -3.93<br>X2 = 4.606<br>p < . 0319 |
| **Directivity** | 119 | 1.1784 | 171 | 1.6758 | -8.84<br>X2 = 9.324<br>p < .0023 |
| **Intentionality** | 579 | 5.7335 | 508 | 4.9783 | -5.41<br>X2 = 4.638<br>p < .0313 |
| **Normativity** | 67 | 0.6635 | 56 | 0.5488 | -1.10<br>*X2 = 0.984<br>Not significant |
| **Potentiality** | 226 | 2.2380 | 60 | 0.0588 | -104.39<br>X2 = 96.350<br>p < .0001 |
| **TOTAL** | 1459 | 14.4477 | 1331 | 13.0436 | -7.28<br>X2 = 5.872<br>p < .0154 |

On the other hand, Normativity seems to be the least common category used in both languages, with 67 (4.6 %) and 56 tokens (4.2 %) respectively. The use of this category in both languages is similar, as proved by the chi square data (-1.10) shown in Table 7, which reveals that the difference is not significant statistically speaking. However, what seems to be significant from a statistical perspective is the difference in the frequency of occurrence of Potentiality (-104.39), which shows an overuse of this category in the English political corpora.

English Effectivity elements would be used in the following order: Intentionality > Deonticity > Potentiality > Directivity > Normativity. However, Spanish Effectivity elements would be used following this preference: Deonticity > Intentionality > Directivity > Potentiality > Normativity.

All in all, the main categories used by politician in both languages are Intentionality and Deonticity, which represent the 75 % of the whole number of Effectivity markers identified in the corpora. However, there are significant differences in the occurrence of Potentiality, which is more often used in English; and Normativity, whose frequency is significantly higher in Spanish, and may be associated with a more direct rhetorical style to encourage the audience to think and act in a particular manner.

**Table 8.** Effectivity results in English and Spanish political discourse.

| EFFECTIVITY | POLITICAL | | PRESS | | PO vs. PR | |
|---|---|---|---|---|---|---|
| LANGUAGE<br>Words | EN<br>100,985 | ES<br>102,042 | EN<br>100,669 | ES<br>100,800 | Log L. & Freq Comp | |
| | N<br>R/‰ | N<br>R/‰ | N<br>R/‰ | N<br>R/‰ | EN | ES |
| **Deonticity** | 468<br>4.6344 | 536<br>5.2527 | 271<br>2.6920 | 326<br>3.2341 | -52.54<br>X2 = 52.516<br>p < .0001 | -49.14<br>X2 = 51.160<br>p < .0001 |
| **Directivity** | 119<br>1.1784 | 171<br>1.6758 | 84<br>0.8344 | 28<br>0.2778 | -5.96<br>X2 = 6.034<br>p < .01 | -112.45<br>X2 = 102.759<br>p < .0001 |
| **Intentionality** | 579<br>5.7335 | 508<br>4.9783 | 34<br>0.3377 | 16<br>0.1587 | -585.36<br>X2 = 484.543<br>p < .0001 | -577.26<br>X2 = 461.954<br>p < .0001 |
| **Normativity** | 67<br>0.6635 | 56<br>0.5488 | 45<br>0.4470 | 57<br>0.5655 | -4.28<br>X2 = 4.321<br>p < . 0376 | -0.03<br>*X2 = 0.009<br>Not significant |
| **Potentiality** | 226<br>2.2380 | 60<br>0.5880 | 196<br>1.9470 | 20<br>0.1984 | -2.04<br>X2 = 2.133<br>p < . 0.1442 | -20.44<br>X2 = 20.000<br>p < .0001 |
| TOTAL | 1,459<br>14.4477 | 1,331<br>13,0436 | 630<br>6.2581 | 447<br>4.4345 | -335.62<br>X2 = 328.981<br>p < .0001 | -448.93<br>X2 = 439.514<br>p < .0001 |

## 4.4 Political and Press Discourse: Comparison

After having discussed the results for the conservative and liberal speeches and opinion columns in English and Spanish independently, Table 8 presents the summary of the results for the two languages and text types, without specific distinction of the ideological slant. The distribution of Effectivity markers can be found in Figure 1.

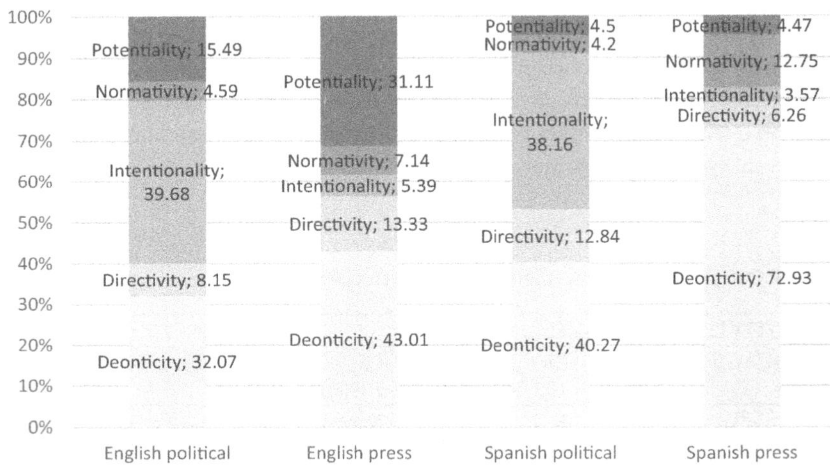


**Figure 1.** Distribution of Effectivity markers in English and Spanish, political and press discourse.

Spanish authors show a higher use of Deonticity markers in both political and press discourse than their English counterparts. The opposite is found in Intentionality and Potentiality, whose use is higher by English authors in both corpora.

Differences are found between languages and genres in Directivity and Normativity. Directivity is more frequent in Spanish political discourse, and in the English press. Therefore, Spanish politicians and English newspapers tend to be more directive. Conversely, Normativity elements appear more frequently in English political discourse than in English press discourse, while, in contrast, they are more frequent in Spanish press discourse than in Spanish political discourse.

Again, adding up all the examples, it can be observed that English discourse shows a higher preference for effectivity than Spanish discourse in both domains.

## 5 Conclusions

This chapter has presented a description of how Effectivity markers are used in English and Spanish political and press discourse, either spoken or written, by liberal and conservative authors. After the examination of the results from a corpus of about 400,000 words (200,000 for each language, half of them for each discourse type and, in turn, half of them for each ideological slant), some interesting conclusions can be drawn that answer the research questions asked at the beginning of the chapter.

Regarding the existence of any differences in the frequency of use of effective stance expressions in press vs. political texts, it can be said that there is a marked overuse of effective stance expressions in political discourse in total figures, and in Deonticity and Intentionality in particular. There is also a significant overuse in political discourse of Directivity and Potentiality, which is even more marked in Spanish. Therefore, discourse domains and genres do have a significant effect on the use of effective stance expressions.

Regarding the existence of any differences in the frequency of use of effective stance expressions in relation to ideological slant in press discourse, it can be concluded that there is an overuse of effective stance expressions in Normativity in *The Times*, and in Directivity in *The Guardian*, in the case of English, and that there is an overuse of effective stance expressions in Deonticity in *El País* and Intentionality in *ABC*, in the case of Spanish.

Regarding the existence of any differences in the frequency of use of effective stance expressions in conservative and liberal parties, an overuse of effective stance expressions was found in Potentiality in the English political conservative corpus, and in Intentionality in the liberal one. In the case of Spanish, there is an overuse of effective stance expressions in Intentionality in the texts from the Spanish liberal party.

Regarding the existence of any differences in the frequency of use of effective stance expressions between English and Spanish, an overuse of Deonticity markers was found in Spanish, while Intentionality and Potentiality were more frequently used in English. Inside political discourse, the difference in the total number of effective stance expressions in both languages is less significant than in press discourse. However, there is an overuse of Potentiality elements in English. In press discourse, there is an overuse of effective stance expressions in English, which is based mainly on Deonticity and Potentiality elements.

Finally, it can be concluded that the analysis of the authors' positioning regarding the realization of events in order to influence how or whether events take place has thrown interesting results that help understand this subtle linguistic mechanism in these types of texts.

## References

Biber, D., and Finegan, E. (1989). 'Styles of Stance in English: Lexical and Grammatical Marking of Evidentiality and Affect', *Text*, 9 (1) (Special Issue on the Pragmatics of Affect), 93–124.

Biber, D., Johansson. S, Leech, G., Conrad, S., and Finegan, E. (1999). *Longman grammar of spoken and written English.* London: Pearson Education Limited.

DuBois, J. W. (2007). 'The Stance Triangle'. In R. Englebretson (ed.), *Stancetaking in Discourse: Subjectivity, Evaluation, Interaction*, pp. 139–182. Amsterdam/ Philadelphia: John Benjamins.

Englebretson, R. (2007). 'Introduction'. In R. Englebretson (ed.), *Stancetaking in Discourse: Subjectivity, Evaluation, Interaction*, pp. 1–26. Amsterdam/ Philadelphia: John Benjamins.

Hunston, S., and Thompson, G. (eds) (2000). *Evaluation in Text: Authorial Stance and the Construction of Discourse.* Oxford: Oxford University Press.

Hyland, K. (1998). *Hedging in Scientific Research Articles.* Amsterdam: John Benjamins.

Langacker, R. W. (2009). *Investigations in Cognitive Grammar*. Berlin: Mouton de Gruyter.

Langacker, R. W. (2013). 'Modals: Striving for Control'. In J. I. Marín-Arrese, M. Carretero, J. Arús, and J. van der Auwera (eds), *English Modality: Core, Periphery and Evidentiality* pp. 3–55. Berlin: Mouton de Gruyter.

Marín-Arrese, J. I. (2011). 'Effective vs. Epistemic Stance and Subjectivity in Political Discourse: Legitimising Strategies and Mystification of Responsibility'. In C. Hart (ed.), *Critical Discourse Studies in Context and Cognition*, pp. 193–224. Amsterdam: Benjamins.

Marín-Arrese, J. I. (2021). 'Stance, Emotion and Persuasion: Terrorism and the Press, *Journal of Pragmatics*, 177, 135–148.

Martin, J. R., and White, P. (2005). *The Language of Evaluation. Appraisal in English.* New York: Palgrave.

Ochs, E. (ed.) (1989). 'The Pragmatics of Affect', *Text*, Special Issue, 9.

Elena Domínguez Romero & Victoria Martín De La Rosa

# Epistemic Stance in Opinion Newspaper Articles and Political Speeches: An English/Spanish Contrastive Approach[1]

**Abstract:** This paper draws from previous research on stance (Marín-Arrese 2015, 2017a, 2017b, 2021) to explore epistemic stance in opinion newspaper articles and political speeches across discourse domains and genres, languages (Spanish and English) and ideology. The focus will be on analysing the similarities and differences in the distribution and use of specific epistemic stance realisations on a 405,964-word corpus comprising opinion newspaper articles (*The Times* and *The Guardian*, on the British side, and *ABC* and *El País*, on the Spanish side) and political speeches differing in language and ideological orientation (Conservative and Labour in Britain versus conservative PP and liberal PSOE in Spain). Results shed light on the motivations leading journalists' and politicians' choices regarding epistemic stance realisations to come across as reflective individuals holding personal beliefs/attitudes or negotiating meaning.

**Keywords:** *stance, epistemicity, opinion newspaper discourse, political discourse, ideology*

## 1 Introduction

This paper focuses on one subtype of stance, namely the epistemic, which includes those linguistic devices used to provide justificatory support for the proposition (Marín-Arrese 2011a, 2011b, 2021; Boye 2012). Epistemic stance comprises the two categories that constitute the general domain of epistemicity: epistemic modality and evidentiality (Chafe and Nichols 1986; Willett 1988; Aikhenvald 2004; Wiemer and Stathi 2010; Boye 2012; Marín-Arrese 2013, 2021; among others).

We aim to determine the similarities and differences in the distribution and use of the epistemic stance realisations found in opinion newspaper articles and political discourse from an English-Spanish contrastive perspective. Additionally, the study looks into the extent to which these linguistic realisations may reflect

1 This research has received support from the project Stance and Subjectivity in Discourse: Towards an Integrated Framework for the Analysis of Epistemicity, Effectivity, Evaluation and Inter/Subjectivity from a Critical Discourse Perspective (STANCEDISC), Ref. PGC2018-095798-B-I00, funded by the Ministerio de Ciencia, Innovación y Universidades (Spanish Ministry of Science, Innovation and Universities).

similarities and differences in the expression of ideology in these discourse domains and genres. Pursuing this line, one of our aims will be to determine how the parameter of ideology is linguistically encoded in opinion newspaper articles and political speeches. Second, we will see whether ideology is invoked differently in English and Spanish as a culture-specific issue. Quantitative differences are expected to be found:

(1) Across languages: English will rely on epistemic expressions more frequently than Spanish (Marín-Arrese 2015)
(2) Across discourse domains: Regarding the patterns of distribution of epistemic markers across discourse domains, it is expected that:
    a) epistemicity, mainly epistemic modals, will be more frequent in newspaper than in political discourse because the meaning - with an absent audience - needs to be negotiated. This brings on stage the importance of the interactional dimension for newspaper discourse
    b) epistemic markers of cognitive attitude and personal factive markers, which reveal a reflective individual trying to build some 'bonding' or common ground (Simon-Vandenbergen and Aijmer 2007) with the audience, will be more frequent in political discourse, where a more attitudinal dimension is pushed forward
(3) Across ideologies, conservative papers and parties will be more inclined to use epistemic markers, although, in line with the first hypothesis, this will mainly apply to English.

The paper sets forth an English-Spanish contrastive analysis of epistemic stance carried out on a 405,964-word corpus comprising two socio-cultural varieties of discourse, namely opinion newspaper articles and political speeches, differing in language and ideological orientation.

Following this introduction, the theoretical framework guiding the analysis, the data and the method are described. Then, the examples of epistemic stance expressions retrieved from the corpus are classified and analysed. Finally, overall results leading to conclusions and lines for further research are discussed.

## 2 Theoretical Framework

As we explain in our book chapter on epistemic and effective stance in political discourse about the European refugee crisis (Martín et al. 2020), there is a tradition in discourse studies in which, as Martin and White (2005: 92) note, "all utterances are seen in some way as stanced or attitudinal". The multifaceted nature of stance has been associated with evaluation, subjectivity, and positioning in interaction (Biber and Finegan 1989; Ochs and Schieffelin 1989; Hunston and Thompson, 2000; Du Bois, 2007; Englebretson 2007; Marín-Arrese 2013; among others). Within the various perspectives on stance, Englebretson (2007: 6) observes that they have five crucial conceptual principles in common:

(1) stance-taking occurs on three (often overlapping) levels – stance is a physical action, stance is personal attitude/belief/evaluation, and stance is social morality
(2) stance is public, perceivable, interpretable and available for inspection by others [...]
(3) stance is interactional – it is collaboratively constructed among participants, and concerning other stances [...]
(4) stance is indexical (cf. Haviland 1989; Silverstein 1976), evoking aspects of the broader sociocultural framework or physical contexts in which it occurs
(5) stance is consequential – i.e., taking a stand leads to real consequences for the persons or institutions involved [...]

In this chapter, we approach language use as a clear manifestation of the double nature of human beings, both as reflective individuals and as social beings at the same time (Kecskes, 2019). On this basis, we approach stance as a form of social action, involving the expression of the speaker/writer's personal beliefs concerning the status of the event and their commitment concerning the communicated proposition. Specifically, we draw on a model for the analysis of stance taking in discourse, which posits two macro-categories of stance, the epistemic and the effective (Marín-Arrese 2009, 2011a, 2021). These categories draw on Langacker's (2009; 2013) distinction between the epistemic and the effective level in the language's grammar. These categories reflect the systematic opposition between striving for control of conceptions of reality and striving for control of relations at the level of reality. Marín-Arrese (2013: 414) defines these categories of stance in the following terms:

> **Epistemic stance** pertains to the positioning of the speaker/writer with respect to knowledge concerning the event and their commitment to the validity of the information. These are stance acts assessing the reality of the event designated or the likelihood of its realization, and/or specifying the sources whereby the speaker/writer feels entitled to make an assertion, which may involve an estimation of their evidentiary reliability.

Epistemic stance strategies comprise the use of epistemic modals, evidentials, and expressions of cognitive attitude and factivity to convey speaker/writer's beliefs, knowledge or evidence that support the truth of a proposition or the validity of its content (Kiparsky and Kiparsky 1970; Capelli 2007; Marín-Arrese 2009, 2011a, 2011b; Boye 2012). It is divided into three subcategories: epistemic modality, which concerns the estimation of the chances for (or against) the truth of the proposition (Nuyts 2001; Carretero and Zamorano-Mansilla 2013); factivity, which pertains to the factual status of a proposition; and evidentiality, which concerns the kind or source of evidence that language users (claim to) have for or against the proposition (Willett 1988; Aikhenvald 2004; Wiemer and Stathi 2010; Boye 2012; Marín-Arrese 2013; among others). The three categories are divided into subcategories based on subjectivity and degree of commitment in epistemic modality and factuality, and on the mode of access to evidence in the case of evidentiality (cf. Marín-Arrese 2011a, 2011b).

> **Effective stance** pertains to the positioning of the speaker/writer with respect to the realization of events, to the ways in which the speaker/writer carries out a stance act aimed at determining or influencing the course of reality itself. (Marín-Arrese 2013: 414)

Effective stance strategies comprise the "speaker/writer's expression of norms, obligations and compelling or enabling circumstances, and of his/her inclination, decision or intention to carry out an event" (Marín-Arrese 2013: 411).

Epistemic and effective stance strategies may be exploited by journalists and politicians as legitimisation strategies for purposes of persuasion or manipulation, with the specific aim of persuading hearers/readers of the benefits of particular policies and action plans. This framework offers a dialogistic construction of social practice where the speaker/writer positions himself/herself and others in the running discourse to achieve social acceptance and social success (Bakhtin 1981). In this light, communication recognises our interconnectedness, which implies a movement from ego to others since discourse is based on consensus (Habermas 1981).

## 3 Corpus description and method

This chapter sets forth an English-Spanish contrastive analysis of epistemic stance on a 405,964-word corpus comprising two socio-cultural varieties of discourse, namely opinion newspaper articles and political speeches. The first 201,899-word subcorpus consists of opinion articles extracted from four quality papers, two British, *The Guardian* and *The Times* (100,699 words), and two Spanish, *El País* and *ABC*, (101,230 words), differing in language and ideological orientation. The second 204,065-word subcorpus comprises English and Spanish political speeches with different ideological orientations mainly extracted from the homepages of four major parties: two British, Conservative and Labour (100,985 words), and two Spanish, conservative PP and progressive PSOE (103,080 words).

The paper draws on a model for the analysis of stance-taking in discourse based on the epistemic macro-category of stance (Marín-Arrese 2011b). The analysis will be carried out through an annotation system and its corresponding tag set, which divides expressions of epistemic stance into epistemic modality, evidentiality and factivity. Epistemic modality refers to the speaker's/writer's "[...] evaluation of the chances that a certain hypothetical state of affairs under consideration (or some aspect of it) will occur, is occurring or has occurred in a possible world" (Nuyts 2001: 21). This includes degrees of speaker certainty: high certainty or necessity (must, in all likelihood...), medium certainty or probability (will, probably...), and low certainty or possibility (may, could...). (Marín-Arrese 2011b: 272; Van der Auwera and Plungian 1998). Evidentiality refers to the speaker's/writer's source of information, which may result from a perceptual act (I saw, we have seen...), or a mental process (I believe, I think...). Personal factivity (I know, we know...) and impersonal factivity (the truth is, the fact is...) constructions account for the proposition's truth.

# 4 Results

## 4.1 Epistemic Stance. Newspaper Discourse

### *4.1.1 EP-IIE (Indirect Inferential Evidential)*

Inferential evidential expressions indicate personal indirect access to information through inferences triggered based on perceptual or conceptual evidence, or inferences based on knowledge acquired through social communication sources, such as reports, documents, or other speakers (Marín-Arrese 2021).

In the English subcorpus, there are no significant differences in the use of IIE markers between the English conservative *Times* and the progressive *Guardian*, with 67 and 60 tokens retrieved from each of the subcorpora, respectively. In both cases, the markers *seem, appear* and *clearly* stand out as the most frequently used. Examples (1) and (2) show the writer's high justificatory support towards the proposition. In the first example, the writer seems to be relying on common knowledge shared with the audience. In the second, the writer's alignment with the proposition is high because of the use of the adverb *clearly*. In the third example, however, the use of seem points to a lack of external evidence turning the inferential reasoning into an impression, which results in the writer's low commitment to the message conveyed. In this vein, example (4) relies on a report-based inference.

(1) *Still, one of the reasons I think about this a lot is because, **clearly**, resilience is needed to make it through an education system that encourages children to see their worth in terms of grades achieved* […]. <GUARDIAN>
(2) *He's **clearly** unable to persuade Meghan that there is much enjoyment in being a royal.* <TIMES>
(3) *Quite a few **seem** to think both of those things, which I'm not sure makes much sense.* <TIMES>
(4) *There are various studies that **appear** to back up these insights, too.* <GUARDIAN>

In the Spanish subcorpus, the results obtained for the progressive newspaper *El País* are very similar to the results obtained for the English newspapers (60 tokens retrieved from *El País* subcorpus). However, the use of these markers is notably less frequent in the case of the conservative Spanish newspaper *ABC* (40 tokens retrieved from the *ABC* subcorpus). Among the most frequent markers used to express indirect inferential evidentiality in Spanish, *parece* (it seems), *parece ser* (it seems to be), *al parecer* (apparently), *evidentemente* (clearly, obviously) and *está claro* (it is clear) are to be highlighted.

In examples (5) and (6), the journalists construct their inferential reasoning based on some pieces of cognitive evidence. The justificatory support is low in both cases, although the degree of commitment seems to increase slightly in example (6), using the determinant *todo* (everything). In example (7), the writer's inferential reasoning is introduced through the choice of the adverb *evidentemente* (evidently), which signals that the judgement offered is evident to the readership. In (8), although the inferential reasoning is based on the choice of the same adverb *evidentemente* (evidently), the inferential process is more openly established as the source of the cognitive evidence is not made explicit. In (9), it is interesting to see that a cognitive-based inferential reasoning is in place although the original meaning of *claro* (clear) points to a perceptual meaning 'allowing light to pass through'. This marker, which builds on the sense of sight as an element to be trusted, enables the writer's alignment with the proposition.

(5) ***Parece** poco probable que así lo haga, pues ha centrado su campaña en situar al Partido - el aparato - como el obstáculo a superar* <EL PAÍS>
[It seems unlikely that he will do so […]]
(6) *Lejos de mi ánimo ser agorero, pero todo **parece** indicar que lo que se nos viene encima es de una gravedad descomunal.* <ABC>
[[…], but everything seems to indicate that what is coming […]]
(7) *Errar en el diagnóstico, **evidentemente**, conlleva errar en las recetas.* <EL PAÍS>
[Erring in the diagnosis, obviously, entails erring in the recipes]

(8) ***Evidentemente****, no podemos plantear que todas ellas podrían pasar a estar sometidas a un arresto domiciliario telemático.* <ABC>
[Obviously, we cannot state that all of them could be under a telematic house arrest, […]]

(9) ***Está claro*** *que una parte importante de la ciudadanía no acudirá a votar.* <EL PAÍS>
[It is clear that an important part of the citizenship won't vote]

### 4.1.2 EP- IRE (Indirect Reportative Evidential)

There are very few IRE markers in English in both conservative *Times* and progressive *Guardian* (4 and 6 tokens, respectively). Among the most frequent ones, 'is reported', 'allegedly', 'hears', 'suggests', and 'apparently' can be highlighted.

Example (10) uses 'is reported' to mark some distancing from the original source, which means that the writer adopts a neutral role towards the information given. This means that the writer's degree of alignment or disalignment to the propositional content is not established (Marín-Arrese, Carretero and Usonienė 2022: 128). However, the use of 'allegedly' in example (11) "signals the speaker's/writer's lack of commitment" (Celle 2009). The expression 'one now hears' is used to indicate evidence from the report and conveys the idea that the information is known to the readership in example (12). A feature of indeterminacy applies to example (13), as there is no specific source for the information suggested.

(10) *The prime minister* ***is reported*** *as being against a sugar tax because it smacks of a nanny state.* <TIMES>

(11) *Allman thought he was harassing her and reported him to Edinburgh University for* ***allegedly*** *breaking its code of conduct* […]. <GUARDIAN>

(12) *One now* ***hears*** *politicians on both sides of the Channel arguing that the reason for the current impasse lies in* […] <TIMES>

(13) *Not every darling of the "alt-right" is a fascist or racist, […], as some coverage* ***suggests****.* <GUARDIAN>

Although IRE markers are slightly higher in Spanish, the differences are not significant between English and Spanish progressive and conservative newspapers. The most frequent markers retrieved from the Spanish subcorpora (*ABC* 8 tokens and *El País* 7 tokens) are *supuestamente* (supposedly), *según los datos/las encuestas* (according to the data/surveys), *a la vista de los datos* (in view of the data), *los datos revelan* (the data reveal), and *dicen* (they say/it is said).

Example (14) conveys the journalist's lack of commitment to the propositional content by relying on the epistemic marker of distancing *supuestamente* (supposedly). In examples (15) and (16), specific reference is made to reliable information compiled by reputed organizations. As a result, the journalists show a high degree of authorial commitment to the propositional content.

(14) *Esas cloacas desde las que,* ***supuestamente****, se quería acabar con su proyección imparable, son las que* [...] <ABC>
[Those sewers from which, supposedly, they wanted to end their unstoppable projection, are the ones that [...]]

(15) *Al fin y al cabo,* ***según los datos de la Encuesta Social Europea****, los ciudadanos europeos* <EL PAÍS>
[After all, according to data from the European Social Survey, European citizens [...]]

(16) *Por desgracia,* ***a la vista de los datos****, es fácil suponer que hay más territorios con* [...] <EL PAÍS>
[Unfortunately, in view of the data, it is easy to assume that there are more territories with [...]]

### *4.1.3 EP-EM (Modals)*

Epistemic modality markers, such as 'may', 'might', 'could', and 'probably' are by far the most frequent markers of evidentiality in English newspapers. However, this difference is much more marked in the conservative English newspaper *Times* than in the progressive *Guardian*, with 235 and 163 tokens retrieved from each of the subcorpora, respectively.

Modals provide a certain kind of assessment of the likelihood of an event described. In the examples taken from the English subcorpus, the writer is referring to the likelihood of the existence of an event. The degree of epistemic support for the actual occurrence of an event depends on the epistemic modal chosen; it can vary from full support, where the speaker/writer is certain about the realisation of an event, partial support, where the event is deemed to be likely, and neutral support, where the event is projected as possible/unlikely (Boye 2012: 133). In the case at hand, the choice of the epistemic modals 'maybe', might', and 'could' indicates neutral or lack of epistemic support for the realisation of the event.

(17) *And* ***maybe****, just* ***maybe****, new alliances across party boundaries are now possible in a way that* ***might*** *have seemed too daunting just a month ago.* <TIMES>

(18) *That mess of contradictions* ***might*** *look like good news for the people who think* [...] <GUARDIAN>

(19) *He* ***could*** *make concessions to the protesters,* ***perhaps*** *allowing more democratic accountability in the governance of Hong Kong* [...] <TIMES>

The frequency of use of epistemic markers – *tal vez* (maybe), *quizá* (perhaps), *es poco probable que* (it is unlikely that), and *podría* (could) – is reduced to less than half in the case of Spanish, both in the conservative newspaper *ABC* and in the progressive *El País*, with 96 and 71 tokens in each case. As in the case of English, the epistemic markers used in each of the examples express either partial – *probablemente* (probably) – or neutral support – *podría* (could), *es poco probable* (it is unlikely that), *tal vez* (maybe) – for the propositional content.

(20) *Y así llegamos al reinado de Felipe VI,* ***probablemente*** *el monarca mejor formado y más honesto de la historia.* <ABC>
[And so, we reach the reign of Felipe VI, probably the best trained and most honest monarch in history]

(21) *Con él España* ***podría*** *comenzar un nuevo periodo regenerador y de esplendor,* [...] <ABC>
[With him, Spain could begin a new period of regeneration and splendour, [...]]

(22) ***Es poco probable que*** *triunfe en su propósito* [...]] <EL PAÍS>
[It is unlikely to succeed in his purpose [...]]

(23) ***Se diría que*** *algunos rehúyen la posibilidad misma de encontrarse con la evidencia de que tal vez buena parte de las respuestas ofrecidas en el momento* [...] *en el eran las adecuadas, o las menos malas, o acaso las únicas posibles.* <EL PAÍS>
[It could be said that some shy away from the very possibility of encountering the evidence that perhaps a good part of the answers offered at the time [...] were the appropriate ones, or the least bad, or perhaps the only possible ones]

### *4.1.4. EP-CGA (Cognitive Attitude)*

In English, CGA markers are more frequent in the conservative newspaper *Times* than in the progressive *Guardian*, as tokens retrieved from the first (30) almost double those retrieved from the second (17). CGA markers, such as 'I think', 'I believe', 'I suppose', 'it seems to me', and 'undoubtedly' are commonly used in English newspapers, where the communicated information is maximally subjective with the experiencer (I-clauses or to me-phrases) made explicit (Marín-Arrese, Carretero and Usoniene 2022: 13). Hence, the examples below show a foregrounded writer functioning as the source of information and the point of departure of the propositional content.

Out of the epistemic markers in the examples, the one which transpires a writer who is certain about the propositional content is 'undoubtedly' (24). The marker 'I suppose' (25) is used to signal a writer who frames his/her thoughts tentatively. Finally, the writer admits having no evidence for the propositional content given in 'I have no reason to believe' (26).

(24) *Even the Brexit vote, which* ***undoubtedly*** *delighted a Kremlin eager to see Europe divided and discordant, now looks open to question.* <GUARDIAN>

(25) *Although* ***I suppose*** *the people who run that need to sleep at night, too.* <TIMES>

(26) ***I have no reason to believe*** *that it is going to be any worse at Portsmouth than at Oxford;* <TIMES>

The results obtained for the Spanish newspapers are in line with the results obtained for the English progressive newspaper *Guardian* although, contrary to English, these markers – mainly *creo* (I think) and *sin duda* (undoubtedly) – are more concentrated in the Spanish progressive newspaper *El País* (18) than in the conservative *ABC* (11).

The two Spanish newspapers rely on markers of cognitive attitude, giving total weight to the writer's cognitive position on the propositional content. The examples show a first-person writer who functions as the source of information and approaches the content by using markers such as *creo honradamente* (I honestly think) (27) and making claims towards the certainty of the information *sin duda* (no doubt) (28).

(27) *Desde luego,* ***creo honradamente*** *que no con mociones de censura para la galería.* <ABC>
[Of course, I honestly believe that not with motions of censure for the gallery]

(28) *Y, por último, aunque seguramente sea lo más importante y,* ***sin duda****, es lo más urgente, dejan fuera ese 32% de nacimientos.* <EL PAÍS>
[And, finally, although it is surely the most important and, without a doubt, the most urgent thing, they leave out that 32% of births]

### *4.1.5 EP-PFV (Personal Cognitive Factives)*

Although results are not significant in the case of personal cognitive factives in English newspapers, it should be noted that these markers, mostly 'we know' and 'I know', are more frequent in the English progressive *Guardian* (7) than in the conservative *Times* (4).

In the examples below, the writer is certain about a given representation of the events to the point that the proposition is presented as a piece of knowledge held either by him/herself (29) or shared with the readership (30).

(29) ***I know*** *a lot of her Tory colleagues winced when they got to that passage of Mrs May's little blue book.* <GUARDIAN>

(30) *The uncertainty makes it very difficult for business to plan for the short to medium term, and* ***we know*** *that this has led to delays in decisions concerning future investments* [...] <TIMES>

In Spanish, the number of PFV markers – *sé* (I know), *sabemos* (we know) – retrieved from the conservative Spanish newspaper *ABC* (9) doubles the number of markers retrieved from the conservative English newspaper *Times* (4). However, there are no significant differences between progressive newspapers in English (7) and Spanish (8).

These markers present pieces of knowledge held by the writer, as in (31) *sé perfectamente* (I perfectly know), or shared by the writer and his/her readership, as in (32). Therefore, his/her epistemic support for the propositional content is very high.

(31) ***Sé perfectamente que*** *no será un camino fácil, pero* [...] <ABC>
[I know perfectly well that it will not be an easy road, but [...]]

(32) ***Sabemos que*** *la economía digital concentra los empleos mejor remunerados y el mayor crecimiento en productividad* <EL PAÍS>
[We know that the digital economy concentrates the highest paid jobs and the highest growth in productivity]

### *4.1.6 EP-IFV (Impersonal Cognitive Factives)*

Impersonal cognitive factives, such as 'the fact' and 'the truth', are more frequent than personal cognitive factives in English, with 17 tokens retrieved from the conservative *Times* and 27 from the progressive *Guardian*. The examples below build on markers that present the information as facts or truths, which implies that this information is known to everybody and proved to be true ('the fact', 'it's a little known fact', 'the truth'). As the evidence is presented as a fact or a piece of truth, the writer's commitment to the propositional content is very high.

(33) *Indeed,* ***the fact that*** *the Met paid £100,000 to Lady Brittan in compensation for "trespass" tells its own story.* <TIMES>

(34) ***It's a little-known fact*** *that the Lib Dems actually did even worse in terms of votes cast in the election of 2017 than they did in 2015,* [...] <TIMES>

(35) *All of us need to confront this wilful forgetting around British history and tell* ***the truth****: Britain was built on the back of black slaves;* [...] <GUARDIAN>

Although the Spanish conservative newspaper *ABC* maintains the trend of the conservative English *Times* with 15 tokens, the progressive *El País* reduces the number of tokens (9) to figures similar to those obtained for personal cognitive factives. In Spanish, the most common IFV are *de hecho* (in fact), *en efecto* (indeed), or *en realidad* (actually).

(36) ***De hecho****, gobierna encantado con las de Montoro.* <ABC>
[In fact, he rules enchanted with those of Montoro]

(37) ***En efecto****, salvo excepciones casi contadas con los dedos de una mano, quienes el jueves votaron abandonar la UE no estuvieron movidos por nobles ideales* [...] <EL PAÍS>
[Indeed, with exceptions almost counted on the fingers of one hand, those who voted to leave the EU on Thursday were not moved by noble ideals [...]]

(38) ***En realidad****, pretenden derrocar a un Rey* <ABC>
[In reality, they intend to overthrow a King]

## 4.2 Epistemic Stance. Political Discourse

### *4.2.1 EP-IIE (Indirect Inferential Evidential)*

There are no significant differences between English Conservative (17) and Labour (13) speeches regarding the frequency of use of IIE markers such as 'as we have seen', 'it now appears that', 'it is clear that', 'it seems', or 'seemingly'.

IIE markers comprise lexical expressions which may express either inferential processes resulting from perceptual/conceptual evidence or inference resulting from oral/written documentary evidence (Marín-Arrese 2021). This feature is common to all of the examples listed below. In (39), the source of the evidence remains unclear. It may be perceptual-based, auditory/written-based, or a combination of the two of them. In any case, the justificatory support of the proposition is high because, based on this evidence, the politician feels entitled to make his/her claim inclusive using the marker 'we have seen'. All of the other examples imply a type of inferential reasoning based on some cognitive-based evidence. In examples (40) and (41), the politicians position themselves towards the proposition showing different degrees of commitment: in (39), claiming that, with a high degree of likelihood, Tony Blair and others would have liked Britain to take part in the next phase of the EU integration; and in (40) and (41), with a lower degree of support, sharing an impression or opinion based on implicit evidence. In examples (42) and (43), however, the reasoning-based source of evidence is made explicit so that the degree of commitment to the propositional content is higher:

(39) ***As we have seen*** *in the recent referendums and recent elections, it [casting a vote] does matter and it does make a difference.* <CONSV>

(40) *The government* ***seems*** *much more concerned about cutting deals with each other and for their friends and funders in the City.* <LAB>

(41) *The fact that the wealthy can* ***seemingly*** *dodge their taxes at will has further undermined public confidence in the tax system.* <LAB>

(42) *And it would* ***obviously*** *be absurd, as Theresa May said in her Lancaster House and Florence speeches – which now have the lapidary status of the codes of Hammurabi or Moses – it would be absurd if we were obliged to obey laws over which we have no say and no vote.* <CONSV>

(43) *But* ***it is clear that*** *this Conservative Government has its focus elsewhere.* <LAB>

Significant differences come out when comparing the results of English with those of Spanish. Both conservative (31) and progressive (23) Spanish speeches stand out for doubling these markers' frequency regarding the results obtained for English Conservative and Labour speeches. The most common IIE markers retrieved from the Spanish political subcorpus are *me parece* (it seems to me), *parece* (it seems), *es evidente* (it is evident), *tenemos muy claro* (it is very clear to us), or *lo estamos viendo* (we are seeing it).

Despite the reference to perception-based evidence through the use of the lexical marker *lo estamos viendo* (we are seeing it), example (44) combines perception and conception-based evidence with report-based evidence, by watching any of the media channels or by reading the papers. All the other examples retrieved from the Spanish corpus point in the same direction of creating a common ground either by including the audience in the assessment made *Tenemos muy claro que* (it is very clear to us that) (45), or by presenting some state of affairs as evident *lo que sí que es evidente es que* (what is evident is that) (46).

(44) *En Cataluña* ***se está viviendo*** *una paulatina transformación. Muchos* ***lo estamos viendo*** *con el alma en un puño.* <PSOE>
[Catalonia is experiencing a gradual transformation. Many of us are seeing it with deep anguish]

(45) ***Tenemos muy claro que*** *este partido es una de las columnas vertebrales del sistema democrático español.* <PP>
[It is very clear to us that this party is one of the backbones of the Spanish democratic system]

(46) *Pero* ***lo que sí que es evidente es que*** *después de escucharles a todos hay dos certezas bien claras.* <PSOE>
[But what is evident is that after listening to all of them there are two very clear certainties]

### *4.2.2 EP-IRE (Indirect Reportative Evidential)*

IRE markers in English, such as 'according to' or 'it is said' are not frequent in English Conservative (5) or Labour (4) speeches.

Examples (47) and (48) refer to primary reportative uses that locate the source of information given in a written report. The politician's commitment to the propositional content is high because the organizations issuing the two reports are prestigious in Britain. In (49), the politician marks his/her lack of knowledge about the source of information openly, thus showing a neutral position towards the propositional content.

(47) *And* ***according to a report*** *from Reform and Deloitte, if we fully rolled out artificial intelligence in Government – we could save £17bn.* <CONSV>

(48) ***A recent report*** *by the Westminster Foundation for Democracy found that* [...] <CONSV>

(49) ***It's said that*** *Labour is trying to offer something to everyone over Brexit.* <LAB>

In Spanish, the use of IRE markers, such as *dicen que* or *de acuerdo con*, is practically non-existent in conservative speeches (1). However, the Spanish progressive speeches (11) almost triple the use of these markers in the English Labour speeches and double the results obtained for the English Conservative speeches.

The two examples taken from the Spanish subcorpus work along the same lines. In (50), the politician refers to a non-specific source *dicen* (they say or it is said), which turns the propositional content into the statement's focus. This standard construction of reportative evidentiality is frequently used as a type of impersonal marker to give voice to a generic source (Marín-Arrese 2017b). Conversely, in (51), the politician makes his/her source available by introducing the lexical marker *de acuerdo con* (according to). Because the notoriety of the source – *Financial Times* – is high, the authorial commitment is also high.

(50) *Hay otros que* ***dicen que*** *ante un reto semejante lo hubieran hecho infinitamente mejor* <PP>
[There are others who say that, faced with such a challenge, they would have done infinitely better]

(51) ***De acuerdo con una amplia encuesta*** *del Financial Times, somos la economía preferida por los franceses, ingleses, italianos y alemanes* <PSOE>
[According to a wide survey by the *Financial Times*, we are the economy of choice for the French, English, Italians and Germans]

### *4.2.3 EP-EM (Modals)*

Markers of epistemic modality in English, fundamentally 'can', 'may', 'might', or 'probably' are three times more used in Conservative (92) than in Labour (35) speeches. These EM markers signal the speaker's/writer's degree of epistemic support to the propositions, which range from full support (certainty), to partial support (probability), or neutral support (possibility) (Boye 2012: 133). Full support is found in examples (55) and (56): 'certainly' conveys the politician's belief in the truth of the propositional content and 'can't be trusted' emphasizes his/her degree of confidence in such a truth. Partial support is located in example (54), and neutral support is observed in (52) and (53), where the different propositions are presented as just possible, which implies the politician's lack of commitment.

(52) ***There may be*** *some specific European programmes in which we might want to participate* […] <CONSV>

(53) *No Deal* ***might not be*** *a problem for Boris Johnson* […] <LAB>

(54) […] *our openness to people and ideas that has brought 300 languages on to the streets of London,* ***probably*** *the most diverse capital on earth.* <CONSV>

(55) […] *and whose participating scholars are* ***certainly*** *not confined to the EU.* <CONSV>

(56) *And it* ***certainly can't be trusted*** *with the NHS post-Brexit either.* <LAB>

The trend continues, although with much lower figures, in the case of Spanish. The use of EM markers in Spanish, such as *puede* (can), *podría* (could), *ciertamente* (certainly), *probablemente* (probably), or *quizá* (maybe), is more common in conservative than in progressive speeches (PP 23, PSOE 13).

Full support is found in (60), where the conservative politician is fully aligned with the proposition. Partial support is found in (61), where the proposition is presented as very likely to be true by the labour politician, which still gives the event some strength. Neutral support is found in (57), (58), and (59), with the realisation of the event deemed possible.

(57) *Votar es gratis, sí, pero* ***puede*** *salir carísimo y por eso tenemos que pensar el voto con la cabeza.* <PP>
[Voting is free, yes, but it can be very expensive and that is why we have to be very thoughtful about our vote]

(58) *Cosas que sólo se* ***podrían*** *hacer si se explicaba con claridad por qué eran necesarias.* <PP>
[Things that could only be done if it was clearly explained why they were necessary]

(59) *Pero* ***quizá*** *tras años de oposición y malos resultados electorales haya llegado el momento de optar por otra cosa.* <PSOE>
[But maybe after years of opposition and poor electoral results, the time has come to opt for something else]

(60) *Y lo seremos,* ***ciertamente****, porque, bajo la dirección de nuestra nueva presidenta o presidente, habrá llegado para nosotros* <PP>
[And we will certainly be, because, under the leadership of our new president, it will be here for us]

(61) *Pero* ***probablemente*** *nos estamos jugando algo más; el rostro de nuestra sociedad para mucho tiempo.* <PSOE>
[But we are probably risking something else; the face of our society for a long time]

### *4.2.4 EP-CGA (Cognitive Attitude)*

CGA markers –'I believe', 'I think' – are used three times as often in Conservative speeches (77) than in Labour speeches (19) in English.

The examples retrieved from the English subcorpus, conservative and labour, give prominence to a politician who presents himself/herself as the foregrounded source of his/her thoughts by using cognitive attitude markers such as 'I believe' (62) or 'I think' (63); in other words, 'The speaker/writer is the sole subject of the assessment of validity or attitude [...]' (Marín-Arrese 2010: 32). An extension in the source of believing is found in (64), where the politician includes the audience (*we*). This interactive function of discourse, where the author deletes the (psychological) space between the audience and himself/herself, proves to be very effective in creating some common ground and shared attitudes (Simon-Vandenbergen and Aijmer 2007).

(62) ***I believe*** *that taking such an approach is also how we resolve the Brexit impasse.* <CONSV>

(63) ***I think*** *some might even have been inspired to become professional dancers.* <CONSV>

(64) ***We believe*** *in fact that we can only fully achieve what we want to as citizens of Britain by also recognising we are "citizens of the world".* <LAB>

The trend is broken in the case of Spanish. Markers of cognitive attitude are more widely used in progressive (38) than conservative speeches (24). In the examples below, the validity of the information, as clearly marked by the politician, is subjective (Marín-Arrese 2010: 15) and limited. It is interesting to note that whenever the subject pronoun is included (65), the subjectivity is reinforced to remind the audience that the politician is the only person accountable for the proposition. This is not the case in (66) and (67). In (68), the politician and the audience are included in one single voice or positioning that applies to all socialists.

(65) ***Estoy seguro que*** *nos dicen cosas que necesitamos oír, aunque algunas no nos gusten.* <PP>
[I'm sure they tell us things we need to hear, even if we don't like some of them.]

(66) ***Sin duda alguna,*** *habrá muchas formas de amar a España, muchas, pero ser del Partido Popular es una de las mejores.* <PP>
[Without any doubt, there will be many ways to love Spain, many, but going with the Popular Party is one of the best]

(67) *Lo hemos hecho para evitar su muerte, algo que él* ***seguramente*** *no podrá comprender.* <PSOE>
[We have done it to avoid his death, something that he surely won't be able to understand]

(68) *Los socialistas* ***pensamos que*** *la salida lógica y racional llegados a este punto del desarrollo de la España autonómica, es la reforma federal del Estado.* <PSOE>
[We socialists think that the logical and rational way out at this point in the development of autonomous Spain is the federal reform of the State]

### *4.2.5 EP-PFV (Personal Cognitive Factives)*

In English, personal cognitive factives, such as 'I know' and 'we know', are slightly more frequent in Labour (44) than in Conservative (35) speeches.

These examples present a politician who is certain about the content of the proposition, which, as a result, is expressed as a piece of knowledge that may be shared with the audience, as in (70), or not, as in (69).

(69) ***I know*** *some people have suggested we should just ignore the rules, and tear up today the treaties that we've entered into.* <CONSV>
(70) ***We know*** *this is not the case.* <LAB>

In Spanish, however, the opposite is true. Personal cognitive factives, such as *sé que* (I know that) and *sabemos que* (we know that), are more prevalent in conservative (48) than in progressive (21) speeches.

(71) ***Sé que*** *ha sido muy duro, son nueve meses muy duros.* <PP>
[I know it has been very hard, it's being a very hard nine months]
(72) *Ya* ***sabemos que****, si la economía crece, crea empleo.* <PSOE>
[We already know that if the economy grows, it creates jobs]

### *4.2.6 EP-IFV (Impersonal Cognitive Factives)*

Impersonal cognitive factives – 'it is true', 'it is a fact', 'the fact is', 'the truth is' – are not as common in English as personal cognitive factives. These markers are used twice as often in Conservative (13) speeches than in Labour speeches (6).

Their use emphasizes that the politician's commitment to the proposition is high enough to be presented as an unquestionable truth, as in (73) and (74), or a fact, as in (75) and (76).

(73) *And* ***it is true*** *that full Customs Union membership prevents us from negotiating our own comprehensive trade deals.* <CONSV>
(74) *But* ***the truth is*** *we really don't know much more about where they're actually heading in these talks.* <LAB>
(75) ***The fact is*** *that immigration is a net benefit to this country.* <LAB>
(76) ***It is a fact that*** *conflict and instability abroad make us less safe here at home.* <LAB>

Impersonal cognitive factives *en efecto* (indeed), *en realidad* (actually), *es verdad* (it is true), *verdaderamente* (truly, indeed) are more frequently used in Spanish than in English. However, there are no significant differences in the frequency of use between conservative (12) and progressive (14) speeches in Spanish.

The markers *en realidad* (actually) (77) and *en efecto* (indeed) (78) confirm or emphasize what has been previously pointed out. In the last example, (79), the politician gives the proposition the status of truth.

(77) ***En realidad****, ha sido muy difícil. Gobernar la crisis ha tenido un coste muy alto para el partido.* <PP>
[Actually, it has been very difficult. Governing the crisis has had a very high cost for the party]
(78) ***En efecto****, la crispación es el mayor enemigo del progreso.* <PP>
[Indeed, tension is the greatest enemy of progress]

(79) ***Es verdad que*** *en España hay otro proyecto político, pero en él no cabe la mayoría de los ciudadanos para ser libres e iguales.* <PSOE>
[It is true that in Spain there is another political project, but it does not fit the majority of citizens to be free and equal]

## 5 Analysis of Results

The results confirm our expectations and show that journalistic opinion discourse is much more epistemic in English than Spanish. Specifically, the results obtained for English (6.49) double the results for Spanish (3.48). The conservative *Times* (7.19) is much more epistemic than the progressive *Guardian* (5.79). However, the differences between the Spanish conservative newspaper *ABC* (3.54) and the progressive *El País* (3.42) are not significant.

The results also show that epistemic modals are the most frequent markers – used to express some assessment of the chances that a state of affairs has occurred or will occur in the future – in the conservative *Times* (4.69) and the progressive *Guardian* (3.25) followed by the IIE markers. The differences between the two newspapers are not so marked regarding IIE markers: *Times* (1.32); *Guardian* (1.19).

**Table 1.** Epistemic stance. Newspaper discourse

| EPISTEMIC STANCE – NEWSPAPERS | | | | | |
|---|---|---|---|---|---|
| | N | R | | N | R |
| EP-IIE TIMES | 67 | 1.32 | EP-IIE ABC | 40 | 0.79 |
| EP-IIE GUARD. | 60 | 1.19 | EP-IIE EL PAÍS | 60 | 1.18 |
| EP- IRE TIMES | 11 | 0.21 | EP- IRE ABC | 8 | 0.15 |
| EP-IRE GUARD. | 16 | 0.32 | EP-IRE EL PAÍS | 7 | 0.14 |
| EP-EM TIMES | 235 | 4.64 | EP-EM ABC | 96 | 1.89 |
| EP-EM GUARD. | 163 | 3.25 | EP-EM EL PAÍS | 71 | 1.40 |
| EP-CGA TIMES | 30 | 0.59 | EP-CGA ABC | 11 | 0.22 |
| EP-CGA GUARD. | 17 | 0.34 | EP-CGA EL PAÍS | 18 | 0.36 |
| EP-PFV TIMES | 4 | 0.07 | EP-PFV ABC | 9 | 0.18 |
| EP-PFV GUARD. | 7 | 0.14 | EP-PFV EL PAÍS | 8 | 0.16 |
| EP-IFV TIMES | 17 | 0.33 | EP-IFV ABC | 15 | 0.29 |
| EP-IFV GUARD. | 27 | 0.54 | EP-IFV EL PAÍS | 9 | 0.18 |
| TOTAL EP TIMES | 364 | 7.19 | TOTAL EP ABC | 179 | 3.54 |
| TOTAL EP GUARD. | 290 | 5.79 | TOTAL EP EL PAÍS | 173 | 3.42 |
| TOTAL EP NEWSPAPERS | 654 | 6.49 | TOTAL EP NEWSPAPERS | 352 | 3.48 |

Epistemic modals and IIE markers are also the most common way of expressing epistemic stance in Spanish. However, the difference between the two types of markers is not as significant in Spanish as in English. Contrary to English, IIE markers are more frequent in the progressive Spanish *El País* (1.18) than in the conservative *ABC* (0.79).

CGA markers occupy the third position regarding the frequency of use in English and Spanish journalistic opinion discourse. However, while these markers are more frequently used in the English conservative *Times* (0.59) than in the progressive *Guardian* (0.34), this trend is broken in Spanish. The frequency of use of CGA markers, although very similar to that of the English progressive *Guardian,* is higher in the Spanish progressive *El País* (0.36) than the conservative *ABC* (0.22).

The opposite applies to IFV markers, which are more frequently used in the English progressive *Guardian* (0.54) and the Spanish conservative *ABC* (0.29) than in the English conservative *Times* (0.33) and the Spanish progressive *El País* (0.18).

As with journalistic opinion discourse, the results show that English political discourse is more epistemic than Spanish (3.53 vs 2.51). Specifically, the results obtained for the English conservative party (4.71) double those obtained for both the English Labour party (2.31) and the Spanish conservative Popular Party (2.71) and progressive PSOE (2.32). Interestingly enough, the results obtained for the English and Spanish progressive parties are almost identical, besides being quite similar to the results obtained for the Spanish conservative Popular Party.

**Table 2.** Epistemic stance. Political discourse.

| EPISTEMIC STANCE – POLITICAL DISCOURSE | | | | | |
|---|---|---|---|---|---|
| | N | R | | N | R |
| EP-IIE CONSRV. | 17 | 0.33 | EP-IIE PP | 31 | 0.60 |
| EP-IIE LABOUR | 13 | 0.26 | EP-IIE PSOE | 23 | 0.44 |
| EP-IRE CONRV. | 5 | 0.10 | EP-IRE PP | 1 | 0.02 |
| EP-IRE LABOUR | 0 | 0 | EP-IRE PSOE | 11 | 0.21 |
| EP-EM CONSRV. | 92 | 1.81 | EP-EM PP | 23 | 0.45 |
| EP-EM LABOUR | 35 | 0.70 | EP-EM PSOE | 13 | 0.25 |
| EP-CGA CONSRV. | 77 | 1.52 | EP- CGA PP | 24 | 0.47 |
| EP-CGA LABOUR | 19 | 0.38 | EP-CGA PSOE | 38 | 0.73 |
| EP-PFV CONSRV. | 35 | 0.69 | EP-PFV PP | 48 | 0.93 |
| EP-PFV LABOUR | 44 | 0.88 | EP-PFV PSOE | 21 | 0.41 |
| EP-IFV CONRV. | 13 | 0.26 | EP-IFV PP | 12 | 0.23 |
| EP-IFV LABOUR | 6 | 0.12 | EP-IFV PSOE | 14 | 0.27 |
| TOTAL CONSRV. | 239 | 4.71 | TOTAL PP | 139 | 2.71 |
| TOTAL LABOUR | 117 | 2.31 | TOTAL PSOE | 120 | 2.32 |
| TOTAL EP POLIT ENG | 356 | 3.53 | TOTAL EP POLIT SP | 259 | 2.51 |

In English conservative and progressive political discourse, the use of epistemic modals (Conservative 1.81, Labour 0.70) is closely followed by CGA markers (conservative 1.52, Labour 0.38). PFV markers occupy the third position in terms of frequency of use. However, the differences between the two parties regarding the use of PFV markers are not evident, with higher results for the Labour party (Conservative 0.69, Labour 0.88).

It is worth noting that the most frequent markers in Spanish conservative political discourse are PFVs (Conservative PP 0.93, Progressive PSOE 0.41). The opposite is true for using CGA in Spanish progressive political discourse (Progressive PSOE 0.73, Conservative PP 0.47). IIE markers occupy the third position in terms of frequency of use (Conservative PP 0.60, Progressive PSOE 0.44). Moreover, most striking of all is that the use of epistemic modals falls to ratios of 0.45 for the Spanish conservative Popular Party and 0.25 for the progressive PSOE. However, as said at the beginning of the paper, political discourse is expected to highlight a more reflective nature (attitudinal dimension) than negotiating/shaping meaning with potential readers, which explains the low ratios of epistemic modals in Spanish.

The most significant differences arise in English, between the Conservative and the Labour Party, regarding epistemic modals (1.81 vs 0.70) and CGA markers (1.52 vs 0.38). However, it is also worth noting the difference regarding PFV markers in Spanish conservative and progressive political discourse (0.93 vs 0.41).

**Table 3.** Epistemic stance. Newspaper and Political discourse.

| EPISTEMIC STANCE | TOTAL<br>TIMES + GUARDIAN<br>100,689 | TOTAL<br>ABC + EL PAÍS<br>101,230 | TOTAL<br>CONS + LAB<br>100,985 | TOTAL<br>PP + PSOE<br>103,084 |
|---|---|---|---|---|
| EVIDENTIALITY | 78 + 76 = 154 | 48 + 67 = 115 | 22 + 13 = 35 | 32 + 34 = 66 |
| | N % R<br>154 23.5 1.53 | N % R<br>115 32.7 1.14 | N % R<br>35 9.8 0.35 | N % R<br>66 25.5 0.64 |
| EP. MODALITY | 265 + 180 = 445 | 107 + 89 = 196 | 169 + 54 = 223 | 47 + 51 = 98 |
| | N % R<br>445 68.1 4.42 | N % R<br>196 55.7 1.94 | N % R<br>223 62.6 2.21 | N % R<br>98 37.8 0.95 |
| FACTIVITY | 21 + 34 = 55 | 24 + 17 = 41 | 48 + 50 = 98 | 60 + 35 = 95 |
| | N % R<br>55 8.4 0.55 | N % R<br>41 11.6 0.41 | N % R<br>98 27.6 0.97 | N % R<br>95 36.7 0.92 |
| TOTAL | 264 + 290 = 654 | 179 + 173 = 352 | 239 + 117 = 356 | 139 + 120 = 259 |
| | N % R<br>654 100 6.49 | N % R<br>352 100 3.48 | N % R<br>356 100 3.53 | N % R<br>259 100 2.51 |

Regarding the expression of stance, both journalistic opinion discourse and political discourse are more epistemic in English (Journalistic 6.49; Political 3.53) than in Spanish (Journalistic 3.48; Political 2.51). In turn, journalistic discourse is more epistemic than political discourse in English and Spanish, although the difference is more significant in English. Specifically, the instances of epistemic modality retrieved from the English subcorpora (Journalistic 4.42; Political 2.21) double those from Spanish (Journalistic 1.94; Political 0.95) in newspaper opinion and political discourse. Likewise, the instances of epistemic modality retrieved from the journalistic subcorpora (English 4.42; Spanish 1.94) double those from the political subcorpora (English 2.21; Spanish 0.95) in both languages.

The opposite is true regarding the expression of epistemic stance through factivity. The instances of factive markers retrieved from the political subcorpora (English 0.97; Spanish 0.92) double those from the journalistic subcorpora (English 0.55; Spanish 0.41) in both languages.

## 6 Conclusions

The results tested the three working hypotheses regarding quantitative differences across (i) languages, (ii) discourse domains, and (iii) ideological orientations.

The first was fully supported because English exceeds Spanish in the use of epistemic expressions in the two discourse domains under analysis, opinion newspaper and political discourse, which is in line with the study conducted by Marín-Arrese (2015).

Regarding the first claim of the second hypothesis, where the use of epistemic modals in opinion newspaper and political discourses is compared, results show that opinion newspaper articles resort to epistemic modals more often than political speeches in both languages. However, the difference between discourse domains is more significant in English. This seems to imply the need to evoke a journalist conceptualizer who can better connect and engage with the readership through open statements (1) to accommodate the different views of readers and (2) share some responsibility with them while negotiating meaning. This finding is in line with Marin Arrese's (2017a) claim that direct evaluations are avoided in the interest of more impersonal formulations in newspaper discourse. Then, it can be concluded that this overwhelming use of epistemic modals in newspaper discourse reveals one of the defining features of this type of genre, as "epistemic modals are a very important means of expressing addressee-oriented meaning" (Coates 1987: 120).

With regards to the second claim of the second hypothesis, where newspaper and political discourses are compared regarding their use of markers of cognitive attitude and personal factives, results show that political discourse is more reflective and personal than newspaper opinion discourse in both languages, especially in Spanish. Politicians combine the use of these two markers to create some 'bonding' or common ground with the intended audience (Simon-Vandenbergen and Aijmer 2007), especially in Spanish. In English, although the use of cognitive attitude and personal factive markers equally points to the reflective character of political discourse, this trend is counterbalanced by the more frequent use of epistemic modals. Finally, politicians also use epistemic modals in the two Spanish parties, although in very low ratios.

Regarding the third hypothesis, results confirm that conservative papers and right-wing parties are more inclined to use epistemic markers. In particular, this is overwhelmingly the case in English newspaper discourse, whereas in Spanish, although in favour of the conservative paper, the difference is almost negligible.

Hence, apart from the overwhelming use of epistemic markers in English versus Spanish, the other remarkable differences are a) newspaper discourse is much more epistemic than political discourse across languages; b) the most significant differences across languages surface in the distribution of markers in political discourse. This suggests a somewhat different functioning of how political discourse is accomplished in both countries: favouring a more personal mediation of the information offered (more weight given to the attitudinal parameter) in Spanish, with the politician as the 'onstage conceptualizer' (Langacker 1991), versus a combination of engagement with the audience (interactional parameter) plus some personal mediation of the propositional content given (attitudinal parameter) in English.

## References

Aikhenvald, A. Y. (2004). *Evidentiality*. Oxford: Oxford University Press.

Bakhtin, M. (1981). *The Dialogic Imagination*. Austin, TX: University of Texas Press.

Biber, D., and Finegan, E. (1989). 'Styles of stance in English: Lexical and grammatical marking of evidentiality and affect'. *Text*, 1, 93–124.

Boye, K. (2012). *Epistemic meaning: A crosslinguistic and functional-cognitive study*. Berlin: Mouton de Gruyter.

Capelli, G. (2007). *"I reckon I know how Leopoldo da Vinci must have felt…" Epistemicity, evidentiality and English verbs of cognitive attitude*. Pari: Pari Publishing.

Carretero, M., and Zamorano-Mansilla, J. R. (2013). 'Annotating English adverbials for the categories of epistemic modality and evidentiality'. In J. I.

Marín-Arrese, M. Carretero, J. Arús Hita, and J. van der Auwera (eds.), *English Modality: Core, Periphery and Evidentiality*, pp. 317–355. Berlin: Mouton de Gruyter.

Celle, A. (2009). 'Hearsay adverbs and modality'. In P. Busuttil, R. Salkie and J. van der Auwera (eds.), *Modality in English*, pp. 269–293. Berlin, New York: Mouton de Gruyter.

Chafe, W. L., and Nichols, J. (eds) (1986). *Evidentiality: The Linguistic Coding of Epistemology*. Norwood, NJ: Ablex.

Coates, J. (1987). 'Epistemic modality and spoken discourse'. *Philological Society*, 85 (1), 110–131.

Englebretson, R. (2007). 'Introduction'. In R. Englebretson (ed.), *Stancetaking in Discourse*, pp. 1–26. Amsterdam: John Benjamins.

Habermas, J. (1981). *Theory of communicative action*. London: SAGE.

Haviland, J. (1989). 'Sure, sure: Evidence and affect'. *Text*, 9: 27–68.

Hunston, S., and Thompson, G. (eds) (2000). *Evaluation in Text: Authorial Stance and the Construction of Discourse*. Oxford: Oxford University Press.

Kecskes, I. (2019). *English as a Lingua Franca: the Pragmatic Perspective*. Cambridge: Cambridge University Press.

Kiparsky, P., and Kiparsky, C. (1970). 'Fact'. In M. Bierwisch and K. E. Heidolph, (eds.), *Progress in Linguistics*, pp. 143–73. The Hague: Mouton.

Langacker R. W. (1991). *Foundations of Cognitive Grammar* (Vol. 2). Stanford, CA: Stanford University Press.

Langacker, R. W. (2009). *Investigations in Cognitive Grammar*. Berlin: Mouton de Gruyter.

Langacker, R. W. (2013). Modals: striving for control. In: Marín-Arrese, J.I., Carretero, M., Arús, J., van der Auwera, J. (eds.), *English Modality: Core, Periphery and Evidentiality*, pp. 3–55. Berlin: Mouton de Gruyter.

Marín-Arrese, J. I. (2009). 'Effective vs. epistemic stance, and subjectivity/intersubjectivity in political discourse: A case study'. In A. Tsangalidis and R. Facchinetti (eds.), *Studies on English Modality. In Honour of Frank Palmer*, pp. 23–52. Berlin, New York: Peter Lang.

Marín-Arrese, J. I. (2010). 'Subjectivity and Intersubjectivity in Discourses'. In M. Blanco and J. Marín-Arrese (eds), *Discourse and Communication: Cognitive and Functional Perspectives*. Madrid: Dykinson.

Marín-Arrese, J. I. (2011a). 'Effective vs. Epistemic stance and subjectivity in political discourse: Legitimising strategies and mystification of responsibility'. In C. Hart (ed.), *Critical Discourse Studies in Context and Cognition*, pp. 193–224. Benjamins: Amsterdam.

Marín-Arrese, J. I. (2011b). 'Epistemic legitimising strategies, commitment and accountability in discourse'. *Discourse Studies*, 13 (6), 789–797.

Marín-Arrese, J. I. (2013) 'Stancetaking and inter-subjectivity in the Iraq Inquiry. Blair vs. Brown'. In J. I. Marín-Arrese, M. Carretero, J. Arús Hita, and J. van der Auwera (eds.), *English Modality Core, Periphery and Evidentiality*, pp. 411–445. Mouton De Gruyter: Berlin and New York.

Marín-Arrese, J. I. (2015). 'Epistemicity and stance: A cross-linguistic study of epistemic stance strategies in journalistic discourse in English and Spanish'. *Discourse Studies,* 17 (2), 210–225.

Marín-Arrese, J. I. (2016) 'Epistemicidad y posicionamiento discursivo: Un estudio interlingüístico de la evidencialidad en el discurso periodístico en castellano y en inglés'. In R. González Ruiz, D. Izquierdo Alegría, and O. Loureda Lamas (eds.), *La Evidencialidad en español: Teoría y descripción*, pp. 329–350. Iberoamericana, Madrid and Vervuert: Frankfurt am Main.

Marín-Arrese, J. I. (2017a). 'Stancetaking and Inter/Subjectivity in journalistic discourse: The Engagement system revisited'. In R. Breeze and I. Olza (eds.), *Evaluation in Media Discourse: European perspectives*, pp. 21–48. Bern: Peter Lang.

Marín-Arrese, J. I. (2017b). 'Multifunctionality of evidential expressions in discourse domains and genres: Evidence from cross-linguistic case studies'. In J. I. Marín-Arrese, G. Hassler and M. Carretero (eds.), *Evidentiality revisited: Cognitive Grammar, functional and discourse-pragmatic perspectives*, pp. 195–223. Amsterdam/Philadelphia: Benjamins.

Marín-Arrese, J. I. (2021). 'Stance, emotion and persuasion: Terrorism and the Press'. *Journal of Pragmatics*, 177, 135–148.

Marín-Arrese, J. I., Carretero, M., and Usoniene A. (2022 in press). Evidentiality in English. In B. Wiemer and J. Marín-Arrese (eds.), *Evidential Marking in European Languages*. Berlin: De Gruyter.

Martin, J. R., and White, P. R. R. (2005). *The Language of Evaluation. Appraisal in English*. Basingstoke/New York: Palgrave Macmillan.

Martín de la Rosa, V., Domínguez Romero, E., Pérez Blanco, M., and Marín-Arrese J. I. (2020). 'Epistemic and Effective Stance in Political Discourse: The European Refugee Crisis'. In L. N. Berlin (ed.), *Positioning and Stance in Political Discourse: The Individual, the Party, and the Party Line*, pp. 141–156. Wilmington, DE: Vernon Press.

Nuyts, J. (2001). *Epistemic Modality, Language and Conceptualization: A Cognitive-Pragmatic Perspective.* Amsterdam: John Benjamins.

Ochs, E., and Schieffelin, B. (1989). 'Language has a heart'. In E. Ochs (ed.), *The Pragmatics of Affect*, Special issue of *Text*, 9, 7–25.

Silverstein, M. (1976). 'Shifters, linguistic categories, and cultural description'. In K. Basso and H. Selby (eds.), *Meaning in anthropology*, pp. 11–55. New Mexico: University of New Mexico Press.

Simon-Vandenbergen, A. M., and Aijmer, K. (2007). *The semantic field of modal certainty: A corpus-based study of English adverbs*. Berlin: De Gruyter.

van der Auwera, J., and Plungian, V. (1998). 'On modality's semantic map'. *Linguistic Typology*, 2, 79–124

Wiemer, B., and Stathi, K. (2010). 'The database of evidential markers in European languages. A bird's eye view of the conception of the database (the template and problems hidden beneath it)', *STUF - Language Typology and Universals Sprachtypologie und Universalienforschung*, 63 (4), 275–289.

Willet, T. (1988). 'A Cross-Linguistic Survey of the Grammaticalization of Evidentiality', *Studies in Language*, 12 (1), 51–97.

Anna Ruskan & Audronė Šolienė

# Realizations of epistemicity and effectivity in Lithuanian political discourse[1]

**Abstract:** The present study aims to explore the expression of epistemicity and effectivity in Lithuanian political discourse by comparing the distribution of epistemic and effective stance markers in the speeches of right-wing and left-wing Lithuanian politicians. Drawing on the framework of epistemicity and effectivity developed by Marín-Arrese (2011), the study focuses on modal verbs, complement-taking predicates (CTPs) and adverbials. The data have been drawn from the self-compiled corpus of political speeches collected in the years 2006–2020.

The results show that both right-wing and left-wing Lithuanian politicians employ markers of epistemicity expressing various degrees of the author's commitment, cognitive attitude (e.g. *manau* 'I think'), inferences based on perceptual or conceptual evidence (e.g. *matyt* 'evidently', *akivaizdu* 'evident'), reports (e.g. *sako* 'they say') and reality/actuality comments (e.g. *tiesa* 'in fact') as well as markers of effectivity denoting deonticity and possibility (e.g. *būtina* 'necessary', *galima* 'possible'). However, markers of effective stance are more frequent than markers of epistemic stance in the speeches of both right-wing and left-wing politicians.

**Keywords:** *Lithuanian political discourse, stance, commitment, actuality, cognitive attitude, evidential, deontic, complement-taking predicate, modal verb, adverbial.*

## 1 Introduction

The present study deals with the expression of stance in political discourse produced by Lithuanian politicians belonging to the right-wing and left-wing political groupings. Although political discourse has attracted a great deal of scholarly attention (cf. metaphorical expressions in British and Lithuanian politicians' speeches (Arcimavičienė 2011; Cibulskienė 2012)), stance in Lithuanian political discourse has not been examined yet. The aim of the present study is to identify devices for conveying two types of stance: epistemic and

1 This research has received support from the following project: *Stance and Subjectivity in Discourse: Towards an Integrated Framework for the Analysis of Epistemicity, Effectivity, Evaluation and Inter/Subjectivity from a Critical Discourse Perspective* (STANCEDISC), Ref. PGC2018-095798-B-I00, funded by the Ministerio de Ciencia, Innovación y Universidades (Spanish Ministry of Science, Innovation and Universities).

effective (Marín-Arrese 2011), also referred to as the categories of epistemicity and effectivity, and to explore the dimensions of subjectivity and intersubjectivity, closely connected with the realizations of epistemic and effective stance. The dimension of intersubjectivity is an important feature of political discourse. As noted by Fetzer (2013: 4), "expressing different degrees and different types of commitment provides the political actors with an opportunity to address the epistemological and intersubjective domains of communication". By presenting their beliefs, promises and attitudes, politicians engage with their audience, for "it is the job of the politician to use all possible means inherent in the contextual constraints and requirements of mass media to present her/his political agenda in a credible and responsible manner to a heterogenous audience, whose members are potential voters" (ibid. 10). The study also looks into the expressions of 'non-speaker subjectivity' realized by markers of attribution (Marín-Arrese 2017).

The structure of the study is as follows. Section 2 provides an overview of the notion of stance, its sub-categories found in various frameworks and its means of realization. Section 3 introduces the connection between stance and the dimensions of subjectivity and intersubjectivity. Section 4 addresses the role of stance in discourse and presents a number of studies into stance conducted in different types of discourse, including political discourse. Section 5 describes the data, procedures of data selection and methods applied to the study. Section 6 discusses the distribution, functions and (inter)subjective dimension of the effective and epistemic stance expressions in Lithuanian political discourse as well as instances of attribution and their qualification in terms of non-speaker subjectivity. Section 7 provides the concluding remarks.

## 2 Stance: Notion, Types and Realization

A number of definitions of stance and its various notional categories have been provided in different linguistic frameworks (Biber et al. 1999; Hunston/Thompson 2000; Martin/White 2005; Du Bois 2007; Simaki et al. 2020). Despite the divergent classifications of stance found in the literature and different approaches applied to its exploration, the core notion underlying stance is authorial positioning towards various entities (first-order entities (individuals, places), second-order entities (states-of-affairs) or third-order entities (propositions) (Lyons 1977)), which means that stance is concerned with subjectivity, attitude, assessment, engagement and similar concepts. As claimed by Biber (2006: 99), "stance expressions can convey many different kinds of personal feelings and assessments, including attitudes that a speaker has about certain information, how certain they are about its veracity, how they obtained access to the information, and what perspective they are taking". The broad concept of stance also emerges from Simaki et al.'s (2020) stance categories such as agreement/disagreement, certainty, contrariety, hypotheticality, necessity, prediction, source of knowledge, tact/rudeness, uncertainty, volition, identified in the Brexit Blog Corpus.

Despite the variety of the notional categories of stance, it is broadly classified into two main categories: attitudinal and epistemic[2] (Biber et al. 1999). Attitudinal stance is connected with the author's personal attitudes, emotions and assessments, whereas epistemic stance deals with the author's evaluations of the epistemic status of a proposition (Gray/Biber 2015: 219). This notional dichotomy of stance can be found in Martin and White's (2005) Appraisal theory, too, where attitudinal stance markers are found within the category of Attitude, whereas epistemic stance expressions are placed within the category of Engagement. Acknowledging the multifaceted nature of stance, Simaki et al. (2020) distinguish different targets of stance: (a) objects, scenes and events towards which authors express attitudes, and (b) propositions and speakers' viewpoints on what is talked about. These distinctions reflect the author's positioning with respect to the first-order, second-order or third-order entities mentioned by Lyons (1977). For example, attitudinal stance markers can be found with all types of entities, while epistemic stance markers concern only third-order entities, i.e. propositions, defined as abstract unobservable entities which lie outside space and time (Lyons 1977: 445) and present "a piece of information of the world that may be true or false" (Carretero 2016: 36).

The present study draws on the notional distinctions of stance provided in Marín-Arrese's (2011) framework of effectivity and epistemicity, related to the above discussed notions of attitudinal and epistemic stance. The category of effectivity includes markers of effective stance concerned with "positioning of the speaker/writer with respect to the realization of events, to the ways in which the speaker/writer carries out a stance act aimed at determining or influencing the course of reality itself" (Marín-Arrese 2011: 195). Within the scope of effective stance are such key notions as potentiality, necessity, volition, intentionality and directivity. Attempting to bring some events and actions into effect, the author resorts to devices expressing effective stance, which is closely related to non-epistemic modality, i.e. event modality (Palmer 2001).

---

2 Biber et al. (1999) also distinguish the third sub-category of stance, namely style of speaking. However, this sub-category is less common and has received less attention in the literature.

The category of epistemicity encompasses markers of epistemic stance concerned with "the positioning of the speaker/writer with respect to knowledge concerning the realization of the event, to the ways in which the speaker/writer carries out a stance act aimed at estimating the likelihood of an event and/or judging the validity of a proposition designating the event" (Marín-Arrese 2011: 195). Within the scope of epistemic stance are evaluations concerned with the author's commitment to the truth and factuality of the proposition as well as with sources of knowledge the author uses to justify the propositional content. Thus, epistemic stance is tightly connected with markers of epistemic modality and evidentiality, discussed also by Boye (2012).

Another key issue to consider is the realization of effective and epistemic stance. In the categorization of stance provided by Biber et al. (1999, 2006) and by Gray and Biber (2015), a distinction is drawn between lexical and grammatical expressions of stance. Lexical devices for stance are conveyed by evaluative words, and lexical marking of stance is considered implicit, "involving a single proposition or evaluated entity [...] it requires reference to the context and shared background in order for the reader/hearer to recognize that this is an attitude/evaluation of the speaker/writer" (Gray/Biber 2015: 220–221). A different situation is found with grammatical marking of stance, for it includes overt expressions of "an attitude or assessment relative to some proposition in the immediate discourse" (Gray/Biber 2015: 221). Grammatical means of stance consist of two components, expressed by "two separate grammatical phrases or clauses": a constituent containing a stance marker and a constituent with a proposition framed by the stance marker (ibid. 221). Grammatical means of stance include adverbials (e.g. *certainly, maybe*), modal and semi-modal verbs (e.g. *may, will, must, have to, need to*) as well as *that* or *to*-complement clauses controlled by verbs, adjectives or nouns (e.g. *I see that you're bored. She seems to be at a loss*) The present study will deal with grammatical expressions of effective and epistemic stance.

It is also important to draw a distinction between authorial and non-authorial stance. As shown in the literature (Biber et al. 1999), authorial stance includes those cases of evaluation that belong to the author of the text, as below:

(A) ***Aš tikiu**, kad Lietuva renkasi laisvę.* (CON)
[**I believe** that Lithuania chooses freedom.][3]

3 All translations are our own unless noted otherwise.

Non-authorial stance expresses third parties' positioning towards some entities. In the following example, the thoughts of the third party are presented:

(B) *They **thought** she would not stand the test.* (Biber et al. 1999: 976)

In the present study, cases of non-authorial stance will be considered within the category of attribution discussed by Martin and White (2005) as well as by Marín-Arrese (2017). Martin and White (2005: 111) consider attribution as "those formulations which disassociate the proposition from the text's internal authorial voice by attributing it so some external source", and locate it within the category of Engagement. Attribution is expressed by means of reported speech and thought, conveyed by communication verbs (e.g. *say*, *claim*) and mental state verbs (e.g. *think*, *believe*) or their nominalizations (e.g. *a claim*, *a belief*, *a thought*) or by adverbials (e.g. *according to*). Attribution also includes cases of reportative evidentiality (ibid.), realized by adverbials (e.g. *reportedly*, *allegedly*) or impersonal constructions (e.g. *it is claimed that*) where no specific external source of information is indicated. Marín-Arrese (2017: 30) notices that attribution overlaps with the sub-category of reportative evidentiality and could be treated as a "hybrid category", including markers of Indirect-Reportative Sourced evidentiality (e.g. *according to X*, *they say*, *it is said*, *it is reported*) and markers of Indirect speech or semi-direct speech. The present study considers both markers of reportative evidentiality and reported speech and thought within the category of attribution. This category is integrated in the current analysis because reliance on external sources of information may help in unravelling political argumentation and its connection with the dimension of (inter)subjectivity.

## 3 Stance, Subjectivity and Intersubjectivity

The multifaceted and complex nature of stance emerges from its relationship with the dimensions of subjectivity and intersubjectivity. Both effective and epistemic stance markers may explicitly or implicitly reflect the author's attitudes and beliefs and qualify as markers of subjectivity, or they may express the author's concern with engaging the addressee into discourse and function as expressions of intersubjectivity. The (inter)subjective dimension of markers of epistemic and effective stance has been treated within a dialogic perspective (Martin/White 2005; Du Bois 2007), which assumes the author's engagement with other voices in discourse. Authors might agree with the positions expressed by others, disagree, show their indecision or remain neutral (Martin/White 2005: 193).

The connection between the dimensions of subjectivity and inter subjectivity in expressing stance is apparent in Du Bois's (2007) approach to stance, defined as "a public act by a social actor, achieved dialogically through overt communicative means (language, gesture, and other symbolic forms), through which social actors simultaneously evaluate objects, position subjects (themselves and others), and align with other subjects, with respect to any salient dimension of value in the sociocultural field" (2007: 169–170). Thus, in any act of stance taking, be it effective (attitudinal) or epistemic stance, there is a social actor (the speaker/author) who expresses his/her positioning towards an object (entity) and negotiates this positioning with other subjects (the addressee). Similarly, White (2011: 14) maintains that speakers/writers express their stance and "engage with socially-determined value positions and thereby align and dis-align themselves with the social subjects who hold to these positions".

The present study adheres to the notion and categorization of subjectivity and intersubjectivity characterizing markers of effective and epistemic stance provided by Marín-Arrese (2011: 195), who maintains that "stance involves a subjective component of attitude and evaluation, and a dialogic construction of enunciational position which is intersubjective in nature". The core aspects of the two dimensions are the degree of "salience and explicitness of the role of the conceptualizer" and "personal vs shared responsibility" for the information transmitted (Marín-Arrese 2011: 197). Thus, a distinction is drawn between markers of subjectivity with the author explicitly or implicitly expressed and information available to the author (explicit and implicit personal responsibility) and between intersubjective expressions with the author explicitly or implicitly sharing information with other members of discourse (explicit shared responsibility and opaque personal/shared responsibility). For example, the phrase *I think* marks explicit personal responsibility (explicit subjectivity) and the modal verb *may* denotes implicit personal responsibility (implicit subjectivity). Similarly, *we have to do something* is an expression of explicit shared responsibility (explicit intersubjectivity), whereas *it is necessary to do something* is a marker of opaque personal/shared responsibility (opaque intersubjectivity).

The dimension of subjectivity is also extended to markers of attribution that will be dealt with in this paper. Expressions of attribution should be considered as cases of non-speaker subjectivity, which may also be explicit or implicit (Marín-Arrese 2017: 35). Instances of reported speech and thought as well as markers of reportative evidentiality specifying a source (e.g. *according to*, *they say*) should be treated as realizations of explicit subjectivity, whereas reportative evidentials referring to a non-specific source (e.g. *it is said*, *reportedly*, *allegedly*) should be regarded as instances of implied subjectivity (ibid. 40).

## 4 Stance in Discourse

Due to its diverse content and interactive dimension, stance has been explored in various types of discourse. Much attention has been devoted to the exploration of epistemic and effective stance in English and Spanish journalistic discourse with a focus on generic differences (Hidalgo 2006; Marín-Arrese 2006, 2015, 2017, 2021). Taking into account the distinction between reports and comments, numerous studies have looked into the expressions of deontic modality, epistemic modality and evidentiality (Marín-Arrese et al. 2004; Marín-Arrese 2015, 2017). The contrastive studies have revealed variation across the two languages and cultures: Spanish journalistic discourse displays preference for effective stance realizations, whereas its English counterpart contains more epistemic stance resources.

Stance in political discourse has also become a wide area of investigation since it is expected that stance will be a salient feature of spoken discourse that is "interpersonal and persuasive in nature" (Gray/Biber 2015: 520). Political discourse, where "participants negotiate communicative meaning in discourse, considering both its production and interpretation" (Fetzer 2013: 7), is intersubjective and interpersonal. As shown by studies conducted by Marín-Arrese (2009, 2011), stance resources and their (inter)subjective qualifications may unravel the ideological positioning, political identity and interpersonal styles of politicians. The analysis of the political speeches and parliamentary statements on the war in Iraq produced by Anthony Blair and Gordon Brown shows how the two politicians reach their target audience: Gordon Brown prefers markers of effective stance, whereas Anthony Blair prefers epistemic stance, which "reflects a lesser degree of commitment to the truth of the communicated proposition" (Marín-Arrese 2009: 38). Stance expressions in political speeches can also be subject to intercultural differences in shaping political speeches. For instance, George Bush and Anthony Blair use more expressions of stance in their discourse than José María Aznar López, former President of Government of Spain, which suggests that "there is a tendency in Spanish to uphold truthfulness over politeness, which might have a reflection in the lower use of epistemic stance markers in discourse" (Marín-Arrese 2011: 211).

A wider approach to stance, which incorporates not only the study of epistemic and non-epistemic modal verbs but also personal pronouns and negation, is found in the examination of George Bush's and Barack Obama's speeches addressed to the Arab World (Hidalgo-Downing/Hanawi 2017). Alongside wider studies of stance in political discourse, there are investigations devoted to more specific sub-categories of stance. Fetzer (2014) considers the cognitive verb parentheticals *I think*, *I mean*, *I believe* in monologic and dialogic argumentative political discourse, namely in political speeches and pre-election interviews.

In Lithuanian, stance in various types of discourse resources have been mainly considered within the categories of epistemic modality and evidentiality. In fiction, based on data from the parallel corpus *ParaCorp*, Usonienė and Šolienė (2010) analysed the ratio of verbal and adverbial strategies of expressing epistemic possibility and necessity in English and Lithuanian. In academic discourse, in a cross-disciplinary study, Šinkūnienė (2012) explored hedges making up the category of authorial stance; and Usonienė (2015) addressed the problem of evidential parentheticals and their discourse functions. On the basis of data drawn from journalistic discourse, Wiemer (2007) examined the syntactic status and evidential semantics of the particles *esą* 'they say', *neva* 'as if, allegedly', *matyt* 'evidently'; Usonienė and Šinkūnienė (2017) investigated participial evidential constructions; and Ruskan (2017) dealt with evidential CTPs, used as main clause predicates or parentheticals in printed and online newspapers. The examination of stance resources in political discourse has not been carried out yet. Thus, the aim of the current study is to identify markers of effective and epistemic stance and to compare their distribution in the speeches of right-wing and left-wing Lithuanian politicians, to investigate expressions of attribution and to explore the dimension of subjectivity and intersubjectivity of the markers of effective and epistemic stance as well as of attribution.

## 5 Data and Method

In order to answer the research questions, a self-compiled corpus of political speeches by right-wing and left-wing Lithuanian politicians was used. The speeches collected were delivered in the years 2006–2020. The corpus includes five speeches by five different right-wing politicians (four males and one female) as well as five speeches by five left-wing politicians (four males and one female). The speeches were retrieved from the official websites of the particular parties, the official website of the Government of the Republic of Lithuania, the official webpage of the Parliament of the Republic of Lithuania and other publicly acknowledged sites. It must be admitted that the speeches vary in their length as the availability of political speeches online is really limited; the majority of the political communication output freely available online is interviews or journalistic reports, which is not the focus of this research. Though the individual speeches differ in their wordcount within each sub-corpus, the overall number of tokens in the two sub-corpora is almost the same: the sub-corpus of the right-wing political speeches includes 9,581 words and the sub-corpus of the left-wing political speeches comprises 9,211 words. The overall wordcount is 18,792.

All the politicians with a right-wing political leaning belong to one conservative party *Tėvynės sąjunga – Lietuvos krikščionys demokratai* [*The Homeland Union – Lithuanian Christian Democrats*]. So, in the paper they are referred to as either 'right-wing' or 'Conservatives'. The abbreviation is CON. As for the left-wing politicians, the Lithuanian political spectrum of this political platform is not so uniform. There are several parties manifesting social democratic ideas. In the present data set the speeches by the members of two social democratic parties are included: the party *Lietuvos socialdemokratų partija* [*The Social Democratic Party of Lithuania*] and *Lietuvos socialdemokratų darbo partija* [*The Social Democratic Labour Party of Lithuania*]. For the ease of reference, this left-wing political grouping is referred to as 'left-wing' or 'Democrats'. The abbreviation used in the text is DEM.

The study utilizes quantitative and qualitative methods of research. Since the sub-corpora are of different size, the raw frequency numbers have been normalized per 1,000 words. Moreover, in order to verify whether the similarities and differences in frequency are statistically significant, the log-likelihood (LL) test[4] was performed, which is commonly considered to be a more statistically reliable tool than the chi-square test (cf. Dunning 1993), especially when the dataset at disposal is not large. The higher the LL test value, the more significant is the difference between two frequency scores. A difference in frequency is considered to be statistically significant if the LL test value is 3.84 or higher at the level of $p < 0.05$.

In order to ensure that all relevant markers are identified and classified correctly, the texts collected were carefully read throughout and annotated manually ascribing the following tags:

- Stance: EF-Effective stance, EP-Epistemic stance;
- Different sub-categories of effective stance: POT-Potentiality, DM-Deonticity, DIR-Directivity, INT-Intentionality, NRM-Normativity, VOL-Volition;
- Different sub-categories of epistemic stance: EM-Epistemic modals, CGA-Cognitive attitude, PFV-Personal factives, IFV-Impersonal factives, DPE-Direct perceptual evidential, IIE-Indirect inferential evidential, IRE-Indirect reportative evidential;

4 The log-likelihood calculator is available at http://ucrel.lancs.ac.uk/llwizard.html.

- Subjectivity/Intersubjectivity: SE-Subjective explicit, SI-Subjective implicit, IE-Intersubjective explicit, IO-Intersubjective opaque;
- Attribution: SEA-Subjective explicit attribution, SIA-Subjective implicit attribution.

Example (1) is an illustration of an annotated case:

(1) *Nuosekliai gerėjantis investuotojų požiūris į Lietuvos verslo aplinką –* ***manau,*** <EP, [[CGA], SE> ***tikrai*** <EP, [[PFV]], SE> *neblogas Vyriausybės darbų įvertinimas.*
[The consistently improving attitude of investors towards the Lithuanian business environment is, **I think**, a **really** good assessment of the Government's work.]

The study focuses on Lithuanian modal verbs (e.g. *galėti* 'can/may/might', *turėti* 'have to/must', reikėti 'need', *privalėti* 'be obliged to'), complement-taking predicates (e.g. *manyti* 'think', *tikėti* 'believe', *tikėtis* 'hope', *norėti* 'want', *pavykti* 'succeed', *tiesa, kad* 'the truth is that', etc.) and adverbials (e.g. *galbūt* 'perhaps', *turbūt* 'probably', *matyt* 'evidently', *deja* 'unfortunately', etc.). Some explanations about the data selection criteria are due. Though Lithuanian adverbials cause no difficulties in their interpretation in terms of stance expression, some Lithuanian modal verbs (for example, *galėti* 'can/may/might', *turėti* 'have to/must') are multifunctional and can potentially function in both effective and epistemic domains (Holvoet 2009; Šolienė 2013). So, all the instances with these two verbs were carefully examined and ascribed to the relevant category. It must be noted that the verb *turėti* 'have to/must' was not attested as a marker of epistemic stance in the present data, which is not surprising, since its overall deployment in the epistemic domain is rare and is very much discourse type dependent (Šolienė 2013). Example (2) below illustrates the epistemic reading of the verb *galėti* 'may/might', while example (3) contains the two verbs expressing effective stance (potentiality and deonticity):

(2) *Šios baimės kaina* ***gali būti*** *ne kurios nors partijos pralaimėti rinkimai, o darganota mūsų šalies, mūsų ir ateisiančių po mūsų ateitis.* (CON)
[The price of this fear **might be** not the lost election of any party, but the unknown future of our country, of us as citizens and of those who will come after us.]

(3) *Lietuva* ***gali*** *ir* ***turi*** *laimėti ne tik krepšinio čempionatą.* (CON)
[Lithuania **can** and **has to** win more than just a basketball championship.]

The Lithuanian *turėti* 'have to/must' has retained its pre-modal possessive meaning to the present day; obviously, such possessive uses were discarded from the analysis:

(4) *Savivaldybė* ***turi svertų*** *šiai problemai spręsti.* (DEM)
[The municipality **has** various **means** to address this issue.]

Finally, one more issue to be addressed in the data selection was the acquisitive verb *tekti* 'be gotten'[5]. We did not include into the analysis cases where *tekti* 'be gotten' occurred in the pattern V+NP, which is clearly not a case for the study:

(5) *Mūsų Vyriausybei* ***teko*** *nedėkingas* ***uždavinys*** *gelbėti šalį iš krizės* [...] (CON)
[Our Government **had** the ungrateful **task** of rescuing the country from the crisis [...].]

Only the instances of the patterning V+ INF in which the verb conveyed stance were taken into consideration:

(6) *R. Songaila – man kaip tik* ***teko grįžti*** *iš komandiruotės, kai tai įvyko.* (DEM)
[Mr R. Songaila – I just **had to come back** from my mission when it happened.]

In example (6) *teko grįžti* 'had to come back' encodes obligation.

# 6 Results and Discussion

The Results and Discussion section is comprised of several sub-sections in which the distribution, functions and (inter)subjective dimension of the effective and epistemic stance markers in Lithuanian political discourse as well as instances of attribution and their qualification in terms of non-speaker subjectivity are discussed.

## 6.1 Distribution of Effective Stance and Epistemic Stance

Table 1 below shows the overall frequencies of the markers of effective and epistemic stance in the right-wing and left-wing Lithuanian parties. The results are given in raw numbers and relative frequencies per 1,000 words. Also, the log-likelihood test scores are given.

**Table 1.** The overall frequencies of effective and epistemic stance in the political speeches.

| | CON | | DEM | | LL |
|---|---|---|---|---|---|
| | **Raw fr** | **fr/1,000** | **Raw fr** | **fr/1,000** | |
| Effective stance | 144 | **15.03** | 121 | **13.14** | 1.20 |
| Epistemic stance | 85 | 8.87 | 69 | 7.49 | 1.09 |
| **TOTAL** | **229** | **23.48** | **190** | **20.63** | **2.26** |

5 Usonienė and Jasionytė (2010) single out two verbs of acquisition in Lithuanian *gauti* 'get' and *tekti* 'be gotten'. However, in the present data the verb *gauti* 'get' did not feature as a marker of stance.

The results show that the overall stance marking is more characteristic of the discourse of the Conservatives than of the Democrats; however, the log-likelihood test scores show no statistical significance whatsoever. The representatives of both political groupings tend to resort to devices for expressing effective rather than epistemic stance, which is in line with the studies of Spanish political discourse. Epistemic stance is employed less frequently than effective stance, though it is more salient in the discourse of the Conservatives.

## 6.2 Distribution of the Sub-Categories of Effective Stance

The next step of the analysis was to look into the sub-categories of effective stance. The results are presented in Table 2. The distribution of the sub-categories of effective stance in the political discourse of both political groupings points out that the most dominant notions are potentiality and deonticity, followed by intentionality.

**Table 2.** The distribution of the sub-categories of effective stance.

| | CON | | DEM | | LL |
|---|---|---|---|---|---|
| | **Raw fr** | **fr/1,000** | **Raw fr** | **fr/1,000** | |
| Potentiality | 61 | **6.37** | 32 | **3.47** | **8.09** |
| Deonticity | 39 | 4.07 | 36 | 3.91 | 0.03 |
| Intentionality | 16 | 1.67 | 22 | 2.39 | 1.20 |
| Volition | 6 | **0.63** | 18 | **1.95** | **6.76** |
| Directivity | 17 | 1.77 | 8 | 0.87 | 2.97 |
| Normativity | 5 | 0.52 | 5 | 0.54 | 0.00 |
| **TOTAL** | **144** | **15.03** | **121** | **13.14** | **1.20** |

However, it should be noted that potentiality is almost twice more frequent in the speeches of the Conservative politicians rather than the Democrats (the LL score is 8.09). The high number of the markers of potentiality can be explained by references to possible actions in the future (7) as well as to those that were successfully completed in the past (8)–(9):

(7) *Esminę pažangą kovoje su korupcija* ***galime*** *pasiekti sukurdami tikrą „saulėtekį" verslo sąlygoms, mažindami biurokratinius suvaržymus, kontroliuojančių institucijų, leidimų ir licenzijų brūzgynus.* (CON)
[**We will be able to** make a significant progress in the fight against corruption by creating a real 'sunrise' for business conditions and reducing bureaucratic constraints as well as diminishing the number of control authorities, permits and licenses.]

(8) ***Mums pavyko*** *suvaldyti krizę ir tą patį fiskalinį deficitą tik todėl, kad mūsų koalicija neišsigando politinės atsakomybės, nesislėpė nuo krizės, nepabūgo opozicijos destrukcijos ir visiškai nepagrįstos ir neatsakingos totalinės kritikos.* (CON)
[**We have succeeded** in managing the crisis and the fiscal deficit only due to the fact that our coalition did not shun from the political responsibility, did not ignore the crisis and were not afraid of the destruction imposed by the opposition and their completely unfounded and irresponsible criticism.]

(9) ***Pasiekta,*** *kad ES šiam projektui skirtų negrąžinamą finansinę paramą* (175 mln. EUR). (CON)
[**Our achievement was** that the EU provided non-repayable financial support for this project (175 million EUR).]

The almost even distribution of the devices for deonticity is not surprising since the representatives of both political alignments find it important to talk about obligations imposed on the parties by some authorities as well as about desirable actions, as shown below:

(10) *Kovodami su šešėliu* ***privalome*** *būti dar greitesni, įžvalgesni, išradingesni.* (DEM)
[In our fight against the shadow economy, **we have to be** even faster, more insightful and more inventive.]

(11) ***Turime*** *greičiau tiesti kelius tolyn į Aziją, Tolimuosius Rytus [...].* (DEM)
[**We have to** quickly reach out for Asia, the Far East [...].]

The sub-categories of volition (12) and intention (13) are more salient in the discourse of the Democrats, whereas directives (14) are more dominant in the speeches of the Conservatives:

(12) ***Tikimės,*** *kad atsižvelgs į mūsų pasiūlytus prioritetus ir kad šie prioritetai bei tikslai yra teisingi ir svarbūs visiems.* (DEM)
[**We hope** that our proposed priorities will be taken into account and that these priorities and goals are right and important to everyone.]

(13) ***Siekiama*** *didinti lietuviško turinio apimtis internete: skaitmeninant ir skleidžiant Lietuvos kultūros paveldą.* (DEM)
[**It is aimed** to increase the volume of Lithuanian output on the Internet by digitizing and disseminating Lithuanian cultural heritage.]

(14) ***Nebijokime*** *savęs ir labiau* ***pasitikėkime*** *savimi,* ***pasitikėkime*** *šalia esančiais, ir tada patikėsime savo ateitimi.* (CON)
[**Let's not be afraid** of ourselves, **let's be more self-confident, let's trust** more the ones who are near us and then we will believe in our future.]

The salient positioning of the Conservatives is apparent in (14) containing three expressions of directives, which accounts for the overall higher occurrences of stance markers in their discourse.

## 6.3 Distribution of the Sub-Categories of Epistemic Stance

Table 3 presents the results for the sub-categories of epistemic stance in the speeches by the Conservatives and Democrats. The quantitative results show that the representatives of both political leanings differ greatly in their use of epistemic modals denoting low degree of speaker commitment (the LL score is 7.41) and the deployment of personal cognitive factives (the LL score is 4.51).

**Table 3.** The distribution of the sub-categories of epistemic stance.

| | CON | | DEM | | LL |
|---|---|---|---|---|---|
| | **Raw fr** | **fr/1,000** | **Raw fr** | **fr/1,000** | |
| Evidential inferentials | 22 | 2.29 | 13 | 1.41 | 2.00 |
| Direct evidence | 1 | 0.10 | - | - | 1.35 |
| EP modals | 27 | 2.82 | 14 | 1.52 | 3.70 |
| | 20 (low) | **2.09** | 6 (low) | **0.65** | **7.41** |
| | 3 (medium) | 0.31 | 3 (medium) | 0.33 | 0.00 |
| | 4 (high) | 0.42 | 5 (high) | 0.54 | 0.15 |
| EP cognitive | 25 | 2.61 | 20 | 2.17 | 0.38 |
| EP impersonal factives | 6 | 0.63 | 10 | 1.09 | 1.17 |
| EP personal factives | 4 | **0.42** | 12 | **1.30** | **4.51** |
| **TOTAL** | **85** | **8.87** | **69** | **7.49** | **1.09** |

The representatives of both political alignments most frequently use markers of cognitive attitude and expressions of epistemic modality. The Conservatives employ more devices expressing a lower degree of the speaker's commitment than the Democrats. The salience of the expressions conveying uncertainty could be related to their dialogical potential or implication that the opinion voiced by the author is only one possible view (Martin/White 2005). The dialogical features of these markers emerge in the context of rhetorical questions, where the markers of epistemic possibility are repeated:

(15) ***Gal** pasikeitė ekonomikos perspektyvos? Ne, apie lėtėjimą žinojom jau pavasarį.* ***Gal** pasikeitė prioritetai?* (CON)
[**Maybe** the economic outlook has changed? No, we already knew about the slowdown in the spring. **Maybe** the priorities have changed?]

The analysis of the speeches of the Democrats reveals the even distribution of the markers of epistemic modality. Expressions of cognitive attitude (16) are also more dominant in the speeches produced by the Conservative politicians. However, interestingly, personal and impersonal factives make up a greater bulk of the expressions in the discourse of the Democrats, who rely on their knowledge

(17), appeal to the shared knowledge with the addressee (18) or emphasize the factuality of the proposition (19):

(16) ***Tikiu**, kad mokytojai idealistai kuria Lietuvos ateitį.* (CON)
[**I believe** that teachers, who are idealists, are building the future of Lithuania.]

(17) ***Žinau**, jog atsiras teigiančių, jog troleibusų išlaikymas (kartu su kontaktiniu tinklu) yra brangesnis nei autobusų.* (DEM)
[**I know** that there will be those who claim that the maintenance of trolleybuses (along with the overhead network) is more expensive than that of buses.]

(18) ***Kaip žinote**, Vyriausybės programa yra socialiai orientuota, ir šiuose pasiūlymuose mes laikomės tos orientacijos.* (DEM)
[**As you know**, the Government's program is socially oriented, and we follow that orientation in these proposals.]

(19) *Didžiausia problema yra ta, kad Kainų komisija **iš tikrųjų** jokio dialogo, kaip priklauso pagal įstatymą, su savivaldybėmis neturi.* (DEM)
[The main problem is that the Price Commission does not **in fact** have any dialogue with the municipalities, as required by law.]

The distributional differences can be noticed by the higher number of the occurrences of the inferential markers in the discourse of the Conservatives in comparison to the Democrats:

(20) *Žurnalo [...] indeksas **rodo**, kad Lietuva – palankiausia valstybė investicijoms Baltijos šalyse [...].* (DEM)
[The index of the journal [...] **shows** that Lithuania is the most promising country for investment opportunities in the Baltic States [...].]

(21) ***Akivaizdu**, kad gili ir skaudi ekonomikos recesija sukėlė didelę nedarbo bangą.* (CON)
[**It is obvious** that the deep and severe economic recession has led to a major wave of unemployment.]

Relying on perceptual or conceptual evidence, the politicians draw inferences that strengthen the authorial argumentation or emphasize that it is one of the possible interpretations. The tentative interpretation is expressed by the CTPs or adverbials *matyt* 'evidently' and *atrodo* 'it seems'.

## 6.4 Attribution

Cases of attribution, i.e. references to external sources, are more dominant in the speeches produced by the Conservatives (46 instances against 23 cases used by the Democrats), who show their alignment or disagreement with some sources and thus greater potential for argumentation. The politicians of both political affiliations indicate authoritative sources, i.e. experts, agencies, the government, President, other politicians responsible for the attributed information, as in the examples below:

(22) *Todėl šiandien jau galime pasidžiaugti ir tuo, kad* ***Tarptautinė reitingų agentūra*** *„Moody's" dar kovo 31 d. ne tik pagerino mūsų skolinimosi reitingo perspektyvą, bet ir* ***konstatavo****, kad „Lietuvos ekonomika stabilizavosi greičiau, nei anksčiau manyta ir greičiausiai tarp visų Baltijos valstybių".* (CON)
[So today we can appreciate the fact that, already on 31 March, the **International rating agency** 'Moody's' not only improved our borrowing rating possibilities, but also **stated** that 'the Lithuanian economy has stabilized more quickly than anticipated and the most quickly among all the Baltic States'.]

(23) *Per rinkimus* ***prezidentas teigė****, kad gerovės valstybė yra tokia, kurioje nereikia spygliuotomis, aukštomis tvoromis apsistatyti turtingiesiems nuo skurdžiau gyvenančiųjų.* (DEM)
[During the election, **the President argued** that the welfare state is the one in which the rich do not need to protect themselves with barbed high fences from the poor.]

(24) ***Ekspertai pastebi****, kad Baltijos valstybes globalinė krizė paveikė stipriausiai, jos patyrė giliausią nuosmukį visame pasaulyje.* (CON)
[**Experts observe** that the Baltic States have been affected by the global crisis most severely and have undergone the deepest recession in the whole world.]

(25) *Jau dabar* ***Vyriausybė*** *plėtoja bendradarbiavimą su socialiniais partneriais ir* ***tikisi****, kad tai padarys teigiamą įtaką mūsų veiklai ateityje.* (DEM)
[**The Government** is already collaborating with the social partners and **hopes** that this will have a positive impact on our activities in the future.]

The credibility of the attributed information is strengthened by the authority of the sources. As claimed by Martin and White (2005: 116), "a multiplicity of sources", as in (24), also adds to the plausibility of the propositional content. In (22)–(25), the politicians refer to external sources of information without explicitly conveying their stance. However, the author's stance towards the attributed material may be expressed in the text:

(26) *Permainų Vyriausybė nepraskolino Lietuvos,* ***kaip nesąžiningai tvirtina opozicija*** *– priešingai, šita Vyriausybė traukia šalį iš finansinės prarajos* [...]. (CON)
[The Government of Change did not pull Lithuania into debt, **as the opposition dishonestly claims** – on the contrary, this Government is pulling the country out of the financial crisis [...].]

(27) *Investuotojai, verslininkai* ***vienu balsu kalba****, kad jų veiklą stabdo kvalifikuotų specialistų stygius.* (DEM)
[Investors, businessmen **unanimously speak** that their activities are hampered by a lack of qualified professionals.]

The attributive expressions in (26) and (27) acquire an evaluative dimension because the evaluations *nesąžiningai* 'dishonestly/falsely' and *vienu balsu* 'unanimously' accompanying the verbs of communication *tvirtina* 'claim' and *kalba* 'say' express the author's position towards the attributed information. In

(26), the author disagrees with the opposition's false claim that the Government of changes pulled Lithuania into debt. Similarly in (27), the author shows alignment with businessmen and investors who speak about the lack of specialists in their fields. Martin and White claim that "it is more typical, particularly in argumentative texts such as media commentaries, political speeches or academic articles, for attribution to be much more obviously implicated in issues of alignment and solidarity" (Martin/White 2005: 115). Alongside cases of reported speech, thought, beliefs and wishes, there are markers of attribution that do not carry the author's evaluation because the information is highly warrantable (28)–(29):

(28) ***Kaip žinia**, 2011-ais metais svarbiausias mūsų prioritetas bus laimėti Europos krepšinio čempionatą čia, Lietuvoje.* (CON)
[**Reportedly**, in 2011, our most important priority will be to win the European Basketball Championship here in Lithuania.]

(29) ***„Investuok Lietuvoje" duomenimis**, Lietuva, praėjusiais metais pritraukusi 44-ių tiesioginių užsienio investicijų projektus, ryškiai pirmauja tarp Baltijos šalių.* (DEM)
[**According to the 'Invest in Lithuania'**, Lithuania, which attracted 44 foreign direct investment projects last year, is a clear leader among the Baltic States.]

Thus, in (28) and (29), the author does not express any value position concerning the attributed information but indicates that this information is based on external sources. The adverbial *kaip žinia* 'reportedly' (28) refers to some unspecific external source, whereas (29) exemplifies a specific original source, which is 'defocused' (Marín-Arrese 2017: 35). Although the markers of attribution referring to a non-specific source express the author's detachment from the veracity of the attributed information and do not comment anything about the sources, in some cases they may evoke the author's position as well:

(30) *Užmetama dar stipriau: **neva** norime iš vienų atimti, kitiems atiduoti.* (DEM)
[We are criticized even more severely: **supposedly** we want to reduce benefits for one group of people and to add extras for the other.]

The marker *neva* 'allegedly/supposedly' in (30) shows the politicians' scepticism towards the attributed information.

## 6.5 Subjectivity/Intersubjectivity

The distribution of the markers of effective and epistemic stance in terms of their dimension of subjectivity and intersubjectivity reveals some variation in the discourse produced by the politicians of different political standing (see Table 4).

The Democrats do not show preference for qualifying their effective or epistemic stance as subjective or intersubjective because they use markers of subjectivity as frequently as those of intersubjectivity, while the Conservatives more frequently deploy markers of intersubjectivity, displaying a shared status of information and engagement with the addressee. As claimed by Fetzer and Johansson (2012: 95), "in the particularized context of mediated political discourse, politicians do not only speak on behalf of themselves as individual agents, but also, if not primarily, on behalf of the political party (or government) they are affiliated with and which they represent".

**Table 4.** The distribution of the markers of effective and epistemic stance as well as attribution in terms of the dimension of subjectivity and intersubjectivity.

| | **CON** | | **DEM** | | **LL** |
|---|---|---|---|---|---|
| | **Raw fr** | **fr/1,000** | **Raw fr** | **fr/1,000** | |
| Subjective EXP | 29 | 3.03 | 38 | 4.13 | 1.59 |
| Subjective IMP | 70 | 7.31 | 55 | 5.97 | 1.26 |
| **TOTAL** | 99 | 10.33 | 93 | 10.09 | 0.33 |
| Intersubjective EXP | 46 | 4.80 | 41 | 4.45 | 0.12 |
| Intersubjective OP | 84 | **8.77** | 56 | **6.08** | **4.59** |
| **TOTAL** | 130 | 13.57 | 97 | 10.53 | 3.60 |
| Subjective explicit attribution | 39 | **4.07** | 21 | **2.28** | **4.80** |
| Subjective implicit attribution | 7 | 0.73 | 2 | 0.22 | 2.75 |
| **TOTAL** | **46** | **4.80** | **23** | **2.50** | **6.94** |

In the case of effective stance, the politicians refer to something that they as a party succeeded in doing, and the implication could be that it was also their electorate's success for they supported the party in the elections:

(31) *Apie tai bus rašomi vadovėliai ir disertacijos – kaip atlaikyti 15 procentų recesiją, sumažinti deficitą 9 procentais nuo BVP (t.y. beveik 9 mlrd. Litų) ir „nesubyrėti" – išsaugoti visuomenės, politinį ir socialinį stabilumą, stabilią valiutą stabiliai laiku mokamą pensiją ir atlyginimus. Kaip* ***mums pavyko*** *tai pasiekti – pasaulyje stebisi daug kas.* (CON)
[Textbooks and dissertations will be written on how to withstand a 15-percent recession, reduce the deficit by 9 percent of GDP (i.e. almost 9 billion LTL) and not 'fall apart' – to maintain social, political and social stability, the stable currency and stable and timely-paid pensions and salaries. How **we managed to achieve** remains a mystery to the world.]

(32) *Per dvejus metus* ***pasiekėme****, kad šilumos gamyboje jau vienodomis dalimis (per pusę) naudojamas vietinis biokuras ir importuojamos dujos.* (DEM)
[In two years' time, **we have** already **achieved** the use of local biofuel and imported gas in equal parts (in half) in the process of heat generation.]

The explicit intersubjective effective stance is found in contexts where the politicians describe their intentions regarding some reforms (33), discuss their potentiality and obligation to win in face of the competitive global trends (34) or signal their readiness for changes (35):

(33) *Todėl pradėjome apskričių reformą, kuria* ***siekiame****, kad paslaugų teikimas gyventojams būtų efektyvesnis, kad sumažėtų administracinė našta gyventojams ir būtų kuo efektyviau naudojamos valstybės biudžeto lėšos.* (CON)
[Therefore, we have started the reform of the counties and **we aim** to make the provision of services to the inhabitants more efficient, to reduce the administrative burden on the population and to use the state budget funds as efficiently as possible.]

(34) *Mes* ***galime*** *ir* ***turime*** *laimėti globalioje konkurencijoje, pasaulinės pažangos lenktynėse.* (CON)
[**We can** and **must** win in the global competition, the race of global progress.]

(35) *Taip pat mes* ***esame pasiruošę*** *daryti kompromisus ir išklausyti jūsų pasiūlymus.* (DEM)
[**We are** also **ready** to make compromises and listen to your suggestions.]

The intersubjective dimension of these markers emphasizes a bond with their target audience or those who are still looking for a better political alternative. In case of epistemic stance, the politicians indicate the shared status of their beliefs, truth and knowledge:

(36) ***Esame įsitikinę****, kad nauja AE padės įgyvendinti Nacionalinės energetikos strategijos tikslus ir sumažins priklausomybę nuo elektros ir dujų importo elektros gamybai.* (CON)
[**We are convinced** that the new nuclear powerplant will contribute to the achievement of the aims of the National Energy Strategy and reduce our dependence on electricity and gas imports for electricity generation.]

(37) *2010 metai nebus lengvesni, bet* ***tikime****, jog jie bus kitokie.* (CON)
[2010 will not be an easy year, but **we believe** it will be different.]

(38) *Nors,* ***kaip žinome****, lietuviškos kilmės prekių eksportas į Rusiją pernai sumažėjo 16 procentų.* (DEM)
[Although, **as we know**, exports of Lithuanian goods to Russia decreased by 16 percent last year.]

In the speeches produced by the politicians of both political affiliations, the intersubjective expressions of effective and epistemic stance more frequently remain opaque as to the identity of the conceptualizer, i.e. the author or a virtual/generalized conceptualizer. However, the difference between the explicit and opaque intersubjective markers in the speeches produced by the Democrats is less prominent than in those produced by the Conservatives. The higher frequencies of the opaque intersubjective markers could be attributed to "obfuscating personal responsibility and accountability" for expressing a certain position (Marín-Arrese 2017: 42). Moreover, in Lithuanian, there are a number of markers capable of occurring in impersonal constructions, such as non-agreeing participles used with *that* or *to* clauses (39), non-agreeing adjectives functioning adverbially (40) or impersonal modal verbs of necessity (41):

(39) ***Tikimasi**, kad tuo būdu valstybinis finansavimas susitelks ten, kur pasirinks geriausi studentai ir taip išaiškės stipriausieji universitetai […].* (CON)
[**It is expected** that in this way public financing will reach universities chosen by the best students, which will help identify the strongest universities […].]

(40) *Ir, **aišku**, todėl mes neturime laiko atidėlioti kardinalius sprendimus.* (DEM)
[And, **clearly**, we do not have time to postpone cardinal decisions.]

(41) ***Reikės** pakeisti beveik 1500 teisės aktų, tarp jų daugiau nei 100 įstatymų.* (DEM)
[Nearly 1,500 legislative acts **will need** to be amended, including more than 100 laws.]

There are no marked differences in the overall use of the markers of subjectivity in the speeches produced by the Democrats and the Conservatives. However, the salience of the conceptualizer differs in their speeches. The Democrats more frequently deploy the markers of explicit subjectivity than the Conservatives, highlighting their personal responsibility in expressing effective (42)–(43) or epistemic stance (44):

(42) ***Norėčiau**, kad miesto sveikatos priežiūros ir socialinių paslaugų įstaigose jus pasitiktų šypsenos […].* (DEM)
[**I would like** you to be greeted with smiles in the city's health and social service institutions […].]

(43) ***Tikiuosi**, kad Lietuvos mokslininkai, inžinieriai pasinaudos išskirtine proga – valstybės užsakymu moderniąsias technologijas pritaikyti krašto gynybos ir saugumo poreikiams.* (DEM)
[**I hope** that Lithuanian scientists and engineers will take advantage of an exceptional opportunity – in accordance with the state order, to adapt modern technologies to the needs of national defence and security.]

(44) *Greta korupcijos prevencijos priemonių, **mano nuomone**, būtina optimizuoti ir korupcinio pobūdžio teisės pažeidimų tyrimą.* (DEM)
[In addition to the measures of corruption prevention, it is, **in my opinion**, necessary to optimize the investigation of corruption offenses.]

Like in case of the opaque intersubjective markers, the Conservatives resort more often to markers of implied subjectivity than the Democrats, thus avoiding direct claims of personal responsibility:

(45) *Lietuvai **nereiks** rinktis tarp blogo ir blogesnio kandidato į Prezidentus, o visi ramia širdimi balsuosime už tą kandidatą, kuriuo pasitikime.* (CON)
[Lithuania **will not have to** choose between a bad and a worse candidate for President, and we will all vote for the candidate we trust with peace in our hearts.]

(46) *Bet kaip tik tada buvo patvirtinta ES nuostata dėl streso testų atlikimo ES kaimyninėse valstybėse ir dėl to dabartinis Prezidentas turi puikų pamatą, kuriuo* ***galėtų*** *remtis reikalaujant atidėti jėgainės eksploatavimo pradžią.* (CON)
[But it was only then that the EU's provision for stress tests in the EU's neighbouring countries was approved, and as a result, the current President **could** have solid grounds for demanding to postpone the beginning of the powerplant's operation.]

The examination of the subjective dimension of the markers of attribution has shown that the politicians of both political affiliations employ more expressions of explicit subjectivity since it is important for them to specify the exact sources and indicate either their alignment or disagreement with the attributed position. In the political speeches examined, implicit subjectivity characterizing the markers of attribution is not dominant. However, the speeches of the Conservatives contain more attributive expressions revealing implicit subjectivity.

## 7 Conclusions

The present study complements research into epistemic and effective stance markers in political discourse across languages and cultures (Marín-Arrese 2009, 2011; Hidalgo-Downing/Hanawi 2017). It provides some preliminary findings how Lithuanian politicians of two different ideological standings, i.e. right wing and left-wing politicians, shape their discourse in terms of effective and epistemic stance, refer to external sources as well as qualify their stance as subjective or intersubjective.

Markers of effective stance are more frequent than markers of epistemic stance in the speeches of both the Conservatives and the Democrats, which also correlates with the preference of effective stance expressions in Spanish political and journalistic discourses (Hidalgo 2006; Marín-Arrese 2011). However, it should be noted that the Conservatives tend to express their authorial position more frequently than the Democrats because the overall number of stance devices in their speeches is higher than in those of their political opponents.

Within the domain of effective stance the most common sub-categories in the speeches of both political affiliations are potentiality and deonticity, with directivity being dominant in the Conservative discourse and volitionality more frequently occurring in the Democrats' speeches. Within the area of epistemic stance, the dominant sub-categories are those of epistemic modality, inferential evidentiality and cognitive attitude. Since representatives of both political orientations wish to express their commitment towards the proposition, to draw conclusions and voice a subjective opinion, it is not surprising that these sub-categories are most frequent. Expressions of attribution, i.e. references to specified or non-specified external sources, again are more common in the speeches of the Conservatives, who display their inclination to agree or argue with external sources, i.e. experts, other politicians, etc.

In terms of subjectivity and intersubjectivity, the speeches produced by the politicians of both political leanings show some variation. The Conservatives tend to employ the intersubjective markers of effective and epistemic stance more frequently than the Democrats. Moreover, the differences between the explicit and implicit subjective or intersubjective positioning in the speeches of the Conservatives is more marked than in the speeches produced by the Democrats. The left-wing politicians do not avoid taking personal or shared responsibility explicitly. They use slightly more markers of explicit subjectivity than the Conservatives. The politicians of both political leanings employ more markers of attribution conveying explicit subjectivity, for it is quite common for politicians to make references to specific sources.

## References

Arcimavičienė, L. (2011). 'The Complex Metaphor of POLITICAL ANIMALS in Media Political Discourse: A Cross-linguistic Perspective'. *Kalbų Studijos*, 19, 95–100.

Biber, D., Johansson, S., Leech, G., Conrad, S., and Finegan, E. (eds.) (1999). *Longman Grammar of Spoken and Written English*. London: Longman.

Biber, D. (2006). *University Language. A Corpus-based Study of Spoken and Written Registers*. Amsterdam/Philadelphia: John Benjamins.

Boye, K. (2012). *Epistemic Meaning: A Crosslinguistic and Functional-cognitive Study*. Berlin: de Gruyter Mouton.

Carretero, M. (2016). 'Noun Phrases as Expressions of Evidentiality: An Analysis of four English Abstract Nouns and their Spanish Equivalents'. *Kalbotyra*, 69, 29–58.

Cibulskienė, J. (2012). 'The Development of the JOURNEY Metaphor in Political Discourse: Time-specific Changes'. *Metaphor and the Social World*, 2 (2), 131–153.

Du Bois, J. W. (2007). 'The Stance Triangle'. In R. Englebretson (ed.), *Stancetaking in Discourse*, pp. 139–182. Amsterdam/Philadelphia: John Benjamins.

Dunning, T. (1993). 'Accurate Methods for the Statistics of Surprise and Coincidence'. *Computational Linguistics*, 19 (1), 61–74.

Fetzer, A., and Johansson, M. (2012). 'Cognitive Verbs in Context: A Contrastive Analysis of English and French Argumentative Discourse'. In S. Marzo, K. Heylen, and G. De Sutter (eds.), *Corpus Studies in Contrastive Linguistics*, pp. 89–115. Amsterdam/Philadelphia: John Benjamins.

Fetzer, A. (2013). 'The Multilayered and Multifaceted Nature of Political Discourse'. In A. Fetzer (ed.), *The Pragmatics of Political Discourse: Explorations across Cultures*, pp. 1–18. Amsterdam/Philadelphia: John Benjamins.

Fetzer, A. (2014). '*I think*, *I mean* and *I believe* in Political Discourse: Collocates, Functions and Distribution'. *Functions of Language*, 21 (1), 67–94.

Gray, B., and Biber, D. (2015). 'Stance Markers'. In K. Aijmer, and Ch. Rühlemann (eds.), *Corpus Pragmatics: A Handbook*, pp. 219–246. Cambridge: Cambridge University Press.

Hidalgo, L. (2006). 'The Expression of Writer Stance by Modal Adjectives and Adverbs in Comparable Corpus of English and Spanish Newspaper Discourse'. In A.M. Hornero, M.J. Luzón, and S. Murillo (eds.), *Corpus Linguistics: Applications for the Study of English*, pp. 125–140. Bern/Berlin: Peter Lang.

Hidalgo-Downing, L., and Hanawi, Y. (2017). 'Bush and Obama's Addresses to the Arab World: Recontextualizing Stance in Political Discourse'. In K. Aijmer, and D. M. Lewis (eds.), *Contrastive Analysis of Discourse-pragmatic Aspects of Linguistic Genres*, pp. 187–209. Springer International Publishing AG.

Holvoet, A. (2009). 'Modals in Baltic'. In B. Hansen, and F. de Haan (eds.), *Modals in the Languages of Europe. A Reference Work*, pp. 199–228. Berlin/New York: Mouton de Gruyter.

Hunston, S., and Thompson, G. (2000). *Evaluation in Text: Authorial Stance and the Construction of Discourse*. Oxford: Oxford University Press.

Lyons, J. (1977). *Semantics* (2 vols.). Cambridge: Cambridge University Press.

Marín-Arrese, J.I. (2006). 'Epistemic Stance and Commitment in the Discourse of Fact and Opinion in English and Spanish: A Comparable Corpus Study'. In A.M. Hornero, M. J. Luzón, and S. Murillo (eds.), *Corpus Linguistics: Applications for the Study of English*, pp. 141–157. Bern/Berlin: Peter Lang.

Marín-Arrese, J.I. (2009). 'Effective vs. Epistemic Stance, and Subjectivity/Intersubjectivity in Political Discourse: A Case Study'. In A. Tsangalidis, and R. Facchinetti (eds.), *Studies on English Modality. In Honour of Frank Palmer*, pp. 23–52. Berlin/New York: Peter Lang.

Marín-Arrese, J.I. (2011). 'Effective vs. epistemic stance and subjectivity in political discourse: Legitimising strategies and mystification of responsibility'. In C. Hart (ed.) *Critical Discourse Studies in Context and Cognition*, pp. 193–223. Amsterdam/Philadelphia: John Benjamins.

Marín-Arrese, J.I. (2015). 'Epistemicity and Stance: A Cross-linguistic Study of Epistemic Stance Strategies in Journalistic Discourse in English and Spanish'. *Discourse Studies*, 17 (2), 210–225.

Marín-Arrese, J.I. (2017). 'Stancetaking and Inter/subjectivity in Journalistic Discourse: The Engagement System Revisited'. In R. Breeze, and I. Olza (eds.), *Evaluation in Media Discourse*, pp. 21–48. Bern/Berlin: Peter Lang.

Marín-Arrese, J.I. (2021). 'Stance, Emotion and Persuasion: Terrorism and the Press'. *Journal of Pragmatics*, 177, 135–148.

Marín-Arrese, J.I., Hidalgo Downing, L., and Molina Plaza, S. (2004). 'Evidential, Epistemic and Deontic Modality in English and Spanish: The Expression of Writer Stance in Newspaper Discourse'. In R. Facchinetti, and F. Palmer (eds.), *English Modality in Perspective: Genre Analysis and Contrastive Studies*, pp. 121–139. Frankfurt am Main: Peter Lang Verlag.

Martin, J. R., and White, P. R. R. (2005). *The Language of Evaluation: Appraisal in English*. Basingstoke: Palgrave Macmillan.

Palmer, F. R. (2001). *Mood and Modality* [2nd ed.]. Cambridge: Cambridge University Press.

Ruskan, A. (2017). 'Markers of Evidentiality in Lithuanian Newspaper Discourse: A Corpus-based Study'. In J.I. Marín-Arrese, M. Carretero, and G. Haßler (eds.), *Cognitive Grammar, Functional and Discourse-Pragmatic Perspectives*, pp. 271–295. Amsterdam/Philadelphia: John Benjamins.

Simaki, V., Paradis, C., Skeppstedt, M., Sahlgren, M., Kucher, K., and Kerren, A. (2020). 'Annotating Speaker Stance in Discourse: The Brexit Blog Corpus', *Corpus Linguistics and Linguistic Theory*, 16, 215-248. <https://portal.research.lu.se/portal/en/publications/annotating-speaker-stance-in-discourse(18e17da2-9c3f-4c27-8980-7a04d12aacda).html>

Šinkūnienė, J. (2012). 'Adverbials as Hedging Devices in Lithuanian Academic Discourse: A Cross-Disciplinary Study'. In A. Usonienė, N. Nau, and I. Dabašinskienė (eds.), *Multiple Perspectives in Linguistic Research on Baltic Languages*, pp. 138–168. Newcastle upon Tyne: Cambridge Scholars Publishing.

Šolienė, A. (2013). *Episteminio modalumo ekvivalentiškumo parametrai anglų ir lietuvių kalbose*. [Realizations of Epistemic Modality in English and Lithuanian: Parameters of Equivalence]. Unpublished PhD thesis, Vilnius University.

Usonienė, A., and Jasionytė, E. (2010). 'Towards Grammaticalization: Lithuanian Acquisitive Verbs *gauti* ('get') and *tekti* ('be gotten')'. *Acta Linguistica Hafniensia*, 42 (2), 199–220.

Usonienė, A., and Šolienė, A. (2010). 'Choice of Strategies in Realizations of Epistemic Possibility in English and Lithuanian: A Corpus-Based Study'. *International Journal of Corpus Linguistics*, 15 (2), 291–316.

Usonienė, A. (2015). 'Non-Morphological Realizations of Evidentiality: The Case of Parenthetical Elements in Lithuanian'. In P. Arkadiev, A. Holvoet, and B. Wiemer (eds.), *Contemporary Approaches to Baltic Linguistics*, pp. 437–463. Berlin: Mouton de Gruyter.

Usonienė, A., and Šinkūnienė, J. (2017). 'Potential vs Use: Revisiting an Evidential Participial Construction in Lithuanian'. In J.I. Marín-Arrese, M. Carretero, and G. Haßler, (eds.), *Cognitive Grammar, Functional and Discourse-Pragmatic Perspectives*, pp. 297–340. Amsterdam/Philadelphia: John Benjamins.

White, P. R. R. (2011). 'Appraisal'. In J. Zienkowski, Jan-Ola Östman, and J. Verschueren, (eds.), *Discursive Pragmatics*, pp. 14–36. Amsterdam/Philadelphia: John Benjamins.

Wiemer, B. (2007). 'Lexical Markers of Evidentiality in Lithuanian'. *Rivista di Linguistica*, 19 (1), 173–208.

Aoife Ahern, José Amenós-Pons & Pedro Guijarro-Fuentes

# Expressing Evidentiality in two Languages: Conjectural Future in Catalan/Spanish Bilinguals[1]

**Abstract:** This study focuses on Majorcan Catalan-Spanish bilinguals' use of the future tense (FUT) for expressing conjectural evidential meaning in Spanish and Catalan. Conjectural interpretations of FUT are rare in Catalan while in Spanish they are more frequent than chronological ones. Ninety-seven bilingual speakers, with varying language dominance measures, performed two tasks in both Catalan and Spanish: firstly, choosing between FUT and two other ways of expressing conjecture; and secondly, judging the acceptability of conjectural uses of FUT. The bilinguals' responses were compared to those of a group of 36 monolingual Spanish speakers. Our data indicate that bilinguals use the FUT to express conjecture less often than monolinguals, both in Catalan and in Spanish. However, all the groups show awareness of the aspectual restrictions on FUT as an expression of conjecture. The sensitivity of bilingual speakers to the factors that make conjectural FUT uses appropriate cannot be correlated with language dominance.

**Keywords:** *future tense, aspect, Majorcan Catalan-Spanish bilinguals, language dominance*

## 1 Introduction

This study examines the role of language dominance (LD) in linguistic competence outcomes in adult bilinguals. We take advantage of the unique geolinguistic situation in the Balearic Islands, testing both Spanish and Catalan[2], where speakers may show dominance in either of these two languages. Despite balanced Catalan-Spanish bilingualism being common to many speakers in this context, language dominance can be expected to fluctuate across individuals. Furthermore, although at the community level successful bilingualism has been

---

1 This is part of the research project *Evidentiality and Perspectivisation at the Interfaces of Language* (ƐPSILone), funded by the Spanish Ministry of Science, Innovation and Universities (PID2019-104405GB-I00). We would like to thank the students of the Universitat de les Illes Balears who participated in the study and the faculty members who revised the questionnaire and helped us to collect the data.

2 The language considered within this article is a specific Majorcan variety of the Catalan language. For brevity's sake, throughout this article, we will use the term 'Catalan' to refer to this variety.

widely achieved, cross-linguistic influence can still be expected in developing bilingual grammars.

Looking at some of the origins of such differences in the grammatical development and outcomes in bilinguals, and the degree to which they depend on the order of acquisition of the languages and other measures of relevant dominance (for instance, patterns of use, frequency of use and so on) in one or the other language, may contribute to deepening knowledge about bilingualism in general. In addition, showing what is similar and distinct among our adult bilingual speakers could provide evidence of certain characteristics that differentiate monolingual and bilingual outcomes in adulthood, and details of how relations between grammar, semantics and pragmatics can drive or prevent diachronic change in situations of language contact.

This study offers data from two groups of Catalan-Spanish bilinguals who were born and raised on the Island of Majorca. All the bilingual participants in the present study have been educated, and are literate, in both languages. In one of the groups, Catalan is the dominant language, while in the other group Spanish is dominant.

An important feature of the research reported on herein is that each bilingual adult participant completed the tasks in both languages. Although, to our knowledge, previous studies have focused on just one of the languages of similar populations, comparable data on each of bilinguals' languages are needed to understand more fully how they interact in the individual speaker's mind. By *dominance*, we mean patterns of preferred language use and usage frequency in daily life, following Unsworth's (2015) proposal. Since Catalan-Spanish adult bilinguals tend to be highly proficient in both languages, correlating proficiency and language dominance in this context of balanced bilingualism would probably not be very informative. Given this relatively unique environment, one can quite often find bilinguals who are more dominant in one or the other language while highly proficient and literate in both languages.

More specifically, in exploring the role of language dominance, computed as an external extralinguistic composite variable that includes individual language history, language use, proficiency and attitudes measured via an ethnolinguistic questionnaire (Birdsong et al. 2012), we examine its correlations with the strength or weakness of a particular grammatical domain in the linguistic competence of bilinguals. The focus of our study is one subtle linguistic phenomenon (i.e., the use of future (hereon, FUT) to express conjecture) in both Spanish and Catalan, a task that we undertake in the following sections.

But first, albeit briefly, we surmise some of the potential outcomes of a prolonged language contact situation like the one described herein. On the one hand, Trudgill (1989) proposed that language contact situations yield erosion or simplification of the internal development of languages, resulting in loss of morphology, and increases in regularity, analyticity, transparency, and redundancy; this has been mostly proven by the development of pidgin languages. On the other hand, a different outcome of an intense language contact situation could be convergence. To that end, considering the Quechua-Spanish language contact situation, Sánchez (2003, 2004, 2015) put forward the concepts of functional convergence and functional interference. Whereas functional convergence is "the specification of a common set of features shared by the equivalent functional categories in the two languages spoken by a bilingual" (Sánchez 2003: 15), there is functional interference when "the activation of functional features in one language, triggered by input in the other language, generates syntactic change in the bilingual grammars" (Sánchez 2003: 13).

The process of functional interference happens when language A possesses functional features that are (I) absent in language B; (II) coupled with a different functional category in language B; (III) grouped with other functional features in language B; or (IV) any combination of (I), (II), and (III). The main difference between convergence and interference processes is the ultimate outcome. Whereas convergence produces a new specification of features in the two languages spoken by a bilingual, in functional interference, the set of features and functional categories from language A are adopted in language B.

Within this convergence scenario, there are researchers, such as Thomason and Kaufman (1988: 14), who argue that "anything can be transferred from any language to any other language" (see also Thomason, 2001, 2008); that is, that syntactic transfer is possible. Others, nevertheless, claim that syntax is relatively impermeable to influence from another language. For instance, Prince (1998) and Silva-Corvalán (1998, 2008) argue that transfer is often limited to pragmatic uses. In their view, direct syntactic transfer is uncommon. Specifically, Silva-Corvalán (2008) discusses the English - Spanish contact situation in the United States, characterized by both maintenance of the minority language and shift to English, and ponders about the limits of syntactic convergence, claiming that bilingual speakers do not modify the abstract syntactic structure of the receding language. In sum, this author upholds that the transfer of features from one language to another does not involve syntax, but it can involve lexicon and pragmatics. In the same vein, Sorace, among other authors, following her seminal work (Sorace 2011, 2012 and references therein), has maintained in her *Interface Hypothesis,* that bilingual speakers, particularly near-native speakers, tend towards optionality and/or indeterminacy in linguistic phenomena involving an interface between syntax and other cognitive domains including pragmatics, but that linguistic phenomena involving only core syntactic computations remain fairly stable.

In connection with these claims, the present paper offers original data on the use of FUT for conveying conjecture, as an instance of phenomena at the grammar-pragmatics interface, in bilingual speakers of a seldom-studied language pair. The outline of the paper is as follows. Section 2 first describes the linguistic background in relation to FUT in both Catalan and Spanish, which serves as a basis for the present study. Subsequently, Section 3 addresses the bilingual situation in Mallorca as regards their exposure to language contact, showing that this particular bilingual situation is an ideal one to test the hypothesized relation between language contact and interference and/or convergency. The method used in investigating the degree of bilingual convergence is described in Section 4, which also contains the results of this investigation. Finally, Section 5 discusses the main findings and conclusions.

## 2 Linguistic Background: Conjectural FUT in Spanish and Catalan

Modern Romance languages (except for Romanian and some Italian vernaculars) have in common synthetic, inflectional future forms stemming from the periphrastic Latin obligative construction 'Infinitive + habere'. Futurity can also be expressed in the same languages by other means besides FUT, such as verbs of movement (go and come) or volition, markers of progressive aspect or certain uses of simple present. Full grammaticalization of these alternative devices in the respective languages, however, is uncommon (Dhal, 2000).

Given that the expression of futurity in Romance is etymologically related to modality, it is not surprising that, in most Romance languages, the FUT forms may trigger not only interpretations related to chronology, but also conjectural ones, similar to those of epistemic modal expressions. Additionally, interpreting chronology and conjecture often leads to the identification of additional nuances such as - on the chronological side - directive and volitional meaning (as in the Spanish examples (1) and (2)), as well as - on the conjectural side - concession and mirativity, as in (3) and (4):

(1) *No se lo dirás a nadie; es una orden.* [directive]
[You will not tell anyone; that's an order]

(2) *Te lo traeré mañana, no te preocupes.* [volition]
[I'll bring it to you tomorrow; don't worry about it]

(3) *Será muy guapo, pero es muy antipático.* [concession]
[He may be (S-FUT) very handsome, but he's very unpleasant].

(4) *¡Será tonto…!* [mirativity]
[He's (FUT) such a fool! ]

Within the Romance languages, Catalan has a unique particularity: it possesses a 'go + infinitive' form (*anar* + infinitive) used as a perfective past (5), and also a 'go to + infinitive' form (*anar a* + infinitive), which expresses the preparatory phase of an event (6). The use of *anar a* + infinitive in the present tense to depict an immediate future situation (7) is generally rejected as a loan from Spanish (Badia, 1962; Gavarró and Laca, 2008). This means that Catalan, unlike Spanish, has no GO-FUT form.

(5) *L'any passat es va casar el meu fill.*
[My son got married last year]
(6) *El fet que anava a produir-se al cap de poques hores…*
[The event that was going to happen in a few hours…]
(7) **Ara vaig a ensenyar-vos el secret del joc.*
[Now I'm going to show you the secret of the game]

Thus, in most cases, in Catalan, the simple future (henceforth, S-FUT) is related to chronology. Conversely, conjectural interpretations of the S-FUT in Spanish are frequent, and they correspond to a very high percentage of this tense's usage. If a purely chronological meaning is intended, the GO-FUT form (*ir a* + infinitive) is often preferred in Spanish (Escandell-Vidal, 2010, 2014).

In contrast, the mere existence of conjectural interpretations of the S-FUT in spontaneous Catalan (except for the Valencian varieties) is a debated issue. Conjectural S-FUT (as in (8) below) is found in written language since the 14$^{th}$ century (Pérez-Saldanya 2008: 2637), but it has nevertheless been criticized as a calque from Spanish (Aramon, 1957; Badia, 1962). Constructions with modal verbs, such as *deure* 'must' + infinitive are generally preferred in current usage (9) (Pérez-Saldanya 2008: 2637). This is also possible in Spanish, but the preference is reversed:

(8) *—On serà, Déu meu? —sospirava Maria Àgueda.* (Sebastià Juan Arbó, *Tino Costa*)
[Where may he be (S-FUT), for God's sake? —sighed Maria Àgueda]
(9) *És molt tard. Ja deuen de ser dormint.*
[It's very late. They must already be sleeping]

In the same vein, the use of conjectural S-FUT to express concession (10) and mirativity (11) is possible in Catalan, but it is much less frequent than in Spanish, especially in everyday language:

(10) *Serà que no ho entenc, però posar-se aquest manat de plomes músties…* (Llorenç Vilallonga, *Mort de dama*)
[I may be (S-FUT) that I don't understand it, but to put on this bunch of musty feathers… ]

(11) *Serà poca-solta!*
[S/he's (S-FUT) really stupid! ]

Despite the frequency of conjectural S-FUT, in Spanish this type of interpretation is restricted to certain linguistic conditions, mainly related to lexical aspect (Soto, 2008): it is usually necessary for the verb to have [- telic] and [- dynamic] features. Therefore, states are naturally compatible with such readings. On the other hand, [+ dynamic] verbs in the S-FUT can only be interpreted as conjectural if their location in the future is contextually ruled out. This generally implies that the events denoted are understood as habitual, as in (13). The aspectual restrictions mentioned above can also be overridden by adding the [+ progressive] feature to the predicate. This is often done by means of *estar* + gerund (to be + gerund) (14).

(12) ?? *No contesta. Dormirá en su habitación.* [+ telic] [+ dynamic]
[S/he's not answering (the phone). S/he must be sleeping (S-FUT) in his/her bedroom]

(13) - *¿A qué se dedica Luis?* + *No sé, trabajará en cosas de informática.* [- telic] [+ dynamic] [+ habitual]
[- What does Luis do? + I don't know, he (probably) works (S-FUT) in computing].

(14) *No contesta. Estará durmiendo en su habitación.*
[S/he's not answering (the phone). S/he must be sleeping (PROG FUT) in his/her bedroom]

In Catalan, the aspectual restrictions operating on conjectural S-FUT are similar to those of Spanish. However, as regards conjectural interpretations of the future perfect, or compound future (henceforth, C-FUT), they obtain in both languages without any lexical aspect restrictions. According to Pérez-Saldanya (2008: 2638), C-FUT, in Catalan, is the most frequent FUT form in conjectural interpretations. The C-FUT is unlike the simple form in that it involves the representation of a completed event, or its resulting state, as being previous to a reference point. This facilitates non-future readings regardless of the predicate type, as in utterances (15) and (16), in which conjectural interpretations in Spanish and Catalan are found with telic predicates:

(15) *La puerta no ha sido forzada. El ladrón habrá entrado por la ventana.*
[The door has not been forced. The burglar must have entered (C-FUT) through the window]

(16) *Jo no sé com el seu germà li haurà explicat les coses, però la veritat és que el procedir del seu germà és una mena d'abús de confiança.* (Josep Maria de Sagarra, *Vida privada*)
[I don't know how his brother has explained (C-FUT) the things to him, but the truth is that his brother's conduct is a kind of breach of trust]

A thorough description of the different usages of FUT in the languages of our study is beyond the scope of this paper. However, the overview provided in the previous paragraphs clearly shows that, despite its common origin, the S-FUT tense has developed divergent tendencies in Spanish as opposed to Catalan, particularly in terms of its potential for expressing conjecture and concession. In Catalan, the S-FUT is always understood as referring to future events; the morphological similarity between the perfective periphrastic past *anar* 'go' + infinitive and the aspectual *anar a* 'go to' + infinitive construction strongly limits the availability of the latter to develop futurate readings. Since in Catalan the S-FUT is needed to express chronology, conjectural uses of S-FUT cannot develop: they are rarely seen in spontaneous oral use and, in written language, they are only acceptable if they represent an event that is verifiable in the future. Such a requisite is absent from the Spanish S-FUT, and this paves the way to a much more widespread use of the tense to convey conjectural meaning.

This line of thought is fully compatible with Escandell-Vidal's (in press) cross-linguistic analysis of the Romance S-FUT. She describes the semantics of the tense in terms of features; there are certain core semantic features common to all Romance varieties, and others that differ. On her view, the core meaning of the Romance S-FUT 'encodes an instruction [for the hearer] to build the eventuality described by the sentence radical, or prejacent proposition **p**, as the representation of an [event] situation (ES) that cannot be accessed from an information acquisition situation (IS), in which the discourse situation (DS) is included'. The core semantic features do not specifically relate to time, nor to conjecture, but to the information source: the situation described is (at the IS) only available as an inference of the speaker. This implies that the FUT has an inherent evidential meaning. Despite the existence of common Romance features, the ultimate materializations of the S-FUT tense in the different languages will vary depending on the meaning-values that other cross-linguistically shared features have taken on. These features and their variation are represented in Table 1 below.

**Table 1.** The semantics of the simple S-FUT in Romance (Escandell-Vidal, in press)

| **CORE MEANING** | **IS \| ES**<br>**DS ⊂ IS** | | | | |
|---|---|---|---|---|---|
| **PARAMETERS** | **CATALAN** | **FRENCH** | **ITALIAN** | **SPANISH** | **PORTUGUESE** |
| ES [± Factual] | - | - | - | - | - |
| IS [± Deictic] | - | + | + | + | + |
| IS \| ES [± Forward] | + | + | - | - | - |

Thus, following Escandell-Vidal's proposal, the Romance S-FUT is always non-factual. In all Romance languages but Catalan it is also [+ Deictic]; this means that (in these languages) the IS is related to the speaker's perceptual field. The Catalan S-FUT is the only one in Romance that is independent from the IS; as a result, this language disallows conjectural readings, as opposed to French, Italian, Spanish and Portuguese. However, the French S-FUT imposes a [+ Forward] relation between IS and ES: thus, all eventualities in the French S-FUT call for a future verification. This is not required in Italian, Spanish and Portuguese and, as a result, conjectural uses of the S-FUT may be more pervasive.

Although the present study only probes written language, it is important to take into account that Escandell-Vidal's account specifically refers to spontaneous use. She considers that it is not surprising that the available readings of a tense in a single language partially differ in written and oral usage, because the two modalities tend to reflect different states in the evolution of the system. The uses that are exclusive to the written modality develop later within the linguistic repertoire of individual speakers and tend to show more variability in acceptability judgements tasks (Escandell-Vidal, 2019).

Escandell-Vidal's hypotheses underlie our own study because they provide explicit, falsifiable linguistic criteria for the commonalities and distinctions of the uses of FUT in Romance. They also offer a basis for conceptualizing the development of the grammar of a bilingual's non-dominant language: in subsequent bilingualism, in developing Catalan when Spanish is the dominant language, and vice versa, the [± Deictic] and the [± Forward] features have to be reassembled in order to fully master the cross-linguistic differences in the conjectural uses of FUT (see Lardiere 2008 and 2009 for a full account of the Feature Reassembly Hypothesis in L2 acquisition which may be applicable to the development of grammars in bilingual speakers like those of our study).

However, in bilingual areas such as Majorca and the Balearic Islands, speakers are regularly exposed to the two languages. The question of S-FUT uses in Spanish-Catalan bilinguals is of particular interest because it allows us to examine whether language dominance play a role in the development and distribution of a specific linguistic domain. This may also shed light on how two typologically close language systems interact in the mind of the bilingual speakers.

## 3 Majorcan Catalan-Spanish Adult Bilingualism: Research Hypotheses

Although there is a large body of previous research that has looked at developmental patterns in mainland Catalan-Spanish bilinguals (e.g., Bel, 1996,

2001, 2003; Bosch and Sebastían-Gallés, 2001; Guijarro-Fuentes and Marinis, 2009; Guijarro-Fuentes, 2012; Illamola, 2015; Perpiñán, 2017, 2018), to our knowledge there are relatively few studies that have examined Balearic Catalan/Spanish bilingualism outcomes in adulthood. In that respect, Cuza and Guijarro-Fuentes (2018) and Jimenez et al. (2020a, b)[3] stand out as noteworthy studies examining the effects of bilingualism in adulthood in the morphosyntactic domain.

In a context like Majorca Island, where relatively balanced bilingualism is likely, and both languages are supported and recognised at all levels, it is reasonable to hypothesize that bilingual grammars would differ less from monolinguals than in other cases of bilingualism. With that in mind, the main overarching research question that has inspired the present study was: What is the role of dominance in Catalan or Spanish in relation to the competence and performance outcomes of FUT usages among bilingual speakers tested in adulthood? Also, more specifically, the following questions are addressed:

- Will Catalan/Spanish bilinguals effectively distinguish the partially overlapping restrictions operating in each language?
- How does the ability to distinguish such restrictions interact with language dominance?
- Will the restrictions on FUT uses in each language somehow merge?

In linking the consideration of these questions to broader issues, analysing the data presented herein may contribute evidence of the extent to which the Spanish-Catalan bilinguals under consideration possess two separate language systems. In line with our research question, our main hypothesis is: Language dominance matters. Cross-linguistic influence (CLI) from Catalan-to-Spanish and Spanish-to-Catalan is, *a priori*, possible for all our participants. Perhaps, irrespective of language dominance, some CLI will be noted. We also predict that greater degrees of CLI might correlate with relative dominance, in which case there would be significant differences across our bilingual speakers. In addition, it is hypothesized that the domain of grammar matters. That is, CLI is conditioned by the relative status of FUT in the two grammars; CLI will influence the range of interpretations grammaticalized in FUT, leading to a more restricted distribution. The two languages under investigation belong to the same family and, therefore, are two closely related systems. This, in turn, may trigger interference effects.

---

3 Space limitations prevent us to review these studies. Interested readers are encouraged to read them and any other references therein.

## 4 Methodology

This section presents the details of the empirical study designed to explore the use of the conjectural and concessive S-FUT and C-FUT, and the effects of the interaction of these tenses with lexical aspect, in Catalan/Spanish bilinguals with varying linguistic dominance, compared to monolingual Spanish speakers.

### 4.1 Participants

The 97 bilingual participants in the study were all university students from the Universitat de les Illes Balears at Mallorca (age: 17–19). They were born and raised on the island of Mallorca and had never lived elsewhere. The 36 monolingual participants were university students, aged 18–21, studying at the Universidad Complutense de Madrid; they were all Spanish-born from the areas of Madrid, Castilla-León or Castilla-La Mancha and had never lived elsewhere.

Before doing the language tasks, the bilingual participants completed the *Bilingual Language Profile Test* (BLP, Birdsong et al. 2012), an instrument that assesses language history, language dominance, language use, and attitudes in the two languages of bilinguals through self-reports. The BLP includes series of questions with scalar responses associated with a certain point value. As a result of the test, a global score of language dominance can be calculated (see Birdsong et al. 2012 for details on the scoring procedure).

The test was administered online. Each bilingual participant received a language dominance score. The participants were then distributed in three groups according to that score: 32 clearly Catalan-dominant bilinguals (henceforth, BIL-CAT), 32 Spanish-dominant bilinguals (BIL-SP), 33 more equilibrated bilinguals (BIL-EQ). Due to space limitations, only the BIL-CAT and BIL-SP results will be reported here and compared to those of the monolingual group (MONOL).

Thus, three groups of similar sociolinguistic profile and size are compared: BIL-CAT (N = 32), BIL-SP (N = 32) and MONOL (N = 36). The bilingual groups performed the linguistic tasks both in Catalan and Spanish (separated by a three-week interval, so as to reduce or potentially rule out possible crosslinguistic priming), whereas the monolingual Spanish group only did the Spanish version of the tasks[4].

4 In the monolingual group, the number of participants differed across the tasks: 29 participants did the first task, while 36 participants did the two other tasks. In the two bilingual groups, the number of participants remained the same for the three tasks.

## 4.2 Linguistic Tasks

The study included three tasks in two different versions: one in European Spanish and the other in Balearic Catalan. The items were the same in both tasks. The first task (hereon, Task 1) consisted of an 18-item multiple-choice questionnaire. The items included a brief contextualisation, then a sentence requiring a choice among three verb forms, namely, the GO-FUT, the S-FUT (or, in some cases, the C-FUT) and a modal expression with *quizás / potser* ('maybe') + present (or present perfect, when appropriate). The task included 12 items with conjectural and concessive uses of the tenses and 6 distractors. They were presented to the participants in randomized order.

In Task 1, considering the differences between Catalan and Spanish, the S-FUT and the C-FUT were expected to be the most frequent options in the monolingual Spanish group, whereas in the choices of the two bilingual groups the modal expression option was expected to play a significant role. Monolingual speakers (but not bilinguals) were expected to occasionally choose the GO-FUT form to express conjecture. Taking into account language dominance, we hypothesized that in the BIL-SP group the FUT forms would be more frequent than in the BIL-CAT group. For the two bilingual groups, the use of FUT was expected to be more frequent in the Spanish test than in the Catalan version.

The second and the third task consisted of grammaticality judgement tests. The second task (Task 2) included 19 focus items and 5 distractors, and the third task (Task 3) included 18 focus items and 5 distractors. As in Task 1, the items were presented in randomized order. The items firstly presented a stimulus including a contextualized utterance in which FUT tense appeared, with the focus verb form highlighted by means of block capital letters. Below each stimulus, three judgement options were shown, of which the participants chose one and clicked on a check-box to indicate their choice. The options to choose from were the following: (a) *The verb form in block capitals is right.* / (b) *It sounds strange; I'm not sure that this form is right.* / (c) *The verb form is wrong.*

Task 2 focused on the relative acceptability of conjectural and concessive FUT interpretations in relation to the lexical aspect – Aktionsart – of verbs. This task presented a linguistic context (a brief text) followed by the stimulus and the three judgement options just mentioned. Task 3 presented an "external" stimulus, specifically, an illustration or a simulated newspaper headline and strapline, shown together with a written utterance in which a FUT form appeared in block capitals, and the same judgement options as those in the previous task, shown below the stimulus. While in Task 2 all the FUT forms were S-FUT forms, in Task 3, half of the FUT forms presented were C-FUT forms, and the items did not include any concessive uses, but only conjectural ones, as the task consisted in verbalizing possible interpretations of what the situation shown in the external stimulus was, or how it had arisen.

Thus, Task 2 focused on the effect of the lexical aspect on the acceptability of conjectural and concessive interpretations of the S-FUT (which are felicitous only with atelic verbs, particularly with states), while Task 3 focused on the different acceptability of the S-FUT and the C-FUT for conjectural interpretations (for the C-FUT, conjectural interpretations are felicitous with all predicate types). The item conditions of both tasks are displayed below, in Tables 2 and 3 respectively.

**Table 2.** Task 2 item conditions

| **Item numbers** | **Interpretation of FUT** | | **Lexical aspect of verb in FUT** | | |
|---|---|---|---|---|---|
| | **conjecture** | **concession** | **state** | **activity** | **Telic** |
| 1 and 2 | √ | | √ | | |
| 3 – 5 | | √ | √ | | |
| 6 – 8 | √ | | | √ | |
| 9 – 11 | | √ | | √ | |
| 12 – 15 | √ | | | | √ |
| 16 – 19 | | √ | | | √ |

Considering Escandell-Vidal's (2010, 2014, 2019 and in press) description of the Romance FUT introduced in Section 2, as well as the predictions on the value-mapping contrast between Catalan and Spanish shown in Table 1, our hypotheses for each item set of Tasks 2 and 3 were as follows. In line with the general hypotheses mentioned in section 3, that language dominance will interact with the degree of CLI shown by different speakers, leading to stronger dominance of Catalan correlating with less frequent use of conjectural FUT, the task-specific hypotheses are:

- Stative verbs in S-FUT: Monolingual Spanish speakers will accept these uses with ease. However, considering that in everyday Catalan, conjectural uses of FUT are extremely infrequent, more variability was expected in the two bilingual groups, especially in the BIL-CAT one. The acceptability was expected to decrease in the Catalan version of the task, compared to the Spanish version.
- Activities in S-FUT: All participants will tend to only accept these items in cases where a habitual reading is made accessible in the discourse context (as in items 6 to 9). However, the same differences described above between the MONOL, BIL-SP and BIL-CAT were expected to hold.

- Accomplishments and achievements in S-FUT: All groups are expected to reject simple FUT in sentential contexts consistent with hypothetical and concessive interpretations, because of the telic nature of these lexical aspect classes.
- Compound FUT forms: In the items with compound FUT, it was hypothesized that all groups would tend accept telic and atelic verb forms, although the rate of acceptability should be higher in the MONOL group than in the two bilingual groups. More variability was expected in the BIL-CAT participants, and a lower degree of acceptance in the two bilingual groups when performing the task in Catalan.

**Table 3.** Task 3 item conditions

| **Item numbers** | **Tense** | | **Interpretation of FUT** | | **Lexical aspect of verb in FUT** | | |
|---|---|---|---|---|---|---|---|
| | **S-FUT** | **C-FUT** | **conjecture** | **concession** | **state** | **activity** | **Telic** |
| 25, 33, 41 | √ | | √ | | √ | | |
| 26, 34, 42 | √ | | √ | | | √ | |
| 27, 35, 43 | √ | | √ | | | | √ |
| 28, 36. 44 | | √ | √ | | | | √ |
| 29, 37, 45 | | √ | √ | | | √ | |
| 30, 38, 46 | | √ | √ | | √ | | |

## 4.3 Results

The statistical analyses of the results included Shapiro-Wilk tests, which rejected a normal distribution of the overall results across groups. Therefore, non-parametric tests were employed. The performances across the three groups were compared using Kruskal-Wallis tests; two-group comparisons were also carried out by means of Wilcoxon test.

The results of Task 1 are displayed in Figures 1, 2 and 3. Answer option A consists of choosing the GO-FUT form to express conjecture and concession (this is considered ungrammatical in Catalan, but not in Spanish); option B is the FUT tense; option C is a modal expression with *quizás / potser* ('maybe').

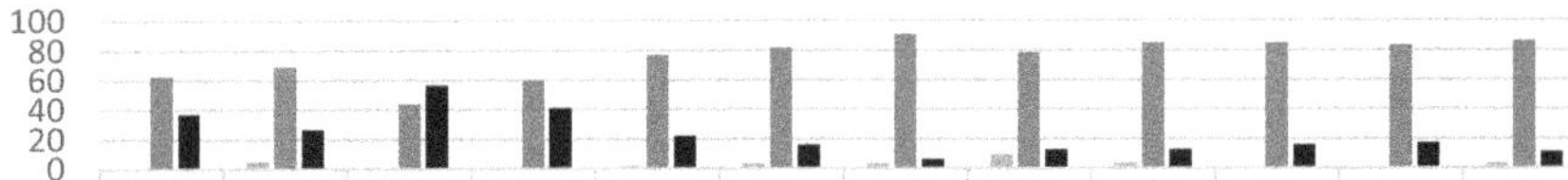

| | CAT | SP | CAT | SP | CAT | SP | CAT | SP | CAT | SP | CAT | SP |
|---|---|---|---|---|---|---|---|---|---|---|---|---|
| | SIMPLE-ST | | SIMPLE-ACT | | PROG-ACT | | PROG-ACCOMP | | COMP-ACT | | COMP-ACHIEV | |
| A | 0,625 | 5 | 0 | 0 | 1,5625 | 3,125 | 3,125 | 9,375 | 3,125 | 0 | 0 | 3,125 |
| B | 62,5 | 68,75 | 43,75 | 59,375 | 76,563 | 81,25 | 90,625 | 78,125 | 84,375 | 84,375 | 82,813 | 85,938 |
| C | 36,875 | 26,25 | 56,25 | 40,625 | 21,875 | 15,625 | 6,25 | 12,5 | 12,5 | 15,625 | 17,188 | 10,938 |

**Figure 1.** Task 1. Results from the BIL-SP group (Tasks in Catalan and in Spanish)

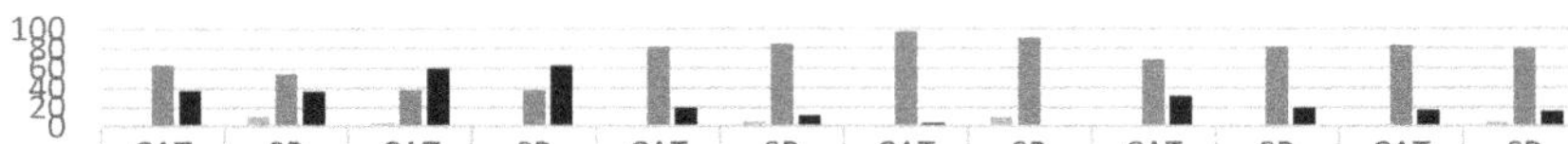

| | CAT | SP | CAT | SP | CAT | SP | CAT | SP | CAT | SP | CAT | SP |
|---|---|---|---|---|---|---|---|---|---|---|---|---|
| | SIMPLE-ST | | SIMPLE-ACT | | PROG-ACT | | PROG-ACCOMP | | COMP-ACT | | COMP-ACHIEV | |
| A | 0 | 10 | 3,125 | 0 | 0 | 4,6875 | 0 | 9,375 | 0 | 0 | 0 | 4,6875 |
| B | 63,125 | 53,75 | 37,5 | 37,5 | 81,25 | 84,375 | 96,875 | 90,625 | 68,75 | 81,25 | 82,813 | 79,688 |
| C | 36,875 | 36,25 | 59,375 | 62,5 | 18,75 | 10,938 | 3,125 | 0 | 31,25 | 18,75 | 17,188 | 15,625 |

**Figure 2.** Task 1. Results from the BIL-CAT group (Tasks in Catalan and in Spanish)

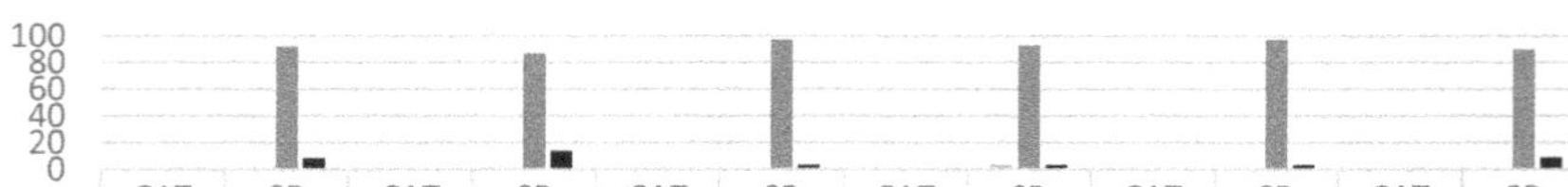

| | CAT | SP | CAT | SP | CAT | SP | CAT | SP | CAT | SP | CAT | SP |
|---|---|---|---|---|---|---|---|---|---|---|---|---|
| | SIMPLE-ST | | SIMPLE-ACT | | PROG-ACT | | PROG-ACCOMP | | COMP-ACT | | COMP-ACHIEV | |
| A | | 0 | | 0 | | 0 | | 3,4483 | | 0 | | 0 |
| B | | 91,724 | | 86,207 | | 96,552 | | 93,103 | | 96,552 | | 89,655 |
| C | | 8,2759 | | 13,793 | | 3,4483 | | 3,4483 | | 3,4483 | | 8,6207 |

**Figure 3.** Task 1. Results from the MONOL group (Task in Spanish only)

Observing these Figures, the MONOL group expressed an overwhelming preference for the simple and compound FUT to express conjecture and concession, without statistically significant differences in the different item conditions ($p < .003$ in the item group comparisons). The use of modal expressions was always marginal (less than 10 % in each item condition, except for with items involving activities in non-progressive forms, where it reached 13.79 %); the choice of GO-FUT forms was almost non-existent (only 3.44 %

in one of the item conditions). The bilingual groups, in contrast, showed more mixed results. The BIL-SP group, when doing the task in Spanish, preferred the FUT tenses in all the item conditions, but with a statistically significant ($p < .003$) lower frequency, compared to the MONOL group. The percentage of modal expression choices was also significantly higher than in the MONOL group, and they occasionally became the preferred option. Additionally, the BIL-SP group exhibited slightly different language-related patterns: when doing the task in Catalan, the percentage of FUT forms was generally lower than in Spanish, although the contrast never reached statistical significance. In the BIL-CAT group, the preference for the FUT forms was (in Catalan and in Spanish) tendentially lower than in the BIL-SP group; the answer pattern in the Catalan and the Spanish version of the first Task was not significantly different.

Interestingly, the GO-FUT form occasionally appeared in the answers of the bilingual groups, not only in Spanish (where such a possibility exists) but also in Catalan (where it is ungrammatical). The percentage is never higher than 9.37 % in Spanish and 4.68 % in Catalan. This is possibly related to the strangeness of the task for the speakers of Catalan (they were driven to choose FUT forms that are extremely uncommon in their language varieties). Variability was generally higher in the answers of the bilingual groups: for example, when performing in Spanish, in the items involving the S-FUT with states, the standard deviation in the BIL-SP group was 17.55 and in the BIL-CAT, 17.88, while in the MONOL group it was 12.55. In the items including activities in the S-FUT, the standard deviation in the BIL-SP group (performing in Spanish) was 24.59, in the BIL-CAT group it was 26.75, and in the MONOL group, 12,89. In the use of the compound forms, however, the contrast is less dramatic: the standard deviation in the BIL-SP group was 22.84, in the BIL-CAT it was 27.99 and in the MONOL group, 19.22.

In sum, all the reported differences between the monolingual and the bilingual groups in the item conditions containing S-FUT were significant ($p < .003$), but none were significant in the items containing the C-FUT. Next let us consider the results of Tasks 2 and 3 which are shown in Figures 4, 5 and 6 (Task 2) and, 7, 8 and 9 (Task 3). In these tasks, recall that option A means that the use of FUT is fully accepted; option B, that the participants are unsure; option C, that they reject it.

| | SIMPLE-ST | | SIMPLE-ACT | | SIMPLE-TELIC | |
|---|---|---|---|---|---|---|
| | CAT | SP | CAT | SP | CAT | SP |
| A | | 91,66666667 | | 56,94444444 | | 15,97222222 |
| B | | 6,111111111 | | 16,2037037 | | 17,70833333 |
| C | | 2,222222222 | | 26,85185185 | | 66,31944444 |

**Figure 4.** Task 2. Results from the BIL-SP group (Tasks in Catalan and in Spanish)

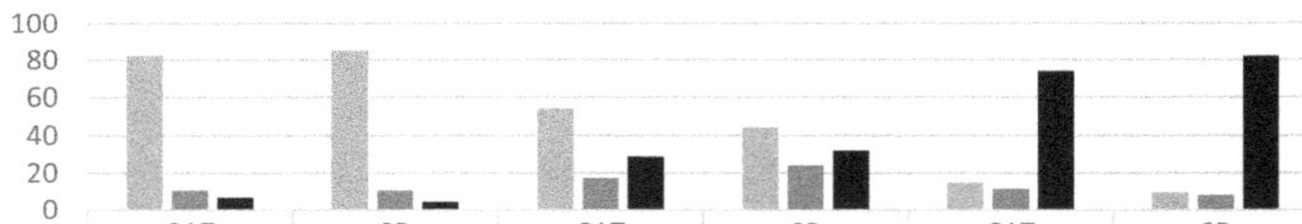


| | SIMPLE-ST | | SIMPLE-ACT | | SIMPLE-TELIC | |
|---|---|---|---|---|---|---|
| | CAT | SP | CAT | SP | CAT | SP |
| A | 82,5 | 85 | 54,16666667 | 44,27083333 | 14,84375 | 9,765625 |
| B | 10,625 | 10,625 | 17,1875 | 23,95833333 | 11,328125 | 8,203125 |
| C | 6,875 | 4,375 | 28,64583333 | 31,77083333 | 73,828125 | 82,03125 |

**Figure 5.** Task 2. Results from the BIL-CAT group (Tasks in Catalan and in Spanish)

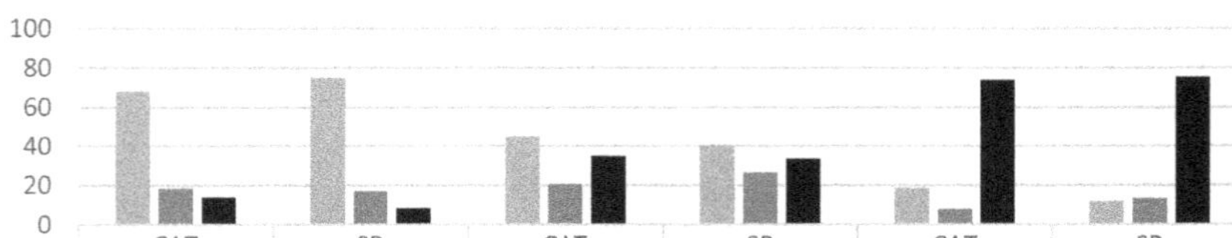


| | SIMPLE-ST | | SIMPLE-ACT | | SIMPLE-TELIC | |
|---|---|---|---|---|---|---|
| | CAT | SP | CAT | SP | CAT | SP |
| A | 68,125 | 75 | 44,79166667 | 40,625 | 18,359375 | 11,71875 |
| B | 18,125 | 16,875 | 20,3125 | 26,04166667 | 7,8125 | 12,890625 |
| C | 13,75 | 8,125 | 34,89583333 | 33,33333333 | 73,828125 | 75,390625 |

**Figure 6.** Task 2. Results from the MONOL group (Task in Spanish only)

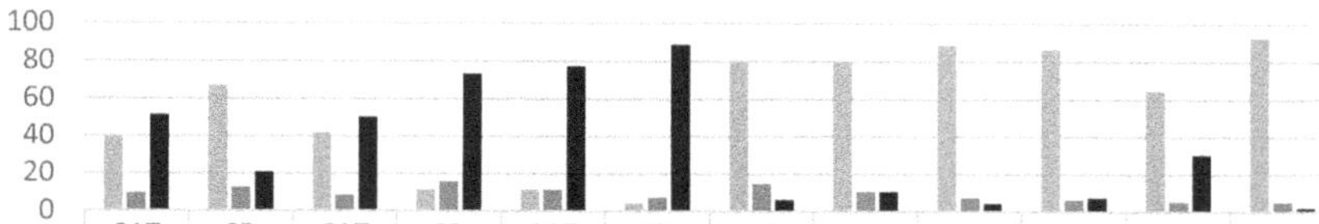


| | CAT | SP | CAT | SP | CAT | SP | CAT | SP | CAT | SP | CAT | SP |
|---|---|---|---|---|---|---|---|---|---|---|---|---|
| | SIMPLE-ST | | SIMPLE-ACT | | SIMPLE-TELIC | | COMP-ST | | COMP-ACT | | COMP-TELIC | |
| A | 39,583 | 66,667 | 41,667 | 11,458 | 11,458 | 4,1667 | 79,167 | 79,167 | 88,542 | 86,458 | 64,583 | 92,708 |
| B | 9,375 | 12,5 | 8,3333 | 15,625 | 11,458 | 7,2917 | 14,583 | 10,417 | 7,2917 | 6,25 | 5,2083 | 5,2083 |
| C | 51,042 | 20,833 | 50 | 72,917 | 77,083 | 88,542 | 6,25 | 10,417 | 4,1667 | 7,2917 | 30,208 | 2,0833 |

**Figure 7.** Task 3. Results from the BIL-SP group (Tasks in Catalan and in Spanish)

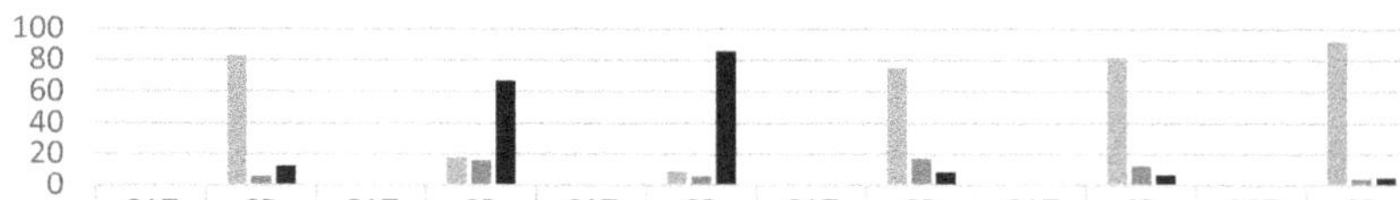


| | CAT | SP | CAT | SP | CAT | SP | CAT | SP | CAT | SP | CAT | SP |
|---|---|---|---|---|---|---|---|---|---|---|---|---|
| | SIMPLE-ST | | SIMPLE-ACT | | SIMPLE-TELIC | | COMP-ST | | COMP-ACT | | COMP-TELIC | |
| A | | 82,407 | | 17,593 | | 9,2593 | | 75 | | 81,481 | | 91,667 |
| B | | 5,5556 | | 15,741 | | 5,5556 | | 16,667 | | 12,037 | | 3,7037 |
| C | | 12,037 | | 66,667 | | 85,185 | | 8,3333 | | 6,4815 | | 4,6296 |

**Figure 8.** Task 3. Results from the BIL-CAT group (Tasks in Catalan and in Spanish)

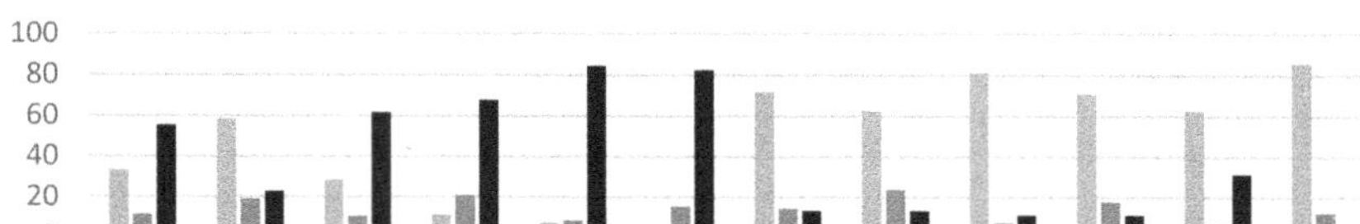


| | CAT | SP | CAT | SP | CAT | SP | CAT | SP | CAT | SP | CAT | SP |
|---|---|---|---|---|---|---|---|---|---|---|---|---|
| | SIMPLE-ST | | SIMPLE-ACT | | SIMPLE-TELIC | | COMP-ST | | COMP-ACT | | COMP-TELIC | |
| A | 33,333 | 58,333 | 28,125 | 11,458 | 7,2917 | 2,0833 | 71,875 | 62,5 | 81,25 | 70,833 | 62,5 | 85,417 |
| B | 11,458 | 18,75 | 10,417 | 20,833 | 8,3333 | 15,625 | 14,583 | 23,958 | 7,2917 | 17,708 | 6,25 | 12,5 |
| C | 55,208 | 22,917 | 61,458 | 67,708 | 84,375 | 82,292 | 13,542 | 13,542 | 11,458 | 11,458 | 31,25 | 2,0833 |

**Figure 9.** Task 3. Results from the BIL-SP group (Task in Spanish only)

In Tasks 2 and 3, the monolingual informants regularly accepted the use of the S-FUT to express conjecture (91 % in Task 2 and 82.4 % in Task 3) with state predicates, while in the bilingual groups, acceptance is lower: 75 % in Task 2 and 58 % in Task 3 in the BIL-SP group, when answering in Spanish; 68 % (Task 2) and 33 % (Task 3), when answering in Catalan. Overall, the contrast between the MONOL group and the bilinguals in this item condition is significant ($p < .003$), as opposed to the difference between the two bilingual groups, which is not significant, regardless of whether the task version was in Catalan or in Spanish.

In the items of Tasks 2 and 3 containing S-FUT with activities and with telic predicates, there were no significant differences across the three groups of informants: as expected, most participants recognized the lexical aspect restrictions and decidedly rejected these combinations, both in Catalan and in Spanish. Finally, the answer patterns in the three groups were not significantly different in the items involving the C-FUT: the percentage of acceptance was always high regardless of the lexical aspect conditions.

Unlike in Task 1, the standard deviation in the answers of the bilingual groups in Task 2 and Task 3 was not systematically higher than in the monolingual group. This may be linked to the kind of information elicited in the tasks: in the first task, the participants were requested to choose between alternative, grammatically possible answers. In the two other tasks, the informants expressed acceptability judgements, but no alternative grammatical possibilities were considered. Thus, acceptability judgements led to stronger response tendencies than usage preferences. In the next section, we discuss what our results suggest in relation to our main research hypotheses.

## 5 Discussion and General Conclusions

Taken together, the results show many areas of convergence, but also clear divergences, in the choices of monolinguals and bilinguals. Firstly, in relation to our hypotheses that '*Cross-linguistic influence (CLI) from Catalan-to-Spanish and Spanish-to-Catalan is, a priori, possible for all our participants;* and that *irrespective of language dominance, some CLI will be noted*', the data supports both. Being in contact with two different languages develops a composite grammatical competence, with clear CLI. All the groups are aware of the lexical aspect restrictions in the availability of conjectural and progressive interpretations of the S-FUT: the percentages of acceptance of states are always much higher than those of the activities, and the rejection of telic predicates is paramount. However, these trends are more prominent in the monolingual group, and less so in the bilingual groups.

Grammatical awareness does not equal usage preference: for the monolingual Spanish speakers, the S-FUT is a default way to express conjecture and concession, whereas for the Catalan/Spanish bilinguals, regardless of the language in which they are performing, this option is less natural; modal expressions come more easily to their minds, and the mere fact of having to choose between alternative uncommon, or even ungrammatical linguistic options, creates some degree of confusion. Thus, as to the hypothesis that '*greater degrees of CLI might correlate to relative dominance, in which case there would be significant differences across our bilingual speakers*' it seems not to have been confirmed in the case of our bilinguals; the semantics of the Catalan and the Spanish S-FUT is the same for them, regardless of the language dominance factor. In the C-FUT, however, this contrast disappears: all participant groups are equally ready to accept this tense for expressing conjecture. This is in line with the fact that the Catalan C-FUT, unlike its simple counterpart, has developed conjectural uses in spontaneous language usage.

Bilingual speakers do not clearly differentiate the possibilities of the Catalan and the Spanish FUT. They tend to transfer the restrictions of the Catalan form to the Spanish morphological equivalent. Thus, in the language competence of our bilingual speakers, the two languages overlap in this respect, and the restrictions of the Catalan form are prevalent. Language dominance plays no clear role. Indeed, compared to the BIL-CAT, the BIL-SP group often shows slightly higher percentages of conjectural S-FUT acceptance and use. Still, these differences are rarely significant. It may tentatively be concluded that, in the minds of our Majorcan bilingual informants, the semantics of the Spanish S-FUT, unlike that of the Madrid and Castilla areas, has a [+ Deictic] and a [+ Forward] features, like the Catalan S-FUT. This supports our third hypothesis: '*The domain of grammar matters. CLI is conditioned by the relative status of FUT in the two grammars; CLI will influence the range of interpretations grammaticalized in FUT, leading to* a *more restricted distribution*'. In the case of the semantics of the S-FUT, the more restricted system (i.e. the Catalan one) is pervasive in what the data suggest constitutes the bilingual groups' representations of this tense's properties. Thus, the language contact situation of these speakers seems to have led them to apply a novel combination within the range of the languages shown in Table 1, where both the deictic and the forward- confirmation restrictions apply to the interpretation of FUT. In other words, in reference to Lardiere's (2009) Feature Reassembly Hypothesis, which was mentioned in section 2, these bilinguals do not show evidence of reassembling features in their less dominant language. They maintain the features of Catalan FUT in Spanish, and simply use this tense in a more restricted way than Spanish dominant bilinguals or Peninsular Spanish monolinguals.

Finally, in relation to the hypothesis that '*The two languages under investigation belong to the same family and, therefore, are two closely related systems. This, in turn, may have an effect on triggering interference effects*', since a single language pair has been studied, our research can only provide tentative confirmation. What our data suggest is that in the case of two closely related languages like Spanish and Catalan, partially overlapping restrictions, such as the ones applying to different linguistic means for expressing conjecture, tend to fully converge.

In sum, the results of this study seem aligned with Kroll et al.'s (2012: 242) general observation about how bilingual speakers' grammatical representations can be expected to differ from those of monolinguals of either of the two languages considered: namely, that 'the bilingual's two languages appear to be open to one another in a manner that enables cross-language exchange when structures are compatible, and that potentially encourages cross-language influences that change each of the languages compared to monolingual speakers of either language'. In the present study, some empirical evidence has been provided that shows how the grammatical means by which bilinguals express conjecture vary in contrast to those of monolinguals, stemming from the contact and interaction that takes place between languages with slightly differentiated restrictions.

## References

Aramon i Serra, R. (1957). 'Notes sobre alguns calcs sintàctics en l'actual català literari'. *Syntactica 1957*, 1–31.

Badia i Margarit, A. (1962). *Gramática catalana*. Madrid: Gredos.

Bel, A. (1996). 'Early negation in Catalan and Spanish'. *Catalan Working Paper in Linguistics*, 5–28.

Bel, A. (2001). *Teoria Lingüística i Adquisició del Llenguatge: Anàlisi Comparada dels Trets Morfològics en Català i Castellà*. Barcelona: Institut d'Estudis Catalans.

Bel, A. (2003). 'The syntax of subjects in the acquisition of Spanish and Catalan'. *Probus* 15, 1–26.

Birdsong, D., Gertken, L.M., and Amengual, M. (2012). 'Bilingual Language Profile: An Easy-to-Use Instrument to Assess Bilingualism'. COERLL, University of Texas at Austin. Web: <https://sites.la.utexas.edu/bilingual/> accessed 13 June 2021

Bosch, L., and Sebastían-Gallés, N. (2001). 'Evidence of early language discrimination abilities in infants from bilingual environments'. *Infancy* 1, 29–49.

Cuza, A. and Guijarro-Fuentes, P. (2018). 'Copula Ser/Estar distribution and use in the grammars of Spanish/Catalan bilinguals'. In A. Cuza and P. Guijarro-Fuentes, P. (eds). *Language Acquisition and Contact in the Iberian Peninsula*. Berlin/New York: Mouton DeGruyter

Dhal, Ö. (2000). 'The grammar of future time reference in the languages of Europe'. In Ö. Dhal (ed.). *Tense and aspect in the languages of Europe*, pp. 309–328. Berlin: Mouton de Gruyter.

Escandell-Vidal, V. (2010). 'Futuro y evidencialidad'. *Anuario de Lingüística Hispánica* XXVI, 9–34.

Escandell-Vidal, V. (2014). 'Evidential futures: The case of Spanish'. In: P. De Brabanter, M. Kissine and S. Sharifzadeh, (eds.), *Future times, future tenses*, pp. 219–247. Oxford: Oxford University Press.

Escandell-Vidal, V. (2019). 'El futuro simple del español. Sistema natural frente a usos cultivados'. *Verba Hispanica*, XXVI, 15–31.

Escandell-Vidal, V. (in press). 'The simple future in Romance. Semantic parameters and linguistic variation'. In De Saussure, L. et al. (ed.) *Cahiers Chronos*, 31. Leiden: Brill.

Gavarró, A. and Laca, B. (2008). 'Les perífrasis temporals, aspectuals i modals'. In J. Solà (dir.), M.R. Lloret, J. Mascaró and M. Pérez Saldanya (eds.), *Gramàtica del català contemporani*, vol 3, pp. 2663–2723. Barcelona: Empúries.

Guijarro-Fuentes, P. (2012). 'The acquisition of interpretable features in L2 Spanish: personal a'. *Bilingualism: Language and Cognition*, 15, 701–720.

Guijarro-Fuentes, P., and Marinis, T. (2009). 'The acquisition of personal preposition a by Catalan-Spanish and English-Spanish bilinguals'. In J. Collentine, B. Lafford, and F. Marcos Marín (eds.), *Selected Proceedings of the 11th Hispanic Linguistics Symposium*, pp. 81–92. Somerville: MA.

Illamola, C. (2015). *Contacto de Lenguas y la Expresión de la Posterioridad Temporal en Español de Cataluña*. Barcelona: Universitat de Barcelona.

Jimenez, A., Pires, A. and Guijarro-Fuentes, P. (2020a). 'Bilingualism and language contact: the case of clitics in Catalan and Spanish'. *International Journal of Bilingual Education and Bilingualism, 23,* 113–131.

Jimenez, A. Pires, A. and Guijarro-Fuentes, P (2020b). 'Transfer and Convergence between Catalan and Spanish in a bilingual setting'. In L.A. Ortiz López, R.E. Guzzardo Tamargo, and M. González-Rivera (eds), *Hispanic Contact Linguistics: Theoretical, Methodological and Empirical Perspectives*, pp. 179–211. Amsterdam: John Benjamins.

Kroll J.F. et al (2012). 'Juggling two languages in one mind: What bilinguals tell us about language processing and its consequences for cognition'. In B.

Ross (ed.), *The Psychology of Learning and Motivation*, pp. 229–262. San Diego: Academic Press.

Lardiere, D. (2008). Feature-Assembly in Second Language in Second Language Acquisition. In J. Liceras, J., H. Zobl, and H. Goodluck (eds.), *Features in Second Language Acquisition*, pp. 106–140. Mahwah, NJ: Lawrence Erlbaum.

Lardiere, D. (2009). Some thoughts on a contrastive analysis of feature in second language acquisition. *Second Language Research*, 25.2, 173–227.

Pérez Saldanya, M. (2008). 'Les relacions temporals i aspectuals'. In J. Solà (dir.), M.R. Lloret, J. Mascaró and M. Pérez Saldanya (eds.), *Gramàtica del català contemporani*, vol 3, pp. 2567–2662. Barcelona: Empúries.

Perpiñán, S. (2017). 'Catalan-Spanish bilingualism continuum: the expression of non-personal Catalan clitics in the adult grammar of early bilinguals'. *Linguistics Approaches to Bilingualism*, 7, 477–513.

Perpiñán, S. (2018). 'Ongoing language change, and crosslinguistic influence in direct object expression in Catalan-Spanish bilingualism'. *Languages*, 3, 1–14.

Prince, E. (1998). 'The borrowing of meaning as a cause of internal syntactic change'. In M. Schmid, J. Austin and D. Stein (eds.), *Historical Linguistics 1997: Selected papers from the 13th International Conference on Historical Linguistics*, pp. 339–362. Amsterdam, Philadelphia: John Benjamins.

Sánchez, L. (2003). *Quechua-Spanish Bilingualism: Interference and Convergence in Functional Categories*. Amsterdam: John Benjamins.

Sánchez, L. (2004). 'Functional convergence in the tense, evidentiality and aspectual systems of Quechua-Spanish bilinguals'. *Bilingualism: Language and Cognition*, 7 (2), 147–162.

Sánchez, L. (2015). 'Crosslinguistic influences in the mapping of functional features in Quechua-Spanish Bilingualism'. In T. Judy and S. Perpiñán (eds), *The Acquisition of Spanish in Understudied Language Pairings*, pp. 19–48. Amsterdam: John Benjamins.

Silva-Corvalán, C. (1998). 'On borrowing as a mechanism of syntactic change'. In A. Schwegler, B. Tranel and M. Uribe-Extebarria (eds.), *Romance linguistics: Theoretical perspectives*, pp. 225–246. Amsterdam: John Benjamins.

Silva-Corvalán, C. (2008). 'The Limits of Convergence in Language Contact'. *Journal of Language Contact*, 2, 213–24.

Simonet, M. (2011). 'Production of Catalan-specific vowel contrast by Spanish-Catalan bilinguals'. *Phonetica*, 68, 88–110.

Simonet, M. (2014). 'Phonetic consequences of dynamic crosslinguistic interference in proficient bilinguals'. *Journal of Phonetics*, 43, 26–37.

Sorace, A. (2011). 'Pinning down the concept of 'interface' in bilingualism'. *Linguistic Approaches to Bilingualism,* 1, 1–33.

Sorace, A. (2012). 'Pinning down the concept of interface in bilingualism: A reply to peer commentaries'. *Linguistic Approaches to Bilingualism* 2, 209–216.

Soto, G. (2008). 'Sobre el llamado futuro de probabilidad'. *Boletín de Filología de la Universidad de Chile*, 43, 193–206.

Thomason, S. and Kaufman, T. (1988). *Language contact, creolization, and genetic linguistics*. Berkeley, Los Angeles, London: University of California Press.

Thomason, S. (2001). *Language contact: an introduction*. Edinburgh and Washington, DC: Edinburgh University Press, Georgetown University Press.

Thomason, S. (2008). 'Social and linguistic factors as predictors of contact-induced change'. *Journal of Language Contact*, Thema 2, 42–56.

Trudgill, P. (1989). 'Language Contact and Simplification'. *Nordlyd,* 15, 115–121.

Unsworth, S. (2015). 'Amount of exposure as a proxy for language dominance in bilingual acquisition'. In C. Silva-Corvalan, and J. Treffers-Daller (eds), *Language Dominance in Bilinguals: Issues of Measurement and Operationalization*, pp. 156–173. Cambridge: Cambridge University Press.

Pascale Leclercq

# L2 acquisition of epistemic/evidential stance-marking by French learners of English: the case of 'I think'[1]

**Abstract:** Speaking about things involves taking a stance towards those things. To express their subjectivity, speakers use a variety of stance-markers, with different discursive functions. For L2 learners, acquiring a relevant repertoire of stance-markers, and making context-appropriate choices, is a crucial process. However, epistemic stance is generally observed to emerge at a late stage of L2 acquisition.

In this study, we adopt a functional and developmental perspective to determine to what extent intermediate and advanced French learners of English use 'I think' in oral narratives and interviews, and to what extent this reveals learner style.

We use two oral discursive tasks: an oral narrative (ten upper intermediate and ten advanced learners, plus a control group of ten English native speakers), where learners are recorded in a French context, and a longitudinal oral interview task (n=5), where intermediate and advanced learners are recorded in a study abroad context on three occasions, plus pre-departure, and post-return.

Our study provides evidence of the influence of the type of discursive task in the way 'I think' is used by French learners of English, while contributing to illustrate the links between the linguistic choices of learners and their study-abroad experience.

**Keywords:** *I think, French, English, second language acquisition, type of discourse, evidentiality, functional approach, longitudinal study, epistemic stance, learner style*

## 1 Introduction

Speaking about a given topic often involves conveying personal feelings, making claims about this topic, evaluating it, or expressing how access to the information was gained. This is what Biber (2006: 99) refers to as the "personal stance of the speaker or writer". Stance-taking is inherent to human speech. It is related to speaker style and identity insofar as it allows the speakers to express their positions and their level of confidence towards a given propositional content

1 Many thanks to the organizers of the STANCEDISC'20 conference (UCM, Madrid), who gave me the opportunity to start exploring the fascinating field of stance studies, and to Amanda Edmonds for her precious comments, which helped me improve the style and clarity of this paper.

(Bucholtz & Hall 2005). For L2 speakers, whose second language identity and style are under construction (see Coupland 1985; Kirkham 2011; Liao 2009; Mullan, 2010, 2012; Grieve 2013, 2015; Compiegne 2020), choice of stance markers and their intended functional load may vary according to proficiency level and discursive situation.

Among the many English verbal stance markers, 'I think' appears as one of the most frequent, and also one of the most polyfunctional. It is often considered as an epistemic/evidential stance marker, but also as a discourse marker. According to the discursive context, it can be used to express epistemic stance, i.e., how certain a speaker is about a state of affairs (Kiesling, 2009; Marín-Arrese, 2015), to express an opinion, to indicate an inference based on the observation of some facts, to mitigate the strength of an assertion, or even to signal a topic shift in conversation.

Epistemic stance is often considered as pertaining to the domain of evaluative discourse. According to Gablasova, Brezina, McEnery & Boyd (2017:614), speakers' epistemic stance "fulfils three major interconnected functions in the interaction: (i) expressing opinion, (ii) maintaining relations between the interlocutors, and (iii) discourse organization". Another closely related domain is that of evidentiality, a semantic concept which refers to the expression of the mode of access to a given piece of information (Aikhenvald 2004). In certain languages such as Turkish or Tibetan, it is an obligatory grammatical category and it is expressed through highly grammaticized morphemes, with specific suffixes for the expression of direct evidentiality (the speaker has witnessed a given state of affairs), hearsay (the speaker has heard about a given state of affairs), or inference (the speaker infers what the given state of affairs might be based on circumstantial evidence or on reasoning). In Romance and Germanic languages, however, evidentiality is an optional category, which can be expressed through a variety of linguistic markers, ranging from lexical means (adverbials, discourse markers) to verbal means (perception and cognition verbs such as 'I think' or 'I guess', modals, verbal morphology such as the conditional in Spanish) (see, among others, Marín-Arrese, 2015; Hassler, 2015; Leclercq 2021, Leclercq & Mélac 2021). In French and in English, some of these markers can also express epistemicity. In particular, the domain of inference sits at the crossroads between indirect evidentiality and epistemic modality, while permitting the expression of the speakers' stance (Hassler, 2015; Guentchéva, 2018).

Since the expression of epistemic stance or evidentiality is by no means compulsory, the use of such markers can to some extent be seen as the linguistic expression of speaker style, which can be considered as a linguistic operationalization of the identity concept, insofar as expressing stance reflects the speakers' subjectivity (Bucholtz & Hall 2005, Coupland 2007).

Previous research has shown that evidentiality and epistemicity are developed quite late by second language learners of French and English, with large inter-individual variation (Baumgarten & House, 2010; Leclercq & Edmonds, 2017; Leclercq & Mélac, 2021; Mifka-Profozic 2017; Gablasova et al. 2017). It is interesting to see how advanced learners develop the use of 'I think', a polyfunctional verbal marker, in different discursive contexts.

We adopt a functional and developmental perspective to determine how the stance marker 'I think' is used at two different proficiency levels (intermediate and advanced) by French learners of English, and with which discursive functions, in two oral discursive tasks: a cross-sectional oral narrative (10 upper intermediate, 10 advanced learners, plus a control group of 10 English native speakers), where learners are recorded in a French institutional context, and a longitudinal oral interview task (n=5), where learners are recorded in a study abroad context on three occasions, plus pre-departure, and post-return. We also seek to find out to what extent the use of the 'I think' evidential/epistemic stance-marker reflects learner style.

## 2 Theoretical Background

As pointed out by Thompson (2002:138), Baumgarten & House (2000), Kärkkäinen (2006) and Aijmer (2009), 'I think' is one of the most frequent epistemic/evidential stance markers in the English language. It is often considered as 'a prototype of subjective language, because it contains reference to the speaker (the first-person pronoun) and a verb that denotes a private or interior cognitive process' (Kärkkäinen 2006: 700). It is particularly frequent in conversation, but it is also found in monologic productions to express speaker's stance. We present the main syntactic structures in which it is found, followed by its main discursive functions.

### 2.1 Syntax

'I think' can be found in three main types of constructions: independent clauses, matrix clauses, and parentheticals (see also Leclercq 2021 for a comparison with the syntactic use of *je pense* 'I think' by French natives).

- *Independent clause construction (IC).* This type of construction includes independent clauses such as (1), in which the speaker states that he or she is engaged in a reflective cognitive process; and short answers, such as (2), in which learner M uses 'I think so' to express her agreement with the interviewer, although the use of 'I think' also functions as a hedge to mitigate her assertion.

(1) *I think about the Chinese people.* (Baumgarten & House 2010: 1187)
(2) **INT1: So hum let's take things back to the second interview right? You met Amanda here heu in November right?*
**M: Yeah I think so.* (MT3, PROLINGSA)

- *Matrix clause construction (MC).* Within this type of construction, 'I think' is a matrix clause followed a complement clause, as in (3) and (4). It generally permits the speaker to express 'epistemic, evidential, or evaluative stance' (Thompson, 2002:131).

(3) *and ehm the dog wakes up in the morning and it's quite ehm it's quite sunny but I think it's frost or ice outside his kennel especially.* (E06, Reksio)
(4) **Y: and I think I'm going to re(ad) to write a lot .* (YT1, PROLINGSA)

- *Parenthetical (P).* The last type of construction is the adverbial phrase, or parenthetical (Thompson 2002:134, also called 'verbal routine' by Baumgarten & House 2010). Parentheticals can take a variety of positions in the sentence, which we will subsume into two subcategories: medial position (5), or final position (6).

(5) *The dog at this point I think got a bit upset with her.* (E07, Reksio)
(6) *So ehm the little girl gets ehm some dirt I think.* (E07, Reksio)

We will now present the different discourse functions that 'I think' can take.

## 2.2 Discursive Functions

While its prototypical meaning refers to 'cogitation' as in (1), it has other uses, namely as an evidential marker as in (3), in which the English speaker indicates that he/she infers, based on observation, that there is frost outside the dog's kennel; as an epistemic marker referring to 'belief', 'opinion' and 'subjective evaluation', as in (5) (Baumgarten & House 2010:1189). It can also be used with a bleached referential meaning (Local 2003) and a pragmatic function of gaining time for online planning, or to keep the speaking turn.

- *Evidential uses.* Evidentiality, often defined as the expression of the mode of access to a given piece of information, includes direct perception, hearsay, or inference. According to Squartini (2008: 925), there are three subcategories of inference: circumstantial inferences, generic inferences, and conjectures (5). He states that all three are "products of the speaker's reasoning process and therefore inferential processes". Circumstantial inferences are based on "external sensory evidence", generic inferences are made based on the speaker's world knowledge, while conjectures are pure reasoning ("all external evidence is missing"). 'I think' may be used as an evidential marker, to express the speaker's inferential reasoning. In (3), the speaker uses 'I think' in a complement clause to indicate that the provided information was inferred from what the speaker remembers viewing in the cartoon (circumstantial evidence), while in (6), the speaker infers, based on their world knowledge and their viewing of the cartoon, that what the character threw on the ground to melt the ice was dirt (generic inference). In (7) however, the conjecture is based on the speaker's reasoning, not on any perceptual evidence. There were no instances of conjectures in our database.

(7) *[The doorbell rings] I was not expecting anybody. It might be Gianni.* (Squartini 2008: 924)

- *Epistemic uses.* Epistemic stance generally refers to the speaker's expression of his or her belief, opinion or evaluation of a given state of affairs. It is considered as part of the modality domain, through which the speaker expresses a degree of certainty concerning a proposition content. We include in this category the expression of opinion and hedging. Expressing an opinion implies to a fairly high degree of assertiveness, as in (8), whereas a lesser degree of certainty suggests hedging on the part of the speaker (see Vincze 2013 on discourse-level uncertainty), as in (9), where Y asserts that he will take part in five dance competitions for his university, before mitigating this claim with a parenthetical 'I think'.

(8) **Y: And uh i think that London is a good place uh is a good place to learn.* (YT1, PROLINGSA)
(9) **Y: Er we will represent like the university in the national level so we'll do like auh five competitions I think in the year.* (YT2, PROLINGSA)

- *Pragmatic uses.* In addition to its use as a hedging device as in (9), 'I think' may be used in conversation to mark online planning, to indicate the end of a speaking turn, to express agreement or negotiate a common stance (Kärkkäinen 2006; Baumgarten & House 2010: 1189), as illustrated in (10), where the American interviewer INT2 uses 'I think' to gain time to decide whether she can wrap up the conversation, or whether she has other questions to ask, as well as to signal alignment with learner A's position.

(10) **A: It's ok for me.*
**INT2: OK well I thi(nk) yeah I think it's ok for us. (AT2, PROLINGSA)*

In (11), the American interviewer INT2 uses 'I think' as a hedge after a long digression from the participant to politely signal that time is running out.

(11) **INT2: okay that's fine okay I think we're going to move on. (YT5, PROLINGSA)*

As acknowledged by Baumgarten & House (2010), differentiating between the epistemic, evidential, and pragmatic functions of 'I think' is not an easy task, especially since they are often overlapping: examples (3), (6) and (9) all express the speaker's inferences based on perceptual evidence or reasoning, but they also express the speaker's opinion, and/or mitigate a claim (hedging).

As for the frequency of use of those different functions, Aijmer (2009), Thompson (2002), and Baumgarten & House (2010) concur to say that most uses are epistemic, while in her conversation data Mullan (2010: 119–23) found that two thirds of her occurrences were discourse markers with a pragmatic function, with the remaining occurrences as epistemic instances, mostly to express speaker opinion. Mullan's work suggests the type of discourse (monologic vs dialogic) might orient the semantic value and discursive function of 'I think'. Mullan (2010, 2012) also attributes speakers' choices to ingrained cultural values. For example, she observes that French speakers have a confrontational conversational style (see also Béal 2010), and that it is important for them to express their opinions and feelings, while Australian speakers are described as 'wishy-washy' by their French counterparts as they often refrain from expressing their opinion. According to Mullan (2012: 203), Australian speakers favour the use of 'I think' as a hedge to mitigate the strength of an assertion.

To sum up, 'I think' appears as a high frequency verbal marker with often overlapping epistemic, pragmatic and evidential values, used in a variety of functions and discursive contexts. The question of how L2 learners of English appropriate this marker at different proficiency levels will now be considered.

## 2.3 'I think' in L2 English

Research on the L2 acquisition of verbal stance markers is scarce, but a few studies on the acquisition of modality and evidentiality provide information as to the way learners use 'I think' in a variety of written and oral tasks, at different proficiency levels.

To start with, research on the L2 acquisition of modality has highlighted the fact that lower-level learners express epistemic stance through cognitive verbs and adverbials rather than modals (Salsbury & Bardovi-Harlig 2000, Fordyce

2009, 2014, Leclercq & Edmonds, 2017), generally through 'I think' and 'maybe'. Aijmer (2002: 71), in her study of modality in advanced Swedish learners' written interlanguage, finds that non-native speakers overuse epistemic modal verbs 'I think' and 'I believe' compared to native speakers. She argues that this might be due to the influence of spoken English.

Taking a developmental approach to the L2 acquisition of the evidentiality, Leclercq & Mélac (2021) show that the use of evidential markers strongly increases with proficiency level in an oral narrative task, with advanced learners slightly overusing evidentials compared to native speakers. At lower intermediate level, French learners of English mostly use perception verbs to express direct perception, while at the upper intermediate level, 'maybe' is the most frequent evidential. At advanced level, 'I think' and 'I guess' are the two most frequently used evidential markers by learners of English in an oral narrative task, while English natives almost never use 'I guess' in their oral narratives. The authors conclude that advanced learners use evidential markers in a similar way to native speakers as regards frequency of use, but that they display different stylistic preferences.

While many of the afore-mentioned studies were based on monologic data, Baumgarten & House (2010) explored the use of 'I think' and 'I don't know' as markers of stance-taking based on elicited conversation data from four English native speakers and eight speakers of English as a lingua franca (i.e., speakers of English whose mother tongue is another language) with various L1s (Indonesian, German, Chinese, Korean, German, French, Nepali and Gujrati). They show that L1 and L2 speakers of English use those two stance markers with high frequency, but L2 speakers use 'I think' in a much larger range of discursive contexts than native speakers. They also observe that, contrary to L1 speakers, L2 speakers often use 'I think' in utterances containing other stance markers, so that it appears as an "additional, overt marker of the speaker's perspective" (2010: 1197). As for Zhang & Sabet 2016, they tap into classroom interaction data from L1 American English speakers, and Chinese and Persian-speaking learners of English, to show that L2 speakers use 'I think' more frequently than native speakers, but with different stylistic preferences (while L1 speakers use 'I think that' the least, it is Persian learners' favourite expression). Unfortunately, no mention is made of the proficiency level of L2 participants in Baumgarten & House (2010) nor in Zhang & Sabet (2016), which makes their results difficult to interpret from a developmental perspective.

Using a social perspective on language use, Gablasova et al. (2017) provide a very innovative account of the use of epistemic stance in spoken L2 English. They use data from the Trinity Lancaster Corpus (TLC), more specifically oral productions from four speaking tasks accomplished by advanced English learners from different L1s and cultural backgrounds. One task involved monologic oral production while the other three tasks elicited interactional discourse. They identified epistemic items in the data, which they classified in three large categories: adverbial expressions (apparently, certainly…), adjectival expressions (likely, possible) and verbal expressions (I think, I believe, I know…). Their results confirm previous findings that 'I think' is the most frequently used marker, accounting for 42.5 % of all epistemic markers. They also show that the monologic task elicits a much lower frequency of epistemic markers (including 'I think') compared with the interactional tasks, probably because expressing subjectivity and managing intersubjective relations is more typical of such tasks. Finally, the authors concluded that advanced learners of English adjusted their style to the requirements of the task as regards the use of epistemic markers.

In a study based on conversation data between Australian and French speakers, either in French or in English, Mullan (2012:216) observed that L2 French speakers most often used "*je pense*" with a pragmatic function (87 %), just like Australian English natives with 'I think', when French natives use "*je pense*" in a more balanced way to either express their opinion (47 %) or for pragmatic purposes (53 %). She suggests this illustrates to what extent L2 speakers are influenced by the pragmalinguistic patterns of their L1, even at an advanced level.

Leclercq (2021) analysed the link between the development of assertiveness and pragmalinguistic competence among L2 learners in a study abroad context. Based on the LANGSNAP data (Mitchell, Tracy-Ventura & McManus 2017), she analysed the use of stance marker "je pense" in interview data from 26 Anglophone learners of French, who spent nine months in France, and 10 French native speakers. Her results confirm Mullan's and show that learners are globally less assertive in their use of "je pense" than native speakers, particularly at the beginning of their stay abroad, and that they develop pragmatic uses of "je pense". She points out that there is a lot of variability in learners' use of "je pense", and highlights the importance of personal style.

In short, Aijmer (2002) and Zhang & Sabet (2016) concur in their finding that L2 speakers of different mother tongues use 'I think' much more than L1 speakers in their productions, while Baumgarten & House (2010), Mullan (2010, 2012), Gablasova et al. (2017), Leclercq (2021) and Leclercq & Mélac (2021) observe different stylistic preferences in the choices of native speakers, and advanced learners, with Gablasova et al. (2017) showing that advanced learners are sensitive to the discursive contexts in which 'I think' is used, and Mullan (2012) and Leclercq (2021) illustrating how L1 patterns influence L2 choices.

## 3 Research questions

In this study, we seek to complement existing research on the use of epistemic stance markers by advanced French learners of English by comparing the use of 'I think' by learners of two proficiency levels (upper intermediate and advanced) in two oral discursive tasks (oral narrative and semi-guided interview). Indeed, as pointed out by Coupland (2007), Gablasova et al. (2017), Baumgarten & House (2010) and Neary-Sundquist (2013), speakers' stylistic choices are intimately linked to discursive context.

While most existing studies have relied on a cross-sectional design, we include longitudinal data from the PROLINGSA (Linguistic Progress during Study Abroad) project to assess:

(A) whether the type of discursive task has an impact on the functions native speakers and learners attribute to the verbal epistemic stance marker 'I think';
(B) to what extent the use of such a marker illustrates the evolution of individual speaker style over the course of a nine-month study abroad programme.

## 4 Data and Method

In this section, we present the design of our two separate studies, based on the Reksio database (Study 1) and the PROLINGSA project (Study 2).

### 4.1 Study 1 Reksio

The first study presents a cross-sectional oral narrative task based on the Reksio stimulus (Watorek 2004), in which speakers are presented with a five-minute long cartoon featuring a little white dog, Reksio, and his master (a curly-haired blond little boy). The cartoon features background music and barking sounds, but no speech, which makes it appropriate for a verbalization task performed by speakers of different proficiency levels and language combinations. Once they had finished watching the movie, speakers were invited by the interviewer to tell them what had happened. In spite of this, the task is mostly monologic, as the interviewers almost never intervene in the narration.

*Participants.* Our database includes 10 English native speakers (E), 10 upper intermediate (UI) and 10 advanced (A) French learners of English. E speakers came from a variety of English-speaking countries, and were recorded on a UK campus, while the L2 recordings were performed on a French campus, where learner participants were enrolled in English studies. Table 1 presents the database and the participants.

**Table 1.** Task 1 – Reksio narrative participants and database description

| Group | N= | Mean Age | Gender | Proficiency test scores** (out of 60) | Length of productions (number of utterances) |
|---|---|---|---|---|---|
| UI | 10 | 21 | 2M, 8F | M 43.9 SD 2.3 Range 40–47 | M 41.6 SD 14.1 Range 30–64 |
| A | 10 | 27 | 7M, 3F | M 54.9 SD 3.17 Range 53–59 | M 57.9 SD 26.2 Range 21–113 |
| E | 10 | 25.4* | 5M, 5F | / | M 115.6 SD 29.7 Range 82–169 |

*Mean age for NS was calculated on 9 participants as one did not specify their age.
** A version of the Oxford Quick Placement test was used.

## 4.2 Study 2 PROLINGSA (Linguistic Progress during Study Abroad)

The second study is based on the longitudinal PROLINGSA project (Leclercq, Edmonds & Sneed German, 2021)[2], which consists in a series of five filmed interviews performed before (Time 1), during (Time 2, 3 and 4) and after (Time 5) a nine-month Erasmus+ stay in the British Isles, with five undergraduate students in Applied Languages, majoring in English and Chinese, Arabic, Italian or Spanish.

We will henceforth refer to Time 1, 2, 3, 4 and 5 as T1, T2, T3, T4, T5. Individual interviews will be referred to through the participant's initial, followed by interview time. For example, participant A's first interview will be labelled AT. Questions focused on the aims pursued by the participants during their Erasmus+ stay, their linguistic experiences, their daily life, their social networking, and their opinion on a variety of topics[3]. This type of conversational data is bound to elicit a large quantity of stance markers, among which 'I think' should feature highly.

Task 2 also enabled us to track the evolution in the use of such markers by five advanced learners, over the course of an academic year abroad. The whole database, presented in Table 2, comprises over twelve hours of videos (total number of words 68,725).

2 The PROLINGSA database is being deposited on the https://hdl.handle.net/11403/prolingsa/v1 repository and the full data set is available upon request.
3 The detailed protocol, including interview questions for the five interview sessions, are available on Ortolang.

**Table 2.** Task 2 – PROLINGSA database description

| Participant | Duration of recording | Length of productions<br># utterances* |
|---|---|---|
| A | T1 27:00<br>T2 35:03<br>T3 24:38<br>T4 17:13<br>T5 34:16<br>Total 2h 18mn 10 s | 645<br>1410<br>734<br>581<br>1189<br>4559 |
| C | T1 26:49<br>T2 26:40<br>T3 12 :18<br>T4 12 :51<br>T5 23 :27<br>Total 1h 42mn 05s | 711<br>805<br>408<br>365<br>579<br>2868 |
| M | T1 18:34<br>T2 15:39<br>T3 13:47<br>T4 15:20<br>T5 20:51<br>Total 1h 24mn 11s | 484<br>729<br>392<br>464<br>719<br>2788 |
| N | T1 23:55<br>T2 44:24<br>T3 23:40<br>T4 22:12<br>T5 37:21<br>Total 2h 31mn 29s | 605<br>1831<br>781<br>612<br>1249<br>5078 |
| Y | T1 44:24<br>T2 56:11<br>T3 48:20<br>T4 43:48<br>T5 53:47<br>Total 4h 06mn 30s | 1524<br>1968<br>1537<br>1426<br>1633<br>8088 |
| Total duration | 12h 05mn 35s | |

* # of utterances includes learner and interviewer speech

*Participants.* All five participants were francophone and had learned English for over 10 years, mostly in a guided context (see Table 3 for a presentation of the participants). Participant Y was an early bilingual in French and Turkish. Depending on the interview, the participants were interviewed by one or two investigators (INT1: French with a C2 command of English, INT2: American native speaker), who followed them over the course of their academic year abroad. The relationship between the investigators and the participants was asymmetrical as the investigators were teachers in the participants' home university, yet the exchanges were warm and relaxed.

**Table 3.** Task 2 - PROLINGSA participants

| Participant code | Gender | Age at T1 | OQPT score/ level at T1 | OQPT score/ level at T5 | Host university location |
|---|---|---|---|---|---|
| A | F | 19 | 36/LI | 45/UI | Ireland |
| C | F | 18 | 28/LI | 40/UI | Ireland |
| Y | M | 19 | 63/A | 48/A | UK |
| N | M | 19 | 67/A | 54/A | Ireland |
| M | F | 19 | 57/A | 48/A | Ireland |

### 4.3 Proficiency assessment

For both projects, L2 proficiency was assessed through a version of the Oxford Quick Placement test, a standardized test that taps into grammatical and collocational competence. In the Reksio task, 10 participants had reached UI level, and 10 were advanced (A). As for the PROLINGSA project, it witnessed the progression of two participants from lower intermediate (LI) to UI (see Table 3). The three advanced participants, while remaining in the advanced range as defined by OQPT, saw their scores decrease after their 9 months Erasmus+ stay abroad. However, the five participants increased their overall lexical range and fluency from T1 to T5 (Gilyuk, Edmonds & Sneed German 2021).

### 4.4 Transcriptions

For Task 1 and 2, all recordings were transcribed using CLAN procedures (McWhinney, 2000). The transcriptions were performed by a team of investigators, and each transcription was reviewed by an expert transcriber. Utterances were segmented on the principle that an utterance can only contain a single verb, except when modal or temporo-aspectual verbs form part of the verb phrase.

### 4.5 Coding scheme

In both datasets, 'I think' occurrences were coded according to their main discursive function (evidential, opinion, hedge, pragmatic) and syntactic construction (independent clause, matrix clause, parenthetical).

- *Evidential*: in this category, we grouped all instances of circumstantial or generic inference, as in (14), where learner Y ironically inferred, based on his observation of a cluttered kitchen, that the real explanation was that his roommate had been quite busy and therefore unable to do the dishes.

(14) **INT2: He keeps the kitchen clean.*
**Y: Yeah er yeah.* [looks unconvinced and laughs]
**Y: Well I think he was busy that er yesterday.* (YT2, PROLINGSA)

- *Opinion*: in this category, we grouped all the instances in which the speaker expressed an opinion, as in (15):

(15) **INT1: What do you think this heu stay abroad experience is going to bring to you?*
**A: Heu I mean I still live heu with heu my mother.*
**A: So I think it will be a good experience to live alone.* (AT1, PROLINGSA)

- *Hedging*: we included in this category occurrences in which the speaker used 'I think' to take a less assertive stance towards the adjacent propositional content, either because of a lack of certainty (16), or to mitigate the strength of the assertion.

(16) *And the owner helped the dog with covering the ground with some leaves like I think and then I'm not sure.* (Reksio, AFE07)

- *Pragmatic marker*: in this category, we included instances of 'I think' which were used by the speaker for discourse management, such as to keep the conversation going, or keeping their speaking turn, as in (17), where learner Y tries to gain time and retain his speaking turn while looking for something to say.

(17) **Y: That would be like yeah challenge.*
**INT2: Uhuh.*
**Y: Er if you say challenge like on the level **I think** yeah i just have like just wait a minute you know we have this book in university.* (YT2, PROLINGSA)

We also coded for syntactic position, in order to more fully investigate the degree of pragmalinguistic competence of our participants:

- *Parenthetical* (P): this category includes occurrences of 'I think' in middle position as in (16), and in final position as in (6).
- *Independent clauses* (IC): this category groups short answers as in (1) and independent clauses such as (2).
- *Matrix clause* (MC): in this category 'I think' features as a matrix clause followed by a complement clause as in (15).

# 5 Data Analysis

## 5.1 Task 1 Cross-Sectional Oral Narrative (Reksio)

First, we would like to point out that there is a very restricted number of occurrences of 'I think' markers in the Reksio database (E: 16, UI: 2, A: 10), as illustrated in Table 4.

Most utterances describe the actions of the main characters, and the expression of personal subjectivity is limited to inferences based on visual perception and world knowledge (12), or metacognitive comments on forgotten episodes (13).

(12) *He realizes that he can't walk because er because the ground is all icy I think.* (Reksio, E07, line 10)

(13) *After that I think they I don't remember what happens but I know that they are getting the skating shoes.* (Reksio, AFE01, line 28)

'I think' is almost exclusively used by native speakers and learners with an evidential meaning, to express the speaker's inferences based on memories of the visualization of the Reksio cartoon.

**Table 4.** Use of 'I think' in Reksio database

| **Participant category** | **'I think' #, SD, range** | **Syntactic structures % (#)** | **Semantic function % (#)** |
|---|---|---|---|
| E<br>N=10 | 18<br>2.15<br>0–7<br>7 users | MC 72 % (13)<br>P 29 % (5):<br>Incl.<br>Middle position 6 % (1)<br>Sentence final 23 % (4) | Evidential 94.44 % (17)<br>Epistemic 5.56 % (1) |
| UI<br>N=10 | 2<br>0.42<br>0–1<br>2 users | MC 100 % (2) | Evidential 100 % (2)<br>Epistemic / |
| A<br>N=10 | 10<br>1.88<br>0–6<br>4 users | MC 80 % (8)<br>P 20 % (2)<br>Incl.<br>Sentence final 100 % (2) | Evidential 80 % (8)<br>Epistemic 20 % (2) |

All groups of speakers favour the use of 'I think' as a matrix clause, but English natives allow more flexibility in the way they position it in the utterance, as they use it as a parenthetical adverbial in middle and final position on five occasions. It is also interesting to note that 7/10 English speakers use 'I think' at least once in their narrative, while this is only the case for 4 A and 2 UI: 'I think' therefore appears as a regular stance-marking option for English natives, while its use is much less homogeneous among learners.

To sum up, native speakers and learners mostly use 'I think' as a main clause followed by a complement clause, to convey an evidential meaning, in the Reksio oral narrative. This is probably due to the fact that oral narratives are a monologic type of discourse, and one in which narrated events do not concern the participant directly. Affordances of the speaker's subjectivity are consequently limited and 'I think' appears in contexts in which speakers indicate the retrieval of memorized evidence based on visual perception (the viewing of the film), through inferential processes, together with relative uncertainty about the related events.

Finally, while 'I think' appears as a regular stylistic feature of native discourse, it is only used by a few learner participants, even at the advanced level. We will now look at the interview data to find out how learners use 'I think' in interactional discourse before, during and after a nine month stay abroad in Ireland or in the UK.

## 5.2 Task 2 Longitudinal Oral Interview Task - PROLINGSA Database

We will first provide a quantitative description of our database, before adopting a more qualitative approach to assess the linguistic changes two learner participants experienced during the PROLINGSA project.

*Quantitative analysis.* Our analysis reveals different patterns of use of 'I think' in the interview data compared to the narrative data from the Reksio task. Graph 1 sums up the total number of 'I think' occurrences used by the five learners over the five interviews. Note that in this analysis, opinion and hedge values have been subsumed under the Epistemic category, as they both reflect the speaker's degree of certainty towards the propositional content.

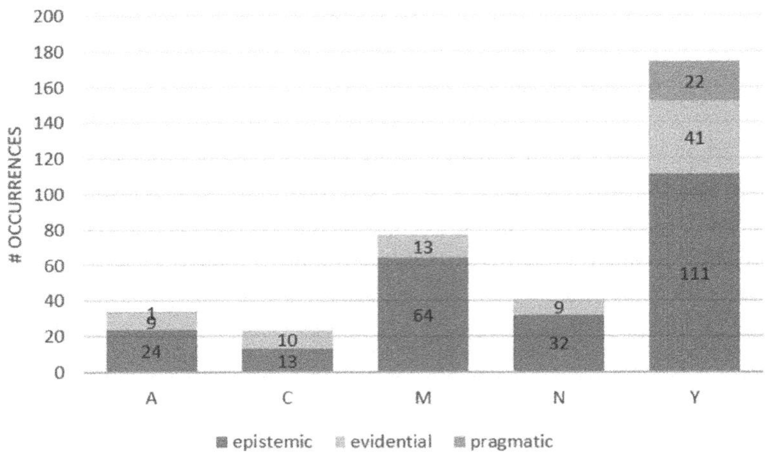


**Graph 1.** Distribution of 'I think' in PROLINGSA database, T1 to T5

It shows that three participants make a relatively moderate use of the 'I think' stance marker: A (34, 0.75 %); C (23, 0.80 %) and N (41, 0.81 %) of total database (Percentages were calculated based on the total number of utterances of the five interviews for all five participants). As for M and Y, they use it more frequently (M: 77, 2.76 %; Y: 174, 2.15 % of total database). All participants use it predominantly with epistemic values, but evidential uses are also frequent (A: 9 (26 %), C: 10 (43 %), M: 13 (17 %), N: 9 (22 %) and Y: 41 (24 %)). Only two participants use 'I think' with a pragmatic meaning (A: 1, Y: 22). The interview task therefore elicits three main types of semantic values, with epistemic values largely outnumbering evidential and pragmatic values, in line with previous research results (Baumgarten & House 2010).

Regarding syntax (see Graph 2), all five participants predominantly use 'I think' as a matrix clause introducing a complement clause, followed by 'I think' as a parenthetical, either mid-clause (MP) or in a final position (SF). We also find a few occurrences of 'I think' as a short answer or an independent clause in the productions of all participants. However, while the productions of the three more advanced participants (M, N and Y) display a high proportion of MC (>70 % of the examples for each of these participants), illustrating the use of more complex syntactic structures, intermediate learners tend to use parentheticals more often (A: 43 %, C:42 %). Style therefore appears to be constrained by proficiency, with advanced learners packaging information in syntactically complex utterances, while intermediate learners use a large proportion of parentheticals.

We will now provide a qualitative analysis of the way M and Y, our two frequent users, use 'I think' to track the way their use evolved over the course of their nine-month stay-abroad in the British Isles.

*Case studies: evolution of speaker style for M and Y - Case study 1 (M).* M, despite her advanced level in English, was neither confident in nor particularly satisfied with the way she spoke English, particularly at T1. Asked by the interviewer how she felt about her English at T1, she replied: '&uh I don 't feel very comfortable speaking English because I know that's &uh that <my> [x2] grammar is not quite good no neither is my accent but as a whole I think I feel yeah not very comfortable but not &uh actually uncomfortable' (AT1). At T4, she declared herself not satisfied with her progress in English: 'I'm not satisfied. I expected so much and it won't be as I expected.'

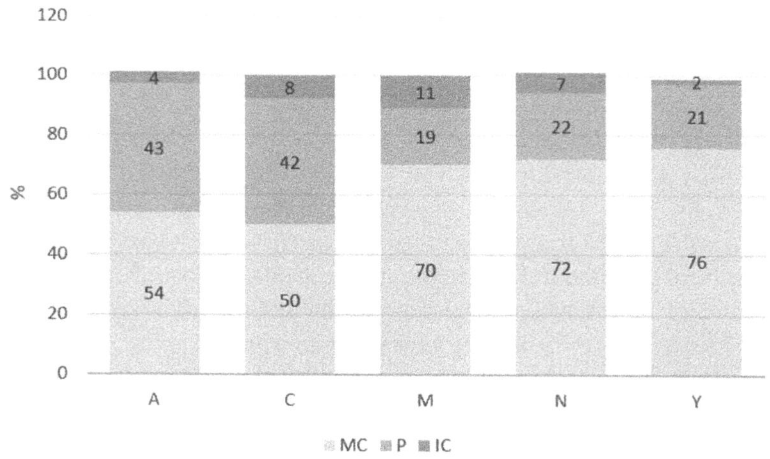


**Graph 2.** Percentage of syntactic constructions for 'I think' per participant, T1 to T5

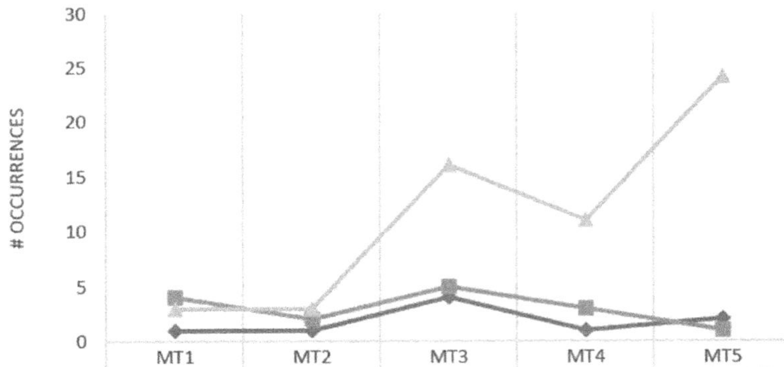


| | MT1 | MT2 | MT3 | MT4 | MT5 |
|---|---|---|---|---|---|
| IC | 1 | 1 | 4 | 1 | 2 |
| P | 4 | 2 | 5 | 3 | 1 |
| MC | 3 | 3 | 16 | 11 | 24 |

**Graph 3.** M's syntactic choices – T1 to T5

However, Graph 3 shows that M developed greater syntactic complexity with the use of 'I think' during and after her nine-month sojourn: at T1 and T2, she uses only a few 'I think', with no specific preference for a type of syntactic structure: she uses it as an independent clause (mostly in short answers), as a sentence final parenthetical, or as a matrix clause in a fairly similar way. From T3 on, her use of 'I think' globally increases, with 'I think' as MC culminating at T5. Graph 3 therefore clearly illustrates the development of syntactic complexity in M's speech, together with an enhanced expression of subjectivity.

Let us now focus on the evolution of the way M uses the different semantic values of 'I think' in the five interviews. In this analysis, we included all evidential and epistemic values, which we subcategorized into hedge and opinion, in order to have an insight into the evolution of the speaker's assertivity.

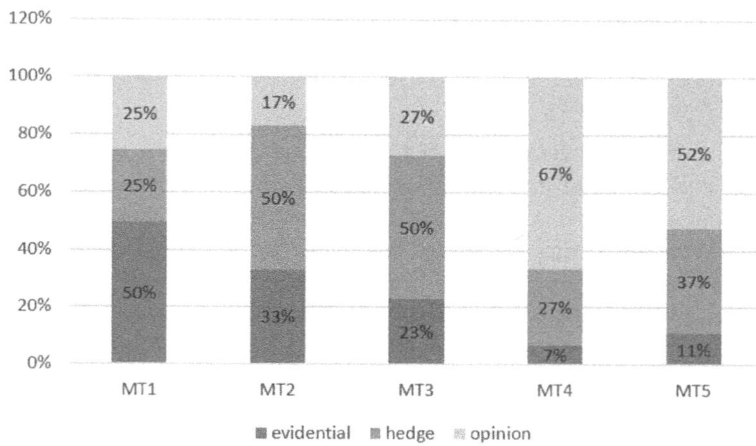


**Graph 4.** M's choice of semantic values for 'I think' - T1 to T5

At T1, M uses 'I think' as an evidential marker and as an epistemic marker (hedge or opinion) in a balanced way. At T2, T3 and T4, M mostly uses 'I think' as a hedging device as in (18).

(18) **INT1: Um and so what in your opinion what are your next challenges with respect to English?*
**M: Um.*
**INT1: Or the next things that you want to try to do.*
**M: Um I think I want to improve my understanding of the Irish accent because sometimes it's so difficult for me .* (MT2, PROLINGSA)

In this example, the use of 'I think' to mitigate her claim that she wants to improve her understanding of the Irish accent indicates that at T2 she does not have a clear idea of what her learning priorities are, or that she lacks the self-confidence to assert them. From T4 however, it becomes clear she uses 'I think' predominantly to express her opinion, suggesting that she took a more assertive stance after a few months in Ireland (T4 took place at the end of March 2019, roughly a month before M's return to France). This is illustrated in (19), where M has been asked to comment on the impact of Brexit on Ireland and uses 'I think' to state her opinion on that matter, while aligning with her interlocutor by responding to their cue ('what do you think') with an immediate uptake ('I think…') (pragmatic function).

(19) **INT1: ok what do you think about it [Brexit]?*
**M: I think for here it's concerning and I'm very curious about what is going to happen with the north and the border and the good Friday agreement and everything.*
(PROLINGSA, MT4)

In brief, our data suggests that M's nine-month Erasmus+ stay in Ireland consolidated her linguistic competence, as illustrated through the development of syntactic complexity with 'I think', while her choice of semantic values for this marker suggests that she gained confidence in her linguistic capacities as well as on her entitlement to give her opinion on a variety of topics. At T5, the interviewers had M watch an extract of the T1 interview to reflect on her linguistic progress: her reaction, transcribed in (20), shows M's surprise at the realization of her progress.

(20) **M: so <I'm> [/] I'm happy.*
**M: and I'm really surprised.*
**M: I think I didn't know how much I improved my confidence when I speak English.*
(PROLINGSA, MT5)

Taken together, M's case study confirms previous research results on the impact of study abroad on the individual's perception of self (see, among others, Papatsiba 2005; Milstein 2005 on self-perceived growth in autonomy and self-efficacy; Grieve 2013, 2015; Compiegne 2020).

*Case studies: evolution of speaker style for M and Y - Case study 2 (Y).* Let us now analyse the developmental trajectory of Y's use of 'I think', as regards syntactic choices and semantic distribution. Y is a very talkative individual, who enjoys reflecting on his study abroad experience, and speaking about his life as an Erasmus+ student in a UK university. His interviews last much longer than the other participants' (see Table 3), thereby yielding affordances for the use of numerous 'I think' stance markers.

Graph 5 shows that Y has a preference for 'I think' as a matrix clause: it is his favourite option even at T1, before departure. His use of 'I think' globally increases over time, and peaks at T5 with a total of 54 occurrences.

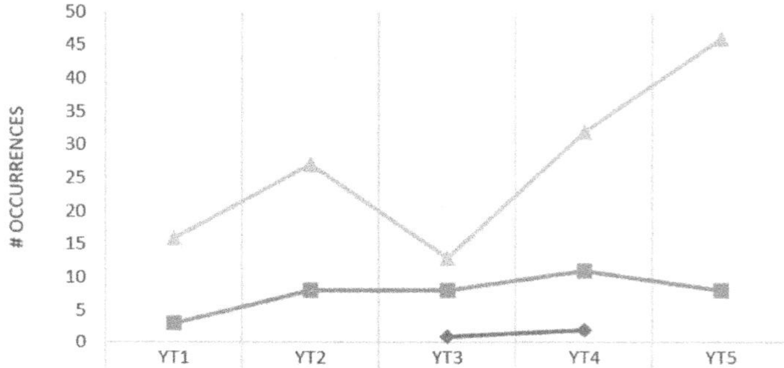


| | YT1 | YT2 | YT3 | YT4 | YT5 |
|---|---|---|---|---|---|
| IC | | | 1 | 2 | |
| P | 3 | 8 | 8 | 11 | 8 |
| MC | 16 | 27 | 13 | 32 | 46 |

**Graph 5.** Y's syntactic choices – T1 to T5

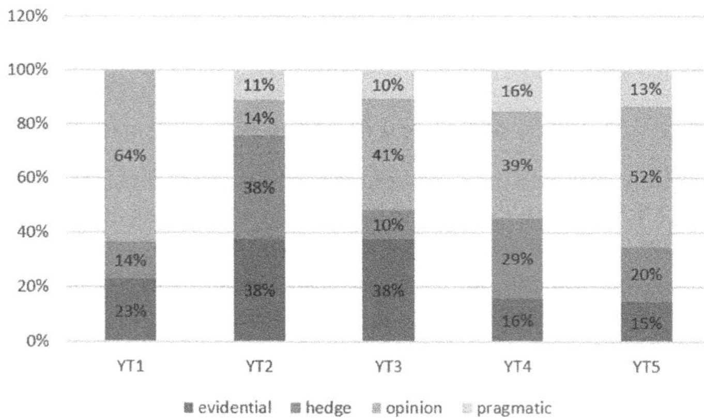


**Graph 6.** Y's choice semantic values for 'I think' - T1 to T5

Let us now turn to the semantic analysis presented in Graph 6.

At T1, before departure, Y mainly uses 'I think' in its more literal meaning: the expression of opinion, as in (21), where Y uses 'I think' to state that his teacher was particularly inspirational.

(21) **INT1: So you had a great English teacher?*
**INT1: So someone who inspired you?*
**Y: I think she's one of the most inspirational teacher that I ever had.* (YT1, PROLINGSA)

The relatively small percentage of hedging (14 %) indicates he mainly uses 'I think' with a fairly high degree of certainty, to express his perspective on events (opinion or source of information). These changes at T2, which took place at the end of October, roughly six weeks after his arrival in the UK: during this interview, 38 % of Ys uses of 'I think' are as hedges, while incorporating pragmatic uses (11 %), signalling a shift to a more intersubjective perspective.

In (22), his use of 'I think' suggests a less assertive stance, and corresponds to a hedging value.

(22) **Y: We have this book (laughs) in Paul Valéry [University].*
**INT1: Oh.*
**Y: I still have it so yeah um I think I'll see like all the vocabulary but…*
*From T2 on, pragmatic values enter Y's stance marking repertoire and he makes good use of them at T2, T3, T4 and T5. This is illustrated in (23) where Y uses 'I think', but also 'yeah', 'but' and 'I don't know' to keep his speaking turn.* (YT2, PROLINGSA)

(23) **Y: Your accent is changing in a weird way.*
**Y: I don't it's just like you know like social instincts.*
**Y: You just get to okay this is just how things are.*
**Y: So just trying to int(egrate) integrate to the group.*
**Y: And so everything's all right.*
**INT1: Mmmm.*
**Y: Uh so yeah but yeah I think yeah yeah I don't know.* (YT3, PROLINGSA)

The proportion of pragmatic occurrences remains fairly constant (10 to 16 %) from T2 to T4. Finally, Y's use of evidential values increases from T1 (23 %) to T2 and T3 (38 %), before falling to 16 % at T4 and 15 % at T5.

Taken together, these results suggest that Y has a globally assertive style, as shown by the high proportion of opinion occurrences (T1: 64 %, T2: 14 %, T3: 41 %, T4: 39 %, T5: 52 %). Moreover, he uses 'I think' with a pragmatic value for discourse management purposes, a type of use he incorporated in his repertoire at T2, after six weeks of immersion. This confirms previous results on gains in pragmalinguistic competence during study abroad (see, for example, Kinginger 2013, Grieve 2013, 2015, Pérez Vidal & Shively 2019; Howard 2021; Leclercq 2021).

## 6 Discussion and conclusion

In this paper, we sought to complement existing research on the acquisition of verbal stance markers. In particular, we wanted to find out whether intermediate and advanced French learners of English were sensitive to the type of discursive context in their choice of semantic values and syntactic preferences for 'I think'. We discuss our main findings in relation to previous research.

*Does the type of discursive task have an impact of the way native speakers and learners use verbal stance marker 'I think'?*

Our data clearly shows that narratives and interview data do not provide the same affordances regarding the use of 'I think'. Whereas narratives elicit the marking of evidential inference based on visual perception of a set of events, and invite speakers to reconstruct the story based on their memories of the viewing, oral interview data, where the interviewers ask the participants questions about their life abroad, provide speakers with more opportunities to express their subjectivity. In conversational contexts, our analysis shows that 'I think' is predominantly used as an epistemic stance-marker, to indicate the degree of certainty with which a speaker relates to a given propositional content, and more specifically to signal the expression of the speaker's opinion, or to mitigate a claim. The two main other uses are evidential and pragmatic, when a speaker seeks to gain time for online planification, or to keep a speaking turn. Our analysis therefore confirms the findings from Gablasova et al. (2017), who found differences in learners' stance-taking choices in monologic and dialogic tasks.

*Does the use of 'I think' illustrate individual speaker style?*

It is difficult to answer this question based on the Reksio data, but the PROLINGSA dataset provides us with a glimpse into how the stylistic preferences of five learners of English evolved over the course of an academic year abroad.

First of all, 'I think' is used by all five learners, although in different proportions according to the participant and to the interview session. On the whole, two profiles emerge: moderate users (A, C and N) and more intensive users (M and Y). Both M and Y developed greater syntactic complexity in their use of 'I think' from T1 to T5. However, a close analysis of the data reveals that while Y is a very self-confident and highly reflexive speaker, feeling entitled to express his stance and opinion on a large variety of topics, M mostly uses those epistemic verbal markers as hedges, to mark her lack of certainty/self-assurance on topics that closely concern her. However, the MT5 data seems to suggest that she gained confidence over the course of her academic year abroad, as reflected in the frequent use of 'I think' to express her opinion. Our two case-studies therefore confirm previous research results on the importance of personal style (Kirkham 2011; Leclercq 2021) and validates Gablasova et al. (2017)'s observation that there is quite a lot of individual variation in the way advanced L2 speakers of English use epistemic stance markers. They called for more fine-grained studies which could "more firmly connect the micro-level linguistic structures (e.g. stance markers) with the higher-order categories such as social identities" (p631). We hope to have shown that learners' style, i.e., the way they use 'I think' reveals something about their degree of assertiveness, and the way they position themselves in discourse relative to others.

To conclude, our study provides evidence of the influence of the type of discursive task in the way 'I think' is used by French learners of English, while contributing to examining the links between the linguistic choices of learners and their study-abroad experience. Our data confirms previous research results that studying abroad permits linguistic development, as regards syntactic complexity, but also the possibility to expand self-confidence in one's linguistic abilities (Papatsiba 2005; Milstein 2005; Kinginger 2013; Compiegne 2020). Each speaker has their own personality, and this is reflected in the way they use verbal epistemic stance markers.

## References

Aikhenvald, A. Y. (2004). *Evidentiality*. Oxford University Press.

Aijmer, K. (2002). 'Modality in advanced Swedish learners' written interlanguage'. In S. Granger, J. Hung and S. Petch-Tyson (eds.), *Computer learner corpora, second language acquisition and foreign language teaching*, pp. 55–76. Amsterdam: John Benjamins.

Aijmer, K. (2009). "'So er I just sort I dunno I think it's just because…': A corpus study of *I don't know* and *dunno* in learners' spoken English". In A. H. Jucker, D. Schreier and L. Hundt (eds.), *Corpora: Pragmatics and Discourse. Papers from the 29th International Conference on English Language Research on Computerized Corpora (ICAME 29)*, pp. 151–168. Amsterdam/New York: Rodopi.

Baumgarten, N., and House, J. (2010). 'I think and I don't know in English as lingua franca and native English discourse'. *Journal of Pragmatics*, 42 (5), 1184–1200.

Béal, C. (2010). *Les Interactions Quotidiennes en Français et en Anglais, de l'Approche Comparative à l'Analyse des Situations Interculturelles*. Bern: Peter Lang.

Biber, D. (2006). 'Stance in spoken and written university registers'. *Journal of English for Academic Purposes*, 5 (2), 97-116.

Bucholtz, M. and Hall, K. (2005). 'Identity and interaction: A sociocultural linguistic approach'. *Discourse Studies*, 7 (4–5), 585–614.

Compiegne, I. (2020). *Study Abroad in the Age of Social Media*. Ph.D. thesis, University of Technology Sidney, Ultimo. Available online: <https://opus.lib.uts.edu.au/handle/10453/142519>, accessed 20 September 2021.

Coupland, N. (1985). 'Hark, hark, the lark': Social motivations for phonological style-shifting. *Language and Communication*, 5 (3), 153–171.

Coupland, N. (2007). *Style: language variation and identity*. Cambridge University Press.

Fordyce, K. (2009). 'A comparative study of learner corpora of spoken and written discursive language: focusing on the use of epistemic forms by Japanese EFL'. *Hiroshima Studies in Language and Language Education*, 12, 135–150.

Fordyce, K. (2014). 'The Differential Effects of Explicit and Implicit Instruction on EFL Learners' Use of Epistemic Stance'. *Applied Linguistics*, 35 (1), 6–28.

Gablasova, D., Brezina, V., McEnery, T., and Boyd, E. (2017). 'Epistemic Stance in Spoken L2 English: The Effect of Task and Speaker Style'. *Applied Linguistics*, 38 (5), 613–637.

Hassler, G. (2015). 'Evidentiality and the expression of speaker's stance in Romance languages and German'. *Discourse Studies*, 17 (2), 182–209.

Gilyuk, V., Edmonds, A., and Sneed German, E. (2021). 'Exploring the evolution in oral fluency and productive vocabulary knowledge during a stay abroad'. *Journal of the European Second Language Association*, 5 (1), 101–114.

Grieve, A. M. (2013). 'Acquisition of the pragmatic marker 'like' by German study abroad adolescents'. In T. Greer, D. Tatsuki and C. Roever (eds.) *Pragmatics and Language Learning*, pp. 161–89. Honolulu: University of Hawai'i, National Foreign Language Resource Center.

Grieve, A. M. (2015). 'The Impact of Host Family Relations and Length of Stay on Adolescent Identity Expression during Study Abroad'. *Multilingua* 34, 623–57.

Guentchéva, Z. (2018). *Epistemic modalities and evidentiality in cross-linguistic perspective* (Empirical approaches to language typology Vol. 59). Berlin Boston: De Gruyter Mouton.

Howard, M. (2021). L'acquisition des langues secondes et la mobilité internationale: s'approprier une langue seconde en immersion. In P. Leclercq, A. Edmonds and E. Sneed-German (eds.). *Introduction à L'acquisition d'une Langue Etrangère*, pp. 373–388. Bruxelles: De Boeck.

Kärkkäinen, E. (2006). 'Stance taking in conversation: From subjectivity to intersubjectivity'. *Text & Talk*, 26 (6), 699–731.

Kiesling, S.F. (2009). 'Style as Stance: Can stance be the primary explanation for patterns of sociolinguistic variation?' In A. Jaffe (ed.), *Sociolinguistic Perspectives on Stance*, pp. 171–194. Oxford University Press.

Kinginger, C. (2013). 'Identity and Language Learning in Study Abroad: Identity and Language Learning in Study Abroad'. *Foreign Language Annals*, 46 (3), 339–358.

Kirkham, S. (2011). 'Personal style and epistemic stance in classroom discussion'. *Language and Literature: International Journal of Stylistics*, 20 (3), 201–217.

Leclercq, P. (2021). 'The Acquisition of Verbal Epistemic Stance Marking during Study Abroad: The Case of je pense in L2 French'. *Languages*, 6 (4), 196.

Leclercq, P., and Edmonds, A. (2017). 'How L2 learners of French and English express modality using verbal means: A crosslinguistic and developmental study'. *International Review of Applied Linguistics in Language Teaching*, 55 (3).

Leclercq, P., Edmonds, A. and Sneed German, E. (2021). *PROLINGSA* [Corpus]. ORTOLANG (Open Resources and TOols for LANGuage), <www.ortolang.fr>, v1, <https://hdl.handle.net/11403/prolingsa/v1>.

Leclercq, P. and Mélac, E. (2021). 'Second Language Acquisition of Evidentiality in French and English: A corpus-based study'. *Language, Interaction, Acquisition*, 12 (2), 251–283.

Liao, S. (2009). 'Variation in the use of discourse markers by Chinese teaching assistants in the US'. *Journal of Pragmatics*, 41 (7), 1313–1328.

Local, J. (2003). 'Variable domains and variable relevance: Interpreting phonetic exponents'. *Journal of Phonetics*, 31 (3–4), 321–339.

Marín-Arrese, J.I. (2015). 'Epistemicity and stance: A cross-linguistic study of epistemic stance strategies in journalistic discourse in English and Spanish'. *Discourse Studies*, 17 (2), 210–225.

MacWhinney, B. (2000). *The CHILDES Project: Tools for Analyzing Talk*. 3rd Edition. Mahwah, NJ: Lawrence Erlbaum Associates.

Mifka-Profozic, N. (2017). 'Processing epistemic modality in a second language: A self-paced reading study'. *International Review of Applied Linguistics in Language Teaching*, 55 (3).

Milstein, T. (2005). 'Transformation abroad: Sojourning and the perceived enhancement of self-efficacy'. *International Journal of Intercultural Relations*, 29 (2), 217–238.

Mullan, K. (2010). *Expressing opinions in French and Australian English Discourse: A Semantic and Interactional Analysis*. Amsterdam: John Benjamins Publishing Company.

Mullan, K. (2012). 'Saying what you think: An analysis of French and Australian English non-native speaker expression of subjectivity'. In N. Baumgarten, I. Du Bois and J. House (eds.), *Subjectivity in Discourse—Unity in Diversity*, pp. 193–227. Bingley: Emerald Group Publishing Ltd.

Neary-Sundquist, C. (2013). 'Task Type Effects on Pragmatic Marker Use by Learners at Varying Proficiency Levels'. *L2 Journal*, 5 (2), 1–21.

Papatsiba, V. (2005). 'Political and Individual Rationales of Student Mobility: A case-study of ERASMUS and a French regional scheme for studies abroad'. *European Journal of Education*, 40 (2), 173–188.

Salsbury, T. and Bardovi-Harlig, K. (2000). 'Oppositional talk and the acquisition of modality in L2 English'. In B. Swierzbin, F.A. Morris, M.E. Anderson, C.A. Klee, and E.E. Tarone (eds.), *Social and Cognitive Factors in Second Language Acquisition: Selected Proceedings of the 1999 Second Language Research Forum*, pp. 57–76. Somerville, MA: Cascadilla Press.

Squartini, M. (2008). 'Lexical vs. Grammatical evidentiality in French and Italian'. *Linguistics*, 46 (5).

Thompson, S. (2002). '"Object complements" and conversation: towards a realistic account'. *Studies in Language*, 26 (1), 125 – 164.

Vincze, V. (2013). 'Weasels, Hedges and Peacocks: Discourse-level Uncertainty in Wikipedia Articles'. In *International Joint Conference on Natural Language Processing*, pp. 383–391. Nagoya, Japan, 14–18 October 2013.

Watorek, M. (ed.) (2004). *Construction du discours par des enfants et des apprenants adultes*. Special issue, *Langages* 38 (155).

Zhang, G. Q., and Sabet, P. G. P. (2016). 'Elastic 'I think': Stretching Over L1 and L2'. *Applied Linguistics*, 37 (3), 334–353.

Cecilia Mihaela Popescu & Oana-Adriana Duță

# From Evidential to Pragmatic Markers: an Insight into the Subjectivization Process of Romanian *Cică* and Spanish *Dizque*

**Abstract:** The paper aims to present a comparative analysis of two lexical particles expressing reportative evidentiality, Romanian *cică* and Spanish *dizque* (see some American and Peninsular varieties), in order to emphasise the convergences and the divergences of their discursive and functional values.

Our approach is motivated first of all by the fact that both items have the same origin and a quasi-identical morphological structure: they are derived from Romance cognates of the Latin verb DICERE 'to say' – the 3rd person singular form, and an agglutinated complementiser, Rom. (*se*) *zice că*/ Sp. *Dice* or *dicen que* 'he/she says that'. Secondly, across the times, these two particles developed a range of similar values (frequently encountered in oral speech and in some complementary textual genres, such as legends, tall stories, rumours, jokes, etc.), that could be distributed, based on the recent frame proposed by Sanromán Vilas (2020), into three groups: (1) evidential, (2) epistemic and (3) discursive and pragmatic values. Hence, the prominent and most frequently used value of the two items is the evidential meaning of hearsay, expressing that the source of the asserted information is not the speaker. The epistemic value is connoted (often simultaneously with the evidential meaning) in different degrees, by the stance of the speaker, who takes a distance from his/her own propositional content, because s/he does not agree with the certainty of this propositional content. Finally, our corpus-based study demonstrates that another kind of values, of a pragmatic and discursive nature (functioning, for example, as objection markers), is emergent in all the linguistic varieties on which our comparative approach focuses. This third category could support the main hypothesis of our study (see also Pop 2017) concerning the existence of pragmaticalization processes that the evidential markers develop in time.

**Keywords:** *evidentiality, pragmaticalization, discursive values, evidential markers*

## 1 State of the Art

### 1.1 A Particular Frame of Reportative Evidence in Romance Languages

The grammatical category of evidentiality is conveyed under a wide range of forms and strategies across linguistic systems. Even though they do not intrinsically encode evidential information (i.e. on a morphological level), Romance languages mark the source of the information conveyed by the speaker, by means of complex lexical (adverbs, expressions that are grammaticalized to a lower or a higher extent, etc.) and pragmatic-discursive strategies, thus falling within the first category of the three-layer typology proposed by Lazard (2001: 360). For instance, in most of the European Romance area (except for Spanish, where the phenomenon is quite recent and not very frequent), conditional forms are often used to convey Reportative Evidentiality – indicating, besides hearsay information or rumours, that the speaker does not commit to the asserted propositional content and distances himself/herself from it. Another pattern of expressing reportative evidentiality, recently indicated in relevant research (see, inter alia, Aikhenvald 2004 and Alcázar 2018: 725–740), is the use of adverbial lexical operators derived from the Romance cognates of the dicendi verb, lat. DICERE [to say]. This is primarily seen with *dizque*, frequently used (see, inter alia, Demonte / Fernández-Soriano 2014 or Vilas 2020: 1–24) in some American (see 1) and Peninsular Spanish varieties or even in Latin American Portuguese varieties.

(1) *sí, sí,* ***dizque*** *estamos progresando,* ***dizque****…*
[yes, yes, people **say** we are progressing, **they say**]
(Company Company 2006: 108, quoted by Remberger 2015: 31).

Other lexemes with the same origin and meaning are found in various Romance varieties (see Cruschina / Remberger 2008; Dumitrescu 2012; Remberger 2015; Zafiu 2020: 190), such as Galician (see ex. 2), Sardinian (see ex. 3), the Sicilian dialect (see ex. 4) or Romanian (see ex. 5):

(2) ***Disque*** *a filla da Antonia marchou á Coruñavivir co mozo.*
[Antonia's daughter **reportedly** went to La Coruña to live with her boyfriend.]
(Cruschina / Remberger 2008: 96).

(3) *In custu castellu* ***nachi*** *bi istaiada su fizu 'e su re…*
[In this castle the son of the king **was said** to live…]
(Archivi del Sud, 1996, quoted by Remberger 2015: 31).

(4) ***Dicica*** *ci avivanu finutu i grana.*
[**It is reported that** they had finished their money.]
(Cruschina / Remberger 2008: 95).

(5) *Amu* ***cică*** *era odată într-o ţară un crai, care avea trei feciori.*
[Once upon a time (**they said**) there was a king who had three daughters.]
(Creangă, *Povestea lui Harap-Alb,* quoted by Remberger 2015: 31).

All these lexical items express, as shown by the English translation of the examples above, indirect reportative evidentiality. A deeper analysis can show that the semantic-pragmatic values of such lexical items deriving from the structure dicendi verb + agglutinated complementiser actually are complex and varied.

## 1.2 Hearsay and Reportative Evidentiality

Given the strongest meaning of these Romance lexical units, their comparative analysis must be transposed to the theoretical framework provided by theories on evidentiality and epistemic modality. Therefore, we should point out some issues defining and characterizing these two domains.

According to the classical definition proposed by Aleksandra Aikhenvald (2004), evidentiality is "a linguistic category whose primary meaning is source of information" (2004: 3), while epistemic modality is a semantic category expressing the degree of certainty of a propositional content and, implicitly, the speaker's attitude regarding the veracity involved by such a propositional content

It should be mentioned that several subclasses have been distinguished within the category of evidentiality, which can be divided into direct evidentiality (based on perception) and indirect evidentiality (inferential and reportative). Our focus here is reportative evidentiality, also referred to as second-hand or third-hand evidence, that can be classified into the following categories proposed by Willett (1988: 96):

- Second-hand evidence – hearsay: the source of the information in the sentence asserted by the speaker is not the speaker, but another person who directly witnessed the event (a direct witness): 's/he says'.
- Third-hand evidence – hearsay: the source of the information in the sentence asserted by the speaker is not the speaker, but another person who did not directly witness the event (an indirect witness): 'I heard', 'I was told', 'it's said', 'people say that' (impersonal).
- Information from the folklore: the source of the information in the sentence asserted by the speaker is represented by pre-established oral customs (fairy tales, mythology, oral literature, proverbs and sayings).

## 1.3 Methodological Outline

The paper aims to present a comparative analysis of two lexical particles expressing primarily reportative evidentiality, Romanian *cică* and Spanish *dizque*, in order to emphasize the convergences and the divergences of their discursive and functional values.

Our approach is motivated first of all by the fact that both items have the same origin and a quasi-identical morphological structure: they are derived from

Romance cognates of the Latin verb DICERE [to say] – the 3rd person singular form, and an agglutinated complementiser, Rom. (*se*) *zice că*/ Sp. *dice* or *dicen que* [he/she says that].

Secondly, across the times, these two particles developed a range of similar values (frequently encountered in oral speech and in some complementary textual genres, such as legends, tall stories, rumours, jokes, etc.), that could be distributed, based on the recent frame proposed by Sanromán Vilas (2020: 1–26), into three groups: (1) evidential, (2) epistemic and (3) discursive and pragmatic values. Hence, the prominent and most frequently used value of the two items is the evidential meaning of hearsay, expressing that the source of the asserted information is not the speaker. The epistemic value is connoted (often simultaneously with the evidential meaning) in different degrees, by the stance of the speaker, who takes a distance from his/her own propositional content, because s/he does not agree with the certainty of this propositional content. Finally, our corpus-based study demonstrates that another kind of values, of a pragmatic and discursive nature (functioning, for example, as objection markers), is emergent in all the linguistic varieties on which our comparative approach focuses. This third category could support the main hypothesis of our study (see also Pop 2017: 171–185) concerning the existence of pragmaticalization processes that the evidential markers develop in time.

## 2 Rom. *cică* and Sp. *dizque* – Functional and Semantic Properties

### 2.1 *Rom.* cică

Proceeding, as shown by the major etymological lexicographical sources of Romanian (also see DELR, vol. II, s.v.*cică*), from the apheresed agglutinated structure '[*se zi*]*ce* + *că*' [it is said + that] made up of the dicendi verb *a zice* [to say]< lat. DICERE used in the 3rd person singular of the present indicative[1] and the complementiser *că* [that], the word *cică* is first attested in Romanian only in the 19th century, more precisely in 1850, in Vasile Alecsandri's works (see RDW, vol. I, s. v. *cică*). Actually, the first lexicalized occurrences of this structure are found in oral and popular texts, in proverbs, sayings, in stories and fairy tales (in Ion Creangă, Anton Pann, Petre Ispirescu, etc.).

1 Zafiu (2020: 191) shows that the short form 'ce' of 'zice' ('says') is attested in records of oral popular texts, such as: 's-o dus ş-au bătut în uşă la-mpăratu. *Ce*: – Poftim, intră! Au intrat' [they went and knocked on the emperor's door. '*says*: - Come in! They came in] (Bîrlea 1966, II: 128, quoted by Zafiu 2020: 191).

From a morphological point of view, the analysed item is an adverb, frequently used in contemporary language in two types of syntactic constructions: as a complex sentence adverb with an impersonal meaning, determining the predication of the sentence or only certain syntactic groups; and as a predicative adverb with an expressed (human) subject (see Zafiu 2020: 189–192).

Functionally, *cică* has lost its original syntactic component, especially when used at the beginning of a sentence (which is probably its most frequent use) (see ex. 5 above), instead activating its pragmatic component, as well as the modal, epistemic one, since it conveys the degree of truth and certainty awarded by the speaker to the asserted propositional content.

The cancellation of the syntactic component, the strong degree of lexicalization and pragmaticalization of the analysed item result from the fact that, in contemporary oral language, in the colloquial, non-standard register, as well as in the area of written orality, *cică* is sometimes accompanied by the complementiser *că* (only two occurrences in CoRoLa) (also see Cruschina / Remberger 2008: 104), as in (6), and very frequently by *să*, as in (7). In other discursive situations, *cică* appears as a verb in an impersonal form, as *cică-se* (= *zice-se că* [it is said that]) (see (8)) or even redundantly preceded by the verb *a zice* [to say] (see (9) below).

(6) *Dragă jurnalule, Sunt foarte foarte supărată pe țara Olanda pentru că e nesimțită și rea și nu o lasă pe țara mea, România, să intre în spațiul Shengen, deoarece* cică că *țara mea este foarte corubtă. Vreau să-i transmit Olandei și pe această cale, în caz că-mi citește jurnalul meu secret (pe care nul citesc decât eu, SRI-ul și tata), să nu o mai bârfească atâta pe țaramea, pentru că…*
[Dear diary, I am very very upset with Netherlands, because this country is evil and jerk and they do not let my country Romania enter the Schengen area, because, **they say that** my country is very corrupt. I would like to hereby inform the Netherlands, in case they read my secret diary (which is only read by myself, the Intelligence Bureau and my dad), that they should no longer gossip about my country, because…]
(*Din cultură îmi plac cel mai mult cărțile*, by Simona Tache (2012), in CoRoLa).

(7) *Auzi, dragă, , îmi zice că* cică să-*mi păstrez și eu una, a zis tanti Coca, un zîmbet ironic i s-a întins pe față.*
[Listen, dear, **he's saying that** I should keep one, Aunt Coca said with an ironic smile covering her face]
(*1989*, by Adrian Buz (2014), in CoRoLa).

(8) *Grosul din ele atârna la mai mult de o tonă (asta,* ***cică-se****, le ajuta la urlat)* [Their biggest part weighed more than a ton (**they say** that helped them scream)]
(*Cei șapte regi ai orașului București*, by Daniel Bănulescu, in CoRoLa).

(9) *Avea nevoie de dînșii în călătoria sa la Împăratul-Roș, care, zice, **cică** era un om răutăcios.*
[He needed them on his journey to the Red Emperor who, it is said, **apparently** was a bad person]
(Creangă, *Povești*, in DLRLC, s.v.*cică*).

## 2.2 *Sp.* dizque

Spanish lexicographical sources are not really generous regarding the etymology of *dizque*. The etymological dictionary of Joan Coromines does not include it, and the *Dictionary of the Real Academia Española* briefly mentions, under etymology, 'de *dice que*'. According to the *Diccionario Panhispánico de Dudas* (2005), *dizque*, proceeding from the archaic apocopated form *diz* ('dice', third person singular in the present tense of *decir*) and the conjunction *que*, is mostly used in Latin America, both as an adverb, with the meaning of 'apparently, allegedly', and as an invariable adjective, always preceding the noun, with the meaning of 'alleged'. The same dictionary also points out that some speakers erroneously interpret it as equivalent to *dicen* [they say] and combine it with the conjunction *que*, which is not necessary, since the form of the adverb already includes the conjunction. Kany (1969: 290) provides a summary of the diachronic pathway of *dizque*, showing that around 1535, Juan de Valdés wrote 'También dezimos *diz que* por *dicen*, y no parece mal' [We also say *diz que* instead of *dicen* and it does not seem wrong], that it was perhaps assimilated to the dialectal, provincial or rustic register at the beginning of the 17th century, when it was classified as a 'palabra aldeana, que no se deve usar en la Corte' [a rustic word, that should not be used in Court] (Kany 1969: 290) and that it was eventually maintained in regional literature and in spoken language, almost always as an archaism in the colloquial style.

According to Gallucci (2017: 245), *dizque* is a marker of free indirect speech, a narrative technique that transcribes the contents of a conscience (thoughts, perceptions, thought or spoken words) so that a confluence occurs between the narrator's and the character's points of view. Therefore, free indirect speech always implies a communicative ambiguity: the receiver cannot know with certainty whether the narrator's words are his/her own or, rather, correspond to an internal monologue of the character (Maldonado 1999: 3551–3552). However, *dizque* is not explicitly mentioned among the elements of free indirect speech – such as the presence or absence of quotation marks, oratio quasi obliqua constructions – listed by Maldonado in the *Gramática Descriptiva de la* Lengua Española (1999: 3551–3555).

The tendency to cancel the syntactic component in the colloquial register, as previously described for Rom. *cică*, is also apparent in the case of *dizque*, basically following the same pattern of the redundant addition of the complementiser *que* in both enclitic and proclitic position ('dizque que', 'que dizque') (see 10). The latter form 'que dizque' has resulted in 'quizque'/'quesque' ['supposedly / allegedly'] (see 11 and 12), a new evidential reportative marker which seems to have 'reintroduced the reportative meaning of the bleached evidential marker *dizque*' (Mora and Maldonado 2015: 174).

(10) *me lo podría decir con todo derecho, no me lo dice* ***que dizque*** *porque me quiere mucho*
[he could say it to me with all due right, but he doesn't tell me that **que dizque (supposedly, he says)** because he loves me]
(CREA Fiction, 1991, quoted by Mora and Maldonado 2015: 176).

(11) *El primer día que fuimos* ***quesque*** *a posar, como dicen, fue, ora verá usté. . .* [The first day that we went to **quesque (so-called)** modelling, as they say, was, let's see.]
(CREA Fiction, 1999, quoted by Mora and Maldonado 2015: 176).

(12) ***Dizque que*** *se pelearon ayer,* ***quesque*** *a eso de las cinco, aunque yo no vi nada.*
[**Dizque (supposedly)** they got into a fight yesterday, **quesque (apparently, they say)** around five, although I did not see anything]
(CREA Fiction, 1999, quoted by Mora and Maldonado 2015: 177).

A query for *dizque* across three corpora of the Real Academia Española (CREA – *Corpus de Referencia del Español Actual*, CORDE – *Corpus Diacrónico del Español* and CORPES – *Corpus del Español del Siglo XXI*) supports the idea that *dizque* is barely used in Peninsular Spanish nowadays, while its evidential and especially epistemic uses are flourishing in Latin American Spanish (Miglio 2010, Demonte / Fernández Soriano 2013, Mora and Maldonado 2015, Marín-Arrese 2020).

## 3 Rom. *cică* and Sp. *dizque* – Pragmatic and Discursive Values

The pragmatic-discursive meanings of *cică* and *dizque* are the outcome of a pragmaticalization process that does not cover a very long timeframe, probably deriving from the inherent anaphoric and modal core meaning of the original structure. For instance, as shown by Reinberger (2015), the evolution of the adverb *cică* towards an evidential discursive unit implies an intermediate step when the analysed item had the verbal meaning of 'someone says that …', i.e. it expressed the act of speech/enunciation followed by the reproduction of another speaker's words. The syntactic and semantic independence implied by any process of pragmaticalization is, in this case, the outcome of a topicalization process, determined by the frequent dislocation of the newly obtained lexeme in an incident or parenthetic position.

In today's Romanian, the primary meanings of *cică* can be structured into three categories, that will be detailed in the following: the evidential reportative meaning, the modal epistemic meaning and the pragmatic-discursive meaning. *Dizque* also covers these three categories, but with a more limited array of pragmatic overtones (see also De La Mora and Maldonado 2015: 175).

## 3.1 Evidential Reportative Meaning

For both Rom. *cică* and Sp. *dizque*, the evidential reportative meaning ('it is said that…', 'people say that…', 'as they say, as they believe' – DLRLC, s. v. *cică*) actually is a continuation of the basic etymological meaning, i.e. the 'reproduction of the words of a previous speaker, from which the speaker takes a certain distance' (Ștefănescu 2007: 123), based on taking information from another source than the speaker, from the 'words of another speaker' (Zafiu 2002: 127–144; GALR 2008 I: 599, II, 717; GBLR 2016: 634).

In Romanian, the impersonal nature of the original construction experienced re-analysis and re-interpretation in the pragmaticalization process: the initial failure to mention the agent translated into the failure to mention the source of the asserted information, introduced by means of the evidential marker *cică*. In a lot of contexts, the meaning of this reportative marker is semantically equivalent to that of a declarative verb (equivalent to: 'he says (or 'they say') that …', DLRLC, s. v. *cică*). However, in other cases, as most indices of reportative evidentiality, *cică* also expresses the speaker's reluctance, lack of commitment and epistemic distance from the reproduced information, that is, it also has a modal-epistemic value. Nevertheless, it should be mentioned that the degrees of certainty vary according to the context and that, as underlined by Zafiu (2020: 190):

> unlike other adverbs and evidential expressions (e.g. 'pasămite', 'chipurile' [allegedly]), that clearly show that the speaker does not commit to the content (and often imply that it is not real), 'cică' generally indicates minimum epistemic distance, that varies and can be conveyed depending on other information[2].

From a syntactic point of view, the evidential reportative meaning of Rom. *cică* is found in two syntactic discursive patterns (close to the construction lying at the source of the analysed word), i.e.:

---

2 Unlike other adverbs and evidential expressions (e.g. *pasămite, chipurile* 'allegedly'), which clearly mark that the speaker is not engaged with the content (frequently implying that it is not real), *cică* generally indicates minimum epistemic distance, which is variable and can be actualized depending on other contextual information (Zafiu 2020: 190).

- sentences where *cică* is a sentence-modifying adverb with an impersonal meaning, frequently used at the beginning or in the middle of the sentence and, most often, right next to the predication:

(13) ***Cică*** *era odată un om însurat, și omul acela trăia la un loc cu soacră-sa.*
[**They say that** a married man once lived, and that he lived with his mother-in-law.]
(Ion Creangă, *Prostia omenească,* in archeus.ro).

(14) *dar habar nu are de legea lui Ohm, că ea nu s-a curentat niciodată, și cine nu a fost zgâlțâit nu știe ce-i ăla gustul curentului. Dar* cică *are toată casa plină de bibelouri, lua-mi-ar bibeloul la muștiuc, cu toate mamele proaste la un loc, care i-au carat sacoșele ca să treacă netoatele lor clasa, că, nu-i așa, fizica nu-i pentru orice cap...*
[but he has no idea about Ohm's law, because she was never electrocuted and those who have not shuddered have no idea about how current tastes. But **she says** all her house is full of small statues, to hell with her statues and all those stupid mothers who lavished her in gifts so that their stupid daughters could pass, because, right, physics is not for everyone]
(*Eu pe cine mai înjur*, by George Safir, in CoRoLa).

- sentences where *cică* functions as a predicative adverb (similarly to 'probably', 'of course', etc.), with an expressed or deducted subject (frequently human), indicating the exact source of information and having the value of a dicendi verb followed by a complementiser (v. Cruschina / Remberger 2008: 109; Zafiu 2020: 190). In such cases, *cică* is an explicit marker of indirect or free indirect speech (exclusively a marker of quotation), that partially maintain the meaning of the dicendi verb in the etymological structure.

(15) *Da, zic căzut și apăsat, te distrează, văd, i-am spus eu pe o bancă în fața teatrului, când* ***cică*** *noi vorbeam despre personaje, te distrează să-mi tot vorbești despre ea, ești detașat, ai control, cred că te simți bine, și după ce-am făcut poze pentru spectacol cu aparatul ei, el stătea cu mâinile lui frumoase și cu degete*
[Yes, I say firmly and bluntly, I see you're enjoying it, I told him on a bench in front of the theatre, when we were **supposedly** talking about characters, you're enjoying talking to me about her, you're detached, you're in control, I think you're feeling well and, after taking pictures for the show with her camera, he was there with his beautiful hands and his fingers]
(in CoRoLa).

(16) ***Cică*** ar fi reclamat cineva că în bloc se aude muzică populară.
[**Allegedly** someone complained about folk music being heard in the building.]
(https://www.digi24.ro/stiri/actualitate/social/mama-unei-fetite-de-2-ani-sanctionata-de-politisti-din-cauza-ca-micuta-face-zgomot-in-apartament-1306345).

(17) *Ia să vezi tu cum se duce el acolo, în aplauzele celor cu anteriele, că e rost de donații babane și* Dumnezeu cică *are nevoie de lovele... Ce-o face cu ele, n-am de unde să știu, e vreun mister spiritual și financiar totodată...*

[You'll see that he goes there. Accompanied by the applauses of churchmen, because huge donations are coming his way and **they say** God needs money… I can't know what He's doing with them, it's a both spiritual and financial mystery…]
(*De-ale chefliilor (proză umoristică)*, by Cristian Lisandru (2011), in CoRoLa).

As for *dizque*, its reportative use is embedded in its own etymology; practically, starting with the 13th century, *dizque* has been used in Spanish to introduce subordinate clauses of reported speech. In example 18 below, *dizque* is used by the speaker to show that the information comes from an external source (a letter sent by the lieutenant), i.e. it is second-hand information. *Dizque* acts, thus, as a reportative marker that the speaker has chosen to use in order to express his viewpoint regarding the propositional content.

(18) *Habrá dos o tres días que por carta del teniente que en mi lugar está en la Villa de la Vera Cruz, supe cómo al puerto de la dicha villa había llegado una carabela pequeña con hasta treinta hombres de mar y tierra, que* ***dizque*** *venía en busca de la gente que Francisco de Garay había enviado a esta tierra*
[It's been two or three days since a letter from the lieutenant who covering for me at Villa de la Vera Cruz informed me that the harbour of this town was approached by a small boat with no more than thirty men, which, they said, were looking for the people that Francisco de Garay had sent to this land]
(CORDE, 1519–1526).

The reported content introduced by *dizque* sometimes appears between quotation marks (examples 19 and 20). In such cases, the source of the information is clearly identifiable and the speaker takes a neutral stance regarding the asserted content, s/he merely reproduces it:

(19) *Al preguntarle un amigo al expresidente Alfonso López Michelsen cómo estaba,* ***dizque*** *que le contestó: "envejeciendo dulcemente"*
[When a friend asked former president Alfonso López Michelsen how he was, **they say** he answered: 'peacefully getting older'] (Press, Colombia, 1998).

(20) *A propósito de rumores, se supo que un grupo de realizadores venezolanos, que filmará una película con Colombia, rechazó la participación de Fanny Mickey en el papel protagónico* ***dizque*** *"porque no era prenda de garantía".* [Speaking of rumours, word came out that a group of Venezuelan film makers, who will shoot a film with Colombia, rejected the participation of Fanny Mickey as the protagonist, **allegedly** 'because she was not reliable']
(Press, Columbia, 1987).

In most cases, however, there is no formal delimitation between the speaker's actual words and the reported speech introduced by *dizque*. Depending on the context, the source of information is more or less apparent – Luciano in example 21, the grammatical subject of the sentence in example 22, probably the grammatical subject of the first sentence in example 23, and a less apparent source in example 24 (in fact, Demonte and Fernández Soriano 2013: 218, who reproduce this example from Travis 2006, choose to leave *dizque* untranslated into English):

(21) *Luciano era un cholito que había llegado a la capital* ***dizque*** *a estudiar.*
[Luciano was a lad who had come to the capital **allegedly** to study.]
(Press, Panama, 2001).

(22) *Se bebía unos tragos de Seco Herrerano* ***dizque*** *para olvidarlo, pero, que va, entonces, se acordaba más de él.*
[[S/he] took some sips of Seco Herrerano, **s/he said** it was to forget him but, alas, at those times s/he remembered him even more.]
(Press, Panama, 1997).

(23) *Siempre tuvieron celos,* ***dizque*** *más me ocupaba de éstos que de ellos.*
[They were always jealous, **allegedly** I was more devoted to those than to them.]
(Olbertz 2007: 155).

(24) *Por ejemplo, el a… aquí el alcalde, todo lo que ha hecho, Y…y ahorita,* ***dizque*** *ya lo están investigando.*
[For example, the mayor here, all that he's done, and now, **dizque** he's under investigation.]
(Travis 2006: ex. 12, quoted by Demonte / Fernández Soriano 2013: 218).

As a reportative evidential encoding source of information, *dizque*, just like Rom. *cică*, can also convey various degrees of certainty of the asserted content and frequently carries an added value of doubt. Studies conducted by Olbertz (2007) for Mexican Spanish and Travis (2006) for Columbian Spanish establish that, when modifying main or subordinate clauses, *dizque* shows an external source of information, functioning as a reportative marker (see examples 21–24 above). On the other hand, when modifying smaller constituents, *dizque* implies a lack of commitment on behalf of the speaker, even indicating that the content of the sentence is false (see 25 below):

(25) *[…] me daba unas aguas para llevar a la casa, en unos frascos grandes y sucios que, según él, debía beber de lunes a sábado, unas, y el domingo, otras.* ***Dizque*** *un elíxir para la eterna juventud […] ¡Nunca me quitó ni una puta arruga!*
[[…] he used to give me some liquid to take home, in some big dirty flasks and he told me I had to drink some from Monday to Saturday and others on Sunday. **He said** they were some elixir for eternal youth […] I did not get rid of one single wrinkle!]
(Travis 2005: 1288).

## 3.2 Modal Epistemic Meaning

The modal-epistemic meaning, marking doubt, lack of commitment, lack of trust in an opinion, is, hence, strongly dependent from the context and, most times, is amalgamated with the previously presented evidential value. Thus, the reportative meaning is gradually giving in to an epistemic meaning 'where the veracity of the message being conferred is called into question by the speaker' (Mora and Maldonado 2015: 169). Generally, for such epistemic-evidential markers, 'the polyphonic component is weaker than in sentences with the saying marker, and the epistemic qualification is very low' (Ştefănescu 2007: 144).

In such contexts, in Romanian, *cică* usually occupies an incident, post-verbal parenthetic position (see 26, 27 and 28) or, more seldom, even a final position (see 29). The speaker's epistemic attitude is present in various degrees; this is clearly seen in (28), for instance, with the immediate use of an adversative phrase that cancels the veracity of the information asserted in the previous sentence.

(26) *Cam aşa, **cică**, arată noua Dacia Logan 2*
[**They say** this is what the new Dacia Logan 2 looks like]
(https://cristianchinabirta.ro/2014/05/24/cam-asa-cica-arata-noua-dacia-logan-2/).

(27) *Ucraina, **cică**, ar trebui să se teamă de o agresiune-militară din partea României!*
[**They say** Ukraine should be afraid of military aggression from Romania!]
(https://www.rumaniamilitary.ro/articolul-de-seara-sa-mai-si-radem-ucraina-cica-ar-trebui-sa-se-teama-de-o-agresiune-militara-din-partea-romaniei).

(28) *Un preot propovăduitor al cuvântului sfânt nu vă va îndruma spre odină. Odihna veşnică o capătă oricine când se culcă în mormânt. Se pare că şi sufletul tău va avea parte de odihna veşnică din rai în care,* cică, *nu se munceşte. Dar pe pământ trebuie să ….*
[A priest preaching about the holy words will not guide you to rest. Eternal rest comes to everyone as they lay in their grave. Apparently, your heart will also get the eternal rest in heaven where, **they say**, one does not work. But, on earth, one must…]
(*Cu Dumnezeu înainte,* by Emil Wagner, in CoRoLa).

(29) *un pix de iscălit ştatul cu venitul minim garantat, o şapcă de şmecher cu cozoroc la spate şi un tricou cu fotografia "demnitarului" care a chelit munţii şi a tulit-o ungureşte, să se ascundă în canalizarea unde Attila era amiral, **cică**!…*
[a pen to sign for the minimum wage payslip, a cool hat turned around and a T-shirt with the photograph of the 'official' who deforested the mountains and ran away to hide in the sewerage where **they say** Attila was an admiral!…]
(*Dumnezeu nu circulă pe Facebook* (I+II=III), in CoRoLa).

In the case of *dizque*, the coexistence of the evidential use with near-epistemic values (some distance regarding the veracity of the proposition) can be traced back to as early as the 16$^{th}$ and 17$^{th}$ centuries. As shown by examples (30) and (31), *dizque* is used by the speaker to contradict the reported information (sometimes along with other lexical means, such as the reiteration of the dicendi verb in 30).

(30) *Dejo aparte los engaños y ficciones del demonio, que* ***dicen que dizque*** *nacieron aquí los primeros padres suyos que los dioses les hicieron, y otras ficciones muchas falsas de que ellos agora se rien y burlan.*
[I leave aside the lies and fictions of the demon, which **say that allegedly** his first parents created by the gods were born here, and many other false fictions they mock nowadays]
(CORDE, 1532, quoted by Demonte / Fernández Soriano 2017: 214).

(31) *[…]* ***diz que*** *era pobre como yo soy abadesa.*
[**dizque** [allegedly] he was as poor as I am an abbess] (i.e., he maintained he was poor, but I am obviously not convinced!)
(José de Valdivieso, 1638, quoted, translated and commented by Miglio 2010: 20).

Historically remote contexts also provide examples of a mirative use, expressing surprising or unexpected information (as in 32). Examples (33) and (34) are a proof of the use of *dizque* in contemporary Latin American Spanish, with the same purpose of expressing the speaker's distrust regarding the propositional content.

(32) *¡Válgame las cuatro patas del caballo de Longino! ¿****Diz que*** *tengo de decir lo que no he visto, ni sé …?*
[By the four legs of Longinus's horse! **Am I really supposed** to say what I did not see and do not know?]
(Tirso de Molina, *Quien da luego da dos veces*, 1616, quoted, translated and commented by Miglio 2010: 20).

(33) *¿Qué ha cambiado la humanidad, si al lado de las Cuatro estaciones, de Vivaldi hemos producido al piloto que lanzó la bomba sobre Hiroshima,* ***dizque*** *en 'defensa' de la autodeterminación de los pueblos y derechos a la libertad individual y colectiva?*
[What has mankind changed if, along with Vivaldi's Four Seasons we have also produced the pilot who launched the bombing on Hiroshima, **allegedly** in 'defence' of the peoples' right to self-determination and individual and collective freedom?]
(Press, Venezuela, 1993).

(34) *LLUVIA DE CÓNDORES: según el título de una conocida novela colombiana, Cóndores no entierran todos los días. Pero parece que sí los regalan a todo el mundo -y eso que* ***dizque*** *que están en vías de extinción-.*
[RAIN OF CONDORS: according to the title of a famous Colombian novel, condors are not buried every day. But they seem to be given as presents to everyone – and **they even say** that they are becoming extinct]
(Press, Columbia, 1991).

As for its position in the sentence, a query in the CREA, CORPES and CORDES corpora shows that, unlike Rom. *cică*, *dizque* never appears in the final position; its most frequent distribution is in subordinate structures (or taking scope over the VO when it simply functions as an adverb), which has led to its classification as a left periphery modal (Demonte / Fernández Soriano 2013, 2014, 2020).

It is noticed that, with such epistemic implications, the analysed items can focus / syntactically determine the entire sentence, acting as a sentence modifier (as in examples 26–34 above) or, very frequently, only a certain segment of the sentence, acting as a constituent modifier and 'modalizing syntactic-nominal (35a, b), prepositional (35c, d), adjectival (35e, ) or adverbial (35g) groups, accompanying them on the left side most frequently' (Zafiu 2020: 190).

(35) a. *Era atlet și a **cică** [profesor de sport].*
[He was an athlete and, **apparently** [a sports teacher].]
(Zafiu 2020: 190).
b. *Mucho ruido y muchos coches; mucha vida nocturna y toda la cosa, pero todos estos **dizque** adelantos no más nos han servido para maldita la cosa.*
[A lot of noise and a lot of cars; a lot of night life and everything, but all this **so-called** progress has not helped us a bit.]
(Kuri 2005, retrievedfrom CORPES).
c. *Și au venit unii, **cică** [de la Protecția Consumatorilor] și ne-au amendat.*
[And some people came, **apparently** [from Consumer Protection] and fined us]
(CoRoLa, in Zafiu 2020: 190).
d. *Lo habían cambiado **dizque** para otra sucursal, y todos nuestros gastos y sofocos se fueron al agua.*
[They had changed it, **allegedly** to another branch, and all our expenses and efforts were in vain.]
(Sabanero 2002, retrieved from CORPES).
e. *Am vorbit cu un meșter **cică** [priceput].*
[I spoke to a foreman, **apparently** [well-trained]]
(Zafiu 2020: 190).
f. *Son amables, limpias y siempre se ponen bonitas antes de venir. Me buscan por **dizque** inocente, me da risa.*
[They are kind, clean and they always freshen up before coming. They are looking for me because I'm **supposedly** naïve, it's hilarious.]
(Rodríguez 2002, retrieved from CORPES).
g. *Au intervenit cu mai multe mașini, **cică** [repede].*
[They intervened with several cars, **apparently** [fast].]
(Zafiu 2020: 190).

The modal-epistemic *cică* triggers various types of presuppositions, depending on the context, most frequently a 'presupposition of the falsity of the asserted sentence' (see Ștefănescu 2007: 123), that is, a counterfactual presupposition[3]. For instance, the presupposition triggered by the sentence in (35e) is *I talked to*

3 Ștefănescu (2007: 144–145) shows that 'a counterfactual presupposition is in opposition with the assertion of the sentence and in a weaker contrast with its explicature'.

*a foreman who was ill-trained/not well-trained* and the presupposition triggered by (35 f) is *I am not naïve.*

## 3.3 Pragmatic-Discursive Meaning

The pragmatic-discursive meaning, with a strong contextual dependence, proves the high degree of pragmaticalization of *cică* in contemporary Romanian. Here are some of the relatively recent functions of the pragmatic marker *cică*:

- *cică* is specifically used in the opening formulae of fairy tales (36) or anecdotes/ jokes (37), also functioning as an *indicator of the fictionality of certain types of discourse* (Pop 2017: 180):

(36) *Amu* ***cică*** *era odată într-o țară un crai, care avea trei feciori.*
[Now, **they say** there was once, in a country, a king who had three sons]
(Ion Creangă, *Povestea lui Harap-Alb,* in www.archeus.ro).

(37) ***Cică*** *doi polițiști mergeau pe stradă ….*
[**They say** two policemen were walking in the street].

- *cică* is used as a marker of non-paraphrastic rephrasing:

(38) *Și-a venit flăcăul,* ***cică,*** *// Un voinic cum altul nu e!*
[And the lad came, **they say** // A strong man like no one!]
(George Coşbuc, DLRLC, s. v. *cică*).

(39) *Și ca s-o auzi și pe* asta, cică *la terapie intensivă au dat peste unul cu pistolul ascuns la piept care s-a dat în spectacol imediat ce a fost descoperit. Și-a scos arma și, deși nu mai avea gloanțe în încărcător, a-nceput să tragă în cei …*
[And, if you have not heard everything, **they say** that they found a guy in intensive care who had a gun hidden in his clothes and made a fool of himself as soon as he was discovered. He took out the gun and, even though there were no bullets left, he started shooting those….]
(*Dansul focului sau 21: roman despre o revoluție care n-a avut loc*, by Adrian Petrescu (2010), in CoRoLa).

(40) *Amu o scornit alta:* ***cică*** *să-i aducă pe fata împăratului-Roș!*
[Now he wants something else: **he says** he wants the daughter of the Red Emperor!]
(Creangă, *Povestiri*, in DLRLC, s. v. *cică*).

- *cică* is used as an objection marker (mostly appearing at the end of the sentence when it has such a meaning, showing the speaker's full disagreement and irritation):

(41) *Ori, dacă nu-s ca ei, le tolerează orice grosolănie, îi încurajează, le injectează nesimțirea până dincolo de os, le cultivă prostul-gust și gustul-prost… ca să-și construiască/definească personalitatea,* cică*! Da?*

[And, if they're not like them, they tolerate all cheekiness, they encourage them, they foster their bad attitude and their bad taste… so that they can build/define their personality, **they say**! Right?]
(*Să nu se împiedice apa în care a plâns Dumnezeu*, in CoRoLa).

(42) *Și așa stăm ca naiba la aprovizionarea cu materiale. Nu sunt bani că nu dăm noi cărbune suficient* ***cică****! Tu'le muma lor la ăștia de la aprovizionare!*
[Anyway, material supply is not going well. There's no money because we don't provide enough coal, **they say**! To hell with the supply people!]
(*Noroc bun, ortacul meu!*, in CoRoLa).

- *cică* is used as a marker of accumulation and pursuit of the discursive topic (metatextual value):

(43) *Aceluia îi dă fata;* ***ba cică****-i mai dă și jumătate din împărăția lui*
[He'll give his daughter to that one; **even more, they say** he'll also give that man half of his kingdom]
(Creangă, *Povestiri*, in DLRLC, s. v. *cică*).

- as an indicator of astonishment:

(44) *E oare cu putință? auzi! Apoi* ***cică*** *să nu te strici de râs!*
[Is it possible? Hear that! Then **how could one** not laugh like hell!]
(Creangă, *Povestiri*, in DLRLC, s. v. *cică*).

*Dizque* also develops a range of pragmatic-discursive values, although to a lower extent than *cică*, mostly as a discursive connector or as a counterfactual marker. Here are some occurrences of its emergent pragmatic values:

(45) a. *Para demostrárselo, continuaba la anécdota, había pedido lo comunicasen con el mandatario dominicano, quien, enterado por el embajador de lo que sucedía,* ***dizque*** *saludó al canciller español desde el Palacio Nacional diciéndole por el teléfono (…)*
[In order to prove that, the anecdote went on, he had asked to communicate with the Dominican commissioner who, after having found out what was happening from the ambassador, **was said to** welcome the Spanish chancellor from the National Palace, telling him on the phone (…)].
b. *En la cama no sirve para nada. Empecé a besarla desde la marquesina y me quitó de encima, después adentro y* ***dizque*** *espérate que primero tengo que quitarme la ropa (…)*
[She's no good in bed. I started kissing her on the porch and she pushed me away, then inside and **she said** wait, I have to take my clothes off first.]
[in (45 a and b), *dizque* has a metatextual value, functioning as a marker of accumulation and pursuit of the discursive topic].

(46) *A un suadero de juaco,* ***dizque*** *era mi vida a sus intrinques.*
[To hell with that, **as if** he could play with my life.]
[*dizque* is an indicator of astonishment, sometimes with a counterfactual value].

## 4 Final Considerations

The functioning of the discursive units (Rom.) *cică*, (Sp.) *dizque*, as well as (Gall.) *disque*, (Sard.) *nachi* or (Sicil.) *dicica* shows that certain universal linguistic categories (such as evidentiality, the reportative, the epistemic) are similarly conveyed in more or less related languages.

However, it is seen that *dizque* is barely used in contemporary Peninsular Spanish, but widely deployed all across Spanish-speaking countries in Latin American. Nevertheless, its meanings are specific and well-established, conveying either a modal epistemic attitude of the speaker or reportative evidentiality. On the other hand, *cică*, although its diachronic evolution is quite recent and its diatopic variation is not as wide as *dizque*, has numerous, complex and frequent semantic and pragmatic meanings in contemporary spoken Romanian, both in the colloquial non-standard register and in written orality.

In conclusion, the adverbial lexical operators deriving from the Romance cognates of the dicendi verb, Lat. DICERE 'to say' include an evidential component and a modal one, that are activated depending on the context. It was seen that topicalization plays a major part not only in the pragmaticalization process, but also in the weaker or stronger activation of one or another of the two semantic components mentioned above.

## References

Aikhenvald, A. (2004). *Evidentiality.* Oxford: Oxford University Press.

Alcázar, A. (2018). '*Dizque* and other emergent evidential forms in Romance languages'. In A. Aikhenvald (ed.), *The Oxford Handbook of Evidentiality*, pp. 725–740. Oxford: Oxford University Press.

Cruschina, S., and Remberger, E.M. (2008). 'Hearsay and reported speech: evidentiality in Romance'. *Rivista de Grammatica Generativa* 33, 95–116.

Cruschina, S., and Remberger, E.M. (2017). 'Before the complementiser: Adverb types and root clause modification'. In M. Hummel, S. Valera (ed.), *Adjective Adverb Interfaces in Romance*, pp. 81–109. Amsterdam: John Benjamins.

De la Mora, J., and Maldonado, R. (2015). 'Dizque: Epistemics blurring evidentials in Mexican Spanish'. *Journal of Pragmatics* 85, 168–180.

Demonte, V., and Fernández Soriano, O. (2017). 'De la parentetización a la gramaticalización. El evidencial/modal *dizque* en español'. In A. Gallego, Y. Rodríguez, and J. Fernández-Sánchez (eds.) *Relaciones sintácticas. Homenaje a José Ma. Brucart y M. Lluïsa Hernanz*, pp. 209–224. Bellaterra: Universidad Autónoma de Barcelona.

Demonte, V., and Fernández Soriano, O. (2014). 'Evidentiality and illocutionary force. Spanish matrix 'que' at the syntax-semantics interface'. In A. Dufter and A.S. de Toledo (eds), *Add Left Sentence Peripheries in Spanish: Diachronic, Variationist, and Typological Perspectives*. Amsterdam: John Benjamins.

Demonte, V., and Fernández Soriano, O. (2013). 'Evidentials dizque and que in Spanish: Grammaticalization, parameters and the (fine) structure of Comp'. *Linguística. Revista de Estudos Linguísticos da Universidade do Porto* 8, 211–234.

Demonte, V., and Fernández Soriano, O. (2020). '*Dizque*: Un evidencial reportativo modal en la periferia izquierda de la oración'. In E. Hernández, and P. Martín Butragueño (eds.) *Las palabras como unidades lingüísticas*, pp. 185–218. Madrid/ Ciudad de México: Consejo Superior de Investigaciones Científicas/ El Colegio de México.

Dumitrescu, D. (2012). 'Rum. *cică* vs. Esp. *dizque:* polifonía e intertextualidad'. In C.U. Lorda Mur and C. Ubaldina (eds.), *Polifonía e intertextualidad en el diálogo*, pp. 317–338. Madrid: Editorial ARCO/LIBROS, S. L.

Florea, S. (2020). 'Reportative evidentiality and attribution in Romanian fairy tales'. *Poznań Studies in Contemporary Linguistics* 56(1), 1–33.

Gallucci, M.J. (2020). 'El discurso referido en la tradición gramatical hispánica'. *Cuadernos de Lingüística de El Colegio de México* 4(2), 213–256.

Guţu-Romalo, V. (coord.) (2005). Academia Română, Institutul de Lingvistică "Iorgu Iordan - Al. Rosetti", *Gramatica Limbii Române* (GALR),vol. I.: *Cuvântul*, vol. II: *Enunţul*. Bucureşti: Editura Academiei Române.

Kany, C. (1969). *Sintaxis hispanoamericana*. Madrid: Gredos.

Lazard, G. (2001). 'On the grammaticalization of evidentiality'. *Journal of Pragmatics* 33, 359–367.

López Izquierdo M. (2006). 'L'émergence de *dizque* comme stratégie médiative en espagnol médiéval'. *Cahiers d'études hispaniques médiévales*, 29, 483–495.

Maldonado González, C. (1999). 'Discurso directo y discurso indirecto'. In Bosque, I., Demonte, V. (eds.), *Gramática descriptiva de la lengua española*, pp. 3551–3595. Madrid: Espasa-Calpe.

Marín-Arrese, J.I. (2020). 'Pragmatics and Semantics: A focus on Evidentiality'. In D.A. Koike and J.C. Félix-Brasdefer (eds.) *The Routledge Handbook of Spanish Pragmatics*, pp. 111–128. London & New York: Routledge.

Miglio, V. (2010). 'Online databases and language change: the case of Spanish dizque'. In S.Th. Gries, S. Wulff, and M. Davies (eds), *Corpus-linguistic applications*, pp. 7–28. Amsterdam: Brill/Rodopi.

Pichler Ciglič, B. (2018). '¿Cómo traducir la evidencialidad? La expresión de la fuente de información en algunas variantes del español de América y sus equivalentes en esloveno'. *Colindancias* 9, 249–267.

Pană-Dindelegan, G. (coord.) (2016). *Gramatica de bază a limbii române*. Bucureşti: EdituraUniversEnciclopedic.

Pop, L. (2017). 'Du marqueur discursif à marqueur textuel: *cică* ('on dit que, dit-on') du roumain'. *Pragmalingüística Monográfico* 1, 171–185.

Remberger, E.M. (2009). 'The syntax of evidential markers: The Romanian hearsay marker *cică*', communication *Tagungzur Generativen Grammatik des Südens*, Leipzig, 22–24 Mai 2009 (handout).

Remberger, E.M. (2015). '"I didn't say it. Somebody else did." – The Romanian hearsay marker CICĂ'. In *Redefining community in Intercultural context*, Vol.4/ 1. Selection of papers presented within 4th RCIC Conference, Brasov, 21 May, 2015.

Sanromán Vilas, B. (2020). 'Do evidential markers always convey epistemic values? A look into three Ibero-Romance reportatives'. *Lingua* 238, 1–26.

Squartini, M. (2001). 'The internal structure of evidentiality in Romance'. *Studies in Language* 25, 297–334.

Squartini, M. (2005). 'L'evidenzialità in rumeno e nelle altre lingue romanze'. *Zeitschrift für romanische Philologie*,121, 2, 246–268.

Ştefănescu, A. (2007). *Conectori pragmatici*. Bucureşti: Editura Universităţii din Bucureşti.

Willett, T. (1988). 'A crosslinguistic survey of the grammaticization of Evidentiality'. *Studies in Language* 12/1, 51–97.

Zafiu, R. (2020). 'Cică'. In G. Pană Dindelegan (coord.), *Dicţionar de interpretări gramaticale. Cuvinte mici, dificultăţi mari*. Bucureşti: Univers Enciclopedic.

Zafiu, R. (2002). '*Evidenţialitatea* în limba română actuală'. In G. Pană Dindelegan (ed.), *Aspecte ale dinamicii limbii române actuale*, pp. 127–144. Bucureşti: Editura Universităţii din Bucureşti.

## Corpora and Dictionaries

Archeus.ro = Electronic resources for Romanian language, <http://www.archeus.ro/lingvistica/CautareTextWikisource?query=MERSI&pageNo=1>

CoRoLA = *Computer-based corpus of reference for contemporary Romanian language*, <http://corola.racai.ro/>

DEX (1998). Academia Română, Institutul de Lingvistică Iorgu Iordan, *Dicţionarul explicativ al limbii române*. Bucureşti: Univers Enciclopedic.

DLR (2010). Academia Română, Institutul de Lingvistică "Iorgu Iordan – Alexandru Rosetti" (eds), [1958–2009], *Dicţionarul limbii române. Serie nouă*. Bucureşti: Editura Academiei Române.

DLRLC (1955–1957). Macrea, D., E. Petrovici (coord.), Al. Rosetti et al. (authors), *Dicționarul limbii române literare contemporane*. București: Editura Academiei Române.

RDW (1986–1989). Tiktin, H., P. Miron, *Rumänisch-Deutsches Wörterbuch*, Wiesbaden: Harrassowitz.

Real Academia Española. CORPES – Corpus del español del siglo XXI. <http://web.frl.es/CORPES/view/inicioExterno.view>

Real Academia Española. CORDE – Corpus Diacrónico del Español. <http://corpus.rae.es/cordenet.html>

Real Academia Española. CREA – Corpus de Referencia del Español Actual. <http://corpus.rae.es/creanet.html>

# Section B. Stance, Evaluation, Metaphor

Laura Hidalgo-Downing & Paula Pérez-Sobrino

# "Pushing Britain off the Precipice": A CDA Approach to Negative Evaluative Stance in Opinion Articles on Brexit[1]

**Abstract:** This chapter studies the construal of negative evaluative stance in opinion articles on Brexit from a Critical Discourse Analysis perspective. We present a system for the annotation and analysis of evaluative stance in discourse which contemplates the following categories: (a) Function: classifying, predicational and attitudinal evaluation, each prototypically related to a Part of Speech; (b) Figurativity: metaphoric and non-metaphoric, and (c) Value: positive and negative. The model is used to analyse the frequency and role of markers of evaluative stance in two samples of British opinion articles on Brexit from *The Times* and *The Guardian*. Our research questions are the following: (1) What is the frequency of lexical units expressing evaluative stance in the corpus and in each newspaper? (2) What is the distribution of evaluative stance categories in general and by newspaper? (3) How is negative evaluative stance towards Brexit and the role of relevant social actors expressed?

**Keywords:** *evaluative stance, evaluative metaphor, opinion articles, evaluative stance, annotation protocol, negative news values, critical discourse analysis*

## 1 Introduction

The study of the expression of evaluation in opinion and comment articles in the press is an under-researched area (for an exception, see, for example, Blanco 2015) and so is the study of how news values such as negativity are construed by means of linguistic choices in the media (Bednarek and Caple 2014: 139). Most research on journalistic genres has focused on the news (see, for example, Bell 1991, Fowler 1991, Fairclough 1995, van Dijk 1988, Ungerer 2000, Bednarek 2007, Richardson 2007), with a few studies addressing the comparison of epistemic and

1 We are grateful to the Spanish Ministry of Science, Innovation and Universities for their funding of the research project "Stance and Subjectivity in Discourse: Towards an Integrated Framework for the Analysis of Epistemicity, Effectivity, Evaluation and Inter/Subjectivity from a Critical Discourse Perspective" (PGC2018-095798-B-I00). The present study has also received funding from other research projects funded by the State Agency of Research - Spanish Ministry of Science, Innovation and Universities (FFI2017-82730-P, PID2020-118349GB-I00 and PID2021-123302NB-I00).

deontic stance in press and opinion articles in English and Spanish newspaper discourse (see, for example, Marín-Arrese, Hidalgo-Downing & Molina Plaza 2004, Hidalgo-Downing 2006, Marín-Arrese and Núñez-Perucha 2006, Marín-Arrese 2021) and some studies on opinion genres such as blogs (see, for example, Simaki et al. 2018, 2020). However, it is surprising that opinion articles have not received greater attention regarding the study of evaluative stance, since, as a genre, they are a natural site for the expression of evaluative assessments and opinions (van Dijk 1995: 21). Furthermore, the study of a controversial topic such as Brexit, which requires a positioning on the part of speakers/writers, also lends itself easily to a critical discourse approach to the analysis of evaluation in this genre. However, most recent research on Brexit has focused on the study of the metaphors used to frame this topic (see, for example, Musolff 2017, Charteris-Black 2019) and on evaluation at the utterance level in blogs (Simaki et al. 2018, 2020).

Moreover, there are hardly any studies showing the frequency and distribution of negative and positive values in different types of discourses and genres (for exceptions, see Biber et al. 1999, and Fuoli, Littlemore and Turner 2021). Biber et al. (1999: 512–513) show that within the category of adjectives, the most frequent evaluative adjectives in the four discourse types they analyse (conversation, fiction, news and academic) are positive adjectives (*good, best, right, nice, important, special*). These results are in line with studies in psychology, which show that the positive is favoured over the negative in actual language use, both regarding clause polarity and regarding connotation of lexical items (Givón 1993, García, Garas & Schweitzer 2012). However, other studies suggest that certain genres may show a preference for negative evaluation (Fuoli, Littlemore and Turner 2021, Maíz-Arévalo and Sánchez-Moya forthcoming). Fuoli, Littlemore and Turner (2021) have shown that in a corpus of film reviews there is a higher frequency of negative evaluative metaphors, which are also typically more creative than non-negative evaluative metaphors, while Maíz-Arévalo and Sánchez-Moya (forthcoming) have found that in a corpus of fora discourse on various topics related to social issues, negative evaluation is more frequent than positive evaluation. This makes it necessary to study in greater depth the preferences for the use of positive and negative evaluative terms in different genres and in relation to the topics addressed.[2]

2 Charteris-Black (2019: 311) in his study of the metaphors of Brexit points out that during the period of the negotiation of Brexit there were no positive evaluations by the press.

The present article aims to contribute to research in this area by discussing from a Critical Discourse Analysis (henceforth CDA) perspective how choices in evaluative stance contribute to the construal of the news value of negativity in two samples of 20 opinion articles from the British newspapers *The Times* and *The Guardian* on Brexit. *The Times* and *The Guardian* are both upmarket broadsheets with a middle class-upper class readership (Bell, 1991: 109). While *The Times* is considered a conservative newspaper, *The Guardian* is considered progressive. The interest in comparing these two newspapers is rooted in the fact that, in spite of their different ideological standpoints, both newspapers are pro-remain with regard to Brexit.

For this purpose, we first present a scheme for the annotation and analysis of evaluative stance in discourse which has been developed under a research project on the study of stance across various genres (Hidalgo Downing et al. forthcoming); we then apply this scheme to the identification and analysis of the expressions of evaluative stance in the two samples, with special attention to the construal of negative evaluation. The motivations for choosing Brexit as a topic of analysis are, first, that it has been one of the most discussed (if not the most discussed) in the British press since the 2016 referendum; second, that it requires, on the part of the journalist, a clear positioning which has ideological implications; and third, that it is an interesting topic for the study of evaluation from a Critical discourse perspective because it is characterised by the news value of negativity (as a conflictive issue) and relevance (see van Dijk 1988, Bell 1991, Bednarek and Caple 2014). Because both *The Times* and *The Guardian* are pro-remain newspapers (Charteris-Black 2019: 310), a higher frequency of negative evaluation is anticipated, which is expected to highlight the negativity news value of the topic. However, the fact that *The Times* is a conservative newspaper while *The Guardian* is progressive may reveal subtle differences in the construal of the topic.

Our research questions are the following: (1) What is the frequency of lexical units expressing evaluative stance in the corpus and in each newspaper? (2) What is the distribution of evaluative stance categories in general and by newspaper? (3) How is negative evaluative stance towards Brexit and the role of relevant social actors expressed?

Our working hypothesis with regard to research question (2) is that we expect a higher frequency of the Predicational strategy, of Adjectives, of non-metaphoric evaluation and of negative value. Research question (3) will be discussed by analysing word frequency lists of the categories of evaluative stance and of examples in context.

## 2 Theoretical Framework

### 2.1 A CDA Perspective on Negativity as a News Value in Opinion Articles

The genre of opinion articles includes both editorials and comment articles (op-ed articles, columns and other comment articles) and is described as an argumentative genre with the main purpose of expressing opinions (van Dijk 1995: 21). Opinion articles as a genre are defined by Alonso Belmonte as follows:

> Editorials and comment articles are (…) public, mass communicated types of opinion discourse which play a definitive role in the formation and altering of public opinion, promote social interaction among journalists, readers and the rest of participants in the language event and influence social debate, decision making and other forms of social and political action. (Alonso Belmonte 2008: 2)

While editorials (or leading articles) are not signed by individual journalists and express the opinion and positioning of the newspaper on a specific topic, comment or opinion articles are typically signed and written by guest journalists. However, even if there may be subtle differences between editorials and comment or opinion articles, it has to be pointed out that in both cases the expression of a positioning can hardly be ascribed to the individual journalist alone. Rather, "Positions defended by the press are not personal opinions, but manifestations of more complex, socially shared and dominant ideological frameworks that embody institutional relationships and power" (van Dijk 1989b: 232). Although this ideological construal is more obvious in news articles and editorials, it can be argued that opinion and comment articles also contribute to construing a specific ideological stance which will be in line with the interests of the newspaper for which the article is written and with a great part of the target audience of that newspaper. In this sense, readers are construed in media discourse (van Dijk 1988, Bednarek 2007: 15). This implies an active process of creating opinion since "the news media do not passively describe or record news events in the world, but actively (re-) construct them, mostly on the basis of many types of source discourses" (van Dijk 1989a: 203).

In this article we adopt a critical perspective to the analysis of evaluative stance in opinion articles by focusing on the way in which the news value of negativity is construed by means of specific linguistic choices (Bednarek and Caple 2014). Bednarek and Caple (2014) argue for a Critical Discourse perspective to the analysis of news values and point to the need of establishing connections between specific news values and the potential linguistic choices which may be at play in each of the values. News values can be defined as what is newsworthy and include, for social actors and events, parameters such as "Proximity (geographical or cultural 'nearness'); Negativity (negative aspects, e.g. conflict, death, disaster, accidents, negative consequences); Eliteness (elite status); and Superlativeness ('the more X, the more newsworthy'), to name but a few" (Bednarek and Caple 2014: 136).

We are here interested in exploring the value of Negativity in the representation of Brexit as a conflictive topic. Bednarek and Caple (2014: 136) argue that linguistic choices may highlight or background specific news values, since news values are construed via language. However, they also point out that within CDA very little attention has been paid to the linguistic realisation or construal of news values and, in order to guide analysts, they propose a list of linguistic resources for the construal of news values (Bednarek and Caple 2014: 139) and suggest that only by means of detailed text analysis is it possible to see what values are foregrounded or backgrounded.

With regard to the news value of Negativity, it is the news value par excellence (van Dijk 1988, Bednarek 2007: 16), "what comes to people's minds as the basic news value" (Bell 1991: 156). Bednarek and Caple (2014: 155) list the following linguistic resources as potential realisations of negativity:

- Negativity (the negative aspects of an event).
- Negative evaluative language (language expressing the speaker's/writer's negative opinion/disapproval 'this is bad'); e.g. Terrible news; a tragedy; gaffe; wannabe. Reference to negative emotions (emotions that are generally regarded as negative experiences); e.g. Distraught: worried; breaking our hearts; shock; disappointment. Negative lexis (lexis describing actors/happenings that would be considered negative by the social mainstream), including 'disaster vocabulary' (…); e.g. Damaged; killed; deaths; bodies; crimes; the IRA; destruction; confusion; offence; road closures… (Bednarek and Caple 2014: 155)

Our study proposes a scheme for the annotation and analysis of evaluative stance which includes categories that account for what Bednarek and Caple (2014: 155) call evaluative language. We describe the scheme of evaluative stance in Section 2.2. below.

## 2.2 Annotating and Analysing Evaluative Stance in Discourse

In this section we present a scheme for the annotation and analysis of evaluation (Hidalgo-Downing and Pérez-Sobrino 2022, Hidalgo-Downing et al. forthcoming) developed under a research project on stance across genres. The categories we propose in our scheme are inspired in previous work carried out in the field of stance (Biber et al. 1999, Du Bois 2007, Englebretson 2007), evaluation and Appraisal (Hunston and Thompson 2000, Martin and White 2005, Bednarek 2008, Hunston 2011, Thompson and Alba-Juez 2014, White 2016) and Critical discourse studies (van Dijk 1995, van Leeuwen 2008, Reisigl and Wodak 2009). We take up the definitions of stance and stance-taking developed by authors such as Du Bois (2007) and Englebretson (2007) and approach evaluation as one of the main dimensions of stance. According to Du Bois, stance can be defined as follows:

> Stance is a public act by a social actor, achieved dialogically through overt communicative means, of simultaneously evaluating objects, positioning subjects (self and others), and aligning with other subjects, with respect to any salient dimension of the sociocultural field. (Du Bois, 2007: 163)

In addition to being a social act, stance can also be described as the set of linguistic resources available to speakers and writers to evaluate entities and events and to express positioning and relations of (dis)alignment with real or potential addressees (see also Martin and White 2005, Simaki et al. 2020). Within the study of stance, three main trends can be identified: the study of epistemic and evidential stance, the study of affect and emotion and the study of evaluation (Englebretson 2008: 17).

We are here concerned with the study of stance and evaluation. Within this approach, the notions of positioning and (dis)alignment are crucial for the interpretation of evaluation in discourse. Thus, for a word to express evaluation it is not enough to have a positive or negative connotation as part of the meaning of the word, but there must be an indication of a positioning in the context of the discourse for that word to count as evaluative. That is, in the case of words with inscribed positive or negative evaluation, especially nouns such as *war, peace, happiness*, the connotation of the word itself does not guarantee that the word will express an evaluative positioning in all contexts (also see the distinction between evaluative words and negative lexis by Bednarek and Caple (2014) in section 2.1 above).

In our approach to evaluative stance, we adopt the word and the phrase as units of analysis. Most instances of evaluation will be words, such as for example, evaluative adjectives (*reactionary, impressive, dishonest, bad*), nouns (*disaster, catastrophe*), verbs (*damage*) or adverbs (*happily, sadly*). Lexical units that are made up of more than one word, such as for example, phrasal verbs (*broke down, snatched away*), compound words (*civil war*) and hyphenated words (*life-destroying, self-delusion*) are counted as words. However, in some cases it is necessary to consider phrases as the units of analysis, for example in some cases of evaluative metaphors (*storming out in a huff, chronic illness, spread their poison*).

Our annotation scheme of evaluative stance contemplates the following categories: part of speech (PoS), function, figurativity and value. Within the dimension which we have termed Function, we distinguish between three main categories: (1) Classifying, typically realised by Nouns, Noun Phrases, Verbs and Verb Phrases; (2) Predicational, typically realised by Adjectives and Adjective Phrases and some Adverbs (adverbs of manner) and (3) Attitude, typically realised by attitudinal adverbs and adjectives in specific grammatical structures. While Classifying and Predicational functions express evaluation towards entities and events, Attitude expresses evaluation of propositions. We define each category in greater detail and illustrate them with examples from our sample. The Classifying and Predicational strategies are inspired in Nomination and Predicational strategies in CDA (van Leeuwen 2008: 40–41, Reisigl and Wodak 2009: 95). Predicational strategies are the prototypical form of evaluation and, in our scheme, they refer to the positive and negative evaluative assessments of qualities or properties of entities and events on the basis of values and beliefs which are shared by communities of speakers. They are prototypically realised by adjectives (*good, bad, irrational, toxic*) and manner adverbs (*vigorously, dispassionately*). The Classifying function is realised by nouns and verbs. Following van Dijk (1995: 29), although the main function of nouns is to categorise entities and events, nouns can also express opinions. Van Dijk (1995: 29) provides the example of the word 'thief', which can be used in discourse to refer to an individual either by describing a fact (as established, for example, by a court of law) or an opinion. The difference between these two uses of a noun can only be determined in context. Verbs are used in a similar way to categorise and provide an evaluation on events. The Function Attitude includes what Biber et al. (1999: 856) call attitudinal stance adverbials, which are typically sentential adverbs (*unfortunately, sadly*) and adjectives in the structure it + be + Adjective (*It is worth noting, it was terrible to see….*).

Regarding the dimension of Figurativity, we distinguish between non-metaphoric evaluative expressions and metaphoric evaluative expressions. Under the term 'metaphoric' we are only considering metaphors and not other types of figurative language such as metonymy, irony or hyperbole, although these figures of speech may be present in the corpus. For the identification of metaphoric expressions, we have followed MIP (Pragglejazz 2007) and MIPVU (Steen at al. 2010), that is, after reading the whole texts, we have checked the meaning of the word in context and have used the MacMillan dictionary to confirm that the meaning of the expression is not listed as the first lexical entry in this dictionary. In this way, we have guaranteed that the meaning of the expression in discourse is not a basic meaning listed as the main dictionary entry. This criterion has led to discarding metaphors which are very conventional and which do not serve to express a positioning of the writer or a relation of (dis)alignment with specific sets of values. The sentences in (1) and (2) below are from an article which discusses the social impact of racism within Brexit and they illustrate evaluative uses of metaphor.

(1) *This is not some new **virus**.* (EOG-5)
(2) *it's a susceptibility to a chronic **illness** that has crippled us for years.* (EOG-5)

The first lexical entry for 'virus' in the MacMillan dictionary is "a simple living thing that is smaller than bacteria and that can enter your body and make you ill" and the first lexical entry for illness is "the state of feeling ill or having a disease". These meanings are different from the meanings of 'virus' and 'illness' in the context of the examples (1) and (2) above, which metaphorically describe the target domain 'racism'. Consequently, we annotate 'virus' and 'illness' in these examples as metaphoric, and as evoking negative evaluation. The basic criterion for the identification of a metaphor as evaluative is that it consists of a mapping of a source domains which transfers positive or negative properties to the target domain. However, in some cases, value arises in context. With regard to the dimension value, we distinguish between positive (*impressive, good, vigorously*) and negative (*disaster, dishonest, toxic, dispassionately*) value.

## 3 Data and Method[3]

### 3.1 Corpus

Our data[4] consists of two sets of opinion articles from the newspapers *The Times* (9893 words, 869 words by article on average) and *The Guardian* (10575 words, 977 words by article on average) that have Brexit as a central topic. Each sample

3 For a detailed description of the method developed for the analysis of evaluation in discourse which includes the inter-rater reliability process, the criteria for evaluative stance, the steps in the implementation of the protocol and the theoretical and methodological grounding of the decisions, see Hidalgo-Downing and Pérez-Sobrino (2022) and for a detailed explanation of the complete protocol and its application to four genres see Hidalgo-Downing et al. (forthcoming).

4 [4] The complementary materials for the present study can be consulted in the following: publicly accessible repository: <https://osf.io/bpxju/>

contains 10 opinion articles which have been extracted from a larger corpus of newspaper opinion articles (100,000 words). In order to sample Brexit-related opinion articles from the full corpus we selected those with the word Brexit in the title, subtitle or text of the article. The corpus of opinion articles was annotated independently by both authors of this study following the protocol for identification of evaluative stance in discourse developed in our project (Hidalgo Downing at al. forthcoming).

## 3.2 Methodology

Given the inherent degree of subjectivity in the annotation of evaluative stance, an inter-rater reliability test was carried out to reduce the analyst bias. Around 20% of the Brexit corpus was randomly sampled and annotated in 4 rounds by the two researchers. Researchers first annotated the text assigned for each round independently (around 900 words), and then met for a joint discussion of their annotations. Diverging interpretations that were resolved after the discussion led to a subsequent refinement of the protocol; conflicting cases that led to ambiguous and multiple possible interpretations were discarded from the analysis. We have applied Fleiss kappa (Fleiss 1971) to measure the degree of agreement between the researchers when applying the protocol to annotate evaluative stance because the task involved two raters annotating a potentially different set of items. Table 1 shows the results of the inter-rater reliability test.

As can be extracted from Table 1, there was perfect agreement for PoS and function in rounds 1, 3 and 4 ($\kappa$=1, $p$<.001). There was a notable exception in round 2 for function ($\kappa$=0.4, $p$<.001) and 3 for PoS ($\kappa$=0.4, $p$<.05), due to the fact that we were still refining the units of analysis (i.e. what should count as evaluative stance).

**Table 1.** Cohen's Kappa results for inter-rater reliability across dimensions of analysis and rounds

| Round | PoS | Function | Metaphor | Value |
|---|---|---|---|---|
| 1 | $\kappa$=1, $p$<.001 | $\kappa$=1, $p$<.001 | $\kappa$=0.86, $p$<.001 | $\kappa$=0.86, $p$<.001 |
| 2 | $\kappa$=1, $p$<.001 | $\kappa$=0.4, $p$<.001 | $\kappa$=0.75, $p$<.01 | $\kappa$=1, $p$<.001 |
| 3 | $\kappa$=0.4, $p$<.05 | K=1, $p$<.05 | $\kappa$=1, $p$<.05 | $\kappa$=1, $p$<.05 |
| 4 | $\kappa$=1, $p$<.001 | $\kappa$=1, $p$<.001 | $\kappa$=1, $p$<.001 | $\kappa$=1, $p$<.001 |

The observation of the crucial role of the concepts of "alignment" and "disalignment" (see Section 3 above) in determining evaluative stance and value helped to solve discrepancies in the identification of what counted as evaluation and, in particular, for value. Refinements adopted in round 2 for the dimension of 'value' proved useful to reach perfect agreement between rounds 2 and 4 ($\kappa=1$, $p<.001$).

Additionally, an improvement in the inter-coder agreement for metaphoricity can also be appreciated between rounds 2 and 3, when we adopted the criterion of MIP (Praggeljaz 2007, later revised by Steen et. al. 2010 in MIPVU) to contrast contextual meaning and basic meaning to code metaphorical expressions (see Section 2 above). This decision proved useful, as we reached perfect inter-coder agreement in rounds 3 ($\kappa=1$, $p<.05$) and 4 ($\kappa=1$, $p<.001$).

Statistical tests were carried out using R 4.0.2 (R Core Team, 2020). To assess the inter-rater reliability, we used the package "irr" (v. 0.84.1; Gamer, Lemon, Fellows, Singh 2019); "ggplot2" for barplots (v. 3.3.3, Wickham 2016); and "vcd" to visualise residual-based shadings in mosaic plots (v. 1.4–8, Zeileis, Meyer, and Hornik 2007). The annotated corpus, the datasets and the full reproducible R script is available in: https://osf.io/bpxju/

## 4 Results and discussion

This section presents the quantitative results of the frequency and distribution of the categories in the sample, together with a discussion and an illustration of some of the relevant categories with examples drawn from the sample. The section is divided in subsections which address each of the research questions which were outlined in the Introduction above.

### 4.1 Frequency of evaluative stance

The first research question addresses the frequency of lexical units expressing evaluative stance in the corpus and in each newspaper.

*Headline finding: The Guardian contains more expressions of evaluative stance than The Times*

**Table 2.** Frequency of evaluative expressions in the whole corpus and by newspapers

| **Source** | **Size of corpus (N words)** | **Evaluative expressions (N words)** | **% of evaluation** |
|---|---|---|---|
| The Guardian | 10575 | 568 | 5.37 |
| The Times | 9893 | 369 | 3.73 |
| Overall | 20468 | 937 | 4.58 |

Table 2 shows the frequency of evaluative expressions in the whole sample and in each of the newspapers. Results show that the frequency of evaluative stance is much higher in *The Guardian*. This result may be interpreted as suggesting that opinion writers in *The Guardian* are making a stronger act of positioning and evaluation in their negative representation and assessment of Brexit than writers in *The Times*, even if both newspapers are pro-remain. This would suggest that the negative assessment of Brexit from the perspective of pro-remain supporters does not involve a homogenous position, but, rather, that it is a question of degree; these two positionings can be interpreted as being in line with the ideological orientation of the newspapers as more or less conservative in general terms and, consequently, as more or less explicitly critical of Brexit. However, a careful reading of the use of evaluative stance markers in context is needed to confirm this. This point is taken up in section 4.3 below. Here it is shown that while the articles in *The Guardian* focus on the evaluation of Brexit itself, the articles in *The Times* seem to focus on the Brexit negotiations, for example the possibility of a no deal and the cost of the separation from the EU.

## 4.2 Distribution of evaluative stance categories

Research question 2 addresses the distribution of evaluative stance categories in the corpus and by newspaper.

*Headline finding: Negative evaluation is more frequent in both newspapers than positive evaluation. The Guardian contains almost twice as many expressions of negative evaluation than The Times.*

Figure 1 below shows the distribution of the categories in the complete sample of opinion articles. Regarding PoS, the most frequent category is adjectives followed by nouns. In terms of Function, the most frequent category is Classifying (which includes nouns and verbs), followed by Predicational (adjectives and adverbs); regarding figurativity, over a fourth of the evaluative expressions (28 %) are coded as having potential for metaphorical interpretation, which surpasses Steen et al.'s (2010) findings for press (16.4 %), although their corpus did not include opinion articles. Finally, negative evaluation is the most frequent value. These results show the crucial role played in opinion articles by the classifying function, which highlights the evaluative representation of entities and events. The higher frequency of negative value reflects the positioning of two newspapers towards the topic, though differences between the two positions are discussed in section 4.3 below. These trends are replicated in each newspaper individually, as shown in Figure 2 below. In terms of PoS, function and figurativity, *The Guardian* is more productive than *The Times*; and, for value, *The Guardian* doubles the number of negative evaluative expressions found in *The Times*. Interestingly, and in spite of these differences, the frequency of positive evaluative stance is similar in both newspapers.

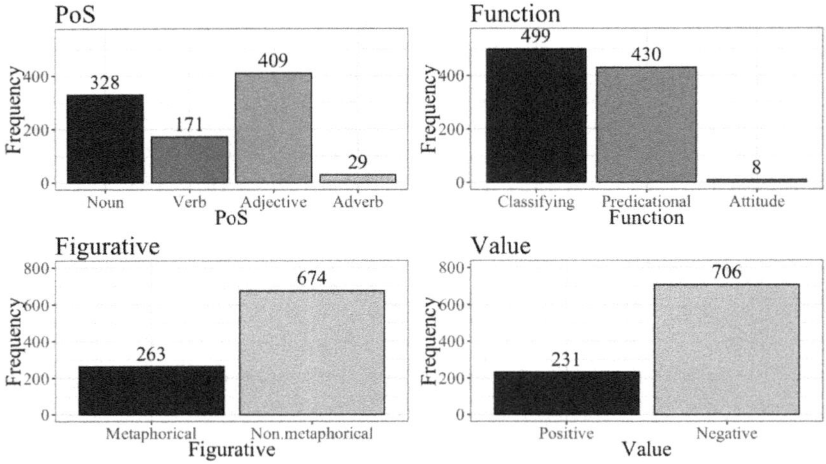


**Figure 1.** Distribution of evaluative stance categories in the complete corpus of opinion articles

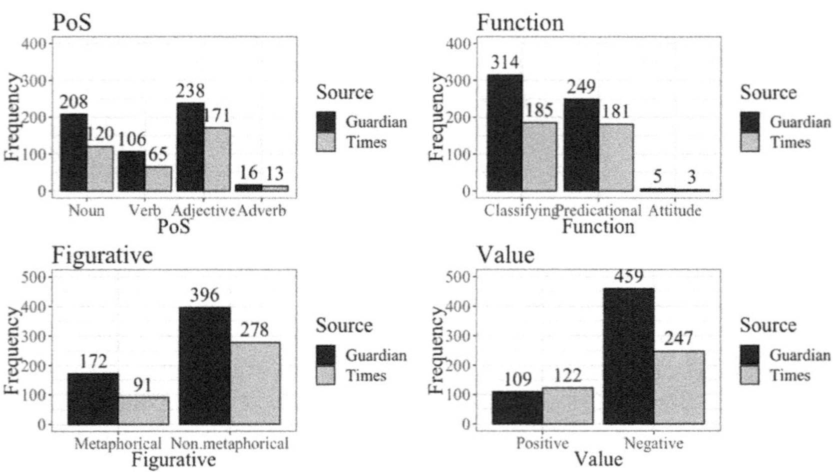


**Figure 2.** Distribution of the evaluative stance categories in *The Times* and *The Guardian*

Figures 3, 4 and 5 show the correlations between PoS and value, function and value and metaphoricity and value respectively. We discuss briefly each of these in turn below.

*Headline finding: The Guardian is more likely to express negative evaluation through classifiers whereas The Times makes a more prominent use of positive adjectives*

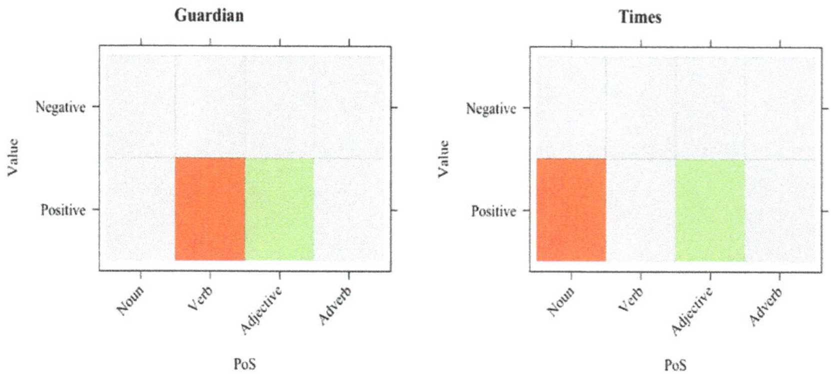


**Figure 3.** Pearson residuals from the Chi-square test showing the distribution of associations between PoS and Value for each newspaper (green = stronger association than chance; red = weaker association than chance)

Figure 3 shows that each newspaper makes use of specific PoS for positive and negative evaluation in different ways, in a statistically significant manner (Guardian: $X^2(3)=22.27$, $p<.001$; Times: $X^2(3)=21.75$, $p<.001$). The plot in Figure 3 presents Pearson's residuals, a statistical test that shows the values that are most likely to show each PoS, in a statistically significant way. In order to interpret the plot, green squares (which represent values over 2) mean that there are more observations in the cell than what would be expected if there was a balanced distribution between PoS and value (null model), and therefore constitute an over-represented combination of PoS and value. Red (values under -2) means there are fewer observations than would have been expected, and therefore reveal an under-represented combination of PoS and value in the corpus. In other words, our findings show that both *The Guardian* and *The Times* make an abundant use of adjectives to project positive evaluation (green squares).

Conversely, the data from *The Guardian* shows that it is highly unlikely for verbs to express positive evaluation, whereas in the case of *The Times*, that is the case for nouns (red squares).

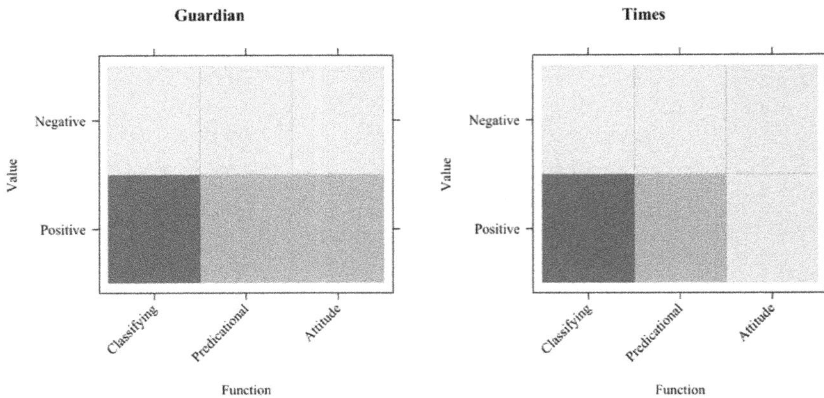


**Figure 4.** Pearson residuals from the Chi-square test showing the distribution of associations between Function and Value for each newspaper (green = stronger association than chance; red = weaker association than chance)

Figure 4 shows the relation between evaluative function (Classifying, Predicational, Attitude) and positive and negative value, which was also statistically significant in both newspapers (Guardian: $X^2(2)=1.94$, $p=.16$; Times: $X^2(2)= 22.59$, $p<.001$). In line with the findings for adjectives reported in Figure 3, the Pearson residuals shown in Figure 4 indicate that both newspapers favour the use of Predicational to convey positive evaluation; as well as Attitude in the case of *The Guardian*. Both newspapers are also similar in their comparatively much lower use of classifiers to convey negative evaluation.

*Headline finding: The Times is not likely to project positive evaluation through metaphor*

Finally, only *The Times* displayed an overall statistically significant different use of metaphorical expressions to express evaluation (Times: $X^2$ $(2)= 8.11$, $p<.001$) but not *The Guardian* (Guardian: $X^2$ $(2)=1.94$, $p=.15$). This means that, in the case of *The Guardian*, there is a balanced presence of metaphors to convey positive and negative evaluation.

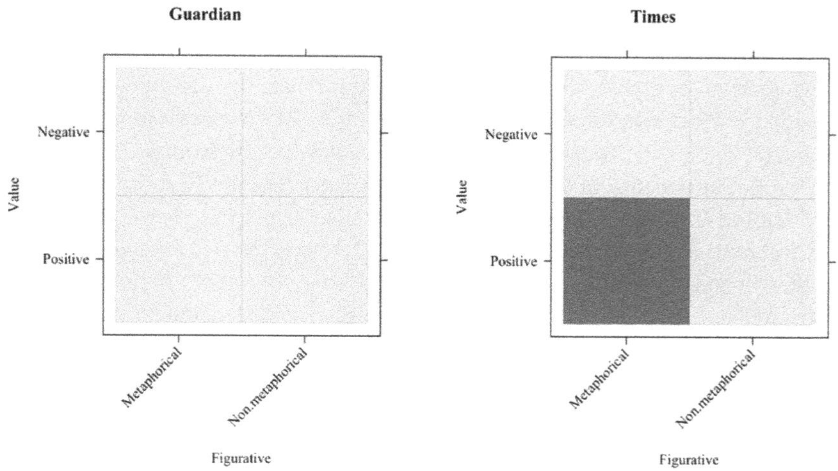


**Figure 5.** Pearson residuals from the Chi-square test showing the distribution of associations between Figurativity and Value for each newspaper (green = stronger association than chance; red = weaker association than chance)

With respect to the most significant trends observed in *The Times*, Figure 5 shows that there is a comparatively much lower chance of finding metaphorical expressions used to evaluate Brexit positively. Qualitative differences between the two newspapers are discussed in section 4.3 below.

## 4.3 The expression of negative evaluative stance towards Brexit

In this section we report the qualitative findings of our study and we address research question 3, that is, how negative evaluative stance towards Brexit and relevant social actors is expressed. Our goal is to discuss the way in which evaluative expressions are used to construe and evaluate Brexit and related social actors and events, which include (but are not limited to) the negotiations with the EU, the politicians involved in the process, most notably Theresa May and Boris Johnson in particular, and the government in general. Specific choices in *The Guardian* and *The Times* are discussed below.

We have collected the most frequently used negative words in the two samples and have analysed the uses of some of these words in context. In order to measure the degree of negativity of the word, we have relied on the valence ratings provided in Warriner, Kuperman and Brysbaert (2013). Valence is understood as the degree of pleasure (or lack of it) evoked by a word, going from *unhappy* (1) to *happy* (9). For the sake of clarity, we have only extracted the 10 most frequently used lemmas projecting negative evaluation. Given the limited size of the corpus, inferential tests are not viable; we will therefore restrict our analysis to a qualitative analysis of the most notable examples.

Figures 6, 7 and 8 below show graphs with the most frequent words (nouns, adjectives, and metaphoric expressions, respectively) used in *The Times* and *The Guardian* to express negative evaluation.

### *4.3.1 Negative PoS*

Figure 6 below shows the most frequent negative nouns distributed according to their valence.

*Headline finding: Overall, The Guardian makes use of more negative nouns and adjectives than The Times*

There is a direct relationship between frequency and negativity of evaluative nouns in both newspapers; in other words, the most frequently used nouns coded as negative are also comparably more negative. Overall, *The Guardian* makes use of more negative nouns (2.73) than *The Times* (3.61).

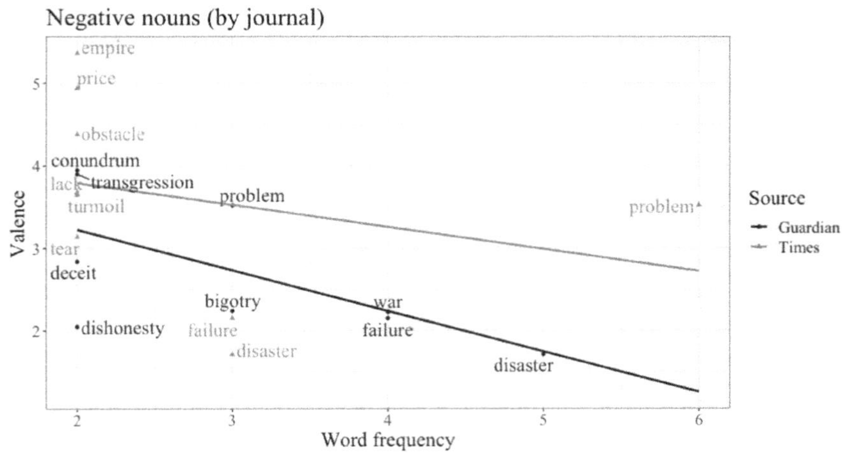


**Figure 6.** Most frequent negative nouns, by journal

*The Guardian* is extremely critical towards the role carried out by politicians during Brexit. Of the three most frequent negative evaluative nouns shown in Figure 6 for *The Guardian*, one refers to the politicians (*failure*), another one to the situation of the conservative party (*war*) and the third one refers to Brexit (*disaster*). Examples (3) and (4) illustrate uses of the word *failure* used to refer to May (example (3)) and to the Labour party (example (4)).

(3) *The prime minister's **failure** to embrace pragmatism sealed her fate. Her successor will have to deploy very different skills.* (EOG-6)
(4) *Though the Labour party's acceptance of Brexit and its **failure** to come up with much of an alternative might seem maddening.* (EOG-26)

One of the articles in *The Guardian* focuses on the internal division within the Tory party which seems to have become foregrounded by Brexit, and which is represented by means of an extended 'civil war' metaphor, as illustrated in example (5). Examples such as this are interesting because Brexit is analysed in the opinion articles at different levels, showing the implications that this process has on the internal politics of the parties and the government and not only on the external politics with the EU.

(5) *She is the no man's land candidate, standing between factions and representing none, deferring the **civil war**. It will be **fought** one day. Maybe then the Tories will work out what it is they are actually **fighting** over.* (EOG-26)

The noun *disaster* is used both by *The Guardian* and *The Times*, but in different ways. *The Guardian* uses the noun *disaster* to categorically define and evaluate Brexit, as in examples (6) and (7) below. Example (6) is long, but it is a good illustration of the type of evaluative stance carried out by *Guardian* opinion journalists. The extract contains numerous examples of evaluative expressions, all of which are negative, and which include nouns (*disaster*), adjectives (*reactionary, harder, not easier*), verbs (*narrow, shrink, curb*) and adverbs (*desperately*). The verbs are metaphoric expressions. It is a good example of the way in which evaluative language has a cumulative effect in certain parts of texts. This extract belongs to the opening of the article. All the evaluative expressions refer to Brexit and its effects for the future of the UK. Example (7) is shorter but shows a similar positioning to Brexit.

(6) *If the last three years have confirmed your fear that Brexit is a **disaster** in the making, a **reactionary** project that will **damage** our economy, **narrow** the horizons of future generations, **shrink** Britain's influence and **curb** our ability to cooperate on grave and urgent questions that go beyond national boundaries, that it will make life **harder**, not **easier**, for those who most **desperately** need change, that it is an enterprise championed by Farage and the two men he admires most, Donald Trump*

*and Vladimir Putin – if you believe all that, how best to say it in the polling booth?* (EOG-1)

(7) *Brexit, as it is being played out, is a* ***disaster, boring*** *beyond words and full of words that mean* ***zilch***. (EOG-14)

Turning now to *The Times*, the noun *disaster* is not used in this newspaper to refer to Brexit directly, but to the no-deal option, as in example (8), or just as a possibility, not a categorical statement, as in example (9). Example (8) is also interesting because it shows some of the evaluative strategies that are typically found in *The Times*, that is, the use of negative evaluation to assess a no-deal Brexit (*unwelcome, disruptive*) but also to assess the EU (*intransigence*). Additionally, positive evaluative words (far *better* for the future of this *great* country) are used to highlight the greatness of the UK as a nation independently of Brexit.

(8) *A no-deal Brexit is unwelcome. It will be* ***disruptive*** *for our neighbours as well as ourselves. But preparing for it, as Johnson is doing, is the only possible chance that he has of persuading the EU to reconsider its* ***intransigence****. Despite its* ***difficulties****, it would be far* ***better*** *for the future of this great country than capitulation. There is a way to avoid* ***disaster***. (EOT-29)

(9) *A start would be regular briefings for foreign diplomats. Ambassadors in London frequently misread the latest eddy in Brexitland politics as a decisive* ***triumph*** *or* ***disaster***. (EOT-13)

In example (9) the assessment of Brexit as a disaster is placed alongside its potential assessment as a triumph, again showing a typical argumentative strategy used in *The Times* to balance arguments for and against, expressed by means of positive evaluations and negative evaluations. A recurrent noun used in *The Times* to construe Brexit and potential deals negatively is the word *problem*, as in (10):

(10) *The* ***problem*** *is that a no-deal Brexit is not cost free.* (EOT-8)

### *4.3.2 Negative Adjectives*

Figure 7 below shows the most frequent negative adjectives and their distribution by valence. Unlike nouns, word frequency does not seem to affect the negativity of the adjectives used. Again, *The Guardian* makes use of more negative adjectives than *The Times* (3.18 and 3.80, respectively), although the difference is less visible than it was for nouns.

When considering the choice of negative adjectives in *The Guardian* and *The Times*, the adjective *bad* is used in both newspapers. In *The Guardian*, it is used to

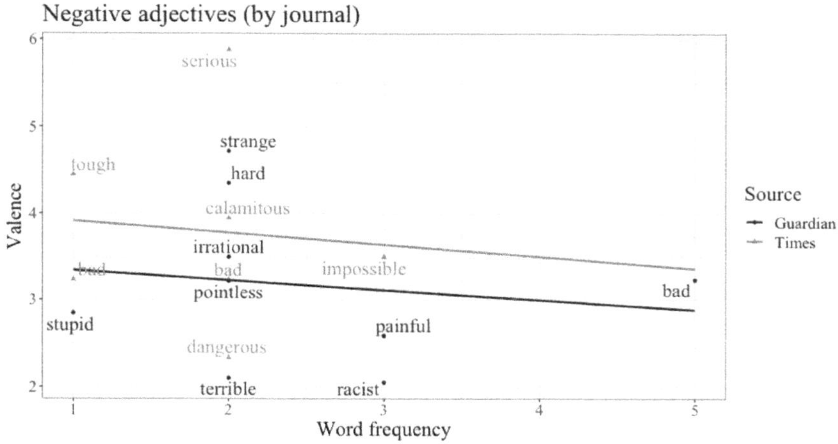


**Figure 7.** Most frequent negative adjectives, by journal

assess in general terms whatever deal is reached by the UK with the EU, as shown in example (11), and to negatively evaluate politicians, as shown in example (12):

(11) *But really this is all about feelings – and I wonder why politicos (sic.) are so **bad** at even beginning to understand this.* (EOG-14)

(12) *Having hyped up "no deal is better than a **bad** deal", May led Britain to the entirely predictable humiliation of a **bad** deal.* (EOG-8)

In *The Times*, the adjective *bad* is not used to assess Brexit, but other matters, on occasions in a structure in which a positive and negative evaluation co-exist, as in example (13) below:

(13) *But Onward had **good** as well as **bad** news for them.* (EOT-6)

Two other relevant negative adjectives in *The Guardian* are *racist* and *painful*. *Racist* is used to describe the half of the UK population who have voted for Brexit, who are represented in a very negative light, as illustrated in example (14):

(14) *So half the country are **racist**, old, **small-minded**, **poor** people who were **seduced** by a combination of Aaron Banks and **delusions of empire**.* (EOG-14)

The adjective *painful* is used to refer to the negative economic effects of Brexit by focusing on the process of separation from the EU, as shown in example (15).

(15) *most now want to leave the EU with as "clean" a break as possible, however **painful**.* (EOG-9)

In *The Times*, two relevant adjectives are *impossible* and *calamitous*. *Calamitous* is used to assess the possible Brexit deals in general terms and more specifically, the no-deal Brexit, as shown by example (16):

(16) *there is no **good** Brexit deal to be done, that Brexit is a **calamitous lose-lose** proposition and that the politically **toxic** challenge of sharing out the losses would be easier once we had left the EU.* (EOT-47)

The adjective *impossible* is also used to refer to the conditions of the Brexit agreement and possibilities of deals, as in example (17), highlighting the difficulties of the negotiations process:

(17) *the reason for the current **impasse** lies in the way that the negotiations were sequenced, which has made an agreement almost **impossible** to achieve.* (EOT-47)

### 4.3.3 Negative Metaphors

*Headline finding: There is a direct relationship between frequency and negativity of metaphors (source domains) in both newspapers. Overall, The Guardian makes use of more negative metaphors than The Times.*

Figure 8 below shows the most frequent negative metaphors distributed according to their valence.

We observe again a negative relationship between word frequency and word valence that is stronger in *The Times* than in *The Guardian*. The average valence

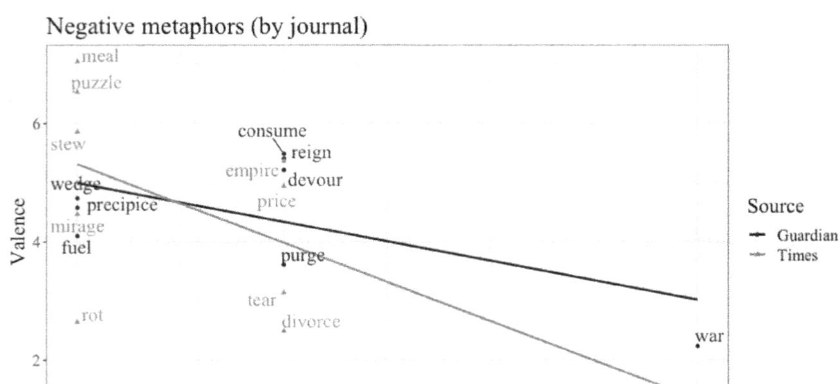


**Figure 8.** Most frequent negative metaphorical source domains, by journal

of the metaphorically-related words in both newspapers is similar but slightly lower in *The Guardian* (4.42) compared to *The Times* (4.72), in consonance with previous trends. With regard to the choice of negative evaluative metaphors, the average values are slightly higher than for PoS and function, indicating that the valence of the words is not felt to be as negative as some of the nouns and adjectives discussed above. However, the metaphoric noun *war* in *The Guardian* has a very marked negative valence, and it is also the most frequent one in this newspaper. In turn, the metaphoric words used in *The Times* (*divorce, empire*) do not have such a strong negative value. As commented above in the analysis of example (5), the noun *war* is used to represent the internal situation of division within the Conservative party led by May. The other most frequent evaluative metaphors used in *The Guardian* assess the behaviour of politicians in a very negative light and thus are profound criticisms of their role in Brexit. Examples (18) and (19) illustrate the uses of the verbs *purge* and *devour* in *The Guardian*:

(18) *Cameron won't* ***purge*** *his Brexit rebels, but there will be a reckoning.* (EOG-10)
(19) *As for Johnson, he can be left to the tender mercies of the Conservative party. It is good at* ***devouring*** *its own.* (EOG-6)

With regard to the specific evaluative metaphors used to depict Brexit, there are three that stand out, *the precipice* in example (20), *the cliff-edge* and *the gang-plank* in example (21). These three metaphors foreground the situation of the UK in Brexit as one of loss of agency in a situation which can only have a negative outcome. Indeed, the UK is represented as having been forced into this position by the incompetence of politicians.

(20) *Having hyped up "no deal is better than a bad deal", May led Britain to the entirely predictable* ***humiliation*** *of a bad deal. That her party's zealots increasingly embraced* ***pushing Britain off the precipice*** *was unsurprising: she kept* ***throwing them red meat****, and they had only grown* ***fatter*** *and* ***hungrier****.* (EOG-8)
(21) *Parliament has a little over one week to.... come up with a plan that saves us from the* Brexit ***cliff edge****. (...) Negotiations to see whether a compromise is possible are the only alternative to what the former Brexit minister, Lord Bridges, has described as the British public being asked* ***to walk a gangplank into thin air****.* (EOG-9)

In *The Times*, Brexit is represented metaphorically as a *divorce*, a *puzzle* and a *headache*, and the no-deal option is described as a *mirage*.

(22) *Many now say that the big mistake was the decision to negotiate only the* ***divorce*** *issues during the two-year Article 50 process and postpone detailed discussion of the future relationship until after Britain had left the EU.* (EOT-47)

(23) *The backstop question presently reminds me of one of those* ***impenetrable brain-teaser puzzles*** *they run on Radio 4's Today show.* (EOT-10)
(24) *The* ***superficially tempting*** *option of a no-deal Brexit is a* ***mirage****.* (EOT-8)

The DIVORCE metaphor is one of the most frequent ones used in the press to refer to the process of separation from the EU, and in *The Times* it is used to refer to the economic conditions of the separation. On the other hand, the PUZZLE metaphor is used to refer to the Irish border backstop issue. In any case, the evaluative metaphors chosen by *The Times* journalists seem to be less dramatic than those chosen by the journalists in *The Guardian*. In the DIVORCE scenario or in trying to solve a puzzle, the involved entities are not rendered powerless and without agency, as in the PRECIPICE and CLIFF-EDGE metaphor scenarios. On the contrary, the role of the UK as a negotiator is foregrounded and the sense of a potential positive outcome (after the divorce is settled or once the puzzle is solved) is present, unlike in the CLIFF-EDGE and PRECIPICE metaphors. These choices seem to support the claim that the perceived negativity in *The Guardian* is stronger than in *The Times*. Finally, *The Times* also uses evaluative metaphors to evaluate the EU and British politicians. The EU is described as a new *empire* (25) and Boris Johnson as *stewing* in his own contradictions (26):

(25) *The principal blame will lie not with Johnson and his colleagues but in the vain heart of the new* ***empire****— Brussels.* (EOT-48)
(26) *Would it be better to let Mr. Johnson* ***stew*** *in his own contradictions.* (EOT-13)

## 5 Conclusions

This section provides some concluding remarks and suggestions for further research. In this chapter, we have explored how the news value of negativity is realised by means of specific linguistic choices within the domain of evaluative stance in two samples of opinion articles from *The Times* and *The Guardian*.

With regard to research question (1) What is the frequency of lexical units expressing evaluative stance in the corpus and in each newspaper?, the results of our analysis have shown that negative evaluation is higher than positive evaluation in both samples, though *The Guardian* shows a higher frequency of negative evaluative words than *The Times*. These results have been interpreted in the light of the ideological orientation of the newspapers. That is, even if both newspapers are pro-remain, *The Guardian* seems to be displaying a stronger negative positioning towards Brexit as a political move, while *The Times* has chosen to balance positive and negative assessments while foregrounding the negative effects of the economic conditions of Brexit and the separation from the EU.

With respect to research question (2) What is the distribution of evaluative stance categories in general and by newspaper?, results have shown that *The Guardian* has a higher frequency of negative classifiers (nouns and verbs) and a higher frequency of negative evaluative metaphors, while *The Times* shows a preference for positive adjectives when compared to *The Guardian*. Close examination of examples from the samples has revealed that the use of positive adjectives in *The Times* forms part of a strategy of presenting arguments for and against an issue, which seems to point at a positioning towards Brexit which tries to find a balance between positive and negative consequences. However, *The Guardian* seems to adopt a clearer negative stance towards Brexit in general terms.

Finally, in answer to question (3) How is negative evaluative stance towards Brexit and the role of relevant social actors expressed?, our findings have shown that negative evaluative words in *The Guardian* have a higher negative valence than those in *The Times*. This finding confirms the claim that the positioning of the journalists writing for *The Guardian* is more strongly expressed than in *The Times*. This is clear, for example, in the choice of evaluative metaphors, which are much more dramatic in *The Guardian* than in *The Times*. Additionally, while both newspapers criticise the politicians and their role in Brexit, *The Guardian* is particularly aggressive, while *The Times* criticises both British politicians and the EU.

This study has also shown that further research is needed in several topics touched upon in this chapter. First, it is necessary to investigate the frequency of positive and negative evaluation in different genres in relation to evaluation of specific discourse topics, and, more specifically in larger corpora of opinion and comment articles. Second, as pointed out by Bednarek and Caple (2014) further research is needed to describe in greater detail how news values are realised by means of specific linguistic choices in media texts. Third, within studies of evaluative language, it is necessary to pay greater attention to parts of speech such as the noun and the verb, which do not express evaluation in such a prototypical way as the adjective. Finally, more studies on the nature and role of evaluative metaphors in discourse are needed.

## References

Alba-Juez, L. and Thompson, G. (eds) (2014). *Evaluation in Context*. Amsterdam: John Benjamins.

Alonso Belmonte, I. (2008). 'Newspaper editorials and comment articles: a "Cinderella" genre?', *RAEL: Revista Electrónica de Lingüística Aplicada extra*, 1, 1–9.

Bednarek, M. (2007). *Evaluation in Media Discourse*. London: Continuum.

Bednarek, M. and Caple, H. (2014). 'Why do news values matter? Towards a new methodological framework for analysing news discourse in Critical Discourse Analysis and beyond', *Discourse & Society*, 25(2), 135–158.

Bell, A. (1991). *The Language of News Media*. Oxford: Blackwell.

Biber, D., and Finegan, E. (1988). 'Adverbial stance types in English', *Discourse Processes*, 11, 1–34.

Biber, D., Johansson, S. Leech, G, Conrad, S. and Finegan, E. (1999). *The Longman Grammar of Spoken and Written English*. London: Longman.

Caple, H. and M. Bednarek (2013). 'Delving into the Discourse: Approaches to News Values in Journalism Studies and Beyond', Working paper, *Reuters Institute for the Study of Journalism*, 18–19.

Charteris-Black, J. (2019). *Metaphors of Brexit No cherries on the cake?* Basingstoke: Palgrave, MacMillan.

Du Bois, J. W. (2007). 'The stance triangle' In Robert Englebretson (ed) *Stancetaking in Discourse*, pp. 139–182. Amsterdam: John Benjamins.

Englebretson, R. (ed.) (2007). *Stancetaking in Discourse*. Amsterdam: John Benjamins.

Fairclough, N. (1995). *Media Discourse*. London: Arnold.

Fleiss, J. L. (1971). 'Measuring nominal scale agreement among many raters', *Psychological Bulletin*, 76 (5), 378–382.

Fowler, R. (1991). *Language in the News. Discourse and Ideology in the Press*. London: Routledge.

Fuoli, M., Littlemore, J. and Turner, S. (2021). 'Sunken Ships and Screaming Banshees: Metaphor and evaluation in film reviews', *English Language and Linguistics*, 1–29.

Gamer, M., Lemon, J., Fellows, I., Singh, P. (2019). 'irr: Various Coefficients of Interrater Reliability and Agreement'. R package version 0.84.1. https://CRAN.R-project.org/package=irr

García, D., Garas, A. and Schweitzer, F. (2012). 'Positive words carry less information than negative words', *EPJ Data Sci*, 1(3), <https://doi.org/10.1140/epjds3Z>, accessed 30 November 2021.

Givón, T. (1993). *English Grammar. A Function-Based Introduction. Volume I*. Amsterdam: John Bejamins.

Hidalgo-Downing, L. (2006). 'The expression of writer stance by modal adjectives and adverbs in a comparable corpus of English and Spanish newspaper discourse'. In A. M. Hornero, M. J. Luzón and S. Murillo (eds.) *Corpus Linguistics. Applications for the Study of English*, pp. 125–140. Frankfurt: Peter Lang.

Hidalgo-Downing, L and Pérez-Sobrino, P. (2022) 'Developing an annotation protocol for evaluative stance and metaphor in discourse: theoretical and methodological considerations', *Text and Talk*. Advanced online publication.

Hidalgo-Downing, L, Pérez-Sobrino, P., Filardo-Llamas, L., Maíz-Arévalo, C., Núñez-Perucha, B., Sánchez-Moya, A., Williams Camus, J.T. (Forthcoming). 'A protocol for the annotation of evaluative stance and metaphor across four discourse genres', *Revista Española de Lingüística Aplicada*.

Hunston, S. and Thompson, G. (2020). *Evaluation in text*. Oxford: Oxford University Press.

Hunston, S. (2011). *Corpus Approaches to Evaluation: Phraseology and Evaluative Language*. London: Routledge.

Ljung, M. (2000). 'Newspaper genres and newspaper English'. In F. Ungerer (ed.) *English Media Texts Past and Present*, pp. 131–150. Amsterdam: John Benjamins.

Marín-Arrese, J. I. (2021). 'Stance, emotion and persuasion: Terrorism and the press', *Journal of Pragmatics*, 177, 135–148.

Marín Arrese, J. I. and Núñez Perucha, B. (2006). 'Evaluation and Engagement in Journalistic Commentary and News Reportage', *Revista Alicantina de Estudios Ingleses*, 19, 225–248.

Marín Arrese, J. I., Hidalgo-Downing, L. and Molina Plaza, S. (2004). 'Evidential, epistemic and deontic modality in English and Spanish. The expression of writer stance in newspaper discourse'. In R. Facchinetti, and F. Palmer (eds.) *English Modality in Perspective*. Pp. 121–140. Frankfurt: Peter Lang.

Musolff, A. (2017). 'Truth, lies and figurative scenarios. Metaphors at the heart of Brexit', *Journal of Language and Politics*, 16(5), 641–657.

Pérez Blanco, M. (2016). 'The construction of attitudinal stance: A corpus-based contrastive study of negative evaluative adjectives in English and Spanish opinion discourse', *Languages in Contrast*, 16(1), 31–53.

Pragglejazz (2007). 'A method for identifying metaphorically used words in discourse', *Metaphor and Symbol*, 22(1), 1–39.

R Core Team (2020). *R: A language and environment for statistical computing. R Foundation for Statistical Computing*, Vienna, Austria. <https://www.R-project.org/>.

Reisigl, M., and Wodak, R. (2009). 'The discourse historical approach'. In R. Wodak and M. Meyer (eds.) *Methods for Critical Discourse Analysis*, pp. 87–121. London: Sage.

Richardson, J. E. (2007). *Analysing Newspapers. An Approach from Critical Discourse Analysis*. Basingstoke: Palgrave, MacMillan.

Sánchez-Moya, A. and Maíz-Arévalo, C. (forthcoming). '"Histrionic, appalling, a major turkey": the expression of evaluative stance in the discourse of online forums'. In J. Marín Arrese, Juana, L. Hidalgo-Downing and J. R. Zamorano Mansilla (eds.) *Stance, Inter/Subjectivity and Identity in discourse*, Frankfurt: Peter Lang.

Simaki, V., Paradis, C., Kerren, A. (2018). 'Evaluating stance-annotated sentences from the Brexit Blog Corpus: A quantitative linguistic analysis', *ICAME journal*, 42(1), 133–166.

Simaki, V., Paradis, C., Skeppstedt, M., Sahlgren, M., Kucher, K., Kerren, A. (2020). 'Annotating Speaker Stance in Discourse: The Brexit Blog Corpus', *Corpus linguistics and linguistic theory*, 16(2), 215–248.

Steen, G., Dorst, A., Herrmann, B., Kaal, A., and Krennmayr, T. (2010). 'Metaphor in usage', *Cognitive Linguistics*, 21(4), 765–796.

Ungerer, F. (ed.) (2000). *English Media Texts Past and Present*. Amsterdam: John Benjamins.

Van Dijk, T. A. (1988). *News as discourse*. Lawrence Erlbaum Associates, Inc.

Van Dijk, T. A. (1989a). 'Mediating racism. The role of the media in the reproduction of racism'. In R. Wodak (ed.) *Language, Power and Ideology: Studies in political discourse*, pp. 199–226. Amsterdam: John Benjamins.

Van Dijk, T. A. (1989b). 'Race, riots and the press. An analysis of editorials in the British press about the 1985 disorders', *Gazette*, 43, 229–253.

Van Dijk, T. A. (1995). 'Power and the news media'. In D. Paletz (ed) *Political Communication and Action*, pp. 9–36. Cresskill, NJ: Hampton Press.

Van Leeuwen, T. (2008). *Discourse and Practice: New Tools for Critical Analysis*. Oxford: Oxford University Press.

Wickham, H. (2016). *ggplot2: Elegant Graphics for Data Analysis*. Springer-Verlag: New York.

Zeileis, A. Meyer, D., and Hornik, K. (2007). 'Residual-based Shadings for Visualizing (Conditional) Independence', *Journal of Computational and Graphical Statistics*, 16(3), 507–525.

Begoña Núñez-Perucha & Laura Filardo-Llamas

# From "Roaring Lion" to "Chlorinated Chicken": Evaluative Stance and Ideological Positioning in a Corpus of British Political Discourse

**Abstract:** This paper aims to analyse the linguistic mechanisms used by British Conservative and Labour politicians to express their evaluative stance. Although much work has been done in Critical Discourse Analysis (CDA) and Political Discourse Analysis (PDA) in relation to the evaluative potential of metaphor (Hart 2008; Charteris-Black 2005 2019, among others) and to the analysis of epistemic and effective stance (Marín-Arrese 2011, 2015), to our knowledge, no comprehensive analysis has focused on the study of evaluative stance. Drawing on the model of positioning and (inter)subjectivity developed as part of the STANCEDISC Project (Marín-Arrese and Hidalgo-Downing, 2019), this paper uses a mixed methods approach to investigate the type of evaluative strategies in each set of speeches, their value-connotation, and their connection with the specific features of representation and ideological positioning that characterise PD (Chilton 2004; Filardo-Llamas and Boyd 2018).

**Keywords:** *Critical Discourse Studies, stance, evaluation, metaphor, political discourse*

## 1 Introduction

Since the classical rhetorical tradition, political discourse (PD) has been characterised by persuasion. It is precisely its persuasive nature that "makes it especially suited for the expression of evaluation, since politicians need to create a distinct profile for themselves in order to persuade their audience to vote for them" (Díez-Prados and Cabrejas-Peñuelas 2018: 179). In the field of linguistics, the study of evaluation in PD has followed two major trends: a trend based on pragmatics and a trend adhering to the appraisal framework (see Cabrejas Peñuelas and Díez Prados 2014 for an overview).

On the one hand, studies which follow a pragmatics-based approach have primarily focused on the use of evaluative markers as a mechanism for saving the positive face of politicians in response to face-threatening questions (Harris 1991; Simon-Vandenbergen 1996; Becker 2009). On the other hand, a number of studies have applied the appraisal framework (Martin and White 2005) to explain uses of evaluative language in PD. These include, among others, Opstaele's (2008) comparison of Barack Obama's and Hillary Clinton's speeches,

Aloy Mayo and Taboada's (2017) corpus-based exploration of the 2014 midterm US elections in *Cosmopolitan*, or Berracheche's (2020) study of how appraisal can help us identify party positioning.

Indeed, the appraisal framework has been widely acknowledged as a valuable tool for studying evaluation within the Critical Discourse Analysis (CDA) paradigm (see Hart 2014a; Coffin and O'Halloran 2012; Bloor and Bloor 2007; Bednarek and Caple 2014). While the analysis of stance includes both evaluation and positioning, the latter has been explicitly approached from a critical perspective, particularly in relation to effective and epistemic stance (see, for instance, Marín-Arrese 2011, 2015). Although these studies have examined the linguistic features used by politicians to position themselves towards events and viewpoints presented in their discourse, to our knowledge, no comprehensive analysis has focused on the way evaluative stance is not only discursively manifested but also ideologically determined and oriented. This chapter tries to fill this gap by exploring the linguistic mechanisms used by British Conservative and Labour politicians to express their evaluative stance. In doing so, it addresses the following research questions:

1. How is evaluation expressed by Conservative and Labour politicians? More specifically, how do they differ in the categories of evaluative markers that they use and in the values (positive or negative) ascribed to them?
2. What role does evaluation play in the construction of their ideological positioning? In other words, how is evaluation used to legitimise the party's ideology?

In order to carry out this analysis, a sample of political speeches delivered by British politicians between 2016 and 2019 was chosen from the PD corpus compiled as part of the STANCEDISC project[1] (see section 3 for further details about the data). Due to the fact that the Conservative party was in office during this period, and after the UK voted to leave the EU, it is hypothesised that Labour politicians will make a higher use of negative evaluation devices with the aim of delegitimising the Conservative party and its political actions. A contextual dimension is thus incorporated to the analysis, with the aim of establishing a relation between the linguistic cues present in the text and the ideological function performed by evaluative lexis.

1 *Stance and Subjectivity in Discourse: Towards an integrated framework for the analysis of epistemicity, effectivity, evaluation and inter/subjectivity from a critical discourse perspective* (STANCEDISC). Project funded by the Spanish Ministry of Science, Innovation and Universities (Ref. PGC2018-095798-B-I00).

This chapter is organised as follows. After this brief introduction, section 2 provides an overview of the concept of stance, particularly focusing on the model followed in this research as well as its connection with evaluation studies in CDA. Section 3 describes the data and the methodology used for the analysis of both sets of political speeches. Section 4 presents the findings from a qualitative and a quantitative perspective together with an interpretation of those results in relation to ideology. Finally, the conclusion section summarises the main results while highlighting their contribution to the field of PD analysis.

## 2 Theoretical Framework

### 2.1 Evaluation and Stance

The concept of stance has been approached from different perspectives within discourses studies, each highlighting particular linguistic dimensions and resources. In its origin, stance was defined as "the lexical and grammatical expression of attitudes, feelings, judgements, or commitments concerning the propositional content of a message" (Biber and Finegan 1989: 93). This definition was further developed by Biber et al. (1999: chapter 12), who distinguished three types of stance: i) epistemic stance, which referred to "the status of information in a proposition", thus including expressions of certainty, doubt, actuality, precision and limitation; ii) attitudinal stance, which comprised markers reporting "personal attitudes or feelings", and, iii) style of speaking stance or "comments on the communication itself". Kiesling (2009) incorporates the interpersonal dimension and defines stance not only as the way people relate to their talk (epistemic stance) but also as the way they relate to their interlocutors (interpersonal stance).

From a systemic functional linguistic perspective, stance has been equated with the language of evaluation (Martin 2000; Martin and White 2005). In an attempt to provide a detailed account of the linguistic resources used by speakers/writers to convey assessments and engage with prior or potential interlocutors, appraisal theory divides these resources into three semantic domains: i) attitude, or meanings by which (positive or negative) values or assessments are attached to participants and processes by reference to emotional responses or to culturally-determined value systems (e.g. *I admire, he's proud*); ii) engagement, or resources whereby speakers or writers position themselves with respect to the propositions or proposals expressed in the text; this domain includes various lexico-grammatical resources traditionally analysed as pertaining to the domains of evidentiality, epistemic modality or hedging (e.g. *I think, perhaps, it seems that…*); and iii) graduation, or values expressed by speakers/writers to graduate the impact, force or focus of their utterances or semantic categorisations (e.g. *slightly, effectively*). In appraisal theory all these lexico-grammatical resources are characterised as evaluative. Like Martin (2000), Thompson and Hunston (2001) place emphasis on the semantics of evaluation and regard evaluation as the "broad cover term for the expression of the speaker or writer´s attitude or stance towards, viewpoint on, or feelings about the entities or propositions that he or she is talking about" (p. 5).

Undoubtedly, evaluation and positioning are key components of stance, to such an extent that the three terms have become inextricably intertwined in the existing literature. Du Bois (2007: 141) claims that "the act of taking a stance necessarily invokes an evaluation at one level or another, whether by assertion or inference". This author views stance as a form a social action, as "a public act by a social actor, achieved dialogically through overt communicative means, of simultaneously evaluating objects, positioning (self and others), and aligning with other subjects, with respect to any salient dimension of the sociocultural field" (p. 163). The act of stance-taking is, according to Elder (2020: 73), also an act of "positioning oneself with respect to the content of what is said, and/or with respect to one´s interlocutors". Consequently, in spite of the complex nature of stance and the multifarious terminology associated with it, it seems reasonable to suggest that a comprehensive view of stance should account for both how one positions oneself towards the content of their propositions and proposals, and how the discursive 'objects' are linguistically evaluated. In other words, stance can be understood as an umbrella term comprising positioning and evaluative resources.

The framework for the study of evaluation presented in this chapter draws on the stance model carried out within the STANCEDISC project, which combines work on stance and evaluation from a CDA perspective (see Marín-Arrese 2011; Marín-Arrese et al. 2020; Hidalgo-Downing et al. forthcoming). According to this model, there are three types of stance:

i) Epistemic stance, whereby the speaker/ writer shows their concern with "knowledge about the events designated" (Marín-Arrese 2011: 193), as manifested by means of epistemic modals, verbs of cognition, evidentials and reporting verbs.
ii) Effective stance, which refers to the ways by which the speaker/writer aims to "exert control or influence on the course or reality itself" (Marín-Arrese 2011: 193). This type of stance is mostly realised by modals expressing deonticity, possibility, necessity and volition as well as predicates expressing desirability, requirement or intention and commitment.

iii) Evaluative stance, which refers to the assessment of entities, participants or events as well as the expression of attitudes or opinions about a whole proposition (Hidalgo-Downing et al. forthcoming). This type of stance links evaluation to positioning and alignment, following Du Bois (2007).

## 2.2 Evaluative Stance and Ideological Positioning

As previously mentioned, evaluative stance is concerned with assessment and alignment. As such, it is realised in discourse by means of lexical choices having a positive or a negative value. As described in Hidalgo-Downing et al. (forthcoming), evaluative markers fall into three categories: classifying, predicational and attitudinal. Classifying expressions are those which "classify entities or events according to social systems of beliefs". These terms are typically nouns and verbs (e.g. this is *chaos*). Predicational expressions are those which "qualify entities or events according to social systems of beliefs", as is the case of adjectives (e.g., *excellent*, *terrible*) or nouns having a modifying function (e.g., a *key* feature). Finally, attitudinal expressions or evaluative resources express the speaker´s attitudes or opinions about a whole proposition. Attitude is prototypically realised by sentential adverbs, such as *luckily*.

It should be noted that in the framework adopted here (Hidalgo-Downing et al. forthcoming; Hidalgo-Downing and Pérez-Sobrino, this volume), classifying and predicational expressions capture the CDA distinction between nomination and predicational strategies, that is, strategies referring to how actors, actions, events or objects are named and characterised in discourse, respectively (see, for instance, Wodak 2001, among others). Additionally, expressions can be metaphoric or non-metaphoric. In fact, Deignan (2010) observes that the evaluative function of metaphor has been widely acknowledged since the 1960s (p. 357). After reviewing existing research on how evaluation is conveyed by metaphor, Deignan (2010) identified four uses of metaphor: creating entailments, exploiting metaphorical scenarios, choosing meaningful source domains and exploiting the connotations of a word´s literal meaning. As will be shown in the analysis section, metaphoric evaluative stance is primarily conveyed by creating entailments, which, in turn, derive from particular source domains strategically chosen to promote the party´s ideology.

The connection between evaluative stance and ideology is another important theoretical foundation for the present study. Within CDA, cognitive-linguistics and socio-cognitive approaches have shown that linguistic choices, and among them, evaluative language, can result in the construction of social identities (Filardo-Llamas and Boyd 2018; Filardo-Llamas and Morales-López 2021), in ideological representations and values of ingroups (Núñez-Perucha 2011) and in alternative construals of reality, which, in turn, encode particular (de)legitimised views (Hart 2014a, 2014b, 2018). Amongst the construal operations identified in the literature, two are of particular interest for the study of evaluation in political discourse: framing and positioning. Positioning strategies are the ones related to the situation of the speaker in relation to a given temporal, spatial or axiological coordinate (Chilton 2004; Hart 2014b; Cap 2013). It is the axiological dimension of positioning that is important for the study of evaluation, given its role in the construal of alien or shared ideological beliefs and values relative to the dominant ideology of the deictic centre (Cap 2010: 399; 2013). In the study of PD, evaluation has been considered a positioning strategy showing the politicians' (inter)subjective alignment or disalignment with (discourse) participants and events in an axis which ranges across the good-bad parameters (Thompson and Hunston 2000; Chilton 2004; Englebretson 2007; Hart 2014a; Lawrence 2017). These good-bad values are closely related to van Dijk´s (1998: 301) ideological square based on the "positive self-presentation and negative other-presentation" of participants and events. Indeed, it can be argued that evaluation is ideologically motivated inasmuch as what the speaker/writer thinks or feels about something reveals their ideology and its underlying value-system. As Thompson and Hunston (2001: 6) rightly note, "every act of evaluation expresses a communal value-system, and every act of evaluation goes towards building up that value-system. This value system in turn is a component of the ideology which lies behind every text".

As will also be shown in the analysis, ideology is articulated on the basis of group values, which, in turn, determine the purpose and features of evaluation. The importance of context and shared knowledge shall thus be addressed when identifying the value system underlying lexical choices. Positive and negative evaluation do not only reflect the politician´s value-system, but they also contribute to reinforcing the party´s ideology and a sense of commonality.

## 3 Corpus and Methodology

### 3.1 Data and Selection Criteria

The data comprises two sets of political speeches delivered by members of the British Conservative and Labour Parties between 2016 and 2019, a time during which the Conservative party was in power. The EU or Brexit referendum took place on 23rd June 2016 and Britain voted to leave the EU. The official withdrawal process started in 2017, but Theresa May failed to win the backing of the UK

Parliament on her Brexit deal and resigned as Prime Minister in 2019. She was then succeeded by Boris Johnson.

As previously mentioned, all the speeches belong to the 200,000-word STANCEDISC corpus. For the purposes of this study, a sample was compiled according to the following selection criteria: First, each set should contain approximately 15,000 words. The number of words rather than the number of speeches was considered the main selection criterion. As a result, the number of speeches varies across the sample. Second, in order to avoid stylistic influence, different politicians, who were not necessarily the leaders of the party, were selected. Finally, for consistency reasons, it was decided that all the speeches should belong to the same genre. Consequently, all the speeches chosen were given at party conferences, which ensured contextual homogeneity.

The Conservative set (henceforth STANCECON) contains 15,537 words and includes speeches given by David Davis, Secretary of State for Exiting the European Union (October 2016); Boris Johnson, as leader of the Conservative Party (October 2017); Theresa May, PM and Conservative leader (October 2018); and, Jacob Rees-Mogg, Leader of the House of Commons (September 2019). The Labour set (STANCELAB) consists of 14,546 words and represents the voices of Jeremy Corbyn, Leader of the Labour Party (September 2018); Emily Thornberry, MP, Shadow Foreign Secretary (September 2018); Diane Abbott, Shadow Home Secretary (September 2019); Dawn Butler, Shadow Secretary of State for Women and Equalities (September 2019); Jennie Formbie, General Secretary (September 2019); Keir Stammer, Shadow Brexit Secretary (September 2019); and Ian Lavery, Chairman of the Labour Party (September 2019). In the analysis section, the source for each example is indicated by the surname of the politician and the year in which the speech was delivered in brackets.

## 3.2 Methodology

The analysis used a mixed methods procedure, thus combining the quantitative analysis of the evaluative categories under investigation and the qualitative analysis of their discursive and ideological functions.[2]

---

2 For a detailed description of the method developed for the analysis of evaluation in discourse which includes the inter-rater reliability process, the criteria for evaluative stance, the steps in the implementation of the protocol and the theoretical and methodological grounding of the decisions, see Hidalgo-Downing and Pérez-Sobrino (2022) and for a detailed explanation of the complete protocol and its application to four genres see Hidalgo-Downing et al. (forthcoming).

First, all the speeches were manually tagged according to the type of evaluative strategies (classifying, predicational and attitudinal), metaphoricity (metaphoric or non-metaphoric) and value conveyed by the expression (positive or negative). Next, details such as the title of the speech and its source were removed in order to upload the texts to the MonoConc software. This was used to make the quantitative analysis as accurate as possible. In this regard, two tools of the MonoConc programme were used: i) the frequency option, which provided the word count and frequency of each category, and, ii) the concordance search, which showed the occurrence of each category in context, thus allowing us to examine common patterns regarding types of evaluative expressions as well as the participants or actions being evaluated. Once quantitative results were obtained, a qualitative analysis was conducted of the most frequent evaluative lexical choices identified in the samples. This qualitative analysis was aimed at explaining the co-textual behaviour of each realisation of evaluation identified in our model.

## 4 Analysis

### 4.1 Evaluative Strategies in British Political Speeches

The quantitative analysis of evaluative strategies in both samples shows that the Conservative politicians make a higher use of evaluation. In terms of function, as illustrated by Figure 1, the predicational function is the most frequent one, followed by the classifying function. In this regard, it is worth noting that classifying expressions are much more numerous in the Conservative set. By contrast, attitudinal expressions display a scarce use in both samples.

As for the categories of figurativity and value, non-metaphoric expressions and positive evaluation are the most frequent types in both sets of speeches. Besides, the same number of negative expressions was found in the two samples, as shown in Figures 2 and 3:

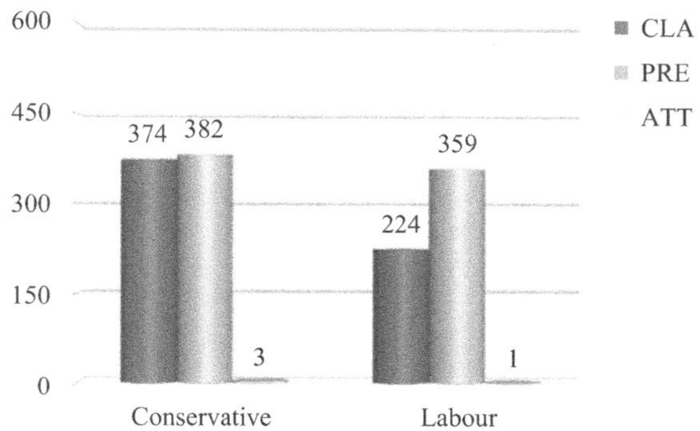


**Figure 1.** Functions of stance markers in the Conservative and Labour samples.

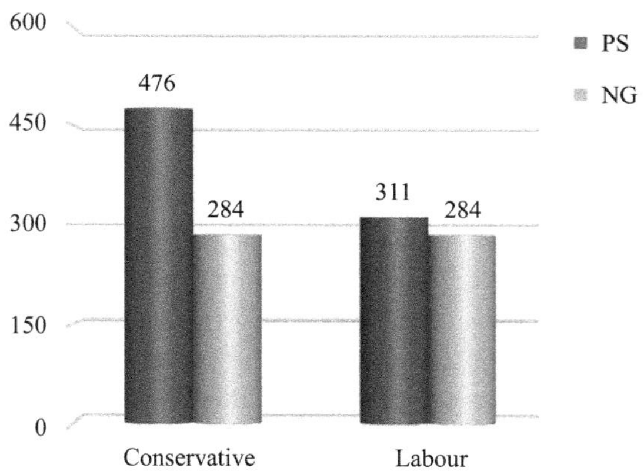


**Figure 2.** Metaphoric and non-metaphoric stance markers in the Conservative and Labour samples.

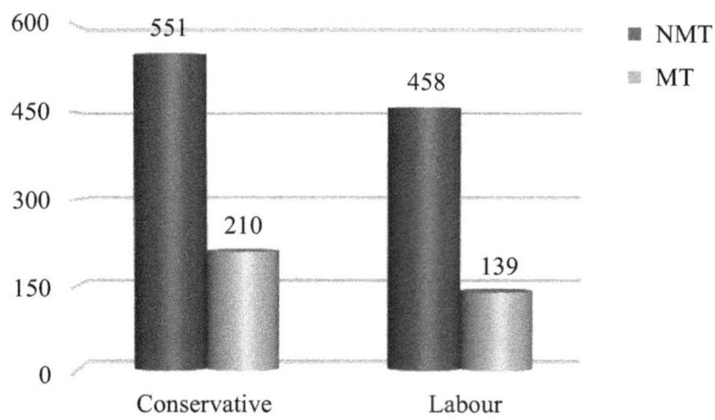


**Figure 3.** Positive and negative values of stance markers in the Conservative and Labour samples.

The following subsections examine the linguistic realisations and use of these evaluative strategies in the politicians′ construction of ideological positioning.

## 4.2 Evaluation in the Conservative Sample

The analysis of predicational evaluation in the STANCECON sample shows a prominence of the adjectives *great* (n=21), *good* (n=14, of which n=4 function as nouns), *clear* (n=8), *new* (n=5) and *strong* (n=3). A closer analysis of the words with which these adjectives collocate shows that they are used to evaluate four main entities: the message delivered by the Conservative party, typically evaluated through the adjective *clear*; Conservative policies, mainly in relation to the Brexit deal, usually through the adjectives *great*, *good*, or *new*; the Conservative party, usually through the adjective *great*; and the British nation, as we can see in examples (1)-(4).

(1) *For each of the four nations that make up our* **great** **<EV, AP, PRE, NMT, PS>** *United Kingdom.* (Davis 2016)
(2) *We are one of the* **great** **<EV, AP, PRE, NMT, PS>** *quintessential <EV, AP, PRE, NMT, PS> European nations.* (Johnson 2017)
(3) *And let's make Britain* **greater** **<EV, AP, PRE, NMT, PS>** *still.* (Davis 2016)
(4) *Security for the nation with* **strong** **<EV, AP, PRE, NMT, PS>** *defences against threats <EV, NP CLA, NMT, NG> from abroad, and protection against threats <EV, NP, CLA, NMT, NG> at home.* (May 2018)

A close reading of the examples above shows that it is frequent for positive predicational evaluation to occur in the near co-text of a first-person plural pronoun *we*, hence anchoring the evaluation to the deictic centre, which is occupied by the British people and/or the Conservative party (examples 1 and 2). This use of *we* tends to be combined with a positive predicational evaluation of entities with which the politician – and hence the party s/he stands for – can establish some relation, either because it is part of their national or political identity (*the nation*, in examples 1 and 2) or because it is the result of the political actions performed by them (in example 3). Likewise, as we can see in example 3, it is very frequent to find instances of positive predicational evaluation combined with an amplifying use associated to the comparative form. This contributes not only to evaluating positively the entity, but also to entailing a comparison with the past. As a consequence, the existence of the entity and any policy which might contribute to improving it are legitimised via an inferential process in which current or future actions are improved with respect to those of the past.

The analysis of negative predicational evaluation clearly shows that an opposition schema underlies PD, mostly equivalent to the 'us vs them' conceptualisation (van Dijk 1998). Thus, antonyms of the previously mentioned adjectives were found to indicate negative evaluation, including examples like *wrong* (n=4), *bad* (n=4), or *worse* (n=4). As was the case of positive evaluation, negative evaluation was used to legitimise Conservative policies by relying on a delegitimisation of Labour behaviour (see examples 5 and 6) or on an explicit reference to the negatively perceived past (as in example 7). As can also be seen in the last example, the evaluative opposition between the self and the others is frequently made explicit in discourse by relying on a co-textual relation of antonymy.

(5) *Ladies and gentlemen, Britain showed them it could be done. We proved them* ***wrong*** ***<EV, AP, PRE, NMT, NG>*** *then, and with your help, Britain will prove them* ***wrong*** ***<EV, AP, PRE, NMT, NG>*** *again.* (Davis 2016)

(6) *However* ***bad*** ***<EV, AP, PRE, NMT, NG>*** *the Labour approach is, we must do more than criticise it.* (May 2018)

(7) *This time it must be* ***different*** ***<EV, AP, PRE, NMT, PS>****. Because we are all* ***worse off*** ***<EV, AP, PRE, NMT, NG>*** *when any part of us is held back. That means doing things* ***differently*** ***<EV, ADV, PRE, NMT, PS>.*** (May 2018)

Other examples of negative evaluation can be found in the predicational use of some evaluative adjectives accompanying verbs indicating states or possession. This can be seen in example 8, where a positioning of the speaker is observed in relation to the policies implemented or proposed by the Labour party.

(8) *A kind of manifestation of Heisenberg's uncertainty principle. It would be* ***disastrous*** ***<EV, AP, PRE, NMT, NG>.*** *And in leaving Britain in this limbo <EV, NP, CLA, MT, NG> – locked <EV, VP, CLA, MT, NG> in the orbit of the EU but unable to take back control.* (Johnson 2017)

Finally, negative predicational evaluation can be observed when referring to the current or future (financial) situation of the UK, as shown by the use of adjectives evoking negative social perceptions about how to spend money, such as *endless* (May 2018) expensive promises of the Labour government. Other examples include the use of the adjective *unfair* to refer to debts (Johnson 2017) or to prices (May 2018). In other cases, the negative evaluation comes from the combination of adjectives indicating quality, often in their comparative or superlative form, hence emphasising the perceived positive value of the new desired political outcome (see example 9 below).

(9) *A* ***fairer*** ***<EV, AP, PRE, NMT, PS>*** *economy in the home of the free market – where enterprise creates wealth to fund* **great** ***<EV, AP, PRE, NMT, PS>*** *public services.* (May 2018)

The analysis of classifying strategies shows that when they have a non-metaphoric construal and positive value, they perform two main discursive functions. First, they contribute to building a shared interpersonal identity as *Conservative(s)* (n= 9). This interpersonal construction of identity is sometimes combined with a legitimation of the self's actions, and it may appear in the near co-text of what could be called an evaluation flag, that is, a word that could indicate that there is potential evaluation in the text. This is the case of the word *as* in example 10, which does not only indicate that a self-identity is discursively constructed, but it also allows for an inferential justification of the political actions of the self because they represent the core positive values of the party.

(10) *No institution embodies our principles* ***as Conservatives <EV, NP, CLA, NMT, PS>*** *more profoundly <EV, ADV, PRE, NMT, PS> or more personally <EV, ADV, PRE, NMT, PS> than our National Health Service.* (May 2018)

Additionally, classifying positive evaluation is used when introducing the self's positive characteristics, as we can see in the use of abstract nouns such as *determination* (n=4), *decency* (n=2), *opportunity* (n=3) or *success* (n=3), which have inscribed evaluation. Other similar abstract nouns can be found in examples 11–13, although their use is not as frequent. These abstract terms have two main uses: i) indicating the positive qualities or behaviour of the Conservative party (example 11), the British people (example 12) or particular members of society, such as workers in the NHS, teachers of the armed forces (example 13); and ii) referring to the political situation at the time and to the political debate on Brexit, as in examples 12 and 13. In these two examples, the use of the *of* Prepositional Phrase illustrates another case of evaluation flag inasmuch as it establishes a "conceptual link" (Radden and Dirven 2007: 159) between qualities and those members of society who have them.

(11) *To champion <EV, VP, CLA, MT, PS>* ***decency <EV, NP, CLA, NMT, PS>*** *in our politics.* (May 2018)

(12) *It would be tough <EV, AP, PRE, NMT, NG> at first, but the* ***resilience <EV, NP, CLA, NMT, PS>*** *and* ***ingenuity <EV, NP, CLA, NMT, PS>*** *of the British people would see us through <EV, VP, CLA, MT, PS>.* (May 2018)

(13) *The* ***compassion <EV, NP, CLA, NMT, PS>*** *of our NHS staff, the* ***dedication <EV, NP, CLA, NMT, PS>*** *of our teachers, the* ***bravery <EV, NP, CLA, NMT, PS>*** *of our police, and the matchless <EV, AP, PRE, NMT, PS>* ***courage <EV, NP, CLA, NMT, PS>*** *of our armed forces.* (May 2018)

Regarding the use of classifying expressions for non-metaphoric negative evaluation, several lexical choices were found in the STANCECON sample. These can be grouped into two types of nouns depending on the foregrounded aspect in the discursive construction of political opposition. On the one hand, we find nouns used to classify opponents depending on their political identity. Unlike references to the self as members of a political party, when pointing at the other it is not the name of the party that is used but nouns like *lefties* (Johnson 2017), *Marxist* (Rees-Mogg 2019) or *semi-Marxist* (Johnson 2017). In fact, besides their representational function, classifying uses of evaluation can also be ascribed an indexical function (Chilton 2004). On the other hand, we can find nouns which contribute to reifying the negative properties which characterise the others while backgrounding their identity as individuals or members of a group (Radden and Dirven 2007), as shown in example 14. Likewise, in example 15 we can see a similar backgrounding of the identity of political opponents who are referred to as *threat[s]* rather than as individuals. As Hart (2014: 127–129) notes, reification and abstraction strategies are frequent when negatively evaluating others' actions.

(14) *Let's make a positive <EV, AP, PRE, NMT, PS> case for our values that will cut through the* ***bitterness <EV, NP, CLA, NMT, NG>*** *and* ***bile <EV, NP, CLA, MT, NG>*** *that is poisoning <EV, VP, CLA, MT, NG> our politics.* (May 2018)

(15) *Security for the nation with strong <EV, AP, PRE, NMT, PS> defences against* ***threats <EV, NP, CLA, NMT, NG>*** *from abroad, and protection against* ***threats <EV, NP, CLA, NMT, NG>*** *at home.* (May 2018)

Metaphoric evaluation tends to rely on conventional metaphors coming from the WAR, BUILDING or MOVEMENT domains, as in *winning* (n=5), *building* (n=5) or *leading* (n=1). It should be noted that these were tagged as positive metaphoric evaluation only when they were combined with the pronoun *we* and they were followed by a clearly identifiable political goal (as can be seen in example 16). While it is more common to find these conventional metaphors to indicate positive evaluation, these domains are also activated to refer negatively to the others as *enemies* (May 2018), when talking about the *barriers to trade* (Davis 2016) or *destroying jobs* (May 2018), both of which are implicitly attributed to Corbyn's proposed policies. Example 17 is particularly interesting as it shows how the negative metaphoric evaluation stems from the co-textual relation between two near synonyms – *fall* and *collapse*– and the reference to cultural knowledge (*the fall of the Berlin Wall*), in such a way that the word *collapse* has to be metaphorically understood.

(16) *And together we will* ***build <EV, VP, CLA, MT, PS>*** *a brighter <EV, AP, PRE, NMT, PS> future for the whole United Kingdom.* (May 2018)
(17) *The defining <EV, AP, PRE, NMT, PS> event for a new generation of voters was not the fall of the Berlin Wall, but the* ***collapse <EV, NP, CLA, MT, NG>*** *of the banks.* (May 2018)

While several conventional metaphors were found in the STANCECON sample, Johnson's speech is a particularly interesting source for the analysis of creative metaphor as a mechanism of evaluation. Examples of metaphor with a positive value include the use of the word *lion* and the verb *roar* to refer to the desired actions of the British people (example 18). More interesting is the use of creative metaphor with a negative value, as can be seen in the description of Jeremy Corbyn as a *zombie* in example 19.

(18) *That role is played by the people of this country. But it is up to us now […] to let* ***that lion <EV, NP, CLA, MT, PS> roar <EV, VP, CLA, MT, PS>***. (Johnson 2017)
(19) *It is back from the grave. Its* ***zombie fingers <EV, NP, CLA, MT, NG> straining <EV, VP, CLA, MT, NG>*** *for the levers of power and that is why we cannot rest.* (Johnson 2017)

As far as attitudinal evaluation is concerned, only three instances of attitudinal evaluation appear in the STANCECON sample. Examples of expressions of attitude include the use of adverbs like *frankly* (May 2018), or the first-person singular pronoun *I* with the verb to be and attitudinal *delighted* followed by a clause (Davis 2016), as seen in example 20. Those two cases show the positive positioning of the politician towards the content of the following clause, which is usually related to the contextual situation. Only one instance of negative attitudinal evaluation could be found in *I worry*, which shows Theresa May's stance towards Corbyn's lack of *leadership* (example 21):

(20) *I* ***am delighted <EV, AP, ATT, NMT, PS>*** *that many who argued for Remain are now focussed on making a success of Brexit.* (Davis 2016)
(21) *That used to be Labour's position too. But when I look at its leadership today,* ***I worry <EV, VP, ATT, NMT, NG>*** *it's no longer the case.* (May 2018)

### 4.3 Evaluation in the Labour Sample

As previously mentioned, predicational markers are by far the most frequent category and contribute to creating a positive presentation of the ingroup versus a negative presentation of the outgroup. The most frequent evaluative expressions having a predicational function are *great* (n= 17), *real* (n=7), *incredible* (n= 8) and *good* (n= 6). As shown by examples (22–24), *great*, *incredible* and *good* are used to refer to the nation, the party or to their actions, thus typically collocating with inclusive *we* pronominal forms. On the other hand, *real* tends to collocate with nouns referring to the social or economic sphere (*real change*, *real alternative*, *real investment*), thus implying a negative evaluation of the Tory party´s actions. Example (25) shows how *real* is chosen to characterise the change that Britain needs, while presupposing that the Tory government has made no change at all or that such a change was not authentic.

(22) *Winning the next election will be because of people in this room and people up and down our* **great <EV, AP, PRE, NMT, PS>** *nation.* (Lavery 2019)
(23) *So my last thank you is to all of you, our* **incredible <EV, AP, PRE, NMT, PS>** *members.* (Formby 2019)
(24) *We are all* **good <EV, AP, PRE, NMT, PS>** *people.* (Butler 2019)
(25) *Labour stands for <EV, VP, CLA, MT, PS> the* **real <EV, AP, PRE, NMT, PS>** *change Britain needs.* (Lavery 2019)

As was the case in the Conservative sample, the adjective *great* is commonly used in a comparative or superlative form, which contributes to amplifying the positive qualities of the ingroup´s actions. However, whereas the Conservative party uses these forms to highlight the positive changes resulting from the party´s actions (*Let´s make Britain greater still*, example 3 above), the Labour party employs them to assess the groups' goals. By doing so, it legitimises the course of action from the present into the future while implying that there are still achievements to obtain, as can be seen in example 26.

(26) *(…) we can unite our fractured <EV, AP, PRE, NMT, NG> world, and we can show that the* **greatest <EV, AP, PRE, NMT, PS>** *achievements of our socialist <EV, AP, CLA, NMT, PS> movement lie not in our past, but in our future.* (Thornberry 2018)

By contrast, the Tory party and their actions are characterised in negative terms as *bad* (n= 3) or resulting in *violent* (n= 2) crime. As we can see in example 28, it is common to find compound patterns of negative predicational evaluation consisting of two pre-modifying negative expressions joined by *and*. Further, *bad* tends to occur as part of an overall us vs them discursive strategy, often inscribed in a comparative framework. Here the contrast between the ingroup´s positive self-representation and the outgroup negative characteristics is conveyed by means of nominalised adjectives as evident from example 29 below. Interestingly, *bad* collocates with *men*, whereas *good* collocates with *people*, thus placing *the people* closer to the speaker´s deictic centre and, in turn, creating an axiological distance with respect to the group of *bad racist men* formed by Boris Johnson and Trump. Indeed, the prevalence of predicational uses of evaluation is closely related to the representational function of PD, and particularly to positioning strategies within the axiological axis (Chilton and Schäffner 1997; Filardo-Llamas and Boyd 2018).

(27) *The Tories are carrying out their plan before our very eyes. We are letting these* ***bad <EV, AP, PRE, NMT, NG>*** *men drag us into <EV, VP, CLA, MT, NG> this* ***dark <EV, AP, PRE, MT, NG>*** *place.* (Butler 2019)

(28) *They [Tories] are the ones who have CREATED the conditions for rising* ***serious <EV, AP, PRE, NMT, NG>*** *and* ***violent <EV, AP, PRE, NMT, NG>*** *crime.* (Abbot, 2019)

(29) *Boris Johnson, Donald Trump – these are just some of* ***the bad <EV, AP, PRE, NMT, NG>*** *racist <EV, AP, PRE, NMT, NG> men combining, and we are* ***the good <EV, AP, PRE, NMT, PS>*** *people who need to associate.* (Butler 2019)

In a similar vein, classifying expressions are used to categorise situations, actions or to express abstract values. As was the case with predicational markers, classification also functions to create polarisation and highlight the difference between the Tory and the Labour party, the former being negatively classified. The most recurrent non-metaphoric classifying terms are *austerity* (n= 12), *threat(s)* (n=10), both being far more frequent than in the Conservative sample, and *scandal* (n=5). These expressions are often used to characterise the times of Tory government or to demonise this party:

(30) *Eight years of destructive <EV, AP, PRE, NMT, NG>,* ***austerity <EV, NP, CLA, NMT, NG>*** *and obsessive <EV, AP, PRE, NMT, NG> outsourcing have left other councils teetering on the precipice <EV, VP, CLA, MT, NG>, too, and this Government must be held to account for their social vandalism.* (Corbyn 2018)

(31) *The predators <EV, NP, CLA, NMT, NG> are circling <EV, VP, CLA, MT, NG> and the privatisation we've already seen is nothing in comparison to the* ***threat <EV, NP, CLA, NMT, NG>*** *posed by a Johnson-Trump trade deal.* (Formby 2019)

(32) *And then there's the* ***scandal <EV, NP, CLA, NMT, NG>*** *of the Tories'£6 billion cuts to social care, leaving 400,000 fewer older people receiving care.* (Corbyn 2018)

In contrast to the Conservative sample, where the outgroup´s identity was backgrounded by reification and abstraction strategies, in the Labour sample the identity of the participant(s) or source of the situation negatively assessed is made explicit thanks to the use of individualisation and collectivisation strategies (van Leeuwen 1996: 48). Specifically, the social actors belonging to the outgroup (i.e. the Tory party and allies), and to whom the negative evaluation is flagged, are either individualised (*the threat posed by a Johnson-Trump trade deal*) or represented as a collective group (*this Government, The Tories*).

Interestingly, this negative representation of the political scenario is used as part of an argumentative strategy justifying the need for transforming Britain. Most of the metaphoric classifying expressions associated with Labour actions rely on conventional metaphors that contain the source domains of BUILDING and WAR. As far as actions are concerned, the most frequent types fall into two categories: metaphoric expressions associated with transformation or change, which represent the party's actions in a positive way and WAR metaphoric expressions that present the Labour party (or its leader) as heroes fighting a struggle. In this regard, the most frequent classifying verbs are *rebuild* (n=12), *transform* (n= 7) and *fight(ing)* (n= 9). As shown by example 33, *rebuild* and *transform* tend to occur together, thus representing Labour as the architect of the change that Britain needs.

(33) *Labour's job is now to win support for a deal that meets the needs of the country, combined with our plan to* ***rebuild <EV, VP, CLA, MT, PS> and transform <EV, VP, CLA, MT, PS>*** *Britain with*
*investment in our people and economy.* (Corbyn 2018)

(34) *We will work with Jewish communities to eradicate antisemitism, both from our party and wider*
*<EV, AP, PRE, NMT, PS> society. And with your help I will* ***fight <EV, VP, CLA, MT, PS>*** *for that with every breath I possess.* (Corbyn 2018)

(35) *Labour government will reverse the privatisation of our NHS and return our health service into expert public control. That's something worth <EV, AP, PRE, NMT, PS>* ***fighting for <EV, VP, CLA, MT, PS>***. (Starmer 2019)

Relying on these conventional metaphors as evaluative strategies contributes to reinforcing the positive representation of the ingroup and to persuading the audience that a different Britain is possible. Although BUILDING and WAR metaphors were also found in the Conservative sample, their ideological potential has been exploited by the Labour party in a different way. Rather than building a brighter future or representing the outgroup in negative terms, Labour emphasises the transformative nature of their actions and their heroic role in this transformation.

Classifying metaphoric expressions conveying negative evaluation are less numerous. In this case, it is worth noting how the use of the WEAPONS and MOVEMENT source domains gives rise to metaphoric expressions characterising the Tories′ actions in a negative way, as shown by examples 36 and 37, and the creative use of metaphor scenarios (Musolff 2016).

(36) *Election after election, Tories* ***weaponise <EV, VP, CLA, MT, NG>*** *immigration, they* ***weaponise <EV, VP, CLA, MT, NG>*** anti-foreigner sentiment. (Abbot 2019)

(37) *But this Conservative Government has* ***pushed*** *our NHS* ***into*** *crisis <EV, VP, CLA, MT, NG>, with more people waiting longer in A&E and to see a GP and over four million people on hospital waiting lists.* (Corbyn 2018)

(38) *(…) 20 years since a Labour government started the Devolution Revolution which the Tories are trying to ignore as they* ***hurtle towards <EV, VP, CLA, NMT, NG>*** *a false <EV, AP, PRE, NMT, NG> choice between the 'Chequers Deal' and 'No Deal'.* (Thornberry 2018)

Example 39 below shows how the negative evaluation of the Tory party is conveyed in a subtler way relying on negative entailments triggered by the creative exploitation of the restaurant scenario. In particular, the food expression *a side order of chlorinated chicken* is metaphorically mapped onto the political domain to present the choice of Liam Fox, Secretary of State for International Trade at that time, as dangerous and illegal. This negative evaluation is activated by the expression *chlorinated chicken*, given that the practice of washing chicken with chlorine has been banned in the UK (also in Europe) since 1997[3].

(39) *Liam Fox is itching to scrap workers' rights and privatise the NHS* ***with a side order of chlorinated chicken*** **<EV, NP, CLA, MT, NG>**. (Corbyn 2018)

Finally, attitudinal resources are by far the least frequent (n= 1) and express the politician´s attitude regarding how he would like his party members to act in the future. This can be seen in the use of the adverb *hopefully* in example 40.

(40) *In the next Labour government, our very own Jon Ashworth, as Health Secretary, and Sarah Jones, as Housing Minister, will be carrying forward the struggle <EV, NP, CLA, MT, PS> to protect and extend democratic <EV, AP, CLA, NMT, PS> rights.* ***Hopefully, <EV, ADV, ATT, NMT, PS>*** *without becoming martyrs <EV, NP, CLA, MT, NG> in the process.* (Corbyn 2018)

## 5 Conclusions

This chapter has examined the way evaluation is expressed by Conservative and Labour politicians in two samples of political speeches delivered between 2016 and 2019. The mixed methods approach used in the study has revealed that Conservative politicians make a higher use of evaluative stance markers. Regardless of the frequency of use, more similarities than differences have been found in the categories of evaluative markers and in the ideological functions that evaluation serves.

---

3 See Schraer and Edgington (2019). Chlorinated chicken. How safe is it?. BBC News, 5th March 2019. <https://www.bbc.com/news/uk-47440562>. Last accessed 2nd April 2020.

In terms of categories, the most frequent one is predicational evaluation, which, in the two samples, was conveyed by means of adjectives, often used in comparative or superlative forms. The use of predicational expressions was employed by the politicians to legitimise their own actions and delegitimise those of others. Likewise, classifying expressions were also used with a (de)legitimising function. These markers included a wider array of lexical choices, ranging from nouns and verbs with inscribed positive or negative evaluation to metaphoric expressions. Interestingly, in both samples, creative uses of metaphor tended to be associated with negative evaluation, as was the case of the representation of Corbyn as a zombie in the Conservative sample, or the reference to the restaurant scenario when describing Liam Fox's actions in the Labour one. By contrast, conventional metaphors, such as those related to the BUILDING, WAR or MOVEMENT source domains were used to convey both positive and negative evaluation. More differences, however, were found in the use of nouns, where the name of the political party was more frequently used than any other classifying lexical choice by Conservative politicians, hence allowing the inferential association of political parties – and related beliefs – to positive or negative values. This was found to be consistent with a backgrounding of the other´s identity by means of reification and abstraction strategies in the Conservative sample, as opposed to the use of individualisation and collectivisation strategies to make the other´s identity explicit in the Labour set. In any case, the use of party names to activate negative evaluation has shown that evaluation is not only inscribed, but it can also be contextually evoked, particularly when building the self and the other´s intersubjective political identity. It shall be finally noted that the lack of attitudinal expressions can be explained if we take into account that PD is characterised as persuasive discourse ultimately aiming at developing a collective consciousness based on the representation of the party's members and values rather than expressing the politicians' individual comments on whole propositions.

Overall, in the two sets, evaluation was subordinate to the ideological square underlying PD, thus contributing to the positive self-representation and negative other-representation. It can be thus argued that in PD evaluative stance resources serve a persuasive goal in the sense that they function strategically to strengthen ingroup solidarity and to persuade the audience to believe that a given party is the best political option. In this way, evaluative stance also becomes the means to promote and legitimise the party´s ideology.

## References

Aloy Mayo, M. and Taboada, M. (2017). 'Evaluation in Political Discourse Addressed to Women: Appraisal Analysis of *Cosmopolitan's* Online Coverage of the 2014 US Midterm Elections'. *Discourse, Context & Media* 18, 40–48.

Becker, A. (2009). 'Modality & ENGAGEMENT in British and German in TV Interviews'. *Languages in Contrast* 9 (1), 5–22.

Bednarek, M. and Caple, H. (2014). 'Why do News Values Matter? Towards a New Methodological Framework for Analysing News Discourse in Critical Discourse Analysis and Beyond'. *Discourse & Society* 25(2), 135–158.

Berracheche, A. (2020). 'Appraisal and Party Positioning in Parliamentary Debates: A Usage-Based Critical Discourse Analysis'. *International Journal of English Linguistics* 10(6), 322–334.

Berlin, Lawrence N. (ed) (2017). *Positioning and Stance in Political Discourse: The Individual, the Party, and the Party Line.* Delaware: Bernon Press.

Biber, D. and Finegan, E. (1989). 'Styles of Stance in English: Lexical and Grammatical Marking of Evidentiality and Affect', *Text* 9 (1), 93–124.

Biber, D., Johansson, S., Leech, G., Conrad, S., and Finegan, E. (1999). *Longman Grammar of Spoken and Written English.* Harlow, Essex: Pearson Education.

Bloor, M., and Bloor, T. (2007). *The Practice of Critical Discourse Analysis. An Introduction* London: Routledge.

Cabrejas-Peñuelas, A. B. and Díez-Prados, M. (2014). 'Positive Self-evaluation versus Negative Other-evaluation in the Political genre of Preelection Debates', *Discourse & Society* 25 (2), 159–185.

Cap, P. (2010). 'Axiological Aspects of Proximization', *Journal of Pragmatics* 42(2), 392–407.

Cap, P. (2013). *Proximization. The Pragmatics of Symbolic Distance Crossing.* Amsterdam: John Benjamins.

Charteris-Black, J. (2005). *Politicians and Rhetoric: The Persuasive Power of Metaphor.* Basingtoke: Palgrave.

Charteris-Black, J. (2019). *Metaphors of Brexit: No Cherries on the Cake?* Basingtoke: Palgrave.

Chilton, P. and Schäffner, C. (1997). 'Discourse and Politics'. In T. A. van Dijk (ed.), *Discourse as Social Interaction,* Vol. 2, pp. 206–230. London: SAGE.

Chilton, P. (2004). *Analysing Political Discourse: Theory and Practice.* London: Routledge.

Coffin, C. and O'Halloran, K. (2005). 'Finding the Global Groove: Theorising and Analysing Dynamic Reader Positioning Using Appraisal, Corpus, and a Concordancer', *Critical Discourse Studies* 2 (2), 143–163.

Deignan, A. (2010). 'The Evaluative Properties of Metaphor'. In G. Low, Z. Todd, A. Deignan and L. Cameron (eds.), *Researching and Applying Metaphor in the Real World*, pp. 357–374. Amsterdam: John Benjamins.

Díez-Prados, M. and Cabrejas-Peñuelas, A.B. (2018). 'Evaluation of "Status" as a Persuasive Tool in Spanish and American Pre-electoral Debates in Times of Crisis', *Atlantis* 40 (2), 160–195.

Du Bois, J. W. (2007). 'The Stance Triangle'. In R. Englebretson (ed.), *Stancetaking in Discourse. Subjectivity, Evaluation, Interaction*, pp. 139–182. Amsterdam: John Benjamins.

Elder, C. (2020). 'Trump vs Clinton: Implicatures as Public Stance Acts'. In L.N. Berlin (ed.) *Positioning and Stance in Political Discourse. The Individual, the Party, and the Party Line*, pp. 71–91. Delaware, US: Vernon Press.

Englebretson, R. (2007a). 'Stancetaking in Discourse. An Introduction'. In R. Englebretson (ed.) *Stancetaking in Discourse. Subjectivity, Evaluation, Interaction*, pp. 1–25. Amsterdam: John Benjamins, 2007.

Englebretson, R. (ed) (2007b). *Stancetaking in Discourse. Subjectivity, Evaluation, Interaction.* Amsterdam: John Benjamins.

Filardo-Llamas, L. and Boyd, M. (2018). 'Critical Discourse Analysis and Politics'. In J. Flowerdew and J. Richardson (eds.), *The Routledge Handbook of Critical Discourse Studies,* pp. 312–327. London: Routledge.

Filardo-Llamas, L., and Morales-López, E. (2021). 'Introduction'. In L. Filardo-Llamas, E. Morales-López, and A. Floyd (eds.), *Discursive Approaches to Socio-political Polarization and Conflict*. London: Routledge, Conflcit, pp. 1–22.

Harris, S. (1991). 'Evasive Action: How Politicians Respond to Questions in Political Interviews'. In P. Scannell (ed.), *Broadcast Talk*, pp. 76–99. London: Sage.

Hart, C. (2008). 'Critical Discourse Analysis and Metaphor: Toward a Theoretical Framework', *Critical Discourse Studies* 5(2), 91–106.

Hart, C. (2014a). *Discourse, Grammar and Ideology: Functional and Cognitive Perspectives.* London: Bloomsbury.

Hart, C. (2014b). 'Construal Operations in Online Press Reports of Political Protests'. In C. Hart and P. Cap (eds.), *Contemporary Critical Discourse Studies,* pp. 167–188. London: Bloomsbury.

Hart, C. (2018). 'Cognitive Linguistic Critical Discourse Studies'. In J. Flowerdew and J. Richardson (eds.), *The Routledge Handbook of Critical Discourse Studies,* pp. 77–91. London: Routledge.

Hidalgo-Downing, L and Pérez-Sobrino, P. (2022). "Developing an Annotation Protocol for Evaluative Stance and Metaphor in Discourse: Theoretical and Methodological Considerations". Text and Talk. Advanced online publication.

Hidalgo-Downing, L, Pérez- Sobrino, P., Filardo-Llamas, L., Maíz- Arévalo, C., Núñez-Perucha, B., Sánchez-Moya, A., Williams Camus, J.T. (forthcoming).

"A protocol for the Annotation of Evaluative Stance and Metaphor across Four Discourse Genres". *Revista Española de Lingüística Aplicada.*

Hidalgo-Downing, L. and Pérez-Sobrino, P. (this volume). "Pushing Britain off the precipice': A CDA approach to negative evaluative stance in opinion articles on Brexit'. In J. Marín Arrese, L. Hidalgo-Downing and J.R. Zamorano (eds.), *Stance, Inter/Subjectivity and Identity in Discourse*. Frankfurt: Peter Lang.

Kiesling, S, F. (2009). 'Style as Stance: Stance as the Explanation for Patterns of Sociolinguistic Variation'. In Jaffe, A. (ed.), *Stance: Sociolinguistic Perspectives,* pp. 171–194. Oxford: Blackwell.

Marín-Arrese, J. (2011). 'Effective vs. Epistemic Stance and Subjectivity in Political Discourse: Legitimising Strategies and Mystification of Responsibility.' In C. Hart (ed.), *Critical Discourse Studies in Context and Cognition,* pp. 193–224. Amsterdam: Benjamins.

Marín-Arrese, J. (2015). 'Epistemic Legitimisation and Inter/Subjectivity in the Discourse of Parliamentary and Public Inquiries: A Contrastive Case Study', *Critical Discourse Studies* 12(3), 261–278.

Marín-Arrese, J., and Hidalgo-Downing, L. (2019) 'Stancetaking in Discourses: Epistemicity, Effectivity, Evaluation', paper presented at the *43rd AEDEAN Conference* held at the University of Alicante. November 13.

Martin, J.R. and P.R.R. White (2005). *The Language of Evaluation: Appraisal in English* Palgrave: New York.

Musolff, A. (2016). *Political Metaphor Analysis. Discourse and Scenarios.* London: Bloomsbury.

Núñez-Perucha, B. (2011). 'Critical Discourse Analysis and Cognitive Linguistics as Tools for Ideological Research: A Diachronic Analysis of Feminism'. In C. Hart (ed.), *Critical Discourse Studies in Context and Cognition,* pp. 193–224. Amsterdam: Benjamins.

Opstaele, S. (2008). *Hillary Clinton vs. Barack Obama. A Linguistic Study of Appraisal in Political Speeches.* Masters Dissertation, University of Ghent.

Simon-Vanderbengen, A. (1996). 'Image-building through Modality: The Case of Political Interviews', *Discourse & Society* 7, 389–415.

Thompson, G. and Hunston, S. (2000), 'Introduction'. In S. Hunston and G. Thompson (eds.), *Evaluation in Text: Authorial Stance and the Construction of Discourse*, pp. 1–27. Oxford: Oxford University Press.

Van Leeuwen, T. (1996). 'The Representation of Social Actors'. In C. R. Caldas-Coulthard and M. Coulthard (eds.), T*ext and Practices. Readings in Critical Discourse Analysis*, pp. 32–70. London and New York: Routledge.

Wodak, R. (2001). 'The Discourse Historical Approach'. In R. Wodak and M. Meyer (eds.), *Methods of Critical Discourse Analysis,* pp. 63–94. London: SAGE.

Alfonso Sánchez-Moya & Carmen Maíz-Arévalo

# "Histrionic, Appalling, a Major Turkey": The Expression of Evaluative Stance in the Discourse of Online Forums

**Abstract:** Digital communication is characterised by the possibility of user anonymisation, a de-centralised dialogicity among participants and the lack to perceive any type of censorship when sharing personal opinions and judgments (Janssen & Kies 2005; Morrow 2006; Boyd & Ellison 2007), features that have an impact on how evaluative stance is transmitted. Previous research has examined the multiple possibilities through which Internet users engage in the expression of digital stance (e.g. Page 2012; Drasovean and Tagg 2015). This paper sets out to analyse evaluative stance in online discourse based on the model designed by Hidalgo-Downing et al. (2020). To this end, we analysed a 100,000-word dataset of publicly-available forum posts dealing with a plethora of social issues. In line with related research (Cooper et al. 2019; Jaki et al. 2019; Maíz-Arévalo et al. 2019), the expression of stance in the online forum threads under scrutiny is predominantly instantiated through negative evaluation.

**Keywords:** *evaluation, forums, metaphor, stance, online discourse.*

## 1 Introduction

The discourse of online forums is generally characterised by an organic nature in its communicative unfolding. This is partly influenced by the affordances of the medium itself. A key feature of communication in online forums is the possibility users have to quote (entirely or partially) the information provided by users engaged in digital discussion. Although communicative turns cascade in an asynchronous fashion, online conversation in this sort of setting becomes very dynamic, and the discussion evolves in ways that are sometimes unrelated to the original purpose of a given thread. Similarly, the evaluative scope of these conversations also becomes blurry, which turns the process of tracing discursive evaluation into a very slippery endeavour.

The aim of this chapter is to explore the discursive mechanisms in which evaluative stance is instantiated in online forums. The two main research questions guiding this study can be worded as follows:

(RQ1) What is the distribution of the categories of evaluative stance in the corpus of online forums?

(RQ2) How is the genre of online forums characterised in terms of choices in evaluative stance?

Based on previous studies that examine the nature of evaluative stance in online forums (Jaki et al. 2019; Lorenzo-Dus & Nouri 2020; Prażmo 2020), it was hypothesised that negative value would prevail in this communicative context. It was harder to establish expectations around the type of lexical expressions used to convey evaluative stance, as well as the degree of metaphoricity found therein.

In the attempt to answer the questions above, a corpus of 28 complete forum threads was collected, which amounts to a total of 103,749 words (see Section 3). Forum posts were collected across a wide range of British sites (co.uk) which had been posted between 2006 and 2019. In the attempt to provide a broader analysis on how evaluative mechanisms are discursively transmitted in the digital environment that online forums embody, topics of discussion span from sports and entertainment to socio-political issues. Online posts under analysis had to comply with certain ethical requirements. Thus, data under scrutiny was publicly-available, not password protected, and fully anonymised.

This chapter is structured as follows. Once the introductory details have been put forward, section 2 provides the main theoretical anchorage this research relies on. It deals with the communicative and discursive nature of online forums, especially those pertaining to the expression of evaluative stance. Attention is also paid to previous research investigating the discursive mechanisms used to convey stance in online contexts. Section 3 offers a description of the corpus under scrutiny and key methodological issues we took into account. Section 4 presents findings from a mixed-methods perspective, dwelling on the mechanisms used to convey evaluative stance in this corpus of online discourse. Section 5 wraps the study up by offering general conclusions as well as limitations and pointers for future research.

## 2 Literature Review

Online forums constitute a very interesting arena for social interaction and communicative purposes. Apart from retaining the multiple advantages of online communication, these spaces are still of use for those who see them as one of the few remaining environments that allow for anonymous interaction (Li & Bernoff 2011; Pendry & Salvatore 2015).

In many cases, online forums become safe spaces in which sympathy and support are almost instantly found. This is particularly relevant when online users seek to find privacy and anonymity around issues that still carry social stigma (Pendry & Salvatore 2015), and, in many cases, social devaluation

(Crocker et al. 1998). This is one of the reasons why many studies have explored the role that online forums have when sharing socially sensitive issues such as infertility (Lee 2017), partner violence (Sánchez-Moya 2019; Nacey 2020), eating disorders (Figueras-Bates 2015) or other health problems (Landqvist 2016).

However, recent research is calling attention to the effects that this environment has to foster the expression of opinions and beliefs in very straightforward ways, no matter how radical these might be (Prażmo 2020). The linguistic radicalisation found in many of these online forums proves conducive to behavioural radicalisation, which can lead to societal disruptions in offline realms (Baumgarten 2017; Lorenzo-Dus & Nouri 2020).

Communicatively speaking, online forums are spaces for the public exchange of computer-mediated communication in an asynchronous way (Marcoccia 2003). In most cases, and despite different visual features, they show a standardised architecture and offer a somewhat simple but effective set of tools to engage in communicative exchanges online. As pinpointed by Androutsopoulos (2006), web forums are organised in threads that group together around a specific topic. Forum threads vary in length and might become more or less active over time depending on the topic they address. The liveliness of a forum thread is usually marked by the frequency of the interaction that individual users provide, becoming an interesting arena for interpersonal exchange among users (Androutsopoulos 2006). Nonetheless, this also poses problems when accounting for the internal coherence of a forum thread (or even a forum post in itself).

In fact, when thinking of a forum post and its internal composition from a more micro-discursive perspective, it is certainly useful to refer to what has been identified as conversational fragmentation (Marcoccia 2003; Androutsopoulos 2006), which very accurately illustrates how conversation unfolds in online forums. In other words, as Herring (2001) argues, it is not possible to equate forum threads to conversational turns, since one post may include two or more "conversational" moves that refer to different points in previous posts. Thus, forum threads offer a plethora of simultaneous (albeit asynchronous) multiple communicative exchanges enacted by many online users. Despite the communicative richness of these online polylogues, this fragmentation is one of the most salient challenges that discourse analysts face when attempting to analyse forum posts in a thread.

## 2.1 Research on Evaluative Stance in Online Discourse

Topic fragmentation in online exchanges becomes particularly challenging when seeking to provide a systematic account of evaluative stance in discourse.

The annotation of stance in forum discourse is specially daunting due to the complexity to identify the stance focus (based on Du Bois's (2007) "stance object")[1], since some comments contain more than one utterance or action with different stance foci (Kiesling et al. 2018). This basically assumes that stance may shift throughout the same post giving rise to complex, sometimes contradictory, expressions of stance. Interestingly, Kiesling et al. (2018) proposed a very useful technique to be able to provide a more accurate tracing of evaluative stance in this context, which relies on a (re)segmentation process of the original online posts and inter-coder reliability. This model offers great potential to provide a more precise recollection of stance in online contexts, although it does not delve into a more detailed linguistic approximation to evaluative stance.

Despite the challenges this may pose, discourse analysts have come up with taxonomies to scrutinise evaluative stance in online settings. For the purposes of this study, we have concentrated on research that also takes discursive value (namely positive or negative) into account. Research on the expression of positive evaluation in online forums is usually related to the exploration of narratives focusing on the positive impact that any social issue may have on forum users. Topics vary to a great extent, ranging from the positive effects of video games on players' lives (Bourgonjon et al. 2016) or the positive correlations between students' participation in online discussion forums and a better academic achievement (Alzahrani 2017). Although previous research has also studied the discursive realisation of positive speech acts, such as compliments on Facebook (Maíz-Arévalo & García-Gómez 2013; Placencia & Lower 2013) or Instagram (Matley 2018), it is not easy to spot studies where language-driven explorations of positive evaluation are undertaken.

Conversely, and quite possibly due to the more worrying implications for societal radicalisation fuelled in many online forums, studies that offer a detailed analysis of how negative evaluation is discursively enacted in social media in general (Cooper et al. 2019) and online forums in particular (Jaki et al. 2019; Lorenzo-Dus & Nouri 2020; Prażmo 2020) are frequent.

An interesting (and very proximate to this study) example of how negative evaluation is expressed in online forums is offered by Baumgarten (2017) in her analysis of a right-wing extremist online forums. Broadly speaking, she employs

---

1 Based on the definition put forward by Du Bois (2007), our approach to evaluative stance (Hidalgo Downing et al. 2020) entails that authors must express an attitude towards or belief about a topic, a social actor or event and, further, show agreement, adherence or support (this is, alignment) or distance and/or disagreement (disalignment).

the framework of Appraisal Theory (Martin & White 2005) to investigate post authors' alignment and disalignment with a very complex array of third parties that are targeted in the posts under scrutiny. More specifically, Baumgarten's study focuses on the expression of affect and emotivity (Attitude) which allows for identifying evaluation towards something or someone by looking at how different types of positive and negative feelings are articulated. As suggested by her results, disalignment towards third parties in this online forum mostly relies on negative judgement and negative appreciation. Furthermore, evaluation is seen to emphasise flaws and faulty behaviour in groups of social actors (with Muslims and Jews as the main two outgroups that are negatively characterised), institutions and organisations (such as the EU). As suggested by this and related research (Cohen et al. 2014; Prażmo 2020), this negativity has been reported to have an impact on offline settings by perpetuating and amplifying discrimination and denigration towards the otherness, which at the same time fuels socio-political polarisation.

In this chapter, we apply the annotation scheme developed by Hidalgo-Downing et al. (2020), which consists of a fine-grained, four-dimensional approach to analyse evaluative stance in discourse, as detailed in the next section. This approach relies on lexical evaluative expressions to start with (which can be classifying, predicational or attitude). It then moves to identifying evaluative metaphor (expressions that are based on cognitive mappings) and eventually categorises the value of the evaluative proposition (positive or negative).

## 2.2 Identifying Evaluative Stance in Online Discourse: an Analytical Proposal

One of the first layers in the analytical scheme developed by Hidalgo-Downing et al. (2020) focuses on evaluative expressions on the basis of their lexical realisation. In this proposal, a major distinction is established between classifying and predicational evaluation. Classifying evaluation consists in using lexical expressions (typically nouns and verbs) to classify entities or events according to social systems of beliefs. This classification can be positive or negative. Examples (1) and (2) from two forums on housing and economics respectively illustrate positive and negative classifying evaluation:

(1) *UK looks like* ***a renters paradise*** <EV, NP, CLA, MT, PS> *though i.e. you can rent* ***very high-end*** <EV, AP, PRE, NMT, PS> *property for* ***relative peanuts*** <EV, NP, CLA, MT, PS>. [ENGF-24]

(2) *This will be* ***a total disaster*** <EV, NP, CLA, NMT, NG> *for small business in the US and for the US economy in general.* [ENGF-10]

On the other hand, predicational evaluation qualifies entities or events according to social systems of belief, prototypically by means of adjective phrases, as in the following example where one user expresses their opinion on musicals. As example (4) shows, predicational evaluation can also be negative or positive, as in the following case where a user positively evaluates the ring her husband has bought for her.

(3) *Musicals based on* ***great*** <EV, AP, PRE, NMT, PS> *novels or plays are* ***pretentious*** <EV, AP, PRE, NMT, NG>*but that doesn't mean they are* ***worthless*** <EV, AP, PRE, NMT, NG>; *it depends on the music.* [ENGF-12]

(4) *As anticipated my hubby to be managed (sic) to find a* ***stunning*** <EV, AP, PRE, NMT, PS> *ring pretty easily* [ENGF-20]

Besides classifying and predicational evaluation, there is a third major category in this scheme: attitude. Attitude differs from the previous two kinds of evaluation in that the lexical evaluative expressions are used to express an opinion about a whole proposition instead of a phrase, as in the classifying and predicational functions. This function is typically performed by sentential adverbs, as illustrated by example (5), where the user negatively evaluates the proposition by means of the adverb "sadly" or by example (6), where the evaluation, inserted mid-sentence rather than at its very beginning, is positive:

(5) ***Sadly*** <EV, ADVP, ATT, NMT, NG>, *I'm pretty sure it's not only Hampshire. At least we have pretty good access to GPS.* [ENGF-04]

(6) [...] *a gothic church is featured and it is set in France and,* ***amazingly*** <EV, ADVP, ATT, NMT, PS>, *it has a Hunchback connection as the priest in it is Cedric Hardwicke* [...]. [ENGF-28]

Another level of annotation in our model (Hidalgo-Downing et al. 2020) focused on the identification of evaluative metaphor. Evaluative expressions were deemed metaphorical when they consisted of a mapping between a source domain with a positive or negative value mapped onto a target domain. Additionally, there were cases in which the value was context dependent. Thus, not all metaphors were tagged as evaluative, especially those that were part of stock phrases such as "gutted Northumbrian" or "white nationalism". Nevertheless, interesting cases of metaphorical fossilisation are also included in this section to observe their potential for the expression of evaluation. The following examples seek to shed light on the different types of conventionalised metaphors and their evaluative load. In example (7), we see a case of an idiomatic expression that was not annotated for the purposes due to the lack of evaluation it entails. Examples (8) and (9), however, illustrate cases in which conventional metaphors were deemed to add evaluative stance, both in negative and positive terms respectively.

(7) *First things first Obama winning is not done and dusted. Ever heard of the Bradley effect? If not look it up.* [ENGF-10]
(8) *It is all over, I caanot [sic] see the bradely effect being so large* ***to knock him out*** <EV, VP, CLA, MT, NG> *of the white house* [ENGF-10]
(9) *Has he shown* ***a cool head*** <EV, NP, CLA, MT, PS> *under pressure and* ***good*** <EV, AP, PRE, NMT, PS> *judgement? Or has he been* ***erratic*** <EV, AP, PRE, NMT, NG> *and* ***irresponsible*** <EV, AP, PRE, NMT, NG>? [ENGF-10]

The final layer in our proposed framework to trace evaluation in discourse deals with the identification of value (positive or negative). It should be noted that "positive and negative evaluation is performed by a speaker/writer towards an object/entity/event mentioned or evoked in the discourse [and] not the evaluation the analyst assigns to that object/entity/event" (Hidalgo-Downing et al. 2020: 8). Terms with inscribed (explicit) evaluation, such as "good", "bad", "right", "wrong", or "problem" were also tagged accordingly.

## 3 Methodology

### 3.1 Corpus Collection

As already mentioned in the Introduction, both researchers collected a corpus consisting of the posts to 28 complete forum threads initiated by a myriad of different users and topics. The total number of words for this ad hoc corpus was 103,749, which means that the average word count per thread was around 3,705 words. The corpus collection lasted for 3 months (in 2019), and threads were collected randomly. The following three criteria were considered in order to guarantee a degree of uniformity in the entire corpus.

First, all the forums had to include the extension co.uk in their web address to ensure they belonged to the British Isles, even if it is virtually impossible to ensure that all the users are employing the UK variety of English. Still, it was deemed this could add an overall sense of internal validity to the collected corpus. Likewise, and especially due to the fact that evaluative expressions are in many cases influenced by cultural aspects, it was believed that collecting forum threads from co.uk domains would also pave the way for a more homogenous understanding of evaluation as specifically conveyed in this context.

Secondly, all the forums had to be publicly accessible and available. This allowed us to comply with the ethical considerations put forward by authors such as Mann & Stewart (2000) and Kozinets (2010: 143), who argues that there is no risk of vulnerability provided the analysts research "activities typical of normal daily behaviour and where the research does not involve the collection of identity in association with response data".

Third, the corpus needed to include as many different topics as possible, to ensure a varied sample where evaluation strategies could be studied independently of the topic under discussion. Thus, the data collected include very different topics like leisure activities (e.g. music, films, book clubs, etc.), politics (e.g. Obama's election), social issues (e.g. gay marriage, climate change), sports, business, education, etc. The threads also belong to different forums altogether, so as to prevent the particular style of one specific forum (e.g. Reddit) from somehow biasing the results. In addition, it is important to mention that the threads belong to different time periods, more specifically from 2006 to 2019. We thought that this might include an interesting time variable, also allowing for a diachronic analysis of evaluative strategies in future studies. Likewise, all the quoted examples have been reproduced in their original form, without modifying them in any sense.

## 3.2 Corpus Annotation

We annotated the corpus by using tags reflecting the multi-layered nature of our scheme. Thus, we marked <EV> to signal evaluative stance. When identifying evaluative stance by PoS and function, we used <NP>, <AP>, <ADVP>, <VP> and <CLA>, <PRE> or <ATT> accordingly. <MT> or <NMT> were used to mark the presence or lack of evaluative metaphor and <PS> or <NG> were used to indicate the third level of our scheme and the positive or the negative value of the evaluative expression. In the process of tagging and identifying evaluative stance in the discourse of online forums, we faced several remarkable challenges (similarly adverted by Kiesling et al., 2018). The main one was related to delimiting the scope of evaluative expressions, which was frequently blurry due to the organic nature of online discourse. This can be illustrated in examples (10) and (11) below[2], taken from a forum thread that encouraged forum users to share their views on Obama becoming the President of the United States.

(10) Original post in thread (#1)
*In 72 hours Senator Obama will be chosen as President of the United States. For me personally and Millions of others I feel a* ***new*** *<EV, AP, PRE, NMT, PS> era could be upon us, he seems to move away from the previous 40 years of* ***inward looking*** *<EV, AP, PRE, MT, NG> presidents that think everything starts and ends at the borders.*
*So what big differences will he make?*
*Peace in the middle east?*

2 Please note that both posts have been literally reproduced from the original thread, and no spelling corrections or typographic alterations have been modified.

*Brining Iran onside?*
*Iraq? Afganistan?*
*What will this mean to African Americans?*
*From what I have seen on the BBC, CNN and others, if the world was voting it would be a landslide for obama, they did a poll in France and 97% would have voted him in!!!*
*Your thoughts?*
*[NAME] [ENGF-10]*

(11) Reply to original thread (#35)
*Don't get how this is going to affect small businesses too much if the economy turns around much quicker and isn't it somewhat of a* ***farce*** *<EV, NP, CLA, NMT, NG>that business income is regarded as personal income in the USA anyway which presumably means that you can deduct mortgage interest and the like as a business expense. We can't do that over here. [ENGF-10]*

Interestingly, these two posts are part of an online exchange whose central communicative topic had a political drive (Senator Obama becoming President of the United States), with a greater focus on issues related to international relationships (Peace in the Middle East, Iran, Iraq) or race (African Americans). As the exchanges unfold, however, related topics begin to arise, opening up to different topics within the spectrum of economics (business, mortgage interest, etc). The organic character of this thematic flow within the same thread is inherently present in online forums, but becomes a challenge when trying to define the evaluative scope of each thread.

Similarly, another decision we had to take was related to annotating evaluative expressions that went beyond the main topic in the thread and focused on different social actors engaged in online discussion. "Meta evaluation", as we labelled these instances, was mainly identified when users assessed other users participating in the thread (or elsewhere in the forum site) or different traits of these users (from their nicknames to their writing styles). Example (12) below illustrates a clear case of this type of evaluation, which arguably embodies a very specific type of evaluation within this genre that is less salient in other contexts.

(12) *I took your statement as an opportunity to review your posts on Climate-debate. com, and* ***low*** <EV, AP, PRE, NMT, NG>*and behold (and I do mean* ***low*** <EV, AP, PRE, NMT, NG>*), guess what I found: that Saint arthur8 needs to look in the mirror to see just how* ***thin*** <EV, AP, PRE, NMT, NG> ***her saintly veneer*** <EV, NP, CLA, MT, NG> *really is.* ***Your pomposity*** <EV, NP, CLA, NMT, NG> *becomes quite clear when one reads your* ***persistent*** <EV, AP, PRE, NMT, NG>*use of phrases like "someone who is an* ***alarmist*** <EV, AP, PRE, NMT, NG> ***troll*** <EV, NP, CLA, NMT, NG>*", "put them on the unemployment heap", "climate nuts", and "****alarmist*** <EV, AP, PRE, NMT, NG>*views", when describing others* [...]. [ENGF-13]

As the example above shows, an online user is providing a fine-grained evaluative description of another user's posts (and the type of comments therein) on a website that fosters online discussion around climate change. Even if the initial thread does address an environmentally-related topic, the conversation ends up in a rather off-topic fashion. It was instances like the ones above that posed a methodological challenge (since they basically evaluate different events or social actors than those specific in the thread title). These cases of evaluation were finally annotated on the assumption that these exchanges represented the naturally-occurring type of online exchanges under analysis.

# 4 Results and Discussion

## 4.1 Lexical Evaluative Expressions: Classifying, Predicational and Attitude

Results reveal that evaluative stance in online forums is predominantly conveyed through predicational markers in 67 % of the instances (N=1386), which suggests a higher focus on properties, features or attributes of the entity under evaluation. To a lesser extent, a quarter of evaluative stance in the analysed sample is achieved by means of classifying markers (25 %). Thus, predicational and classifying evaluation amount to more than 92 % of the cases, the remaining being tokens of attitude (8 %). This might be due to the more salient use of adjective phrases and noun phrases than adverb phrases in general terms. This is illustrated in Figure 1 below.

Examples below seek to illustrate textual evidence of the three main types of lexical evaluative expressions in this annotation scheme. Both examples (13) and (14) include prototypical cases of classifying strategies. Thus, items such as "prejudice" and "problem" are identified as evaluative noun phrases with a classifying function. At the same time, these terms have inscribed (explicit) negative evaluation, showing in this case a negative alignment from the user with the topic under discussion (gay marriage). Likewise, examples (13) and (14) also illustrate clear cases of evaluation instantiated through predicational strategies. Adjectives such as "unfortunate" or "wrong" are straightforward realisations of predicational strategies. In some cases, as exemplified by "I don't believe it's acceptable", the value of predicational function can only be ascertained by means of the context.

(13) *The **prejudice*** <EV, NP, CLA, NMT, NG> *that exists is indeed a **most unfortunate*** <EV, AP, PRE, NMT, NG> *thing. Nevertheless, there is still a substantial gay community existing within the Christian community* [ENGF-01]

(14) *I don't have* ***a problem*** <EV, NP, CLA, NMT, NG> *with churches being forced to perform gay weddings. It is* ***wrong*** <EV, AP, PRE, NMT, NG> *for them to discriminate between heterosexual and homosexual couples. I don't believe it's* ***acceptable*** <EV, AP, PRE, NMT, NG>*to force anyone to do anything.* [ENGF-01]

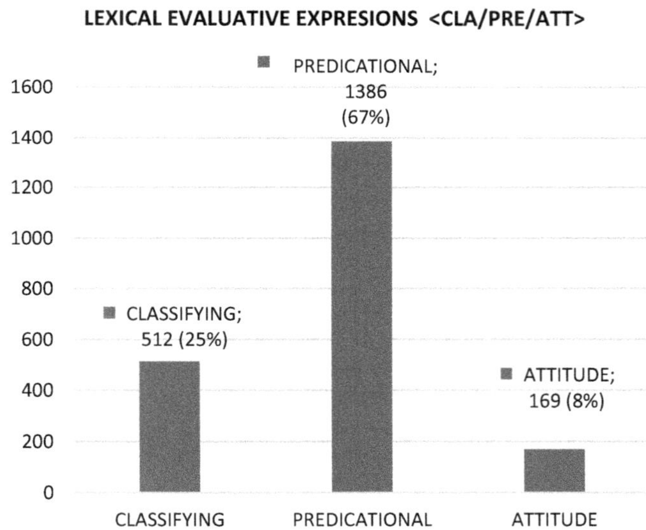


**Figure 1.** Distribution of evaluative expressions in online forums (N and %)

As Figure 1 above suggests, we found a total of 8 % of instances (N=169) that employed attitudinal strategies. As pointed in Section 2 above, this is mostly accomplished through sentential adverbs (such as "sadly" or "amazingly") in which the adverb evaluates a given proposition. This becomes more interesting, however, if we take into consideration that the tag 'attitude' was also used for adjective phrases that form part of "an expression which provides a comment on the whole sentence/propositions" (Hidalgo-Downing et al. 2020: 5). This is usually realised by means of structures such as "it + verb to be + adjective + that…". Examples (15) and (16) below illustrate this type of attitudinal evaluation as manifested in the corpus.

(15) *It isn't* ***fair*** <EV, AP, ATT, NMT, NG> *that he has so much more than I do* [ENGF-14]

(16) *it is only* ***clear*** <EV, AP, ATT, NMT, PS> *that there are some Conservatives (doubtless along with some Liberal Democrats and some Labourites) who are* ***uncomfortable*** <EV, AP, PRE, NMT, NG> *with the issue of gay marriage.* [ENGF-01]

An interesting observation that would need further exploration was related to the levels of linguistic creativity present in these three possibilities when conveying lexical evaluation. Forum users have a wider range of lexical options available when expressing evaluation by means of predicational strategies, especially considering this is mostly instantiated through adjectival phrases or adverbs of manner (as in "clumsily collected votes"). Example (17) below illustrates a common trend to express predicational evaluation, which at the same time shows how an adjectival chain can be used to express evaluative stance. This example is also interesting to illustrate the importance of context when identifying evaluative stance in online forums. Thus, the adjective "religious" cannot be considered negative per se. Nonetheless, it was deemed negative in this case due to its communicative context (an online forum where academics meet to discuss climate change).

(17) *Is this just more of your* ***absurd*** <EV, AP, PRE, MT, NG>, ***WACKY*** <EV, AP, PRE, NMT, NG>, ***unfalsifiable*** <EV, AP, PRE, NMT, NG>, ***religious*** <EV, AP, PRE, NMT, NG> *dogma... or can you explain how you calculated the "rate of climate change" all throughout earth's history?* [ENGF-13]

(18) ***re-pubic-lick-uns*** <EV, NP, CLA, NMT, NG>, *listening to rich people, lower wages & make it hard for low & mid-class people to have health insurance. Rich "don'T rump" is the epitome of wage & health care low & mid-class "take away & give to the rich"* [ENGF-14]

Additionally, as example (18) demonstrates in sardonic and jocular ways, it was interesting to observe creative uses of evaluative classifiers. The possibility of engaging in freer, more creative uses of linguistic forms is rooted in the discursive and communicative features of online forums (see Section 2.1 above), and linguistic creativity (in this particular corpus more visible in classifying nouns) plays a great role in achieving evaluative effects. Examples of this sort posed challenges for our annotation scheme, especially at the lexical level. For instance, the term "re-pubic-lick-uns" employs the adjective "pubic" and the verb "lick" to criticise the republicans, making it complex to categorise lexically in the light of our annotation scheme. Despite the evaluative function that terms of this sort may evoke, the inability to annotate them following the annotation scheme we developed was the main reason to leave them out.

## 4.2 Evaluative Metaphor

Broadly speaking, the expression of evaluative stance in these online forums is done more frequently in non-metaphoric ways (74.62 %, N=778). However, evaluative metaphors account for 25.48 % of cases (N=266). Interestingly, these results mirror those we obtained in a preliminary study (Maíz-Arévalo et al. 2019) only based on 12,744 words of two online forum threads. In a similar vein, evaluative stance was achieved non-metaphorically (72 %) in that study, whereas evaluative metaphor was observed in 28 % of the total. Figure 2 below summarises the distribution of metaphorical / non-metaphorical evaluation as manifested in the corpus at hand.

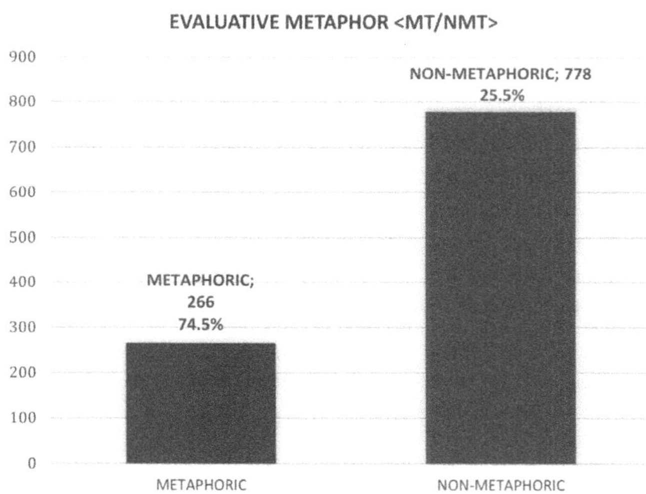


**Figure 2.** Distribution of evaluative metaphor in online forums (N and %)

Examples (19) and (20) below illustrate metaphorical evaluation. In (19), "stab" is used metaphorically to send a rather abstract message (or warning) to the police and their actions concerning street drinking in the UK (the main topic of the thread). Similarly, as can be seen in (20), the user employs three metaphors to describe the need for change in US politics triggered by Obama's election as president. In the first metaphor ("hit the ground running"), the user employs an idiomatic, conventional metaphor that emphasised the need for the recently elected president to proceed quickly and energetically. The second metaphor is also idiomatic and serves to personify the country as a fallen animated being that needs to regain its stand-up position ("get the usa back on its feet"). Finally, the third metaphor ("build bridges not blow em up"), albeit idiomatic, is arguably more creative as the user plays with the contrast between "building" and "blowing up bridges" -i.e. restoring good relationships rather than the opposite.

(19) ***One little stab*** <EV, NP, CLA, MT, NG> *at the police :I'm pretty sure it is an* ***offence*** <EV, NP, CLA, NMT, NG> *for kids to gather in crowds more than three on the streets and i think it is an* ***offence*** <EV, NP, CLA, NMT, NG> *to drink on the streets*

(20) *well its over I wish him good luck, I hope obama can bring some change to the usa ,lets face he can not make it much worse, the usa and the world to be honest need him* ***to hit the ground running*** <EV, VP, CLA, MT, PS> *and* ***get the usa back on its feet*** <EV, NP, CLA, MT, PS>, ***build bridges***<EV, VP, CLA, MT, PS> *not* ***blow em up*** <EV, VP, CLA, MT, NG>. [ENGF-10]

The use of metaphor (mostly nominal) is less frequent than expected, and both conventional and more creative metaphors are salient throughout the corpus. Although a more detailed account of this tendency would benefit from additional research, conventional metaphors seem to outnumber more creative ones. Users might be using these metaphorical expressions unaware of their metaphorical nature and driven by the evaluative function that these idiomatic expressions trigger. Besides example (20) above, another example of a creative elaboration of a conventional metaphor is (21), where the user rephrases creatively the idiomatic (and metaphoric) expression "a brain the size of a walnut" to refer to Ronald Reagan:

(21) ***Old*** <EV, AP, PRE, NMT, NG> ***walnut brain*** <EV, NP, CLA, MT, NG> *himself Ronald Regan whose claim to fame was playing a cowboy in* ***dreadful*** <EV, AP, PRE, NMT, NG> *B movies.* [ENGF-10]

However, some conventional metaphors can be contextually triggered, as illustrated in example (22) to refer to US conservative politician Sarah Palin, after a TV interview where she stated that "Africa was a country". In a very heated discussion in the forum, her detractors make use of numerous metaphors concerning shooting, as she is a notorious hunter. Thus, one of the users suggests that her not being elected was a bullet dodged by the world:

(22) *An* ***interesting*** <EV, AP, PRE, NMT, PS> *clip from Fox news about Palin -* ***really scary*** <EV, AP, PRE, NMT, NG> *stuff: Palin thought Africa was a country. I think the world* ***dodged a bullet*** <EV, VP, CLA, MT, NG> *on that one!* [ENGF-10]

## 4.3 Evaluative Value

Echoing results in similar research (Cohen et al. 2014; Baumgarten 2017; Prażmo 2020), the evaluative value of the forum threads under scrutiny is overwhelmingly negative. In fact, negative evaluation accounted for approximately 60 % of the cases (N=1184). Conversely, positive value was identified in 41 % of the cases (N=836). This result is also supported by the preliminary analysis we carried out (Maíz-Arévalo et al. 2019), where negative evaluation amounted to 66 % of the total. Figure 3 below illustrates the distribution of negative and positive evaluation present in the sample of online discourse we analysed.

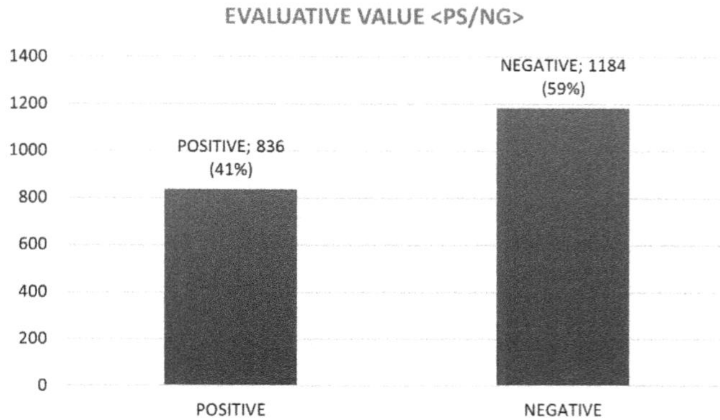


**Figure 3.** Distribution of evaluative value in online forums (N and %)

As discussed in section 2 above, the main reason for this tendency is surely connected to one of the main appeals that these online settings have: the possibility forum users have to vent their anger or complaints with the lack of inhibition fostered by anonymity. For example, in (23) the user piles up negative evaluations in a single comment when assessing Billy Wilder's production of The Private Life of Sherlock Holmes:

(23) *Firstly, I felt Wilder was* ***very disrespectful*** <EV, AP, PRE, NMT, NG> *in his interpretation of the Holmes and Watson characters. Holmes is played out as slightly effete and possibly gay? Watson is played again like other interpretations to be* ***buffoonish*** <EV, AP, PRE, NMT, NG>? *Even though I was never myself an expert or a huge fan, I thought the plot was* ***weak*** <EV, AP, PRE, NMT, NG> *for a Sherlock Holmes adventure* [ENGF-27]

Apart from the predicational strategies that display a negative tone ("disrespectful", "buffoonish", "weak"), this example also illustrates the challenges we found when annotating evaluative online discourse. Far from aligning with our own views, it could be argued that the terms "effete" and "gay" are employed here with negative connotations. It is precisely this representation what seems to support this post's author's assessment of this film production as "disrespectful". Another case of negative evaluation being piled up is example (24) below, where the user combines both predicational evaluation ("massive", "unusual", "silly", "childish", "sloganizing") and classifying one ("cloud cuckoo land") to negatively evaluate the political doings of the Bush administration:

(24) *What actually happens is that government gets bigger whilst taxes are cut to deliver on the promise. This leads to massive borrowing - which ends in tears about five years*

*later. It's also a very unusal [sic] economy that is able to cut taxes then go to war - it was* ***cloud cuckoo land*** <EV, NP, CLA, MT, NG>; ***silly*** <EV, AP, PRE, NMT, NG>, ***childish*** <EV, AP, PRE, NMT, NG>, ***sloganizing*** <EV, AP, PRE, NMT, NG> *stuff.* [ENGF-10]

Another interesting observation that would need more systematic analysis was that positive evaluation is achieved less creatively (in linguistic terms) than negative evaluation in online discourse. Although this observation would benefit from further insights, this tendency can be illustrated in the following examples. Excerpt (25) below shows part of the initial post in a thread whose main theme is asking forum participants to comment on adaptations from classic novels into musicals.

(25) *The trend of adapting classic novels into musicals / It started with Les Miserables and the popularity of that show has spawned musical adaptations of other classic novels [...]/ What do you think of the practice? Have you enjoyed any of the above musicals? Are there any novels which you think would make a* ***good*** <EV, AP, PRE, NMT, PS> *musical?* [ENGF-12]

Examples (26) and (27), extracted from this same thread, are worth contrasting. On the one hand, example (26) presents an overall positive description of novel-musical adaptation practices. As can be seen, this user opts for evaluative predicational resources (by means of adjectival phrases), using the same adjective twice ("powerful") within the same description. On the other hand, example (27) shows how another user shares his/her negative impression on several adaptations. Contrary to the previous case, lexical evaluation here is achieved through classifying ("a major turkey", "something of a sour note") and various predicational devices ("histrionic", "boring", "appalling"), which adds a more colourful, creative outlook to the overall expression of evaluation in this particular case.

(26) *Yeah, I wasn't talking about the film version, though. I actually saw it on Broadway four times. The very first time was a* ***powerful*** <EV, AP, PRE, NMT, PS> *experience, especially when you see the chandelier come crashing down. The music is so* ***gorgeous*** <EV, AP, PRE, NMT, PS> *and* ***powerful*** <EV, AP, PRE, NMT, PS>, *especially if you're listening to the original cast recording.* [ENGF-12]

(27) *The film version didn't have a* ***good*** <EV, AP, PRE, NMT, NG> *reception, only 33% on Rotten Tomatoes, with an average score of 5/10. "The music of the night" has hit something of a* ***sour*** <EV, AP, PRE, NMT, NG>*note. Critics are calling the screen adaptation of Andrew Lloyd Webber's popular musical* ***histrionic*** <EV, AP, PRE, NMT, NG>, ***boring*** <EV, AP, PRE, NMT, NG>, *and lacking in both romance and danger. I quiet like Abba, but the cast, plot and characters of the film version of Mama Mia was* ***appalling*** <EV, AP, PRE, NMT, NG>. *Moulin Rouge was also a*

***major turkey*** <EV, NP, CLA, NMT, NG>. *Modern film musicals just don't seem to work, unless they go all out for irony, like "The Producers".* [ENGF-12]

This tendency to find a broader range of linguistic creativity when users express negative evaluation is also found in seemingly more serious threads, such as those included in the online forum Climate-Debate.org. As example (28) below shows, one frequent way to mark a negative stance in more creative ways is precisely through metaphors that become integrated in rather ardent discussions about specific, scientific terminology.

(28) *It's not* ***a terminology war*** <EV, NP, CLA, MT, NG>. *You did not invent the term "ocean acidification." It is an intentionally* ***deceptive*** <EV, AP, PRE, NMT, NG> *term created by the* ***warmazombies*** <EV, NP, CLA, MT, NG> *for* ***fear-mongering*** <EV, NP, CLA, NMT, NG>. [ENGF-13]

In a similar vein, as example (29) below illustrates, it is also interesting to observe the salient role of metaphors when users discuss several topics related to the forum thread (from the accuracy of the posted content to issues of digital etiquette in the forum). In some cases, the activation of a type of metaphor to express indirect, subtle evaluation ("if you can find a public online climate debate site where everyone sips their tea with their pinkies out a perfect ninety degree [sic] angle") seems to trigger the use of metaphor that creates a mini-narrative of metaphor scenarios (Musolff, 2006). In this particular case, and quite likely due to the effect evoked by "sipping the tea with a perfect ninety-degree angle", the online forum itself becomes a mind feast, where everything on the table represents the multiple types of arguments, voices and opinions with which you can stuff your face in this online space.

(29) *Perhaps you should look at everyone (including me) on this site and realize that this is not the National Science Foundation or NASA. It's a public debate sight where anyone from 2 to 102 years old can join in. Granted, I too wish that we all came here with the same attitudes and education levels, but we don't. So there's gonna be a lot of disagreement and "I'm right - you're wrong" going on and, you know what, it doesn't matter who's* ***right*** <EV, AP, PRE, NMT, PS> *or who's* ***wrong*** <EV, AP, PRE, NMT, NG>. *That's just how it is. So, every now and then, everyone is gonna* ***blow off some steam*** <EV, VP, CLA, MT, NG>. *If you don't like it, start another thread of your own. In the meantime, if you can find a public online climate debate site where everyone sips their tea with their pinkies out a perfect ninety degree [sic]* ***angle*** <EV, NP, CLA, MT, NG>, *let me know and I'll give it a try. Until then, welcome to* ***the mind feast*** <EV, NP, CLA, MT, PS> *of Climate-debate.com. You're probably not gonna like everything on the table, but I'm sure you'll find plenty to stuff your face with and you can just ignore the rest (including me if you like).* [ENGF-13]

## 5 Concluding Remarks

In this chapter, and using the annotation scheme for the identification of evaluation proposed by Hidalgo-Downing et al. (2020) for that end, we have provided an exploration of the different discursive mechanisms used to express evaluative stance in online forums. As present in related research (Kiesling et al. 2018), one of the main challenges we encountered in this process was finding limits for the stance focus, which becomes particularly slippery when the discursive nature of online discourse is taken into account.

According to our analysis of the dataset at hand, evaluative stance in online forums is lexically instantiated via predicational strategies (67 % of the total), which grammatically corresponded to adjectival phrases. Classifying strategies were found to amount to 25 % and attitudinal markers were the least frequent ones (8 %). Metaphoric evaluation in this sample was identified in 25 % of the total cases, a similar proportion to what we observed in a small-scale preliminary study based on one two forum threads (circa 12,000 words). This study contributes to similar research in these lines (Jaki et al. 2019; Lorenzo-Dus & Nouri 2020; Prażmo 2020) on the type of evaluative value found in this set of forum threads. The value of evaluative stance was predominantly negative (59 %), which might also be explained by some of the affordances (namely anonymity) users seek when engaged in communicative exchanges in online forums (Prażmo 2020).

An interesting observation that would benefit from further research is connected to the tendency to express negativity in sharper, wittier, and generally more creative ways. As we illustrated, and according to the model we followed, negative evaluation seems to be achieved more multifariously (through classifying, predicational and attitudinal ways) than positivity. Likewise, levels of metaphoricity seem to be higher when users engage in discussion that has a negative motivation, with users relying on the role of metaphor scenarios to achieve their communicative goals.

Interesting though these observations may be, they would benefit from more systematic analysis to find out how frequent this correlation occurs in the corpus under scrutiny. Relatedly, findings would yield more robust claims by providing a more detailed account of the cross-variable effect on evaluative stance. To put it differently, future studies will necessarily need to focus on how negative/positive or metaphorical/non-metaphorical each type of lexical evaluation is, an endeavour that has not been pursued here.

## References

Alzahrani, M. G. (2017). 'The Effect of Using Online Discussion Forums on Students' Learning'. *Turkish Online Journal of Educational Technology-TOJET*, 16 (1), 164–176.

Androutsopoulos, J. (2006). 'Multilingualism, diaspora, and the Internet: codes and identities on German-based diaspora websites', *Journal of Sociolinguistics*, 10 (4), 429–450

Baumgarten, N. (2017). 'Othering practice in a right-wing extremist online forum'. *Language@ internet*, 14 (1) <https://www.languageatinternet.org/articles/2017/baumgarten> accessed 22 February 2021.

Bourgonjon, J., Vandermeersche, G., De Wever, B., Soetaert, R., & Valcke, M. (2016). 'Players' perspectives on the positive impact of video games: A qualitative content analysis of online forum discussions'. *New Media & Society*, 18 (8), 1732–1749.

Boyd, D. M., & Ellison, N. B. (2007). 'Social network sites: Definition, history, and scholarship'. *Journal of Computer-Mediated Communication*, 13 (1), 210–230.

Cohen, K., Johansson, F., Kaati, L., & Clausen Mork, J. (2014). 'Detecting linguistic markers for radical violence in social media'. *Terrorism and Political Violence*, 26, 246–256.

Cooper, T., Stavros, C. & Dobele, A.R. (2019). 'Domains of influence: exploring negative sentiment in social media'. *Journal of Product & Brand Management*, 28 (5), 684–699.

Crocker, J., Major, B. & Steele, C. B. (1998). 'Social stigma'. In D. Gilbert, S.T. Fiske, G. Lindzey (Eds.), *Handbook of Social Psychology*, pp. 504–553. New York: McGraw-Hill.

Drasovean, A., & Tagg, C. (2015). 'Evaluative language and its solidarity-building role on TED. com: an appraisal and corpus analysis' *Language@ Internet*, 12 <https://www.languageatinternet.org/articles/2015/drasovean > accessed 17 January 2021.

Du Bois, J. W. (2007). 'The stance triangle'. In R. Engelbretson (Ed.), *Stancetaking in Discourse*, pp. 139–182. Amsterdam: John Benjamins Publishing Company.

Figueras-Bates, C. (2015). '"I am a waste of breath, of space, of time" metaphors of self in a pro-anorexia group'. *Qualitative Health Research*, 25 (2), 189–204.

Janssen, D., & Kies, R. (2005). 'Online forums and deliberative democracy'. *Acta política*, 40 (3), 317–335.

Jaki, S., De Smedt, T., Gwóźdź, M., Panchal, R., Rossa, A., & De Pauw, G. (2019). 'Online hatred of women in the Incels. me forum: Linguistic analysis and automatic detection'. *Journal of Language Aggression and Conflict*, 7 (2), 240–268.

Hidalgo-Downing, L., Pérez-Sobrino, P., Filardo-Lamas, L., Maíz-Arévalo, C, Núñez-Perucha, B., Sánchez-Moya, A., & Camus, J. W. (2020). 'An annotation protocol for evaluative stance in discourse'. <https://doi.org/10.31219/osf.io/asd5r > accessed 25 January 2021.

Herring, S. C. (2001). 'Computer-mediated discourse'. In D. Schiffrin, D. Tannen, & H. Hamilton (Eds.), *The Handbook of Discourse Analysis*, pp. 612–634. Oxford: Blackwell.

Kiesling, S. F., Pavalanathan, U., Fitzpatrick, J., Han, X., & Eisenstein, J. (2018). 'Interactional stancetaking in online forums'. *Computational Linguistics*, 44 (4), 683–718.

Kozinets, R. V. (2010). *Netnography: Doing ethnographic research online*. London: Sage Publications.

Landqvist, M. (2016). 'Sense and sensibility–online forums as epistemic arenas'. *Discourse, Context & Media*, 13, 98–105.

Lee, M. (2017). 'Don't give up! A cyber-ethnography and discourse analysis of an online infertility patient forum'. *Culture, Medicine, and Psychiatry*, 41 (3), 341–367.

Li, C., & Bernoff, J. (2011). *Groundswell: Winning in a World Transformed by Social Technologies*. Cambridge (MA): Harvard Business Press.

Lorenzo-Dus, N., & Nouri, L. (2020). 'The discourse of the US alt-right online–a case study of the Traditionalist Worker Party blog'. *Critical Discourse Studies*, 1–19.

Mann, C., & Stewart, F. (2000). *Internet communication and qualitative research*. London: Sage Publishers.

Maíz Arévalo, C., Núñez Perucha, B. & Sánchez Moya, A. (2019). Evaluation and attitude across discourse domains: Advertising, fora and scientific discourses. Paper presented at the 43rd AEDEAN Conference held at the University of Alicante. November 13.

Marcoccia, M. (2003). 'On-line polylogue: Conversation structure and participation framework in Internet newsgroups', *Journal of Pragmatics*, 36, 115–145.

Matley, D. (2018). '"This is NOT a# humblebrag, this is just a# brag": The pragmatics of self-praise, hashtags and politeness in Instagram posts', *Discourse, Context & Media*, 22, 30–38.

Morrow, P.R. (2006). 'Telling about problems and giving advice in an Internet discussion forum: Some discourse features'. *Discourse Studies*, 8 (4): 531–548.

Musolff, A. (2006). 'Metaphor scenarios in public discourse'. *Metaphor and Symbol*, 21 (1), 23–38.

Nacey, S. (2020). 'Figurative production in a computer-mediated discussion forum'. In J. Barnden & A. Gargett (Eds.), *Producing Figurative Expression: Theoretical, experimental and practical perspectives*, pp. 363–388. Amsterdam: John Benjamins.

Page, R. E. (2012). *Stories and Social Media: Identities and Interaction*. London: Routledge.

Pendry, L.F., & Salvatore, J. (2015). 'Individual and social benefits of online discussion forums'. *Computers in Human Behavior*, 50, 211–220.

Placencia, M. E., & Lower, A. (2013). 'Your kids are so stinkin' cute!:-): Complimenting behavior on Facebook among family and friends'. *Intercultural Pragmatics*, 10 (4), 617–646.

Prażmo, E. (2020). 'Foids are worse than animals. A cognitive linguistics analysis of dehumanizing metaphors in online discourse'. *Topics in Linguistics*, 21 (2), 16–27.

Sánchez-Moya, A. (2019). *Exploring digital discourses on intimate partner violence: a socio-cognitive approach* [Doctoral dissertation, Universidad Complutense de Madrid/Vrije Universiteit Amsterdam]. ISBN: 978-94-6380-076-1.

Julia T. Williams Camus

# Evaluative Stance in Science Popularisations in the English Press[1]

**Abstract:** Whereas the traditional view of popularisation considered journalists as mere translators of scientific "facts" for lay readers, current approaches acknowledge a more active role for journalists in science reporting in the press. Press popularisations are not neutral accounts of scientific achievements, and a degree of evaluation can be expected in these texts. Discourse-oriented studies of science popularisations have indicated that evaluation is achieved through various linguistic strategies including the use of metaphor. Within a broader project investigating evaluative stance categories in five discourse domains, this paper explores evaluative stance and metaphor in a corpus of popularisation articles on scientific advances drawn from *The Guardian* and *The Times*. Evaluative expressions were identified and tagged for function (classifying, predicational, attitudinal or graduation), grammatical category (noun phrase, adjective phrase, adverb phrase), metaphoricity, and value (positive or negative). The study presents the most frequent evaluative categories and considers the role of metaphorical language in this genre.

**Keywords:** *evaluative stance, metaphor, popularisation discourse, science reporting, corpus linguistics, English press*

## 1 Introduction

The research project entitled *STANCEDISC: Stance and Subjectivity in Discourse: Towards an Integrated Framework for the Analysis of Epistemicity, Effectivity, Evaluation and Inter/Subjectivity from a Critical Discourse Perspective* analyses stance in four different genres that include opinion articles, political discourse, fora on social issues and science popularisation articles (Hidalgo-Downing et al. 2020). As part of this broader project, the present chapter analyses evaluative stance in science popularisation articles in the English press.

For many years, traditional accounts of popularisation have greatly simplified the process and have regarded it as a kind of translation between

1 The author is affiliated to the *Universidad de Cantabria* and is grateful to the Spanish Ministry of Science, Innovation and Universities for their generous financial support for the research project "Stance and Subjectivity in Discourse: Towards an Integrated Framework for the Analysis of Epistemicity, Effectivity, Evaluation and Inter/Subjectivity from a Critical Discourse Perspective" (PGC2018-095798-B-I00).

registers. However, this view does not consider the reduction in content and its adaptation to a new environment. Truly, it is more than a linguistic exercise. Therefore, popularisation can best be regarded as a variety of genres, spoken and written, which involve a recontextualisation of scientific discourse and a transformation of specialised knowledge into everyday or lay knowledge. This recontextualisation involves three different tasks: re-*elaboration*, which involves adding and eliminating information to make the conceptual network of scientific knowledge more accessible to the public; *denomination*, which involves modifications of scientific terminology at the local level and *textualisation*, which involves discourse resources that help to refocus the content for a new audience in a different genre (Cassany, López and Martí 2000: 80). In the traditional view, journalists writing press popularisations were also considered as mere translators of scientific "facts" for the lay public. But current approaches generally acknowledge a more active role played by journalists in the reporting of science. Thus, in the context of the press, the purpose of the resulting piece is not only to transmit scientific information, but also to entertain and to inform the public of both the relevance and value of a given scientific achievement to their lives (Fahnestock 1986; Radford 2009). Crucially, journalists must be explicit in their claims about the value of scientific discoveries they pass along because they cannot rely on the audience to recognise the significance of the information (Fahnestock 1986).

One important aspect of press popularisations is that they are polyphonic texts (Calsamiglia & López Ferrero 2003, Elorza & Pérez-Veneros 2014). In addition to the voice of the journalists, the presence of scientists, politicians, and representatives of charities and associations is also found in the text to contextualise scientific information, to position themselves on controversial topics and to evaluate scientific achievements. This last-mentioned function can sometimes be problematic, as scientists often criticise journalists for hyping the results of their investigations. However, Tim Radford, a former science editor at *The Guardian,* considers this to be a necessary evil in the publication of popularisation articles: "while overstatement is not necessarily a good tactic, understatement is synonymous with no statement at all" (Radford 2009: 146). As science normally moves at a glacially slow pace, with no revolutionary developments making the headlines on a daily basis, Radford may have a point since scientific news needs to be made newsworthy in order to attract the attention of newspaper editors and, ultimately, the readers. However, journalists are not the only ones to blame for exaggerating scientific achievements. Scientists themselves may also sometimes play up the implications of their work as a means of self-promotion and to attract funding for their research. Thus, it is evident that press popularisation articles cannot be viewed as completely neutral accounts of scientific achievements, and a degree of evaluation on the part of the writer and the other voices involved can be expected in these texts. In fact, previous discourse-oriented studies on science popularisation articles indicate that evaluation is achieved through a number of linguistic strategies such as framing (Dhal 2015) attribution of source (Elorza & Pérez-Veneros 2014) and use of metaphor (Williams Camus 2016).

In contrast to research articles, where scientists make a strategic use of hedges and other resources to avoid overstating their claims, popularisation articles have been said to seek to glamorise material for a wider audience, upgrading their uniqueness, rarity and originality because, as argued by Fahnestock (1986), the purpose of popularisation articles is to celebrate science. She argues that science accommodators achieve this by making two appeals to their audiences. The 'wonder' appeal praises something by attaching to it a category that has a recognised value for an audience. On the other hand, the 'application' appeal involves claims that highlight the value of something because it leads to further benefits. Fahnestock (1986) observes that for popularisations to achieve the laudatory effect, communication to a knowledgeable scientific audience is released from the requirement of mitigation strategies because these would reduce the news-value of a statement for a lay audience by undermining its certainty. The research questions that have guided the analysis are as follows:

(1) What are the most frequent categories used for evaluation?
(2) Is there a preference for metaphorical or non-metaphorical evaluative language?
(3) What is the source of the evaluation in the popularisation genre?

The chapter is organised as follows. Section 2 describes the corpus used in the study and the analytical methods. Section 3 presents the quantitative results. Section 4 is devoted to a detailed analysis of the different evaluative patterns identified in the study. Section 5 summarises the main findings and identifies aspects to be developed in later studies employing a larger corpus.

## 2 Materials and Methods

### 2.1 Corpus

The corpus used in this study was drawn from the English press and consists of 164 articles compiled from *The Guardian* (57,760 words) and *The Times* (52,026) and published between the years 2002 and 2019. Articles eligible for inclusion had to report scientific advances and had to appear in the science section of the newspapers. The articles deal with various scientific topics including health, biotechnology and the environment. For the purposes of this study, a smaller sample corpus was randomly selected and analysed to examine the potential challenges in the analysis of evaluative stance in the genre of popularisation articles. This sample consisted of 15 texts from each of the newspapers: *The Guardian* (11,859 words) and *The Times* (7,088).

## 2.2 Definitions

In this study, evaluative stance is regarded as "a social act which expresses a positioning of a speaker/writer towards a specific topic, entity, social actor or event; by means of this positioning, the speaker/writer aligns or disaligns with real or potential addressees and communities of speakers according to shared systems of beliefs, expressing a positive or negative value towards the topic, entity or event" (Hidalgo et al. 2020: 2). Evaluative stance thus defined is realised in discourse by the selection of specific lexical items which express an assessment of words or phrases in the local context. The evaluative expressions perform a number of functions: (1) the *classifying* function categorises entities or events according to social systems of beliefs and is typically realised by nouns and verbs; (2) the *predicational* function, which qualifies entities or events according to social systems of belief, is typically performed by adjectives; (3) the *attitudinal* function expresses a position adopted towards a whole proposition and is typically performed by sentential adverbs (Hidalgo et al. 2020: 2). The first two functions can be metaphorical or non-metaphorical and all three functions may express positive or negative value explicitly or implicitly (Hidalgo et al. 2020: 2). Lexical expressions of stance may be strengthened or attenuated by intensifiers and downtoners, a subfunction denominated Graduation in line with certain categories in Appraisal Theory (Martin & White 2005).

## 2.3 Procedure

This study applied the general analytical procedure adopted in the broader project investigating evaluative stance categories in four different discourse domains (Hidalgo-Downing et al. 2020, Hidalgo-Downing and Pérez-Sobrino, this volume) as follows:

(1) Read the entire text to identify the main event or topic and the main related participants.
(2) Identify lexical items used to express evaluation of the main event and the related participants/social actors.

(3) Code the lexical items for part of speech: noun phrase (NP), verb phrase (VP), adjective phrase (AP) and adverb phrase (ADVP).
(4) Code for function: classifying (CLA), predicational (PRE), or attitude (ATT).
(5) Code for Value: positive (POS), negative (NG).
(6) Metaphorical: Expressions with a classifying and predicational role were also coded as metaphorical (MT) or non-metaphorical (NMT).

Lexical items of stance may be amplified or mitigated by Martin and White's (2005) category of graduation markers and these have been coded in the analysis: intensifiers (MOR) or downtoners (LESS).

Although the overall project does not consider second-degree evaluative stance, in the case of popularisation articles it is an aspect that should be taken into account because this polyphonic genre includes numerous quotations from experts and spokespeople representing different organisations who provide their views on the implications and value of a given scientific achievement. Thus, all items were coded for the source of the evaluation: journalist (1) or others (2).

## 3 Quantitative Results

Although the number of evaluative expressions in *The Guardian* was almost double the figure in *The Times*, the frequency was similar when the results were normalised per 1,000 words (Table 1).

**Table 1.** Distribution of evaluative stance in the sample corpus

| **Source** | **Nº of words** | **Evaluative expressions** | **Normalised per 1,000 words** |
|---|---|---|---|
| *The Guardian* | 11,859 | 163 | 13.74 |
| *The Times* | 7,088 | 87 | 12.27 |
| Total | 18,947 | 250 | |

As shown in Table 2, second-degree evaluation was about twice as frequent as first-degree evaluation both overall and in the two newspapers separately. These evaluative stance expressions were most often present in quotations not only from the scientists participating in the research, but also from other experts in the field, spokespersons from different charities and associations and other stakeholders that may be affected by the research outcomes. These figures suggest that journalists are not particularly inclined to evaluate different aspects of the reported research explicitly.

**Table 2.** Distribution of first- and second-degree evaluative stance expressions in the corpus

| **Source** | **First-degree** | **Second-degree** | **Total** |
|---|---|---|---|
| *The Guardian* | 56 (34 %) | 107 (66 %) | 163 |
| *The Times* | 32 (37 %) | 55 (63 %) | 87 |
| Total | 88 (35 %) | 162 (65 %) | 250 |

Table 3 represents evaluative stance expressions in terms of function and graduation markers. The categories were not equally distributed in the corpus but, in general, there were no major differences between the two newspapers.

**Table 3.** Distribution of evaluative stance by function and graduation markers

| | *The Guardian* | | *The Times* | | **Combined** | |
|---|---|---|---|---|---|---|
| **Function** | No. | % | No. | % | No. | % |
| CLA | 58 | 35.6 | 31 | 35.6 | 89 | 35.6 |
| PRE | 76 | 46.6 | 39 | 44.8 | 115 | 46.0 |
| ATT | 1 | 0.6 | 1 | 1.1 | 2 | 0.8 |
| *Subtotal* | *135* | *82.8* | *71* | *81.5* | *206* | *82.4* |
| **Graduation markers** | | | | | | |
| MOR | 28 | 17.2 | 12 | 13.8 | 40 | 16.0 |
| LESS | 0 | 0 | 4 | 4.6 | 4 | 1.6 |
| *Subtotal* | *28* | *17.2* | *16* | *18.4* | *44* | *17.6* |
| **Total** | **163** | | **87** | | **250** | |

In terms of function, the most frequent category was predicational, followed by expressions with a classifying function, whereas stance expressions with an attitudinal role were extremely rare in the corpus. The 44 graduation markers identified showed a similar proportional distribution in *The Guardian* and *The Times* (17.2 % and 18.4 %, respectively). However, it is notable that boosters far outnumbered downtoners and no instance of the latter occurred in *The Guardian*.

With regard to grammatical category, evaluative stance was most frequently expressed through adjectives, followed by nouns, verbs and adverbs (Table 4). Only about a quarter of the evaluative expressions were classed as metaphorical. In terms of value, the expressions were more frequently positive, although in *The Times* positive and negative values were evenly distributed. Thus, the most frequent pattern for evaluative stance in the corpus was predicational function, adjectival phrase, non-metaphorical and positive value (PRE, AP, NMT, PS).

**Table 4.** Distribution of evaluative stance by part of speech, metaphoricity and value

| | *The Guardian* | | *The Times* | | **Combined** | |
|---|---|---|---|---|---|---|
| **Part of Speech** | No. | % | No. | % | No. | % |
| NP | 43 | 31.9 | 24 | 33.8 | 67 | 32.5 |
| VP | 15 | 11.1 | 7 | 9.8 | 22 | 10.7 |
| AP | 71 | 52.6 | 39 | 54.9 | 110 | 53.4 |
| ADVP | 6 | 4.4 | 1 | 1.4 | 7 | 3.4 |
| **Total** | **135** | | **71** | | **206** | |
| **Metaphoricity** | | | | | | |
| MT | 40 | 29.6 | 18 | 25.4 | 58 | 28.2 |
| NMT | 95 | 70.4 | 53 | 74.6 | 148 | 71.8 |
| **Total** | **135** | | **71** | | **206** | |
| **Value** | | | | | | |
| PS | 82 | 60.7 | 36 | 50.7 | 118 | 57.3 |
| NG | 53 | 39.3 | 35 | 49.3 | 88 | 42.7 |
| **Total** | **135** | | **71** | | **206** | |

# 4 Evaluative Stance Patterns in the Corpus

## 4.1 Predicational Function

Table 5 provides a summary of the different patterns in which the predicational function was identified in the corpus.

The predicational function was most frequently realised by adjective phrases. In *The Guardian*, of 76 predicational role expressions 71 were adjective phases and only 5 were adverb phrases whereas in *The Times,* only one adverb phrase was found in a total of 39 instances. In the 6 adverb phrases identified, there was an even distribution of both negative and positive values (3 each) and first- and second-degree stance (3 each), and only one instance was metaphorical.

**Table 5.** Patterns identified for the predicational function

| | *The Guardian* | *The Times* | **Combined** |
|---|---|---|---|
| ADVP, MT, NG, 2 | 1 | 0 | 1 |
| ADVP, NMT, NG, 1 | 1 | 1 | 2 |
| ADVP, NMT, PS, 1 | 1 | 0 | 1 |
| ADVP, NMT, PS, 2 | 2 | 0 | 2 |
| *Subtotal* | *5* | *1* | *6* |
| AP, MT, NG, 2 | 2 | 0 | 2 |
| AP, MT, PS, 1 | 1 | 0 | 1 |
| AP, MT, PS, 2 | 1 | 0 | 1 |
| AP, NMT, NG, 1 | 13 | 6 | 19 |
| AP, NMT, NG, 2 | 16 | 12 | 28 |
| AP, NMT, PS, 1 | 13 | 6 | 19 |
| AP, NMT, PS, 2 | 25 | 14 | 39 |
| *Subtotal* | *71* | *38* | *109* |
| **Total** | **76** | **39** | **115** |

The absence of metaphoricity was also true for adjective phrases, with only 4 instances, all of which appeared in *The Guardian* and could be subsumed under the MOVEMENT source domain. Of the four occurrences, two were positive (*closer, groundbreaking*) and two negative (*distant, remote*); only one was classed as first-degree stance and three as second-degree stance. Interestingly, three instances appeared in a single article. The adjective *groundbreaking* (example 1) was placed in the lead, thus underlining the potential benefit of the development whereas the quote from the co-author (example 2) serves to play down the immediate possibility of applying the technique to enhancing genetic traits in embryos:

(1) ***Groundbreaking*** *project corrects faulty DNA linked to fatal heart condition and raises hopes for parents who risk passing on genetic diseases.* [ESG-40]

(2) *Asked about the potential for gene editing to produce designer babies, Rossant, a co-author of the NAS report on gene editing, said it was a* ***distant*** *prospect.* [ESG-40]

Non-metaphorical adjective phrases were most frequently (58 instances) conveyed by positive evaluation (38 in *The Guardian* and 20 in *The Times*) and this was twice as frequent in second-degree as in first-degree stance (39 vs 19) with similar proportions in both *The Guardian* and *The Times*. Negative evaluation was expressed in 47 instances of non-metaphorical adjective phrases (29 in *The Guardian* and 18 in *The Times*). This negative evaluation was somewhat higher in second-degree than in first-degree stance (28 vs. 19). Interestingly, whereas positive evaluation in second-degree stance was much more frequent than negative evaluation (39 vs 28), in first-degree stance positive and negative evaluation were exactly the same (19 instances each).

A close analysis of the instances of second-degree positive stance revealed that it was equally distributed between scientists or other agents involved in the research being popularised (13 in *The Guardian* and 7 in *The Times*) and experts outside the research (12 in *The Guardian* and 7 in *The Times*). Those involved in the research used adjectives to highlight the degree of its importance (*important* (5), *vital*, *key*, *crucial*, *significant*); to indicate an emotional response (*enthusiastic*, *exciting*, *striking*); to signal the originality and/or applicability of the research (*radical*, *first*; *usable*, *valuable*); and to indicate ethical suitability (*permissible* (2), not *unacceptable*, *clear*). Other experts cited in the texts also used evaluative expressions to convey degree of importance (*important* (4), *vital*, *significant*, *watershed* moment, *invaluable*) and an emotional response (*striking*, *interesting*, *intriguing*, *exciting*). No instances referring to originality, applicability or ethics were identified, but they also used expressions to assess the solidity of the arguments or outcomes (*unassailable*, *convincing* evidence, *good* results, *fantastic*) or the implications of the findings for science and society (*fresh* hope, *long-awaited* advance, *potential* insights).

With regard to first-degree positive stance, the analysis revealed that journalists resorted to evaluation in five of the six categories mentioned above: namely, importance (*important* implications, *significant* study); emotion (*striking* effect); originality (*radical* (2) therapies, *first* demonstration); solidity of evidence (*comprehensive* (2) and *conclusive* study, *firmest* biological evidence) and implications for science and society (*positive* note). However, they also emphasised, on the one hand, elements or techniques used in the research (*powerful* (5) gene editing tool, *crucial* part of the gene) or, on the other, the reputation of the scientists or the publication (one of the world's *foremost* cancer biologists, *prestigious* journal).

The close analysis of the negative non-metaphorical predicational expressions produced interesting findings. A total of 28 of these were second-degree stance (16 in *The Guardian* and 12 in *The Times*). However, these were found to be concentrated in a small number of articles (6 in *The Guardian* and 5 in *The Times*), and, in fact, in both newspapers most of these expressions were present in only two texts.

The second-degree negative expressions were related to (1) the negative impact on society or the environment (*devastating* (2), *damaging*, *dangerous*, *under threat*, *catastrophic*, *condemning*); (2) problematic methods (*superficial* and *unconvincing* comparison, *vague* research, *difficult* to tell); (3) deficiencies in findings and interpretation (*spurious* correlation, *unreliable* or *exaggerated* findings, *random*, *not real*, *complex* and *inconsistent* results, *simplistic* interpretation, not paradigm *shifting*); (4) uncertainty or lack of clarity regarding future research (*unclear* (2), *unexpected*, *unpredictable*); (5) ethics (*bad* practice, *unacceptable* risk); (6) emotions (*alarmist* titles, *alarming* declines).

(3) *The dangers of screens have been* ***exaggerated*** *by* ***cherry-picking*** *of* ***vague*** *research that throws up* ***spurious*** *correlations, according to researchers at Oxford University, who said ministers should devote more effort to things that were known to have a bigger impact, such as helping children eat breakfast and get a good night's sleep.*
*He said it was* ***unclear*** *if this was statistical noise or a real effect, but argued: "If [glasses-wearers] are getting teased in the playground, how do we balance that against the benefit of being able to see? The same applies to social media."* [EST18]

In example 3, the researchers of a study question the previously reported results on the effects of screens on mental health. The extract combines three negative adjectives with another two negative items for a cumulative critical effect.

(4) *The study was published in the journal Science and has been hailed for* ***potential*** *insights into the story of human migration but disputed by some experts, who claim that the findings are* ***unreliable*** *or* ***exaggerated****.*
*But Ben Potter, a professor of archaeology at the University of Alaska Fairbanks, queried the dating of the oldest artefacts and called the comparison of the weapon heads "****superficial*** *and* ***unconvincing****". He said that the findings overall were "****intriguing****, but not paradigm* ***shifting****".* [EST76]

In example 4, where it is the research being reported that is being questioned by other experts in the field, the extract accumulates a total of six negative evaluative expressions that counter the single positive note of '*potential* insights'.

The frequency of first-degree negative expressions was lower, with 13 instances in *The Guardian* and six in *The Times*. In this case, the analysis revealed that the journalists used these expressions differently in the two newspapers. In *The Guardian*, the negative adjectives were: *controversial* (5) referring to techniques and procedures, *devastating* (3) and *lethal* in relation to diseases and illnesses, *deadly* mutations, *dramatic* style, *poor* record in treating anorexia and *terrified* about losing weight. Most of these can be considered as recurrent in popularisation discourse and could be regarded almost as clichés. Thus, it could be argued that journalists avoid a direct and explicit involvement in the negative reporting of scientific stories. In contrast, in *The Times*, of the six instances only one could be considered clichéd (*catastrophic* effects). The negative evaluation in the remaining cases could be seen as a rhetorical strategy used by the journalists to attract the reader's attention, since the negative lexis clusters at the beginning of the articles, sometimes in combination with other stylistic resources. For instance, the headline in text EST-63 presents an oxymoron: *Sweet smell of global warming*. In the lead, the negative adjective further develops this incongruity:

(5) *IT MAY be* ***disastrous*** *for ice sheets, rainforests and coastal cities but scientists have discovered climate change will make flowers more fragrant.* [EST-63]

In the lead of another article, the journalist classes the formation of elephant all-male gangs as an *unusual* occurrence, which is then repeated in the explanation in the second paragraph of the main text. Similarly, the tune of a Hawaiian bird presented in the headline (example 6) is more fully described through 'less *interesting*' in the third line of the article:

(6) *Birdsong gets more* ***boring*** *as species shrink.* [EST81]

## 4.2 Classifying Function

Table 6 summarises the different patterns with the classifying function identified in the corpus.

As shown in table 6, the classifying function is mainly realised by noun phrases (67 instances) with 43 in *The Guardian* and 24 in *The Times*. In contrast to the predicational function, for noun phrases with the classifying role there was a greater presence of metaphors, which outnumbered non-metaphorical expressions both overall (42 vs. 25), and in the two newspapers (27 vs. 16 in *The Guardian*; 15 vs. 9 in *The Times*). Positive evaluation was more frequent than negative evaluation overall (42 vs. 25) and in both newspapers (28 vs. 15 in *The Guardian*; 14 vs. 10 in *The Times*). Second-degree stance was higher than first-degree stance overall (39 vs. 28) and in *The Guardian* (27 vs. 16) but not in *The Times* (12 each). The preference for metaphorical evaluation held true for first-degree (18 vs. 10) and second-degree (24 vs. 15) stance, and for positive (27 vs. 15) and negative (15 vs. 10) stance. When source was analysed in terms of value, first-degree stance was found to be strongly positive (22 vs. 6) whereas for second-degree stance positive and negative evaluation were almost the same (20 vs. 19). Thus, the general pattern for the classifying function was noun phrase, metaphorical, positive value and second-degree stance (NP, MT, PS, 2).

**Table 6.** Patterns identified for the classifying function

| | ***The Guardian*** | ***The Times*** | **Combined** | **Row Sum** |
|---|---|---|---|---|
| Noun Phrase Metaphorical | No. (%) | No. (%) | No. (%) | |
| NP, MT, NG, 1 | 1 | 2 | 3 | 15 |
| NP, MT, NG, 2 | 10 | 2 | 12 | |
| NP, MT, PS, 1 | 10 | 5 | 15 | 27 |
| NP, MT, PS, 2 | 6 | 6 | 12 | |
| *Subtotal* | *27 (46.6)* | *15 (48.4)* | *42 (47.2)* | |
| Noun Phrase Non-metaphorical | | | | |
| NP, NMT, NG, 1 | 1 | 2 | 3 | 10 |
| NP, NMT, NG, 2 | 3 | 4 | 7 | |
| NP, NMT, PS, 1 | 4 | 3 | 7 | 15 |
| NP, NMT, PS, 2 | 8 | 0 | 8 | |
| *Subtotal* | *16 (27.6)* | *9 (29.0)* | *25 (28.0)* | |
| Verb Phrase Metaphorical | | | | |
| VP, MT, NG, 1 | 0 | 1 | 1 | 5 |
| VP, MT, NG, 2 | 3 | 1 | 4 | |
| VP, MT, PS, 1 | 3 | 0 | 3 | 6 |
| VP, MT, PS, 2 | 2 | 1 | 3 | |
| *Subtotal* | *8 (13.7)* | *3 (9.7)* | *11 (12.4)* | |
| Verb Phrase Non-metaphorical | | | | |
| VP, NMT, NG, 1 | 2 | 0 | 2 | 7 |
| VP, NMT, NG, 2 | 1 | 4 | 5 | |
| VP, NMT, PS, 1 | 1 | 0 | 1 | 4 |
| VP, NMT, PS, 2 | 3 | 0 | 3 | |
| *Subtotal* | *7 (12.1)* | *4 (12.9)* | *11 (12.4)* | |
| **Total** | **58** | **31** | **89** | |

The frequency of classifying verb phrases was much lower than that of noun phrases both overall (22 vs. 67) and in the two newspapers. In this case, however, metaphorical and non-metaphorical expressions were evenly distributed (11 vs. 11) overall and reasonably so in both newspapers (8 and 7 in *The Guardian* and 3 and 4 in *The Times*). In addition, in contrast to the noun phrases, negative value slightly exceeded positive value overall (12 vs. 10), although the figures for the newspapers varied considerably (6 vs. 9 in *The Guardian* and 6 vs. 1 in *The Times*). Second-degree stance was higher than first-degree stance overall (15 vs. 7) and in both newspapers (9 vs. 6 in *The Guardian* and 6 vs. 1 in *The Times*). The fairly even distribution of metaphorical and non-metaphorical expressions was maintained in both first-degree (4 vs. 3) and second-degree (7 vs. 8) stance. When source was analysed in terms of value, first-degree stance slightly favoured positive evaluation (4 vs. 3) but second-degree stance favoured negative evaluation (6 vs. 9).

### *4.2.1 Metaphorical Classifying Expressions*

For the contextual analysis of metaphorical expressions, noun and verb phrases were considered together. As can be seen in the distribution of the 53 occurrences shown in Table 7, there were 35 in *The Guardian* and 18 in *The Times*. Positive exceeded negative evaluation (33 vs. 20) and second-degree outnumbered first-degree stance (31 vs. 22). With regard to source domain, the outstanding representation was of MOVEMENT metaphors (37 instances) with the remaining 16 expressions drawn from a variety of domains usually represented by isolated cases.

The analysis of the 33 instances of positive evaluation revealed that there was little variation and most could be classed as MOVEMENT metaphors (29 instances) with only four drawn from other source domains. The most recurrent metaphorical expression is *breakthrough*, which seems to be favoured by journalists. The three instances in *The Guardian* occurred in the same text. A leading expert in the field who did not participate in the reported research qualified the scientific achievement as a 'tour de force' and a *breakthrough*. Although the actual quotation appeared at the end of the article, the journalist recycled the expression as part of his own discourse in a subheadline and through indirect quotation in the body of the text. In *The Times* the *breakthrough* motif was also repeated in two of the three texts containing the expression. Of the five instances only one was attributed to experts through indirect quotation (example 7), and three of the four employed by journalists were placed in prominent positions such as the headline and lead (example 8):

(7) *The **breakthrough** could also revolutionise transplant surgery, scientists said* [EST5: 3rd paragraph]

(8) **Breakthrough** for Dundee cancer research [Headline]
*Scientists have made a **breakthrough** in understanding the tumour-suppressing p53 gene that acts as a "call centre" for co-ordinating responses to the disease at a molecular level.* [Lead: EST33]

**Table 7.** Summary of the metaphorical expressions identified in the corpus

| | **Domain** | **Metaphorical Expression** | *The Guardian* | | *The Times* | | **Row Sum** |
|---|---|---|---|---|---|---|---|
| | | | **Degree** | | **Degree** | | |
| | | | **1st** | **2nd** | **1st** | **2nd** | |
| Positive | MOVEMENT source domain | *Breakthrough* | 1 | 2 | 4 | 1 | 8 |
| | | *Landmark* | 5 | – | – | – | 5 |
| | | *Milestone* | 1 | – | – | – | 1 |
| | | *Advance* | 1 | 2 | – | 1 | 4 |
| | | *Step* | 2 | 1 | – | 1 | 4 |
| | | *Path* | – | – | – | 1 | 1 |
| | | *Pave the way* | 1 | 1 | – | 1 | 3 |
| | | *Lead* | – | 1 | – | – | 1 |
| | | *Propel* | 2 | – | – | – | 2 |
| | Other | *Gift* | – | – | 1 | – | 1 |
| | | *Peak* | – | 1 | – | – | 1 |
| | | *Jigsaw* | – | – | – | 1 | 1 |
| | | *Players* | – | – | – | 1 | 1 |
| | *Subtotal* | | *13* | *8* | *5* | *7* | *33* |
| Negative | MOVEMENT source domain | *Long way* | – | 3 | – | – | 3 |
| | | *Hurdles* | 1 | 1 | – | – | 2 |
| | | *Bottleneck* | – | 1 | – | – | 1 |
| | | *Knocked off track* | – | 1 | – | – | 1 |
| | | *Not on the horizon* | – | 1 | – | – | 1 |
| | Other | *Horror story* | – | 1 | – | – | 1 |
| | | *Red Carpet* | – | 1 | – | – | 1 |
| | | *Gilded age* | – | 1 | – | – | 1 |
| | | *Male Gangs* | – | – | 1 | 1 | 2 |
| | | *Cultural collapse* | – | – | – | 1 | 1 |
| | | *Bee sting* | – | – | 1 | – | 1 |
| | | *Stifle* | – | 3 | – | – | 3 |
| | | *Hit* | – | – | – | 1 | 1 |
| | | *Tricking* | – | – | 1 | – | 1 |
| | *Subtotal* | | *1* | *13* | *3* | *3* | *20* |
| | **Total** | | **14** | **21** | **8** | **10** | **53** |

Journalists in *The Guardian* also evaluated discoveries through metaphors indicating reference points, *landmark* (5) and *milestone* (1). These instances were all first-degree stance and appeared in three articles, with at least one item placed prominently in the headline or lead to contribute to the newsworthiness of the piece:

(9) *Deadly gene mutations removed from human embryos in* ***landmark*** *study* [headline] *Scientists have modified human embryos to remove genetic mutations that cause heart failure in otherwise healthy young people in a* ***landmark*** *demonstration of the controversial procedure.* [Lead: ESG-40]

(10) *While none of the research so far has created babies from modified embryos, a move that would be illegal in many countries, the work represents a* ***milestone*** *in scientists' efforts to master the technique and brings the prospect of human clinical trials one* ***step closer****.* [ESG-40]

In contrast, the metaphorical expressions of *advance* (4 instances) and *step* (4) from the MOVEMENT source domain seem to be preferred by scientists and experts quoted in the articles; in two instances of first-degree stance, one for each item, the journalist had drawn on the conceptualisation in the quotation, as can be seen in examples 10 and 11:

(11) *"If all of this holds up for different genes and is also true when the mutation is inherited from the mother, it will be a major* ***step*** *forward," said Janet Rossant, senior scientist and chief of research emeritus at the Hospital for Sick Children in Toronto.* [ESG-40]

The six MOVEMENT metaphors expressed as verb phrases, together with the instance of *path*, could be regarded as future-oriented metaphors. The use of *have a clear path* by a scientist indicated that research could proceed from work with cells to trials with animals and possibly humans. The most frequent verbal metaphor, *pave the way* (3), is a fairly conventional expression to introduce the eventual application of a research outcome. Similarly, *lead* made a connection between a given discovery and potential development in treatment. Finally, *propel*, used twice in the same text, introduces the nuance of speed. These verbal metaphors were used both by the researchers (12) and other experts (13) as well as by journalists (14), and may occur in close proximity to other MOVEMENT metaphors, as seen in (12) and (14):

(12) *Andrew Tobin, a molecular pharmacology expert at Glasgow University and a co-author of the study, said: "We are tremendously excited about these new findings, and hope they* ***pave the way*** *for the first* ***step*** *in the eradication of malaria."* [EST-77]

(13) *Rebecca Park, a consultant psychiatrist who studies eating disorders at the University of Oxford, said that while the work did not provide an instant solution, it may* ***lead*** *to new ways of treating anorexia.* [ESG-75]

(14) *Scientists have genetically engineered pigs to be immune to one of the world's most costly animal diseases, in an* ***advance*** *that could* ***propel*** *gene-editing technology into commercial farms within five years.* [ESG-57]

Although the distinction between first- and second-degree stance is not clear cut and the numbers are small, it appears that journalists, on one side, and scientists and other experts, on the other, have different metaphorical preferences regarding the use of MOVEMENT expressions with a positive evaluative function.

Interestingly, three of the four positive metaphorical expressions drawn from outside the MOVEMENT domain were more creative and appeared in direct quotations from scientists and experts at the end of the articles:

(15) *Paul de Zylva, campaigner at Friends of the Earth, said: "This is the strongest ever evidence of harm to bees from neonicotinoid pesticides in British fields. [It] adds a huge new* ***peak*** *to the existing mountain of evidence showing the risk these chemicals pose to our bees."* [ESG-15]

(16) *Dr Meek said: "P53 is a protein of huge interest to cancer researchers yet there is still a lot that we don't fully understand. Our work has linked several pieces of the* ***jigsaw*** *by describing how this process in a particular part of p53 has a significant effect on its activity."* [EST-33]

(17) *Efforts to obliterate malaria have generally focused on creating a vaccine, but Professor Tobin said: […] "It is likely that drugs like the one we are developing will be important* ***players*** *in the elimination of a disease that has plagued mankind since antiquity."* [EST-77]

The remaining metaphor *gift* was employed by the journalist in a witty play on words which serves as an attention-grabbing headline:

(18) Funnel-web spider's lethal poison may hold ***gift*** of life [EST-05]

With regard to negative metaphorical stance, it should be noted that 16 of the 20 instances were second-degree stance with only four classed as first-degree. This suggests that negative metaphorical stance is not frequently expressed by journalists. The metaphorical expressions in this group showed greater variety than positive stance metaphors. However, eight expressions could be grouped together as MOVEMENT metaphors. These included the variants *a long way* (twice) and *a way to go* (once) and the related *not on the horizon*, and signalled that the desired outcome was still out of reach (example 19). In addition, *hurdles* (2) and *bottleneck* (example 20) were used to reflect difficulties encountered when performing research while the verbal phrase *knocked off track* (example 21) conveyed criticism on the part of scientists of a moratorium that may be imposed to halt the research on gene drives.

(19) *Asked about the potential for gene editing to produce designer babies, Rossant, a co-author of the NAS report on gene editing, said it was a* ***distant*** *prospect. "We are*

*still a long way from serious consideration of using gene editing to enhance traits in babies," she said.* [ESG-40]

(20) *"That is something that is going to stay with us with Crispr or any other tool we develop that cuts DNA. It is a major* ***bottleneck*** *in the field of genetics – the possibility that the cell, after the DNA is cut, may introduce harmful mistakes."* [ESG-47]

(21) *Research on a radical new way to combat malaria and other devastating diseases could be* ***knocked off track*** *if a UN biodiversity conference imposes a moratorium on the work, a group of scientists have said.* [ESG-65]

Of the negative metaphors drawn from other domains, the six in *The Guardian* were all instances of second-degree stance. In the text that included the expression *knocked off track*, three instances of the verb *stifle* also appeared in quotes in which scientists expressed their concern about restraint on research. In another text, a report from an ethics committee was criticised through the paradoxical use of '*a red carpet*' and '*a gilded age*', which would normally have positive associations, to express ethical concerns about unrestricted use of reproductive genetic engineering and increased inequality. A final original example uses *horror story* to reflect the unforeseen persistent effects of agricultural practices on bees:

(22) *Environmental campaigners said the new research exposed the full impact of neonicotinoids. "The* ***horror story*** *is clear: we have contaminated our land and water with persistent neonicotinoid pesticides," said Matt Shardlow, CEO of the charity Buglife.* [ESG-35]

In *The Times*, the six negative metaphors in noun and verb phrases were all drawn from outside the MOVEMENT domain. They occurred in texts dealing with the negative effects of human activities and/or climate change on humans and different animal or plant species.

Interestingly, of three instances of first-degree stance, two were used rhetorically in the headlines to attract the reader's attention:

(23) *Bees feel the* ***sting*** *of climate change* [EST-75]

(24) *Indian elephants form all-male* ***gangs*** *in face of threats from humans and habitat.* [EST-07]

In example 23, the journalist puns on the word *sting*, since the topic of the article is bees, in a parallel of the biter being bitten. In example 24, the journalist exploits the negative term *gang*, which also appears in an indirect quote summarising the researchers' main claim.

(25) *The findings coincide with Britain's mild winter, which is already "****tricking****" some species, including hydrangeas and witch hazels, into blooming as if it were spring.* [EST-63]

In example (25), the journalist broadens the implications of the research (carried out in Spain) by relating it to the British context. The use of *trick* and the scare quotes appear to imply a potential negative effect.

Two final negative metaphors, the noun phrase *cultural collapse* and the verb *hit* were second-degree stance. In the former, the researchers make an elegant summary of the reduction of birdsong complexity and diversity through loss of culturally transmitted behaviour. In the latter, the journalist indirectly quotes the researchers in the headline through the standard collocation of *hit* and *hard* to reflect the impact of climate change on crowded cities, and this is then paraphrased non-metaphorically as 'affected badly' in the lead.

### *4.2.2 Non-metaphorical Classifying Expressions*

Apart from a reference to Crispr, a gene editing technique, as a 'game-changer' and to a rare positive effect of climate change as a 'bonus', most of the positive expressions referred to the value of the researcher's contributions. This was done through a number of conventional expressions (a *first* (3), *tour de force* (2), *feat*) when the research was outstanding, or through more modest expressions that were often modalized (*hope* (2), important *piece of evidence*, clinical *potential*, *encouragement*). In example 26, the nouns 'treatment' and 'cure' were also considered evaluative:

(26) *"We believe that this could provide a **treatment**, if not a **cure**, depending on when it's injected," said Mark Zylka, a neurobiologist at the University of North Carolina.* [ESG-72]

Positive non-metaphorical evaluation was marginally carried out through verbs, which underlined the contribution of the research to knowledge (*add*, *fill* a gap) or referred to its emotive impact on other scientists (*impressed*), and in one case predicted increased productivity through the application of a new technique:

(27) *According to Shoukhrat Mitalipov, who led the latest research, gene editing could **bolster** the number of healthy embryos available for doctors to implant.* [ESG-40]

The detailed analysis of the negative non-metaphorical classifying expressions produced interesting findings. Of the 17 expressions identified 12 were second-degree stance and only five were first-degree evaluation. Negative nouns referred to the negative effects mainly of climate change (*chaos, confusion, implications, risks, double whammy, fear*) and in one instance of disease (*burden*); to problematic methods (*cherry-picking*); to uncertainty or lack of clarity regarding research (*open question*); or to institutional obstacles for research (*distraction*).

Negative verbal phrases referred to phenomena being held responsible (*blame* (2)) for negative effects or placing living creatures in peril (*endanger*); to publication of research resulting in negative effects (*dash* hopes (2), *exaggerate* danger).

(28) *"the current model of farming based on huge monocultures treated with dozens of pesticides is causing **devastating** environmental harm, **undermining** vital ecosystem services that keep us all alive."* [ESG-35]

In example 28, the verbal phrase introduced by *undermining* expands on the negative adjective by specifying the elements affected by the environmental harm.

## 4.3 Attitudinal Function

As mentioned above, the presence of the attitudinal function was extremely rare with only two instances identified in the corpus, one in each newspaper, and one realised by an adjective phrase and the other by an adverb phrase. Both instances were non-metaphorical, second-degree stance, and expressed positive reactions. In the first case, new findings were considered to shed light on the current situation in the field:

(29) *"It is **clear** that we have until now underestimated the dramatic impact that local policies could make in reducing urban warming,".* [EST-65]

The second instance reflects the scientist's expectations with regard to future prospects:

(30) *"**Hopefully** over time such findings will lead to novel treatment approaches and begin to shift a culture of blame, that sufferers should just be able to snap out of it."* [ESG-75]

## 4.4 Graduation

A total of 44 graduation markers were identified in the articles (Table 8). The vast majority (40) of these were boosters (28 in *The Guardian* and 12 in *The Times*), with only a token representation (4 instances) of downtoners, all of which appeared in *The Times*. Intensifying graduation markers occurred more frequently in second-degree than in first-degree stance (31 vs. 9) whereas the downtoners were equally distributed between the two types (2 instances each).

**Table 8.** Distribution of graduation markers in the corpus

| | *The Guardian* | *The Times* | **Combined** |
|---|---|---|---|
| MOR, 2 | 23 | 8 | 31 |
| MOR, 1 | 5 | 4 | 9 |
| LESS, 2 | 0 | 2 | 2 |
| LESS, 1 | 0 | 2 | 2 |
| **Total** | **28** | **16** | **44** |

The contextual analysis showed that the boosters performed three functions. The most frequent (18 instances) was to combine with other evaluation patterns to intensify the discursive effect of the evaluation: adjective predicational phrases (9) and noun classifying phrases (9). With regard to metaphoricity, only four instances occurred with metaphorical expressions, all of which were noun classifying phrases. The exponents of the boosting function were varied: *huge* (3), *major* (2), *most* (2), with *big, critically, high, highly, impressive, large, particularly, profound, remarkably, tremendously, very,* and *widely* all used once. Of the 18 instances 16 appeared in second-degree stance (example 31) and only three in first-degree evaluation (example 32).

(31) *"They've got* ***remarkably good*** *results, it's a* ***big advance****." said Richard Hynes.* [ESG-40]

(32) *The technique could hold* ***huge*** *clinical* ***potential****, but it is also controversial because it involves altering the "germline", meaning that any changes would be passed down to future generations.* [ESG-43]

A second function (13 instances) was to emphasise the size of an impact or trend and manifested as *dramatic* (3), *dramatically* (3), *huge* (4) and *sharp*, *sharply* and *tremendously* (once each). This function was equally distributed between first-degree (example 33) and second-degree stance (example 34):

(33) *Populations of each have fallen* ***sharply*** *in the past 20 years, largely as a result of avian malaria, a parasite that has increased its range because of higher temperatures attributed to climate change.* [EST-81]

(34) *Writing in the journal Nature, the researchers describe how gene editing* ***dramatically*** *reduced the number of embryos that carried the dangerous mutation.* [ESG-40]

The third function (9 instances) only occurred in second-degree stance and was realised through forms of the lemma *strong* (5) together with *clearly*, *dramatic*, *hard,* and *major*. The boosters served to reflect the solidity of evidence, beliefs or argument:

(35) *Even so, he said, the work added* ***strong*** *biological evidence to his extreme male brain theory.* [EST-38]

(36) *"We* ***strongly*** *believe that policy decisions – such as restricting the use of neonicotinoids – must be based on sound science which gives strong evidence. And while this CEH study provides more useful information, we still don't have that definitive evidence for the impact of neonicotinoids."* [ESG-35]

(37) *"The NAS report came out* ***strongly*** *against any form of gene editing designed to simply enhance human potential," she added.* [ESG-40]

For the four downtoners, the analysis showed that two (*less*, *rare*) were combined with the predicational evaluative pattern and both were first-degree stance:

(38) *The likelihood of the increased fragrance of flowers is a* ***rare positive*** *note in the world of climate science.* [EST-63]

The other two instances realised by the adjective *tiny* qualified statistical lexical elements (*effect* and *association*) and were second-degree stance:

(39) *"Our findings demonstrate that screen use itself has at most a* ***tiny*** *association with youth mental health," Andrew Przybylski, who led the study, said.* [EST-18]

## 5 Discussion and Conclusions

This study has analysed evaluation in popularisations of scientific research in a corpus (30 articles) drawn from two English newspapers, *The Guardian* and *The Times*. The main aim was to establish the categories used for evaluation and to identify any trends in the data that would serve for a more exhaustive analysis in the complete corpus containing 150 texts. The study sought to answer questions on 1) the most frequent categories employed; 2) preference for metaphorical or non-metaphorical language; and 3) the source of evaluation – journalists (first-degree) or scientists and other stakeholders (second-degree).

The results showed a predominance of the predicational over the classifying function, with only a minimal presence of attitudinals. For grammatical category, adjectival phrases were preferred over noun phrases, with verbs and adverbs having far smaller representations. Positive evaluation predominated over negative evaluation. Thus, in answer to the first question on the most frequent categories employed in science popularisations, evaluation in this genre showed a preference for a predicational role realised through adjectival phrases of positive value. This overall trend was generally maintained in the two newspapers, except that in *The Guardian* a stronger tendency was observed towards positive evaluation, a finding that was supported by the greater use of boosters in this newspaper. With regard to the second question, the data on metaphoricity showed that non-metaphorical language was preferred to metaphorical expressions overall and in both newspapers. Although the STANCEDISC research project as a whole focused on evaluation by the writer of the text (first-degree stance), investigation of the evaluative source was included in this part of the project because of the polyphonic nature of science popularisations (Calsamiglia & López Ferrero 2003, Elorza & Pérez-Veneros 2014). The findings for the third question showed that evaluation was predominantly second-degree stance and attributed to scientists, experts, spokespersons for associations, or other stakeholders related to the research.

More detailed contextual analyses of the different functions, with cross comparisons of the categories for metaphoricity, positive versus negative evaluation and first-degree versus second-degree stance, revealed interesting exceptions to the main trends. The predicational function displayed the overall pattern for evaluation: overwhelmingly expressed through adjectival phrases, it was strongly non-metaphorical with a preference for second-degree stance and positive evaluation. However, this positive preference was due to external sources since journalists expressed positive and negative evaluation equally (20 vs. 21). The classifying function, which was expressed through noun and verb phrases, deviated from the overall pattern in that metaphorical outnumbered non-metaphorical expressions. Moreover, although positive evaluation exceeded negative expressions overall, this preference was enhanced in first-degree stance (26 vs. 9) and attenuated in second-degree stance, where positive and negative were almost equal (26 vs. 28). Similarly, metaphoricity, which almost exclusively had a classifying role, was expressed equally in positive and negative terms in second-degree stance (15 vs. 16), but was highly positive in first-degree stance (18 vs. 4). Thus, it seems that journalists are reluctant to evaluate research negatively and resort to attribution to external sources to realise this function.

The study has two main limitations. Firstly, the small numbers in some of the categories (attitudinal function, adverbs, verbs and downtoners) makes generalisation rather difficult, but this should be solved in the analysis of the complete corpus. More problematic was the difficulty encountered in the assignment of evaluative source, particularly in indirect quotations where the distinction between journalist and external source becomes blurred in the summarising and paraphrasing of the scientific content and the choice of terms. In conclusion, this study has served to identify the main categories employed for evaluation in science popularisations and has revealed preferences and trends that it is hoped will be confirmed or qualified in a full analysis of the corpus.

## References

Calsamiglia, H. and van Dijk, T. (2004). 'Popularization discourse and knowledge about the genome'. *Discourse and Society*, 15 (4), 369–389.

Calsamiglia, H. and López Ferrero, C. (2003). 'Role and Position in Scientific Voices: Reported Speech in the Media'. *Discourse Studies*, 5 (2), 147–173

Cassany, D., López, C. and Martí, J. (2000). 'La transformación divulgativa de redes conceptuales científicas. Hipótesis, modelo y estrategias'. *Revista Iberoamericana de Discurso y Sociedad*, 2 (2), 73–103.

Dahl, T. (2015). 'Contested Science in the Media: Linguistic Traces of News Writers' Framing Activity'. *Written Communication*, 32 (1), 39–65.

Elorza, I. & Pérez-Veneros, M. (2014). 'Constructing stance by means of attribution. How is the 'evaluative space' filled in science popularizations in English?'. In D. Glynn & M. Sjölin (eds.), *Subjectivity and Epistemicity. Corpus, Discourse and Literary Approaches to Stance*, pp. 281–301. Lund: Lund University Press.

Fahnestock, J. (1986). 'Accommodating science: The rhetorical life of scientific facts'. *Written Communication*, 3 (3), 330–350.

Hidalgo-Downing, L. and Pérez-Sobrino, P. (this volume). "Pushing Britain off the precipice': A CDA approach to negative evaluative stance in opinion articles on Brexit'.

Hidalgo-Downing, L., P. Pérez-Sobrino, L. Filardo-Llamas, C. Maíz-Arévalo, B. Núñez-Perucha, A. Sánchez-Moya, J. T. Williams Camus (2020). 'An annotation protocol for evaluative stance in discourse'. *Open Science Framework pre-print*. <https://osf.io/asd5r>, accessed 18 June 2021.

Martin, J. R., & White, P.R.R. (2005). *Language of evaluation: Appraisal in English*. New York: Palgrave Macmillan.

Radford, T. (2009). 'A workbench view of science communication and metaphor'. In B. Nerlich, R. Elliott and B. Larson (eds.), *Communicating Biological Sciences. Ethical and Metaphorical Dimensions*, pp. 145–152. Surrey: Ashgate.

Williams Camus, J. T. (2016). 'Get the metaphor right! Cancer treatment metaphors in the English and Spanish press'. *Alfinge: Revista de Filología*, 28, 109–138.

Celeste Moreno Palmero

# Siamo in Cura, non in Guerra: WAR Metaphors, Political Discourse, and Evaluation during the Covid-19 Pandemic

**Abstract:** The present paper analyses political tweets regarding the Covid-19 crisis. It focuses on four leaders–Trump, Johnson, Sánchez, and Conte–and in a particular time frame: March 2020. The goal of this paper is twofold: on the one hand, it endeavours to confirm whether war metaphors are pervasive in the discourse of the pandemic, on the other, it seeks to transcend the conceptual approach to metaphor and situate it within the context of evaluation in discourse. In order to do so, once war metaphors are individuated, we identify the evaluative processes implied in their use. Our claim is that war metaphors played an essential role not only by framing a novel situation as a conflict, but also by allowing the situation to be evaluated in a way that would provoke the audience to act.

**Keywords:** *conceptual metaphors, war metaphors, appraisal theory, twitter, political discourse, covid-19, attitude, evaluation, social esteem, social sanction, appreciation.*

## 1 Introduction

In early March 2020, authorities worldwide were facing a challenge without precedent as a deadly new virus spread across the globe. Governments soon understood the need to establish drastic measures and they began implementing a series of restrictive policies designed to limit the spread of the virus. Citizens across the world faced lockdowns in their homes for months at a time. Although the move was justified, the audience was unprepared to process the complexity of a pandemic and its consequent sacrifices. Communicating the urgency of the moment to the population of an entire country, particularly in the midst of persistent misinformation, posed a challenge requiring rapid, effective action.

Aware that they would need a widely disseminated, nearly infallible argument in order to reach everyone, world leaders turned quickly to social networks to convey their messages. And thus the war on Covid-19 began, and a barrage of martial vocabulary— such as frontline, enemy, battle, or fight—were incorporated into the jargon of the pandemic.

War metaphors have been always prominent within situations of social emergency (Blankshain and Lupton 2020; Chiang and Duann 2007; Flusberg et al. 2018; Wicke and Bolognesi 2020; Wilson Rose 1989). From the war on drugs or the war on hunger to the war on terror, we find countless examples of politicians using this device when trying to implement new policies or rules. War metaphors are also prevalent when describing diseases and epidemics (Wicke and Bolognesi 2020).

Generally speaking, metaphors have always been considered an ideal vehicle for ideological purposes given their ability to illustrate novel events in terms of familiar ones, facilitating the understanding of complex situations (Lakoff and Johnson 1980; Kövesces; Chilton 2004; Charteris-Black 2004). Yet metaphor can also be employed to evaluate events and persuade people to act in certain ways. In fact, metaphor not only allows us to understand events, it also has the capacity to transform social beliefs and provoke attitudes in receivers (Charteris-Black 2004). Particularly in the context of a health crisis with no precedents, evoking the appropriate evaluation was paramount.

In the present work, we study how political leaders evaluated the health crisis in terms of a war framing, and the particular outcomes arising from such evaluation. The politicians under study are: Boris Johnson (UK), Pedro Sánchez (Spain), Giuseppe Conte (Italy), and Donald Trump (USA). We focus specifically on Twitter to understand how these world leaders convey their message through this platform, which—due to its principles of linguistic economy—constitutes an optimal format with which to demonstrate the use of war metaphors and the approach employed.

This study takes a multidisciplinary methodology in which we analyse metaphors and their evaluative prospection (Hunston and Thompson 2000; Martin 1998; Martin and White 2005) and the way they frame the entire pandemic within a war frame. We are interested in the way war metaphors were employed by politicians in order to provoke a reaction that would effectively manipulate citizens into embracing the war scenario and *fighting back against the enemy* (Charteris-Black 2004; Chilton 2004; Martin and White 2005). These are the main research questions that this paper posits:

a) How do these four politicians construe the war metaphor?
b) How do these world leaders express attitude through the use of war metaphors?
c) What types of evaluations are most common and what are their potential effects?

Thus, along with the identification and study of war metaphors through a critical approach (Chilton 2004), the present paper attempts to engage in a closer look at the appraisal strategies (Martin and White 2005) employed by leaders in order to reach their performative goals.

# 2 Theoretical Framework

## 2.1 Political Discourse

Political discourse has the ability to set agendas, fuel conversation, position the self and others in specific relationships, and provoke assumptions about realities that we are obliged to accept even if only temporarily (Chilton 2004: 45). We can identify this type of discourse by its two constituents: its actors, such as prime ministers, presidents or other members of the government; and its recipients, the citizens (Van Dijk 2000). Political discourse, thus, is a matter of a very particular interpersonal communication: that of establishing institutionalised meaning.

Politicians address their people on a daily basis to tackle all sorts of issues, from local affairs to more global initiatives. Their public voice is paramount in their work as leaders. Whenever and whatever they talk about, their discourse always has an elevated potential to persuade. Political discourse is never naïve, and—whether hidden or not—always has manipulative and persuasive goals as part of its agenda.

## 2.2 Twitter as a Political Tool

Political discourse favours channels that are institutionalised, such as political speeches or press conferences. However, in the digital era to which we belong, the speed of any message's transmission is directly proportional to its efficacy. And while traditional television press conferences and newspaper articles still work to deliver politicians' statements, more and more often we find their voices channelled through the most popular social media, such as Facebook, Instagram, and Twitter. Twitter in particular has become a perennial favourite among many heads of state—Donald Trump being perhaps the most salient example in recent years. In fact, Twitter has emerged as one of the most accurate vehicles for concise and succinct ideological messages, and has increasingly become a powerful channel for political communication (Tasente 2020: 67). It can also be utilised as an ideological tool, for it is "the fastest and most critical campaign tool for reaching and mobilizing people, for gathering data and responding to the public" (Bouvier 2015: 157).

With only a limited number of characters per tweet, Twitter allows for communications that, while brief, prove extremely efficient. It is also an optimal vehicle for creating personae with solid self-representation and self-affirmation (Tasente 2020). It demonstrates commitment, and it provides high cultural capital. These factors make this platform an efficient channel for evaluation and legitimisation (Bouvier 2015). Its textual economy compels users to employ language of the most carefully crafted kind. The platform thus necessitates the use of powerful rhetoric devices from anyone wishing to achieve persuasive goals.

## 2.3 Conceptual Metaphors: the Case of War Metaphors

Among the most powerful strategies one can use to convey a convincing, yet condensed message is metaphorical thinking (Charteris-Black 2004), which provides us with the capacity to extend the boundaries of our conceptual knowledge. Metaphorical thinking facilitates the conceptualisation of complex events, in terms of simpler and more structured ones (Lakoff and Johnson 1980). The effectiveness of the use of metaphors resides in the fact that with them, text producers can influence the behaviour of text receivers. In fact, the powerful effect of metaphors is usually associated with persuasion and manipulation:

> Metaphor is a figure of speech that is typically used in persuasion; this is because it represents a novel way of viewing the world that offers some fresh insight. Because metaphor is persuasive it is frequently employed discursively in rhetorical and argumentative language such as political speeches. (Charteris Black 2004:7)

Using war metaphors to depict an adverse situation is part of a long tradition in political discourse (Flusberg et al. 2018; Wicke and Bolognesi 2020). War metaphors allow us to conceptualise a complex event in terms of a much simpler and more readily accessible concept: that of physical conflict. Thus, we evoke *enemies* in our conversations about social ills or negative events, *battles* to describe our approach to a particular adverse situation, and *heroes* to define the people charged with their resolution (Lakoff and Johnson 1980). Within medical argot, use of war metaphors is commonplace: Medicine wages war on death by conquering illness. Doctors fight disease, using their armamentarium of drugs. To cure is to defeat death. We target drugs to specific areas of the body, as if they were bullets or missiles sent on a search and destroy mission (Wilson Rose 1989:41).

The use of war metaphors in medicine implies an underlying sense of risk requiring action and urgency. War metaphors when used in this context elicit anxiety because of the tremendously high stakes: feelings of despair, loss of resources, or worse, loss of lives (Flusberg et al. 2018: 4). The evident need for prompt action, the willingness for sacrifice, and the acceptance of loss are germane to the war concept, and likely the main reason that these metaphors are such popular subjects of study in the field of critical discourse (Blankshain and Lupton 2020; Chiang & Duann 2007; Flusberg et al. 2018). Indeed, the rhetorical invocation of the military has been proven to elicit a positive response in the audience (Blankshain and Lupton 2020). In the context of a health crisis, the PANDEMIC IS WAR metaphor—with its well-defined structure and clear division between 'good' and 'evil' engaged in a struggle to achieve very diverse goals (Flusberg et al. 2018: 4)—constitutes a powerful tool for persuasive discourse.

Particularly compelling in any discussion of war metaphors is the notion of achievement. Indeed, war metaphors allow politicians to evoke fear (Flusberg et. al, 2018:12) and prove to be key to thread recognition, as in the case of the Covid-19 public health emergency. They allow speakers to confer structure upon an unprecedented event through the crafting of a clear timeline and plan of action within the conflict (Flusberg et al., 2018: 16).

## 2.4 Appraisal Theory: Evaluation in Discourse

Given their capacity to simplify conceptualisation, war metaphors can aid in the creation of a clear plan for the resolution of the events. In fact, they can be used to describe an ideologically favourable assessment of said plan. We need to keep in mind that, beyond their conceptual role, metaphors are also useful evaluative instruments:

A metaphor is an incongruous linguistic representation that has the underlying purpose of influencing opinions and judgements by persuasion; this purpose is often covert and reflects speaker intentions within particular contexts of use (Charteris-Black 2004: 21).

Metaphors in political discourse cannot, and should not, be detached from their evaluative purpose. So while it is paramount to establish the conceptual value with which a metaphor contributes to the organisation of novel knowledge; it is even more important to acknowledge its evaluative roles in discourse. Metaphors within the Appraisal framework have been defined as "the process whereby meaning is cooked twice as it were, introducing a degree of tension between wording and meaning" (Martin and White 2005: 10). This tension is reflected in the way speakers use metaphors to evaluate, given that metaphors and their linguistic features usually carry connotations that support their interpretation as attitudinal meanings (Katajamäki and Koskela 2018: 141). In order for a metaphor to be effective, shared cognitive knowledge along with a common ideological frame are expected (Lakoff and Johnson 1980). Therefore, the choice of metaphors and their use as means of evaluation may indicate how institutionalised discourse transforms or reproduces social identities, power-relations, and values (Katajamäki and Koskela 2018: 141).

Evaluation has been defined as a cognitive mental process that facilitates the understanding of an event (Martin and White 2005). With Appraisal Theory we study the way in which language is employed to evaluate, and more importantly, to construct interpersonal positioning, to create consensus, to negotiate social relationships with the receiver, and to create solidarity (Martin & White 2005). In a way, these can be considered coercive strategies, employed by the speakers in order to affect the emotions, behaviours and beliefs of the receivers (Hart 2010: 62–63), and move them to act.

Within Appraisal Theory we find three main approaches to the study of stance in discourse: attitude, engagement, and graduation. For the purpose of this paper, we will be focusing only on Attitude, "a framework for mapping feelings" (Martin and White 2005: 42) because a particular attitude in discourse can help politicians to achieve their goals when it comes to restrictive policies:

> Through expressing one's feelings and opinions, one can build a particular kind of relationship with the reader/hearer by confirming solidarity with their views or by leading or persuading them towards a certain viewpoint and by fine-tuning the level of certainty in statements (Ngo and Unsworth 2015: 1).

Within the Attitude system, we find three semantic regions related to emotion, ethics and aesthetics: affect, judgment, and appreciation (Martin and White 2005: 42). Affect allows us to express positive or negative emotions: "do we feel happy or sad, confident or anxious, interested or bored?" (Martin and White 2005: 42). Judgment allows us to evaluate people's behaviour, with admiration or critique, praise or condemnation. Finally, appreciation deals with "evaluations of semiotic and natural phenomena, according to the ways in which they are valued or not in a given field" (Martin and White 2005: 42). All three categories have different levels of positive and negative subclasses.

Evaluation of people, or judgment, comes in two types: social esteem and social sanction. Esteem evaluates normality (or what a culture considers normal), capacity (one's capacity to do something), and the tenacity (or dependability) of a person. Sanctions, on the other hand, have to do with one's honesty, ethical position regarding a social issue, or propriety (Read and Carroll 2012: 425). Alternatively, we have appreciation, which focuses on the evaluation of natural events, objects, and abstract constructs. Although appreciation may be related to aesthetics, such is not always the case. Indeed we can find instances in which social valuation of an event or process is represented.[1]

1 Information retrieved on Feb, 9th, 2021 from <https://www.grammatics.com/appraisal/appraisaloutline/unframed/appraisaloutline.htm#:~:text=APPRECIATION1%20is%20the%20system,such%20as%20significant%20and%20harmful>.

## 2.5 Evaluative Metaphors in Discourse

When studying political discourse as it deals with a global crisis, interpersonal meaning, positioning, and, more importantly, solidarity will be key elements in the constitution of an institutionalised frame. In a study that focuses on metaphors, we need to keep in mind that "the framing power of metaphors does not just depend on the conceptual structures involved, but emerges in the dynamic interaction of people 'talking and thinking' in interaction" (Semino et al. 2018: 631).

In this particular scenario, with the use of war metaphors, world leaders in question are creating a mental model in which a virus becomes an active war enemy whose defeat involves us all. This type of evaluation has the metafunctional goal of creating an ideational model of evaluation, not only by evoking evaluation, but also by provoking an attitudinal response through emotive coercion. In fact, "ideational meaning can be used not just to invite but to provoke an attitudinal response in readers" (Martin and White 2005: 64).

For that reason, beyond the identification and analysis of war metaphors in political discourses regarding Covid-19, we want to look at evaluation through the lenses of Appraisal Theory to shed light on the evaluative power of metaphorical thinking. Considering the context, appealing to solidarity constitutes a powerful tool for politicians exhorting citizens to "play their part" and "fight this virus". In order to do so, an array of evaluative meanings is set into motion to provoke citizens to act. Judgement and appreciation have the ability to institutionalise a position, an aspect that proves to be crucial when asking people to follow a new set of restrictive rules such as those imposed as a result of the pandemic:

> One way to think about judgment and appreciation is to see them as institutionalised feelings, which take us out of our everyday common sense world into the uncommon sense worlds of shared community values. In these terms, judgment reworks feelings in the realm of proposals about behaviour – how we should behave or not; some of these proposals get formalised as rules and regulations administered by church and state. Appreciation on the other hand reworks feelings as propositions about the value of things – what they are worth or not. (Martin and White 2005: 45)

In sum, evaluative metaphors, particularly military ones, can evoke evaluation and thus more successfully accomplish persuasive goals. Others have previously noted, not without certain consternation, that the use of war metaphors regarding the Covid-19 crisis is rather widespread (Blankshain and Lupton 2020; Chiang and Duann 2007; Dotti 2020; Musu 2020). Our analysis thus seeks to confirm the prevalence of war metaphors over other types of metaphors, and whether a particular evaluative position is delineated when using war metaphors to talk about the current pandemic.

# 3 Data and Method

## 3.1 Corpus

Given our intention to examine the extent to which evaluative war metaphors were employed to provoke people to act, the origins of Covid-19 ideological discourse are of paramount importance for the purposes of this paper. Hence, the period under analysis includes the early stages of the Covid-19 crisis: the first few weeks after the virus started to spread outside China (from March 1st to March 31st). This is the period when governments began employing the idea of war as a way to persuade citizens to behave accordingly and to embrace what would inevitably be viewed as draconian lockdown measures. The type of discursive framing that politicians will favour and that will become the source of the Covid-19 lexicon is particularly evident during this period. Terms such as *curfew*, *frontline workers*, or *battle*—the use of which has become daily—originated in those early days.

Corpus linguistics always faces the challenge of determining an appropriate corpus size. For the purpose of this paper, we narrow our analysis down to the four Western countries in which the virus emergency developed most rapidly: the USA, Italy, Spain, and the UK.[2] Once we determined the set of politicians under study, we performed an advanced search for Twitter activity from March 1st to March 31st, 2020 for each of the users (Giuseppe Conte, Boris Johnson, Pedro Sánchez, and Donald J. Trump). Having individuated all tweets from this period for each participant, we selected and organised those that specifically regarded Covid-19, identifying metaphors according to the parameters employed in Critical Metaphor Analysis (Charteris-Black 2004). Next, we singled out the specific war metaphors present in the texts. With that information at hand, we proceeded to evaluate those sixty-eight tweets that had at least one instance of war metaphor.

Once this stage was completed, we carried out an appraisal analysis following protocols developed by Martin and White (2005) for the analysis of the attitudinal system. In order to do so, we proceeded to analyse the type of evaluation presented in the aforementioned war metaphors at the core of this study.

2 The country choice comes also in base of the language spoken by this researcher. An interesting study including other countries in the world would shed light into the question of whether the notion of war is similar in different cultures. Similarly, a parallel study could compare male vs. female politicians to see if the war metaphor is equally employed.

## 4 Analysis and Discussion

In order to determine whether politicians were employing war metaphors and their evaluative values, we need to examine the frequency and ways in which these leaders used Twitter. Naturally, the degree of activity varies from one politician to the other: Donald Trump was its most prolific user (until his account was suspended) and Giuseppe Conte the most frugal. Even so, the data show that each employed Twitter on a daily basis as a vehicle for communication about the Covid-19 crisis. Indeed, with the exception of Donald Trump, Covid-19 was the most prominent topic in their tweets during the period under study (March 1st to March 31st):

**Table 1.** Number of tweets by topic: Covid-19 vs. other issues

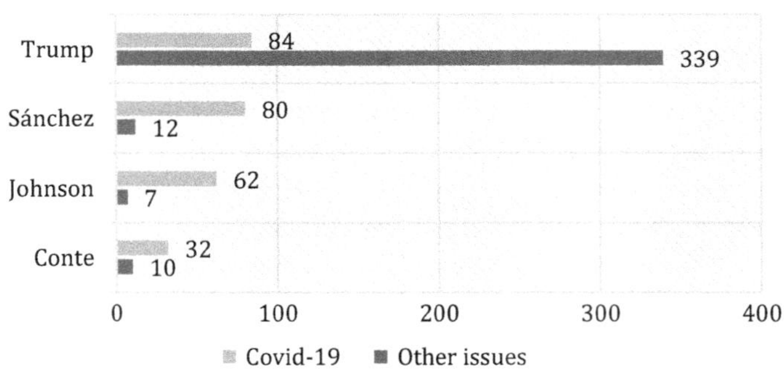


When it comes to the type of language employed to describe the crisis, we find a stable and extensive use of war metaphors among all the participants: Trump (14 %), Sánchez (25 %), Johnson (22 %), and Conte (20 %).

**Table 2.** Tweets regarding Covid-19 with and without war metaphors

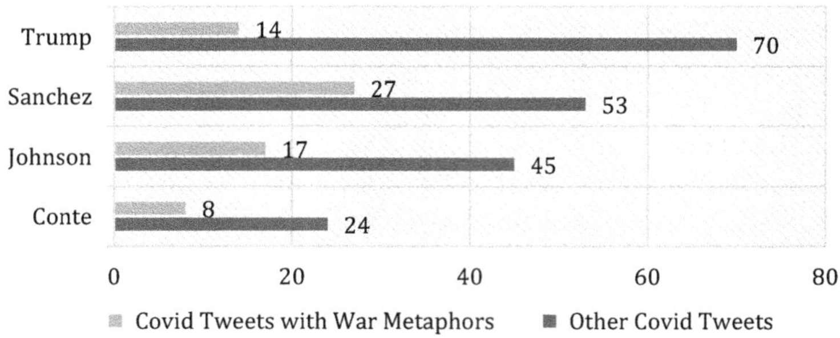


## 4.1 War Metaphors

War metaphors are consistent for all four of the world leaders and constitute the preferred metaphor with which to conceptualise the Covid-19 health crisis. These data correspond with a trend that has been found in similar studies in which war metaphors were the frame most frequently employed (Wicke and Bolognesi 2020). In fact, while container and movement metaphors are also common, they do not play as determining a role as that of reframing the whole event as a war, and on many occasions they are deployed within a war scenario.

Cognitive linguists assert that the core importance of metaphorical thinking is not the language itself, but the cognitive process by which we are able to conceptualise one mental domain in terms of another (Lakoff 1993: 20). In the early stages of a global crisis it is crucial to find reference points that facilitate the interpretation of complex, novel events. When politicians stated that we were at war with a virus, they employed "a metaphor in which a highly complicated and unfamiliar concept (in this case SARS-CoV-2) becomes conceptualised in terms of a more familiar concept (in this case war) to allow auditors to more readily understand the unfamiliar concept" (Bates 2020: 2). Further, the war metaphor acts as a vehicle to frame adversarial relationships, evoking fear that can motivate people to behave in particular ways: such as paying closer attention to the circumstances, taking action, or even re-evaluating their beliefs (Flusberg et al. 2018).

Indeed, war scenarios facilitate our understanding of ourselves more as soldiers than as mere citizens. Recognizing this, politicians can call for obedience and appeal to our patriotism in ways other metaphors would not allow (Musu

2020). Thus, by deploying a wartime discourse early on, these politicians created a scenario in which we are all at war with an invisible or hidden enemy:

(1) *The world is at **war** with **a hidden enemy**. WE WILL **WIN**! (Trump, Mar 17th)*
(2) *We're getting better at testing. This crisis is so difficult because the **enemy** is invisible. The answer is to remove the cloak of invisibility to identify the virus, and to be able to know which of us is carrying it and who has actually had it and got over it. (Johnson, Mar 19th)*
(3) *Ebbene, che tutti sappiano che lo Stato è al loro fianco, non lilascerà soli. Lo Stato non è solo strutture e istituzioni. Lo Stato siamo noi: 60 milioni di cittadini che **lottano** insieme, con forza e coraggio, per **sconfiggere** questo **nemico invisibile**. (Mar 17th)*
[Well everyone should know that the State is on their side, it will not leave them alone. The state is not just structures and institutions. We are the state: 60 million citizens who **fight** together, with strength and courage, to **defeat** this **invisible enemy**].

In these examples, the conceptualisation centres around the idea that Covid-19 is an active enemy and we (all the citizens) belong to an army of active soldiers combating together. Metaphorical entailments such as *fight, enemy, win, beat,* or *defeat* appear frequently in the language of these four leaders and contribute to the establishment of a war scenario. Interestingly, the virus is portrayed as an invisible or hidden enemy, immediately flagging this war as unconventional (Bates 2020: 5). Although politicians understand that this conflict will be very different from others, they persist in their use of military rhetoric despite the fact that our subsequently construed duty as soldiers consists primarily in sheltering in place (or in other words, doing nothing):

(4) *We will get through this together, and we will **beat** the virus. **To win this fight**, we need everyone to follow our advice: as far as possible, **we want you to stay at home**. The more effectively everyone does this, the faster this country will recover.*

Yet the conceptualisation of such a simple action as a heroic *fight*, is far more persuasive than (for instance) employment of container or natural phenomena metaphors. Indeed, lexical metaphors evoking the idea of a battlefield or a fight recur pervasively. Almost all of the tweets in this corpus contain at least one lexical metaphor directly related to the idea of combat or fight. This discursive choice appeals to sentiments of solidarity:

(5) *I want to say a huge thank you on behalf of the whole country to everyone working in our NHS, of every specialism and role, in our **fight against the coronavirus pandemic**. We've never needed you more than we do today.*
(6) *Ognuno di noi, con la propria determinazione, può offrire un prezioso contributo per **vincere questa battaglia**. Facciamo risuonare ancora il nostro Inno. Possono*

*separarci una porta, un balcone, una strada. Ma niente e nessuno potrà separare i nostri cuori. Uniti ce la faremo. (Conte, Mar 14th)*
[Each of us with our own determination, can make a valuable contribution **to winning this battle.** Let's play our hymn again. A door, a balcony, a road can separate us. But nothing and no one will be able to separate our hearts. United we will make it].

As in all wars, we can also find our particular heroes, *the frontline workers*, as they have come to be known in the mainstream. Thus, *weapons, heroes,* and *frontlines* are common tropes in this corpus:

(7) *Contamos con uno de los mejores sistemas sanitarios del mundo, sostenido por grandes profesionales. Ellos y ellas son nuestro* ***escudo*** *más seguro ante una emergencia sanitaria como la que vivimos. Desde el Gobierno reconocemos y agradecemos su enorme trabajo frente al #coronavirus. (Sánchez, Mar 10th)*
[We have one of the best health systems in the world, supported by great professionals. They are our safest **shield** in the face of a health emergency like the one we are experiencing. From the Government we recognise and appreciate their enormous work in front of the #coronavirus].

(8) *Today I spoke with American physicians and nurses to thank them for their tireless work. Doctors and nurses are at* ***the front lines of this war*** *and are true American* ***HEROES!*** *With their help, America will* ***WIN****. (Trump, Mar 18th)*

(9) *Gracias, de corazón, a todas y todos los profesionales de la salud. Sois ejemplo de* ***heroicidad****, entrega y trabajo. Hoy, el país entero os aplaude. (Sánchez, Mar 14th)*
[Thank you very much, with all my heart, to all the health professionals. You are an example of **heroism**, commitment and hard work. Today, the entire country applauds you].

However, the use of war metaphors is not merely an expression of gratitude toward these workers, but an effective appeal to the general public to play its role in this battle/combat/fight. In the following examples, war metaphors are combined with the notion of active responsibility for that very purpose:

(10) *Her Majesty The Queen speaks for us all. We all have a vital role to play. We will do whatever it takes* ***to beat*** *this together. (Johnson, Mar 19th)*

(11) *This afternoon, we're announcing new guidelines for every American to follow over the next 15 days as* ***we combat*** *the virus. Each and every one of us has a critical role to play in stopping the spread and transmission of the virus. (Trump, Mar 19th)*

(12) *Non possiamo* ***abbassare la guardia****.* ***Combattiamo la sfida*** *più importante degli ultimi decenni, la più grave dal dopoguerra e per* ***vincerla*** *serve il contributo responsabile di 60 milioni di italiani. Uniti ce la faremo.*
[We cannot let our guard down. **We are fighting the most important challenge** of recent decades, the most serious since the war and to **win** it we need the responsible contribution of 60 million Italians. United we would do it]

In pursuit of more than the simple expression of an opinion, these politicians were employing persuasive language and emotive coercion to convince people to perform certain actions (stay home, wear a mask, keep the distance, and trust us). The key to the performative success of this language lies in its appeals to our feelings. By employing military metaphors and declaring war on Covid-19, these leaders coaxed disparate individuals into a unified, institutionalised group whom they expected to abide by *wartime* rules. All these tweets have been carefully crafted (probably by a team of public relations professionals) to engender an institutionalised attitude toward the crisis—one that naturalises a reading position that "will be fairly directive in the kinds of attitude it wants readers to share" (Martin and White 2005: 63). In this context, metaphors have the effect of intensifying emotive coercion and constitute an optimal tool for invoking attitude (Martin and White 2005: 67).

## 4.2 Evaluation in Discourse: Evaluative War Metaphors

Discerning how this persuasive agenda was executed requires examining the evaluative aspects of these war metaphors in order to understand the extent to which they provoke—rather than evoke—an active evaluation. As mentioned before, Appraisal Theory provides profound insight into the ways language, and more specifically lexical metaphors, can spur evaluation in the audience (Katajamäki and Koskela 2018). In a total of sixty-eight tweets, we found ninety-six metaphorical expressions with a type of evaluation that included positive judgements (+capacity, +tenacity) and negative appreciation. As we can observe, in the tables, the most frequent metaphorical expressions are related to positive judgment (a total of sixty-eight) that can be either praising the capacity of the people, as we as their tenacity to defeat the enemy:

**Table 3.** Type of attitudes in metaphorical expressions

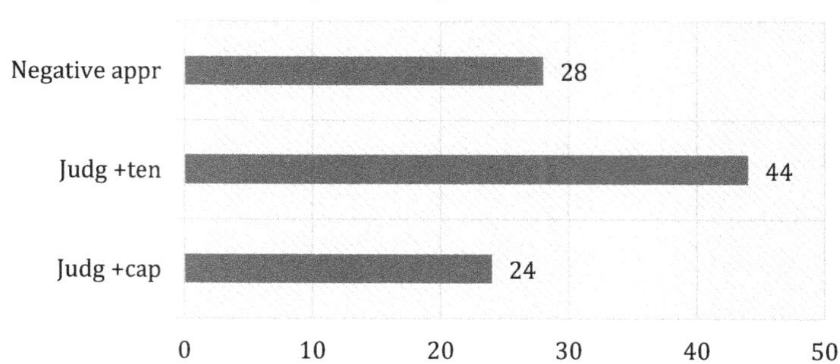

Indeed, as we see in the following table, *to win, to beat* and *to fight* are the more prominent metaphorical expressions, employed by these politicians. There is a distinction between verbal expressions and nouns. The data shows that evaluative metaphorical expressions are either negative appreciation (with nouns such as battle, fight, war, or enemy) or positive judgement (with verbs such as to win, to fight, or to beat). For example, in the case of *fight* and *to fight*, we find that the noun is employed to negatively appreciate the pandemic, whereas the verb, *to fight*, is used to emphasise the tenacity of the people (+ten). As a clear trend, positive tenacity is preferred over positive capacity. The following table shows the distribution of metaphorical expressions and their type of evaluative value:

It is interesting to notice that among the four leaders, we find certain differences when it comes to their preferred metaphorical expressions. For example, the only leader that uses the metaphorical expression *war* is Donald Trump (five times); whereas Giuseppe Conte and Pedro Sánchez prefer the term *battle* and Boris Johnson *fight*. However, evaluative strategies appear to be consistent among them:

**Table 4.** metaphorical expressions and their evaluative value

| EXPRESSION | # | JUDGMENT | APPRECIATION |
|---|---|---|---|
| BATTLE | 5 | | NEGATIVE |
| FIGHT | 7 | | NEGATIVE |
| WAR | 5 | | NEGATIVE |
| ENEMY | 6 | | NEGATIVE |
| TO WIN | 22 | POSITIVE (capacity) | |
| TO BEAT | 17 | POSITIVE (tenacity) | |
| TO FIGHT | 8 | POSITIVE (tenacity) | |
| TO COMBAT | 8 | POSITIVE (tenacity) | |
| TO DEFEAT | 2 | POSITIVE (tenacity) | |
| TO SURRENDER | 2 | POSITIVE (tenacity) | |
| VICTORY | 5 | POSITIVE (capacity) | |
| WEAPON | 1 | POSITIVE (tenacity) | |
| SHIELD | 1 | POSITIVE (tenacity) | |
| HEROES | 3 | POSITIVE (tenacity) | |
| ATTACK | 1 | POSITIVE (tenacity) | |
| FRONT LINES | 2 | POSITIVE (tenacity) | |

**Table 5.** Distribution of evaluative expressions by participant

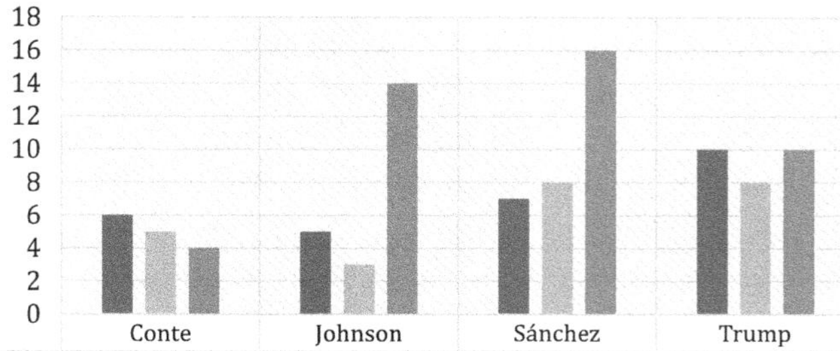


| | Conte | Johnson | Sánchez | Trump |
|---|---|---|---|---|
| neg appr | 6 | 5 | 7 | 10 |
| Judg +cap | 5 | 3 | 8 | 8 |
| Judg +ten | 4 | 14 | 16 | 10 |

Although we can perceive slightly different preferences when it comes to the type of evaluative war metaphors employed, there is a constancy in their evaluative goals. In fact, the first clear strategy consistent amongst the leaders is that of a negative appreciation of the pandemic. This negative valuation is performed by means of the structure of the war metaphor itself, in which the virus is portrayed as an enemy to be defeated:

(13) *The Media should view this as a time of unity and strength. We have* ***a common enemy****, actually,* ***an enemy of the World****, the CoronaVirus. We must beat it as quickly and safely as possible. There is nothing more important to me than the life & safety of the United States! (Trump, Mar 11th)*

(14) *We're getting better at testing. This crisis is so difficult because* ***the enemy is invisible****. The answer is to remove the cloak of invisibility to identify the virus, and to be able to know which of us is carrying it and who has actually had it and got over it (Johnson, Mar 19th)*

(15) *Cada ciudadano y ciudadana debe cuidarse para cuidar así de los demás.* ***Si queremos vencer*** *al #Covid_19 cuanto antes, necesitamos seguir las recomendaciones oficiales. Responsabilidad y disciplina social. Con nuestro esfuerzo personal contribuiremos a la victoria frente al virus. (Sánchez, Mar 21st)*
[Each citizen must take care of themselves to take care of others. **If we want to beat** *# Covid_19* as soon as possible, we need to follow the official recommendations. Responsibility and social discipline. With our personal effort we will contribute to victory against the virus.]

This negative valuation proves key to effecting a political agenda with regards to virus containment measurements: that is, getting people to play their part. As Blankshain and Lupton (2020) observe, "labelling something as 'war' provides those in power more leeway in their policy actions". For instance, curfews, which have been imposed throughout the world for more than a year now, are only possible if we have already accepted that we live in times of war. Moreover, being at war fosters a strong sense of commitment and partisanship. However, as mentioned before, the only leader that uses the metaphorical expression "war" is Donald Trump, while the other leaders favour the notion of battle or fight:

(16) *The world is at* ***war*** *with a hidden enemy. WE WILL WIN! (Trump, Mar 27th)*

(17) *I want all Americans to understand: we are at* ***war*** *with an invisible enemy, but that enemy is no match for the spirit and resolve of the American people…(Trump, Mar 18th)*

(18) *Esta* ***batalla*** *la vamos a ganar con el compromiso y la responsabilidad de todos y todas. Protégete para proteger a los demás. (Sánchez, Mar 15th)*
[We are going to **win** this battle with the commitment and responsibility of everyone. Protect yourself to protect others]

(19) *Questo è il momento della responsabilità, da parte di tutti. Questa* ***battaglia*** *si vince solo con l'impegno di ognuno di noi (Conte, Mar 8th)*
[This is the moment of responsibility, on the part of all. This **battle** can only be won with the commitment of each of us]

(20) *However tough the months ahead we have the resolve and the resources to win* ***the fight****. And, to repeat, this government will do whatever it takes. (Johnson, Mar 18th)*

Yet in order to create that institutionalised community, leaders require a solid network of interconnected meanings that will support their claims. To do so, a negative evaluation of the event is not enough and positive judgment—that is, appealing to the people—emerges as a potential game changer. As noted by Martin and White (2005: 54), "capacity is to ability, as tenacity is to inclination" and these two positive axes of judgement are key when appealing to the public to play their part, because citizens are expected to have both the ability to win this battle and the resolve to fight courageously (by staying home, wearing a mask, and maintaining social distancing).

If on one side of the spectrum we find an evil virus that has declared war upon us, on the other we will find the courageous people willing to risk their lives and freedom in order to win the battle. In fact, positive judgment is pervasive in all the tweets we analysed: citizens are encouraged to embrace an active role in the war, so that they can be admired and praised (Martin 1995: 30). Lexical metaphors such as *fight, or combat,* are indirect appeals to an innate desire to be seen as courageous. In many instances, this positive judgment focuses on social esteem by emphasizing the tenacity of citizens plunged into a state of war:

(21) *We will get through this together, and* ***we will beat the virus****. To win this fight, we need everyone to follow our advice: as far as possible, we want you to stay at home.*

*The more effectively everyone does this, the faster this country will recover. (Johnson, Mar 22nd)*

(22) *Quiero enviar un mensaje de confianza, de serenidad y unidad a la ciudadanía española ante el #coronavirus. Para* ***combatir*** *esta emergencia de salud pública haremos lo que haga falta, cuando haga falta y donde haga falta. Juntos superaremos esta crisis. (Sánchez, Mar 10th)*
[I want to send a message of confidence, serenity and unity to the Spanish citizens in the face of #coronavirus. To **combat** this public health emergency, we will do what it takes, when it is needed, and where it is needed. Together we will overcome this crisis]

We need to keep in mind that positive judgements such as tenacity emerge through pursuit of goals in a specific manner (Katajamäki and Koskela 2018: 151). In these examples, political leaders invoke tenacity when they refer to combating or fighting the enemy. Similarly, when describing health workers in a context of war as heroes, front line soldiers or strategic weapons, politicians are employing positive evaluations that emphasises their tenacity:

(23) *Contamos con uno de los mejores sistemas sanitarios del mundo, sostenido por grandes profesionales.* ***Ellos y ellas son nuestro escudo*** *más seguro ante una emergencia sanitaria como la que vivimos. Desde el Gobierno reconocemos y agradecemos su enorme trabajo frente al #coronavirus (Sánchez, Mar 13th)*
[We have one of the best health systems in the world, supported by great professionals. **They are our safest shield** in the face of a health emergency like the one we are experiencing. From the Government we recognise and appreciate their enormous work against the #coronavirus]

(24) *Today I spoke with American physicians and nurses to thank them for their tireless work. Doctors and nurses are at the front lines of this war and are true* ***American HEROES!*** *With their help, America will WIN. (Trump, Mar 18th)*

The use of social esteem, in fact, increases the patriotic appeal of these exhortations to *fight*. Hence, when people were asked to stay home, wear a mask, or maintain distance from our families and friends, we felt that it was a war sacrifice, and that we, as soldiers in this conflict, needed to do our part. The target of judgement in these tweets are the countries' citizens, which may be considered both a group of individuals, but also an institutionalised entity: we the people, the country. The ultimate goal being a victory. In fact, the notion of victory in enhanced throughout these tweets by means of metaphorical expressions such as *win* (22 times) *or victory* (5 times). Assuming that everyone plays its role, as courageous soldiers, we will win this battle:

(25) *We are marshalling the full power of government and society to achieve* ***victory*** *over the virus. Together, we will endure, we will prevail, and we will* ***WIN!*** *#CARESAct… (Trump, Mar 27th)*

(26) *We have the resolve and the resources to* ***win*** *the fight against #Coronavirus (Johnson, Mar 19th)*

(27) *Non possiamo abbassare la guardia. Combattiamo la sfida più importante degli ultimi decenni, la più grave dal dopoguerra e per* ***vincerla*** *serve il contributo responsabile di 60 milioni di italiani. Uniti ce la faremmo (Conte, Mar 16th)*
[We can't let our guard down. We are fighting the most important challenge of recent decades, the most serious since the war and to **win** it we need the responsible contribution of 60 million Italians. United we would do it]

(28) *La* ***victoria*** *depende de cada ciudadano y ciudadana. El heroísmo es también lavarse las manos, quedarse en casa y protegerse uno mismo para proteger a la sociedad. Tardaremos semanas, pero pararemos al #Covid19 con unidad y disciplina social, cumpliendo cada uno con nuestro deber. (Sánchez, Mar 13th)*
[**Victory** depends on each citizen. Heroism is also washing your hands, staying home, and protecting yourself to protect society. It will take weeks, but we will stop # Covid19 with unity and social discipline, each one fulfilling our duty.]

With the use of this evaluative strategy, leaders are highlighting our capacity, as nations or individuals, to be able to win a war against Covid-19. This type of evaluation is, perhaps one of the most effective and, definitely, one of the most recurrent strategies among these tweets. With it, patriotism is enhanced, and optimism spread as the only possible way to overcome this difficult situation.

In sum, metaphors of war, as we have seen, play a role a) in the establishment of a particular frame that would facilitate the interpretation of a novel event; and b) as evaluative items with a persuasive goal in mind. Looking at the intersection of Conceptual Metaphor and Appraisal Theories we get a complete picture of the process of persuasion and evaluation in political discourse. We are not simply identifying a conceptual frame of war inherent to the sanitary crisis; we are also using the study of evaluation in language to demonstrate its high degree of efficiency. Analysing metaphor beyond the realm of its conceptual nature provides a more complete understanding of the process of co-construction of interpersonal meaning, emotive coercion, and ideological agendas.

## 5 Conclusions

The present paper looked at institutionalised media discourse and the ways in which politicians employed evaluative metaphors to incite their audiences to action. In the midst of a health crisis, people were asked to embrace highly restrictive policies in order to halt the crisis. World leaders started to make their voices heard by means of their social networks, press conferences, and public statements. We focused on one such social network, Twitter, for its very political nature.

Our study revealed the prominence of the employment of war metaphors across the four leaders under study. We were also able to confirm that one of the goals of war metaphors within this appraisal and attitude-taking context was to evoke—or rather provoke—a particular behaviour in the audience. And that was carried out by means of the evaluation exercised by these metaphors. Given the institutionalised nature of these texts, it not surprising that the most common evaluative strategies were judgement and appreciation. The latter was carried out by means of a negative valuation of the health crisis as a war, and a virus as our enemy. Judgment focused on providing positive social esteem and social sanction. This is done by means of metaphorical and non-metaphorical expressions working in conjunction. The employment of war metaphors facilitates evaluation that is inclined to positive judgement.

In sum, war metaphors were the common thread that unified a discourse of partisan commitment to overcome the challenges that the current pandemic began to cast over the entire planet. Such metaphors are the very fabric that binds the ideational selection in these four presidents' discourses; in fact, war metaphors situated the mental event within specific coordinates that encouraged people to behave in a particular way.

As we saw in the introductory section, many critical voices have emerged arguing against the use of war metaphors to engage with Covid-19. However, the present study suggests that, given their evaluative power, the war metaphor played an important role to emphasise the importance of the current crisis and our roles in stopping its spread. Other alternatives could have been employed to appeal to the people and make them abide by the restrictive rules imposed in the last year; nonetheless, we do not know to what extent other types of metaphors would have been as effective in provoking the particular assessment that this frame did. What we know is that the employment of war metaphors during the early stage of this pandemic provoked a definite assessment of the situation as one in which everyone needed to play an important role.

As the pandemic unfolds, with new challenges and hopes, politicians may or may not want to change their strategic language. As the persuasive goals and ideological interests shift, so too does the way institutional discourse conveys messages. With new challenges ahead as new variants emerge and sceptical people abandon their role, the stances leaders adopt will be critical in determining the way the remainder of the pandemic unfolds.

## Appendix: Corpus

| | | TWEET | JUDGMENT | | AP |
|---|---|---|---|---|---|
| | | metaphorical expressions in **bold** | CAP + | TEN + | VAL - |
| ITALY | | CONTE | | | |
| 8-Mar | 1 | Questo è il momento della responsabilità, da parte di tutti. Questa **battaglia** si **vince** solo con l'impegno di ognuno di noi | 1 | | 1 |
| 9-Mar | 2 | Questa **battaglia** si **vince** con il contributo di TUTTI. Agiamo responsabilmente. | 1 | | 1 |
| 14-Mar | 3 | Ognuno di noi, con la propria determinazione, può offrire un prezioso contributo per **vincere** questa **battaglia.** Facciamo risuonare ancora il nostro Inno. Possono separarci una porta, un balcone, una strada. Ma niente e nessuno potrà separare i nostri cuori. Uniti ce la faremo | 1 | | 1 |
| 16-Mar | 4 | Non possiamo abbassare la guardia. **Combattiamo** la **sfida** più importante degli ultimi decenni, la più grave dal dopoguerra e per **vincerla** serve il contributo responsabile di 60 milioni di italiani. Uniti ce la faremmo | 1 | 1 | 1 |
| | 5 | Ebbene, che tutti sappiano che lo Stato è al loro fianco, non li lascerà soli. Lo Stato non è solo strutture e istituzioni. Lo Stato siamo noi: 60 milioni di cittadini che **lottano** insieme, con forza e coraggio, per sconfiggere questo **nemico invisibile**. | | 1 | 1 |

| | | TWEET | JUDGMENT | AP |
|---|---|---|---|---|
| | 6 | L'Europa **batte** un colpo! Forte, sonoro, adeguato alla gravità dell'emergenza sanitaria che stiamo affrontando e dello shock economico che ne consegue. Bene la BCE | 1 | |
| 23-Mar | 7 | Quelli che stiamo vivendo sono giorni pesanti, difficili. Ognuno di noi sta compiendo piccoli e grandi sacrifici, rinunciando ad abitudini e affetti. Ma questa è una **battaglia** che si **vince** restando uniti. | 1 | 1 |
| 28-Mar | 8 | L'Unione europea ha un appuntamento con la storia e la storia non aspetta, bisogna esserne all'altezza. La reazione all'emergenza #Coronavirus deve essere forte, vigorosa e coesa. Mi **batterò** per i cittadini italiani fino all'ultima goccia di sudore. | 1 | |
| UK | | JOHNSON | | |
| | 1 | Coronavirus may very well be a challenge in the weeks and months ahead. But I have no doubt that with the help of the NHS and its incomparable staff, this country will get through it — and **beat** it. | 1 | |
| 18-Mar | 2 | However tough the months ahead we have the resolve and the resources to **win** the **fight.** And, to repeat, this government will do whatever it takes. | 1 | 1 |
| 18-Mar | 3 | We have the resolve and the resources to **win** the **fight** against #Coronavirus | 1 | 1 |

| | | TWEET | JUDGMENT | AP |
|---|---|---|---|---|
| 19-Mar | 4 | I want to say a huge thank you on behalf of the whole country to everyone working in our NHS, of every specialism and role, in our **fight** against the coronavirus pandemic. We've never needed you more than we do today. | 1 | |
| 19-Mar | 5 | We're getting better at testing. This crisis is so difficult because **the enemy is invisible**. The answer is to remove the cloak of invisibility to identify the virus, and to be able to know which of us is carrying it and who has actually had it and got over it. | | 1 |
| 19-Mar | 6 | I say to business, stand by your employees, stand by your workers, because we will stand by you.<br>I have absolutely no doubt that we will turn the tide of this disease and **beat** it together. | 1 | |
| | 7 | Her Majesty The Queen speaks for us all. We all have a vital role to play. We will do whatever it takes to **beat** this together. | 1 | |
| 20-Mar | 8 | We can **beat** this together, but only if we follow government advice and look out for each other. | 1 | |
| 20-Mar | 9 | NHS staff are doing extraordinary work across the country to help our **fight** against coronavirus. We now need to play our part in supporting them by following the government's guidance and working from home if you possibly can. | 1 | |

| | | TWEET | | JUDGMENT | AP |
|---|---|---|---|---|---|
| 21-Mar | 10 | Josephine sets a great example to us all by postponing her birthday party until we have sent coronavirus packing. Together we can **beat** this. In the meantime let's all wish her happy birthday (twice) whilst washing our hands. | | 1 | |
| 22-Mar | 11 | We will get through this together, and we will **beat** the virus. To **win** this **fight,** we need everyone to follow our advice: as far as possible, we want you to stay at home. The more effectively everyone does this, the faster this country will recover. | 1 | 1 | 1 |
| 22-Mar | 12 | We need you to do your bit to help us **beat** #coronavirus<br>Please RT. | | 1 | |
| 25-Mar | 13 | Fantastic to see so many people doing their bit in the **fight** against #coronavirus<br>If you want to volunteer to help the NHS, you can do so here: https://goodsamapp.org/NHS | | | 1 |
| 26-Mar | 14 | Governments around the world must step up to help us **defeat** #coronavirus. I've announced a further £210m of aid funding for vaccine research following today's G20 call, meaning the UK is going above and beyond in the search for a vaccine. | | 1 | |
| 26-Mar | 15 | On behalf of the whole country, I want to thank all the incredible nurses, doctors, NHS support staff & carers who are working flat out to **fight** coronavirus | | 1 | |

| | | TWEET | JUDGMENT | AP |
|---|---|---|---|---|
| 27-Mar | 16 | Over the last 24 hours I have developed mild symptoms and tested positive for coronavirus. I am now self-isolating, but I will continue to lead the government's response via video-conference as we fight this virus.<br>Together we will **beat** this.<br>#StayHomeSaveLives | 1 | |
| 28-Mar | 17 | Thank you to everybody who's doing what I'm doing, working from home and stopping the virus spreading from household to household. We're going to **beat** it, and we're going to **beat** it together. Stay at home, protect the NHS and save lives. #StayHomeSaveLives | 2 | |
| SPAIN | | SANCHEZ | | |
| 10-Mar | 1 | Quiero enviar un mensaje de confianza, de serenidad y unidad a la ciudadanía española ante el #coronavirus. Para **combatir** esta emergencia de salud pública haremos lo que haga falta, cuando haga falta y donde haga falta. Juntos superaremos esta crisis. | 1 | |
| 10-Mar | 2 | Contamos con uno de los mejores sistemas sanitarios del mundo, sostenido por grandes profesionales. Ellos y ellas son nuestro **escudo** más seguro ante una emergencia sanitaria como la que vivimos. Desde el Gobierno reconocemos y agradecemos su enorme trabajo frente al #coronavirus. | 1 | |

| | | TWEET | JUDGMENT | | AP |
|---|---|---|---|---|---|
| 10-Mar | 3 | Cada persona puede ayudar a **vencer** la emergencia del #coronavirus siguiendo las recomendaciones de los expertos. Haciéndolo protegemos nuestra salud, la de nuestros familiares y conciudadanos. Habrá semanas difíciles, pero lo superaremos si todos y todas asumimos nuestro papel. | 1 | | |
| 11-Mar | 4 | Solo con la implicación y responsabilidad de toda la sociedad, y trabajando de forma coordinada desde las distintas administraciones superaremos esta situación. Estamos listos, @DrTedros, para **luchar** unidos frente al #COVID19. Juntos lo lograremos. | | 1 | |
| 12-Mar | 5 | No escatimaremos esfuerzos para reducir las consecuencias del #Covid_19. Hoy aprobamos un primer paquete de medidas para:<br>-**Combatir** la enfermedad<br>-Respaldar a las familias<br>-Proteger el empleo, a pymes y autónomos<br>-Atender a los sectores más afectados | | 1 | |
| 12-Mar | 6 | Cada ciudadano y ciudadana debe cuidarse para cuidar así de los demás. Si queremos **vencer** al #Covid_19 cuanto antes, necesitamos seguir las recomendaciones oficiales. Responsabilidad y disciplina social. Con nuestro esfuerzo personal contribuiremos a la **victoria** frente al virus. | 1 | | |

| | | TWEET | JUDGMENT | | AP |
|---|---|---|---|---|---|
| 13-Mar | 7 | La **victoria** depende de cada ciudadano y ciudadana.<br>El **heroísmo** es también lavarse las manos, quedarse en casa y protegerse uno mismo para proteger a la sociedad.<br>Tardaremos semanas, pero pararemos al #Covid19 con unidad y disciplina social, cumpliendo cada uno con nuestro deber. | 1 | 1 | |
| 14-Mar | 8 | Gracias, de corazón, a todas y todos los profesionales de la salud. Sois ejemplo de **heroicidad,** entrega y trabajo.<br>Hoy, el país entero os aplaude. | | 1 | |
| 14-Mar | 9 | Mañana me reuniré por videoconferencia con los presidentes autonómicos para garantizar la coordinación frente al #COVID19.<br>Debemos **vencer** al virus desde la unidad de acción de todas las Administraciones Públicas. No es una opción, es nuestra obligación.<br>#EsteVirusLoParamosUnidos | 1 | | |
| 14-Mar | 10 | Lo conseguiremos. España tiene la capacidad de levantarse cuantas veces haga falta. Cuántas más vidas nos ahorremos, cuántos más enfermos evitemos, cuánto menos tiempo de vida sacrifiquemos, más rotunda será nuestra **victoria.** Unidos, saldremos adelante. | 1 | | |
| 15-Mar | 11 | Esta **batalla** la vamos a **ganar** con el compromiso y la responsabilidad de todos y todas. Protégete para proteger a los demás. | 1 | | 1 |

| | | TWEET | JUDGMENT | | AP |
|---|---|---|---|---|---|
| 15-Mar | 12 | He contactado por videoconferencia con los presidentes y presidentas de CC.AA. y ciudades autónomas. Todos se suman al llamamiento de unidad de acción para **vencer** al #COVID19 y actuarán en sus territorios con responsabilidad y lealtad en la aplicación del RD de Estado de Alarma. | | 1 | |
| 16-Mar | 13 | Estoy al habla con todos los grupos para trasladarles la máxima lealtad mutua e informarles sobre las medidas para **ganar** al #COVID19. El Gobierno siempre se guiará por los principios de cooperación, colaboración y solidaridad entre todos los españoles. | 1 | | |
| 16-Mar | 14 | Trabajamos sin descanso para frenar el #COVID19. Esta tarde he conversado también con el director de la #OMS, @DrTedros, ambos estamos comprometidos en reforzar la coordinación, colaboración y comunicación permanente en la **lucha** a escala española y global contra el coronavirus. | | 1 | |
| 17-Mar | 15 | Amigo Antonio, pueblo de Portugal. Juntos tomamos esta decisión para cuidarnos y cuidar a nuestros compatriotas. **Ganaremos** al #COVID19 con el esfuerzo de todos y todas. Y cuando todo pase, volveremos a abrazarnos como países hermanos que somos. | 1 | | |

| | | TWEET | JUDGMENT | AP |
|---|---|---|---|---|
| 17-Mar | 16 | Todos somos uno en esta **lucha.** Aprobamos una gran inyección económica para apoyar a las familias más vulnerables, a todos los trabajadores y trabajadoras, para garantizar la liquidez y los pagos a las empresas y los autónomos de nuestro país. | | 1 |
| 17-Mar | 17 | Estos días aflora una conducta social modélica. Orgullo de una sociedad solidaria que se organiza para **combatir** la adversidad y para dar aliento. Orgullo de nuestros sanitarios, de la cadena humana que garantiza la movilidad y abastece nuestras tiendas. | 1 | |
| 18-Mar | 18 | Hago un llamamiento a la unidad política y a la unidad social. Todos y todas debemos estar a la altura, dar lo mejor de nosotros mismos. España es un país que ha decidido **no rendirse**. A una sociedad así no puede pararla nada. Ni el virus más dañino. | 1 | |
| 21-Mar | 19 | Gracias, científicos, por vuestro trabajo para **vencer** al coronavirus. Este Gobierno os necesita y os escucha. Hoy hemos constituido el Comité Científico del #COVID19 con expertos en distintas áreas de la medicina y la ciencia en la **lucha** contra el virus. | 1 | 1 |
| 21-Mar | 20 | Lo peor está por llegar. Recibiremos el impacto de la ola más dura, que nos pondrá al límite. Para **vencerla,** los españoles y españolas deben permanecer unidos, en sus casas, mientras su país les protege, les cuida y la combate con tesón. Lo lograremos | 1 | |

| | | TWEET | JUDGMENT | AP |
|---|---|---|---|---|
| 21-Mar | 21 | El confinamiento es decisivo para **vencer** al #COVID19. También lo es extender los test a la mayor parte de la población. Así sabremos quiénes están infectados, podrán aislarse y romperemos la cadena de propagación del virus. En eso estamos trabajando. | 1 | |
| 22-Mar | 22 | Este martes, el Consejo de Ministros solicitará al @Congreso_Es la ampliación de la declaración del estado de alarma hasta el 11 de abril. Una medida drástica, que afecta por completo a la vida de la gente, pero efectiva en la **lucha** contra el #COVID19. | | 1 |
| 24-Mar | 23 | He conversado con el presidente de Corea del Sur, Moon Jae-in, con quien he abordado la **lucha** contra la epidemia del #COVID19 que afecta a nuestros países. La próxima reunión del #G20 será una oportunidad para impulsar la cooperación internacional y combatir unidos esta crisis. | | 1 |
| 24-Mar | 24 | Todos nuestros esfuerzos están volcados en la **lucha** contra el #COVID19. Hoy aprobamos en #CMin nuevas medidas que protegen a los colectivos más vulnerables, al empleo y la actividad productiva. No dejaremos a nadie atrás. | | 1 |
| 25-Mar | 25 | Comparezco ante el @Congreso_Es para pedir una prórroga del Estado de Alarma, del confinamiento. Para solicitar tiempo, porque es imprescindible para **vencer** al virus seguir privándole de su principal **arma** de difusión: nuestros propios contactos sociales. | 1 | 1 |

| | | TWEET | JUDGMENT | AP |
|---|---|---|---|---|
| 26-Mar | 26 | El @Congreso_Es da luz verde a la prórroga del estado de alarma. España gana un tiempo esencial para seguir **combatiendo** al #COVID19. Gracias a los grupos que lo han hecho posible. Sigamos trabajando para acabar con el virus desde la unidad y la lealtad. #EsteVirusLoParamosUnidos | 1 | |
| 28-Mar | 27 | Es momento de intensificar la **lucha.**El #CMin aprobará mañana un permiso retribuido recuperable para que los trabajadores y trabajadoras de actividades no esenciales no tengan que desplazarse a sus centros de trabajo desde el 30 de marzo al 9 de abril. | 1 | |
| | | TRUMP | | |
| 5-Mar | 1 | Congress has agreed to provide $8 Billion to **fight** Coronavirus! This means @CDCgov @HHSGov and @DHSgov will have the resources they need to Keep America Safe and keep the risk to workers and families very low. This is great news for our Health, our Economy, and our Nation! | 1 | |
| 8-Mar | 2 | We have a perfectly coordinated and fine tuned plan at the White House for our **attack** on CoronaVirus. We moved VERY early to close borders to certain areas, which was a Godsend. V.P. is doing a great job. The Fake News Media is doing everything possible to make us look bad. Sad! | 1 | |

| | | TWEET | JUDGMENT | | AP |
|---|---|---|---|---|---|
| 11-Mar | 3 | The Media should view this as a time of unity and strength. We have a common **enemy,** actually, an **enemy** of the World, the CoronaVirus. We must **beat** it as quickly and safely as possible. There is nothing more important to me than the life & safety of the United States! | | 1 | 2 |
| 16-Mar | 4 | This afternoon, we're announcing new guidelines for every American to follow over the next 15 days as we **combat** the virus. Each and every one of us has a critical role to play in stopping the spread and transmission of the virus | | 1 | |
| 17-Mar | 5 | The world is at **war** with **a hidden enemy**. WE WILL **WIN!** | 1 | | 2 |
| 18-Mar | 6 | I want all Americans to understand: we are at **war** with an **invisible enemy**, but that **enemy** is no match for the spirit and resolve of the American people… | | | 2 |
| 18-Mar | 7 | Today I spoke with American physicians and nurses to thank them for their tireless work. Doctors and nurses are at the front lines of this **war** and are true American **HEROES!** With their help, America will **WIN.** | 1 | 1 | 1 |
| 18-Mar | 8 | I only signed the Defense Production Act to **combat** the Chinese Virus should we need to invoke it in a worst case scenario in the future. Hopefully there will be no need, but we are all in this TOGETHER! | | 1 | |
| 19-Mar | 9 | We are going to **WIN,** sooner rather than later! | 1 | | |

| | | TWEET | | JUDGMENT | AP |
|---|---|---|---|---|---|
| 19-Mar | 10 | THANK YOU to our Police Officers, Fire Fighters, and EMS who help us **defeat** the Virus every day. Our proud nation is grateful for the unwavering dedication and sacrifice of our First Responders and their families. TOGETHER we will **beat** this! | | 2 | |
| 19-Mar | 11 | America's Private Sector is stepping up to help us be STRONG! Many of the Nation's distillers, large and small, are producing and donating hand sanitizer to help **fight** #COVID19. THANK YOU! | | 1 | |
| 27-Mar | 12 | The world is at **war** with a **hidden enemy**. WE WILL **WIN!** | 1 | | 2 |
| 27-Mar | 13 | We are marshalling the full power of government and society to achieve **victory** over the virus. Together, we will endure, we will prevail, and we will **WIN!** #CARESAct | 2 | | |
| 28-Mar | 14 | With the **courage** of our doctors and nurses, with the skill of our scientists and innovators, with the determination of the American People, and with the grace of God, WE WILL **WIN** THIS **WAR.** When we achieve this **victory,** we will emerge stronger and more united than ever before! | 2 | 1 | 1 |
| | | | 24 | 44 | 28 |

## References


Bates, B. R. (2020). 'The (In)Appropriateness of the WAR Metaphor in Response to SARS-CoV-2: A Rapid Analysis of Donald J. Trump's Rhetoric'. *Frontiers in Communication*. V. 5. Article 50.

Blankshain, J. and Lupton, D. (2020). *This is the problem with calling it a 'war' against coronavirus*. <https://www.washingtonpost.com/politics/2020/04/20/this-is-problem-with-calling-it-war-against-coronavirus/>

Bouvier, G. (2016). 'What is a discourse approach to Twitter, Facebook, YouTube and other social media'. *Journal of Multicultural Discourses*, 10 (2), 149–162.

Charteris-Black, J. (2004). *Corpus approaches to critical metaphor analysis*. Houndmills, Basingstoke, Hampshire: Palgrave Macmillan.

Chiang W-Y., Duann, R-F. (2007). 'Conceptual metaphors for SARS: "war" between whom?' *Discourse & Society* 18 (5), 579–602.

Dotti, G. (2020). Siamo in Cura, Non in Guerra! <http://www.quotidianosanita.it/lettere-al-direttore/articolo.php?articolo_id=83899 >

DuBois, J. (2007). 'The stance triangle'. In Robert Englebretson (ed.), *Stancetaking in Discourse: Subjectivity, Evaluation, Interaction*, pp. 139–182. Amsterdam: John Benjamins.

Fillmore, C. J. (1982). 'Frame semantics'. The Linguistic Society of Korea (eds.) *Linguistics in the Morning Calm*, pp. 111–37. Seoul: Hanshin.

Flusberg, S., Matlock, T. and Thibodeau, P. (2018). 'War metaphors in public discourse'. *Metaphor and Symbol*, 33, 1–18.

Hart, C. (2010). *Critical Discourse Analysis and Cognitive Science: New Perspectives on Immigration Discourse*. London: Palgrave Macmillan

Hodgkin, P. (1985). 'Medicine is war: And other conceptual metaphors'. *British Medical Journal*, 291, 1820–1821.

Hunston, S. and Thompson, G. (Eds.) (2000). *Evaluation in Text Authorial Stance and the Construction of Discourse*. Oxford: Oxford University Press.

Katajamäki, H. and Koskela, M. (2018). 'Lexical Metaphor as Judgement: Attitudinal Positioning of Editorial Writers in Business Newspapers' Fachsprache. *Journal of Professional and Scientific Communication* 40.3–4, 140–160.

Lakoff, G. (1993). 'The contemporary theory of metaphor'. In A. Ortony (Ed.), *Metaphor and thought*, pp. 202–251. Cambridge: Cambridge University Press.

Lakoff, G. and M. Johnson (1980). *Metaphors We Live By*. Chicago: The University of Chicago Press.

Martin, J.R. (1995). 'Reading Positions/Positioning Readers: JUDGEMENT in English' Prospect'. *A Journal of Australian TESOL* 10 (2), 27–37.

Martin, J.R., and White, P.R.R. (2007). *The Language of Evaluation: Appraisal in English*. London: Palgrave Macmillan.

Musu, C. (2020). War Metaphors Used For COVID-19 Are Compelling But Also Dangerous. <https://theconversation.com/war-metaphors-used-for-covid-19-are-compelling-but-also-dangerous-135406>

Ngo, T., Unsworth, L. (2015). 'Reworking the appraisal framework in ESL research: refining attitude resources'. *Functional Linguist*. 2, 1–24.

Semino, E. (2021). "Not Soldiers but Fire-fighters"–Metaphors and Covid-19. *Health Communication*, 36(1), 50–58

Semino, E., Demjén, Z., & Demmen, J. (2018). 'An integrated approach to metaphor and framing in cognition, discourse, and practice, with an application to metaphors for cancer'. *Applied linguistics*, 39(5), 625–645.

Stephen J., Flusberg T., Thibodeau P. (2018). 'War metaphors in public discourse'. *Metaphor and Symbol*, 33:1, 1–18.

Read, J., Carroll, J. (2012). 'Annotating expressions of Appraisal in English'. *Lang Resources & Evaluation* 46, 421–447.

Ross, J. W. (1989). 'THE MILITARIZATION OF DISEASE: Do We Really Want a War on Aids?' *Soundings* (Nashville, Tenn.), 72(1), 39–58.

Tasente, T. (2020). 'Twitter Discourse Analysis of US President Donald Trump'. *Technium Social Sciences Journal*, Vol. 2 (1), 67–75.

Van Dijk, T. A. (1998) *Ideology: A Multidisciplinary Approach*. London: SAGE.

Van Dijk, T. A. (2000) *Ideology and Discourse: A Multidisciplinary Approach*. Barcelona: Open University.

Van Dijk, T. A. (2005). Contextual knowledge management in discourse production. In R. Wodak and P. Chilton (eds) *A New Agenda in (Critical) Discourse Analysis*, pp. 71–100. Amsterdam/Philadelphia: John Benjamins Publishing Company.

Wicke, P. and Bolognesi M. (2020) Framing COVID-19: How we conceptualize and discuss the pandemic on Twitter. *PLoS ONE* 15(9), e0240010.

Xiang Huang

# Metaphor, Stance and Obesity in the *People's Daily* (2010–2020)[1]

**Abstract:** In this chapter, I examine how metaphor is used as a stance strategy, more specifically, as a positioning resource in health communication around obesity in the *People's Daily*, China's major official newspaper. By analysing 98 obesity-related editorials from the *Daily*, I identify three major metaphor groupings in the editorials: *JOURNEY*, *WAR* and *MONEY*. The metaphors help the editorials position themselves both at the epistemic level (knowledge-related) and affective level (emotion-related) around obesity. At the epistemic level, expertise in health is asserted by the editorials, while at the affective level, a sense of danger and threat is constructed around obesity and further projected onto the reader. Moreover, I find that the self-positioning of the editorials entails other-positioning, especially of individuals with obesity. Such a positioning act of both oneself and others aims to build solidarity in society for common efforts in dealing with obesity, reflecting a collectivist stance taken by the *Daily*.

**Keywords:** *obesity, metaphor, stance, self-positioning, other-positioning, health communication, the People's Daily, Chinese*

## 1 Introduction

*Féipàng shì huì hūxī de tòng, tā huó zài wǒ shēnshang suǒyǒu jiǎoluò.*
[Obesity is a breathing pain; it lives at every corner of my body].[2]

As illustrated in a popular quote from *Baidu*, China's major search engine, the experience of obesity is communicated effectively through metaphors. It is estimated that about 46 % of adults and 15 % of children are obese or overweight in China (Wang et al. 2019). The rapid rise in obesity rates has rendered obesity (or losing-weight) a hot topic in everyday life and a proliferation of media reports on obesity in China. Yet, the way in which obesity is represented in Chinese

1 I would like to thank Mario Bisiada for very insightful and constructive comments on an earlier draft of this chapter. Mario Bisiada also helped in proofreading this chapter, which structured and improved the present article.

2 This quote is a lyrics adaptation and becomes popular with the Chinese sitcom *iPartment*. All translations in this chapter are done by the author unless otherwise noted. Metaphorical expressions in the data analysis are shown in bold.

media, especially through the discursive strategy of metaphors, has not been properly elucidated.

In this chapter, I explore the use of metaphor in the context of health communication around obesity in the *People's Daily*, one of China's major official media outlets. I investigate the use of metaphors as a stance strategy, or more specifically, as a positioning resource in the *Daily* and consider the joint effects of self-positioning and other-positioning through metaphors in health communication. Along with the worldwide obesity stigma (Puhl and Heuer 2009), discourse studies looking into the negative stance on obesity and individuals with obesity in the media have gained momentum in recent years (mainly conducted on Western media, e.g., Atanasova and Koteyko 2017, 2020; Brookes 2021; Malterud and Ulriksen 2010; Wanniarachchi et al. 2020). Investigating the underexplored Chinese media can help advance this growing interest and may offer interesting cross-cultural comparisons. The aims of this chapter can be summarised as follows:

- To identify metaphors used in the *Daily* to represent obesity;
- To explore the stance activities through positioning enacted by the metaphors.

In the following sections, I first introduce my theoretical account of stance and metaphor in health communication (Theoretical Background). Then, I explain how I proceed in my metaphor and stance analysis (Research Methods) before explaining metaphors and their positioning activities in my data (Results and Case Studies). In the final section, I offer a discussion of the findings in relation to wider socio-cultural discourses, especially the modernity discourse in Chinese society and present some conclusive remarks.

## 2 Theoretical Framework

Stance-taking is one of the fundamental properties of human communication (Jaffe 2009: 3). Although some forms of communication (e.g., debating) are more stance-saturated, communication is never completely neutral, because "neutrality is itself a stance" (ibid). However, despite its ubiquity, there is no agreed-upon academic definition of stance (Englebretson 2007). Within the field of Applied Linguistics, according to Biber and Finegan (1989: 93), stance is "the lexical and grammatical expression of attitudes, feelings, judgements, or commitment concerning the propositional content of a message". Broadly following the more recent stance theory of Du Bois (2007: 163), I understand stance as a linguistically articulated form of social actions, which simultaneously incorporate three acts: evaluating an object, positioning subjects, and aligning oneself with other subjects. The "three acts in one" or 'tri-act' nature of stance (Du Bois 2007: 162) has received wide scholarly attention (e.g., Du Bois 2014; McEntee-Atalianis 2013).

Based on the 'tri-act' of stance and its intersubjective nature, in this chapter, I am particularly interested in the component of 'positioning'. I am primarily concerned with how discourse participants (the subjects) position themselves through, for example, showing their knowledge, characters, roles, beliefs, attitudes, feelings, etc. towards certain objects. Apart from positioning themselves with respect to the objects, the subjects also tend to position other co-participants in the communication. Especially in asymmetrical contexts with hierarchical roles, self-positioning by individuals that casts them into higher hierarchical roles tend to entail or index other-positioning of some of the involved individuals into lower roles. For example, Jaffe (2009: 119) has found that hierarchically superior teachers can scaffold or project students' stance. Such stance activities through education-based language are then exploited also when used metaphorically to establish differences in authorities in political discourse (Bisiada 2018).

Health communication, for example, medical consultation, has long been recognised as an asymmetrical context between empowered doctors and disempowered patients (Ariss 2009; Bonnin 2019). In this chapter, I shift my attention to mass media representation of health issues which I believe consists of another major asymmetrical context in health communication. As Seale (2002: preface) reminds us of the role of media in health communication: "people's response to illness, healthcare and health-related behaviour generally are profoundly influenced by mass media representations", media, as the primary source of health information in modern society, play a pivotal and powerful role in introducing health issues to the public and further affect the public view on the issues. Convinced by their presumed advantage in health knowledge and motivated by their influence on public opinion, the media can be said to 'speak for' (Coupland and Coupland 2009: 230) the public on health issues. The *People's Daily* in this study, in particular, as one of the most influential media in China, has additional access to speak for their readers through, for example, forming influential views on health-related topics, saying what is healthy and what is not, and establishing certain health agendas for the public.

Existent stance studies mainly focus on self-positioning (e.g., Baynham 2011; Myers 2010), leaving other-positioning, along with its interaction with self-positioning insufficiently explored, especially in the field of health communication. As far as I am concerned, the most relevant work on other-positioning surrounding the obesity issue I have identified is Coupland and

Coupland's (2009: 227) study on stance-attributing around body shape and weight loss in lifestyle magazine texts and doctor-patient dialogues in geriatric medicine. Their study finds that instead of within individuals' authorial control, personal stances on their age, health and body are sometimes constructed for and attributed to them in their sociocultural contexts. Therefore, in this chapter, advancing Coupland and Coupland's (2009) call for more attention to the 'speaking-for' phenomenon in stance activities, I investigate self-positioning and other-positioning for two reasons:

Firstly, solely focusing on self-positioning tends to play down or obscure the power negotiation or struggle in health communication and distil the complexity of stance activities among subjects with different hierarchical roles; while solely focusing on other-positioning would miss the complete stance picture: when a speaker or writer positions others, this necessarily entails a positioning of themselves (Coupland and Coupland 2009: 232). By simultaneously looking into both self-positioning and other-positioning, we can see how particular social knowledge, roles, statuses and relationships are designed and asserted by certain subjects and further attributed to other subjects in the context of health communication. We can also further understand how some stances are normative in certain socio-cultural contexts as suggested by Coupland and Coupland (2009).

Secondly, a joint look at self-positioning and other-positioning can practically help us reduce the prevalent asymmetry in health communication. Relating to the present study, given the fact that obese individuals are found to face stigmatisation in society in general (Brookes and Baker 2021), reducing the asymmetry can be expected to empower obese individuals and further achieve better health communication effects surrounding obesity. Just as "giving voice to the concerns of previously silent and underrepresented groups is an initial step for the empowerment of the groups" (Serrano-García and Bond 1994: 433), taking this voice away from obese individuals through acts of positioning may marginalise this group even further. As obese individuals may not yet be able to claim ownership of their experience and speak for themselves as envisaged by the consumers/survivors/ex-patients movement (Bassman 2001), research into how media speak for them and position them can yield insights into the way they are viewed by the general public and how weight is viewed in society. Such an effect is not only exclusive to obese individuals. With prevalent self-starvation among people who are indeed physically healthy yet claim and see themselves as obese and concerned for their not-thin-enough bodies, exploring how obesity is talked about and how obese individuals are spoken for in the media may help mitigate the widespread body anxieties and contribute to a more egalitarian society.

For a detailed description of self- and other-positioning, I draw on Ochs's (1990: 2) differentiation between two stances, i.e., epistemic stance (i.e. "a socially recognised way of knowing a proposition") and affective stance (i.e. "a socially recognised feeling, attitude, mood or degree of emotional intensity"). Marín-Arrese (2009: 23) makes a distinction between epistemic stance, which refers to the "knowledge of the speaker/writer regarding the realisation of the event and/or to his/her assessment of the validity of the proposition designating the event"; and effective stance, which "pertains to the realization of events and situations, to the ways in which the speaker/writer expresses the necessity or possibility of the event occurring, […] or his/her emotive/affective position with regard to the event". Put simply, epistemic stance is knowledge-related, referring to the propositional position a subject takes towards an object ('what the object is' and how certain one is of this denotational view); while affective stance is emotion-related, referring to the emotional position a subject takes towards the object ('how one feels about the object' and further solidarity signalled).

Drawing on the two stances, I choose metaphors as my perspective of stance analysis because metaphors have been asserted to have evaluative properties (Deignan 2010). As defined by Semino et al (2018: 5), metaphor involves "talking and, potentially, thinking about something in terms of another, where the two things are different but some form of similarity can be perceived between them". In the field of health communication, epistemically, metaphors can facilitate public understandings of health issues and have the potential to translate some complex and abstract health issues into simpler and more concrete information (e.g., Castaño 2020; Charteris-Black 2012; Demmen et al. 2015). Obesity is a complex biological, socio-economic, political and cultural issue with an array of causes and consequences. Metaphors, based on their framing effects (Semino et al., 2018), can enable us to talk and think about obesity by highlighting certain aspects and de-emphasising other aspects of it. For instance, obesity is often metaphorically referred to as a disease (e.g. as in the popular term of *féipàng* ***liúxíng bìng*** [obesity **epidemic**]) or a war (e.g. as in the title of the book *Men and* ***War*** *on Obesity* by Monaghan 2008), or a journey (e.g. as in the headline, i.e., *jiǎnféi/zhī/**lù**/wèishéme/cháng/**bàntúérfèi*** [Why the **journey** of losing-weight is often given up **halfway**?] from my data). These metaphors allow people to use their previous knowledge about disease, war, or journey to understand complex issues surrounding obesity and further give different answers to "What is obesity?".

Further, metaphors can evoke emotional reactions and affectively influence people's stance towards issues. Compared with literal language, the use of metaphorical language "gives our expression colour, shape and character" (Mohammad et al. 2016: 23), thus strengthening people's emotive reactions to the issues (Citron and Goldberg 2014). The more emotive evaluation function of metaphors is observed by Taylor (2018) in immigration discourse. The emotive function is mainly achieved through the emotional connotations associated with the metaphor itself. For instance, referring to losing weight as a *JOURNEY* could conjure an emotional call for perseverance, care, or encouragement towards the obese individuals, while referring to it as a *WAR* would trigger a feeling of threat, insecurity and perhaps stigmatisation and discrimination of obese individuals (Atanasova and Koteyko 2020). However, as argued by Semino et al (2018: 3), "the framing effects of metaphors are a context- and usage-dependent phenomenon"; while *WAR* metaphors are normally criticised in health communication and increasingly called to be replaced by *JOURNEY* metaphors (e.g., in the case of the HIV cure research by Nie et al. 2016), the way in which *WAR* metaphors empower or disempower groups involved largely relies on the context. Similarly, Flusberg et al. (2018) also argue that *WAR* metaphors in public discourse are closely related to the context in which they are used, which decides the positive or negative results of the metaphor uses. My subsequent analysis will show the context-dependent framing effects of *JOURNEY* and *WAR* metaphors in the Chinese context.

In all, metaphors provide a useful perspective to explore stance both at epistemic and affective levels. Although an array of published work has explored the negative stance towards obesity in the Western media (e.g., Baker et al. 2020; Brookes and Baker 2021; Saguy and Almeling 2008), there has been only occasional consideration of the role metaphors play in positioning different subjects around obesity. The rare exceptional studies can be seen in Atanasova and Koteyko (2020), who find that being framed under the *WAR* metaphors, obese individuals are represented as the 'targets' of public measures against obesity and further positioned as a threatening 'other' group (Atanasova and Koteyko 2020: 238). However, there remain some unanswered questions, e.g., for the side of influential media, how do they use metaphors to position themselves to justify their negative evaluations towards other subjects around obesity, especially the obese individuals? How are the positioning activities conducted in the specific Chinese sociocultural context? Bearing the questions in mind, I shift my attention to obesity represented in Chinese media. In the next section, I explain my research methods.

# 3 Research Methods

## 3.1 Data Collection

98 editorials (95,928 Chinese characters) from the online webpage of the opinion part of the *People's Daily* (http://opinion.people.com.cn/) are collected. I looked at editorials in the decade of 2010–2020, so as only to explore the most recent discourse. In detail, I extracted editorials based on my manual search of keywords, i.e., *féipàng* [obesity/fat], *chāozhòng* [overweight], and *jiǎnféi* [losing-weight] on the website. I manually read all editorials and selected the ones which fulfilled two criteria: first, the article should be about obesity in the health sense of human beings (eliminating, for instance, editorials of 'slimming' governmental institutions); second, the article should discuss obesity in an in-depth way instead of only mentioning it as an example (e.g., slimming pills advertising).

## 3.2 Metaphor and Stance Analysis

I first used the Chinese Lexical Analysis System developed by the Institute of Computing Technology, Chinese Academy of Sciences (http://ictclas.nlpir.org/index.html) to demarcate lexical units, which later functioned as the unit for metaphor analysis.

I identify metaphors according to the Metaphor Identification Procedure Vrije Universiteit (MIPVU, Steen et al. 2010), which has been proven reliable in identifying linguistic metaphors in Chinese texts (Lu and Wang 2017; Wang et al. 2019). I first read all editorials for a general understanding of their contents and meanings; I then manually search for metaphorical words or phrases. Following MIPVU, when a lexical unit was not meant literally, such as *gémìng* [revolution] in *yāowéi/shàng/de/**gémìng*** [a **revolution** on the waistlines], it is checked with *xiàndài hànyǔ cídiǎn* [Contemporary Chinese Dictionary] (the 7th edition), one of the most authoritative dictionaries of Mandarin Chinese as a reference for the establishment of its basic meanings. *gémìng* here describes a fight to get rid of or remove surplus body fat as similar to its dictionary meaning of *cuīhuǐ jiù de fǔxiǔ de shèhuì zhìdù, jiànlì xīn de jìnbù de shèhuì zhìdù* [destroying the old and decayed social systems and building up new and advanced social systems]. I see its contextual meaning is more abstract than its literal meaning and regard it as metaphorical in this context. Later, I generally adopt the Discourse Dynamics Approach (Cameron et al. 2009) in my recursive metaphor analysis. Each metaphorical expression was recursively and heuristically categorised into different groupings, such as *JOURNEY*, *WAR*, *MONEY*, *PERSONIFICATION* and *DEHUMANIZATION*.

Once the metaphorical expressions are identified and grouped, the next step is analysing the stance, more specifically, the self-positioning and other-positioning the expressions convey. I have to acknowledge that the phenomenon of positioning is not obviously identifiable, as it appears to depend on immediate context and on my own assumption about the sociocultural values embedded in the context. This involves closely reading the metaphorical expressions to understand their recursive positioning activities based on my own interpretation of their context. As stance in nature "is a meaning, a type of meaning, or several types of meaning, rather than a form" (Hunston 2007: 54), I conduct context-specific qualitative analysis in revealing the positioning activities.

To illustrate how I do the stance analysis, here is an example from the data:

(1) *yī /fāng miàn /......jiā zhǎng /，yào /**zhú bù** /gǎi biàn /zì jǐ /de /jiàn kāng guān /。yòng /chī hǎo /dài tì /chī chēng zhe /，yòng /yíng yǎng /wǔ cān /tì dài /"duō chī yī wǎn fàn "/，hé lǐ /diào zhěng /hái zǐ /de /shàn shí /，ràng /tā men /de /tǐ zhòng /**huí guī** /zhèng cháng* 。

[On the one hand..., parents need to change their views on health **in a step-by-step way**. (They should) replace full-eating with good-eating and 'one more bowl of rice' with nutritious lunch. (In this way they can) reasonably adjust their kids' diets and make the kids' bodily weight **return to** the normal.] (*The People's Daily*, 26 July 2016)

Example 1 uses *JOURNEY* metaphors to depict the problem of childhood obesity, implying the parents need to find their way to set up their health view in order to get their kids' bodily weights, which have been in an 'abnormal' place, 'return' to the 'normal'. A health expert voice can be seen across the texts through an imperative tone (e.g., the use of words like 'need', 'change', 'replace', and 'adjust', etc.). The textual voice positions itself as guiding the parents in their way of feeding their kids properly. In more detail, epistemically, the *JOURNEY* metaphors use the readers' knowledge of journeys to describe the process of losing weight, implying that weight loss depends on a right direction and also requires persistence, patience and energy on the side of the travellers. Affectively, a solidarity is built among the editorial and the parents as getting kids' weights 'return to the normal' is a shared goal and target between them. Therefore, we can see how the editorial positions itself as having expert knowledge (knowing the solution of solving childhood obesity) and meanwhile position the parents as needing more epistemic guidance on diet. In the next section, I present detailed stance activities conveyed through major metaphor groupings and their systematic metaphors (for more detail on the methods in metaphor groupings and the proposal of systematic metaphors, see Huang and Bisiada 2021).

## 4 Results and Case Studies

My analysis resulted in the identification of 857 metaphorical expressions subsumed under the following metaphor groupings (with figures showing the observed instances): *JOURNEY* (179), *WAR* (146), *MONEY* (97), *ENVIRONMENT* (54), *ARCHITECTURE* (49), *DEHUMANIZATION* (48), *PERSONIFICATION* (47), *MACHINE* (37), *DISEASE* (34), *EDUCATION* (30) and Others[3] (136). It needs to be noted that these figures are only to be seen as a way of describing my results (i.e., helping me to identify the major metaphors) instead of a significant contribution to my results. The figures reveal three dominant groupings, i.e., *JOURNEY*, *WAR* and *MONEY* and my stance analysis hence focuses on systematic metaphors within the three groupings. I start with *JOURNEY* metaphors.

*JOURNEY*. *LOSING WEIGHT IS A NATIONAL JOURNEY TOWARDS HEALTH* is exploited by the editorials in describing a national-level journey of losing weight. *JOURNEY* in this study takes a broad concept, which includes movement, direction, physical activities, etc. As shown in example 2, a question is asked on why losing weight is usually given up halfway, implying the epistemic complexity of losing weight. To answer the question, a cognitive frame of 'walking together' as the answer is given across the editorials. The frame conceptualises the process of losing weight as a group journey and represents different stakeholders around obesity, especially the government and individuals with obesity as co-travellers on the journey. Different travellers are evaluated as possessing different epistemic knowledge of the 'journey'. For example, when discussing obesity as a serious public health problem, governments are positioned as health authorities with leading roles on the 'journey' (see example 3). Such positioning serves to bestow a health expert status and a guiding responsibility on governments, thereby also establishing the group in need of guidance (the group who is likely to lag behind, here can be reasonably understood as obese individuals). Nevertheless, a stance of solidarity between different 'travellers' is formulated by stressing the togetherness among them along the journey.

(2) *jiǎn féi /zhī /**lù** /wéi hé /zǒng /shì /**bàn tú ér fèi**?*
[Why is the **journey** of losing-weight always given up **halfway**?] (*The People's Daily*, 2 April 2019)

(3) *zài /jiàn kāng /wèn tí /shàng， zhèng fǔ /yīng /zhǔ dòng /chéng dān /zé rèn /， cǎi qǔ /guǒ duàn /xíng dòng /bú /ràng /rèn hé /yī gè /qún tǐ /**diào duì*** 。

3 Other less frequent groupings include *AGRICULTURE*, *SENSORY*, *OBSTACLE*, *ARTS-ENTERTAINMENT*, *RELIGION* and *EMOTION*.

[For the issue of health, governments should actively take their responsibilities and take decisive actions to make sure no group **lag behind**.] (*The People's Daily*, 24 November 2016)

However, though the 'walking-together' frame itself does not trigger negative evaluation towards obese individuals, the frame taps into traumatic historical memories of China and sets up a dichotomy between the new 'walking-together' path and an old path characterised by 'Sick Man of East Asia' (see example 4). The impulse to avoid the 'old path' has affectively attributed a sense of humiliation to obese individuals:

(4) *nà /dǐng /zǎo /yǐ /bèi /**tī jìn** /tài píng yáng /de /"dōng yà bìng fū "/de /mào zǐ ， qiān wàn /bú yào /zài /**jiàng lín** /dào /guó rén /de /tóu /shàng /。*
[The hat of 'Sick Man of East Asia', which has been **kicked into** the Pacific Ocean, should never **fall down** again on compatriots' heads.] (*The People's Daily*, 24 December 2013)

In example 4, the use of the emotionalised term 'Sick Man of East Asia', an expression of prejudice, contempt and insult towards China, conveys a collective sense of disgrace and humiliation of the colonial and semicolonial eras in China's national history (Yang 2020). The term is predominantly present in discussing topics related to China's hard-won achievements in curing the national trauma (kicking the 'hat' to the Ocean) and the determination to forever bid farewell to the humiliating past. Thus, obese individuals, who are somehow deemed as the embodiment of the 'sick man' are prone to be evaluated negatively. Again, the common goal of shaking off national humiliation sets up a solidarity among the subjects, reflecting an intersubjective alignment and creating a bigger 'we' (e.g., by bestowing readers with a health initiative and responsibility). The alignment is reinforced in extending obesity as a trap on dual journeys of improving individual and national competitiveness (example 5):

(5) *zhè xiē /"féi pàng /**xiàn jǐng** "/……shì bì /xuē ruò /gè rén /jìng zhēng lì /**yǔ** /guó jiā / jìng zhēng lì。*
[These 'obesity **traps**'…definitely will weaken both individual and national competitiveness.] (*The People's Daily*, 1 June 2012)

Therefore, within *JOURNEY* metaphors, by utilising a 'walking-together' frame and relating the frame to the national 'old path' with humiliation and the new path of improving national competitiveness, the editorials warrant their negative stance towards obesity in the name of both the past and future of the nation. By negatively evaluating obesity and differently depicting stakeholders like the government and the obese individuals, the editorials implicitly encode their own authority as if having a bird-view of the journey (knowing the past, the present and the future of the journey). In this way, the editorials perform the dual act of self-positioning and other-positioning. Next, I turn to *WAR* metaphors to see more varied positioning-activities.

*WAR. LOSING WEIGHT IS A FIGHT FOR NATIONAL SECURITY* is exploited by the editorials in descriptions of the harm of obesity and justification of a war needed to fight against obesity. Similar to *JOURNEY* metaphors, *WAR* metaphors take a broad view, which includes other related concepts of violence, fighting, aggression, conflict, and destruction, etc. I include any metaphorical meaning related to the above concepts into the group of *WAR*. The *WAR* metaphors index the editorials' negative evaluation of obesity, as seen in the following examples (6–8):

(6) *chāo zhòng /féi pàng /yǐ /chéng wéi /**wēi xié** /qīng shǎo nián /shēn xīn /jiàn kāng /de /zhòng yào /gōng gòng /wèi shēng /wèn tí*。
[Overweight and obesity have become a key public hygiene issue, **threatening** the physical and mental health of teenagers.] (*The People's Daily*, 14 December 2020)

(7) *nóng cūn /qīng shǎo nián /ér tóng /zhèng /miàn lín /féi pàng /de /**qīn xí***。
[Teenagers and children in rural areas are facing the **invasion** of obesity.] (*The People's Daily*, 26 July 2016)

(8) *xīn wén zhōng /"běi jīng /chāo /bàn shù /chū zhōng /nán shēng /bú /huì /zuò /yǐn tǐ xiàng shàng /"xiàng /guó rén /qiāo xiǎng /le /**jǐng zhōng***。
[The news that over half of boys in middle schools in Beijing cannot do pull-ups is an **alarming siren** to compatriots.] (*The People's Daily*, 24 December 2013)

The above examples set up the epistemic authority of the editorials, showing the editorials are familiar with expert knowledge of obesity, i.e., how serious the obesity issue is and how different groups of people (e.g., teenagers and children in rural areas) are influenced by it. Based on the expert epistemic stance, what is more interesting is the other-positioning embedded in the *WAR* metaphors. The *WAR* metaphors do not stop at telling readers that obesity is an enemy which needs to be fought against, but further project the readers' role towards obesity. First of all, fighting against obesity has been embedded as a given and shared war goal among the readers. As shown in example (9), a war-strategic period is projected onto the readers:

(9) *jīn hòu /shí nián /dào /èr shí nián /， shì /gǎi shàn /guó mín /yíng yǎng /jiàn kāng /de /guān jiàn /**zhàn luè /shí qī***。
[The coming one and two decades is a key **war-strategic** period for improving nationals' nutrition and health.] (*The People's Daily*, 22 February 2013)

In example (9), the term *zhànlüè* can be literally translated as 'war-strategic'. The term of *zhànlüè/shíqí* [war-strategic period] depicts the process of improving nationals' nutrition and health as a war in the timeframe of the coming decades.

Being in the timeframe and part of the nationals, readers are implicitly positioned as soldiers in the war.

Across the above examples, the editorials, by using *WAR* metaphors, take authoritative stances for themselves, which are carried by the textual voice's taking a higher epistemic position (explaining the magnitude of the obesity issue and setting health agendas). By the *WAR* metaphors, the editorials display an expert awareness of obesity, but also imply the readers' relatively lay-people status (being unaware of the harm of obesity) and anticipates reader's compliance to take required actions (to take part in the war and to savage their bodies). In this way, the editorials position themselves as informing (on the seriousness of obesity, in examples 6–8) and instructing (on how to fight against obesity, in example 9), finally achieving an authoritative status for themselves in terms of the obesity issue.

Based on their authoritative epistemic status, the editorials claim their mastery of the 'best solutions' to solve the obesity issue by attributing roles, tasks and responsibilities to various stake-holders. For example, parents are attributed the role of 'weapons' in solving childhood obesity:

(10) *jiě jué /rì yì /yán zhòng /de /ér tóng /féi pàng /wèn tí ， zuì jiā /de /**wǔ qì** /shì /tā men /de /fù mǔ。*
[To solve the increasingly serious childhood obesity problem, the best **weapon** is their parents.] (*The People's Daily*, 28 February 2014)

Example 10 renders parents morally responsible for childhood obesity. Meanwhile, parents are empowered (cast as the 'best weapons') in the fight against their kids' obesity. The editorial shows an appreciation of the parents' key roles in solving childhood obesity, and also motivates the parents to play their part as 'weapons'. In this way, through evaluating the role of parents, the editorial implicitly aligns itself with parents to face their common enemy of childhood obesity.

Further, the issue of improving the health of children shifts into a policy discourse and the editorial claims its credibility from a national-policy source as shown in example 11:

(11) *quán miàn /shí shī /《guó jiā xué shēng tǐ zhì jiàn kāng biāo zhǔn》/， bǎ /jiàn kāng /sù zhì /zuò wéi /píng jià /xué shēng /quán miàn /fā zhǎn /de /zhòng yào / zhǐ biāo ， chōng fèn /fā huī /**zhǐ huī bàng** /de /zuò yòng ， jiāng /tǐ yù /nà rù / zhōng kǎo。*
[Comprehensively implement National Student Physical Health Standard and put health quality as an important indicator in evaluating students' overall development. Fully play the role of **command baton** to put physical education into high-school entrance examinations.] (*The People's Daily*, 8 August 2019)

In example 11, the editorial turns into the document of national standard and further legitimises its position and asserts its credibility. There is an interesting element of syntactic ambiguity regarding the subject of 'implement' and 'play the role'. The unspecified actor here can be generally understood as 'we', or the state. Thus, the textual voice speaks on a national level, which provides a basis for the editorial to introduce its best practice from a grander national-level. The 'command baton' is a local and prevalent metaphor in Chinese education, which refers to requirements of high-school (or college) entrance examination, a war where students are positioned as soldiers who need to closely follow the 'baton' in order to pass the examination. Identifying functions of the baton can make other-positioning on students more warranted in the sense that the editorials position themselves as 'speaking in the name of the nation' and meanwhile also 'for the students' good'. Similarly, a syntactic ambiguity can also be found in example 12:

(12) *bǎ /duàn liàn /bǔ /huí lái /，bǎ /wěi suō /de /jī ròu /chōng shí /qǐ lái ，bǎ /qiáng jiàn /de /tǐ pò /zhǎo /huí lái /，rú cǐ /cái /néng /**dǐ yù** /，**kàng yù** /hé /**jī bài** /kě néng /fǎn fù /fā zuò /de /xīn guàn fèi yán /yǐ jí /qí tā /jí bìng。*
[Make up for exercise, flesh out the atrophied muscles, get the strong bodies back, only in this way can we **defend**, **resist** and **defeat** the recurring COVID-19 and other diseases.] (*The People's Daily*, 30 April 2020)

In example 12, despite the lack of an overt subject in the example, an unspecified 'we', which refers to general readers can be inferred. The editorial aligns itself with readers in the implied 'we'. Yet meanwhile, again, an authoritative stance is carried out by the textual voice's frequent use of imperatives ('make up for', 'flesh out', 'get…back') and links a strong body to the defeat of the recurring Covid-19 (as obese individuals are found to face higher risk of serious illness and death from Covid-19). In this way, the obligation to fight against Covid-19 by improving their health (here specifically referring to keeping or losing bodily weight) is projected onto readers. However, different from the rigid tone in *WAR* examples above, some empathetic emotional stance can be observed in the editorial as shown in example 13:

(13) *yě xǔ /，wǒ men /yīng gāi /hé /shēn tǐ /**hé jiě** /，zhì shǎo /bú yào /ràng /suǒ wèi /de /biāo zhǔn /bǎ /zì jǐ /shù fù /dé /tòu bú guò qì /lái。*
[Maybe we should **come to peace with** our bodies, at least do not let the so-called standards fetter ourselves that we cannot breathe.] (*The People's Daily*, 12 October 2015)

Different from the above examples which encourage fighting against obesity, example 13 talks about a different solution of the war, i.e., a peace, or a reconciliation between one and one's body. In other words, instead of a clear win-lose dichotomy between obesity and people, a stop or a cease-fire can be called between the two sides. The use of explicit 'we' suggests an alignment between the editorial and the readers. By calling for a peace between people and obesity, the editorial shows it has access to the challenging experiences and frustrating feelings of people in losing weight. In this way, readers find the editorial trustworthy as it shows understanding of their situations in losing weight where a reconciliation is necessary sometimes (e.g., some individuals are found to be extremely hard to lose weight due to genetic reasons). In all, through using *WAR* metaphors, the editorials take an authoritative epistemic position for themselves in an 'expert' discourse, informing readers of the magnitude of the war against obesity and necessary strategies adopted to win the war or stop the war. Meanwhile, readers are positioned as laymen in obesity and are attributed various roles and responsibilities in the obesity issue, especially relating to how they should practice their bodies in the fight against obesity (e.g., to actively take part in the war or to come to peace with obesity). I move on to discuss *MONEY* metaphors to see their positioning and potential differences with those shown in the *JOURNEY* and *WAR* metaphors.

*MONEY. LOSING WEIGHT IS AN INVESTMENT BOTH AT THE INDIVIDUAL AND NATIONAL LEVEL* is employed in the editorials to represent losing weight as a money-driven investment in a market. First, in some ways like the authorial voice delivered in *WAR* metaphors, a national-level market is built by the textual voice of speaking for the nation as shown in example 14:

(14) *féi pàng /……huì* ***/xiāo hào*** */dà liàng /de /shè huì /cái fù /，dǎo zhì /zhōng guó /'yīn pàng ér kùn /'。*
[Obesity… will **cost** a large amount of social wealth, leading to a poor China caused by obesity.] (*The People's Daily*, 22 February 2013)

In example 14, the editorial, in the way of speaking at a national level, positions itself as an arbiter of the money issue associated with obesity, counting how the nation will bear costs due to the obesity issue of its nationals. It depicts a would-be-poor China caused by obesity, projecting a shared concern for the readers in terms of the nation's future where everyone is involved. In the following examples, a different sense of market which relates more to personal value is observed:

(15) ***xiāo hào*** */jiàn kāng /，yǐ /chéng wéi /yī xiē /rén /fèn dòu /de /****dài jià****。*
[For some people, **consuming** health has become the **cost** of fighting.] (*The People's Daily*, 7 October 2016)

In example 15, the editorial shows an insider-status as if knowing how hard someone's fighting is (here generally referring to the daily life of making a living, which typically includes working to support themselves and families or pursuing further education). It delivers a caring tone in referring to the challenges people face in their daily life which to some extent takes a form of a fight. For winning in the fight, some people are found to overuse their bodies and hence consume their health as a price they pay in the fight. However, in example 16, a stance of moral failure is projected to the health-consuming people:

(16) *tǐ zhòng jì /，běn gāi /shì /yī gè /shàn yú /zì wǒ /guǎn lǐ /zhě /shēng huó /zhōng /de /* ***biāo pèi*** 。
[Weight scales should become **standard fit** in the life of people who are good at self-management.] (*The People's Daily*, 22 September 2014)

Standard fit refers to a standard specification, compact or structure of a certain product. In example 16, the life of people is referred to as a product and weight scale is positioned as a must-have in the product. In this way, people, as the designers of the product, i.e., their lives, are positioned as being in agentive control of their own weights to meet the standard fit. Further, the stance of needing to control one's bodily weight is built into the discourse, which can be seen in the implied meaning that people who do not have weight scales are out of self-management and hence are not 'standard' enough. For those who do not meet the standard, personal cost and investment are called upon as shown in examples 17–18:

(17) *zhè xiē /xí guàn /shì /cuò wù /de /，jié guǒ /shì /bì xū /jiū zhèng /de，nà /jiù /xū yào /**huā /chéng běn** /，shēn xīn /de /tòng kǔ /jiù shì /bì xū /fù chū /de /**chéng běn /zhī yī*** 。
[These habits are wrong so that their outcomes need to be corrected. In this way, a **cost** is needed and the physical and mental misery is a **must-pay.**] (*The People's Daily*, 22 September 2014)

(18) *duì /zì jǐ /de /jiàn kāng /，zài /nián qīng /shí /jiù yào /**tóu zī** /，ér /zhè zhǒng /**tóu zī** /yě /bìng /bú nán* 。
[In terms of personal health, one needs to **invest** in health when one is young and such an **investment** indeed is not difficult.] (*The People's Daily*, 29 November 2019)

Further, the editorials attribute the role of chief executive to readers, comparing body management to running a business, where readers themselves are part of their own products (i.e., the stock) as shown in examples 19–20:

(19) měi /gè /rén /shì /zì jǐ /jiàn kāng /dì yī /**zé rèn rén** 。
[Everyone should be the **chief executive** for his health.] (*The People's Daily*, 14 August 2019)

(20) *měi /gè /pàng zǐ /dōu /shì /**qián lì gǔ**。*
[Each fat person is a **potential stock**[4].] (*The People's Daily*, 11 December 2015)

In the above examples, obese individuals are attributed a motivational stance to lose weight aimed at improving their market value. They are positioned as active and agentive in their attempts at weight loss. It implies a self-market frame, where exercise for keeping healthy bodily weight is metaphorically referred to as a form of 'producing value' for oneself.

To sum up, the *MONEY* metaphors place the responsibility for mitigating obesity on individuals. The editorials count the costs of obesity and encourage individuals to control their weights as investments to gain profits both for themselves and the nation. Obese individuals are attributed the moral failure of lacking self-management and are thus cast as low-valued both to themselves and to the nation.

## 5 Discussion and Conclusion

This chapter illustrates how obesity-related editorials in the *People's Daily* metaphorically position themselves as well as various stakeholders around obesity. I have discussed three major metaphors in the editorials: *JOURNEY*, *WAR* and *MONEY* metaphors. Overall, I find these metaphors generally have negatively evaluated obesity and obese individuals, especially the *WAR* and *MONEY* metaphors. Though *JOURNEY* metaphors represent the seemingly neutral 'walking together' scenario, if related to China's historical trauma of the 'Sick Man of East Asia', the *JOURNEY* metaphors may also negatively evaluate obese individuals.

Moreover, I have found that through using the metaphors, the editorials position themselves and others on the obesity issue in certain ways. In particular, I find metaphors help the editorials speak for various stakeholders around obesity, thus mapping their own epistemic understanding and affective feelings of obesity onto the stakeholders. In detail, at the epistemic level, the use of metaphors helps the editorials set up their expert role in obesity and suggest the layman status of the general reader (especially the obese individuals) in health; at the affective level, metaphors, especially *WAR* metaphors, attribute a sense of danger and threat towards obesity. Joint work of stance at the two levels finally contributes to a solidarity among all societies in dealing with obesity. The solidarity orientation can be related to the highly collectivist culture in China, especially in the context

4 The phrase, i.e., 'potential stock' can be generally understood as 'diamonds in the rough'.

of health communication (Tang and Peng 2015). Influenced by the culture, society-level and long-term solutions are preferred in the discussion of health issues in Chinese media, especially the official media. For example, Zhang et al. (2015) find the coverage of depression in the *Daily* tends to make societal-level responsibility attributions. The collectivist culture influences the media to report and discuss health issues from a summative viewpoint at a collective or a national level, as shown in the obesity case in our data.

Metaphors are effective positioning resources in health communication around obesity. Such positioning references reproduce ideologies and sociocultural values, providing opportunities for ideological transfer through stance attribution (Coupland and Coupland 2009). I argue that, in my data, the ideologies transferred can be mainly seen in China's modernity discourse, which has uplifted obesity from an individual health issue to a national development issue. Traumatic memories of past wars and humiliating experiences of being seduced in recent modern history have contributed to an emerging national prosperity discourse in China. Obesity, which can be taken as an index of weakness and counter-prosperity, offers a good site to observe the modernity discourse in China. Therefore, the negative representation of obesity in the editorials is not necessarily bad, as in the Chinese context it can help to motivate the public to take more initiative at taking care of their health. However, we need to bear in mind that along with the negative representation of obesity comes the stigmatisation and marginalisation of obese individuals in society. As a joint consensus statement has been made that "changes to language used at the point of care can alleviate the stigma of obesity" (Albury et al. 2020: 447), linguistic study on how negative stance is projected to individuals living with obesity could help solve this social problem. I believe metaphors can be used as a useful resource in looking into the disempowered obese individuals and further studies can look into how metaphors can be used in a more sensitive way to achieve better health communication outcomes surrounding obesity.

To sum up, this chapter contributes to contemporary studies on stance and metaphor, highlighting the importance of metaphors as a dual-positioning resource (self-positioning and other-positioning) in public health communication in media. I have to acknowledge the inevitable subjectivity in my metaphor and stance analysis and the relative limited size of my data. Yet this chapter represents an initial effort to explore the positioning effects of metaphors in the context of health communication on obesity in Chinese media. Further studies might seek to explore how metaphors are used by obese individuals to position themselves and how these positions compare with the ones projected onto them in the media. Future studies can also work on larger discourse data to quantitatively find positioning-patterns in obesity-related discourse in the Chinese context.

## References

Albury, C., Strain, W. D., Brocq, S. Le, Logue, J., Lloyd, C., & Tahrani, A. (2020). 'The Importance of Language in Engagement between Health-care Professionals and People Living with Obesity: A Joint Consensus Statement'. *The Lancet Diabetes and Endocrinology*, 8(5), 447–455.

Ariss, S. M. (2009). 'Asymmetrical Knowledge Claims in General Practice Consultations with Frequently Attending Patients: Limitations and Opportunities for Patient Participation'. *Social Science and Medicine*, 69(6), 908–919.

Atanasova, D., & Koteyko, N. (2017). 'Obesity Frames and Counter-frames in British and German Online Newspapers'. *Health (United Kingdom)*, 21(6), 650–669.

Atanasova, D., & Koteyko, N. (2020). 'Fighting Obesity, Sustaining Stigma: How Can Critical Metaphor Analysis Help Uncover Subtle Stigma in Media Discourse on Obesity'. In Z. Demjén (ed.), *Applying Linguistics in Illness and Healthcare Contexts*, pp. 223–243. London: Bloomsbury Publishing.

Baker, P., Brookes, G., Atanasova, D., & Flint, S. W. (2020). 'Changing Frames of Obesity in the UK Press 2008 – 2017'. *Social Science & Medicine*, 264(September), 113403.

Bassman, R. (2001). 'Whose Reality is It Anyway? Consumers/Survivors/Ex-Patients', *Journal of Humanistic Psychology*, 41(4), 11–35.

Baynham, M. (2011). 'Stance, Positioning, and Alignment in Narratives of Professional Experience'. *Language in Society*, 40(1), 63–74.

Biber, D., & Finegan, E. (1989). 'Styles of Stance in English: Lexical and Grammatical Marking of Evidentiality and Affect'. *Text*, 9(1), 93–124.

Bisiada, M. (2018). 'A Cross-linguistic Analysis of the 'Homework' Metaphor in German and English Political Discourse'. *Discourse and Society*, 29(6), 609–628.

Bonnin, J. E. (2019). *Discourse and Mental Health: Voice, Inequality and Resistance in Medical Settings*. Routledge.

Brookes, G. (2021). '"Lose Weight, Save the NHS": Discourses of Obesity in Press Coverage of COVID-19'. *Critical Discourse Studies*, 1–19.

Brookes, G., & Baker, P. (2021). 'Fear and Responsibility: Discourses of Obesity and Risk in the UK Press'. *Journal of Risk Research*, 1–16.

Cameron, L., Maslen, R., Todd, Z., Maule, J., Stratton, P., & Stanley, N. (2009). 'The Discourse Dynamics Approach to Metaphor and Metaphor-led Discourse Analysis'. *Metaphor and Symbol*, 24(2), 63–89.

Castaño, E. (2020). 'Discourse Analysis as a Tool for Uncovering the Lived Experience of Dementia: Metaphor Framing and Well-being in Early-onset Dementia Narratives'. *Discourse and Communication*, 14(2), 115–132.

Charteris-Black, J. (2012). 'Shattering the Bell Jar: Metaphor, Gender, and Depression'. *Metaphor and Symbol*, 27(3), 199–216.

Citron, F. M., & Goldberg, A. E. (2014). 'Metaphorical Sentences are More Emotionally Engaging than Their Literal Counterparts'. *Journal of Cognitive Neuroscience*, 26 (11), 2585–2595.

Coupland, J., and Coupland, N. (2009). 'Attributing Stance in Discourses of Body Shape and Weight Loss', In A. Jeff (ed.), *Stance: Sociolinguistic Perspectives*, pp. 227–249. Oxford: Oxford University Press.

Deignan, A. (2010). 'Evaluative Properties of Metaphors'. In G. Low, Z. Todd, A. Deignan, & L. Cameron (eds.), *Researching and Applying Metaphor in the Real World*, pp. 357–373. John Benjamins Publishing.

Demmen, J., Semino, E., Demjén, Z., Koller, V., Hardie, A., Rayson, P., & Payne, S. (2015). 'A Computer-assisted Study of the Use of Violence Metaphors for Cancer and End of Life by Patients, Family Carers and Health Professionals'. *International Journal of Corpus Linguistics*, 20(2), 205–231.

Du Bois, J.W. (2007). 'The Stance Triangle'. In R. Englebretson (ed.), *Stancetaking in Discourse: Subjectivity, Evaluation, Interaction*, pp. 139–182. John Benjamins Publishing.

Du Bois, J. W. (2014). 'Towards a Dialogic Syntax'. *Cognitive Linguistics*, 25(3), 359–410.

Englebretson, R. (2007). *Stancetaking in Discourse*. John Benjamins Publishing.

Flusberg, S.J., Matlock, T., & Thibodeau, P.H. (2018). 'War Metaphors in Public Discourse'. *Metaphor and Symbol*, 33(1), 1–18.

Huang, X., & Bisiada, M. (2021). 'Is Obesity Just a Health Issue? Metaphorical Framings of Obesity in the People's Daily'. *CADAAD Journal*, 13(2), 18–40.

Hunston, S. (2007). 'Using a Corpus to Investigate Stance Quantitatively and Qualitatively'. In R. Englebretson (ed.), *Stancetaking in Discourse: Subjectivity, Evaluation, Interaction*, pp. 27–48. John Benjamins Publishing.

Jaffe, A. (2009). *Stance: Sociolinguistic Perspectives*. Oxford University Press.

Jaffe, A. (2009). 'Stance in a Corsican School: Institutional and Ideological Orders and the Production of Bilingual Subjects', In A. Jeff (ed.), *Stance: Sociolinguistic Perspectives*, pp. 119–145. Oxford: Oxford University Press.

Lu, X., & Wang, B.P.Y. (2017). 'Towards a Metaphor-annotated Corpus of Mandarin Chinese'. *Language Resources and Evaluation*, 51(3), 663–694.

Malterud, K., & Ulriksen, K. (2010). '"Norwegians Fear Fatness More than Anything Else"-A Qualitative Study of Normative Newspaper Messages on Obesity and Health'. *Patient Education and Counseling*, 81(1), 47–52.

Marín-Arrese, J.I. (2009) 'Effective vs. Epistemic Stance, and Subjectivity/Intersubjectivity in Political Discourse: A Case Study', In Tsangalidis A and Facchinetti R (eds), *Studies on English Modality*, pp. 23–52. Berlin: Peter Lang.

McEntee-Atalianis, L. J. (2013). 'Stance and Metaphor: Mapping Changing Representations of (Organizational) Identity'. *Discourse and Communication*, 7(3), 319–340.

Mohammad, S. M., Shutova, E., & Turney, P.D. (2016). 'Metaphor as a Medium for Emotion: An Empirical Study'. *Proceedings of the Fifth Joint Conference on Lexical and Computational Semantics*, 23–33.

Monaghan, L. F. (2008). *Men and the War on Obesity: A Sociological Study*. Routledge.

Myers, G. (2010). 'Stance-taking and Public Discussion in Blogs'. *Critical Discourse Studies*, 7(4), 263–275.

Nie, J. B., Gilbertson, A., de Roubaix, M., Staunton, C., van Niekerk, A., Tucker, J. D., & Rennie, S. (2016). 'Healing without Waging War: Beyond Military Metaphors in Medicine and HIV Cure Research'. *American Journal of Bioethics*, 16(10), 3–11.

Ochs, E. (1990). 'Cultural Universals in the Acquisition of Language'. *Papers and Reports on Child Language and Development*, 29, 1–19. Standford University, California.

Puhl, R. M., & Heuer, C. A. (2009). 'The Stigma of Obesity: A Review and Update'. *Obesity*, 17(5), 941–964.

Saguy, A. C., & Almeling, R. (2008). 'Fat in the Fire? Science, the News Media, and the "Obesity Epidemic"'. *Social Forum*, 23(1), 53–83.

Seale, C. (2002). *Media and Health*. Sage.

Semino, E., Demjén, Z., Hardie, A., Payne, S., & Rayson, P. (2018). *Metaphor, Cancer and the End of Life: A corpus-based Study*. Routledge.

Serrano-García, I., & Bond, M. A. (1994). 'Empowering the Silent Ranks: Introduction'. *American Journal of Community Psychology*, 22(4), 433–445.

Steen, G. J., Dorst, A. G., Berenike Herrmann, J., Kaal, A. A., Krennmayr, T., & Pasma, T. (2010). *A Method for Linguistic Metaphor Identification: From MIP to MIPVU*. John Benjamins Publishing Company.

Tang, L., & Peng, W. (2015). 'Culture and Health Reporting: A Comparative Content Analysis of Newspapers in the United States and China'. *Journal of Health Communication*, 20(2), 187–195.

Taylor, C. (2018). 'Representing the Windrush Generation: Metaphor in Discourses Then and Now'. *Critical Discourse Studies*, 17(1), 1–21.

Wang, B.P., Lu, X., Hsu, C., Lin, E.P., & Ai, H. (2019). 'Linguistic Metaphor Identification in Chinese', In S. Nacey, A. G. Dorst, T. Krennmayr, & W. G. Reijnierse (eds.), *Metaphor Identification in Multiple Languages: MIPVU around the World*, pp. 247–265. John Benjamins Publishing.

Wang, Y., Xue, H., Sun, M., Zhu, X., Zhao, L., & Yang, Y. (2019). 'Prevention and Control of Obesity in China'. *The Lancet Global Health*, 7(9), e1166–e1167.

Wanniarachchi, V. U., Mathrani, A., Susnjak, T., & Scogings, C. (2020). 'A Systematic Literature Review: What is the Current Stance towards Weight Stigmatization in Social Media Platforms?'. *International Journal of Human Computer Studies*, 135(July 2019), 102371.

Yang, J. S. (2020). 'From Discourse of Weakness to Discourse of Empowerment: The Topos of the "Sick Man of East Asia" in Modern China'. In I. Amelung (ed.), *Discourse of Weakness in Modern China: Historical Diagnoses of the "Sick Man of East Asia"*, pp: 25–78. Schwächediskurse und Ressourcenregime.

Zhang, Y., Jin, Y., & Tang, Y. (2015). 'Framing Depression: Cultural and Organizational Influences on Coverage of a Public Health Threat and Attribution of Responsibilities in Chinese News Media, 2000–2012'. *Journalism and Mass Communication Quarterly*, 92(1), 99–120.

# Section C. Stance, Engagement, Evaluation and Emotion

Carolina Figueras

# Empathy in Online Mental Health Communities

**Abstract:** Empathy is usually separated into two major components: affective or emotional (the capacity to share the emotional experience felt by others) and cognitive (the recognition of the other person's emotions, a process that likely requires perspective taking). The focus of the present contribution is how empathy is conversationally managed in two mental health online communities: a chat room and a forum for recovery from an eating disorder (ED). The analysis revealed that in the ED chat room participants resorted to primal responses, formulations of understanding, and parallel assessments to claim understanding and display emotional empathy when responding to a troubles-telling. In contrast, ED forum members tended to produce complex discursive operations to persuade recipients to modify their ED thoughts, feelings and behaviours. This goal called for cognitive empathy displays, such as echoic formulations and resolutive second stories, by which the empathizer echoed the other person's mental representations and offered alternative epistemic and emotional stances.

**Keywords:** *eating disorders, empathy, emotions, online support groups, e-mental health interventions.*

## 1 Introduction

In the last decades, a growing body of research has been dedicated to understanding empathy from a wide range of disciplines (evolutionary psychology, cognitive psychology, clinical and abnormal psychology, neuroscience, psychology of development, philosophy of mind, linguistics, sociology, etc.). The burgeoning interest in empathy has given rise to an array of empirical and interdisciplinary methods of analysis to account for this multifaceted phenomenon (Brunsteins 2018). Relatedly, the complexity of the empathic experience has sparked a longstanding debate about the limits and interfaces of this psychological construct with other associated intersubjective phenomena (e.g., mindreading, perspective taking, sympathy or emotional contagion). Some authors have opted to differentiate empathy as a distinctive construct (e.g., Batson 2011), whereas others have argued in favour of an overarching category, empathy, that includes other mental processes, such as emotional contagion, sympathy or compassion (Preston and de Waal 2002).

Beyond the particular issue of its boundaries and relations, the ability of empathy usually incorporates two aspects, according to the extant literature in neuroscience: cognitive and affective (emotional) (Shamay-Tsoory 2011; Walter 2012). The former refers to the subject's capabilities to recognise and to understand the mental and emotional states of another person, an operation that requires taking her/his perspective (Baron-Cohen and Wheelwright 2004); the latter, instead, points to the subject's emotional response to the affective state displayed by the recipient (Eisenberg and Fabes 1990). Whereas emotional empathy alludes to the automatic capacity to react and to respond with stimulation to the perceived emotional states of the other, cognitive empathy engages more complex cognitive processes and triggering mechanisms (Barlińska et al. 2018).

Against this backdrop, the main goal of the present chapter is to reflect on the repertoire of discursive resources to construe empathy when interacting in online mental health groups. This work fits into the fruitful line of research on empathy in social interaction, developed in recent years in the areas of discourse and conversation analysis. Proof of the interest in this subject is the investigation on the role of empathy as related to claiming experiential knowledge in conversation (Heritage 2011), and to responding to affective-laden stories in everyday interaction (Kupetz 2014, 2019), as well as the efforts to systematise the characteristic empathy displays arranged in institutional talks (Hepburn and Potter 2007; Pudlinski 2005; Ruusuvuori 2005, 2007; Stommel and Te Molder 2018; Voutilainen et al. 2011).

While it is true that the study of empathy in institutional interactions has gained some traction in the field of discourse analysis, there is still little attention being paid to the role of empathy in computer mediated communication. Specifically, the question of how empathy is construed and communicated in online mental health communities should be further explored, due to the exponential increase in searches of these online platforms in the last decade (Prescott et al. 2020). So far, the few studies tackling the issue of digital empathy (e.g., Grondin et al. 2019; Hargreaves et al. 2018; Pfeil and Zhaphiris 2007; Preece and Gozhati 2001) have noted that the specific features of computer mediated communication tend to shape the empathic interaction. Factors such as the type of digital medium used for the exchange, its synchronic or asynchronic nature, its distinctive technological affordances, or its own rules to post on the site might affect how the interpersonal communication is perceived by the empathizer and the target of empathy (Grondin et al. 2019). Compared to the embodied practices of doing empathy in face-to-face interaction (cf. Kupetz 2014, 2019), the only markers of empathy in computer mediated communications are textual and graphic elements (such as emoticons, emojis and other visual elements; cf. Grondin et al. 2019).

Despite the limitations of the medium, empathic communication is extraordinarily high in online support groups (Preece and Ghozati 2001: 254). As a matter of fact, one key gratification from the use of these communities is the perceived empathy their members report when interacting with similar others (Hodges et al. 2010; Nambisan 2011). The importance of perceived empathy is such that it can affect the success of the treatment and the chances of recovery (Nambisan 2011: 298). On that account, peer empathy could eventually supplement the empathy provided by caregivers, which is expensive and time consuming (Nambisan 2011). This potential to deliver more integral mental health interventions justifies the need to better understand the singular and distinctive ways of doing empathy in online peer-to-peer communication. The present study seeks to contribute to this discussion.

Applying discourse and conversational analysis methods, my specific goals are twofold: to discern the differences in empathic responses according to the communicative setting, and to investigate some of the linguistic resources used to communicate emotional and cognitive empathy in interaction. It is not my purpose, though, to compile a comprehensive list of empathic resources. Instead, I narrow the analysis to the diverse methods and resources assembled by empathizers when negotiating the meanings of mental illness and recovery in two different online platforms: a chat room and a forum dedicated to eating disorders (EDs). In this study, I am only concerned with empathic responses in online mental health settings. The interactional construction of empathy in these particular contexts will be the topic of another study.

## 2 Methods

### 2.1 Corpus

The corpus for the present investigation comprised messages gathered from two different English-speaking digital platforms: a real time chat channel with the hashtag *#eating_disorders*, and an asynchronic online forum for EDs that is part of a large social news aggregation and discussion website.[1] The rationale

1 Both sites are public, so that anyone can get access to the repository of threads and posts and read the message boards online. Users resort to 'throwaway accounts' and pseudonyms, which are practices that facilitate anonymous discourse and help to shield individuals with stigmatized conditions, such as EDs (van der Nagel and Frith 2015). In order to further ensure that participants are protected and that their anonymity is

to select these two sites was to examine whether empathic practices in mental health communities were distinctively different or shared some key aspects. In fact, each site has specific affordances that shape the kind of interaction being developed. The ED chat room is regulated by moderators, whose role is basically to promote and to engage users in discussions on topics related to EDs, whilst simultaneously banning any content that might be harmful to participants or distressing for them. The ED forum for its part belongs to an extensive social networking platform with different topical moderated forums that has become increasingly popular with young adults.

I collected two samples of messages, one for each online mental health community. I included opening posts that explicitly posed a problem (troubles-telling), requested advice, or asked for information. The sample from the ED chat room included conversations from May 9th of 2018 to January 2nd of 2019, and from January 1st to February 18th of 2021 (total number of words: 61,971). Both time periods were selected to detect potential differences in empathy displays between the first and the latest interactional activity in the channel. The sample from the ED forum, in turn, contained 50 threads published during the month of February of 2021 (total number of words: 64,020).

## 2.2 Procedure and Analysis

Instances of empathic expressions were identified by going through the data. Empathic moves were broadly understood as a verbal display of understanding, affiliation, compassion or alignment with the emitter's troubles-telling. The codification of these empathy displays was conducted taking into account the list of forms of communication identified as empathy, support or affiliation in the previous literature (Burleson 2003; Burleson et al. 2002; Couper-Kuhlen 2012; Fiehler 2002; Figueras 2021; Heritage 2011; Kupetz 2014; Pudlinski 2005; Sanahuges and Curell 2020).

All representative instances of empathy were subjected to a fine-grained, small-scale and local qualitative analysis with the methods of discourse analysis, in the specific version of discursive psychology (Edwards and Potter 1992).

secured, the names of the sites have been concealed. Likewise, I removed any individual identifiers and those specific details that might identify individuals or organizations. Finally, I entered random phrases from the personal profiles collected for the present study into Google and I checked to see if they could be traced back to the personal profiles in the two sites investigated. Results of these searches did not return to the original post or to the site.

This analytic perspective is concerned about the ways psychological states are displayed in talk. Rather than regarding mental processes as the primary explanations for human action, discursive psychology focuses on conversation to scrutinise the actions and practices that the talk is doing, how it is constructed, and what resources are available to perform this activity. Taking this approach, empathy displays were not investigated in terms of changes of inner states but more in conversational terms, as social practices construed with and within discourse.

## 3 Results and Discussion

### 3.1 Types of Understanding and Types of Empathy

As Meneses and Larkin (2017) reason, empathy is a form of interpersonal or social understanding that connects to the exercise of reaching a substantial insight into another person's experience while, at the same time, being cognizant of the difference between the self and the other. Three prevailing ways of knowing what other people are feeling can be differentiated: intuiting, sharing and imagining (Meneses and Larkin 2017). Although all three have experiential validity, only sharing and imagining are common modes of understanding in the psychological definitions of 'empathy'. While sharing is a common mode of empathic understanding in the two online mental health communities examined here, imagining has a more prominent presence in the ED forum. Imagining is closely associated with the intellectual understanding (perspective taking) characteristic of cognitive empathy processes.

In reality, the empathic responses in both support groups are contingent on the discursive construction of two different insights into the other's ED experience: shared emotions and shared understandings. The ED operated as the binding or collective experience that all members had in common, which meant that participants in both platforms were personally implicated and emotionally invested in the business of sharing those ED insights. This personal involvement sometimes was more emotional (shared emotions), as for the ED chat room exchanges, and sometimes was more reasoned (shared understandings), as in the ED forum, when responders opposed two mental and emotional models of the illness experience: the ED and the recovery mindset (Figueras 2020, 2021). In any case, what is relevant in this discussion is the ways to discursively construe understanding in both online communities, and how they relate to two kinds of empathy displays: emotional and cognitive.

Following Sacks (1992), a contrast should be established between claiming understanding and demonstrating understanding. These two types of displays are connected to the specific ways of asserting membership categories, epistemic (a)symmetries, and particular rights and obligations (Mondada 2011). In both the ED chat room and the ED forum all their members were entitled to experience, given that they had a common epistemic access to the sensations, behaviours, body perceptions, feelings and thoughts associated with the ED. Hence, they all owned a collective network of meanings resulting from their personal firsthand experiences. However, not all of the experiential knowledge circulating in either group was uniformly distributed among its members. Some posters (the moderators, for instance) had more experiential rights than others, mainly because they were more advanced in the process of recovery from an ED (Figueras 2021). This differential expertise was made available in discourse through a variety of manifestations of emotional and intellectual understandings. In other words, the interplay of epistemic symmetries and asymmetries in online mental health support groups revealed fundamental differences in the types of empathy displays that interactants produced.

The first distinction to be made is between emotional empathy displays (based on shared emotions) *vs* cognitive empathy displays (built on shared understandings). Following Meneses and Larkin (2017), the more intellectual aspects of empathy are the basis for the phenomenon of shared understanding, whereas its emotional aspects are more closely related to the experience of shared emotions. Reasoning (e.g., generalisation, projection), mindreading and argumentation are operations involved in communicating cognitive empathy, as it will be argued in section 3.2. Reacting with primal responses to the troubles-telling (1), exhibiting alignment with the troubles reported in the opening message (2), taking the same emotional stance as the first poster (3), and/or describing one's own ED practices as proof of understanding (4) are considered in the present study some of the discursive moves to claim understanding. In any of these cases, the responder is doing emotional empathy.

(1) a. 😭 [ED chat room]
b. *that's good!* [ED chat room]

(2) a. *omg this is literally EXACTLY what I do too* [ED forum]
b. *I'm so sorry it is!! You're not alone, though!* [ED forum]
c. *This is my entire existence too* [ED forum]

(3) a. *I feel the same and I'm actually chubby* 😭😭😭 [ED chat room]
b. *I have the same feelings. Disgusted with myself, unable to control yourself and ashamed.* [ED chat room]

(4) *Omg I feel the same way I don't eat for a couple of days except no one notices I just starve myself in secret* [ED forum][2]

The most basic emotional displays that convey empathy are primal responses (Sanahuges and Curell 2020), which equate to non-elaborated reactions that are placed at the beginning of the post to communicate the immediate reply to the troubles-telling message. Primal responses included primary sound objects (onomatopoeias, such as 'awww', 'ugh'; interjections, like 'oops'; or emojis, like the heart ❤, or the raising hands 🙌), and secondary sound objects, corresponding to more substantive lexical forms ('Soooo good!!!', 'That's good', 'YESSSSSSSSS…', 'Oh, yeah'). These elements, more common in the ED chat room than in the forum, could be considered tokens of response cries, that is, "signs meant to be taken to index directly the state of the transmitter" (Goffman 1981: 116).

Response cries represent the most typical and embodied resources to bring about empathic alignments between interlocutors (Heritage 2011). In the case of computer mediated communication, they can be associated with certain textual features of a non-propositional nature (such as emojis), that make them more suitable to convey bare or raw emotional reactions to a reported event. Naturally, they evoke a more primal or basic form of empathic expression. By being part of the into-the-moment communication characteristic of the ED chat room, these textual cues indicated that responders were fully engaged and emotionally connected to any member of the group who was wrestling with the ED.

In both online communities, the significance of 'sharing emotions' was linked to the business of building relationships with other sufferers, participating in another's person story and forming an impression of emotional connectedness with others. Members of each group expressed a feeling of emotional togetherness that stemmed from the similarities, real or presumed, regarding the experience of the illness. Sharing-as-knowing was a powerful tactic to create familiarity and solidarity among strangers. Reporting on personal feelings when responding to the call for support by another member stood as proof of understanding the recipient's emotional condition.

The motivation for empathy, however, might not be necessarily altruistic in the majority of the interactions held in the two online ED communities examined here, but directed toward the ultimate goal of relieving one's own distress (fear, anxiety, guilt). After all, when responders reacted to the troubles-telling, they might not have been led by the distress they experienced by seeing

2 The examples are reproduced with all the errors in grammar and spelling that were present in the original posts.

another person suffering, but by their own struggles with the illness (cf. Batson 2011). This underlying egotistic motivation explains why so many responders in both online communities rendered formulations of understanding and parallel assessments only to claim understanding, but not to demonstrate it.

According to Mondada (2011), formulations of understanding are the most explicit mechanisms to claim understanding, albeit they are commonly used for doing something more than just showing understanding. In the ED chat room, as well as in the ED forum, statements of the kind reproduced in (5–6) were in service of coping with the responder's own strains with the illness, rather than to show that a process of understanding had really taken place:

(5) *Totally understand and personally also feel what you're saying. Eating feels like work almost all the time, so I've started a couple of things in particular (food/mood journaling, cooking larger batches of comfort food, ~daily walks around the block) to help get back on track and kind of guide myself along while tracking progress.* [ED forum]

(6) *I understand what you're going through. I'm like that with most clothes. Shopping makes me depressed a lot of the time too. And I say I can't find my size when it's because I don't want to try a bigger size. So I get what you're going through* [ED chat room]

In the excepts in (5) and (6), ED members resort to an empathic formulation introduced by a verb of acknowledgment ('I understand…'), in order to transform prior talk (the troubles-telling act) and express explicit understanding of the target's feelings and experiences. Notwithstanding this claim of epistemic rights, no meanings of deep comprehension were delivered in those responses. Resorting to the verb 'to understand', that denotes the achievement of a mental state (the result or success of a process) does not offer any guarantee that a real move of taking the other person's perspective has occurred. In these replies, the poster is, rather, conveying emotional empathy based on the realisation of two activities: claiming understanding (with the preface containing the verb of acknowledgment) and sharing her/his own emotional state. These two moves result in an affiliative action that matches the evaluative/affective stance of the target. The responders in (5) and (6) do shared feelings and, hence, their posts stand as displays of emotional empathy.

According to Håkansson and Montgomery (2003), both empathizers and targets express their own emotions, although the targets do not usually refer to the empathizers'. The opposite is generally true for empathizers. In this manner, the empathy experience is shared by the participants, but the focus is more on the target's situation than the empathizer's (Håkansson and Montgomery 2003). Yet, emotional empathy displays that appear in both the ED chat room and the ED forum arose from an epistemic and emotional symmetry between the empathizer and the target. This is emphasised by the fact that responders of (5–6) focused almost exclusively on their own experience when giving feedback. They did not make reference to any other subject's mental or affective state but their own.

The examples in (5–6) also reveal the role that parallel assessments fulfil in the construction of emotional empathy in mental health support groups. As Heritage (2011) points out, parallel assessments describe similar experiences to the one reported by a first speaker, but without getting into the trouble that was reported. When ED responders resorted to parallel assessments in their replies, they narrowed their interest to the core elements of the original post (the one announcing the troubles-telling) that aligned with their own dealings with the illness. Their messages contained self-references and second stories without any (re)elaboration of the original poster's experience. The second story was usually introduced as a parallel experience that was oriented to prove the responder's understanding of the first story, the troubles-telling, resulting in conversations with different individual voices, each one reporting on its own (similar) circumstances.

Inasmuch as the responses in (5–6) were delivered without problematizing the trouble that was being collectively shared (cf. Arminen 2004), they should be considered instances of claiming, rather than demonstrating understanding. Thereby, the myriad of parallel assessments so often exchanged in both groups (particularly, in the chat room) symbolically represented the stand-alone tales in a collective ED lived experience. Participants in this kind of interaction became both the actors and the audience when enacting their stories, as was the case in the thread with the title "Does anyone else have 'safe clothing"?', posted in the ED forum. The first message is reproduced in (7), and a selection of the 47 responses that were offered to the original post are copied in (8a-g):

(7) *i have specific clothes i always feel safe in but then i have other clothes that i cannot wear bc they make me feel so fat. like i cannot wear sweatpants with an elastic waist band bc it touches me*

(8) a. *i am the same. i only feel 'safe' in elastic waists when they are loose on me even if they fit just fine, my brain perceives it as a sausage casing and it is just the worse.*
 b. *yes, exactly! i only wear one brand of leggings consistently and even then, sometimes some batches are just..*
 c. *I hate any jeans or slacks with no stretch in the waistband. When I sit and it tugs at my abdomen.....rage fuel. I can't stand it*
 d. *i only feel safe in one pair of sweatpants (usually paired with a crop top.) or really tight high waisted shorts with a large hoodie- my safe clothing isn't typical i know :/*
 e. *my 'safe' clothing is warm knee high socks and legging under bell bottom jeans*
 f. *Yes. I can't wear jeans because I'm afraid of seeing my legs.*
 g. *I have a weird flip flop between safe clothes. I either want a lot showing or none at all*

The private ED practice disclosed in (7) opens a response space that has to be fulfilled by other members. The specific emotions described in this troubles-telling sequence (feeling 'safe' with certain clothes, as opposed to feeling 'so fat' with others) constitute a relatable ED episode to which other sufferers can align. The personal tribulations exposed by the emitter of (7) set the stage for the audience to react with emotional empathy. The particular strategy to enact empathy in this case was issuing responses that contained parallel assessments. Responders in (8a-g) shift the focus from the experiential world of the first poster to their own experiential worlds (Kupetz 2014). Telling their side means not only describing recognizable ED habits and behaviours (such as wearing certain kinds of clothes) but also verbalizing those feelings and emotions that are triggered by the illness (e.g., 'I always feel safe', 'I hate', 'rage fuel', 'I'm afraid'). By doing so, that is, by showing shared feelings (emotional involvement), ED members sought to legitimise and normalise their private labours coping with the ailment.

The display of emotional empathy was more prevalent in the ED chat room, due to the particular affordances of the site. Chat rooms are designated virtual channels in which messages are spontaneous and instantly visible and readable, which means that subscribers of the ED channel could have conversations in real time. The messages were, in general, shorter and with a sharp focus on the trouble at hand (chiefly, issues with food intake). Forums, in contrast, are better suited for asynchronic interactions, a feature that allows participants to discuss pressing issues in more depth. This fundamental distinction accounts for the orientation of each of the two platforms explored in this chapter. While subscribers of the ED chat room leaned towards dealing conversationally with the emotional stresses caused by the illness, members of the ED forum were more inclined to manage and to negotiate the workings of recovery in their interactions.

These different orientations translate into distinct ways of talking about EDs with other members, as it has been underscored in the literature (Figueras 2018, 2021; Wolf et al. 2013). Members of the ED chat room seemed to be more self-focused (although they sustained high levels of sympathy and concern for others in similar situations) and gravitated more around their own preoccupations, feelings of distress, and arduous efforts to control eating. Instead, the space of the ED forum was populated by several recovered individuals who actively promoted and advocated for a life without the disorder. As a result of these positionings toward the ED, distinguishable ways of doing empathy can be found in each site, as it is argued in the next section, dedicated to the speech act of advice.

## 3.2 Empathy and Advice

One of the main features of online mental health communities is the fundamental role that advice solicitation and advice provision play in users' interactions (cf. Figueras 2020, 2021; Kouper 2010; Morrow 2006; Stommel and Lamerichs 2014). It comes as no surprise that advice exchange constitutes one of the main activities in the two support groups explored in the present study. Focusing on the advice-giving act, its realisation involves transferring information, recommendations and a proposed course of action (Kouper 2010). On the one hand, offering advice seems to be based on an asymmetric epistemic relationship, an imbalance in power and expertise between the interactants (Feng and MacGeorge 2006). On the other hand, it might be received as an imposition by the part on the advisor and, as a result, regarded as face threatening, particularly among peers (Kouper 2010; Locher 2006; Locher and Limberg 2012). To make the advice more acceptable to the recipient, advisors in online mental health communities often resort to empathy moves (Figueras 2020, 2021).

Two main types of advice-giving acts, with their corresponding different empathy moves, could be distinguished in each site (the ED chat room and the ED forum): giving tips to deal with the symptoms (ED chat room) and providing elaborate and reasoned advice to overcome the illness (ED forum). Regarding the former, the ED chat room, its more synchronic nature facilitated the exchange of pieces of information to manage specific symptoms of the disorder on the spot, such as what to do right after a binge, how to control the imminent urge of purging, or how to overcome the fear of eating the next meal. Thus, for instance, the poster of (9) asked specifically for advice to manage food portions and responders offered a list of practical tips (10a-c):

(9) *Advisee: I dont know how to have a small portion of 'bad foods', and once i have too much, i say 'may as well keep going' and purge it. Does anyone have advice?*

(10) a. *Eat a little protein with it your body tells u to stop because it has the nutrition*

b. *Have you tried Almond butter or peanut butter for some fat*

c. *I learned in health class and gym class that it's good to eat slowly. When eating fats your brain doesn't register that you are full because you are eating so fast. So if you eat slowly then you won't end up over eating.*

Since other members of the ED chat room usually experienced similar struggles with the ED, tips were often supplemented with a battery of emotional empathy tactics, such as inserting expressions of alignment and affiliation (11a), making formulations of understanding (11b), acknowledging and validating the advisee's feelings (11c), or extending a common experiential ground (with the first person plural) whereby coping strategies could be shared (11d):

(11) a. *I relate. Hang in there. I'm here to talk if you want.*
b. *I understand that. It's the same with me*
c. *It's easy to get overwhelmed with things. [...] And, tbh, I'm not too good at coping when I feel overwhelmed. But, the best advice that I have for you is to remember to take deep breaths. Try to clear your thoughts the best you can and try to think logically.*
d. *We can do this though. I ate because I was in a good mood and it made me spiral into a bad one. But we have to remind ourselves that food is not a bad thing.*

The unifying theme in these ED interactions was the management of the behaviours, thoughts, feelings and social pressures of living with an ED. Interactants publicly admitted to performing a set of eating practices labelled as the clinical symptoms of an ED (whether anorexia, bulimia or otherwise). The fact that all of them self-identified as ED sufferers justified why providers of tips positioned themselves in an epistemic and emotional symmetry in relation to the recipient (the initial poster). One way to honour that symmetry was by claiming their inability to dispense practical advice, as was the case in the messages reproduced in (12):

(12) a. *I'm not sure if I can help but I can definitely relate*
b. *I'm sorry if I don't have any advice atm but I'm always here to listen*
c. *I might not have the best advice but I can listen and try my best to help you*
d. *I will be here for you and others too, I can't give advices too, but i hope I can help just a little*

The utterances in (12a-d) pose a dichotomy between advice, understood in practical terms as help to solve particular ED problems ('try my best to help you', 'I hope I can help'), and listening abilities ('I'm always here to listen'). The posters could do the latter but were doubtful about the former, thus constructing themselves more as passive receptors of the troubles-telling than as active givers of sound advice.

The analysis of the corpus made clear that the main interactional activity in the ED chat room revolved around the allocation of emotional resources to support other members and the exchange of small tips to carry on with the daily life of an ED patient. Conversely, this channel was not a discursive space in which participants imagine and collaboratively construe and negotiate the new realities of recovery, as in the ED forum. Given that the orientation of the interactants was more focused on the day-to-day operations of enduring a full-blown ED, it is not surprising that the exhibitions of empathy in the ED chat room were rather emotional than cognitive. In that particular site, then, the responses were aimed at regulating the emotional content of those messages expressing distress, for the most part, as opposed to fulfilling an agenda of long-term recovery from the ED. However, when enrolled in the process of recovery, ED members of support groups tend to gravitate towards a more disruptive advising exchange (cf. Figueras 2020, 2021), as they seek to modify the mental and emotional states of the advisee, an endeavour that opens up the venue for cognitive empathy displays.

## 3.3 Cognitive Empathy Displays

A review of the literature suggests that the construct of cognitive empathy encompasses abilities such as knowing another person's emotional and/or cognitive internal state, figuring how another person is thinking and feeling, and/or envisioning how one would think and feel if she/he was in the target's situation (Batson 2011). This exercise of imagining what the mental and emotional contents of the other person's mind are draws on her/his words and her/his actions, as well as the empathizer's knowledge of the target's character, values, and desires.

Conceptualizing the mental states of others has been considered a particular form of perspective taking. Likewise, the capacity to adopt the perspective of the other represents the key component of empathy (Decety 2005). It has been characterised as an 'imagine-self' perspective (imagining how one would personally feel about a situation), as well as an 'imagine other' perspective (imagining what the target of a story might be feeling or experiencing; Batson 2011). To adopt an imagine-self perspective is in some respects similar to the act of projecting oneself into another's situation, which is essentially what an elaborate act of advice giving is (Figueras 2020, 2021). The following posts, taken from the ED forum, are instances of this kind of discursive operation:

(13) *If you didn't specifically tell them that it's your safe food then how would they know? If they tend to forget, I would create a fridge shelf that is only for you and write your name in a sticky note there or something.*

(14) *I wouldn't give up my dream of having children because of your ED*

In both excerpts, the responder delivers her/his advice by impersonating an imagined 'I' that locates her/him in the very centre of the advisee's trouble. By discursively simulating that they can put themselves in the other person's shoes ('I would/wouldn't…'), the posters in (13) and (14) are able to create an impression of empathic understanding that makes the recommendation more suited and tailored to the advisee's needs and expectations.

Rendering advice aimed at changing the advisee's thoughts, feelings and attitudes, as is the case in the ED forum, requires, on the part of the advisor, to come up with a model of the other person's mental and emotional states. She/

he faces two challenging tasks when strategizing her/his advice: a) imagining the advisee's state of mind; and b) making a mental simulation of the model that the advisee is building of the advisor (Martinovski et al. 2004). Both tasks triggered mindreading (theory of mind) processes: the advisor has to be able to represent the mental states of others in terms of intentions, desires and beliefs, as well as to understand and predict others' behaviours (Abu-Akel and Shamay-Tsoory 2013).

In order to persuade the advisee to make significant changes in her/his attitudes and behaviour towards the ED, advisors in the ED forum often resorted to empathy displays that prepared the speech act of advice provision, as the message in (15), posted on the ED chat room, exemplifies:

(15) *Hello @X I am sorry to hear you are struggling so much, just remember that your struggles are valid. It is truly devastating when our eds start affecting aspects of our lives like health, studies and family, but they eventually will, and if they go on too long, they are not going to affect them in a good way.*
*Although I do not mainly struggle with restriction, I can advise you to take care of yourself in non-ed related ways, make it a point to give yourself the care and love you oh so crave, then it gets easier to let go of ed, even if it is just a part of it, because the truth is that sometimes we simply need tools to keep our lives afloat, because when we get out of this dark web, it would be nice to have something to get back to. Think about the 80-year old you, what would you want them to remember? what would they tell you to do?*
*I think it is important to know what your ed replaces, and give it to yourself, love? safety? care? attention? and do it for you!*

The response in (15) combines both emotional and cognitive empathy displays. The advisor opens her/his post by replying directly to the advisee's (using the tag @X). With this manoeuvre, she/he frames her/his message as a personal response to the specific query posed by the advisee. Next, she/he inserts an expression of care and concern that prefaces a validating move to acknowledge the legitimacy of the target's struggles ('just remember that your struggles are valid'). Then, she/he claims understanding of the destructive effects of an ED on the person's life by performing an evaluative assertion ('It is truly devastating') and by resorting to the first-person plural to emphasise the reality of the common experience ('our lives'). This battery of strategies instantiates emotional empathy displays that prepare the advice-giving act which is realised in the second paragraph: 'I can advise you…'

Giving advice requires knowledge of the other person's reality. Although the advisor in (15) is well versed on the emotional toll of the ED, based on her/his own personal history, she/he needs to make a disclaimer implying that she/

he might be lacking the experiential knowledge to advise someone struggling with restriction. In spite of her/his insufficient expertise in a specific domain of the ED experience, she/he asserts her/his epistemic rights as an ED patient with the recourse to vivid metaphors to refer to the illness ('this dark web') and the use of the first-person plural to create an emotionally congruent stance with the advisee ('we simply need tools', 'when we get out'; Figueras 2021).

In addition, with the use of the imperative form 'think', the advisor induces the recipient to perform some mental tasks. First, she/he poses a hypothetical question ('Think about the 80-year old you, what would you want them to remember?'), in order to transport the recipient to an imagined future self ('the 80-year old you') who would be judged by others for her/his past self. This exercise of simulating or pretending works in conjunction with another inquiry about the advisee's insight into the symbolic meaning that the ED plays for her/him ('what would they tell you to do?'). In reality, these queries materialise the advisor's claims of knowing the mental state of any ED experiencer, which is why they can work as the preamble to the advice-giving act performed at the end of the post ('do it for you'). All the linguistic devices deployed in (15) constitute the discursive tools to produce cognitive empathy, inasmuch as they bring together the self-perspective and the other-perspective. As Decety (2005: 144) contends, "empathic understanding requires the inclusion of other characteristics within the self". It is, precisely, the process of perspective taking which creates an explicit representation of the other person.

Perspective taking is a major component of mindreading. It represents the complex socio-cognitive process by which speakers are capable of recognizing others' point of view, whether it be the same or different from their own (Healey and Grossman 2019: 59). Consistent with this view, empathy should be considered a representational capacity, a motivated behaviour that can be triggered voluntarily (Decety 2005: 153).

Empathy should not be reduced to a simple resonance of affect between empathizer and target, but rather understood as a complex ability to make second-order representations of the other which are available to consciousness (Decety 2005: 153). When analysing the interactions in the ED chat room, a recurrent response offered by other members to the troubles-telling or advice seeking post was rendering an account based on self-perspective (as in 10a-10g). Self-perspective facilitated emotion sharing (emotional empathy, to be more precise), but it was not enough for empathic understanding.

In addition to shared emotion and self-awareness, demonstrating understanding requires consciously adopting the perspective of the other. Affective resonance triggers automatic empathic consideration for the target's emotional state, while perspective taking induces empathic understanding. Empathic understanding entails incorporation of known information about the target in order to imagine her/his emotional and/or mental state (Grondin et al. 2019). The object of understanding may be the other's thoughts, feelings, desires, beliefs, situation, perspective, or experiences (Håkansson and Montgomery 2003), as is the case for many of the interactions in the ED forum.

Reasoning, imagining, simulating, predicting, or inferring another person's experience are central to the empathy process (Meneses and Larkin 2017). This combination of tasks reveals what the advisor is doing with her/his talk in the troubles-telling sequences produced in the ED forum. Since cognitive empathy involves the effort of comprehending the internal world of the other person, the question, from a discursive standpoint, is how the interactants whose intention is to impact and modify the recipient's cognitive and emotional environment, support their conversational activity with cognitive empathy moves. Since careful advice calls for cognitive empathy (Figueras 2021), the issue at hand is to determine the specific strategies that demonstrate understanding when providing advice in an ED support group. For limitations of space, I will focus on only two strategies to demonstrate empathic understanding: echoic formulations and resolutive second stories.

I call 'echoic formulations' those discursive moves oriented to surmise the thoughts and feelings of the recipient. Echoic formulations contain explicit enunciations of the imagined mental representations held by the recipient. Advisors attribute those mental representations to the advisee making ostensively clear, at the same time, that they distance themselves from those beliefs. Initially, the advisor seems to take the advisee's epistemic and evaluative stance, but then she/he makes a move to disaffiliate herself/himself from this perspective and to offer an alternative positioning. An example of this kind of discursive operation can be found in (16):

(16) *Part of the instinctual habit you're describing is the learnt association between ['keep my calories low ---> lose/maintain weight']* THOUGHT ATTRIBUTED TO THE ADVISEE. *In order to break this, you must recognise that this not a perfect association. ['It's all well and good *telling* myself that',]* THOUGHT ATTRIBUTED TO THE ADVISEE *you'll say, and [I get it]* CLAIM OF UNDERSTANDING. *You need to make it experiential in order for it to factor into your habit-making. What would be ideal is if you could force yourself to have a few days 'off' where you eat whatever you want within reason and see for yourself that you wont gain weight. However, [THAT'S EASIER SAID THAN DONE FOR SOMEONE WITH AN ED.]* DEMONSTRATING UNDERSTANDING

*[People who struggle with problems like yours often employ Cognitive Behavioural Therapy. Is this an option for you?]*ADVICE-GIVING ACT

The kind of mental representations that are being echoed in (16) are not all of the advisee's thoughts, but only those that belong to the category of 'ED thoughts'. These particular mental representations are beliefs that are discursively construed as 'wrong' (as is in 16) or 'false' by the ED members themselves. This privileged access to the advisee's ED thoughts comes from the experiential rights claimed by those members in recovery. The fact that the recovering person has lived through analogous situations, and that she/he is now trying to prevail over the ED, legitimises her/his claim to epistemic superiority over the recipient.

The empathic strategy put forward by the advisor in (16) consists of attributing a set of particular assumptions to the advisee but ostensibly indicating that they are part of a more general mindset of distorted beliefs shared by any ED sufferer (including the advisor's past self with the illness). With this tactic, the advisor achieves two goals: a) she/he grants validity for her/his interpretation of what the mental state of a recovering person is; b) she/he demonstrates understanding (she/he does cognitive empathy). Invested with the authority of someone with real insight into the phases of illness and recovery, the advisor is able to produce deontic statements ('you need to') that pose the advisee the challenge of cognitive restructuring, that is, the reorganisation of automatic thoughts and the reorientation of emotional stimuli (Vartanian et al. 2004). This exercise of demonstrating understanding with an elaborate cognitive empathy display paves the way for the indirect advice delivered at the end of the post: 'Is [Cognitive Behavioural Therapy] and option for you?'.

Cognitive empathy seems to be part of the act of advice provision in contexts in which, as the ED forum, there is the need to encourage others to challenge implicit cognitions and to modify maladaptive schemas. The goal sought with the response in (16), as in many other exchanges in the forum, is to change those automatic associations (such as 'keeping calories low' and 'maintaining weight', for instance) that influence feelings and behaviour.[3] From this stance, cognitive empathy in the ED forum invokes an epistemic asymmetry between the empathizer and the target. The grounds for these contrasting epistemic statuses are the differences of knowledge regarding the phases of illness and recovery. These asymmetric experiential rights between the interactants also play a role in the construction of resolutive second stories.

3 This kind of rationale was probably borrowed from the cognitive-behavioural therapy that many recovering ED patients likely underwent during the time they participated in online support groups.

With resolutive second stories, the responder mirrors the experience of the illness reported by the first poster and makes it the foundation to describe an alternative reality. In the ED forum, this other state of affairs is the conceptual domain of recovery. In a similar fashion as echoic formulations, these second accounts of the ED serve the purpose of overcoming the recipient's resistance to get treatment. One example of this kind of narrative is illustrated in (17):

(17) *I've been there- I went from basically starving myself, to becoming paleo to allow myself to eat, to adding in fear foods (rice, sugar) while calorie counting. It's a prison. You're not going to forget your calorie counting overnight. I frequently redownloaded and deleted my fitness pal for months after saying I wanted to stop counting calories. This isn't a matter of willpower — that's part of what makes eating disorders so horrible — they're MEAN. They tell you something's wrong with you and make you feel bad about yourself. Your BMI, fat percentage, etc, don't matter. Your fear of gaining weight and the coping mechanisms you use to deal with that fear are what matter. The eating disorder is mental. It's hard to navigate all this without a therapist. Before I sought help, I would try to recover, but my thoughts were so disordered that I constantly relapsed. [So number one- get professional help from someone who specializes in this; you don't have to recover alone.]*ADVICE-GIVING ACT
*Your therapist will be able to help you break down your fears and learn techniques that will help you cope. When you start spiralling and thinking negative thoughts, it helps me to think of them as something a bully is saying to someone else. Like, it's so easy to tell yourself, 'you're disgusting,' and think it's just a truth. But what if you heard someone say that to your friend?*

The linking of the advisor's experience to the troubles-telling is crucial to offer mutual support when the advisee is undergoing the difficult process of recovery. By reflecting on the concerns expressed in the first message, empathic responders project a strong alignment with the recipient. Likewise, in tying-up their responses to the initial poster's message (in 17 with expressions such as 'I've been there'), the ordeal of the mental condition (metaphorically described in 17 as 'a prison') is recounted in a thoughtful, knowledgeable, and transformative way (see Arminen 2004). The value of second stories that narrate the transition from the illness state to the successive stages of recovery is that the tale reframes the thoughts, feelings and behaviours characteristic of the ED. As a result, in second stories like (17) the ED reaches, at least symbolically, a resolution.

The empathic component of a response of this kind lies in demonstrating an understanding of the pains caused by the disorder, owning them, and taking the ordeal of the illness as a starting point to rewrite the recipient's story. Both the advisee's and the advisor's ED experiences are blended together by resorting to mechanisms such as the second person singular with generalised reference: 'They tell you something's wrong with you and make you feel bad about yourself. Your BMI, fat percentage, etc, don't matter. Your fear of gaining weight and the coping mechanisms you use to deal with that fear are what matter'. With this empathy device, deployed to demonstrate understanding, the experience is construed as reciprocally shareable (see Figueras 2021). The responder thus exhibits deep knowledge of the cognitive and emotional mechanisms developed during the course of the ED, and of the coping strategies that have to be devised and learned in the process of recovery.

Following the advisor's account, the turning point to break the cycle of the ED ('I constantly relapsed') was to find a therapist. Consequently, she/he urges the advisee to 'get professional help'. The acceptance of treatment introduces a new perspective (the recovery mindset), described in the second paragraph of this post, from which emotions and thoughts are questioned, contradicted and reorganised. As illustrated in (17), second stories advocating for recovery may afford the recipient with figurative, symbolic interpretations (such as 'something a bully is saying to someone else') that transvaluate the adaptative meanings that the ED has acquired for the recipient.

## 4 Conclusions

The present study explored some of the linguistic resources to do empathy in two different online mental health communities: an ED chat room and an ED forum. The analysis of responses to troubles-telling in both sites shed light onto the distinct nature of the empathy displays produced by members of each community. In the chat room, the predominant way of enacting empathy was through displays of shared emotions. In that context, empathy could be read as a type of emotional capital that interactants built and relied on when navigating difficult interactions aimed at releasing the tensions of living with an ED. Primal responses, formulations of understanding, and parallel assessments were three common strategies deployed by responders to claim understanding of the troubles voiced by the first poster (Sacks 1992). The three empathy displays represented the discursive realisation of emotional empathy, understood as the capacity to share the emotional experience felt by others or, more specifically, the ability of appropriating the emotions sustained by the other person. These affective reactions when acknowledging and replying to troubled members created a shared network of mutually recognizable feelings, behaviours and beliefs characteristic of ED rituals and practices.

Emotional empathy is critically different from cognitive empathy. In many cases, the former implies appropriating the other person's feelings (on a gross level); the latter, instead, refers to the capacity to engage in the cognitive process of adopting another individual's psychological perspective (Dvash and Shamay-Tsoory 2014). Cognitive empathy involves the intellectual recognition of the other person's mental and emotional states. Discursively, it projects onto perspective taking moves, by which the empathizer echoes the other person's mental representations. This is the kind of exercise found in the ED forum through two main discursive strategies: echoic formulations and resolutive second stories. Both empathy displays were realised in the ED forum when delivering advice. Taking into account this specific speech act, a distinction was made in the present study between the interactive tasks of providing tips to manage the symptomatology of the ED *vs* rendering thoughtful advice to overcome the illness and initiate the process of recovery. Exchanging tips was a conversational routine for the members of the ED chat room. It did not require the drawing of elaborate hypotheses about the contents in the recipient's mind, as opposed to the kind of discursive operations that were essential in the ED forum to guide and persuade advisees to modify their ED thoughts and feelings. In this case, advisors had to demonstrate understanding of both the illness and the recovery positionings.

The contrast between the empathy displays (emotional *vs* cognitive) performed in each of these two sites revealed a substantial difference when communicating empathy between self-perspective and other-perspective. The orientation to the self that is the basis of emotional empathy displays seemed to be characteristic of participants who were still deep into the illness experience. The orientation to the other, alternatively, came from a different positioning of the empathizer toward the illness: from the position of self-focus to the position of other-focus of one who has access to the experiences of illness and recovery (Popham 2017).[4] As a result, members of these communities could construe distinguishable levels of empathy in their online communications. Therefore, empathy should be conceived in terms of different levels of understanding that are projected into distinctive discursive operations and moves.

In this regard, and as Kupetz (2014: 28) suggests, displays of empathy can be organised in an apprehension-comprehension continuum. In our data, one end

4 These results could be related to the differences between the cognitive abilities of ED patients compared to non-ED individuals. According to Kerr-Gaffney et al. (2019), the review of the literature indicates that those with anorexia nervosa have lower cognitive empathy abilities. That might explain the self-focus style of the messages in the ED chat room.

is represented entirely by emotional empathy displays (primal responses) and the opposite end by full displays of cognitive comprehension (echoic formulations, resolutive stories). In between these two extremes, there will be more nuanced instances of empathy to be defined and (re)negotiated for each communicative setting. Understanding these differences in the expression of empathy in online mental health communities is essential to better patient 'quality-of-life' in clinical treatments for EDs.

## References

Abu-Akel, A., and Shamay-Tsoory, S. (2013). 'Characteristics of theory of mind impairments in schizophrenia'. In D. Roberts, and D. Penn (eds.), *Social cognition in schizophrenia: from evidence to treatment*, 196–214. Oxford: Oxford University Press.

Arminen, I. (2004). 'Second stories: the salience of interpersonal communication for mutual help in Alcoholics Anonymous', *Journal of Pragmatics*, 36(2), 319–347.

Barlińska, J., Szuster, A., and Winiewski, M. (2018). 'Cyberbullying among adolescent bystanders: Role of affective versus cognitive empathy in increasing prosocial cyberbystander behavior'. *Frontiers in Psychology*, 9: 799.

Baron-Cohen, S., and Wheelwright, S. (2004). 'The empathy quotient: An investigation of adults with Asperger syndrome or high functioning autism, and normal sex differences', *Journal of Autism and Developmental Disorders*, 34(2), 163–175.

Batson, C. D. (2011). 'These things called empathy: Eight related but distinct phenomena'. In J. Decety, and W. Ickes (eds.), *The social neuroscience of empathy*, 3–16. Cambridge, MA: MIT Press.

Brunsteins, P.C. (2018). 'Empathy and vicarious experience. Congruence or identical emotion?', *Philosophies*, 3(2): 6.

Burleson, B.R. (2003). 'Emotional support skills'. In J.O. Greene, and B.R. Burleson (eds.), *Handbook of communication and social interaction skills*, 551–594. Mahwah, NJ: Lawrence Erlbaum Associates.

—— Feng, B., and MacGeorge, E.L. (2002). 'Supportive communication'. In M.L. Knapp, and J.A. Daly (eds.), *Handbook of interpersonal communication* (3rd ed.), 374–424. Thousand Oaks, CA: Sage.

Couper-Kuhlen, E. (2012). 'Exploring affiliation in the reception of conversational complaint stories'. In A. Peräylä, and M.L. Sorjonen (eds.), *Emotion in interaction*, 113–146. New York: Oxford University Press.

Dvasg, J., and Shamay-Tsoory, S.G. (2014). 'Theory of mind and empathy as multidimensional consrtructs. Neurological foundations'. *Top Lang Disorders*, 34(4), 282–295.

Decety, J. (2005). 'Perspective taking as the royal avenue to empathy'. In B. F. Malle, and S. D. Hodges (eds.), *Other Minds: How Humans Bridge the Divide Between Self and Others*, 143–157. New York, NY: The Guildford Press.

Edwards, D., and Potter, J. (1992). *Discursive psychology*. Sage: London.

Eisenberg, N., and Fabes, R. A. (1990). 'Empathy: Conceptualization, measurement, and relation to prosocial behavior'. *Motivation and Emotion*, 14(2), 131–149.

Feng, B., and MacGeorge, E.L. (2006). Predicting receptiveness to advice: Characteristics of the advice-giver, and the recipient. *Southern Communication Journal*, 71(1), 67–85.

Fiehler, R. (2002). 'How to do emotions with words: Emotionality in conversation'. In S.R. Fussell (ed.), *The verbal communication of emotions: Interdisciplinary perspectives*, 79–106. Mahwah, NJ: Lawrence Erlbaum Associates.

Figueras, C. (2018). 'Evidentiality in Illness Narratives: structures with Spanish verb *ver* in autobiographical narratives of eating disorders'. *Pragmatics And Society*, 9 (3), 356–380.

—— (2020). Cognitive and affective dimensions of mitigation in advice. *Corpus Pragmatics*, 4 (1), 31–57.

—— (2021). 'Mitigation in discourse: Social, cognitive and affective motivations when exchanging advice'. *Journal of Pragmatics*, 173, 119–133.

Goffman, E. (1981). *Forms of Talk*. Philadelphia: University of Pennsylvania Press.

Grondin F., Lomanowska A.M., and Jackson P.L. (2019). 'Empathy in computer-mediated interactions: A conceptual framework for research and clinical practice'. *Clinical Psychology: Science and Practice*, 26 (4), 17.

Håkansson, J., and Montgomery, H. (2003). 'Empathy as an interpersonal phenomenon'. *Journal of Social and Personal Relationships*, 20(3), 267–284.

Hargreaves, S.A., Bath, P., Duffin, S., Cert, P.G., and Ellis, J. (2018). 'Sharing and Empathy in Digital Spaces: Qualitative Study of Online Health Forums for Breast Cancer and Motor Neuron Disease (Amyotrophic Lateral Sclerosis)'. *Journal of Medical Internet Research*, 20(6), e222.

Healey, M.L., and Grossman, M. (2019). 'Cognitive and affective perspective taking: Evidence for shared and dissociable anatomical substrates'. *Frontiers in Neurology*, 9, 491.

Hepburn, A., and Potter, J. (2007). 'Crying receipts: Time, empathy, and institutional practice'. *Research on Language and Social Interaction*, 40, 89–116.

Heritage, J. (2011). 'Territories of knowledge, territories of experience: Empathic moments in interaction'. In T. Stivers, L. Mondada and J. Steensig (eds.), *The Morality of Knowledge in Conversation*, 159–183. Cambridge: Cambridge University Press.

Hodges, S.D., Kiel, K.J., Kramer, A.D., Veach, D., and Villanueva, R. (2010). 'Giving Birth to Empathy: The Effects of Similar Experience on Empathic Accuracy, Empathic Concern, and perceived empathy'. *Personality and Social Psychology Bulletin*, 36(3), 398–409.

Kerr-Gaffney, J., Harrison, A., and Tchanturia, K. (2019). 'Cognitive and affective empathy in eating disorders: A systematic review and meta-analysis'. *Frontiers in Psychiatry*, 10: 102.

Kouper, I. (2010). 'The pragmatics of peer advice in a LiveJournal Community'. *Language@Internet*, 7. Retrieved from <https://www.languageatinternet.org/articles/2010/2464>

Kupetz, M. (2014). 'Empathy displays as interactional achievements — Multimodal and sequential aspects'. *Journal of Pragmatics*, 61, 4–34.

—— (2019). 'Embodying empathy in everyday and institutional settings: On the negotiation of resources, rights and responsibilities in comforting actions'. In E. Reber, and C. Gerhardt (eds.), *Embodied activities in face-to-face and mediated settings: Social encounters in time and space*, 329–367. London, UK: Palgrave Macmillan.

Locher, M. A. (2006). *Advice online*. Amsterdam: John Benjamins.

Locher, M. A., and Limberg, H. (2012). 'Introduction to advice in discourse'. In H. Limberg, and M. A. Locher (eds.), *Advice in Discourse*, 1–27. Amsterdam: John Benjamins.

Martinovski, B., Mao, W., Gratch, J., and Marsella, S. (2004). 'Mitigation theory: and integrated approach'. In *Proceedings of Cognitive Science*. Stresa: Italy. Retrieved from <http://ict.usc.edu/pubs/Mitigation%20Theory-%20An%20Integrated%20Approach.pdf>

Meneses, R.W., and Larkin, M. (2017). 'The experience of empathy: Intuitive, sympathetic, and intellectual aspects of social understanding'. *Journal of Humanistic Psychology*, 57(1), 3–32.

Mondada, L. (2011). 'Understanding as an embodied, situated and sequential achievement in interaction'. *Journal of Pragmatics*, 43, 542–552.

Morrow, P.R. (2006). 'Telling about problems and giving advice in an Internet discussion forum: some discourse features'. *Discourse Studies*, 8(4), 531–548.

Nambisan, P. (2011). 'Information seeking and social support in online health communities: impact on patients' perceived empathy'. *Journal of the American Medical Informatics Association*, 18, 298e–304.

Pfeil, U., and Zhaphiris, P. (2007). 'Patterns of empathy in online communication'. In *Proceedings of the SIGCHI Conference on Human Factors in Computing Systems,* 919–928. New York: Association for Computing Machinery.

Popham S. (2017). 'Developing empathy and expertise in online health forums'. Paper presented at *Professional Communication Conference (ProComm). IEEE International*, Jul 23–26, 2017. Madison, WI. Retrieved from: <https://ieeexplore.ieee.org/abstract/document/8013966>

Preece, J., and Ghozati, K. (2001). 'Observations and Explorations of Empathy Online'. In. R. R. Rice and J. E. Katz, *The Internet and Health Communication: Experience and Expectations*, 237–260. Sage Publications Inc.: Thousand Oaks.

Prescott, J., Rathbone, A.L., and Hanley, T. (2020). 'Online mental health communities, self-efficacy and transition to further support'. *Mental Health Review Journal*, 25(4).

Preston, S.D., and de Waal, F. (2002). 'Empathy: Its ultimate and proximate bases'. *Behavioral Brain Science*, 25(1), 1–20.

Pudlinski, C. (2005). 'Doing empathy and sympathy: Caring responses to troubles tellings on a peer support line'. *Discourse Studies*, 7(3), 267–288.

Ruusuvuori, J. (2005). 'Empathy and sympathy in action: Attending to patients' troubles in Finnish homeopathic and GP consultations'. *Social Psychology Quarterly*, 68, 204–222.

—— (2007). 'Managing affect: Integration of empathy and problem-solving in health care encounters'. *Discourse Studies*, 9, 597–622.

Sacks, H. (1992). *Lectures on Conversation*. Basil Blackwell: Oxford.

Sanahuges, C., and Curell, H. (2020). 'Responding to trouble: An interactional approach to empathy in Catalan and English'. *Corpus Pragmatics*, 4, 449–472.

Shamay-Tsoory, S. G. (2011). 'The neural bases for empathy'. *The Neuroscientist*, 17(1), 18–24.

Stommel, W., and Lamerichs, J. (2014). 'Interaction in online support groups: advice and beyond'. In H. E. Hamilton, and W. S. Chou (eds.), *The Routledge Handbook of Language and Health Communication*, 198–211. London: Routledge.

Stommel, W., and te Molder, H. (2018). 'Empathically designed responses as a gateway to advice in Dutch counseling calls'. *Discourse Studies*, 20(4), 523–543.

van der Nagel, E., and Frith, J. (2015). 'Anonymity, pseudonymity, and the agency of online identity: Examining the social practices of r/Gonewild'. *First Monday*, 20(3).

Vartanian, L., Polivy, J., and Herman, P. (2004). 'Implicit cognitions and eating disorders: Their application in research and treatment'. *Cognitive and Behavioral Practice*, 11(2), 160–167.

Voutilainen, L., Peräkylä. A., and Ruusuvuori, J. (2011). 'Recognition and interpretation: Responding to emotional experience in psychotherapy'. *Research on Language and Social Interaction*, 43, 85–107.

Walter, H. (2012). 'Social cognitive neuroscience of empathy: Concepts, circuits, and genes'. *Emotion Review*, 4(1), 9–17.

Wolf, M., Theis, F., and Kordy, H. (2013). 'Language use in eating disorder blogs: Psychological implications of social online activity'. *Journal of Language and Social Psychology*, 32(2), 212–226.

Jennifer Moreno, Vicent Montalt & Ana Muñoz-Miquel
*Universitat Jaume I*

# Narrative-Based Medicine: The Use of Metaphors and Technical Terms in Spanish Patients' Narratives

**Abstract:** Writing can be a useful tool to anyone wishing to express feelings and emotions, especially when facing a difficult situation. The need to humanise the practice of medicine and enhance the relationship between patients and doctors has led to the emergence of narrative-based medicine as a new way to foster patient-centred care. Patients' narratives can help both patients, who can express how a certain disease affects them, and medical professionals, who can gain a deeper understanding of their patients' experiences and feelings. From a discursive perspective, certain elements can have an impact on how we face a situation, which may be also reflected in the way we express it in writing. An example is the use of metaphors in narratives, through which attitudes of patients towards their disease can be somehow appreciated. Based on the results from a pilot study where a bilingual corpus of narratives was studied, in this paper we analyse how metaphors are used, as opposed to specialised medical terms, in a corpus with over 100 narratives of patients with haematological diseases written in Spanish in order to reflect on the ways in which metaphors drive the construction of illness experiences.

**Keywords:** *narrative-based medicine, disease, patient-centred care, patients' narratives, metaphors, medical terms, corpus analysis, haematological diseases.*

## 1 Introduction

The biomedical model of the medical practice has dominated the healthcare field for a long time. It is centred in the biophysical aspect of medicine or, in other words, in how an organ is affected by a certain disease. Within the biomedical model, diagnostic tests play a key role, since they are the main and, in most cases, the only evidence which doctors consider when prescribing a treatment. However, in the last few decades, a general discontent of society towards the way patients are treated and diagnosed by health professionals, who seem to lean only towards evidence-based medicine when addressing a patient, led to the appearance of a humanist movement in the US (Jonsen 1998).

Such movement claimed the importance of humanities in the medical field, and emerged as a response to the need to bring harmony between the biomedical and the human approaches within the practice of medicine. Therefore, its main aim was that of providing a balance between the objective and the subjective dimensions of medicine, for which Engel proposed the creation of a *biopsychosocial model* in 1977. The aim of this model was that of integrating the psychosocial perspective into the medical field so that patients' feelings and experiences towards their disease would not be left behind. This would mean that doctors would not only take evidence-based medicine into account when addressing patients, but they would also listen to their experiences, fostering patient-centred care. Therefore, this model would allow patients to feel involved in their treatment at the same time that it could also benefit the biomedical model, as doctors would get to learn more about a certain disease (Montalt 2021). The integration of the psychosocial perspective into the biomedical model, which answered to Engel's vision of disease, more complete and holistic, led to the appearance of what is known as *health humanities*.

## 1.1 Health Humanities

The main aim of the health humanities is to raise awareness of the role of human values in healthcare. According to Jones and Tansey (2015), these aim at highlighting the importance of empathy and analysis to provide a patient-centred care by taking into account patients' feelings and their experiences with their disease to make them acquire an active role in their healing process. For such purpose, not only evidence-based medicine is to be considered when treating and diagnosing, but also non-clinical factors, which are vital when it comes to treating patients and not merely diseases, since two patients can have a different experience with a same disease.

For instance, if someone suffers from glaucoma, an injury on their optic nerve and a possible sight loss would be a result of such *disease*. However, the patient's own experience towards how their life is being affected by such sight loss would be what is referred to as *illness*. In this context, it is important to emphasise on the distinction between disease and illness since, as Moreno (2020) states, even if both of them are used in general language, from the perspective of the health humanities, they illustrate the double approach in the medical field – the biological and the humanistic. It is thus crucial to understand the slight difference between these terms; whereas the term *disease* refers to the disorder affecting an organ, structure or function in someone's body, *illness* refers to how such disorder affects that person. Therefore, by making this distinction, the patient-centred clinical method aims at enhancing the relationship between patients and health professionals.

In this context, narrative medicine emerged with the aim of promoting interaction between doctors and patients. It embodies a whole of skills necessary to tell stories and narrate experiences in the medical context, and it refers to writing as a tool to build bridges between patients and health professionals. It includes narratives written either by patients or health professionals, being the first group the subject matter for the present study.

## 1.2 Patients' Narratives

According to Charon (2001), narration is a way of freedom. It can help patients to express feelings which cannot be measured, helping them give voice to their suffering and reflect on the subjective part of their disease. The idea of introducing narrative in the medical practice would turn patients into the narrators of their own experience, allowing doctors to learn how patients feel, instead of just knowing something about them (Sayligil 2017), for which it could be considered, at the present time, as the culmination of narrative medicine.

During the 1980s, the conceptualisation of the patient-centred clinical method, whose aim was, according to Brown, Thorton and Stewart (2012), to place communication at the heart of the medical practice by encouraging patients to share their experiences of illness and, therefore, draw a balance between the biomedical and the humanist approach. Writing as a tool in the medical context was also supported by authors such as Weatherall (1995), since it was acknowledged to help establish a relationship between the biomedical and the personal facts of disease.

As Moreno (2020) mentions, it is worth referring to Lisansky's three levels of content in patients' narratives. According to Ramírez Villaseñor (2005), the first level belongs to those narratives in which patients talk about their symptoms. For example, in the case of the patient with glaucoma that we mentioned before, if he wrote about his experience with the disease, the part in which he talked about his difficulties to see properly would correspond to the first level of content. The second level of content embodies those aspects which have to do with the patient's routine during his treatment. In this case, this level would include the patient with glaucoma's reference to the fixed times he has to take tablets or drops every day. Finally, the third and last level would correspond to personal information given by the patient concerning their illness. For instance, in the case of our patient with glaucoma, at this level he would refer to how glaucoma is affecting him psychologically, knowing that he has to stop doing certain activities or that he may end up completely blind. In this context, it is necessary for patients to get to the third level when writing if they want to allow doctors to learn about their experience with illness.

As we have just mentioned, patients' narratives can be a powerful tool for health professionals too, who may be able to expand their knowledge about a certain disease and to provide patients with an individualised treatment. However, patients' narratives are useful to patients themselves, since narrating promotes self-reflection, allowing them to have a better understanding of their own experience with the disease. According to Charon (2006), other patients can also benefit from reading patients' narratives, given that most times patients need to learn different opinions from people going through the same situation.

In fact, patients' narratives seem to be gaining relevance; as Montalt (2021) points out, patients seem to be increasingly willing to tell their own stories on different platforms and, according to Moreno (2020), the great variety of channels that patients can use to narrate their experiences stands in the way of defining structural patterns for patients' narratives.

Bearing the above in mind, one of the works of reference considered for the present study was that carried out by Montalt (2017), in which he explores the presence of discursive elements in Rodhes' work (2015) and outlines future research gaps. Semino (2017) also uses narratives written by patients diagnosed with cancer to analyse the presence of metaphors, which was the main reference used by Moreno (2020) and Moreno et al. (2022), who use patients' narratives to build a bilingual corpus, German-Spanish, to analyse convergence and deviation points in terms of structural patterns and linguistic elements such as metaphor and specialised medical terms. Such works have been the basis for the present study, in which both the use of metaphor and technical terms are analysed in Spanish narratives.

The main aim of choosing metaphors and technical terms is the fact that both are examples of the biomedical and the humanistic sides of medicine. In this way, technical terms would represent the objective side of medicine, or, in other words, the disease, whereas metaphors may reflect the subjective side of medicine, which would be the illness.

Our interest in the first type of elements may somehow reflect the impact of the biomedical model in patients, as they get used to listening to doctors using specialised terms when addressing to them. On the other hand, our interest in learning about the role of the humanistic part of medicine has led us to analyse the presence of metaphors too, which may suggest the necessity of understanding patients to foster patient-centred care.

### 1.3 Metaphors in the Medical Field

When using metaphors, we establish a relationship between two concepts or domains, source and target domains. Usually, the target domain refers to a more complex idea, often an abstract concept difficult to describe. Therefore, the source domain, according to Semino, Demjén and Demmen (2016) is used to easy the understanding of the target domain.

However, as Lakoff & Johnson (1980) claim, the use of metaphor will depend on the speakers' own conception of the world and, therefore, the way metaphors are used may differ from one individual to another. This is particularly interesting in the medical field, since the metaphor used to refer to illness could vary according to different factors, such as patients' age, sociocultural background, culture or mother tongue.

In the medical context, it is important to highlight Semino's view, shown in the International Workshop MetaforUP held at the University of Navarra in 2018. The author claims that we use metaphors to talk about subjective and difficult experiences, being cancer one of them. This would explain the great interest that the use of metaphor has in the medical context, since disease is often something difficult to describe, for which the use of metaphors is somehow necessary.

An example of the great interest towards the use of metaphors in medicine which has arisen over the years is the work of Sontag (1978), where the author analysed the main metaphors used when talking about cancer. Sontag (1978) claimed that, in spite of the advances in medicine, which resulted in a wide range of health conditions being curable, the metaphors used to refer to cancer reflected the general negative conception of this disease, understood as a synonym of death.

Based on Sontag's work, several studies have adopted the linguistic approach to analyse the use of metaphor in the medical context. For example, in 2017, Sapiño et al. analysed the use of metaphor by young cancer survivors in both English and Spanish to explore possible differences in its use in comparison to adult patients. In 2019, Demjén et al. analysed the use of metaphors in patients suffering from schizophrenia. Patients were asked to listen to other patients' narratives containing two types of metaphors – empowering and disempowering metaphors. This research showed that patients who listened to patients' stories containing empowering metaphors felt less afflicted than those who listened to the stories containing disempowering metaphors.

However, the main inspiration for the present work was, together with Moreno's work (2020), Semino's project 'Metaphor, Cancer and the End of Life' (2017), in which, after carrying out an analysis of 1.5 million words retrieved from online sites, a Metaphor Menu for people living with cancer was made available for patients to choose that metaphor they feel more comfortable with when talking about their illness experience. In this menu, several metaphors used to talk about cancer are explained so as to allow patients to choose the situation they identify better with.

## 1.4 Technical Terms

Technical terms include those expressions or terms which are commonly used by professionals of a certain field. In the case of medicine, technical terms would include terms related to disease and to the human body, such as lymphoma or epithelioma, which are types of cancer.

Technical terms are often used by health professionals and are usually only employed by people with the same degree of specialisation. However, technical terms often have popular versions which are more common among unspecialised population. That is the case, for example, of *postpartum*, which would be the word used by health professionals when communicating in medical settings. However, non-specialised patients would prefer to use *after childbirth* instead.

Our interest in analysing the use of technical terms by patients is the fact that we believe that it can somehow reflect the impact of the biomedical model in society; even if patients are not specialised in the field, they tend to use more and more often this kind of terms, not only when they speak to doctors, but also when they talk about their disease out of the medical consultation.

Going back to our example of the patient with glaucoma, if we asked him about what glaucoma exactly consists of, the chances of hearing 'optic nerve' or 'ocular hypertension' are many, even if he is not completely sure of what the optic nerve is in charge of. This may happen because of the influence of the biomedical model; we think it is normal to hear doctors using technical terms when talking to us about our disease. Hence, in the end, we adopt them as part of our usual vocabulary, ignoring the fact that sometimes we may use them with people who may have never heard of such term or disease before. This happens especially often when patients suffer from a chronic disease.

## 1.5 Previous Studies

Moreno (2020) and Moreno *et al.* (2022), who were also inspired by Semino's work, analysed patients' narratives from a double linguistic and cultural approach to observe the main differences in both Spanish and German, using two small corpora, defining possible structural patterns and focusing on the use of certain linguistic elements such as metaphors and technical terms.

That research showed that it was not possible to determine a structural pattern common for both languages, although some sections were mostly present for narratives within the same corpus. Regarding the use of linguistic elements, it was observed that the types of metaphors identified were different in both corpora, despite having some of them in common. For the German corpus,

14 different types of metaphors were identified, whereas the Spanish corpus counted on 12. However, in spite of having fewer categories, metaphors appeared more often in texts written by Spanish patients. In contrast, the analysis revealed that German patients tended to use more technical terms.

Based on the results obtained in such case study in which two small corpora of 8 texts each, were analysed, the present study focuses on the use of both metaphors and technical terms in the Spanish language to observe whether these are used in the same way.

Bearing all the above in mind, and picking up the thread of the need for a balance between the biomedical and the humanist values within the medical context, some burning issues come still to mind:

- In the first place, one of our main units of interest is metaphor. Taking the previously-mentioned study as a reference, are all the metaphor categories in our first study present in a larger corpus? Are there any additional categories? Would it be possible to create a metaphor menu for Spanish patients? Would such menu be similar in English and Spanish?
- Secondly, regarding technical terms, as we showed in our previous study, German patients are often well-informed about what their disease and treatment consists of. This was reflected on their narratives, which seemed to have been written by experts in the field. This was not the case for the Spanish corpus, where technical terms were scarce. Therefore, taking this into account, why do German patients use more technical terms than Spanish patients? If so, to what extent do Spanish patients prefer like using technical terms in their narratives? Would the previously-observed tendency be the same in other corpora and diseases?
- Lastly, as we mentioned before, the biomedical model has the leading role in the practice of medicine. Could that be somehow reflected on patients' narratives, for example in the presence of technical terms and metaphors?

In order to provide an answer to those questions, the present study presents an analysis of a corpus of over 50,000 words written by Spanish patients suffering from haematological diseases paying special attention to metaphors and technical terms.

## 2 Aims

Based on the pilot study where two corpora, one in German and one in Spanish were analysed, for which a brief summary has also been provided, the main objectives of the present analysis are the following:

- First aim: To observe whether the metaphorical density or, in other words, the presence of metaphors in the corpus, is the same as in our previous study.
- Second aim: To observe and whether the metaphor categories remain the same as in our previous study for the Spanish language.
- Third aim: To find out about the presence and use of technical terms, for example observing if these are accompanied by explanations.

For the present study, we use the same type of texts, which have been retrieved from the same webpage as those used in the pilot study mentioned above.

## 3 Materials and Method

### 3.1 Materials

For the present study, a corpus of 50,000 words has been used. The corpus was compiled between July and November 2020, and all texts were retrieved from the official website of the Josep Carreras' Leukaemia Foundation (https://www.fcarreras.org/es). This Foundation has been working for over 30 years to raise awareness of haematological diseases such as Leukaemia, among others, and to help patients with psychological or financial support. In addition, since 1991, this Foundation manages the official bone donors registry in Spain, known as REDMO, in order to help patients from all over the world to find a compatible bone marrow when necessary. This Foundation offers a section on its website where patients, ex-patients and patients' relatives can share their story. This is the main website in Spain devoted to patients with haematological diseases and, therefore, it has been our main source for texts written in Spanish.

The section devoted to patients' narratives included a total of 460 texts by the time the compilation of this corpus had finished, with a total of around 300,000 words. However, for the present analysis, 50,000 words have been analysed due to the fact that our main objective is to observe whether there would be much difference. For the selection of the texts, these were all numbered from 1 to 460. With the aid of a webpage which selects random numbers[1] a total of 122 texts containing over 50,000 words have been chosen and used in the present study.

In order to study the texts, we have also used some corpus analysis tools such as UAM Corpus Tool[2] and Sketch Engine.[3] The first one has been used to identify metaphors and types, as well as technicisms, while the second one has been

1 www.generarnumerosaleatorios.com

2 UAM Corpus Tool: http://www.corpustool.com

3 Sketch Engine: https://www.sketchengine.eu

used to obtain more general information about the corpus, such as extension of the texts.

### 3.2 Method

In order to carry out our analysis, which focuses, mainly, on metaphors and technical terms, we have used UAM Corpus Tool. This tool offers several features, although the most useful one for our study was the annotation tool. Here, you can create layers to write notes all along the texts. We have created two main layers: technical terms and metaphors, for which additional sublayers indicating the metaphor category have been set.

Technical terms have been analysed in a general way and only those technical words used to refer to haematological diseases have been taken into consideration. This is important to be highlighted, since some patients have suffered from other diseases apart from a haematological one which have nothing to do with it and, therefore, have not been marked as technical term.

Regarding metaphors, our main basis has been the pilot study in which two small corpora, one in German and one in Spanish, were analysed to identify types of metaphors. Since the texts used in such pilot study were hazardously retrieved from the same webpage, we have wanted to keep using the same categories. Such categories are:

- War: metaphors using war lexicon have been included in this category. Some examples of them are warrior, fight, fighter, battle, beat (in Spanish *guerrero, luchar, luchador, batalla, vencer*).
- Challenge: in this category, metaphors regarding the disease as a challenge or a test have been included, such as *carrera* (race) or *maratón* (marathon),
- Person/being: this category embodies those metaphors used to refer to the disease as a person or as a companion.
- Lottery/Raffle: metaphors referring to the hazardousness of the disease have been taken into consideration for this category.
- Punishment: this category includes those metaphors referring to the disease as a kind of punishment or karma for a bad action patients have done.
- Journey: this category embodies metaphors which refer to the disease as a part of life or a stage on the way.
- Lesson: here, metaphors referring to the disease as a learning or a kind of moral have been taken into consideration.
- Change: this category includes those metaphors which refer to the disease as a life shift or turn.

- Fate: this category includes metaphors which refer to the disease as something that life had planned for them.
- Present/Luck: here, metaphors referring to the disease as something that has had a positive impact on their life have been included.
- Nightmare: this category embodies those metaphors used to refer to the disease to a hard time which seems not to be real.
- Stroke: metaphors about the disease appearing as a stroke, something unexpected and hurting, are embodied in this category.

These categories have been set by adding different sublayers to the metaphor layer. Therefore, when identifying a metaphor, it could be easily classified according to the categories described above.

Finally, we used the tool "statistics" provided by UAM Corpus Tool in order to take record of the data obtained. This tool offers the possibility to have the information for every layer set individually, in the way of graphic or table, or to get the information of a layer and its sublayers, as in the case of metaphors. In addition, it can be used to compare the information extracted corresponding to different layers.

## 4 Results and Discussion

Before moving on to discuss further details of the results of the study concerning our hypothesis, we have considered it to be appropriate to depict some of the general characteristics that have been found when carrying out the present analysis and which concern the macrostructure of the narratives of our corpus.

As it has been said before, the total of 50,343 words analysed correspond to 122 different texts. It means that the average length of texts is of approximately 413 words, which differs much from the average length of the texts which were taken into consideration for our case study of reference, where the average length per text was of 778 words.

In addition, whereas all the texts observed in such study had been written in the first person, here we have found substantial differences, since many of them have been written by relatives or by an unknown third person, especially in the case young patients.

Regarding the organisation of the texts, a common structural pattern has not been observed. The narratives studied are very different from each other, although most of them make reference to at least one of the following: diagnosis, treatment, or life after disease.

## 4.1 First Aim

Our first aim was that of observing whether the metaphorical density is the same as in our previous study. In order to do so, we have established a relationship between the total number of metaphors which were identified and the total number of texts. If we take into consideration the 460 metaphorical structures which have been identified and the 122 texts which shape our corpus, each text contains, in average, around four metaphors.

At first glance, this result differs much from what our first hypothesis expected, although it seems logical that, if we take into consideration the fact that the average length per text was also shorter than what had been observed in our previous study, the fewer words, the fewer chances for metaphor.

However, if we focus on the percentage that metaphors represent in both cases, in the previous study, metaphors represented 1.02 % per text, whereas in the present study, they represent 0.96 % (being, in this case, 9.2 metaphorical structures per 1000 words).

## 4.2 Second Aim

Our second aim was that of observing whether the metaphor categories remain the same as in our previous study for the Spanish language. For such purpose, we have first identified the metaphors present in the corpus and, in the second place, we have classified them into categories according to the lexicon used for their construction.

As we said before, a total of 460 metaphorical structures have been identified within the corpus, which correspond to 14 different categories, being three of them newly delimited. In addition, one of the former categories was deleted, since no metaphors were identified for such category. These three new categories are that of disease as a halt/stop, that of disease as a tunnel/well and that of achievement. In the case of the halt/stop category, metaphors where disease is referred to as a stop sign for patients are embodied. Here, also those metaphors referring to disease as a break have been included. On the other hand, the tunnel/well category include those metaphors which refer to disease as a labyrinth, a tunnel or a dark place they cannot escape. Finally, the achievement metaphor has been used when patients overcome a stage of the disease or when they finish the treatment. The representation of these categories is shown, together with the previously-known categories, in Table 1.

As we can see, the types of metaphors found for the existing categories was very similar to those found in previous studies. The war metaphor prevails over the rest, representing over one third of the total number of metaphors found, which means that disease is appreciated by many patients as a battle, where there is place just for one winner and where patients claim their responsibility for the therapy outcomes. Some of the examples found are "*sabía que tenía que volver a desempolvar el florete*" (I knew I had to dust the foil off), "*le hará luchar como un valiente*" (It'll make him fight like a brave man), "*sabrá luchar con garra*" (He'll know how to fight with energy).

**Table 1.** Types and percentage of metaphors (Total)

| METAPHOR-TYPE | N | % |
|---|---|---|
| - lottery/raffle | 6 | 1.3 |
| - challenge | 78 | 17.0 |
| - war | 173 | 37.6 |
| - travel | 60 | 13.0 |
| - change | 24 | 5.2 |
| - present/luck | 16 | 3.5 |
| - fate | 9 | 2.0 |
| - nightmare | 7 | 1.5 |
| - stroke | 21 | 4.6 |
| - person/being | 23 | 5.0 |
| - lesson | 9 | 2.0 |
| - achievement | 6 | 1.3 |
| - tunnel/well | 19 | 4.1 |
| - halt/stop | 9 | 2.0 |
| **TOTAL:** | **460** | **100.0%** |

In the second place, we find the challenge metaphor. Often, patients perceive their disease as a kind of test life is making them go through. Some patients refer to their disease as a long-distance race, or some of them even as a challenge to measure their psychological strength. Some examples of the challenge metaphor are "*superamos con éxito la prueba*" (we succeeded in passing the test), "*me preparaba para una carrera de fondo*" (I was getting ready for a long-distance race). This metaphor has been usually found together with the achievement metaphor, used by patients to describe what meant for them overcoming their disease.

Thirdly, we find the journey metaphor, by which patients refer to disease as the long path they have to travel to reach a destination and from which there are plenty of things to enjoy, being one of these, for example, the people they met during their healing process. Some of them even compare it to a stage which is a part of the path of life, as it is the example of "*no ha sido un camino fácil*" (the way hasn't been easy), or "*tienes que seguir adelante*" (you have to keep going).

Patients also use the stroke metaphor to refer to their disease as the way life had to hit them ("*fue un golpe muy duro*" – It was a hard stroke) sometimes with a certain purpose. As the result of such stroke, sometimes the change metaphor ("fue una señal para cambiar" – It was a warning to change) or even the lesson metaphor ("fue una lección sobre las cosas importantes de la vida" – it was a learning about what matters in life) have been used.

Some patients have also attributed their experience with disease to fate ("*pensé que ya todo estaba escrito*" – I thought it was all written down), and some of them have perceived their disease as a way to stop and take a break from their routines and worries ("*hay que disfrutar este kit kat que te da la vida*" – We have to enjoy the kit kat that life gives you).

The tunnel/well metaphor has been used to describe disease as a dark place they could not escape despite them trying to ("*hemos caído 1000 veces*" – We've fallen 1000 times / "*pronto verán la luz al final del tunel*" – They'll see the light at the end of the tunnel). The nightmare metaphor can be compared to this one since in both cases patients see disease as a bad place or a bad dream, something that seems unreal or where they feel lost and abandoned ("*era como una pesadilla*" – It was like a nightmare).

The person/being metaphor, which also appeared in previous studies, is one of the most commonly used in the present corpus. Often, patients refer to disease as a living thing, such as an insect, a monster, or sometimes even as a companion ("*mi alien se ha adaptado a mi cuerpo*"- *my alien has adapted to my body* / "espero que el bicho me deje" – I hope this bug leaves me alone).

Finally, both the lottery/raffle ("*nunca pensé que podría tocarme a mí*"- I never thought it could be me) and the present/gift metaphors "la enfermedad me regaló otras cosas" – The disease gave me other things have been used together to express that disease can happen to anyone, as you do not have it as a punishment for something you might have done wrong. In some cases, this "prize" is even perceived as a present or something, in spite of the disease itself, with a positive impact in their lives.

Therefore, we can see that two additional categories have been found for the Spanish language. Diagram 1 shows metaphor categories in a more visual way.

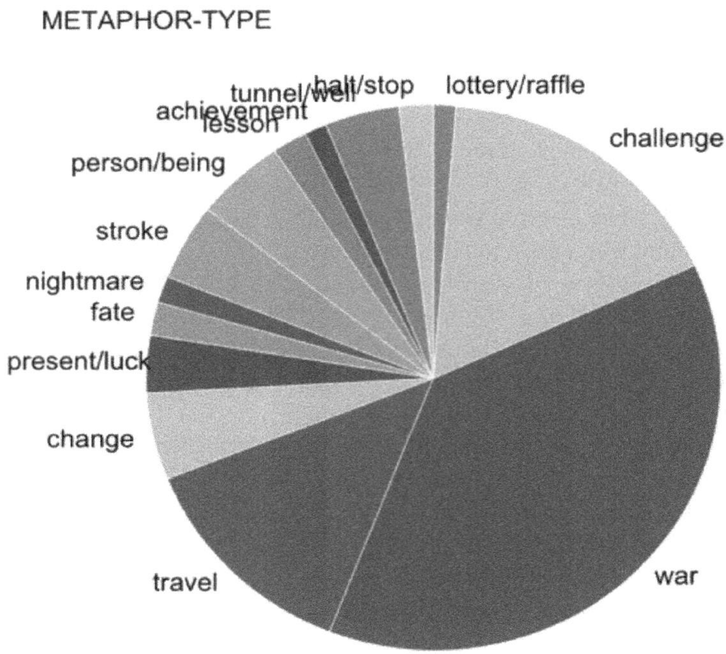


**Diagram 1:** Visual representation of metaphor categories

Considering the previously-discussed results, if we take a look at the Metaphor Menu created by Lancaster University, we can see that some of the metaphors which appear there have not been found in our narratives, such as the rollercoaster metaphor, where patients describe cancer as a scary ride which finally comes to an end, or the garden with weed metaphor, where the weed-killer damages both the healthy plants and the weed but only the healthy ones end up growing again. However, we should take into account that, for the creation of such menu, over 1,000,000 words in English were analysed. In addition, all types of cancer were taken into consideration.

Since the present study is a part of a doctoral dissertation which is still being carried out, we should consider that those three could be key facts when obtaining results. Would our results be different if the 300,000 words originally compiled were analysed? Or would our results depend on the language and not of the wordcount? What if we had not focused on just one type of cancer? These are questions which certainly cannot be answered yet.

### 4.3 Third Aim

Our third aim was that of observing whether technical terms are widely or poorly used. Although we do not have exact data regarding the use of technical terms in previous studies, we know that, in Spanish narratives, technicisms were not as common, for example, as in German narratives. We also know, as we mentioned before, that the metaphor rate was higher than the rate of specialised terms in Spanish narratives.

In order to achieve our third objective, technical terms present in every text have been identified, where no subcategories have been delimited. Some examples of the structures identified for the technical term parameter are: *leucemia linfoblástica aguda* (acute lymphoblastic leukaemia), *leucemia mieloide* (myeloid leukaemia), *linfoma* (lymphoma), *ganglios linfáticos* (lymph nodes), punción lumbar (spinal tap), *ciclo de quimioterapia* (cycle of chemotherapy), *trasplante de médula ósea* (bone marrow transplant), *período de consolidación* (period of consolidation), *linfocitos* (lymphocytes), or *trasfusión de sangre* (blood transfusion).

Table 2 shows the number of technical structures found in the narratives. A total of 1,297 technical structures have been identified, which results in an average of approximately 11 technical structures per text. Considering the total number of words analysed, which was 50,343, the global representation of technical terms within the corpus, which means a total of 2,268 words, adds up to 0.045 %.

We would like to point out that we are aware of the fact that both parameters analysed in the present study, metaphors and technical terms, are completely different and cannot be quantitatively compared as a whole. However, going back to the balance issue between the biomedical and the humanist parts of medicine, we have considered it interesting to offer a wider perspective in which these parameters are embodied and analysed qualitatively.

Metaphors are complex textual phenomena which are difficult to quantify by counting them per word. Therefore, the group of words taken into consideration when analysing them have been referred to as *metaphorical structures.* Each narrative contains an average of 4 metaphorical structures, while the number of technical terms per text adds up to 11. When considering the number of structures, we could say that the rate of technical terms is higher than the rate of metaphors, or in other words, that the influence of the biomedical perspective is strongly reflected on patients' narratives and, therefore, on their experience with illness.

**Table 2.** Detailed information on technicisms

| Length | |
|---|---|
| Number of segments | 1297 |
| Tokens in segments | 2731 |
| Words in segments | 2268 |
| **Text Complexity** | |
| Av. Word Length | 7.2 |
| Av. Segment Length | 1.75 |
| Min. Segment Length | 1 |
| Max. Segment Length | 12 |
| **Lexical Density** | |
| Lexemes per segment | 1.73 |
| Lexemes % of text | 98.77 |

However, if we look at Table 3, which shows the total number of words that metaphors represent, we can see that, when measured in words, the presence of both parameters is not that different. This has made us reflect about the fact that it may not be worth analysing linguistic elements quantitatively, but only qualitatively.

**Table 3.** Detailed information on metaphors

| Length | |
|---|---|
| Number of segments | 463 |
| Tokens in segments | 2328 |
| Words in segments | 2075 |
| **Text Complexity** | |
| Av. Word Length | 4.65 |
| Av. Segment Length | 4.48 |
| Min. Segment Length | 1 |
| Max. Segment Length | 23 |
| **Lexical Density** | |
| Lexemes per segment | 4.21 |
| Lexemes % of text | 94.02 |

The representation of metaphors in the whole corpus is of 0.041%, being this still a bit lower than that of technical terms, which represent, as we already mentioned, 0.045%. Therefore, even if, as we already remarked, such parameters are different and cannot functionally be compared, we could say then that there is a similarity between the use of objective (technical terms) and subjective elements (metaphors). Would this be a reflection of the place that humanities are trying to fight for within the medical field? Or would this just depend on the number of words analysed? In the study mentioned before in which two corpora in two different languages were compared, the German language proved a prevalence of objective terminology over figures of speech such as metaphors. Would this correlation depend then on the language? Or would it be linked to patients' sociocultural background?

## 5 Conclusion

The aim of the present study was that of analysing the use of metaphors and technical terms in narratives written by Spanish patients suffering from haematological diseases in order to compare the results to what was observed in our previous research and to observe possible differences in the use of objective and subjective elements.

In the first place, we have observed important differences regarding the macrostructure. While no structural pattern was observed, in this case, many of the texts were not written in the first person. In addition, not all of them included parameters such as introduction, diagnosis, treatment, and living after the disease, and the average extension was much shorter than what had been previously confirmed.

In the second place, a similar correlation between the number of words and the presence of metaphors has been observed. However, three new metaphor categories have been identified in the narratives, being 14 the whole of categories for the Spanish language spotted so far, not a great difference taking into account that the number of the present corpus was larger than the one used in our previous research.

Concerning the use of technical terms, where our aim was to observe whether those were widely or poorly used by patients, we have observed a rather high tendency towards the use of technical terms. Although in our previous study the presence of metaphors prevailed over that of specialised terms, we have observed an opposite direction in the present study, being technical terms prevalent in this case. However, when considering the total number of words analysed, we observed that both parameters were at a similar level. In this context, we are aware of the difficulties posed when analysing certain structures. Therefore, the annotation protocol used in the case study taken as a reference was refined for the present analysis.

Regarding the results, we are aware of the fact that the results obtained in the present study might have been influenced by several factors such as patients' sociocultural background, age or gender, or even the type of disease (some haematological diseases are chronic while others are not). Nevertheless, since the webpage from which the corpus has been retrieved does not provide this type of information, it is impossible to take them into consideration. Moreover, given the main purpose of the study in which this work is framed, which is that of helping both translators and health professional working with patients of different origins and cultures, having access to patients' perception and knowledge of their disease may help them to improve their medical practice and to foster patient-centred attention.

Our final and future aim is that of analysing metaphors and technical terms in several languages, such as Spanish, English and Italian, in order to determine how linguistic and cultural differences can have an impact on the way patients feel and write and how both the human and the biological sides of disease are represented in those languages.

Therefore, despite being this a recently-explored field and having still many questions to answer, it is a fact that narrative medicine, and especially patients' narratives, still has much to offer to the medical field when it comes to raising awareness of the importance of fostering patient-centred care.

## References

Brown, J., Thorton, T. and Stewart, M. (2012). *Challenges and solutions: narratives of patient-centered care*. United Kingdom: Radcliffe.

Charon, R. 2001. 'Narrative Medicine. A Model for Empathy, Reflection, Profession, and Trust'. *The patient-physician relationship. American Medical Association. JAMA*. 2001; 286 (15): 1897–1902.

Charon, R. (2006). *Narrative Medicine: Honoring the Stories of Illness*. New York: Oxford University Press.

Demjen, Z., Koller, V. and Semino, E. (2016). 'Metaphors for 'good' and 'bad' deaths: a health professional view'. *Metaphor and the Social World,* 6(1), 1–19.

Lakoff, G and Johnson, M. (1998). *Metaphors We Live By*. University of Chicago Press.

Engel, G. (1977). 'The need for a new medical model: a challenge for biomedicine.' *Science, New Series, Vol. 196*. American Association for the Advancement of Science, 129–136.

Jones, E. M. and Tansey, E. M. (eds) (2015). *The Development of Narrative Practices in Medicine c.1960–c.2000*. Wellcome Witnesses to Contemporary Medicine, vol. 52. London: Queen Mary, University of London.

Jonsen, A. (1998). *The birth of bioethics*. Oxford University Press.

Montalt, V. (2017). 'Traducir el trauma y el estigma a escritura autobiográfica: una lectura de James Rhodes'. *eHumanista/IVITRA*, 319–336.

Montalt, V. (2021). 'Medical humanities and translation'. In *The Routledge Handbook of Translation and Health*. London and New York: Routledge, 130–148.

Moreno, J. (2020). 'La metáfora en las narrativas de pacientes: estudio de corpus desde una doble perspectiva lingüística y cultural'. *Unpublished Master's thesis.* Castelló de la Plana: Universitat Jaume I.

Moreno, J., Muñoz-Miquel, A. and Montalt, V. (2022). 'Las narrativas de pacientes desde una perspectiva interlingüística e intercultural: estudio de caso de un corpus en español y alemán'. In *Comunicando en salud para la nueva ciudadanía.* Valencia: Tirant lo Blanch, 341–356.

Ramírez Villaseñor, I. (2005). 'La narrativa del paciente como herramienta terapéutica.' *Pan-American Family Medicine Clinics, Vol.* <http://www.apamefa.com/publicacoes/vol012005/vol012005_La_narrativa_del_paciente.pdf>

Rhodes, J. (2015). *Instrumental. A Memoir of madness, medication and music.* Edinburgh: Canongate

Sapiña, L., Domínguez, M. and Montalt, V. (2017). 'More than a Battle. Intercultural and interlingual issues in the use of metaphors in the narratives of Young cancer survivors'. *Genealogies of Knowledge I: Translating Political and Scientific Thought across Time and Space Conference,* University of Manchester, 7–9 December 2017. Abstract available at <http://genealogiesofknowledge.net/wp-content/uploads/2017/11/book-abstracts-gok2017-final.pdf>

Sayligil, O. (2017). *Patient Centered Medicine*. IntechOpen.

Semino, E. (2008). *Metaphor in Discourse*. Cambridge: Cambridge University Press

Semino, E., Demjén, Z. and Demmen, J. (2016). 'An integrated approach to metaphor and framing in cognition, discourse and practice, with an application to metaphors for cancer.' *Applied Linguistics*, Vol. 39, 625–645.

Semino, E., Demjén, Z., Hardie, A., Payne, S. and Rayson, P. (2017). *Metaphor, Cancer and the End of Life: A Corpus-Based Study.* University of Lancaster. <https://www.researchgate.net/publication/321599735_Metaphor_Cancer_and_the_End_of_Life_A_Corpus-Based_Study>

Semino, E. (2017). 'Corpus linguistics and metaphor'. In Dancygier, B. (ed.) *The Cambridge Handbook of Cognitive Linguistics*, 463–476 Cambridge: Cambridge University Press.

Sontag, S. (1978). *La enfermedad y sus metáforas*. Debolsillo. 2011 Edition.

Weatherall, D. (1995). *Science and the Quiet Art. Medical research and patient care*. United Kingdom: Oxford University Press.

Ma. Paula Roverso & Julia T. Williams Camus

# Authorial Stance and Identity Roles in Research Article Introductions in Two Medical Subdisciplines

**Abstract:** This study uses Tang and John's taxonomy (1999) to explore and analyse the creation of writer identity through the use of first-person pronouns in a corpus of 60 research article introductions from two medical subfields. The introductions were analysed for moves and steps according to a slightly modified version of Swales' Create-a-Research-Space model (1990, 2004). Then, the different first-person pronouns were identified with the software AntConc 3.5.8 (Anthony 2019) and Tang and John's taxonomy (1999) was used to analyse the different identity roles in relation to the move-step analysis. The results indicate that, in general terms, the frequency of self-reference was similar in the two subdisciplines. The pronoun 'we' was the most frequent manifestation of self-reference and was predominantly used in Move 3 to introduce the study. The analysis of the identity roles revealed that all the roles with the exception of author as guide were present in the two subfields, although some subtle differences were noted for the architect, opinion holder and originator roles.

***Keywords*** *Authorial stance, identity roles, first-person pronouns, research article introductions, Create-a-Research-Space model, English for Publication Purposes, Academic writing.*

## 1 Introduction[1]

Recent decades have witnessed a growing interest in the analysis of the discourse of research articles (RAs) in different disciplinary fields. Scholars in the field of English for Specific Purposes (ESP) have focused on the rhetorical patterns of the different sections of the RA, mainly for pedagogical purposes. The introduction section has attracted the most attention because writing introductions is regarded as a challenging task for both professionals and novice writers or students

1 The authors of this article are affiliated to the *Universidad de Cantabria* and assert equal contribution and joint first authorship. Julia T. Williams Camus is grateful to the Spanish Ministry of Science, Innovation and Universities for their generous financial support for the research project "Stance and Subjectivity in Discourse: Towards an Integrated Framework for the Analysis of Epistemicity, Effectivity, Evaluation and Inter/Subjectivity from a Critical Discourse Perspective" (PGC2018-095798-B-I00).

wishing to publish their research in well-known international journals (Swales 1990). Introductions are a crucial section because this is where writers present themselves to the research community and where they not only have to save their own face and appear as credible researchers, but they also have to protect other researchers' face when citing and evaluating previous literature in the field.

One especially problematic aspect for writers is to decide how much to express their voice and authorial stance and how to do it (Flowerdew 1999; Pho 2012). Thus, the different manifestations of authorial stance in academic writing have become a focus of attention in different disciplinary fields (Mur-Dueñas and Šinkūnienė 2016). The use of personal pronouns is one of the possible manifestations of authorial stance among the different discoursal choices that writers have at hand. They are a way to present themselves to the research community and to project their identity in their writing (Kuo 1999). A substantial number of studies have shown that first-person pronouns are a valuable resource to construct identity in academic writing (Basal and Bada 2011; Carciu 2009; Chávez Muñoz 2013; Cheng and Lau 2020; Harwood 2005a, 2005b; Hyland 2001, 2002; Kuo 1999; Lóres-Sanz 2011; Martínez 2005).

In their analysis of student essay writing, Tang and John (1999) have shown that the study of these pronouns constitutes a fertile ground for the exploration of author identity. They identified six writer identity roles and placed them along a continuum of increasing authorial power from author as representative, through author as guide, as architect, as recounter, to author as opinion holder and as originator. Different researchers have used and validated Tang and John's taxonomy in different disciplinary fields. For example, Chávez Muñoz (2013) used a modified version of this taxonomy to explore the different functions of personal pronouns in English and Spanish in three different fields (Linguistics, Psychology and Educational Research). Sheldon (2009) also used this taxonomy to compare the use of personal pronouns employed in RAs in Applied Linguistics and Language Teaching written in Spanish and English. Cheung and Lau (2020) added two new roles to the taxonomy – author as 'researcher' and as 'explainer' – to compare the identity roles in RAs in two different disciplines (Literature and Computer Science). In the field of medicine, Carciu (2009) employed Tang and John's taxonomy to analyse and contrast the use and the rhetorical function of personal pronouns across the different sections of medical RAs written in English by Anglo-American and Spanish scholars.

However, to our knowledge, no study has compared these manifestations in RA introductions in different medical subfields. Therefore, the purpose of this study is to explore and analyse authorial presence through the use of first-person pronouns in relation to the rhetorical moves of RA introductions in two medical subfields, neurology and paediatrics. Moreover, it aims to explore the different identity roles of authorial stance played by the first-person pronouns in the two subfields and to determine whether there is any variation between them.

## 2 Analytical Framework

### 2.1 Swales' Create a Research Space Model

Swales (1981) analysed forty-eight RA introductions from different disciplines to describe the rhetorical organisation of RAs with the aim of helping second language learners to improve their reading and writing skills (Moreno and Swales 2018). In that study, he introduced a model of RA introductions with a sequence of four moves: (1) establishing the field, (2) summarizing previous research, (3) preparing for present research and (4) introducing present research.

In Swales (1990: 141) the author introduced a revised model, denominated CARS, which reduced the four moves to three and was based on the ecological metaphor of competing for a research space: (1) establishing a territory, (2) establishing a niche and (3) occupying the niche (Swales 1990). The author points out that the amount of rhetorical work for the writer will depend on the competition that exists in the field, the importance of the niche and other factors, such as the researcher's reputation within the scientific community. Move 1, which reflects the author's need to establish a territory, a field of investigation, can be realised by three different steps: (1) claiming centrality, (2) making topic generalisations and/or (3) reviewing items of previous research. Move 2, in which authors use the information of move 1 to demonstrate that there is a niche to be occupied, can be realised by four steps: (1a) counter claiming, (1b) indicating a gap, (1c) question-raising, or (1d) continuing a tradition. Swales (1990) explains that moves 2 and 3 are closely related because, when move 2 is present, move 3 occurs to fill the space created. Move 3 can be accomplished by four possible steps: (1a) outlining purposes, (1b) announcing present research, (2) announcing principle findings, or (3) indicating RA structure.

In 2004, Swales proposed a new revised and improved model based on the results of different studies. He defines the term '*move*' as "a discoursal or rhetorical unit that performs a coherent communicative function in a written or spoken discourse" (Swales 2004: 228). He specifies that a move is a functional unit not a formal one and can consist of one or more sentences. The main difference between a move and a step is that the interpretation of a text fragment at step level is usually more specific than the interpretation at move level (Moreno and Swales 2018).

Because of certain difficulties in move 1 in analysing RA introductions, Swales (2004) decided to reduce the three steps to just one: topic generalisations of increasing specificity. For move 2, he reduced four steps to three, maintaining step 1a (indicating a gap) and 1b (adding to what is known) and including a new optional step 2 (presenting positive justification). Finally, in the new model, move 3 acquires greater complexity, consisting of one obligatory step (1 announcing present research descriptively and/or purposively) three optional steps (2 presenting research questions or hypothesis, 3 definitional clarifications and 4 summarizing methods); and three steps that can occur in some fields, but not in others (5 announcing principal outcomes, 6 stating the value of the present research and 7 outlining the structure of the paper).

## 2.2 Tang and John's Taxonomy of Identity Roles

In their study, Tang and John (1999) analysed the use of first-person pronouns in students' academic essays to explore how they expressed writer identity. They examined twenty-seven students' essays at the National University of Singapore and created a taxonomy to analyse the different identity roles. This taxonomy includes six possible roles of first-person pronouns in academic writing arranged in a continuum from the least to the most powerful role of authorial stance (Figure 1).

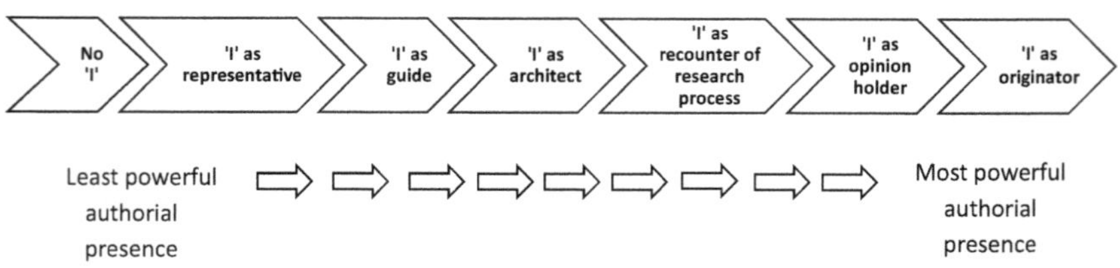


**Figure 1.** Identity roles of first-person pronouns in academic writing (Adapted from Tang & John 1999)

Clearly, the lack of the first-person pronoun 'I' corresponds to the least powerful role of authorial stance. It is followed by the role of 'representative', which uses generic first-person plural pronouns to express universal and/or common knowledge, and to refer to people in general or to the members of the discourse community. The role of 'guide' is employed to help to locate the reader and the writer in the same time and place and to engage the reader in the writing. When the personal pronoun takes the role of 'architect', it organises the material in the writing and helps to indicate structure. As its name suggests, the role of 'recounter' is used to describe the different steps of the research procedure. The role of 'opinion holder' shares an attitude or view towards something established and evaluates others' contributions. Finally, the role of 'originator', the most powerful role of authorial stance, is used to express commitment to and/or a claim to the content presented in the writing.

## 3 Corpus and Methods

This study is based on a corpus of sixty RA introductions from two different medical subfields, neurology and paediatrics. The total corpus is made up of 22,370 tokens: 10,788 from neurology and 11,582 from paediatrics. The articles were drawn from six different international journals published in English between the years 2017 and 2018. Ten articles were taken at random from each of the six journals which had achieved the best positions in the Scimago Journal and Country Rank website for the two subdisciplines in North America, Europe and the United Kingdom. For selection, besides the rank position, the journals had to have free access to all, or some articles and they had to belong to the general areas of neurology and paediatrics. For neurology, the selected journals were *JAMA Neurology* (JN), *Journal of Neurology* (JON), *The Lancet Neurology* (TLN); and for paediatrics: *JAMA Pediatrics* (JP), *The European Journal of Pediatrics* (TEJOP) and *BMC Pediatrics* (BMCP). It is important to mention that although the six journals publish different types of texts, only articles presenting original research were considered for this study.

In a previous study (Roverso and Williams Camus in press), the rhetorical analysis of the 60 RA introductions was carried out using an adapted version of Swales' CARS model (Figure 2). In this model we selected features from the 1990 and 2004 CARS models and from Swales and Feak (2012) and redefined a step we thought useful for the subfields under study. For move 1, we included the two steps in Swales and Feak (2012) because we considered them to be more appropriate for our study: an optional step 1a that contributes to establishing the territory by showing that the topic is relevant, central or problematic; and an obligatory step 1b, where writers review the literature by citing previous research in the field. In move 2, we maintained steps 1a (indicating a gap) and 2 (presenting positive justification) from Swales (2004), but in 1A we added the word 'need' because many articles expressed the niche in this way. We included step 1b (question-raising) from 1990 and redefined steps from previous models as a new step 3 (continuing own research), where authors indicate that the new study represents a continuation of the same authors' previously published research. Finally, in move 3, we maintained the seven steps in the 2004 model for a more complete analysis.

The results of that study indicated that both subdisciplines respected Swales' CARS model, except for one text in neurology with no move 2 or 3 and one in paediatrics with no move 3. In these cases, an overlap was observed between the Introduction and Methods sections and the information typical of the missing moves was located in the description of the methodology.

For the analysis of first-person pronouns, we first conducted a quantitative analysis using the software AntConc 3.5.8 (Anthony 2019) to detect all the occurrences of the pronouns in the different moves of the RA introductions in the two subfields. Since all the RAs in the corpus were written by two or more authors, the search was performed with the plural forms of the personal pronouns: 'we', 'our' and 'us'. Then, we applied Tang and John's taxonomy of identity roles in a qualitative contextual analysis to identify the different discoursal functions performed by these pronouns in the different rhetorical moves. All instances of the first-person pronouns were manually coded into one of the roles of authorial stance.

Creating a Research Space model (1990 – 1994 – 2004)

**Move 1 – Establishing a research territory (citations required)**
Step 1A by showing that the general research area is important, central, interesting, problematic or relevant in some way (optional)
Step 1B by introducing and reviewing items of previous research in the area (obligatory)

**Move 2 – Establishing a niche (citations possible)**
Step 1A Indicating a gap or need
Step 1B Question-raising
Step 2 (optional) Presenting positive justification
Step 3 Continuing own research [this study]

**Move 3 – Occupying the niche / Presenting the present work**
Step 1 – (obligatory) Announcing present research descriptively and/or purposively
Step 2* – (optional) Presenting research questions or hypotheses
Step 3 – (optional) Definitional clarifications
Step 4 – (optional) Summarizing methods
Step 5 – (PISF**) Announcing principal outcomes
Step 6 – (PISF) Stating the value of the present research
Step 7 – (PISF) Outlining the structure of the paper

* Steps 2–4 are not only optional but less fixed in their order of occurrence than the others
** PISF: Probable in some fields, but unlikely in others

**Figure 2.** Adapted Swales' CARS model for our study.

# 4 Results

## 4.1 Quantitative Analysis

The analysis shows that most of the RA introductions in the two medical subdisciplines employed first-person pronouns since twenty-one (70 %) of the introductions in neurology and twenty-three (77 %) in paediatrics contained at least one instance (Figures 3 and 4). The total number of instances of first-person pronouns was forty-six in neurology and forty-eight in paediatrics, that is a mean of 2.19 and 2.09 respectively for articles that included these pronouns. This represents a frequency of 4.26 instances per 1,000 running words for neurology and 4.14 for paediatrics. These figures are slightly lower than the 5.72 reported by Carciu (2009: 77) for haematology.

Regarding the number of personal pronouns employed in each introduction (Figure 5), the two subdisciplines contained similar numbers since they mostly presented one to three pronouns. However, we found slight differences between them, since in paediatrics there were nine introductions that contained two personal pronouns compared with six in neurology. In addition, of the small number of introductions with more than three pronouns, two paediatrics introductions had four first-person pronouns and one neurology introduction contained five and another had six.

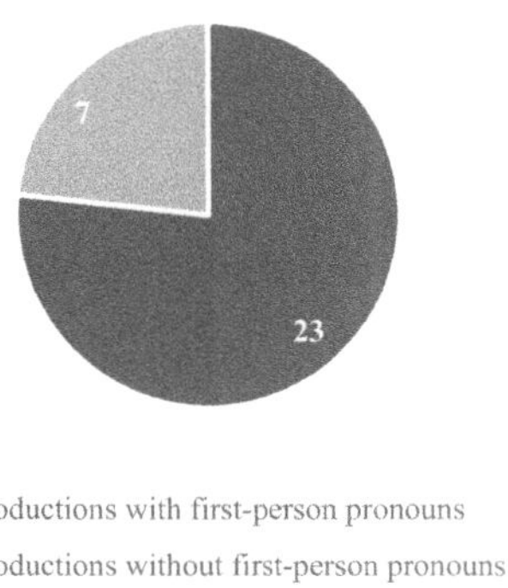


**Figure 3.** First-person pronouns in neurology RA introductions

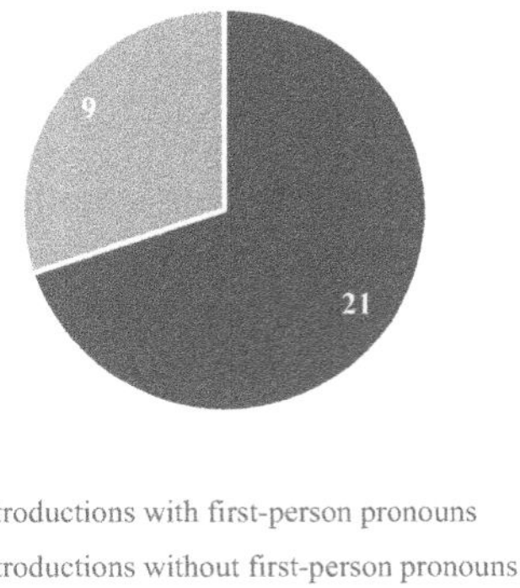


**Figure 4.** First-person pronouns in paediatrics RA introductions

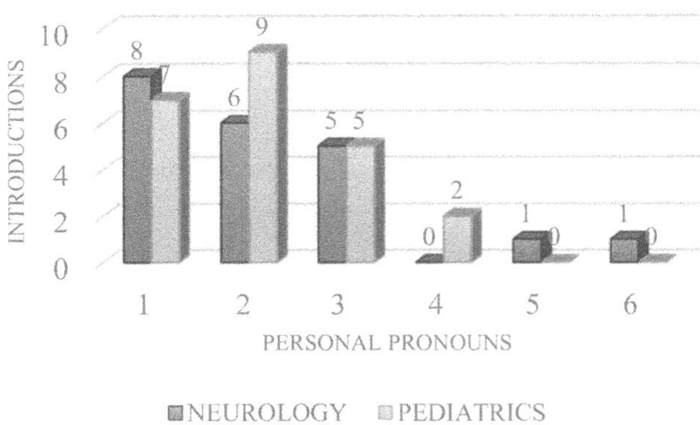


**Figure 5.** Number of first-person pronouns in each introduction in the two subfields

## 4.2 Distribution of First-Person Pronouns by Rhetorical Structure

Table 1 shows the distribution of the different pronoun forms in relation to the rhetorical moves. The plural subject pronoun 'we' was found to be the most frequently used in the two subfields: thirty-nine occurrences in neurology and thirty-five in paediatrics. In both subfields, most of these instances were found in move 3, where authors occupy the niche and present their study (Examples 1 and 2).

(1) ***In this study, we document*** *evolution of falls over 54 months from diagnosis in an incident cohort of PD.* (JON 15)

(2) ***In this study, we assessed*** *the association between prenatal exposure to PM2.5 (particulate matter with an aerodynamic diameter ≤2.5 μm) and TL at birth.* (JP 35)

**Table 1.** First-person pronouns in the different rhetorical moves in the two subfields.

| | Neurology | Paediatrics |
|---|---|---|
| Plural subject pronoun WE | 39 | 35 |
| - Move 1 | 9 | 2 |
| - Move 2 | 1 | 6 |
| - Move 3 | 29 | 27 |
| Possessive adjective OUR | 7 | 12 |
| - Move 1 | - | 1 |
| - Move 2 | 3 | 6 |
| - Move 3 | 4 | 5 |
| Object pronoun US (Move 2) | - | 1 |
| Total | 46 | 48 |

However, there were some subtle differences in the use of this pronoun in the other moves. For example, in neurology five introductions used it nine times in move 1 to establish the research territory (Example 3) whereas in paediatrics it was only employed in this move twice in different texts (Example 4). In examples 3 and 4, it can be observed that authors used it in step 1b to present their own previous studies related to the topic of the new investigation.

(3) *In 2011,* ***we reported that*** *acute stroke hospitalization rates were increasing among young adults aged 15 to 44 years.* [4] (JN 6)

(4) ***We and others have previously demonstrated*** *differences in skeletal development in African American children compared with non-African American children.* [5,6] (JP 36)

Moreover, while in paediatrics there were six instances in which this pronoun was employed in move 2 (Example 5), in neurology there was only one (Example 6).

(5) ***Yet, we do not know*** *whether this is applicable to preschool children.* (TEJOP 50)

(6) ***We now*** *extend these findings by taking a more nuanced and detailed approach to the data.* (JON 15)

Example 5 from paediatrics appears in step 1a to indicate a gap in knowledge whereas example 6 from neurology belongs to step 3 in which the authors establish that they are continuing their own research. It should be noted that in the latter the authors have used exclusive 'we' referring only to themselves as writers whereas in the former it is inclusive 'we' referring to both authors and the discourse community in order to share responsibility for the lack of knowledge with the discipline (Harwood 2005b: 348).

There was also a minor difference in the use of the possessive 'our' since the frequency in paediatrics was higher than in neurology (twelve versus eight). One instance occurred in a paediatrics introduction (Example 7), where it combined with 'we' in step 1b of move 1 to present previous research:

(7) *We reported high risks of concerning health care practices and morbidities following infant male circumcision* ***in our community based study in rural Ghana*** *[6].* (BMCP 58)

The remaining instances are fairly evenly divided between move 2 and 3 in both subfields (three and four, respectively in neurology; six and five in paediatrics). However, for move 2 there were twice as many instances in paediatrics as in neurology. This is because paediatrics made far more use of the pattern of 'to [the best of] our knowledge' (six cases) followed by a negative quantifier (Example 8) whereas there was only one instance of this pattern in neurology.

(8) *Despite a growing body of literature related to ATV-related injuries in youth [1, 7, 10–15],* ***to the best of our knowledge,*** *none have been designed specifically to determine if the risk of moderate to serious injuries is higher in younger age groups, compared to adults or older adolescents [7, 11].* (BMCP 55)

In neurology, the other two occurrences included the possessive with 'understanding' (Example 9).

(9) ***Although insights into our understanding*** *of the epidemiology of motor neuron diseases, and amyotrophic lateral sclerosis in particular, have been provided by population based registries in Europe over the past two decades [10,11] and in the USA more recently, [12] these epidemiological surveillance systems are not available in other parts of the world.* (TLN 30)

As seen with the subject pronoun 'we', the possessive 'our' can be either exclusive or inclusive. In the repeated pattern with 'our knowledge', exclusive 'our' acts as a hedge for the writers' assertion and to indicate caution (Kuo 1999: 133); in contrast, the two instances with 'our understanding' have inclusive 'our' either as part of a question-raising statement or to establish a gap in knowledge as in example 9, where the 'unfair' unavailability of important data-collection systems globally is seen to be the shared responsibility of the discourse community (Harwood 2005b: 348).

In move 3 most instances appeared in step 1 to introduce the study combining with 'aim' or 'objective' (Example 10), although two appeared in step 2 and step 6.

(10) ***Our primary objective*** *was to examine the incidence of sedation related adverse events and identify risk factors associated with these events.* (JP 32)

(11) ***Our study considers*** *motor neuron diseases across the whole age spectrum including spinal muscular atrophy, a rare disorder in the first years of life affecting proximal limbs and respiratory muscles.* (TLN 30)

Finally, the object pronoun 'us' was used once in move 2 step 3 in a paediatrics introduction to indicate that the authors were extending their previous research with an intraosseous device designed for adults to the paediatric context (Example 12):

(12) *Previous favorable experience with the adult NIO* ***led us to evaluate*** *the performance of the pediatric NIO-P [22].* (TEJOP 41)

## 4.3 Identity Roles

The distribution of identity roles in relation to the rhetorical moves is shown in Table 2. Neither of the subfields used first-person pronouns in the role of 'guide' to engage the reader in the argument. This role usually occurs when authors are presenting a theoretical argument as in physics or mathematics or when commenting on data presented in figures and tables (Harwood 2005b: 361), but this is not the case of RA introductions in medical fields.

The most frequent role by far in both subcorpora was that of 'recounter', followed by 'originator', 'architect', 'opinion-holder' and finally 'representative'.

*Role 1 – Representative.* The role of 'representative', the least powerful role of authorial stance, was only found in two introductions in neurology and in one in paediatrics. In both subfields the inclusive personal pronouns included authors, readers and the scientific community as a whole and were used in move 2 to establish a gap in knowledge. In the two neurology introductions this identity took the format of the possessive adjective 'our' (Example 13) whereas in paediatrics it was expressed through the pronoun 'we' (Example 14).

**Table 2.** Identity roles of authorial stance in relation to the different moves in the two subfields

| | **Neurology** | | | **Paediatrics** | | |
|---|---|---|---|---|---|---|
| | **Move 1** | **Move 2** | **Move 3** | **Move 1** | **Move 2** | **Move 3** |
| 1. Representative | - | 2 | - | - | 1 | - |
| 2. Guide | - | - | - | - | - | - |
| 3. Architect | - | 1 | 6 | - | - | 2 |
| 4. Recounter | - | - | 24 | - | - | 27 |
| 5. Opinion holder | - | - | 2 | - | 2 | 2 |
| 6. Originator | 9 | 1 | 1 | 3 | 10 | 1 |

(13) *The association between GS or CD and ALS may have implications* ***for our understanding*** *of a pathogenic mechanism, as well as for future ALS treatment options.* (JON 19)
(14) *Yet,* ***we do not know*** *whether this is applicable to preschool children.* (TEJOP 50)

As mentioned in the previous section, the inclusive 'we' in example 14 with this role allows the responsibility for imperfections in the state of the discipline to be shared (Harwood 2005b: 348). However, as in example 13, it also allows authors to point out the potentially positive implications of the new research for the discourse community (Harwood 2005b: 353).

*Role 3 – Architect.* The role of 'architect' was found with more frequency in neurology than in paediatrics (seven versus two instances). In both subfields it was mostly employed in move 3 to occupy the niche (examples 15, 16 and 17).

(15) *In this study,* ***we document*** *evolution of falls over 54 months from diagnosis in an incident cohort of PD.* (JON 15)
(16) *In this report,* ***we summarize*** *the main outcomes of Connect for Health.* (JP 39)
(17) *In the current article,* ***we report*** *the results of nutrient intake from the first stage of the intervention programme, that is before introducing education of the preschool staff and parents, and before modifying children's diets.* (BMCP 60)

In this move, the role was realised in similar ways in the two subdisciplines since both generally employed communicative verbs in the present tense – of which the most frequent was 'report' (three instances) with 'describe', 'document' and 'summarize' used once each – but also included procedural verbs (e.g. 'identify' and 'examine').

In one case in neurology the role occurred in move 2 step 3 to show that the authors were building on their previous research (example 18). In this example the authors not only refer to the discourse through the deictic 'now' and indicate how the new study fits with their previous research, but also give a positive justification for the study with the lexical items 'more nuanced' and 'detailed'.

(18) ***We now extend these findings*** *by taking a* ***more nuanced and detailed approach*** *to the data.* (JON 15)

*Role 4 – Recounter of the research process.* As mentioned above, this role was the most frequent in both subcorpora (twenty-four in neurology and twenty-seven in paediatrics), but it was also exclusive to move 3. When Tang and John's classification was applied in the analysis of roles, we found a subtle difference in the way this role was employed to introduce the new study, that is descriptively or purposively. Therefore, we decided to divide it into two subcategories as follows:

*Role 4.1. Authors presenting their study purposively.* The more tentative role of 'recounter' where the authors present the aims and purposes of the study is used with the same frequency in the two subfields since it is present in eight instances in move 3 in each subcorpus. In the case of neurology, all the instances had the verb 'aim' in the past simple tense (Example 19) whereas in paediatrics this verb occurred only in three instances. Another four employed phrases such as 'our aim was to' or 'our primary objective was to' (Example 20). The other instance proved rather more difficult to assign to the purposive or descriptive perspective and will be dealt with in the discussion.

(19) *In this study, **we aimed** to compare the risk of recurrence in children with PCAIS with that seen in children with ACAIS.* (JN 9)

(20) ***Our primary objective was to** examine the incidence of sedation related adverse events and identify risk factors associated with these events.* (JP 32)

*Role 4.2. Authors presenting their study descriptively.* Most authors preferred the stronger factual perspective of 'recounter', with this role appearing in eleven neurology and sixteen paediatrics introductions. In both subfields, first-person 'we' were generally accompanied by procedural verbs in the simple past tense (Examples 21 and 22), with only one instance each of the present perfect and present simple.

(21) ***We** additionally **investigated** whether concentrations of NfL in CSF would correlate with those in plasma.* (TLN 23)

(22) ***We** then **conducted** this propensity weighted comparative effectiveness analysis testing the hypothesis that ICP monitoring is associated with improved functional survival of children with severe TBI.* (JP 31)

The most frequent verbs employed were 'investigate' (seven instances) and 'conduct' and 'test' (four instances each) with 'compare', 'examine' and 'use' each appearing twice. These six verbs accounted for 63 % of all instances of these procedural verbs.

It should be noted that most of the statements realizing this role represent step 1 of move 3. However, there were also a small number of cases in which methodological aspects of the study were presented in the introduction in a step 4:

(23) ***We used innovative techniques** that have significantly increased the feasibility of such investigations.*[8] (JP 36)

*Role 5 – Opinion holder.* First-person pronouns with the role of 'opinion holder' occurred in two neurology and four paediatrics introductions. In neurology, the two instances were in move 3 step 2 to state the study hypotheses (Examples 24 and 25).

(24) ***We postulated*** *that moderate or higher (≥50%) restenosis would be more frequent after stenting than endarterectomy and might predispose to a higher risk of recurrent stroke during long-term follow-up.* (TLN 30)

(25) ***We hypothesised*** *that accelerated long-term forgetting would also be a feature of presymptomatic autosomal dominant Alzheimer's disease in human beings, with mutation carriers forgetting more material over 7 days compared with non-carriers, despite similar learning and short interval (30 min) retention.* (TLN 26)

In paediatrics two similar instances also appeared in move 3 (Example 26):

(26) ***We assumed*** *that (1) pulmonary exacerbations and lung function decline are related to worsening of CFQ-R respiratory health domains; (2) the number of medications/ inhalation therapies are associated with higher CFQ-R treatment burden scores.* (TEJOP 45)

However, another two instances occurred in move 2 step 1b, where the role is employed to establish the niche by making a hypothetical statement or by raising questions about the previous literature (Examples 27 and 28):

(27) *In this regard,* ***we hypothesized*** *that exposure to PM air pollution during pregnancy may contribute to telomere setting at birth.* (JP35)

(28) ***We*** *therefore* ***questioned*** *whether BMI z scores could be misclassifying a significant fraction of adolescents as overweight.* (JP 37)

In all cases the verbs used in this role expressed mental states or activities. The most frequent was 'hypothesize' (three instances) and 'assume', 'postulate' and 'question' were all used once. The role of opinion-holder is one in which writers assume responsibility for their statements, but at the same time are exposing themselves to potential criticism since their opinions may enter in conflict with those of other authors or the general consensus (Vassileva 1998).

*Role 6 – Originator.* As occurred with the role of 'recounter', when Tang and John's classification was applied to the corpus, we found that the role of 'originator', the most powerful role of authorial stance, could be divided into three subcategories depending on the function and move structure.

*Role 6.1. Making self-citations.* In this subcategory, writers claim authority by presenting their previous research in a factual manner through self-citation. There were nine instances of this role in five neurology introductions and six instances in five articles in paediatrics. In the case of neurology, they all appeared in move 1 to establish the research territory (Examples 29 and 30).

(29) *In 2011,* ***we reported*** *that acute stroke hospitalization rates were increasing among young adults aged 15 to 44 years.*[4] (JN 6)

(30) ***We previously showed*** *that mHTT concentrations in blood leucocytes were associated with clinical severity cross-sectionally, 11 but that this was probably due to peripheral mHTT production rather than CNS pathology.* (TLN 23)

In paediatrics, this role was divided between move 1 (three instances) and move 2 (three instances). The contexts in move 1 were similar to those in neurology (Example 31):

(31) ***We and others have previously demonstrated*** *differences in skeletal development in African American children compared with non-African American children.*[5,6] (JP 36)

In move 2, the self-citations were references to previous publications that formed part of a broader research programme leading to the presentation of the new study (Example 32):

(32) *Previous favorable experience with the adult NIO* ***led us to evaluate*** *the performance of the pediatric NIO-P [22].* (TEJOP 41)

The verbs appearing in these citations were almost always past simple and included reporting verbs ('report' five, 'show' two, and 'demonstrate'), procedural verbs ('assess', 'develop' and 'link') and observational verbs ('identify' and 'observe').

Participation in published research is one of the strongest demonstrations of authorial stance, showing that the writers are to be taken seriously in the scientific community. It should be noted that in medicine self-references usually remain hidden behind numbers in brackets or in superscript. Therefore, when authors use first-person pronouns to present their previous research, they make a strategic choice whereby they establish their professional credibility (Hyland 2003: 251).

*Role 6.2. Expressing the gap.* In this subcategory, authors make a claim to originality that is realised in an indirect and tentative manner. This role appeared in only one introduction in neurology, but in eight in paediatrics. All except one instance in paediatrics occurred in move 2 to create a gap in knowledge (Examples 33–35).

(33) *However,* ***to our knowledge,*** *no previous study has examined imaging correlates of anti-LGI1 encephalitis and their association with cognitive deficits and clinical outcome in detail.* (JN 5)

(34) ***To our knowledge,*** *no study has evaluated an appropriately powered, controlled comparison of FBT and PBT with longer follow-up.* (JP 33)

(35) *(…)* ***we are not aware of*** *systematic studies addressed to assess potential influential factors at district level.* (BMCP 53)

As can be seen in these examples, the gap is created by means of negative elements linked to the authors' knowledge of the existing situation. In this way, authors state that they have found no previous research within the scope of their study, thereby indirectly establishing its originality. At the same time, the 'knowledge' element serves as a shield to protect them against potential criticism that the review of the literature may not have been exhaustive.

The remaining instance, which occurred in move 3 in a paediatrics introduction, will be commented on in the discussion.

*Role 6.3. Expressing the value of the study.* In the third subcategory, authors make a claim regarding the value of the outcome of their study. The only instance of this predictive use of the originator role appeared in a neurology introduction (Example 36):

(36) *Furthermore,* ***we hope that this study will provide*** *the basis for further investigation into the mechanisms of stroke unique to each distribution that may influence their rates of recurrence.* (JN 9)

This case represents move 3 step 6, where the authors claim that their data and findings will contribute to further research in the field. Framing this claim with the verb 'hope' makes this value statement both predictive and tentative.

Figure 6 summarises the revised model of Tang and John's identity roles that have emerged in the analysis of our corpus in the two subdisciplines of neurology and paediatrics.

| **Identity roles of authorial stance** |
|---|
| 1- 'I' as the representative |
| 2- 'I' as the guide |
| 3- 'I' as the architect |
| 4- 'I' as the recounter of the research process |
| - 4.1. Tentative |
| - 4.2. Factual |
| 5- 'I' as opinion-holder |
| 6- 'I' as originator |
| - 6.1. Factual |
| - 6.2. Tentative |
| - 6.3. Predictive |

**Figure 6.** Adapted model of Tang and John's taxonomy

## 5 Discussion

The results of the combined application of identity roles and rhetorical move analysis to the corpus revealed certain patterns in the correlation of moves and roles and a number of difficulties in the assignment of an identity role to some instances of the possessive.

One pattern that emerged involved move 1, step 1b with the factual perspective of the originator role. In reporting their own previous research, the authors' presence can be selected to show that they are active in the field and making a valuable contribution (Hyland 2003: 251). The strong authorial stance adopted in this pattern is somewhat attenuated by the associated verbs which are generally neutral communicative verbs, especially 'report', or objective procedural verbs, such as 'assess', 'develop' and 'identify'. A difficulty in assignment arose in one instance in which the possessive 'our' complemented the subject pronoun (example 37):

(37) ***We reported*** *high risks of concerning health care practices and morbidities following infant male circumcision in* ***our community based study*** *in rural Ghana [6].* (BMCP 58)

While 'we' is clearly exclusive, the possessive broadens the scope to one of 'representative' by including the authors as members of the community and thus underlining the value of their study to the community as a whole. However, for simplicity both 'we' and 'our' were classified as 6.1 originator-factual.

The second pattern, which correlated move 2, step 1a with the tentative perspective of the originator role, consisted of phrases such as 'to our knowledge' or 'to the best of our knowledge' combined with negative quantifiers 'no' or 'none' and occurred seven times. The potential for novelty is indicated by the negative marker, which establishes the gap in knowledge (step 1a), but this is hedged by the personal reference, which protects the writers' face as their review of previous research may have been flawed. This negative evaluation of the state of affairs in the field anticipates a positive response in move 3 (see examples 8, 33 and 34).

The two exceptions to this correlation were an instance of the subject pronoun instead of the possessive in this step through 'we are not aware' (example 35) and one instance of 'to our knowledge' that occurred in move 3 step 1 together with the subject pronoun (example 38).

(38) *However,* ***to our knowledge, we carried out*** *the first nutrition intervention programme for Polish preschool children, which aimed to modify diet and physical activity in preschool children in order to improve their nutritional status and physical fitness.* (BMCP 60)

In this case, the combination of the subject pronoun with a procedural verb indicates the descriptive 'recounter' role while the hedging phrase attenuates the authors' claim to the 'first nutrition intervention programme' in Poland and thus was assigned to the originator-tentative role. This represents a shortened form of the standard formula which might have been written:

> * However, **to our knowledge**, no nutrition intervention programmes have been performed in Polish preschool children. [move 2: step 1a] Therefore, **we designed** and **carried out** such a programme which aimed to modify diet and physical activity in preschool children in order to improve their nutritional status and physical fitness. [move 3: step 1]

In the published form, the claim to originality is explicit and positive whereas in the revised standard formula, it is implicit and the hedge serves to protect the authors' face.

As shown in the previous section, the third pattern correlated move 3, usually step 1, with the descriptive 'recounter' role and almost always involving procedural verbs in the past simple. However, in the analysis a difficulty arose in role assignment when the possessive combined with the subject pronoun (example 39).

> (39) ***We therefore investigated*** *the risk of sICH following cSAH in: (1) a cohort of patients from* ***our comprehensive stroke service*** *presenting with acute symptomatic cSAH due to suspected CAA and (2) a pooled analysis which included* ***our cohort*** *and all other available published data on cSAH in suspected CAA cohorts.* (JON 20)

Although the whole statement is clearly a descriptive step 1, as seen in example 37, the possessive extends the scope of the exclusive pronoun 'we' to add the nuance of authors as representatives of their institution 'our comprehensive stroke service'. This sense of identification is further strengthened when the possessive combines in a second shortened 'our cohort'. Despite this secondary role, for consistency all three instances of the personal reference were classified under the 'recounter' role.

Another problematic case of role assignment occurred in move 3 when the possessive appeared in the subject position combined with a present tense verb, thus representing a double divergence from the standard pattern of we + past tense.

> (40) ***Our study considers*** *motor neuron diseases across the whole age spectrum including spinal muscular atrophy, a rare disorder in the first years of life affecting proximal limbs and respiratory muscles.* (TLN 30)

In this statement the authors provide a detail on the design of the new study in comparison with previous research. The present tense could suggest the role of architect, but this is unlikely with the possessive as subject. If the subject pronoun 'we' had been used, the tense would most probably have been past simple 'In this study, we considered…' and therefore assignment to the descriptive 'recounter' role would have been clear. Despite the divergence from the norm, we finally decided to assign it to 'recounter'.

As seen in the previous section, in the purposive 'recounter' role there were two clear syntactic patterns: (1) subject pronoun 'we' + 'aimed to/at'; (2) possessive 'our' + 'aim' or 'objective' + was + infinitive. Again, a difficulty arose with a double first-person reference in the same statement (example 41):

(41) *In the International Collaborative Infantile Spasms Study (ICISS), **we aimed to test our hypothesis** that combining hormonal and vigabatrin therapy would achieve spasm cessation for 4 weeks (between day 14 and 42 of treatment) in a greater proportion of infants than with hormonal therapy alone.* (TLN 21)

Here the assignment of the 'recounter' role is clear but the second reference through the possessive and 'hypothesis' suggests a similar relationship between the parts as in 'we hypothesised' (see Example 25), indicating a secondary role of 'opinion-holder' and perhaps claiming this as their contribution to the field.

There was also one exception to the two above-mentioned patterns (example 42):

(42) *As more and more individuals with DS are diagnosed with CD, **we were motivated to examine** if concurrent CD influences the risk of death in DS.* (BMCP 54)

If we consider this example with examples 43–45, we can establish clear differences in the roles to be assigned:

(43) ***Our primary objective** was **to examine** the incidence of sedation related adverse events and identify risk factors associated with these events.* (JP32)

(44) *Using data from a population-based cohort study of infants with CHD (the EPICARD study), **we examined** the association between PTB and the risk of infant mortality for newborns with CHD for: i) all CHD combined, ii) "isolated" CHD (excluding CHD associated with chromosomal or other anomalies) and iii) "isolated major CHD" (isolated CHD excluding ventricular septal defects).* (BMCP 57)

(45) ***We examine** baseline characteristics of emergent fallers and non-fallers over 54 months to identify features that precipitate and alternatively protect from falls.* (JON 15)

Example 43 is a characteristic instance of purposive 'recounter'. Similarly, example 44 is typical of the descriptive 'recounter' role. Example 45 is more problematic because of the present tense, which draws the procedural verb from the experimental world into the realm of discourse (Carciu 2009) and is, thus, assigned to the role of 'architect' with the writer signalling to readers what to expect in the later sections of the article. However, because of the passive verb structure, example 42 does not fit so easily into any of these roles: the past tense precludes 'architect'; the passive hinders the descriptive 'recounter' role, where we anticipate active procedural verbs; and the semantic status of 'motivate' and its association with future intention – as occurs with 'aim' – brings it closest to purposive 'recounter'.

## 6 Conclusion

This chapter has provided a comprehensive description of the results obtained when Tang and John's (1999) identity role model was applied in conjunction with an adapted version of Swales move and step model to a corpus of medical RA introductions. In the two medical subfields under study there was scant presence of inclusive first-person pronouns and, therefore, the role of 'representative'. In these introductions there were no instances of the 'guide' role, but the other four roles were found in both subcorpora. Thus, our analysis has confirmed the general usefulness of Tang and John's model for the analysis of authorial presence; however, the results also revealed a number of correlations between the first-person roles and certain moves and steps. This led us to propose more nuanced subcategories in the two most frequent roles in the corpus. Thus, the 'recounter' role could be conveniently divided into purposive and descriptive subclasses, which confirms the usefulness of Swales (1981: 22) original distinction for the move introducing present research. In our medical introductions this was reflected in a tentative perspective indicating the authors' intentions and a descriptive factual perspective on the study. Similarly, the strongest identity role of originator could be divided according to move structure with the factual subcategory corresponding to self-citation in move 1, the tentative subcategory to expression of hedges in move 2 and a predictive subcategory when an evaluation of the contribution of the study was made in move 3. These fairly consistent correspondences could be added to the two models to enhance their pedagogical application in designing materials to develop awareness of authorial stance in specific courses aimed at novice writers in the field.

## References

Anthony, L. (2019) AntConc 2.5.8 [Computer Software]. Tokyo, Japan: Waseda University. Available in: <https://www.laurenceanthony.net/software>

Basal, A. and Bada, E. (2011). 'Use of first person pronouns: A corpus based study of journal articles', *Energy Education Science and Technology Part B: Social and Educational Studies*, 4 (3), 1777–1788.

Carciu, O. M. (2009). 'An intercultural study of first-person plural references in biomedical writing', *Ibérica*, 18, 71–92.

Chávez Muñoz, M. (2013). 'The "I" in interaction: authorial presence in academic writing', *Revista de Lingüística y Lenguas Aplicadas*, 8, 49–58.

Cheung, Y. L. and Lau, L. (2020). 'Authorial voice in academic writing: A comparative study of journal articles in English Literature and Computer Science', *Ibérica*, 39, 215–242.

Flowerdew, J. (1999). 'Problems in writing for scholarly publication in English: The case of Hong Kong', *Journal of Second Language Writing*, 8 (3), 243–264.

Harwood, N. (2005a). "*Nowhere has anyone attempted . . . In this article I aim to do just that*' A corpus-based study of self-promotional *I* and *we* in academic writing across four disciplines', *Journal of Pragmatics*, 37, 1207–1231.

Harwood, N. (2005b). "We Do Not Seem to Have a Theory … The Theory I Present Here Attempts to Fill This Gap': Inclusive and Exclusive Pronouns in Academic Writing', *Applied Linguistics*, 26 (3), 343–375.

Hyland, K. (2001). 'Humble servants of the discipline? Self-mention in research articles', *English for Specific Purposes*, 20, 217–226.

Hyland, K. (2002). 'Authority and invisibility: authorial identity in academic writing', *Journal of Pragmatics*, 34, 1091–1112.

Hyland, K. (2003). 'Self-Citation and Self-Reference: Credibility and Promotion in Academic Publication', *Journal of the American Society for Information Science and Technology*, 54 (3), 251–259.

Kuo, C. (1999). 'The Use of Personal Pronouns: Role Relationships in Scientific Journal Articles', *English for Specific Purposes*, 18 (2), 121–138.

Lorés-Sanz, R. (2011). 'The construction of the author's voice in academic writing: the interplay of cultural and disciplinary factors', *Text and Talk*, 31 (2), 173–193.

Martínez, I. (2005). 'Native and non-native writers' use of first person pronouns in the different sections of biology research articles in English', *Journal of Second Language Writing*, 14 (3). 174–190.

Moreno, A. I. and Swales, J. M. (2018). 'Strengthening move analysis methodology towards bridging the function-form gap', *English for Specific Purposes*, 50, 40–63.

Mur-Dueñas, P. and Šinkūnienė, J. (2016). 'Self-reference in research articles across Europe and Asia: A review of studies', *Brno Studies in English*, 1 (42), 71–92.

Pho, P.D. (2012). 'Authorial stance in research article abstracts and introductions from two disciplines'. In N. Baumgarten, I. Du Bois and J. House (eds.), *Subjectivity in Language and in Discourse*, 97–114. Bingley: Emerald.

Roverso, M.P. and Williams Camus, J.T. (in press). 'Rhetorical structure of research article Introductions in two medical subfields'.

Sheldon, E. (2009). 'From one *I* to another: Discursive construction of self-representation in English and Castilian Spanish research articles', *English for Specific Purposes*, 28, 251–265.

Swales, J. M. (1981). *Aspects of article introductions*. Birmingham, UK: The University of Aston, Language Studies Unit.

Swales, J. M. (1990). *Genre Analysis: English in academic and research settings*. Cambridge: Cambridge University Press.

Swales, J. M. (2004). *Research Genres: Explorations and Applications*. Cambridge: Cambridge University Press.

Swales, J. M. and Feak, C. B. (2012). *Academic writing for graduate student: Essential tasks and Skills (3rd ed.)*. Ann Arbor: University of Michigan Press.

Tang, R. and John, S. (1999). 'The 'I' in identity: Exploring writer identity in student academic writing through the first person pronoun', *English for Specific Purposes*, 18, S23–S39.

Vassileva, I. (1998). 'Who am I/who are we in academic writing? A contrastive analysis of authorial presence in English, German, French, Russian and Bulgarian', *International Journal of Applied Linguistics*, 8 (2), 163–190.

Jacqueline Aiello

# The Discursive Realisation of a Progressive Congresswoman: Stancetaking Across Contexts and Media[1]

**Abstract:** This paper aims to provide novel insights into contemporary political identities and discourse with a study of the stancetaking moves and discursive strategies that American freshman Congresswoman Alexandria Ocasio-Cortez employed in her first term to impute stances of alignment and disalignment across contexts and media. It adopts a critical discourse analytical approach to examine Representative Ocasio-Cortez's stancetaking trajectory and, specifically, the features that characterise the stance dimensions, reframing practices, and self- and other-positioning strategies in selected responses that she articulated within the tweets she posted and the remarks she delivered before the US House of Representatives in reaction to attacks perpetrated by the media and her political opponents against her and her political platform. The results of this investigation do not only unveil the nature of Representative Ocasio-Cortez's stancetaking moves to align with 'the people' and disalign with the opposition in different situations and for different audiences but it also unearths the strategies and practices that she has deployed in the attempt to maintain her authenticity and legitimacy, to safeguard the coherence of her personal narrative and political self, and to situate herself within a larger national and historical storyline.

**Keywords:** *critical discourse analysis, left-wing populist discourse, identity construction, legitimisation, political discourse, political identity, (re)framing, social media communication, stance dimensions, stancetaking.*

## 1 Introduction

In 2017, the progressive political action committee Justice Democrats recruited Alexandria Ocasio-Cortez for the Democratic primary race for New York's fourteenth congressional district (NY14) seat, in line with its mission to challenge "out-of-touch incumbents" in primary races and to elect "better Democrats" in order to "usher in a new generation of diverse working-class Democrats". Ocasio-Cortez fit this description to a tee. Born in the Bronx in 1989 to a Puerto Rican-born mother and a Bronx-born father of Puerto Rican descent, Ocasio-Cortez resided in the Bronx before moving to the suburbs in Westchester County.

1 This paper is an earlier, adapted version of an updated and expanded chapter entitled "'Get used to me slaying': The discursive realization of a 'clapback queen'", which appears in *The Discursive Construction of the Modern Political Self* (2022, Routledge).

Although she accrued some political experience as an intern in the foreign affairs/ immigration constituent office of late Senator Ted Kennedy and as an organizer on Bernie Sander's 2016 Presidential campaign, Ocasio-Cortez famously tended bar and waited tables in Manhattan before embarking on her primary campaign.

Despite being a political unknown when she joined the race against a renowned 10-term incumbent, Ocasio-Cortez's campaign garnered a lot of attention and her campaign video, *The Courage to Change,* released just a month before the primary, became a viral hit. On 26 June 2018, Ocasio-Cortez shocked the establishment when she unseated her opponent and subsequently became the youngest female Congressperson in American history. With a platform that champions progressive policies and disparages contemporary capitalism, since joining Congress, Ocasio-Cortez was defined by *Time* magazine as "the second most talked-about politician in America" after Donald Trump, and by the *New York Times* as "the most exposed and fixated-on House freshman in history." She has become a magnetic, polarizing figure in the US political landscape who is at once one of the most visible symbols of left-wing populism and one of the most persistent targets of attacks by the right. In early 2019 it was reported that Fox News, the mainstream media bastion of American conservativism, mentioned Ocasio-Cortez over three thousand times in just six weeks (Hagle 2019), a staggering amount for a freshman Representative. In response, Ocasio-Cortez has not cowered silently. Rather, she has consistently reacted to these attacks, fuelling the popularity of her newly constructed political identity and her political agenda.

This paper delves into these attacks and responses with a study of the stancetaking moves and discursive strategies that Ocasio-Cortez employed in her freshman term to impute stances of alignment and disalignment across contexts and media. It adopts a critical discourse analytical (CDA) approach to examine her stancetaking trajectory and, specifically, the features that characterise the stance dimensions, reframing practices, and self- and other-positioning strategies in selected responses that she articulated within the tweets she posted and the remarks she delivered before the US House of Representatives in reaction to attacks perpetrated by the media and her political opponents against her and her political platform. For the Representative, these discourses serve to maintain her authenticity and legitimacy, to safeguard the coherence of her personal narrative and political self, and to situate herself within a larger national and historical storyline.

## 2 Stance

According to Du Bois (2007: 163), stance is "a public act by a social actor, achieved dialogically through overt communicative means, of simultaneously evaluating objects, positioning subjects (self and others), and aligning with other subjects, with respect to any salient dimension of the sociocultural field". Stances, which rely on the context of the utterance (Kiesling et al. 2018), encode speakers' attitudes towards the stance object, their moods, evaluations, points of view, and opinions at different levels of language including lexis, grammar, style, and pragmatics (Ushchyna 2014). Kiesling (2011: 1) has theorised that stance is at the core of what drives language users to employ particular discourses, sociolinguistic variables, or lexical items since it underpins the type of person that users wish to project with talk, and (groups of) language users tend to prefer certain stances such that "the language forms used to create this stance becomes associated, or indexed, with some aspect of the speaker's identity or the speech event".

Further insights in this light can be gleaned by investigations into style, which have unearthed the relationship(s) between identity and stance. Style has been retheorised "as a multimodal and multidimensional cluster of linguistic and other semiotic practices for the display of identities in interaction" (Bucholtz 2009: 146). A burgeoning strand of research has applied indexicality to the exploration of stylistic practice to unearth the ideologically-bound and fleeting interactional moves through which social actors take stances, create (dis) alignments, and construct personas. Indexical processes may construct identity within interaction directly, where linguistic forms index interactional stances, or indirectly, where ideological associations emerge between these linguistic forms and social types (for instance, some forms come to be seen as inherently feminine or masculine).

Recent studies have begun to unearth how stances are enacted in online contexts. Wang (2020) combines stancetaking and frame theory to analyse participant interactions and different types of alignment – defined as synonymous with Goffman's (1981) notion of footing – in Facebook comments regarding Taiwan's same-sex marriage legislation. Wang (2020) finds that a focus on language affords insights into the mediated performance involved in the production and negotiation of information on social media, of which alignment is the central mechanism. Kiesling et al. (2018) put forth a novel computational operationalisation of interpersonal stancetaking in the study of conversational threads from Reddit. The researchers investigate the thread structure and linguistic properties of stancetaking by undertaking a close analysis of the stance focus – or "the thing that is made most relevant by an utterance" based on Du Bois's (2007) stance object – and three linked stance dimensions: affect – "the polarity or quality of the stance to the stance focus" –, investment – "how strongly invested in the talk the speaker is" –, and alignment – "how much a speaker/writer aligns (or not) to their interlocutor(s), real or imagined" (Kiesling et al. 2018: 688). Kiesling et al. (2018) exhibit evidence that dividing stance into these three dimensions fosters a more productive analysis of relational aspects and meanings of interaction.

A strand of this recent research has shed light onto the role of stances in the identity construction and consolidation of public figures. For instance, Valentinsson (2018) uncovers the stance-taking moves that American celebrity Lady Gaga deploys to fashion an authentic celebrity persona, usefully analysing two different data sources: tweets and interviews. On the one hand, her tweets suggest the celebrity's effort to create a stance of alignment with her fans (above all other audiences) by citing intimate relationships with them, using inclusive plural pronouns, and directly responding to fans. On the other hand, interviews reveal the construction of stances of disalignment with the media by flouting the norms of celebrity interviews and using strategies such as critique, dismissal, and reframing of journalist questions. Usher (2016) instead offers an analysis of the Twitter and Facebook profiles of the political leaders running in the 2015 UK 'short campaign' to examine how they constructed their political personas on social network sites (SNS). Usher (2016: 23) notes that public political personas on SNS "[straddle] lines between authority as public figures and authenticity as users". While the electoral successes of Conservatives suggest that their highly professionalised and resourced SNS use is a winning strategy, Nigel Farage's "digital dog-whistling" garnered him the greatest increase in likes during the campaign and succeeded at attracting attention and increasing visibility of himself and his party (Usher 2016: 38).

The present study builds on this recent work to examine the relationships between stance-taking moves, identity construction, and rapport-building in Representative Ocasio-Cortez's online and off-line talk. In line with Johnstone's recommendation to explore how stancetaking works across situations and audiences (See also Valentinsson 2018), this paper analyses both the tweets she posted since winning the Congressional primary and selected remarks she delivered before the US House of Representatives.

## 3 Data and Analysis

### 3.1 Tweets

The tweets analysed in this study were those posted by Ocasio-Cortez (using the twitter handle @AOC) during a roughly twenty-six-month period that began on 26 June 2018, the day of her Democratic primary, and ended on 19 August 2020, according to CEST. The resulting 3,935 tweets (excluding retweets) amounted to a roughly 167,000-token corpus. The line graph in Figure 1 displays the frequency of tweets per day. Despite a significant peak in number of tweets on the day of her Democratic primary win, during the full period in question, Ocasio-Cortez tweeted on average five times a day.

The corpus was analysed using the online text analysis tool Sketch Engine first to explore the most frequently used lemmas, or basic forms of words, and their original context via the concordance tool. Comparative keyword analysis was also performed against a reference corpus constituted by original tweets from Representatives of the 116th Congress, developed using the larger corpus created by Wrubel and Kerchner (2020). It includes 30,000 tweets (1,050,260 tokens) posted from 26 June 2018 to 19 August 2020, randomly selected from the larger corpus. This reference corpus was deemed fitting because it comprised tweets posted by US politicians, referred to the same context and timeframe, and used the same variety of English (US English).

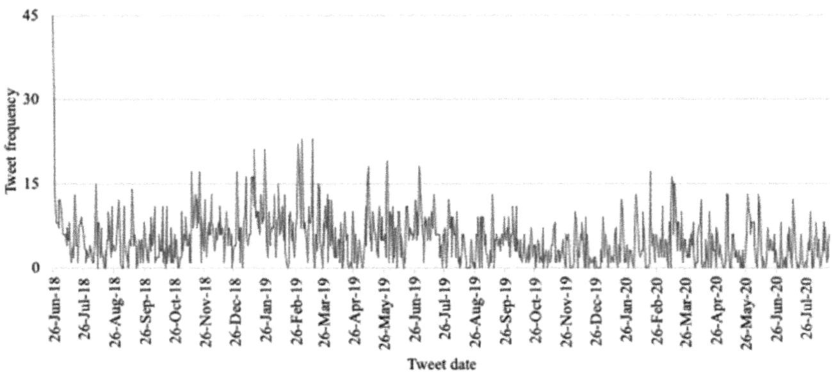


**Figure 1.** Frequency of @AOC tweets by day (from 26 Jun 2018 to 19 Aug 2020)

In order to glean more detailed insights into the stancetaking within Ocasio-Cortez's online communication, a sub-corpus of the top tweets from the larger @AOC corpus was created. To create this sub-corpus, the 3,935-tweet corpus was sorted in ascending order by 'favourite' (or 'like') count and the top forty tweets were selected. Several reasons underpin these selection criteria. First, users generally like a tweet because they like its content (Meier et al. 2014) and it is most resonant with and representative of their views, and most-liked tweets are more visible and impactful. Thus, these tweets also convey the reception by the politician's constituents and larger pool of followers, and therefore are suggestive of the most well-received tweets in the designated timeframe. Second, forty tweets were selected because this amount represents roughly 1% of the larger corpus.

Figure 2 maps the number of likes of each of the top forty @AOC tweets over time. These tweets were favourited by between 305,684 and 771,335 users (whereas the average like count across all tweets posted by the Representative in the full period under study was roughly 40,000 likes). Although the most-favourited tweets occur throughout the twenty-six-month period, there is a higher concentration of tweets in the summer of 2020.

Stance was analysed in the sub-corpus of top tweets by identifying the stance focus of each tweet as well as by exploring the features that characterise the stance dimensions: affect, investment, and alignment (Kiesling et al. 2018), with an emphasis on (dis)alignment driven by the aims of the study. In doing so it adopts a CDA approach with an emphasis on self- and other-positioning strategies and accounts for the (re)framing practices (Goffman 1981) utilised by the Representative.

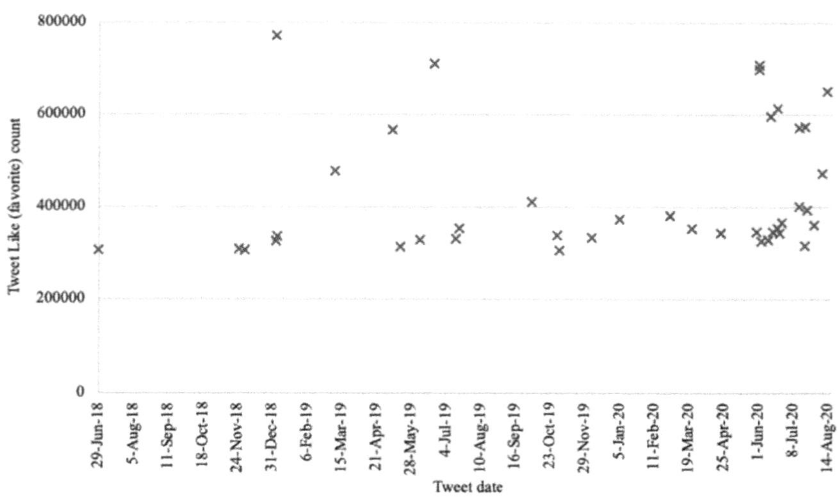


**Figure 2.** Top 40 @AOC tweets: like (favourite) count over time

### 3.2 House Remarks

The second data source consists of the remarks Representative Ocasio-Cortez delivered before the US House of Representatives. Due to space constraints, only two remarks were selected for analysis in this paper. The first comes from her contribution to the Subcommittee on Oversight and Reform, and specifically a 9 April 2019 hearing called "The need for leadership to combat climate change and protect national security". This was chosen because it includes a response to an attack and it involves the Green New Deal, a package of legislation that aimed to address climate change and economic inequality that is Ocasio-Cortez's most renowned policy proposal to date. The second is a point of personal privilege delivered by Ocasio-Cortez on 24 July 2020 on the House floor to address a colleague's remarks. These remarks were selected because they garnered a lot of media coverage.

For both sets of House Remarks, the full interactional setting was reconstructed in order to contextualise Ocasio-Cortez's remarks. The stances of the responses by Ocasio-Cortez were then analysed by identifying stance markers, style and (re)framing practices (Goffman 1981), as well as legitimisation and self- and other-positioning strategies following a CDA approach (van Leeuwen 2007).

## 4 Stances of (Dis)Alignment in @AOC Tweets

### 4.1 Constructing Alignment in the Full Corpus

*Frequency and Comparative analysis.* To obtain a general snapshot of what Ocasio-Cortez aimed to project on Twitter, the corpus of tweets was analysed for the most frequent lemmas and the top twenty results are shown in Table 1. The presence of the terms 'people', 'community', 'family', and 'member' evidence the Representative's attempt to position herself as a member of the NY14 community with deep roots in said community, and 'climate', 'policy', 'healthcare', and 'worker' are indicative of her political platform as a democratic Socialist. Of note are also the presence of "woman", the polysemic "right" and "GOP", the political opposition.

**Table 1.** Most frequent lemmas in full @AOC tweet corpus

| | *Lemma* | *Freq* | | | *Lemma* | *Freq* |
|---|---|---|---|---|---|---|
| 1 | people | 826 | | 11 | woman | 183 |
| 2 | time | 299 | | 12 | member | 180 |
| 3 | community | 287 | | 13 | right | 167 |
| 4 | GOP | 273 | | 14 | policy | 166 |
| 5 | today | 234 | | 15 | healthcare | 161 |
| 6 | Congress | 221 | | 16 | thing | 157 |
| 7 | year | 219 | | 17 | way | 154 |
| 8 | day | 202 | | 18 | worker | 153 |
| 9 | family | 202 | | 19 | life | 152 |
| 10 | climate | 192 | | 20 | power | 149 |

However, when the corpus was compared to the larger reference corpus of Congressional tweets, a different picture emerges. The top twenty results of the comparative keyword analysis are presented in Table 2. Although these results exclude those related specifically to the district (e.g.: Bronx, NY14), which would have otherwise been the top results, the absence of the language of belonging that we witnessed in the preceding table is telling. Based on these analyses, the community-bound nature of Ocasio-Cortez's language can be deemed endemic to politicians and cannot be considered a unique style. Notable, however, are some terms that the Representative has used to describe herself and her campaign, or 'waitress', 'organizing', and 'outspent', which emphasise her humble upbringing, tireless commitment, and self-made success, respectively.

**Table 2.** Results of the comparative keyword analysis

| | *Item* | *Keyness* | | | *Item* | *Keyness* |
|---|---|---|---|---|---|---|
| 1 | GND | 120.5 | | 11 | usury | 48.8 |
| 2 | UBI | 102.6 | | 12 | alright | 48.8 |
| 3 | corp | 66.8 | | 13 | convo | 45.6 |
| 4 | marginal | 60.8 | | 14 | abt | 45.2 |
| 5 | waitress | 60.8 | | 15 | M4A | 43.4 |
| 6 | organizing | 58.7 | | 16 | decarbonize | 42.8 |
| 7 | runaway | 54.8 | | 17 | diff | 42.8 |
| 8 | outspent | 54.8 | | 18 | Twitch | 42.8 |
| 9 | tuition-free | 49.7 | | 19 | classist | 42.8 |
| 10 | pollsite | 48.8 | | 20 | neo-nazi | 42.8 |

Other keywords are specialised, policy-related terms, including 'GND' (Green New Deal), 'UBI' (Universal basic income), 'marginal' (describing tax rates), 'runaway' (describing income gaps), 'tuition-free' (for public colleges), 'usury' (for high interest rates), 'M4M' (Medicare for All), and 'decarbonize' (reduce carbon(aceous) deposits). Given that this corpus is being compared to that of other lawmakers, the emergence of these terms is less suggestive of a high degree of specialisation of Ocasio-Cortez's Twitter discourse and more indicative of her aim to advance her Democratic Socialist and pro-environment political platform. Undoubtedly, the use of these specialised terms does also serve the purpose of legitimating her discourse (van Leeuwen 2007).

Another category of words that transpires in this comparative keyword analysis is abbreviations, indicating that Ocasio-Cortez's use of these shortenings exceeds that of her colleagues on the platform. They include the initialisms specified earlier, clippings such as 'corp' (corporate or corporation), 'convo' (conversation), and 'diff' (different), and omissions of the central vowel in 'abt' (about). Ocasio-Cortez's use of 'alright', the non-preferred spelling of 'all right', can arguably also be considered an abbreviation. This usage suggests command of the Twitter discourse format, given the platform's character limit, but also of informal, online talk. The increased use of these non-standard forms – along with her reference to 'Twitch', a popular livestreaming platform for gamers – fashions a style that is worlds apart from the traditional, stoic, and institutionalised discourse of leaders and is instead geared towards the construction of a stance of relational closeness with her young followers. Her informal and relaxed language use creates an "audience-centered, rapport-building" style (Johnstone 2009: 39) that crafts a perception of Ocasio-Cortez as young, hip, and media-savvy, and aligned with and alert to the interests of her followers.

## 4.2 "Don't hate me cause you ain't me, fellas": disalignment in the sub-corpus

This section examines a sub-corpus of forty most-liked tweets by Ocasio-Cortez to uncover the stance foci and stance dimensions therein, with emphasis on the alignment dimension.

*Stance foci.* The stance foci, which reveal the topics that most resonated with her followers, were twenty-three in all, as illustrated in Table 3. Donald Trump, the president and leader of the opposing party at the time of data collection, and his actions and plans were the most frequent stance focus, followed by the Republican Party (GOP). Together, the political opposition – including Republican Senator Ted Cruz, Trump advisor Brad Parscale, and pro-life legislators – amounted to just shy of half of the stance foci occasioned in the full subset of tweets. Five tweets referred to members of Congress, (the administration of) the United

States, and budgets (allocated by legislators), and two tweets targeted Ocasio-Cortez's critics in the media, including Fox News host Tucker Carlson. Other issues raised in the tweets included police brutality (2 occurrences), women's health issues (3 occurrences), race relations (2 occurrences), misogyny (2 occurrences), and working-class rights (3 occurrences). Another common thread was Ocasio-Cortez herself, which accounted for one eighth of tweets and was manifested in terms of her identity, her political platform and career, and her groundbreaking win.

**Table 3.** Stance foci in top forty @AOC tweets

| *Stance focus* | *Freq* | | *Stance focus* | *Freq* |
|---|---|---|---|---|
| Donald Trump | 10 | | Abortion bans | 1 |
| Trump advisor (Brad Parscale) | 1 | | Birth control | 1 |
| GOP | 5 | | Pro-life legislators | 1 |
| Senator Ted Cruz | 1 | | Communities enabling racism | 1 |
| Members of Congress | 3 | | Redskins | 1 |
| The US | 1 | | Critics (haters) | 1 |
| Budgets (money allocation) | 1 | | Tucker Carlson | 1 |
| Police Brutality | 2 | | Culture of misogyny | 1 |
| AOC's win | 2 | | Yoho incident | 1 |
| AOC | 1 | | Elite (wealthy) | 1 |
| AOC's platform | 1 | | Essential workers | 1 |
| AOC's political career | 1 | | | |

*Affect.* Given that the most frequent stance foci were Ocasio-Cortez's political opposition, it is unsurprising that the tweets under study were predominantly characterised by negative affect. For instance, most negative affect characterised the tweets in which Trump was the object of focus. Suggestive of this affective stance was the Representative's positioning of Trump as entitled ('A man whose entire life was built on a rich blend of daddy's money and financial fraud […]', 15-07-2020), evil ('He holds that Bible like it's burning him', 2-06-2020), unfit for office ('This President needs to be impeached', 21-06-2019), corrupt ('Si es Trump, tiene que ser corrupto 💸', 15-07-2020), and treasonous ('a criminal who betrays our country', 4-10-2019).

Only six tweets are characterised by positive affect and, with the exception of a single tweet about essential workers, they are all self-referential. One such tweet, represented below as tweet (1), connects Ocasio-Cortez's first primary race to her second, two years later:

(1) *When I won in 2018, many dismissed our victory as a "fluke."*
*Our win was treated as an aberration, or bc my opponent "didn't try."*
*So from the start, tonight's race was important to me.*
*Tonight we are proving that the people's movement in NY isn't an accident. It's a mandate.* (24-06-2020)

Although the affective stance towards her victory – alternatingly attributed to herself in the first person singular ('I', 'my', 'me') and the inclusive plural ('our', 'we') – is positive, this positive stance is fashioned in opposition to the derision of her critics, enacted by the use of quotation marks. Indeed, some sort of criticism is embedded even within tweets that show a positive effective stance, such that every single one of the most-favourited tweets analysed contains a covert or overt attack, with the latter far outnumbering the former.

*Investment.* As a whole, the tweets under study are characterised by high investment. Not only do the contents of the tweets suggest a high degree of commitment on the part of the author but there is also little linguistic evidence of hedging devices and uncertainty. In the two brief tweets that follow, the Congresswoman declares what "needs to" happen (tweet 2) and what "should not" exist (tweet 3):

(2) *This President needs to be impeached.* (21-06-2019)
(3) *The United States of America should not have secret police.* (20-07-2020)

Neither of these tweets contain linguistic devices to mitigate the force of the high-value modal elements, nor do they incorporate linguistic justification for Ocasio-Cortez's commitment to the truth of the proposition. Instead, Ocasio-Cortez's tweets are characterised by 'epistemically non-modal' categorical assertions, expressing the strongest possible degree of speaker commitment (Simpson 2005).

Two more tweets, represented below, display the high commitment of the Representative. While the two tweets refer to different scenarios – tweet (4) refers to the death of George Floyd at the hands of police officers while tweet (5) responds to Trump's threat to target Iranian cultural site – they both aim to condemn a crime and, in doing so, follow a similar argumentation structure. In response to a tweet by a CNN correspondent detailing Floyd's autopsy,[1]

1 The 29 May 2020 tweet written by CNN Correspondent Shimon Prokupecz (@ ShimonPro) read as follows: "Important from autopsy: The combined effect of George Floyd being restrained by the police, along with his underlying health conditions and any potential intoxicants in his system likely contributed to his death, according to the criminal complaint."

tweet (4) employs an explicitly expressed topos with the conditional 'if x, then y' ('If you killed a man w/ health conditions, you still killed a man'), followed by an account of what occurred to Floyd on the day of his death as evidence of the standpoint. Tweet (5) instead begins by framing Trump's plan as 'a war crime' following a 'y because x' structure (Reisigl and Wodak 2001), with the standpoint followed by reasoning to support the stance. The tweets both end with a negation – refuting any argument that mitigates or is in support of the antagonists' actions – followed by a final, grave and accusatory affirmation.

(4) *If you killed a man w/ health conditions, you still killed a man. George Floyd couldn't breathe. 3 officers held him down, & one w/ a recorded, violent history kneed his neck as others helped. They waited 9 minutes for his last breath. This was not an accident. It was murder.* (30-05-2020)

(5) *This is a war crime. Threatening to target and kill innocent families, women and children - which is what you're doing by targeting cultural sites - does not make you a "tough guy." It does not make you "strategic." It makes you a monster.* (05-01-2020)

The argumentation schemes employed by the Representative in these two tweets not only create a rational dispute but also communicate high investment. If, as Kiesling et al. (2018: 713) posit, high investment can be identified with the answer to the question "would [the speaker] defend their claims and opinions to the death?", then the structures of the tweets, careful definition of the crime, rebuff of alternative explanations, and final condemnation suggest that Ocasio-Cortez creates stances of high investment.

*(Dis)alignment.* This section analyses how Ocasio-Cortez aligns with her followers and recriminates opposition policies, politicians, and critics to unveil the strategies through which she constructs her persona and style. Over three-quarters (or thirty-one) of the tweets do not have a direct addressee and/or are addressed to a generic, wider audience. Yet, even in these cases the stance focus is the antagonist, and the Representative seems to rally her followers to support her mockery of opponents and recriminations of critics. The tweet that follows provides additional insights:

(6) *I hear the GOP thinks women dancing are scandalous.*
*Wait till they find out Congresswomen dance too!* 💃
*Have a great weekend everyone :)* (4-01-2019)

The pretext for tweet (6) is a video of Ocasio-Cortez dancing with her friends in 2010, while she was an undergraduate at Boston University, that was leaked and shared by the opposition in the attempt to smear the Representative. The text reproduced in (6), along with an 11-second clip, serves as a retort to this attempt. In the clip Ocasio-Cortez light-heartedly yet defiantly points at the camera, performs a light backwards shuffle and lip-syncs to a Motown hit, before bursting into laughter, and hurling herself into her Capitol Hill office. The subdued dance of a member of Congress in formal attire at the most formal setting of the nation, with a plaque of the Representative's name in plain sight, seems not only to suggest that there is nothing wrong with playful dancing, but it is also a sign of change. Indeed, on the one hand, the tweet and accompanying video, the most liked of the sub-corpus, reaffirms that "women dancing are scandalous" is preposterous. On the other, the tweet's youthful, accessible style and playful frame, enacted by the use of emoji and emoticon, the friendly parting phrase with the direct address "everyone", and, above all, by the video, establishes a polar relationship between Ocasio-Cortez and the GOP, where the former is hip and relatable, and the latter is puritan and obsolete.

The remaining tweets, roughly one quarter of the total, directly address one or more people. All of these cases represent censures. To analyse these instances further, we will take two examples into account. In tweet (7), Ocasio-Cortez reprimands the GOP for singling her out during the election of the Speaker of the House. The second phrase constitutes a riposte characterised by several linguistic and semiotic features worthy of exploration. First, it contains non-standard forms, mainly "cause", "ain't" and "fellas", which occur in non-formal youth talk and African American Vernacular English. "Fellas" underscores the primarily male constitution of the GOP and the woman tipping her hand emoji, commonly used to express sassiness or sarcasm, is modified by skin-tone, placing race as an explicit part of communication (Sweeney and Whaley 2019). Thus, Ocasio-Cortez disaligns with the GOP not only because she chastises their actions but because her identity is distinct from – and better than – their old, white maleness.

(7) *Over 200 members voted for Nancy Pelosi today, yet the GOP only booed one: me. Don't hate me cause you ain't me, fellas* 💁🏽‍♀️ (4-01-2019)

(8) *Sen. Cruz, while I understand you judge people's intelligence by the lowest income they've had, I hold awards from MIT Lincoln Lab &others for accomplishments in microbiology. Secondly, I'm surprised you're asking about chromosomes given that you don't even believe in evolution.* (28-02-2020)

In tweet (8), the Representative addresses Republican Senator Ted Cruz, and specifically his condescending response to her tweet criticizing the Trump administration's choice of head to the US coronavirus response effort: "As you are speaking as the oracle of science, tell us, what exactly is a Y chromosome?" (27-02-2020). Unlike Cruz's response, Ocasio-Cortez explicitly names the Senator, including his title, in her tweet. She cites her accomplishments to construct an authoritative stance and to discredit his sarcastic remark but does so after a dependent clause with an ad hominem attack that positions Cruz as a classist. Then, instead of replying to what could be perceived as a misogynist reference to the male sex chromosome, Ocasio-Cortez affirms that Cruz is an evolution denier as a recriminatory resource. In short, Ocasio-Cortez disaligns from Cruz based on her science-based experience and his science scepticism.

The final two tweets under study, of which the text is reproduced below, rely heavily on accompanying visuals.

(9) *Oh look, someone took a photo of what my life is like debating Republicans in committee each week* (14-06-2020)

(10) *Some folks are saying I won for "demographic" reasons.*
*1st of all, that's false. We won w/voters of all kinds.*
*2nd, here's my 1st pair of campaign shoes. I knocked doors until rainwater came through my soles.*
*Respect the hustle. We won bc we out-worked the competition. Period.* (29-06-2018)

Tweet (9) is the reply to a tweet posted by American activist Rashad Robinson, which, without additional comment, consisted of a comic by Will McPhail that pictures a female interview candidate who is sitting across from ten near-identical white, middle-aged, suit-wearing males whose posture and facial expressions communicate arrogance and dismissiveness above the caption: "Describe what you can bring to this company." In the text that Ocasio-Cortez includes in tweet (9), the Representative sets her experience with House Republicans as comparable to that of the woman in the comic and, by doing so, once again, she casts the GOP as constituted by white males only and Republicans as oblivious to both this lack of diversity and to the benefits that diversity affords.

Tweet (10), instead, takes aim at critics of Ocasio-Cortez's first primary win. In the text, she labels the "demographic" rationalization that these critics have advanced for her victory as "false" outright, citing having won with "voters of all kinds" as evidence. The only reason the candidate (and her team) won – emphasized by the explicitly stated "period" – is her hard work, which she had occasioned throughout her campaign. The tweet is accompanied by two images of the tops and bottoms of deeply worn shoes that reframe the statement "I knocked doors until rainwater came through my soles" from a hyperbole to an authentic account. By inviting readers to "respect the hustle" she asks that the role her work ethic and agency played in her win be acknowledged. With this retort, Ocasio-Cortez authenticates her candidacy and situates herself in the tradition of American success stories. Textually and visually, she appeals to the deeply entrenched theme of hard work and dedication at the heart of the all-American 'work ethic' trope and positions herself among archetypal, successful Americans who have pulled themselves up by their own bootstraps. The attached photographs – and, in particular, the hole-laden soles – support this even more persuasively. Democratic presidential nominee Adlai Stevenson's hole in the sole of his shoe was famously depicted in a 1952 Pulitzer-prize winning photograph and, more recently, Barack Obama's worn soles were the protagonists of a famed 2008 photograph by Callie Shell. This tweet therefore both verbally and visually reverberates the message that Ocasio-Cortez fits well within the historical tradition of American leaders.

The comparative keyword analysis of the full corpus of tweets posted by Ocasio-Cortez from 2018 to 2020 revealed use of language that accentuated her humble upbringing, tireless commitment, and self-made success, and these same themes emerged in the analysis of her attempts to create stances of alignment with her followers and disalignment with her opposition. In addition, evidence of the rapport-building style that transpired in the analysis of the full corpus was also present in the sub-corpus, most visibly in her astute use of emoji, emoticons, and visuals. However, it was her expressions of most negative affect with respect to her adversaries and her high investment, enacted by 'epistemically non-modal' categorical assertions (Simpson 2005: 45) and argumentation schemes, that cast Ocasio-Cortez's online discourse as committed, powerful, and genuine. Furthermore, her stances of disalignment with the political opposition and critics paved the way to forge her political identity in contrast with the out-of-touch, obsolete, and bigoted white, male GOP.

## 5 Stances of (Dis)Alignment, Legitimisation and Positioning in House Remarks

This section discusses the language Ocasio-Cortez uses in a very different context and for a very different audience, or the remarks she delivered before the US House of Representatives. In the interest of time, this analysis will home in on two aforedescribed instances. While in the previous section consistent imputations and/or recriminations transpired from the analysis of the sub-corpus of tweets, the instances discussed in this section were purposely selected because they featured this aim.

### 5.1 Subcommittee on Environment

The first instance analysed comes from Ocasio-Cortez's contribution to the Subcommittee on Oversight and Reform. In this April 2019 hearing, expert witnesses are heard on the matter of climate change and the Green New Deal emerged as a point of debate. Specifically, Republican Representative Clay Higgins from Louisiana delivered a statement in which he not only provided remarks displaying climate scepticism and xenophobic overtones, but he also declared: "I will not criticize my colleague from New York for her enthusiasm and her creativity regarding the Green New Deal". In so doing, Clay associates childlike attributes – or "enthusiasm" and "creativity" – to his "colleague from New York", or Ocasio-Cortez. In contrast with his affirmation that he will "not criticize" his colleague, whom he does not name, the belittling attributive terms he uses can be interpreted as ad hominem attacks since they subvert Ocasio-Cortez's credibility, expertise, and competence.

In response, Ocasio-Cortez does not reply to this critique as soon as she has the floor. She first asks a series of questions to the expert witnesses, thereby prioritizing climate change over her retort to criticism, which occurs in the last minute of her five minutes of allotted time, and follows:

1 You know, I would be remiss if I didn't talk or address some of the
2 comments made across the aisle, and while I am incredibly flattered
3 that the ranking member and many members across the aisle seem to
4 be so enamored with a non-binding resolution presented by a freshman
5 Congresswoman sworn in three months ago, I think that ironically,
6 despite that fixation, it doesn't seem that they've actually read the contents
7 of the proposed and presented resolution. And so I would just- I would
8 encourage that we do not need Cliff Notes for a 14-page resolution that
9 was designed to be read in plain English by the American people. So
10 I would encourage my colleagues to actually read the resolution presented
11 so that they can speak to it responsibly and respectfully.

In her retort, the start of her remark is littered with overstatements and hyperbolic expressions – we see "incredibly flattered" (line 2), "so enamored" (line 4) and even "fixation" (line 6) – which create a non-serious frame (Haugh 2010) and serve to mock her opposition. Moreover, by citing both the "non-binding" nature of the Green New Deal (line 4) and the brief duration of her tenure as a US Representative (line 5), she mitigates and even undermines her authority and her proposed policy again with the effect of mocking her opponents. Adding another layer of jocular mockery, she suggests that the politicians who constitute her opposition have not even read the resolution in spite of its brevity and simplicity. By citing "Cliff Notes" (line 8), which provide a dumbed-down version of literature, the brief length of the document ("14-page," line 8), its non-specialised language designed for a non-expert audience ("designed to be read in plain English by the American people", line 9), and suggesting that the politicians have not actually read the resolution they criticised ("to *actually* read the resolution", line 10, emphasis added), Ocasio-Cortez implies that her political opponents are slow-witted, indolent, and bigoted.

Yet, although Ocasio-Cortez indexes a strong disaffiliative stance, in contrast with the findings of the tweet analysis, when this retort is analysed in terms of epistemic positioning strategies, we see examples of subjective and impersonal evidential expressions – or "I think" and "It does not seem" (lines 5–6) – that index an attenuated degree of commitment, or investment. Furthermore, the repeated use of the modal "would" (lines 1, 7, 9), an effective stance marker that attenuates her volition, in the last part of her utterance again serves to mitigate, this time her critique of her opponents.

## 5.2 A Point of Personal Privilege

On 21 July 2020, the political website *The Hill* ran a story that gained substantial coverage for stating that a Republican US Representative from Florida, Ted Yoho, called Ocasio-Cortez a sexist slur at the Capitol building. It further reported that Ocasio-Cortez declared that nothing like this had "ever happened to" her and she "never had" this "kind of disrespect levied at" her (Lillis 2020). The next day, Yoho took to the House floor to deliver a response. In his speech, he referenced his wife and daughters as evidence that he did not use the alleged offensive language. Yoho did not apologise to Ocasio-Cortez nor did he call her by name. Instead, he declared "words attributed to me by the press were never spoken" and "I apologize for their misunderstanding".

The following day, Ocasio-Cortez used a point of personal privilege to address Yoho's remarks on the House floor. An excerpt of this widely covered speech follows:

> …In front of reporters Representative Yoho called me, and I quote, "a fucking bitch." These were the words that Representative Yoho levied against a congresswoman. The congresswoman that not only represents New York's 14th Congressional District, but every congresswoman and every woman in this country. Because all of us have had to deal with this in some form, some way, some shape, at some point in our lives. I want to be clear that Representative Yoho's comments were not deeply hurtful or piercing to me, because I have worked a working-class job. I have waited tables in restaurants. I have ridden the subway. I have walked the streets in New York City, and this kind of language is not new. I have encountered words uttered by Mr. Yoho and men uttering the same words as Mr. Yoho while I was being harassed in restaurants. I have tossed men out of bars that have used language like Mr. Yoho's and I have encountered this type of harassment riding the subway in New York City […] Not only have I been spoken to disrespectfully, particularly by members of the Republican Party and elected officials in the Republican Party, not just here, but the President of the United States last year told me to go home to another country, with the implication that I don't even belong in America.

In a radical departure from what she stated to *The Hill* reporter, in her address Ocasio-Cortez declares that Yoho's comments were neither "hurtful" nor "piercing" (line 8) because she had a working-class job and she had experienced this type of disrespect countless times before. A fundamental component of this argument is, as seen in line 5, "all of us have had to deal with this in some form", with which she aligns herself with every woman. Yet, her careful detailing of the extensive experience she has had with verbal abuse legitimises her stance, helps to position her as an authority on the matter, and therefore brings 'authorisation' (van Leeuwen 2007) to the speech. What's more, in the end of the excerpt, Ocasio-Cortez cites examples of verbal offenses levied by other members of her political opposition, which implicitly and explicitly occasioned her ethnicity.

Unlike her response in the Subcommittee on Oversight and Reform, in this prepared speech, there is high investment and total commitment towards the information provided. The narrative is constructed in terms of evidential constructions for the 'evidentiary justification' of her viewpoint (Marín-Arrese 2015) such as "I have worked" and "I have waited tables" (line 8), "I have ridden" and "I have walked" (line 9). These serve to solidify her reputation as a reliable source of information with privileged access to this experience, a stance that is reinforced with expressions of epistemic certainty such as zero-marked modality (Hart 2011, Marín-Arrese 2011). This speech therefore becomes an opportunity for Ocasio-Cortez to present herself as a passionate voice of the oppressed, whether it be on the basis of gender or race. She lays bare the onslaughts on her identity that she has endured not to present herself as a victim but rather to situate herself as a leading champion of the people.

## 6 Discussion and Conclusions

The analysis in this study has shown divergences but mainly convergences in the stancetaking and discursive strategies Ocasio-Cortez employed to impute stances of (dis)alignment based on her audience and the communicative platform she uses. Ocasio-Cortez's online presence has fuelled her popularity and, as also suggested by Figure 2 in which later tweets received more likes, there is evidence that she is becoming increasingly successful at using this platform. On Twitter, stances were constructed with her opponents through the use of an informal and relaxed style, enacted by the use of emojis, shortenings, and non-standard forms that served not only to show alignment with her Bronx- and Queens-based constituents but also to portray herself as someone who is a skilled and authentic code-switcher across diastratic and diaphasic varieties. Humour used alongside ad hominem attacks enacted mockery and/or recast the target of mockery and rekeyed the frame from serious to jocular. These linguistic devices position her as youthful, in-touch, and relatable. Boulomaic modality, expressing wishes and desires of speakers and recurrent in political discourse, is virtually absent from this sample of tweets. Instead, Ocasio-Cortez's tweets are characterised by 'epistemically non-modal' categorical assertions, expressing the strongest possible degree of speaker commitment (Simpson 2005: 45).

In the Subcommittee hearing, Ocasio-Cortez also used a non-serious frame in her disalignment from and mockery of her opponents, even at the risk of undermining her own authority. However, in her critique of her colleagues, she confuted her status as 'clapback queen' and used stance markers that attenuated her commitment and mitigated her antagonistic stance. Since this was the only response that was delivered before her adversaries neither only in written form (tweets) nor a prepared speech (house remarks), these findings suggest a weakening of her investment when faced with her opponents and/or when delivering impromptu remarks.

Finally, Ocasio-Cortez's House address featured a narrative of personal experience that she used as a legitimisation strategy to strengthen her position of expertise and authority to speak on behalf of all women and those without white male privilege. Her personal narrative resonated with her identity references that she used in different contexts, even on Twitter. That address, however, was the only instance in which she applied a serious frame. This, alongside expressions of epistemic certainty, are used by Ocasio-Cortez to situate herself in the long line of political activists and leaders in the American tradition.

Admittedly, the choice to analyse multiple instances likely jeopardised the depth of analysis and this is a limitation of the present study. This notwithstanding, more than one context and audience allows us to see how versatile the expression of stances can be. Even within one individual who has become so strongly associated with combative responses – i.e., 'clapback queen' – we see evidence of mitigation and attenuation in more formal contexts. These different contexts suggest that Ocasio-Cortez is nimble at responding to, and as the argumentative nature of the top-liked tweets suggest, this may be the root of her popularity.

In sum, as a social media-savvy millennial woman of colour who was suddenly catapulted into the political scene, the discursive realisation of Ocasio-Cortez's political persona has been unexpected in terms of its divergence from traditional approaches. Ocasio-Cortez evolved from political unknown to legitimate threat to the political status quo of the US. She engaged in stancetaking moves that both highlight her alignment with her constituents/followers and that construct disalignment with her opposition to maintain authenticity and legitimacy, to safeguard the coherence of her personal narrative and political self, and to present herself not as a freshman politician but within a larger American national and historical storyline. Her high investment, playful frames, and rapport-building style have not only powered her popularity and exposure but have also served to solidify, reinforce, and embellish the political persona that she sketched – in opposition to the out-of-touch, bigoted white male GOP – as an authentic Bronx-born member of the working class and paladin for the people.

## References

Bucholtz, M. (2009). 'From Stance to Style: Gender, Interaction, and Indexicality in Mexican Immigrant Youth Slang'. In A. Jaffe (ed.), *Stance: Sociolinguistic Perspectives,* pp. 146–170. Oxford: Oxford University Press.

Du Bois, J.W. (2007). 'The stance triangle'. In R. Englebretson (ed.), *Stancetaking in discourse: subjectivity, evaluation, interaction,* pp. 139–182. Amsterdam/ Philadelphia: John Benjamins.

Goffman, E. (1981). *Forms of Talk*. Philadelphia: University of Pennsylvania Press.

Hagle, C. (2019). 'Six Weeks of Fox's Alexandria Ocasio-Cortez Obsession', *Media Matters for America*, <https://www.mediamatters.org/fox-news/six-weeks-foxs-alexandria-ocasio-cortez-obsession-totalitarian-ignorant-scary-and-waging>, accessed 25 February 2021.

Hart, C. (2011). 'Legitimising Assertions and the Logico-Rhetorical Module: Evidence and Epistemic Vigilance in Media Discourse on Immigration'. *Discourse Studies,* 13 (6), 751–769.

Haugh, M. (2010). 'Jocular mockery, (dis)affiliation, and face'. *Journal of Pragmatics,* 42, 2106–2119.

Johnstone, B. (2009). 'Stance, Style, and the Linguistic Individual'. In A. Jaffe (ed.), *Stance: Sociolinguistic Perspectives*, pp. 29–52. Oxford: Oxford University Press.

Kiesling, S. (2011). 'Stance in context: Affect, alignment and investment in the analysis of stancetaking'. Paper presented at *iMean conference*, 15 April 2011, The University of the West of England, Bristol, UK.

Kiesling, S.F., et al. (2018). 'Interactional Stancetaking in Online Forums'. *Computational Linguistics*, 44 (4), 683–718.

Lillis, M. (2020). 'Ocasio-Cortez accosted by GOP lawmaker over remarks', *The Hill*, <https://thehill.com/homenews/house/508259-ocaasio-cortez-accosted-by-gop-lawmaker-over-remarks-that-kind-of>, accessed 19 February 2021.

Marín-Arrese, J.I. (2015). 'Epistemicity and stance: A cross-linguistic study of epistemic stance strategies in journalistic discourse in English and Spanish'. *Discourse Studies,* 17 (2), 210–225.

Marín-Arrese, J.I. (2011). 'Epistemic legitimizing strategies, commitment and accountability in discourse'. *Discourse Studies,* 13 (6), 789–797.

Meier, Florian, et al. (2014). 'More than liking and bookmarking? Towards understanding Twitter favouriting behaviour', *Eighth International AAAI Conference on Weblogs and Social Media.*

Reisigl, M., and Wodak, R. (2001). *Discourse and Discrimination: Rhetorics of Racism and Antisemitism*. London: Routledge.

Simpson, P. (2005). *Language, Ideology, and Point of View*. London-New York: Routledge.

Sweeney, M.E., and Whaley, K. (2019). 'Technically white: Emoji skin-tone modifiers as American technoculture'. *First Monday*, 24 (7), n.p.

Ushchyna, V. (2014). 'Stancetaking in the discourse on risk identities construed'. In M. Thormählen and C. Paradis (eds.), *Subjectivity and Epistemicity: Corpus, discourse, and literary approaches to stance,* pp. 215–238. Lund: Lund University Press.

Valentinsson, M-C. (2018). 'Stance and the construction of authentic celebrity persona'. *Language in Society*, 47, 715–740.

van Leeuwen, T. (2007). 'Legitimation in Discourse and Communication'. *Discourse & Communication*, 1 (1), 91–112.

Wang, P.-H. (2020). 'Stance, framing, and the construction of reality in Facebook comments about Taiwan's same-sex marriage bills'. *Discourse & Society*, 31 (2), 218–234.

Wrubel, L. and Kerchner, D. (2020). '116th U.S. Congress Tweet Ids'. *Harvard Dataverse*, V1.

Boitshwarelo Rantsudu

# Setting the Scene for Other Voices: Strategic Stance-Taking and the Construal of Objectivity in Hard News Reporting

**Abstract:** This chapter explores mechanisms by which journalists embed indirect evaluative standpoints within news headlines and lead sentences to signal an endorsement of, or alignment with evaluations that are introduced into the news stories through attribution. The appearance of evaluative language in hard news reporting has been widely investigated and several studies have documented that within the context of hard news reports, explicit evaluative language is largely confined to words that are attributed to external news sources. White (2000) and Thomson, White and Kitley (2008) point out that the attribution of explicit evaluative news content to external news sources is one way through which journalists assert the objectivity of their reports. Using insights from Appraisal Theory and Critical Discourse Analysis (CDA) to examine news stories from *Daily News* (a state-owned newspaper), and *Mmegi* (a privately-owned newspaper), I show that attribution of evaluations to external news sources is a complex resource, and that journalists succeed in strategically embedding their subjective opinions within an 'objective' hard news report, and in turn advancing the evaluative standpoint of the news sources that they quote (Höglund 2008). Evidently, journalists downplay their evaluative stances and, endorse and align with evaluations that they attribute to external news sources while constructing seemingly objective news reports.

**Keywords:** *stance-taking, evaluation, attribution, hard news reporting, objectivity, subjectivity, Appraisal theory, Critical Discourse Analysis.*

## 1 Introduction

The aim of this chapter is to examine mechanisms by which journalists succeed at setting up indirect evaluations in news headlines and lead sentences in order to strategically advance or distance themselves from evaluative positions that are expressed by external news sources who are quoted in the news reports. This is carried out by examining news reports from *Mmegi* (a privately-owned newspaper), and *Daily News* (a government-owned newspaper). The news texts that are analysed in this chapter are taken from reports of the 2011 nationwide public sector workers' strike in Botswana. The overarching point I make in this chapter is that through mechanisms by which positive or negative viewpoints are indirectly expressed in news openings, news reporters set up a subtle evaluative angle that is later taken up or disputed by external news sources. The strategic use of headlines and lead sentences, combined with the use of attribution, affords new reporters success at taking an evaluative stance, and projecting an adherence to the ideals of objectivity in hard news reporting. As a starting point, let us consider the following excerpt from *Daily News.*

Excerpt 1

(1) a. *Tlokweng Border Gate handles high traffic volume*
  b. *Holidays have always been synonymous with travelling, whether it is within the country or to other parts of the world…*
  c. *Because of the on-going public sector strike, there were fears that some peoples' travel might be affected…*
  d. *He [Mr Abueng] disputed insinuations that civil servants from other departments had been deployed to the border posts to relief the situation. Mr Abueng stated that all of his colleagues were on duty*
  (*Daily News*, 26 April 2011).

In Excerpt 1, the authorial voice begins the news report with a positive view of services that were provided at Tlokweng Border Gate. At the time of this news report, the public sector workers' strike had been going on for nine days and the news report gives an assessment of how the provision of services fared during Easter holidays. There is a noticeable use of intensification in the news headline as the authorial voice describes the level of busyness at the border gate via the phrase *high traffic volume.* By stating that *there were fears that some people's travel might be affected* because of the ongoing strike (line c), the news reporter hints at retrospective *fears* which, by implication, did not materialise. While no explicit evaluative viewpoints are expressed from lines (a) to (c), and the news reporter successfully refrains from direct positive/negative evaluation of events, the news excerpt generally presents a value-laden opinion about the provision of services and the workers' strike. It can thus be suggested that the authorial voice conveys indirect positive evaluation of services at the border gate on the one hand, and a negative evaluation of the strike on the other. These indirect evaluations are all achieved via implication. When an external news source is introduced into the news report in line (d), the words attributed to him are set off with the reporting verb *disputed.* Arguably, this reporting verb underlines questionable views that were/are held by some unnamed parties. Interestingly, the reporting verb *disputed* and the noun *insinuations* seem to provide an evaluative space for an implied 'agreement' or association between the views of the authorial voice and those of the external news source. Overall, the implied association between the authorial voice and the external news source also opens an evaluative space for a negative indirect evaluative stance towards the unnamed parties who had held 'questionable' views about the effect of the strike on the provision of services at the border gate. Such and other similar examples, in which authorial stance-taking is subtly set up and an uptake of the evaluation by external news sources is constructed, are the focus of the present chapter. In order to explore the mechanisms of authorial stance-taking and construal of objectivity in *Mmegi* and *Daily News*, I argue for a consideration of indirectness and attribution as strategies for mitigation of evaluation in hard news reporting.

A key aspect of indirect evaluation is the exclusion and strategic avoidance of direct positive/negative attitude in texts (Martin 2003; White 2006; Coffin and O'Halloran 2006). In instances of indirect evaluation, the expression of positive/negative attitude is achieved via invocations or tokens of evaluation (Martin and White 2005). Such tokens include invocations via experiential information, implication, association, intensification, comparison, metaphor and counter-expectation (Martin and White 2005; Martin and Rose 2007, White 2009). Martin (2003: 173) highlights that evaluation can often be implied even in instances that do not readily lend themselves to attitudinal locutions. In Martin's view, an extended focus on direct realisations of evaluation can lead to a great deal of implied evaluations being missed out. It is therefore important to cast our gaze beyond direct realisations of evaluation if we are to gain a broader understanding of the complexity of evaluation in texts, especially in hard news reporting, the type of texts that I deal with in this chapter. In addition to exploring indirect evaluation, another feature of focus in this chapter is attribution. While the existing body of research indicates a strong and consistent association between the use of attribution and journalists' assertion of objectivity (White 2000; Thomson, White and Kitley 2008), investigation of attribution as an avenue for the reporters' stance (Höglund 2008; Jullian 2011; Rantsudu 2019) has grown in importance in light of recent studies. This chapter therefore addresses the question of journalists' pre-setting of indirect evaluation in the news openings, and a construction of external news sources' uptake of such indirect evaluation. As it will be argued in a later section, the pre-setting of indirect evaluations and the uptake of such evaluations by external news sources is indicative of dynamic interaction of the authorial voice and the voice of external news sources. An investigation of the dynamic interaction of voices is crucial to our understanding of strategic stance-taking via indirect evaluation, and simultaneous construal of objectivity in hard news reporting. In light of the potential complex nature of indirect evaluation, and the dynamic use of attribution to maintain a claim to objectivity, the question dealt with in this chapter is:

- How can evaluation and objectivity be reconciled in hard news reporting, and what strategies do news reporters employ in order to succeed at expressing positive/negative evaluations while maintaining the objectivity ideal?

In order to address this question, I propose that indirectness and attribution should be viewed as strategies for mitigation of evaluation. The next section therefore, provides an overview of the concept of mitigation, and then briefly discusses the mitigating characteristics of indirectness and attribution in hard news reporting.

## 2 Indirectness and Attribution as Strategies for Mitigating Evaluation

As a concept, mitigation has largely been studied from the perspective of Pragmatics with a focus on its association with the notion of *face* in spoken interactions (Rantsudu 2018). Mitigation is said to be concerned with the reduction and avoidance of certain 'unwelcome' effects which a speech act may have on an addressee (Fraser 1980), or the softening of face threatening speech acts during spoken interactions (Brown and Levinson 1987). While a Pragmatic perspective provides a useful starting point for explaining mitigation, it is necessary to adopt a broader perspective into which written texts can be included. In light of this, I argue for an expanded view that treats mitigation as a "superordinate organising concept" (Caffi 1999) under which we can group a number of strategies by which we can account for the interplay between evaluation and objectivity in hard news reporting. Supporting this view, Thaler (2012: 909) argues that the avoidance of unwelcome or negative effects on addressees, as upheld in the Pragmatic tradition, is not sufficient for explaining the concept of mitigation. A broader perspective of mitigation can therefore move us beyond what speakers and writers avoid, to what speakers or writers do in order to mitigate evaluations as they strive to achieve and construe objectivity. According to Fraser, two techniques that a speaker can use to gain some relief and mitigate the effects of what is being said are, indirect speech acts and the creation of *distance* (1980: 344–347). The creation of distance is a strategy that positions the speaker as an individual who functions as "a mere instrument for others who are in authority" (Fraser 1980: 347). An important question that arises here is how notions of *indirectness* and *distance* can be extended beyond speech acts in order to examine their mitigating characteristics in hard news reporting. As a result of continued claims to objectivity in hard news reporting, tokens of evaluation, particularly as used by news reporters, are preferred over direct evaluations. In that case, news reporters cannot be easily accused of bias or partiality (Coffin and O'Halloran 2006). For the discussion of how the creation of *distance* can be a technique of mitigation, Lauerbach (2006) provides a comprehensive account of *distance* by referring to the technique of 'voicing'. Lauerbach (2006: 198) states that the representation of the discourse of others is a useful device that speakers or writers use to distance themselves from the content of what is being expressed. In news media discourse, journalists are able to embed other sources' critical and controversial statements into their reporting in order to create distance from blame allocation and dispute. The distancing strategy of voicing therefore has been shown to absolve news reporters from the responsibility of evaluative statements that are expressed by third parties, particularly in instances where such evaluative statements are contentious. When we consider that expressions of evaluative opinions and adherence to the professional code of objectivity in hard news reporting cannot be viewed as mutually exclusive, it becomes important to explore mechanisms by which the relational tension between objectivity and evaluative stance can be accounted for. On the basis of the foregoing discussion, it can be argued that through various mechanisms of indirectness, and the quotation of external news sources, news writers are able to "get off the hook" (Fraser 1980: 345) and gain relief from the effects of evaluative or subjective opinions.

If we now return to the aim of the present chapter as outlined in the introduction, the question of authorial expressions of indirect evaluation, and the use of attribution demonstrate a multi-layered use of mitigation in hard news reporting. Even more importantly, the authorial setting up of indirect evaluations in news openings, and the construction of an uptake of such indirect evaluations by external news sources, opens the space for the "co-construction" of hard news discourse (Piazza 2009). As was highlighted earlier, my concern in this chapter is with instances where indirect evaluations that are set up in the news openings affords news reporters strategies to advance or distance themselves from evaluative positions that are expressed by external news sources who are quoted in the news reports. In the section that follows, I present two news reports, Text 1 and Text 2, from *Mmegi* and *Daily News* respectively. I also provide a brief account of the analytical approach that I take in this chapter. As previously mentioned, Text 1 and Text 2 are taken from a data set of reports covering the 2011 nationwide public sector workers' strike in Botswana. As part of the strike news data set, the two news reports give an update of the state of service delivery at different border posts in the country during the first week of the strike. The update on the state of service delivery, as reported in the two texts, is placed within the context of the ongoing workers' strike.

# 3 Data and Analytical Approach

## 3.1 The News Reports

Text 1 (Mmegi, 19 April 2011)

(1) *Borders open as workers ignore strike*
(2) *It was business as usual at Tlokweng border post yesterday as the Mmegi team found immigration officers busy stamping passports and ushering in people from South Africa.*
(3) *"We are working, there are no problems here. My officers are working two shifts, in the morning and another in the afternoon, so as you can see they are all here. I don't know what will happen in the next shift," said Donald Abueng, officer-in-charge at the border post.*
(4) *When asked why his officers are not on strike he said he did not know, because: "I can't interview them and ask them why they are not striking as that will be tantamount to harassment and intimidation on my part".*
(5) *"I have realised that people who work tough jobs like immigration officers are passionate about their work and would not want to stay away."*
(6) *He said he was however, keeping watch to see if there are any changes.*
(7) *One of the immigration officers, speaking on condition of anonymity, told Mmegi that he would not go on strike.*
(8) *"I know that my job is about helping people, I know I need to help them and that is it," he told this reporter.*
(9) *In the afternoon when Mmegi called his office, Abueng reiterated that the second shift had started without fanfare. "Everybody reported to work", he said.*
(10) *Contacted for comment, BOFEPUSU spokesman said a quick review of the strike nationwide has revealed that most government workers have responded well to "our call". "They stayed away".*
(11) *"However at the Tlokweng border, and Labour and Home Affairs Headquarters, it would seem they heeded the employer's call not to strike".*

Text 2 (Daily News, 21 April 2011)

(1) *Border posts report normal operations*
(2) *GABORONE: Tlokweng Border Gate, one of the busiest in the country linking Botswana with South Africa, is 100 per cent operational despite the ongoing public servants' strike.*
(3) *Tlokweng border is one of the four border posts which were expected to be badly affected by the strike.*

(4) *Chief immigration officer in charge of the border post, Mr Donald Abueng said the strike had never affected operations since its commencement on Monday.*
(5) *"There is no change in our work, we work in two shifts and all the employees reported for duty on time in the past two days".*
(6) *Mr Abueng said the movement of people in and out of Botswana had been steadily increasing with further increases expected over the coming Easter weekend.*
(7) *Still at the border gate, a Botswana Unified Revenue Service official, Mr Onkemetse Plaatje, said they had been experiencing an unusual movement of people especially those leaving the country.*
(8) *"It appears like it is a holiday, they kept on asking us if we will be on duty during the period of the strike".*
(9) *The Ramatlabama Border Gate Principal Immigration Officer, Mrs Idah Chalegwa also reported a business as usual working environment despite a few of her employees having opted for the strike action.*
(10) *Mrs Chalengwa said even though the rate of movement at the border gate was starting to increase, she had a good number of officers who could be equal to the task even during busy periods such as the Easter holidays.*
(11) *She stated that the five employees who joined the strike did not change anything in their daily operations.*
(12) *Martins Drift Border Gate Principal Immigration Officer, Ms Ontitile Maromoloa said the strike had not affected their daily operations and that everything was normal.*
(13) *She said they were receiving numerous phone calls from foreign tourists who wanted to know about the effect of the strike and whether the employees of the immigration department were also on strike.*
(14) *"The response is that everything is normal", she said.*

## 3.2 Analytical Approach

As can be noticed from the presentation of the news reports, the prominence of external news sources is evident in *Mmegi* and *Daily News*. For the purpose of analysis of the two news reports, news headlines and lead sentences are examined first to determine the types of evaluative tokens that the authorial voice uses to signal expressions of indirect evaluation. At the heart of the discussions on news headlines and lead sentences are the distinctive structural components that serve to launch the reader into the newsworthy details of the subject matter being covered (White and Thomson 2008; Thomson, White and Kitley 2008: 214).

In light of these views I examine news headlines and lead sentences in *Mmegi* and *Daily News* in order to determine their role in indicating subtle judgements about the events being covered. To better understand how indirect evaluation plays out in the headlines and lead sentences, I focus on how two attitudinal targets, that is, the workers' strike and service delivery, are talked about in terms of positive and negative evaluation. In terms of attributed news content, I examine the news reports for signals of the external news sources' uptake of the indirect evaluations that are established in the headlines and lead sentences. I also explore how authorial articulations in the headlines and lead sentences shed light into the news reporters' indirect affinity or distance from the external news sources evaluative positioning.

## 4 Findings and Discussion

In this section I present and discuss findings from an analysis of the two news reports from *Mmegi* and *Daily News*. As mentioned in the preceding section, the news reports, Text 1 (*Mmegi*) and Text 2 (*Daily News*), cover the state of service delivery at different border gates in the country. This section is subdivided into two main parts. Part 1 is concerned with mechanisms by which indirect evaluations are set up by the authorial voice in the news openings. In Part 2, I examine news content that is attributed to external news sources and how the external news sources are framed to take up or dispute the indirect evaluations that are expressed in the news openings.

### 4.1 Part 1: Indirect Evaluations in the News Openings

What follows is an examination of news openings from *Mmegi* and *Daily News* reports in order to determine how the two newspapers set up indirect evaluations in the headlines and lead sentences.

Text 1 *(Mmegi, 19 April 2011)*

(1) *Borders open as workers ignore strike*

(2) *It was business as usual at Tlokweng border post yesterday as the Mmegi team found immigration officers busy stamping passports and ushering in people from South Africa.*

The news headline in Text 1 is somewhat surprising. What is striking about the news headline is that it is constructed as a connotative statement that expresses information that immigration officers, who form part of the wider public service sector, have intentionally disregarded participation in the nationwide public sector workers' strike. While the news headline does not use any explicit words to convey either positive or negative evaluation, it sets a binary evaluative tone that targets service delivery on the one hand, and non-effectiveness of the strike on the other. The news headline conveys two noticeable themes: that *borders are open*, and that *workers have chosen to ignore the strike*. The two themes are conjoined by the conjunction *as*, a conjunction that indicates simultaneous occurrences of an ongoing nationwide strike, and the fully functional state of borders. Through the headline, the public sector workers' strike is portrayed as an event that has no effect on the delivery of services at the borders. The authorial voice constructs the headline in a way that relies on experiential details to achieve an evaluative effect that establishes an implied positive evaluation of service delivery, and an implied negative evaluation of the strike. This finding is consistent with observations made by White (2006: 45), which showed that news content of an apparent informational or experiential nature has the potential to trigger positive and negative attitudinal assessments. When we consider that the strike is organised and led by the workers' unions, it is surprising that the authorial voice sets the tone of the news story to emphasise a generalised message about public sector workers deriding the strike. In addition to reliance on experiential information as a token of evaluation, the authorial voice also invokes evaluation by problematizing the two thematic events of an on-going nationwide strike and the seemingly unexpected functional state of service delivery at Tlokweng border gate, thus constructing a subtle counter-expectation.

Moving on now to consider the lead sentence in line (2), we notice that the authorial voice reinforces the counter-expectation that is flagged in the news headline. Notice that this is achieved via a strategic use of synonymy and interdependence of meaning in which the description of services as constituting the opening of borders is given more evaluative weight through the idiomatic expression *business as usual*. Another interesting aspect in line (2) is the use of a categorical statement that is qualified with what can be referred to as an evidential expression. The verb *find*, which of course is used in line (2) in its past tense form, stands out in the evidential statement as it seems to convey an act of coming across something or an event that is unusual or unexpected. This evidential statement establishes an overall sentiment of counter-expectation in the news opening. It can be argued that as the authorial voice problematises the concurrent events, of the ongoing strike and a positive assessment of service delivery, a disguised question directed to external news sources to either confirm or deny that workers have ignored the strike, can be inferred from the news opening. This is a point that I will return to in Part 2. In the rest of this discussion, I turn to the news opening in *Daily News* to examine how indirect evaluation plays out in its headline and lead sentences. Before proceeding to examine the news opening in Text 2, it is necessary to provide a general context to the news report, and for that, let us consider Excerpt 2 below. Excerpt 2 is taken from one of the news reports that were run on the day the public sector workers' strike commenced. In the news report, *Daily News* had covered a parliamentary question time session during which the responsible cabinet minister was asked by opposition party MPs to outline to parliament measures that the government had put in place to deal with possible disruptions to the provision of services in government departments.

Excerpt 2

(2) a. *On the issue of maintaining essential services and ensuring service delivery Mr Masisi said that was part and parcel of what was negotiated in the rules of the strike.*

b. *He also assured MPs that government would ensure that there was minimal disruption in service delivery and appealed to them to remain calm and reassure their constituents of such…* (*Daily News*, 18 April 2011)

In (a), the authorial voice uses a preface that suggests that maintaining essential services is a highly probable occurrence. This highlights an indirect positive attitude towards service delivery that is conveyed via the pre-quotation segment *maintaining essential services and ensuring service delivery.* These expressions are immediately followed by the words attributed to the cabinet minister, who expresses an implied obligation on the part of the government and the workers' unions to provide services during the strike. The news excerpt indicates some evaluative focus on positive evaluation of service delivery as a target, and the simultaneous reference to the role of the government and public sector workers in maintaining the provision of services during the strike. Interestingly, a pattern of intersecting positive evaluations recurs in line (b) in which self-imposed high obligation on the part of the government can be noticed. This is followed by an indirect expression of a positively anticipated provision of service delivery that is also expressed as a highly probable occurrence. Such high probability is expressed with an emphatic tone of certainty that is marked by the verb *ensure.* As an important target during the strike, service delivery featured in some contentious and tense political debates during the parliamentary session in question. With this brief context, let us now turn to the news opening in Text 2.

Text 2 *(Daily News, 21 April 2011)*

(1) *Border posts report normal operations*

(2) *GABORONE: Tlokweng Border Gate, one of the busiest in the country linking Botswana with South Africa, is 100 per cent operational despite the ongoing public servants strike.*

(3) *Tlokweng border is one of the four border posts which were expected to be badly affected by the strike.*

The news report from *Daily News* opens with a headline that draws attention to the normality of operations at border posts. Notice that responsibility for the information about the normality of operations is ascribed to *border posts*, a categorisation that can be assumed to refer to some credible or official sources. In the context of an ongoing nationwide strike, the description of service delivery as conforming to a *normal* standard can be viewed as a subtle negation of the effectiveness of the strike. In light of potentially contentious information about the positive state of service delivery at the border posts, the authorial voice can be observed to take a strategic distance and a seeming cautionary position towards the information. With respect to lines (2) and (3), we notice an intriguing move from the cautionary positioning that was depicted in the headline as the authorial voice makes a series of categorical statements and describes Tlokweng Border Gate as *one of the busiest in the country*. The adjective *busiest* is quite revealing in two ways. First, it suggests a constant excessive amount of work at the border gate, and secondly, on account of disruptions that were anticipated because of the workers' strike, the adjective intensifies an indirect positive attitude that is directed towards service delivery. Interestingly, intensification of an indirect positive evaluation of service delivery is amplified via the adjective phrase *100 per cent operational*. This is an expression that is synonymous with *normal operations* in the headline. Here the authorial voice is not only setting up an evaluative angle, but there is an implied daring evaluative position that is communicated in line (2). This daring position on the part of the authorial voice opens the space for the expression of counter-expectation that is indicated via the adversative preposition *despite*. Overall, through the realisation of counter-expectation, an indirect positive evaluation of service delivery and a parallel negative evaluation of the strike are maintained. In the case of line (3), the authorial voice makes reference to retrospective anticipation of disruption to services. By stating that *Tlokweng border is one of the four border posts which were expected to be badly affected by the strike*, the authorial voice flags another instance of counter-expectation. The adverb *badly* suggests the magnitude of disruption that would have been expected to affect the provision of services at the borders.

The analysis of news headlines and lead sentences in *Mmegi* and *Daily News* has so far shown that tokens of experiential information, the use of intensification and indications of counter-expectation are the dominant mechanisms by which the newspapers set up indirect evaluations in their news openings. These indirect evaluations are directed towards service delivery at border posts, and the public sector workers' strike. As we proceed to Part 2 below, I focus on the use of attribution and the framing of external news sources' uptake of indirect evaluations that are set up in the news openings. In the discussion that follows, it will be argued that the strategies that the news reporters assume in order to advance or distance themselves from the evaluative positions taken by external news sources depend on the framing of the news sources' uptake of the indirect evaluations established in the news openings.

## 4.2 Part 2: Indirect Evaluation and Attribution

### *4.2.1 Indirect Evaluation and Attribution in Mmegi*

In Part 1, I argued that the news headline in *Mmegi* carries a strikingly surprising evaluative tone that depicts an intentional disregard for the strike by public sector workers. I also made an observation that the state of affairs depicted about the ongoing strike and the fully functional state of service delivery at Tlokweng border gate is problematised in the news opening. As the state of affairs was problematised, indirect evaluations were set up to evaluate service delivery positively while the strike was evaluated negatively. Let us now examine how the indirect evaluations that are set up by the authorial voice in the news opening are taken up or disputed by the external news sources who are quoted in the news report. As could be noticed in the presentation of Text 1 above, there are three external news sources who are quoted in the news report. However, in the discussion that follows, I will refer to words attributed to only two of the news sources to illustrate the arguments I make in this section. These are, the Officer-in-Charge at Tlokweng border gate, and the workers unions' representative (referred to as[1] BOFEPUSU spokesperson in line 10).

The Officer-in-Charge at Tlokweng border gate begins with the emphatic statement *we are working, there are no problems here* in line (3). This is not only a conveyance of a positive attitude towards service delivery, but it can also be viewed as an expression of commitment to duty. By implication, the Officer-in-Charge underlines the immigration officers' decision to abstain from participation in the ongoing strike. The rest of line (3) shows an interesting change of perspective when the Officer-in-Charge expresses uncertainty about how service delivery will fare in the afternoon shift. This is an evaluative sentiment that is carried forth into line (6) in which the Officer-in-Charge seems to anticipate that immigration

1 Botswana Federation of Public Sector Unions

officers are likely to stay away and not report for work. While earlier in line (5) the Officer-in-Charge projects a positive image about immigration officers and the opinion that *they are passionate about their work and would not want to stay away*, the repetition of expressions of uncertainty dominates the evaluative angle that is assumed by the Officer-in-Charge. Arguably, the authorial voice subtly frames the response given by the Officer-in-Charge as an instance of apparent self-contradiction. Notice also that line (4) sustains denotations of uncertainty or 'lack of knowledge' on the part of the Officer-in-Charge. The expression of uncertainty is however, paired with an ironic statement in which the Officer-in-Charge is quoted to have said, *I can't interview them and ask them why they are not striking as that will be tantamount to harassment and intimidation on my part*. The ways by which the responses from the Officer-in-Charge are framed are suggestive of distancing strategies that are assumed by the authorial voice. By framing the Officer-in-Charge as expressing self-contradictions, uncertainty and resorting to ironic statements, the authorial voice implicitly invokes distance and strategically problematises the evaluative position that is taken by the Officer-in-Charge in regard to service delivery and the ongoing strike.

Having discussed the distancing strategies that the authorial voice assumes as the Officer-in-Charge is quoted in the news report, it is now necessary to examine the uptake of indirect evaluation as articulated by the second external news source, that is, the representative of the workers' unions. For this purpose, I will focus on lines (10) and (11).

In line (10) the authorial voice uses the phrase *contacted for comment* to preface the words that are attributed to the representative of the workers' unions. Through this preface, the authorial voice seems to anticipate a different uptake of evaluation from the union representative, thus setting the scene for a viewpoint that contrasts the one expressed by the Officer-in-Charge and disputing the implied message that public sector workers have derided their own strike. The union representative accords an indirect positive evaluation to the strike. This is achieved via the adverb *most*, a non-cardinal description that signifies an intensification of the magnitude of the workers' turn out and participation in the strike. Line (11) is an interesting uptake of the indirect evaluation that was set up in the news opening. It is reproduced below for ease of reference.

(11) *"However at the Tlokweng border and labour and home affairs headquarters, it would seem they heeded the employer's call not to strike"*.

In line (10) we noticed that the union representative presented a positive assessment of public sector workers' participation in the strike. The evaluative sentiment in line (11) is different because the union representative does not use a categorical denouement of the events surrounding service delivery and the strike. Instead, he uses the adversative adverb *however* and the adverbial clause *it would seem* in order to hedge his response.

Before concluding this discussion of indirect evaluation and attribution in *Mmegi*, it is necessary to return to a suggestion I made earlier. I made a case for interpreting the news headline in Text 1 as a disguised question that sought to ask external news sources to either confirm or deny that workers have ignored the strike. I pointed out that the surprising tone that is embedded into the headline is crucial to the creation of an evaluative space and a frame in which external news sources can express their uptake of the indirect evaluations in the news opening. I also suggested that the authorial voice uses the news headline to problematise the events surrounding the on-going workers' strike and the functional state of service provision at Tlokweng border gate. As I argued in the foregoing discussion, problematizing the events afforded the authorial voice strategies to put the external news sources on spot without using explicit forms of evaluation.

### *4.2.2 Indirect Evaluation and Attribution in Daily News*

The uptake of indirect evaluation by external news sources in Text 2 generally displays a successive pattern. Immigration officials from different border gates are quoted in the news report to follow one another as they evaluate the state of service delivery and the strike. The successive pattern of evaluations enables immigration officials to present a collective voice by which they amplify a positive evaluation of service delivery and a negative evaluation of the strike. This represents a stark contrast between the evaluation of service delivery and the strike throughout the news report. In lines (4) and (5) the Chief Immigration Officer (referred to as 'Officer-in-Charge' in *Mmegi*) is quoted to have stated that the strike *had never affected operations* and that *there is no change* in their work. These represent striking categorical pronouncements about service delivery and the workers' strike. While the words that are attributed to the Chief Immigration Officer take the form of experiential information, the adverb *never* and the phrase *there is no change* flag the full operational status of borders and the non-effectiveness of the strike on the provision of services. These evaluative sentiments are marked by intensification. As other external news sources are introduced into the news report they maintain an evaluative disposition that places emphasis on an indirect positive evaluation of service delivery and a negative evaluation of the strike and the public sector workers who have opted to participate in the strike. Lines (9)–(14) capture this evaluative disposition.

The words attributed to all the Principal Immigration Officers are marked with descriptions of service delivery that include, *business as usual*, *the strike had not affected their daily operations* and *everything is normal*. These expressions describe the positive state of service delivery. In addition, there is an adversative construction indicated by the use of the word *despite*. The evaluative disposition in *Daily News* is emphasised via counter-expectation. In terms of indications of authorial affinity or authorial distance, it can be concluded that there is a clear association of evaluations that are set up by the authorial voice and those that are expressed by external news sources. Thus, the authorial voice advances the evaluative positions taken by external news sources.

To conclude this section, it is perhaps necessary to briefly touch on one general aspect of the news reports that have been examined in this chapter. From the presentation of the news reports, it could be noticed that *Mmegi* ran the news report on 19th April 2011, a day following the commencement of the public sector workers' strike, while *Daily News* ran the report on 21st April 2011, three days after the commencement of the strike. While this difference in the dates of coverage may not necessarily be suggestive of major analytical interpretations, it might be related to the differences that have so far become apparent in the ways the newspapers achieve authorial stance-taking and construal of objectivity.

### *4.2.3 Signals of Authorial Stance-Taking*

Perhaps the most striking finding from the analysis of news stories from *Mmegi* and *Daily News* is that the two newspapers invoke dissimilar evaluative angles in their news openings. This was apparent in their use of experiential information, counter-expectation and intensification as tokens of evaluation. Through these tokens of evaluation, the news headlines and lead sentences were generally constructed to depict subtle antithetical constructions. As we saw above, *Mmegi* began by strategically problematizing parallel events – the ongoing workers' strike was being evaluated in contrast to the delivery of services and the functional state of border gates. The binary pattern of evaluations that was used to target service delivery and the strike was either taken up or disputed by external news sources who were quoted in *Mmegi*. In contrast to *Mmegi*, *Daily News* displayed an evaluative pattern that began with a seeming cautionary positioning, followed by a daring stance which was weaved into a series of categorical statements in the lead sentences. Overall, the conveyance of experiential information, counter-expectation, implication and intensification in *Mmegi* and *Daily News* brought out a parallel indirect evaluation of the workers' strike on the one hand, and the delivery of services on the other.

## 4.3 Attribution and the Construal of Objectivity

As explained earlier, attribution is a fundamental characteristic upon which claims for objectivity in hard news reporting are based. However, as I showed in the presentation of the findings, the authorial voice in *Mmegi* and *Daily News* succeeded in setting up indirect evaluations in the news openings, and external news sources, whose voices were quoted in the news reports, took up or disputed the evaluations that were set up by the authorial voice. The news reports from *Mmegi* and *Daily News* therefore demonstrated that objectivity is a complex and dynamic characteristic in hard news reporting. It is encouraging to compare the evaluative patterns from *Mmegi* and *Daily News* with those found by Thomson, White and Kitley (2008: 224) who showed that indirect attitude that gets articulated by the authorial voice does act to support and lay the evaluative groundwork for the attitudes which are elsewhere expressed by external news sources. As news reporters strategically avoid explicit evaluative meanings, their evaluative stance is backgrounded, thus concealing the subjective role of the journalistic author (Thomson, White and Kitley 2008).

# 5 Summary of Findings and Conclusion

The purpose of this final section is to draw the main findings together and consider implications of the findings in relation to the dynamics of strategic stance-taking and construal of objectivity as depicted in *Mmegi* and *Daily News* reports. At the beginning of this chapter, I set out to examine the news reports from *Mmegi* and *Daily News* in order to determine how the two newspapers invoke evaluations in their news openings. In addition, I examined how external news sources who are quoted in the news reports are framed in ways that create an evaluative space for them to express an uptake of the evaluative sentiments that are set up and articulated by the authorial voice in the news openings. I have argued that as the authorial voice sets up indirect evaluations in the news openings, and external news sources are framed to take up or dispute the evaluations set up in the news openings, there were also signals that indicated that the authorial voice either advanced or created distance from the evaluative opinions of the externals news sources. Through such an evaluative pattern, a strategic evaluative stance that is assumed by the authorial voice was paralleled with a construal of objectivity in the news reports.

As I have shown in this chapter, the expression of evaluation is complex, and as such, news reporters rely on the use of indirectness and the creation of distance via attribution in order to mitigate evaluation in hard news reporting.

In order to fully capture the dynamics of stance-taking in hard news reporting it is important to examine the subtle interplay between the authorial voice and external news sources. The news coverage of the state of service delivery at border gates, as reported in Text 1 and Text 2 provided an interesting site to examine such interplay. The various mechanisms by which indirect evaluations were established in *Mmegi* and *Daily News* openings laid an evaluative groundwork for evaluations that were expressed by external news sources.

## References

Brown, P., and Levinson, S. (1987). Politeness: Some universals in language usage. Cambridge: Cambridge University Press.

Caffi, C. (1999). 'On mitigation', *Journal of Pragmatics*, 31, 881–909.

Coffin, C., and O'Halloran, K. (2006). 'The role of Appraisal and corpora in detecting covert evaluation', *Functions of Language*, 13 (1), 77–110.

Fraser, B. (1980). 'Conversational mitigation', *Journal of Pragmatics*, 4, 341–350.

Höglund, M. (2008). 'Using the words of others: 'reporter voice' and the construal of objectivity in the reporting of political conflict in Finland'. In Thomson, E., and White, P.R.R. (eds.), Communicating conflict: Multilingual studies of the news media, pp. 227–252. London: Continuum.

Jullian, P.M. (2011). 'Appraising through someone else's words: The evaluative power of quotations in news reports', *Discourse & Society*, 22 (6), 766–780.

Lauerbach, G. (2006). 'Discourse representation in political interviews: The construction of identities and relations through voicing and ventriloquizing', *Journal of Pragmatics*, 38, 196–215.

Martin, J.R. (2003). 'Introduction', *Text*: *Special issue on Appraisal*, 23 (2), 313–319.

Martin, J.R., and White, P.R.R. (2005). *The Language of Evaluation: Appraisal in English*. Basingstoke: Palgrave.

Martin, J.R., and Rose, D. (2007). *Working with Discourse: Meaning beyond the clause*. London: Bloomsbury.

Piazza, R. (2009). 'News is reporting what was said: techniques and patterns of attribution'. In Haarman, L., and Lombardo, L. (eds), *Evaluation and stance in war news: A linguistic analysis of American, British and Italian television news reporting of the 2003 Iraqi war*, pp. 170–194. London: Continuum.

Rantsudu, B. (2018). *Stance and Objectivity in hard news reporting*. Unpublished Doctoral Thesis. Cardiff University, UK.

Rantsudu, B. (2019). 'Taking a stance through the voice of 'others': Attribution in the news coverage of a public sector workers' strike in two Botswana newspapers'. In Hart, C., and Kelsey, D (eds.), *Discourses of Disorder: Riots, strikes and protests in the media*, pp, 93–108. Edinburgh: Edinburgh University Press.

Thaler, V. (2012). 'Mitigation as modification of illocutionary force'. *Journal of Pragmatics*, 44, 907–919.

Thomson, E.A., White, P.R.R. and Kitley, P. (2008). '"Objectivity" and "Hard news" reporting across cultures: Comparing the news report in English, French, Japanese and Indonesian journalism'. *Journalism Studies,* 9 (2), 212–228.

White, P.R.R. (2000). 'Media Objectivity and the Rhetoric of News Story Structure'. In E. Ventola (ed.), *Discourse and community: Doing Functional Linguistics*, pp. 379–397. Tubingen: Gunter Narr.

White, P.R.R. (2006). 'Evaluative semantics and ideological positioning in journalistic discourse: A new framework for analysis'. In Lassen, I., Strunck, J. and Vestergaard, T. (eds.), *Mediating Ideology in Text and Image: Ten critical studies*, pp. 37–67. Amsterdam: John Benjamins.

White, P.R.R. and Thomson, E. (2008). 'The news story as rhetoric: Linguistic approaches to the analysis of journalistic discourse'. In Thomson, E., and White, P. R. R. (eds.), *Communicating conflict: Multilingual studies of the news media*, pp. 1–23. London: Continuum.

White, P.R.R. (2009). 'Media power and the rhetorical potential of the "hard news" report attitudinal mechanisms in journalistic discourse', VAKKI, 36, <http://www.vakki.net/publications/2009/VAKKI2009_White.pdf>, accessed 11 July 2016.

Mercedes Querol-Julián

# Non-Native EMI Lecturers' Expression of Stance through Subject Pronouns and Modal Verbs

**Abstract:** English-medium instruction (EMI) at university is a common practice in many non-English speaking countries nowadays. Lecturers interact with an (inter)national audience using English as a lingua franca (ELF). However, little research has been done on discursive features and teacher positioning in this context. Bearing in mind the heterogeneous nature of the evaluative dimension of language, this study explores non-native EMI lecturers' expression of stance through two important mechanisms: subject pronouns (*I*, *we* and *you*) and modal/ semi-modal verbs. The research carries out a quantitative analysis of this cluster. The corpus was formed by fourteen lectures from ELFA (English as a Lingua Franca in the Academia). About 1,000 clusters were analysed. The results show that *you can* is by far the most frequent assemblage. The reference of *you* is mostly the learners or indefinite, and the modal verb *can* is used to express possibility and as a hedge to not impose ways of doing or thinking on the learners. The lecturers express solidarity and engagement, show cooperation, open up for negotiation with the learners, and identify with them.

**Keywords:** *EMI, English as a lingua franca, higher education, stance, subject pronouns, modal verbs, ELFA.*

## 1 Introduction and Theoretical Framework

Nowadays, universities more than ever intensify efforts to create higher education spaces to prepare learners for the new challenges of a globalised labour market that demands to master hard and soft skills and English. Universities internationalise to follow the pace of an increasingly globalised world. Nevertheless, international policies in higher education pursue different objectives and outline different ways to internationalise: internationalisation abroad – featured by students (and staff) mobility –, internationalisation at home – attracting international students –, and internationalisation of the curriculum – integrating international and intercultural dimensions into the formal and informal curriculum. This study focuses on internationalisation at home. There are two main trends to attract and accommodate (inter)national students: technological evolution in how instruction is delivered and English-Medium Instruction (EMI) (Querol-Julián & Crawford Camiciottoli 2019). EMI refers to "the use of the English language to teach academic subjects (other than English itself) in countries or jurisdictions where the first language of the majority of the population is not English" (Macaro 2018: 1). In EMI, we teach in English, which does not mean that we teach English, but we enhance improvement in English language ability (Chapple 2015). Although recent publications refer to English-Medium Education in Multilingual University Settings (EMEMUS) (Dafouz & Smit 2020) – a term that embraces the whole education process, the linguistic diversity of the participants and the context –, in this study, we use the term EMI since it examines one feature of "instruction".

The bulk of research conducted on EMI has primarily focused on stakeholders' attitudes, perceptions and beliefs (Aguilar & Rodríguez 2012; Dearden & Macaro 2016). Thus, there is a lack of research on classroom discourse (Macaro et al. 2018) and EMI lecturer's discourse in particular (Morell 2018). Only recently, issues such as the language used in EMI contexts at university have received more attention (Lasagabaster & Doiz 2021; Macaro 2020). The study aims to fill in this research gap by analysing non-native English lecturer's expression of stance through personal pronoun-modal clusters. Three features characterise the study: i) EMI lectures belong to internationalisation at home programmes in a European university where lecturers are non-native speakers of English. Being non-native is the most common EMI lecturer profile in many universities worldwide and the one preferred by students (Inbar-Lourie & Donitsa-Schmidt 2020; Karakas 2017). In this setting, lecturers interact with an international audience using English as a lingua franca (ELF) (Mauranen 2012). ii) Lecturers' expression of stance is paramount to establish and protect relationship in class. This function relates to classroom management that, from a relational perspective, refers to "all teacher actions and associated cognitions and attitudes involved in creating the social emotional aspect of the learning environment" (Wubbels et al. 2015: 363). iii) Bearing in mind the heterogeneous nature of the evaluative dimension of language (Li et al. 2020), this research aims to understand the expression of ELF lecturers' attitude through two linguistic devices: subject pronouns (*I*, *we* and *you*) and modal/ semi-modal verbs. Personal pronouns as a strategy to engage learners with lecture content have significant learning consequences because interactive lectures enhance comprehension (Morell 2007). Biber's (2006) study of modal verbs across university genres in four universities in the United States showed that modal verbs were more frequent in spoken genres, mainly in lectures, during class teaching (instructional register) and class management (regulative register).

There is extensive literature on personal pronouns and modals as linguistic mechanisms to express stance in academic writing (Hyland & Sancho Guinda

2012). Although their investigation in academic speech is not so abundant, some research has focused on the genre of lectures, revealing that the study of modal verbs and personal pronouns is inexorably linked. However, most of the research has been conducted in non-ELF contexts, such as those using Michigan Corpus of Academic Spoken English (MICASE) (Fortanet 2004; Okamura 2009). The use of personal pronouns and modal verbs in EMI settings where English is a *lingua franca* and lecturers are non-native speakers (Dafouz et al. 2007; Crawford Camiciottoli 2004; Morell 2004) have not received much attention yet.

The study's main objective was to disclose the expression of stance by EMI lecturers who are non-native speakers of English through the clusters: *I/ we/ you* + modal/ semi-verbal modal verbs. To meet this objective, we formulated three research questions:

RQ1. What are the most frequent personal pronouns and modal meanings used to express stance?
RQ2. What are the most frequent modal/ semi-modal verbs used to express stance?
RQ3. How do the most frequent personal pronoun-modal clusters express stance?

## 2 Method

We took the data for the analysis from ELFA corpus (English as a Lingua Franca in Academic Settings). ELFA is a corpus designed to investigate English as it is used by speakers with other mother tongues when they participated in different academic events in four universities in Finland. The corpus data consist of both audio recordings and their transcriptions. ELFA perfectly serves the purpose of the present study interested in the linguist expression of stance by EMI lecturers, who are non-native speakers of English and use it as a *lingua franca* to interact in class with their learners. We selected those lectures from ELFA corpus where only one teacher was in class to conduct the study.

A total of fourteen lectures from 6 academic domains (Social Sciences, Natural Sciences, Economics and Administration, Medicine, and Technology) formed the sub-corpus (approximately fourteen hours of recorded speech). Table 1 presents the academic domain and discipline of the lectures. As we can see, there is not a homogeneous distribution of lectures according to their academic domains. Yet, the study's domain/ discipline could not be considered as a variable to compare results.

**Table 1.** Academic domain and disciple of the lectures

| ELFA code | Academic domain | Discipline |
|---|---|---|
| ULECD120 | Economics and administration | Economics |
| ULEC050 | Humanities | Slavonic philology |
| ULEC150 | Medicine | Neurology |
| ULEC180 | | |
| ULEC23A | | Cell biology |
| ULEC090 | Natural sciences | Physics |
| ULEC160 | | |
| ULEC020 | Social sciences | Social history |
| ULEC030 | | Russian studies |
| ULEC060 | | Journalism and mass communication |
| ULECD020 | | |
| ULECD030 | | International relations |
| ULECD040 | | Russian studies |
| ULEC080 | Technology | Forest products chemistry |

We used AntConc (version 3.5.9, Anthony 2020) software to carry out the frequency analysis of the pronoun-modal clusters under examination. A concordance analysis was done with the following search strings that include all possible combinations of the two elements of the cluster, negative and future forms, and contractions.

**Table 2.** Search strings used in the concordance analysis

| | |
|---|---|
| *i/ we/ you* | *can/ cannot/ can't/ could/ couldn't/ might/ mightn't/ must/ mustn't/ should/ shouldn't/ have to/'ve to/ do not have to/ don't have to/ haven't to/ had to/ did not have to/ didn't have to/ had to/ had not to/ need to/ don't need to/ needed to/ did not need to/ didn't need to/ ought to/ ought not to/ oughtn't to/ will/ 'll/ will not/ won't/ would/ 'd/ would not/ wouldn't/ shall/ shall not/ shan't/ want to/ wanna/ do not want to/ don't want to/ wanted to/ did not want to/ didn't want to* |
| *i am/ 'm/ was*<br>*we/ you are/ 're/ were* | *able to/ not able to/ supposed to/ not supposed to/ going to/ not going to/ gonna/ not gonna* |
| *i wasn't*<br>*we/ you weren't* | *able to/ supposed to/ going to/ gonna* |

The sample selection was completed with a manual analysis of all the occurrences automatically retrieved by the software. We made a close reading of all the clusters in context to guarantee that the sample was reliable and contained only and all the target clusters (for example, we deleted direct citations read aloud from books) and interpreter them.

To analyse the most frequent modal meanings used to express stance, we followed Biber et al.'s (1999) classification of modal/ semi-modal verbs into three main semantic meanings:

- permission/ possibility/ ability: *can, could, may, might, be able to*
- obligation/ necessity: *must, should, need to, be supposed to, ought to*
- volition/ prediction: *will, would, shall, be going to, want to*

# 3 Results and Discussion

## 3.1 Personal Pronouns and Modal Meanings

We found a total of 1,073 occurrences of the clusters *I/ we/ you* + modal/ semi-modal verbs in the corpus. Table 3 shows their absolute frequency (normalised to 1,000 clusters) according to the modal meaning of the verbs.

**Table 3.** Absolute frequency of personal pronouns and modal meanings (per 1,000 clusters)

| | I | we | you | Total |
|---|---|---|---|---|
| permission/ possibility/ ability | 37 | 120 | 283 | 440 |
| obligation/ necessity | 28 | 46 | 66 | 140 |
| volition/ prediction | 224 | 83 | 113 | 420 |
| Total | 289 | 249 | 462 | |

As we can see, the non-native EMI lecturers show a preference for *you* modal clusters. These clusters are about twice as frequent as the clusters with *I* and *we* modal pronouns, which recurrence is quite similar, even the number of *I* clusters are slightly higher than *we* modal clusters. Furthermore, *I*, *we* and *you* were used in the corpus in any linguistic context 3,895 times (291, 319, and 390 occurrences respectively per 1,000). That means that *I*, as part of modal clusters, represents 27 % of the total times the pronoun is used in the corpus, *we* does 22 % and *you* 33 %. Interestingly, these results reveal that *you* is also the most frequent personal pronoun used by these lecturers in any linguistic context, although the differences among the three pronouns are not as big as when they are part of modal clusters. Besides, unlike its use in the clusters, the general account shows that *we* is slightly more frequent than *I*.

These results contradict Dafouz et al.'s (2007) findings on the use of personal pronouns in three EMI technology lectures given by non-native English speakers in a Spanish university. These authors observed that *we* – particularly inclusive *we* – was the most frequent pronoun and *I* was the one less used. They analysed how these pronouns were employed in general and not only when they were part of modal clusters. It seems that the lecturers that form our corpus show a preference for *you*, both in general and as part of a modal cluster. Nonetheless, our sample is formed by lectures that belong to different academic domains and disciplines. Although technology is one of them, due to the lack of homogeneity of the sample in this respect, we have not conducted a comparative study between academic domains/ disciplines. Besides, Dafouz et al.'s (2007) sample was very small, with only three lectures. It will be necessary to conduct further research to determine the variable(s) that respond to the differences observed between these two studies.

Our results also contradict those found by Fortanet (2004), who studied the use of personal pronouns in six mathematic lectures given in a university in the United States. She found that *I* was predominantly employed. This study adds a new factor that may influence the interpretation of the results – apart from those already mentioned above and that are also present here –, the lecturers were native or native-like speakers of English, and English was not used as a *lingua franca* in a non-English speaking context. Not having found such predominance of *I* in our study may be revealing aspects regarding the identity that the lecturers chose to project in class. This action could be related to a lack of self-confidence of non-native EMI lectures – being these presumably less skilful than native lectures –. Indeed, lecturers have expressed linguistic difficulties as one challenge during EMI courses (Tazl 2011), and it seems that teachers' English proficiency level may affect attitudes on EMI (Dearden & Macaro 2016; Jensen & Thøgersen 2011). Yet, the lack of predominance of *I* in the corpus could also be related to adopting a learner-centred perspective in EMI lectures. In so doing, lecturers bring learners to the forefront with *you* and inclusive *we* (Dafouz et al. 2007), rather than using the first-person singular pronoun.

Additionally, Morell's (2004) research on the personal pronouns used in three interactive lectures and three non-interactive lectures given by non-native English speakers, who belonged to an English Studies Department in a Spanish university, revealed that *you* and *we* were the most frequent personal pronouns in interactive lectures, and *I* was common in non-interactive ones. Although the sample analysed by this author was small – as they were the ones examined by Dafouz et al. (2007) and Fortanet (2004) –, participants were English foreign language teachers rather than EMI lecturers, and the frequency of personal pronouns referred to any linguistic context, the results were revealing. They showed a connection between interactive lectures, "which had the most student interventions" (Morell 2004: 327), and using *you* and *we* pronouns. Following Morell's (2004) findings, the EMI non-native lecturers analysed in the present study show a feature of interactivity with the common employment of *you* modal clusters. Interaction is one feature of class engagement. In this vein, EMI non-native lecturers' inclination to use *you* modal clusters indicates that attention is placed on the students, which also shows lecturers may be understanding teaching from the engaged model (Light et al. 2009). In this model, learning is seen as active and reflective construction of concepts, and knowledge is socially built up through an intersubjective dialogue of shared meanings between lecturer and learners. The use of this *you* modal cluster may be particularly relevant in constructing interpersonal relations between lecturer and learners, which may lead to class engagement. Two main reasons support this conclusion. First, EMI lecturers (in)directly address their speech to the learners – using *you* –, calling their attention, acknowledging their presence, and showing they are important for them and the group. These are features of teaching with emotional intelligence, which have been proven to impact learning significantly (Mortiboys 2012). Second, lecturers modify their speech with a modal verb that expresses how they see learners as part of the social construct of the class. This outcome relates to the type of modal meaning and the modal/ semi-modal verb that the lecturers decide to choose.

Regarding modal meaning, Table 3 also tells us that the frequency of clusters that express permission/ possibility/ ability and volition/ prediction is almost four times higher than those that show obligation/ necessity. Biber et al. (1999) also identified a low preference for the expression of obligation/ necessity. It seems that these lecturers tend to avoid expressing their commitment openly, or to "impose" learners or anyone, to do, say, think, etc., something. Likewise, they also choose not to reveal their or others' needs. In so doing, they express their stance towards themselves and others, protecting themselves and showing respect for others.

Moreover, the general analysis of these three personal pronouns and the modal meaning indicates that *I* modal clusters mainly convey volition/ prediction. Yet, *we* and *you* modal clusters express permission/ possibility/ ability, which reinforces the interpretation that these lecturers show a protectionist attitude towards their relationship with learners that may aim to engage them in learning during the class. This attitude could be because it is in the modal clusters initiated by these two pronouns (*you*, *we*) – in which lecturers (in)directly refer to learners –, when they primarily mention these social actors' capacity/ ability, rather than when lecturers talk about themselves (in *I* modal clusters).

## 3.2 Personal Pronouns and Modal Verbs

In addition to the approximation to personal pronoun-modal clusters, we observe substantial differences when examining the two elements that form them (Table 4).

**Table 4.** Absolute frequency of personal pronouns and modal/ semi-modal verbs (per 1,000 clusters)

| | | *I* | *we* | *you* |
|---|---|---|---|---|
| permission/ possibility/ ability | *can* | 24 | 94 | 233 |
| | *could* | 8 | 17 | 20 |
| | *may* | 3 | 7 | 20 |
| | *might* | 1 | 1 | 10 |
| | *be able to* | 1 | 1 | 0 |
| | | | | |
| obligation/ necessity | *must* | 2 | 7 | 9 |
| | *should* | 8 | 9 | 0 |
| | *have to* | 16 | 27 | 50 |
| | *need to* | 1 | 3 | 7 |
| | *be supposed to* | 1 | 0 | 0 |
| | *ought to* | 0 | 0 | 0 |
| | | | | |
| prediction/ volition | *will* | 98 | 44 | 34 |
| | *would* | 70 | 8 | 33 |
| | *shall* | 2 | 2 | 0 |
| | *be going to* | 30 | 10 | 5 |
| | *want to* | 24 | 19 | 41 |

Regarding permission/ possibility/ ability verbs, *can* is mostly used by the lecturers of the corpus. Nonetheless, significant differences are observed among the frequency of use of the three personal pronouns and this modal verb, being *you can* by far the most frequent cluster and *I* the less frequent. Additionally, other modal/semi-modal verbs are also relatively frequent with *we* and *you*, i.e., *we could* and *you could/ may/ might*.

(1) *we can measure the amplitude of certain values of S and T, er <P:05> if* ***i can*** *show you. they're different masses* (ULEC090, Natural Sciences)
(2) ***we can*** *er have a small break and then* ***we could*** *talk about the stories that we're going to going to write* (ULEC020, Social Sciences)
(3) *okay now we start our informal part so if you want* ***you can*** *go and er have a coffee* (ULEC050, Humanities)
(4) *in a commercial synthesis* ***you could*** *actually wash the crude-product the mixture of this and this with hot water* (ULEC080, Technology)
(5) *if you know the code* ***you may*** *understand what is it about* (ULEC050, Humanities)
(6) *you see quite a large qualitative similarity between the two so* ***you might*** *ask yourself what is the brain doing actively during rest* (ULEC180, Medicine)

Even though verbs that express obligation/ necessity are hardly used in the clusters analysed, *have to* seems to be the one preferred by these lecturers to express personal obligation, being *you have* the most frequent.

(7) *this would be a good good good thing to check er* ***i have to*** *ask julia whether she did that experiment or not* (ULEC23A, Medicine)
(8) *when they started this thing up and they said well suppose* ***we have to*** *shut this process down* (ULEC080, Technology)
(9) *in er mhm local government there are* ***you have to*** *remember two kinds of er bodies* (ULECD120, Economic and Administration)

Finally, the modal *will* accounts for most of the prediction modals in *I* and *we* clusters, being *I will* two times more frequent than *we will*. This modal verb commonly announces future plans and events. Furthermore, *I would* is also predominant in this cluster; being *would* a modal verb that expresses a directive force that is polite and indirect (Biber 2006). In this corpus, *I would* is commonly followed by *like to*, i.e., *I would like to*. Two clusters with semi-modal verbs of volition, *I am going to* and *I want to*, have a much lower presence.

(10) *the next session will which will be as the matter of fact next thursday erm **i will** lecture the ethical norms of promoting sustainable development* (ULEC030, Social Sciences)
(11) *and what **we will** do today it w- mhm **we will** er er study er we will study mhm local finance in in Poland* (ULECD120, Economic and Administration)
(12) *so **i would like to** conclude i hope you, got enough of this erm there exist experimental models* (ULEC150, Medicine)
(13) *i'm saying you this all of this because **i'm going to** talk about physics later about the res- real research later* (ULEC160, Natural Sciences)

Regarding *you* modal clusters, we find that there is no predominant prediction/volition modals, but *you want to*, *you will* and *you would* have quite similar frequencies. The cluster with the semi-modal verb *want to*, which is quite common with *you* and not much frequent with *I* and *we*, seems to serve different functions. The cluster *you want to* is commonly part of a conditional sentence and shows a hypothetical situation that learners may be involved in; *we want to*, in a similar way that *you want to*, is used during class teaching to attribute desires to learners related to mental processes. The cluster *I want to*, however, expresses in a direct way lecturers' desires in relation to class management.

(14) *you can do it because as **you will** recall when you scatter, electromagnetically particles* (ULEC90, Natural Sciences)
(15) *we shall create our own posters in whatever style **you would** prefer russian avant-garde style malevich kandinsky or. rodchenko and so on and so on* (ULEC050, Humanities)
(16) *if **you want to** do all of this it would be good if you could pulp without adding any sulphur* (ULEC080, Technology)
(17) *there are no temporal correlations down here **we want to** know what is actually causing this difference* (ULEC180, Medicine)
(18) *there was some general stuff that **i want to** go through with you first* (ULEC060, Social Sciences)

In line with the results of our study, Biber's (2006) observed that *will* was the most common modal verb and also found high use of *can* in regulative and instructional registers. Interestingly, Crawford Camiciottoli (2004) studied how three native lecturers and three non-native lecturers used modal verbs in cross-cultural business lectures in an Italian university. She found that *can* and *will* were commonly employed. Yet, non-native lecturers mostly used *can*, and the use of *may* and *might* by native lecturers was also relevant.

### 3.3 Most Frequent Clusters

After this general overview, we make a close analysis of the most frequent collocations found in the corpus: *you can*, *I will* and *we can*.

### 3.3.1 *You can*

The use of the pronoun *you* in the cluster *you can* has two functions. The primary function is an indefinite or impersonal reference. In example (19), the cluster is followed by the verb *drive*, with the semantic meaning of action (Biber et al. 1999). The personal pronoun *you* means "any person". The lecturer may not be actually referring to the learners as having the possibility of driving a trunk in the forest, but when using *you can*, the lecturer may evoke the experience of doing it. The example may be more vivid and real in learners' minds, as they may feel actors of the situation described, contributing to engaging them in the learning process.

(19) *it's easier to move in the forest because the er because the land has is frozen* ***you can you can*** *er drive by trucks in the forest in the wintertime not in the summertime* (ULEC020, Social Sciences)

In example (20), the impersonal reference is not as general as "any person". The pronoun refers to a person with some technical knowledge. In the lesson context, the reference could be interpreted by the students as *we* – *you* and *me*, the learners and the lecturer – (Kamio 2001). The learners may perceive this inclusive *you* as a more direct reference to them, who are valued as being knowledgeable about the topic. The cluster, followed by a verb of communication, attributes the learners the capacity to talk about a technical issue. This acknowledgement may also contribute to creating a positive emotional learning environment that may work favourably in constructing relationships and engagement.

(20) ***you can*** *say that magnetic field lines are equipotentials and what you have on the earth electric field* (ULEC160, Natural Sciences)

The secondary function of *you* in the cluster *you can* we identify in the corpus is a direct reference to the learners. Unlike the primary function that seems to be performed as part of the instructional register during class teaching, lecturers appear to prefer to address their speech to learners during class management directly. As we can see in examples (21) and (22), lecturers describe what learners "*can* do" in class, "come and look" the photographs the lecturer has brought to class (20), or "prepare" a subject at home (22).

(21) *there is a book of russian avant-garde and* ***you can*** *also come here and look at my photographs and i will be happy to discuss them with you* (ULEC050, Humanities)
(22) *now i will give you the subject that* ***you can*** *prepare at home and send me* (ULECD120, Economic and Administration)

It seems that the combination "direct reference to learners (*you*) plus *can* followed by a verb with a semantic meaning of activity" works perfectly during regulative register. However, we also find some examples used during class teaching when learners are the reference of *you*. In these instances, the main verb that follows *can* is mainly mental, as in examples (23) and (24).

(23) *you have an equivalent of that so in the uncorrelated case if* ***you can*** *imagine that this would be sort of neurons and you would activate* (ULEC150, Medicine)
(24) *he key challenges of world religions and security challenge i mean i will it's a huge as* ***you can*** *see erm topic but i will try to summarize as much as i can* (ULECD030, Social Sciences)

### *3.3.2 I will*

The second most common modal cluster found in the corpus is *I will*. First-person subjects have been described as "the most overt expressions of stance" (Gray & Biber 2012: 22). In this cluster, lecturers present themselves as the authoritative voice in class since the reference of *I* is the lecturer in all the instances found in the corpus. This cluster is mainly used during regulative register with verbs of communication, announcing what they will show/ speak/ talk about, etc. (25). The cluster collocates also with main verbs of action (26) and mental (27) or aspectual verbs (28).

(25) *it's actually symmetric H component used in event-oriented model er so also* ***i will i'll*** *show you the DST index in event-oriented* (ULEC160, Natural Sciences)
(26) *this here just shows an example of the specific behaviour of different vesicles and* ***i'll*** *play you some more movies here* (ULEC023A, Medicine)
(27) *it's a huge as you can see erm topic but* ***i will*** *try to summarize as much as i can* (ULEC030, Social Sciences)
(28) *it is not implausible that correlations in the modulation of beta oscillations could reflect this,* ***i will*** *come back to that later erm , first i want to show how we could possibly study this* (ULEC180, Medicine)

During class management (regulative register), we have found few examples of *I will*. Nevertheless, in those cases, main verbs with the semantic meaning of existential/ relationship follow the modal cluster, expressing lecturers' positive state of mind regarding their future interaction with learners when responding to their questions (29) or discussing with them (30).

(29) *if you have questions or comments or protests against something point of views er , please* ***i'll*** *be* ***very grateful*** (ULEC030, Social Sciences)
(30) *come here and look at my photographs and* ***i will*** *be* ***happy*** *to discuss them with you* (ULEC050, Humanities)

### *3.3.3 We can*

Many studies make a fine-grain distinction of the reference of the personal pronoun *we*: *we* for *I*, *we* for *you* (audience), *we* for indefinite *you* or "one", *we* for *they*, *we* for a larger group of people (including the speaker), etc. However, in this study, we follow Crawford Camiciottoli's (2005) and Yeo and Ting's (2014) conclusion that what is important in a lecture context is whether the students are included or excluded as a reference of *we*. Thus, we use the dichotomy of inclusive-*we* and exclusive-*we* to discuss our findings. Results reveal that the lecturers in the corpus only used inclusive-*we* (Dafouz et al. 2007; Fortanet 2004; Morell 2004), showing solidarity with learners, an aspect that may be paramount in the construction of lecturer-learners relationships and an indicator of lecturers trying to foster learners engagement. Furthermore, regarding the use of this cluster, Dafouz et al. (2007) also observed that the three EMI non-native lecturers that participated in their study had a preference for the collocations *we can* and *we will*.

The cluster *we can* is mostly followed by mental verbs. Lectures involve learners – assuming they have the capacity to do it – in the mental processes needed to follow their explanations or draw conclusions (31) and solve problems (32). Learners are also engaged during class instruction (instructional register) in hypothetical situations (33), or real ones (34), with verbs with a semantic meaning of action.

(31) *er the conclusions the physical conclusions which* ***we can*** *get from this from the analysis they depend very much on the modelling of course* (ULEC160, Natural Sciences)

(32) *set up erm a four time er 16 er channel multielectrode array where* ***we can*** *measure er oscillating from brain slices and that allows us to actually measure er in vitro oscillations from four slices* (ULEC180, Medicine)

(33) *what we want to do is to use the non-sulphur process so that* ***we can*** *make additional fuels and chemicals and er compete in other sectors* (ULEC080, Technology)

(34) *we have then developed software for tissue typing where anatomically the different channels are (sitting) so that* ***we can*** *enter the data into a database* (ULEC180, Medicine)

Finally, *we can* also collocates, to a lesser extent, with verbs of communication sharing with learners the authorial voice that is able to formulate technical statements during class teaching (35) or utterances related to class management, such as "invite" others to come to class and "discuss" with them (36).

(35) *what we found is that the plasma membrane doesn't react to glutamate application in the same way so* ***we can*** *really claim that there is an increased spatial association between mitochondria and plasma membrane* (ULEC23A, Medicine)

(36) *erm i-tampere people the writers for i-tampere are meeting at four o'clock over there so i think we can invite them here and* ***we can*** *discuss about different topics with them they can tell what they are writing and so on* (ULECD020, Social Sciences)

## 4 Conclusions

This study has explored non-native teachers' construction of stance in EMI lectures through the cluster *I/ we/ you* + modal/ semi-verbal modal verbs. Results have shown that *you* clusters were mostly used and modal/ semi-modal verbs that expressed permission/ possibility/ ability and volition/ prediction. The most common clusters found in the corpus were: *you can*, *I will* and *we can*. The analysis of the clusters reveals that in the fourteen lectures analysed, EMI non-native lecturers who use English as a *lingua franca* seem to construct and protect interpersonal relations with learners, showing solidarity and respect for them, identifying with them and assuming their capacities, showing features of teaching with emotional intelligence and placing learners at the centre of the teaching-learning process. This attitude was generally showed during class teaching, which may favour learners' engagement. Unsurprisingly, the lecturer's authorial voice – *I* modal clusters and especially *I will* –, however, was listened in general to manage class, e.g., to announce topics to be treated.

Findings also reveal some methodological questions. The stance conveyed through these personal pronoun-modal clusters relates to the type of register – instructional or regulative, i.e., class teaching or class management – in which they operate. Furthermore, results also indicate a connection between the semantic meaning of the main verb that follows the clusters and the register. Therefore, the study of how EMI lecturers express stance through personal pronouns and modal verbs cannot be limited to the analysis of either personal pronouns and modal verbs in isolation or personal pronoun-modal clusters, as it has been done in the present study. Results have revealed that we should: i) focus the analysis on the triad pronoun + modal/ semi-modal verb + main verb, ii) examine the semantic domain of the main verb in detail, and iii) identify the register in which the utterance is expressed.

Finally, further research is needed to confirm the results found in the study, which do not entirely align with previous findings. It will be necessary to research a larger and representative sample of lectures from different academic domains/ disciplines. We see other three main lines of research from this methodological framework, which results will be of interest for the training of EMI non-native lecturers as regards the expression of stance, comparative studies between:

- interactional and non-interactional lecturers, to replicate Morell's (2004) study with a larger sample from different disciplines;
- native and non-native speakers of English, to replicate Crawford Camiciottoli's (2004);
- live online lectures (also called synchronous online lectures or synchronous virtual lectures) and face-to-face lectures, to attend nowadays needs where online teaching has become a common practice for many EMI lecturers.

## References

Aguilar, M., and Rodríguez, R. (2012). 'Lecturer and Student Perceptions on CLIL at a Spanish University', *International Journal of Bilingual Education and Bilingualism,* 15 (2), 183–197.

Anthony, L. (2020). AntConc (Version 3.5.9) [Computer Software]. Tokyo, Japan: Waseda University. <https://www.laurenceanthony.net/software>

Biber, D. (2006). 'Stance in Spoken and Written University Registers', *Journal of English for Academic Purposes,* 5 (2), 97–116.

Biber, D., Johansson, S., Leech, G., Conrad, S., and Finegan, E. (1999). *Longman grammar of spoken and written English.* Essex: Longman.

Chapple, J. (2015). 'Teaching in English is not Necessarily the Teaching of English', *International Education Studies,* 8 (3), 1–13.

Crawford Camiciottoli, B. (2004). 'Interacting with the Audience: Modal Verbs in Cross-Cultural Business Lectures', In R. Facchinetti, and F. Palmer (eds.), *English Modality in Perspective: Genre Analysis and Contrastive Studies,* pp. 27–43. Frankfurt Am Main: Peter Lang.

Crawford Camiciottoli, B. (2005). 'Adjusting a Business Lecture for an International Audience: A Case Study', *English for Specific Purposes,* 24, 183–199.

Dafouz, E., and Smit, U. (2020). *ROAD-MAPPING English Medium Education in the Internationalised University.* London/New York: Palgrave Macmillan.

Dafouz, E., Nuñez, B., and Sancho, C. (2007). 'Analysing stance in a CLIL University Context: Non-native Speaker Use of Personal Pronouns and Modal Verbs', *International Journal of Bilingual Education and Bilingualism*, 10 (5), 647–662.

Dearden, J., and Macaro, E. (2016). 'Higher Education Teachers' Attitudes Towards English Medium Instruction: A Three-Country Comparison', *Studies in Second Language Learning and Teaching*, 6 (3), 455–486.

ELFA (2008). The Corpus of English as a Lingua Franca in Academic Settings. Director: Anna Mauranen. <http://www.helsinki.fi/elfa>

Fortanet, I. (2004). 'The Use of 'we' in University Lectures: Reference and Function', *English for Specific Purposes*, 23, 45–66.

Gray, B., and Biber, D. (2012). 'Current conceptions of stance'. In K. Hyland and C. Sancho Guinda (eds.), *Stance and voice in written academic genres*, pp. 15–33. London: Palgrave Macmillan.

Hyland, K., and Sancho Guinda, C. (eds.) (2012). *Stance and voice in written academic genres*. London: Palgrave Macmillan.

Inbar-Lourie, O., and Donitsa-Schmidt, S. (2020). 'EMI Lecturers in International Universities: Is a Native/Non-native English-Speaking Background Relevant?', *International Journal of Bilingual Education and Bilingualism*, 23 (3), 301–313.

Jensen, C., and Thøgersen, J. (2011). 'Danish University Lecturers' Attitudes towards English as the Medium of Instruction', *Ibérica, Revista de la Asociación Europea de Lenguas para Fines Específicos*, 22, 13–33.

Kamio, A. (2001). 'English Generic we, you, and they: An Analysis in Terms of Territory of Information', *Journal of pragmatics*, 33 (7), 1111–1124.

Karakas, A. (2017). 'Teacher Preferences in Content and Language-Focused Courses in Higher Education: The Case of Turkish EMI Students', *Online Submission*, 7 (2), 127–145.

Lasagabaster D., and Doiz, A. (eds.) (2021). *Language use in English-Medium Instruction at University: International Perspectives on Teacher Practice*. New York: Routledge.

Li, J., Lei, L., and Cheng, L. (2020). 'Mapping Evaluation, Appraisal and Stance in Discourse (2000–2015): A Bibliometric Analysis', *Glottotheory*, 10 (1–2), 31–55.

Light, G., Cox, R., and Calkins, S. (2009). *Learning and Teaching in Higher Education: The Reflective Professional*. London: Sage.

Macaro, E. (2020). 'Exploring the Role of Language in English Medium Instruction', *International Journal of Bilingual Education and Bilingualism*, 23 (3), 263–276.

Macaro, E., Curle, S., Pun, J., An, J., and Dearden, J. (2018). 'A Systematic Review of English Medium Instruction in Higher Education', *Language Teaching*, 51 (1), 36–76.

Mauranen, A. (2012). *Exploring ELF: Academic English Shaped by Non-Native Speakers*. Cambridge: Cambridge University Press.

Morell, T. (2004). 'Interactive Lecture Discourse for University EFL Students', *English for Specific Purposes*, 23 (3), 325–338.

Morell, T. (2007). 'What Enhances EFL Students' Participation in Lecture Discourse? Student, Lecturer and Discourse Perspectives', *Journal of English for academic Purposes*, 6 (3), 222–237.

Morell, T. (2018). 'Multimodal Competence and Interactive Lecturing', *System*, 77, 70–79.

Mortiboys, A. (2012). *Teaching with Emotional Intelligence: A Step–By–Step Guide for Higher and Further Education Professionals*. London: Routledge.

Okamura, A. (2009). 'Use of Personal Pronouns in Two Types of Monologic Academic Speech', *The Economic Journal of Takasaki City University of Economics*, 52 (1), 17–26.

Querol–Julián, M., and Crawford Camiciottoli, B. (2019). 'The Impact of Online Technologies and English Medium Instruction on University Lectures in International Learning Contexts: A Systematic Review', *ESP Today*, 7 (1), 2–23.

Tatzl, D. (2011). 'English-Medium Masters' Programmes at an Austrian University of Applied Sciences: Attitudes, Experiences and Challenges', *Journal of English for Academic purposes*, 10 (4), 252–270.

Wubbels, T., Brekelmans, M., Den Brok, P., Wijsman, L., Mainhard, T., and Van Tartwijk, J. (2015). 'Teacher–Student Relationships and Classroom Management'. In E. Emmer and E. J. Sabornie (eds.), *Handbook of Classroom Management*, 363–386. New York: Routledge.

Yeo, J., and Ting, S. (2014). 'Personal Pronouns for Student Engagement in Arts and Science Lecture Introductions', *English for Specific Purposes*, 34, 26–37.

Mario Serrano-Losada

# *Spoiler Alert*, This is no Spoiler: Mirativity, Assumption and Irony at Play[1]

**Abstract:** The present chapter focuses on the pragmatic parenthetical *spoiler alert*, which is used as a humorous, ironic device to underscore the obvious nature of a statement (e.g., *Four orcas chase a penguin and spoiler alert, it doesn't end well*, NOW). This corpus-based study first traces the history of this relatively recent innovation –which originates as a disclaimer to warn readers of potential plot revelations in online discussion forums– to then explore the meanings and pragmatic functions that this expression has acquired over its short history. Corpus data for this chapter were drawn from COCA and NOW. My analysis shows that, despite its specialised origins in online forums, the expression has attained a remarkably wide dispersion. Moreover, the parenthetical itself has undergone an important semantic shift. A warning expression in origin, *spoiler alert* first acquired mirative extensions, i.e., meaning related to surprise and unexpectedness, to then acquire assumed evidential extensions, expressing evidence based on assumption or logical reasoning. This shift from mirativity to assumed evidentiality was brought about through pragmatic enrichment, as a result of humorous and ironic uses of the parenthetical: *spoiler alert* no longer introduces surprising or revealing information, but a predictable or self-evident fact.

**Keywords** *spoiler alert, pragmatic parentheticals, language change, semantic shift, humour, cooptation, mirativity, evidentiality, assumption.*

## 1 Introduction

The existing inventory of pragmatic markers and parentheticals is in constant flux. Over the last decades, a particularly salient number of parentheticals have emerged: a group of expressions that convey mirative and assumed evidential overtones and which are frequently used with humorous or ironic intentions. This group includes expressions like *spoiler alert*, *plot twist*, *shocker*, *oh wait* and *surprise, surprise* as well as rebukes like *duh* and *no shit* (*sherlock*). Many of them are associated with online communication and seem to be ephemeral – in fact, not all of them have actually diffused into the general language. However, with

1 For generous financial support, I am grateful to the Spanish Ministry of Economy and Competitiveness (grant PID2020-114604GB-100).

the sole exception of Andersen's (2015) study on *duh*, these expressions have received little scholarly attention. The present chapter zooms in on one of these relatively recent and unexplored innovations: the pragmatic parenthetical *spoiler alert*, illustrated in (1):

(1) *Four orcas chase a penguin and* ***spoiler alert****, it doesn't end well.* (NOW:NZ:2020)

In (1), *spoiler alert* is used as a humorous device to underscore the obvious nature of the statement under its scope, by acknowledging that this information is expected or self-evident: it is a well-known fact that orcas are sophisticated predators that prey on fish, penguins, seals and even other cetaceans. The odds that the penguin will be able to escape the four killer whales are thus rather slim.

The aim of this contribution is twofold. First, this corpus-based study aims to trace the history of this expression, which originates as a disclaimer to warn readers of potential plot revelations in online discussions about films and television, as exemplified in (2):

(2) *the following is a sample of what we received. (****Spoiler alert!*** *Many of the following responses contain key plot points.)* (COCA:News:2002)

Example (2) belongs to a piece on the movie *Star Wars: Episode II – Attack of the Clones* published in the *Chicago Sun-Times*. In this excerpt, *spoiler alert* is a disclaimer used to warn its readers about the remainder of the article: what follows the warning may disclose fundamental plot developments which those who have not seen the movie yet might not want to read about.

Second, this study aims to explore the range of meanings and pragmatic functions that *spoiler alert* has acquired over its short history. As will be shown, despite its specialised origins in online forums, the expression has attained a remarkable dispersion across different genres as a parenthetical expression (1). Moreover, this parenthetical has undergone an important semantic shift. A warning expression in origin, e.g. (2), *spoiler alert* first acquired mirative extensions, i.e., meaning related to surprise and unexpectedness, to then acquire assumed evidential extensions, expressing evidence based on assumption or logical reasoning. This shift from mirativity to assumed evidentiality was brought about through pragmatic enrichment, as a result of humorous and ironic uses of the parenthetical. Thus, *spoiler alert* does not necessarily introduce surprising or revealing information; it may also be used to underscore a predictable or self-evident fact, as shown in (1).

This chapter is organised as follows. Section 2 explores the notion of pragmatic parentheticals. Section 3 offers a brief outline of assumed evidentiality and mirativity, the two main semantic categories expressed through *spoiler alert*.

Section 4 introduces the data sources used in the study. While Section 5 explores the origins and the main discourse-pragmatic functions of *spoiler alert*, Section 6 provides an overall discussion of the rise and development of the parenthetical expression, focusing on semantic-pragmatic change. Finally, Section 7 puts forward some concluding remarks and issues for further research.

## 2 (Pragmatic) Parentheticals

As argued above, over its short history *spoiler alert* has become a formulaic expression that is often used parenthetically to express non-propositional, procedural meaning, as illustrated in (1) above. Parentheticals constitute a rather complex category. Broadly speaking, a parenthetical is an expression that is structurally independent from the utterance in which it is interpolated, and which interrupts the prosodic flow of that utterance (Dehé & Kavalova 2007: 1). Such expressions vary greatly as regards their length and category, and their main function is usually to add to, comment on or modify the proposition to which they are attached.

The most prototypical parentheticals are clausal forms like *I mean* or *you know*. However, a wide range of expressions fit the criteria to be considered parentheticals. In recent times, parentheticals have attracted a great deal of attention in the literature, having been examined from different theoretical frameworks both from a synchronic and a diachronic perspective (see, for instance, Dehé & Kavalova 2007; Brinton 2008; Kaltenböck, Heine & Kuteva 2011; Dehé 2014; Brinton 2017).

Any kind of linguistic material has the potential to be used parenthetically. Dehé (2014: 2–6) characterises parentheticals as a heterogeneous class that contains a diverse variety of expressions, ranging from finite clauses (e.g. *I guess*) to interjections (e.g. *huh*) or filled pauses (e.g. *um*). Thus, parenthetical expressions can virtually take any form, and any given segment of discourse could potentially be used parenthetically (Kaltenböck 2007: 29–31; Kaltenböck, Heine & Kuteva 2011: 856, 876).

Interpolated uses of *spoiler alert* like (3) can thus be broadly defined as parenthetical.

(3) *Your dude will love you even if he knows that you poo sometimes! Which, **spoiler alert**, he already knows because you are a fellow human.* (COCA:Web:2012)

Brinton (2017) summarises the main characteristics of what she terms pragmatic parentheticals. I ground my consideration of *spoiler alert* as a pragmatic parenthetical on the following five very general characteristics adduced by

Brinton (2017: 8–10): in its parenthetical form, *spoiler alert* is (i) syntactically independent from its host clause, (ii) it has (limited) positional mobility, as it can appear in initial, medial or final position, (iii) it may constitute a separate intonation unit, (iv) its host clause is complete without the parenthetical expressions and (v) it has semantic secondary status (i.e., it is semantically backgrounded with respect to the host clause). These and other features have been dealt with extensively in the specialised literature.[2]

Several typologies and classifications of parentheticals have been put forward in the literature, and numerous terms have been used to refer to them and the various subtypes of expressions covered by this concept. While the terms *discourse marker* or *pragmatic marker* are generally used to describe shorter, highly frequent expressions such as *oh*, *well* or *like*, longer parenthetical expressions, especially clausal ones like *I mean*, *I think* or *as you know* have received a plethora of names. Such expressions are frequently described as *comment clauses* (see Quirk et al. 1985: 1112–1118; Brinton 2008), but also as *extra-clausal constituents* (see Kaltenböck, Keizer & Lohmann 2016: 1–2), *supplements* (Huddleston & Pullum 2002: 1350–1362) or *pragmatic parentheticals*, as Brinton (2017: 8–10) describes them in her most recent proposal.[3]

In a similar vein, Kaltenböck, Heine and Kuteva (2011: 856) put forward an alternative cover label for such expressions, the abbreviated form *thetical*, given that "not all instances of the category are in fact parenthetical in the sense that they are interpolated in or require an anchor utterance", but can appear as free-standing expressions as well, as illustrated in the dialogue under (4):

(4) - OPHIRA-EISENBERG: *And in the end of That Is All you do mention that he is the only person that will know what happened during the apocalypse.*
- JOHN-HODGMAN: ***Spoiler alert.***
- OPHIRA-EISENBERG: *Yeah. (LAUGHTER)*
- JOHN-HODGMAN: *It's possible that the world might not end on December 21st, 2012.* (COCA:SPOK:2012)

Given that *spoiler alert* can also be used in isolation forming utterances of its own, I will use both terms when describing the grammaticalised expression: *parenthetical* for actual interpolated instances like (1) and (3) and *thetical* for free standing instances of the expression like (4).

2 Not all authors agree on these features. Traugott (2015: 123), for instance, provides counterexamples to each of these characteristics. According to the author, ""Comma intonation" is not required or even characteristic of PMs" (Traugott 2015: 126).

3 For terminological discussions, see, for instance, Heine (2013: 1207–1208) or Beeching (2016: 3–6).

## 3 Evidentiality and Mirativity from a Typological Perspective

In order to understand the meanings of parenthetical *spoiler alert*, it is important to have a working understanding of evidentiality and mirativity, as well as the relationship between these two semantic categories. This section puts forward some basic ideas regarding evidentiality and mirativity. After briefly examining these categories, I turn to the relationship between assumed evidentiality and mirativity.

### 3.1 (Assumed) Evidentiality

Roughly defined as "a linguistic category whose primary meaning is source of information", evidentiality is a morphologically encoded category in about a quarter of the world's languages (Aikhenvald 2004: 3). One of the most quoted examples in the literature appears under Table 1, which illustrates the three main evidential enclitics in Cuzco Quechua. As shown in the table, the same basic utterance (*parashan* 'it is raining') expresses different evidential meanings depending on which enclitic is used. Cuzco Quechua enclitics are used to mark direct evidence (*-mi*), reportative or hearsay evidence (*-si*) and reasoning or inferential evidence (*-chá*). According to Faller (2002: 14), these evidential markers are not obligatory, but their absence implies that the speaker has direct information.

**Table 1.** Cuzco Quechua evidentials (adapted from Faller 2002: 3)

| *Direct evidence* | *Hearsay* | *Inference* |
|---|---|---|
| Para-sha-n-*mi*. | Para-sha-n-*si*. | Para-sha-n-*chá*. |
| rain-prog-3-*mi* | rain-prog-3-*si* | rain-prog-3-*chá* |
| 'It is raining (I see).' | 'It is raining (I was told).' | 'It might/must be raining (I conjecture).' |

Aikhenvald's (2004) detailed crosslinguistic survey on evidentials distinguishes as many as six different semantic parameters, which can be roughly classified as either 'firsthand' (visual and non-visual sensory), or 'non-firsthand' (inference, assumption, hearsay and quotative), that is, as direct or indirect evidentials.

Unlike many of the world's languages which, like Quechua, have complex grammaticalised evidential systems, European languages generally express evidentiality lexically. Such is the case of English, which features abundant indirect evidential strategies (e.g. inferential/hearsay *seem*, Aijmer 2009; reportative *reportedly*, Celle 2009; Rozumko 2019). Whereas inference is based on tangible or visible evidence, assumed evidentiality (or assumption) relies on "evidence other than visible results", which may include assumption proper, general knowledge or logical reasoning (Aikhenvald 2004: 63). The Tariana examples under (5) help to illustrate the concept of assumed evidentiality. Tariana, an endangered Arawak language spoken in the north-west Brazilian Amazonia, possesses a large system of obligatory evidential markers that are appended as clitics on verbs (see Aikhenvald 2003).

(5) a) *nu-nami* *karaka* *di-merita-**mha***
1SG-father's.younger.brother chicken 3SG.NF-fry-PRS.NVIS
[My younger uncle has fried chicken (I smell it, but cannot see it.)]

b) *nu-nami* *karaka* *di-merita-**si-ka***
1SG-father's.younger.brother chicken 3SG.NF-fry-ASSM-RECPST
[My younger uncle has fried chicken (I assume so: he gets so much money he can afford it, and he looks like he has had a nice meal).]
(Aikhenvald 2015: 255)[4]

The two examples in (5) are identical except for the choice of evidential marker. In both, the speaker's uncle has fried chicken, but the source of information differs. Example (5a) illustrates the Tariana non-visual evidential. The speaker makes his/her statement based on olfactory information (s/he can smell the fried chicken). (5b) exemplifies the assumed evidential: the speaker assumes that his uncle has had chicken given, among other cues, the socio-economic status of his uncle.

English provides us with plenty of instances of assumed evidential strategies. Consider the English adverb *obviously* in (6):

(6) [A Virginia Democratic senator celebrates the fact that they have a Republican governor that has been able to find common ground with them:]
***Obviously**, there are places where we differ with Republicans, whether it's gay rights or gun safety or Medicaid expansion, and we'll have ample time to drive those points home.* (COCA:NEWS:2015)

---

4 The following abbreviations are used in this gloss: 1/3 = 1st/3rd person; ASSM = assumed; NF = non-feminine; NVIS = non-visual; PRS = present; RECPST = recent past; SG = singular. According to Aikhenvald (2015: 255): 'the present tense evidential forms *-naka* 'present visual' and *-mha* 'present non-visual' combine the tense and the evidential values. […] the inferred and the assumed evidential have no present tense.'

The emphasised expression in (6), *obviously*, conveys assumed evidential nuances, since it entails assumption or general knowledge. In using this expression, the speaker points to the evidential source of what he is saying, emphasising shared points of view and common places (i.e., it is generally known that Democrats and Republicans hold opposite views on key issues like LGTBI+ rights or gun control). Similarly, parenthetical *spoiler alert* in examples like (1) and (3) signals assumed evidentiality as well.

### 3.2 Mirativity

Closely related to evidentiality is the notion of mirativity. This category conveys "information which is new or unexpected to the speaker" (DeLancey 1997: 33), with overtones of surprise, sudden discovery and counter expectation (see DeLancey 2001; DeLancey 2012; Aikhenvald 2012). Despite their similarities, mirativity is regarded as a category of its own, independent from evidentiality, in the typological literature. Take the Tarma Quechua example in (7):

| | | | |
|---|---|---|---|
| (7) | *turumanya* | *inti-ta-m* | *muyu-ra-ya:-**naq*** |
| | rainbow | sun-ACC-CERT | turn-CONT-PROG-3A/S.MIR |

[(*turns out*) a rainbow was surrounding the sun]
(adapted from Adelaar 2013: 102)[5]

The Tarma Quechua mirative particle *-naq*, which I have rendered in English as *turns out*, marks the statement under its scope as unexpected and thus surprising. Notice that in this Quechuan variety, the mirative combines freely with the evidential marker of certainty (*-m*).[6] The fact that evidential and mirative markers are compatible provides strong evidence for the consideration of the two phenomena as independent grammatical categories. Grammatical mirativity is attested in a vast number of languages; however, it is less widespread than evidentiality in the languages of the world (Aikhenvald 2012: 473).

5 The following abbreviations are used in this gloss: ACC = accusative; CERT = certain; CONT = continuous aspect; PROG = progressive aspect; A/S.= agent; MIR = mirative.

6 According to Adelaar (2013: 102), 'Tarma Quechua has a transparent system of evidentials consisting of three mutually exclusive categories: Certainty, Reported and Conjectural. The 'Certainty' evidential implies a firm conviction on the side of the speaker. It does not always mean that the speaker has witnessed the communicated state or event in person, but the utterance contains information that (s)he can vouch for.'

Languages around the globe have infinite ways to convey the linguistic reflexes of new information, surprise and related meanings like unexpectedness and counter expectation. Just like evidentiality, this semantic category can be expressed through a wide array of linguistic means. The pragmatic parenthetical *turns out* exemplified in (8) illustrates the use of a mirative strategy in English. Likewise, parenthetical *spoiler alert* is oftentimes used with a mirative intent (see Section 5.4.).

(8) *I thought I'd looked everywhere. Everywhere but up,* ***turns out.*** (COCA:2009, in Serrano-Losada 2017: 174)

As hinted above, mirativity has often been accounted for in close connection with –and even as a part of– evidentiality. This is explained by the close ties between both categories: typologically, the connection between them is robust; in fact, most languages that mark mirativity have evidential systems, whether large or small. Moreover, evidential markers can have mirative overtones. The extant literature, however, generally agrees that, in spite of their close ties, there is enough evidence to consider evidentiality and mirativity as independent grammatical categories (see, among others, Aikhenvald 2004: 195–215 for an overview of the relationship between evidentiality and mirativity; Aikhenvald 2012; DeLancey 2012; Peterson 2015).

### 3.3 Assumed Evidentiality and Mirativity

Unlike other evidential categories, assumed evidentiality has been largely overlooked in English linguistics (see Blanco-Suárez & Serrano-Losada 2017). In fact, constructions that could be analysed as expressing this category have been sometimes analysed as mirative expressions. Such is the case of the *no wonder* construction illustrated in (9):

(9) ***No wonder*** *model Sophie Dahl has health problems if she has dieted down from size 16 to size 8* (Gentens et al. 2016: 126)

According to Gentens et al. (2016) and Van linden (2020), such a construction would be an instance of mirativity, as *no wonder* encodes a meaning of lack of surprise. Their analysis is sound insofar as it adapts a label, mirativity, to account for both ends of the spectrum: surprise and the lack thereof. Typological studies, however, consistently define mirativity as the linguistic encoding of surprise and related notions, including unexpectedness, sudden realisation and new information (Aikhenvald 2012), and no mirative markers have been described for meanings related to unsurprise. 'Lack of surprise', then, seems to be something else altogether. Assumed evidentiality would be a viable category when trying to describe such lack of surprise: if something can be described as not surprising, it must be because it is expected. Moreover, if something is expected there must be a source of information involved, whether assumption, general knowledge or logical reasoning. In this chapter, thus, lack of surprise is not considered as a mirative extension; rather, it is understood as involving assumed evidential nuances.

## 4 Data

In order to study the emergence and meaning of *spoiler alert*, data were drawn from Mark Davies' the *Corpus of Contemporary American English* (COCA) and the *News on the Web* (NOW) corpus.

COCA, which includes texts spanning 1990–2019, contains over one billion words distributed across eight different genres: spoken, fiction, popular magazines, newspapers, academic texts, TV and movies subtitles, and blogs and other web pages. The search query for *spoiler alert* throws 473 tokens. These include both instances of warnings such as (2) and (paren)theticals like (1) and (3). The first documentation of *spoiler alert* in COCA, included under (2) above, dates from 2002. Table 2 records the raw number of instances for the search string 'spoiler alert' yielded by COCA. In turn, Figure 1 illustrates the exponential growth of *spoiler alert* across time.

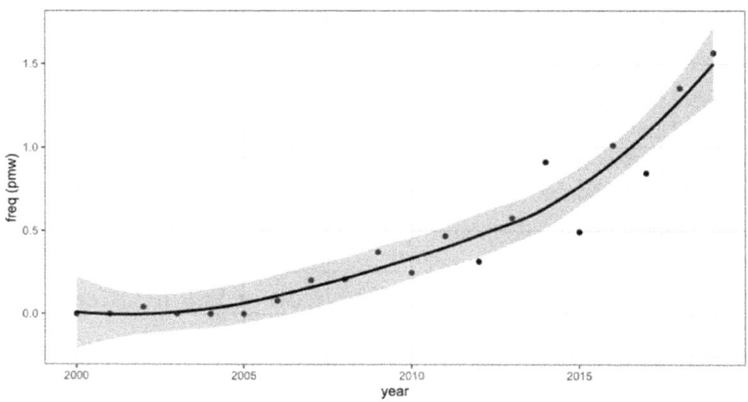


**Figure 1.** Instances of *spoiler alert* in COCA (pmw)

Despite its value, the COCA dataset presents a limitation to study the dispersion of the expression over internet-based genres. While most of the textual genres provide us with a particular date, blogs and web pages do not, as they were only collected and incorporated to COCA in October 2012. Thus, these two text types cannot be considered from a diachronic perspective. This is problematic insofar as the use of *spoiler alert* has its roots in online forums and discussion lists. Nevertheless, early attestations in genres other than blogs and web pages are an indication that the expression has diffused across different text types over the last two decades. Davies' *Corpus of Historical American English* (COHA) was probed for earlier attestations, but it yielded one token alone: the same example included under (2) and coincidentally the first attested example in COCA.

According to the corpus description, NOW contains data from "2010 - yesterday", roughly 12.2 billion words as of 21 March 2020. This corpus includes web news from a wide range of World English varieties. The search string *spoiler alert* throws 11,676 tokens worldwide (5,128 of them in the US). In order to focus on parenthetical uses, I limited my search to < spoiler alert, >, a query that yielded 330 tokens in total. These tokens have been analysed to explore the functions of parenthetical *spoiler alert* across web-based newspapers, blogs and magazines. Despite its restrictions as regards text types, NOW serves as an ideal testing ground to probe ongoing changes and phenomena taking place in the language at present, as is the case with *spoiler alert*.

**Table 2.** Raw frequencies for *spoiler alert* in COCA

| | Academic | Blog | Fiction | Magazine | Movies/ TV | News | Spoken | Web | Total |
|---|---|---|---|---|---|---|---|---|---|
| 2000s | 1 | - | - | 9 | 2 | 7 | 3 | - | 22 |
| 2010s | 2 | 148 | 6 | 61 | 53 | 30 | 40 | 111 | 451 |

## 5 Origin, Meaning, Form and Function of *Spoiler Alert*

Before exploring the meaning, form and function of *spoiler alert* in the corpus data, it is important to pinpoint the origins of the expression.

### 5.1 *Tracing the Origins of Parenthetical* Spoiler Alert

The diachronic study of pragmatic markers and parentheticals entails some limitations. Most pressing is the "primarily oral nature of pragmatic markers" (Brinton 2017: 12), which complicates the diachronic study of such expressions.

In this case, however, the origins of the parenthetical can be traced back to exclusively written sources, more specifically, to internet discussion groups. In an OED blog entry on new word notes, Martin (2018) puts forward a short squib about the meaning and origins of *spoiler alert*:

> the phrase spoiler alert has become commonplace in online discussions of films and television as a way of warning readers that an important detail of the story is about to be divulged. Its roots go back to the early years of internet fandom: the earliest citation comes from a post about the film *Star Trek II: The Wrath of Khan* on a Usenet newsgroup in 1982.

The expression has thus rather specialised origins, as it is said to have first appeared in film discussion forums on USENET – a discussion system that predates the internet – during the 1980s. The earliest citation mentioned by Martin (2018) is reproduced in Figure 2.

As illustrated in Figure 2, disclaimer *spoiler alert* is an expression of warning

**ST-2 A QUESTION – (nf)**
[…] Jun 8 00:47:00 1982

[SPOILER ALERT]

regarding Spock's parting gesture to McCoy, it wouldn't surprize me if that's how they bring him back (if they do); but then, i have a low opinion of ST's script(s). Spock's farewell to Kirk sounded pretty final to me.

**Figure 2.** Earliest attested instance of disclaimer *spoiler alert* (Usenet Newsgroups archives, compiled on Google Groups)[a]

[a] Available at https://groups.google.com/g/net.movies/c/c09z1_ob--M/m/hTh1SpYoSa4J?pli=1 (last accessed February 2021).

used to forewarn the reader about possible surprising bits of information that are about to be divulged. Such pieces of information usually refer to important plot revelation which the readers or audience of books, TV shows or films would rather prefer to remain undisclosed. According to a 1994 article in *The Washington Post*:

(10) *On movie buffs' discussion lists… there is wide use of the term 'spoiler alert', which is a warning inserted before any comment that would give away a film's ending.* (1994 *Washington Post*, s.v. OED, *spoiler*, n.)

The expression, thus, seems to have become increasingly common over the 1990s. Disclaimer *spoiler alert* gained momentum over the years, with the popularisation and expansion of the internet (1990s-2000s), where internet forums, blogs, film and TV reviews abounded. In such platforms, it became commonplace to warn readers of the spoilers that could reveal essential plot points. The disclaimer expression, however, soon started to appear in parenthetical instances, like (12) below.

Although such parenthetical instances at first retain their function as a disclaimer, new parenthetical uses emerge as the expression diffuses through

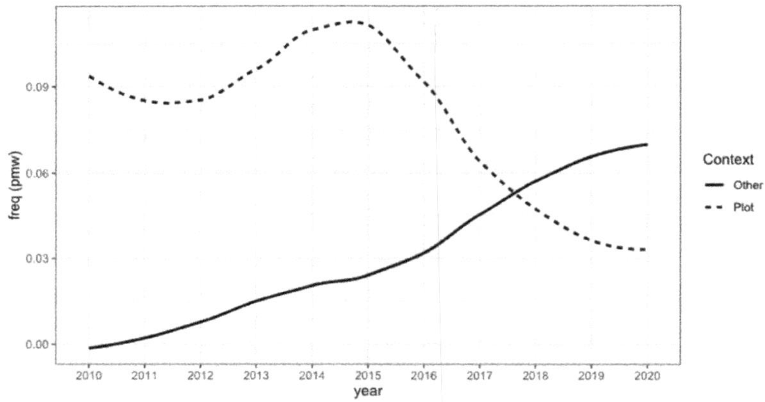


**Figure 3.** Contexts for parenthetical *spoiler alert* (NOW dataset)

other text genres during the 2010s, making it into oral communication. Over this decade, as shown in Figure 3, parenthetical *spoiler alert* began to appear in contexts other than plot discussions (e.g., sports or technology). In such contexts, the warning sense of *spoiler alert* shifted to meanings related to mirativity and assumed evidentiality. In what follows, I provide an overview of the main uses of *spoiler alert*, as transcends from the available corpus data.

## 5.2 *Disclaimer* Spoiler Alert

Disclaimer *spoiler alert* describes those literal instances in which the expression is used as a warning. This first type follows certain typographic conventions, especially in its earlier uses (cf. also Figure 2): it is usually set in all caps, centred, with some blank space following the disclaimer so that readers who do not want to learn about plot developments do not read on. The disclaimer may also appear enclosed in brackets or simply set apart by punctuation (e.g., followed by a colon). Take (11) below:

(11) *ARGH, ETHAN!* ***Spoiler alert****, please! If anyone's reading this page and is concerned about spoilers, PLEASE don't read Ethan's comment. I know it's one thing to say that certain endings of certain stories are telegraphed by their authors (…) but at least put a* *******SPOILER****** *warning on your post, as not everyone has read the book and the movie's only just coming out.* (NOW:US:2010)

Example (11) is an answer to a post on the *Los Angeles Times*. The comment to which the author is replying concluded with a reference to the ending of *Somebody Flew Over the Cuckoo's Nest* ("Has anybody else read/seen *Cuckoo's Nest* that can relate? Obviously the ending is not the same but the premise is: that it's all made up."). The writer in (11), annoyed by the revelation, rebukes the spoiler in Ethan's post, reprimanding him for not having included a disclaimer *spoiler alert* in his comment.

Oftentimes, the expression *spoiler alert* appears as a parenthetical expression (P), whether in the context of film/TV reviews or elsewhere. I have identified three different types of parentheticals: parenthetical disclaimers (Section 5.3), mirative parentheticals (Section 5.4) and assumed evidential parentheticals (Section 5.5).

## 5.3 Parenthetical Disclaimer

Parenthetical disclaimer *spoiler alert* amounts to 29.2 % of all parenthetical instances in the NOW dataset. In (12) below, the parenthetical *spoiler alert* aims to forewarn the reader about an immediate plot revelation (that the skulls in the Indiana Jones film turn out to be alien in origin). However, such parenthetical disclaimers introduce some differences in relation to the non-parenthetical ones.

(12) [An archaeologist in Belize has filed a lawsuit against the makers of the film "Indiana Jones and the Kingdom of the Crystal Skull," alleging that the movie profits off references to an artifact illegally stolen from the country.] *The skull is smaller than the life-size ones seen in the Indiana Jones film (which are also,* ***spoiler alert****, alien in origin).* (Now:US:2012)

Some parenthetical disclaimer instances are sometimes ambiguous, as they do not seem to behave as warnings; rather, they introduce mirative nuances, since they are used to introduce newsworthy information, even breaking news. That is to say, the original disclaimer/warning meaning seems to naturally give way to meanings related to surprise.

Parenthetical *spoiler alert* often appears outside of contexts which refer to narrative plots. In such contexts, the expression is not used as a literal warning to prevent the reader from an actual plot revelation, but to encode a different type of meaning. Such instances of P *spoiler alert* seems to fall into two main types according to its meaning: mirative *spoiler alert*$_1$ ($P_1$) and assumed evidential *spoiler alert*$_2$ ($P_2$).

## 5.4 *Parenthetical* Spoiler Alert$_1$

$P_1$ refers to instances which introduce a mirative nuance, i.e., it introduces new, unexpected information (cf. other similar expressions like parenthetical *turns out*, Serrano-Losada 2017). $P_1$ instances amount to 33.9 % of the total parentheticals in the NOW dataset. The emergence of such mirative uses can be explained as the expression begins to be used out of contexts in which readers are being warned.

(13) *We had the chance to try some of the awesome things the company's Advanced Technology and Projects (ATAP) team is working on, including the Projects Soli, Jacquard and Vault detailed earlier.* ***Spoiler alert****, they were all awesome.* (NOW:US:2015)

(14) *After months of hype, the world finally has human trial data from a front-running vaccine collaboration between the University of Oxford and AstraZeneca Plc.* ***Spoiler alert****, it's good news.* (NOW:US:2020)

Examples (13) and (14) are both used out of the context of film or book discussions. The initial P in both examples is used to introduce a piece of newsworthy, surprising information. In the case of (13), $P_1$ is used to emphasise that all of the projects that the company are working on are awesome; in (14), it is used to reveal important newsworthy information: that the human test trial data for the AstraZeneca vaccine have been positive. Unlike the $P_2$ examples in Section 5.5 below, the use of $P_1$ is not meant as a humorous device. Aimed at surprising the reader, *spoiler alert*$_1$ is simply used to introduce a sudden discovery (cf. '*Turns out*, they were all awesome'; '*turns out*, it's all good news'). Given that $P_1$ usually anticipates forthcoming discourse, it generally appears at left periphery, although it might also appear clause medially, as in (15):

(15) *Brimming with humor, this animated comedy follows a group of children trying to escape the clutches of La Llorona (who,* ***spoiler alert****, is depicted as much more empathetic than usual!)* (NOW:US:2020)

Even though *spoiler alert* in (15) is used in the context of a film review, its use is clearly mirative (cf. 'La Llorona, who, *surprisingly*, is depicted as much more empathetic than usual').

## 5.5 *Parenthetical* Spoiler Alert$_2$

In this use, the P acquires an assumed evidential function. Such instances, which are humorous or ironic in intention, amount to 37 % of the total parentheticals in the NOW dataset. Take examples (16) and (17) below:

(16) *After Robyn arrives, Karen tells her and Gizelle all about Raymond's golf-duel with Michael. Gizelle is pleased with this news, only wishing she'd been there to see it.* ***Spoiler alert****, Gizelle: it wasn't all that.* (NOW:US:2016)

(17) *Like many women, I was raised around the idea that if you put your head down and work hard, your work will speak for itself and you will (eventually) be acknowledged.* ***Spoiler alert****, that's not how the world works (especially in male dominated industries).* (NOW:US:2019)

In (16), the author is discussing the TV show *The Real Housewives of Potomac*. In this specific instance, however, the author is not discussing the plot itself: in her writing, she is addressing Gizelle, one of the cast members. The parenthetical expression is used ironically to emphasise that the golf duel was utterly unremarkable. In (17), the writer is describing the difficulties that women face in the job market. In spite of the common narrative the writer grew up with (that hard work would take her to great places), the truth is that she has faced a completely different reality. P *spoiler alert*$_2$ in (17) is used to introduce a piece of information which the writer considers absolutely obvious: that women face great disadvantages as many are not able to break the glass ceiling, especially in male dominated industries.

Unlike $P_1$, $P_2$ does not introduce surprising information. Rather, it is used to introduce well-known facts or issues considered common knowledge by the speakers/writers. $P_2$ represents an assumed evidential use: the proposition under its scope is anything but surprising. Such interpretations are the result of the humorous or ironic intentions of the speaker. In other words, $P_2$ is used to introduce "an evaluative utterance, the valence of which is implicitly reversed between the literal and intended evaluation" (Burgers 2010: 19).

## 5.6 *Rebuke* Spoiler Alert

A final type[7] of *spoiler alert* is that exemplified in (18):

(18) - DEREK: *Wait a second. So the Library's responsible for hedge witches dying?*
- PENNY: *Yeah, but they don't know that yet.*

---

7 Given the make-up of the NOW corpus and the query carried out in this corpus ('spoiler alert,'), no such examples appeared in this dataset. The COCA data, however, yielded several such instances, both in Movie/TV scripts and in the spoken component.

- DEREK: ***Spoiler alert.***
- PENNY: *Zelda had some other things on her mind at the time.*
- DEREK: *Her dead daughter. Wait, is she, like, down here?*
- PENNY: *I thought you didn't like spoilers.* (COCA:TV:2019)

Like $P_2$, the expression in (18), taken from an exchange from the TV series *The Magicians*, is used with an ironic intent. Such thetical instances are attested in oral conversation, both in scripted dialogue and in unscripted conversation. In these contexts, thetical *spoiler alert* is used as an ironic, mild reproach with assumed evidential meaning: Penny's reply is deemed obvious by Derek, who uses *spoiler alert* as a rebuttal to Penny's evident remark. The expression is thus similar in use to other rebukes like *duh* or *no shit*. In such instances *spoiler alert* has an interactional and intersubjective function.

## 6 Discussion: The Emergence of Parenthetical *Spoiler Alert*

The different functions and meanings of parenthetical *spoiler alert* described in Section 5 point to the existence of a semantic path from warning to mirativity and assumption. Figure 4 schematises the hypothesised semantic changes undergone by the expression.

The corpus data suggest that the disclaimer expression *spoiler alert* is frequently used parenthetically. As shown in Figure 5, earlier instances of the parenthetical are still used as expressions of warning in the context of film, TV or book reviews (I). The parenthetical, however, undergoes a process of semantic generalisation, which allows for mirative nuances to emerge: the expression is no longer used to give notice of an upcoming plot revelation, but to signal information that is surprising or unexpected, emphasising the newsworthiness of the propositions within its scope (II). Mirative nuances are thus inherited from the original disclaimer construction as the parenthetical diffuses to contexts other than plot discussions.

| **I** | > | **II** | > | **III** |
|---|---|---|---|---|
| *spoiler alert* | → | *spoiler alert₁* | → | *spoiler alert₂* |
| [warning] | | MIRATIVITY | | ASSUMPTION |
| | | ↘ | irony | ↗ |
| nonsubjective | > | subjective | > | intersubjective |

**Figure 4.** Semantic change of P *spoiler alert*

The emergence of mirative readings can be understood as the result of a process of subjectification (see Figure 4). As argued by Traugott (2003: 126), this mechanism enables the semantic encoding of erstwhile contextual or pragmatic senses which reflect a speaker oriented perspective. Thus, a nonsubjective meaning (a warning about an upcoming plot revelation) comes to be encoded subjectively (i.e., as mirativity) as the expression generalises to other contexts: when using $P_{1,}$ the speaker expresses their subjective perspective by assessing the proposition as surprising or newsworthy.

In this sense, mirative meaning in $P_1$ is conventionalised and not the result of conversational implicatures. In order to test this claim, I have restated a reduced version of example (15) in (15′) and (15″) below. $P_1$ can be paraphrased using mirative adverbials such as *surprisingly*, *turns out* or *unexpectedly*, as shown in (15′). In fact, it is not possible to cancel out the parenthetical's mirative scope. In this respect, (15″) presents us with a simple entailment test: negating its mirative scope proves odd (if not contradictory).

(15′) *Who, **turns out/surprisingly**, is depicted as much more empathetic than usual!*
(15″) *Who, **spoiler alert**, is depicted as much more empathetic than usual! # Not that this is a newsworthy, unexpected or surprising discovery.*

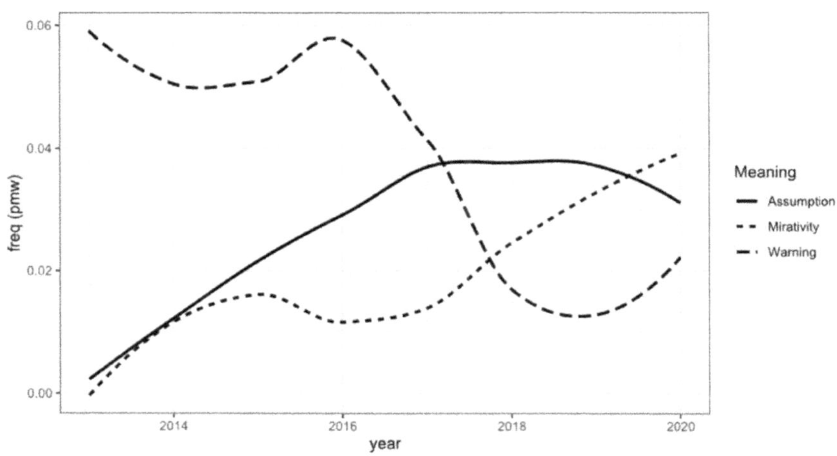


**Figure 5.** Parenthetical *spoiler alert* in the NOW Corpus

As regards assumed evidentiality, such nuances emerge as a result of humorous and ironic uses (III). Consequently, assumptive readings are the result of pragmatic enrichment. When used ironically, the value of the mirative parenthetical is reversed. Thus, if something is not surprising at all it becomes completely expectable. In such instances, it can be interpreted that there are grounds on which to base our assumption, namely, logical reasoning or general or common knowledge. Example (3), restated in a minimal form below, can help us understand this assumed evidential nuance. In (3′), *spoiler alert*$_2$ has been replaced by *obviously*. Unlike $P_1$, however, $P_2$ is not fully conventionalised, and we must rely on the context to disambiguate the ironic intention and thus the assumed evidential meaning of the parenthetical.

(3′) *Which, **obviously**, he already knows because you are a fellow human.*

The cline of subjectification in Figure 4 – nonsubjective > subjective > intersubjective – was put forward by Traugott and Dasher (2002: 40). Alongside its assumed evidential readings, $P_2$ has an interactional and intersubjective function and is aimed at seeking agreement with the interlocutor. By using *spoiler alert*$_2$, the speaker is making their interlocutor a part of their community of practice (i.e., the speaker takes for granted that the interlocutor shares, at least partially, common points of view, experiences or knowledge). Moreover, the assumed evidential expression has face-saving purposes, as the speaker foregrounds that whatever they are saying is either self-evident or well-known by everyone within their sociocultural community.

The question remains as to how to explain the emergence of parenthetical instances out of a former disclaimer expression. The cognitive-communicative strategy of cooptation (see Kaltenböck, Heine & Kuteva 2011; Heine 2013; Heine et al. 2017) may shed some light in this regard. Cooptation has been defined as a "packaging strategy whereby a clause, a phrase, a word, or any other unit is taken from SG [=Sentence Grammar] and is coopted (or re-defined) for use as a thetical" (Heine 2013; Kaltenböck, Heine & Kuteva 2011: 879). Within the framework of discourse grammar (see Kaltenböck, Heine & Kuteva 2011; Heine et al. 2013; Heine et al. 2017), discourse is organised into two interdependent domains: the domain of sentence grammar (SG) and the domain of thetical grammar (TG). The mechanism of cooptation would allow any element to be coopted or redefined for use as a thetical element. That is, any expression would have the potential to be used parenthetically out of Sentence Grammar. While SG "is organized in terms of parts of speech or constituent types such as sentences, clauses, phrases, words, and morphemes, plus the morphosyntactic machinery to relate constituents to one another", TG includes "a catalogue of thetical formulae and constructions as well as the ability to form new theticals via cooptation from Sentence Grammar" (Heine et al. 2017: 816)

The emergence of parenthetical uses of *spoiler alert* could thus be explained via cooptation, i.e., as a sentence element that has been coopted or taken from SG and redefined as a thetical in TG. Consider in this regard the examples under (19):

(19) (a) *So you guys know and this is not a spoiler alert, because we don't know this.* (COCA:Spok:2016)
(b) *Bert's never misspelled a word in his whole life. And spoiler alert, ladies and gents, he's not about to start now.* (COCA:Mov:2019)

In (19a) disclaimer *spoiler alert* is used as a predicative complement. In (19b), however, *spoiler alert* appears parenthetically. From the perspective of Discourse Grammar, parenthetical instances like (19b) could be conceived of as coopted elements, as they are used thetically, freed from the syntactic constraints of SG. In (19b) the coopted parenthetical has acquired secondary status (non-propositional meaning) and could potentially be moved around within the sentence (e.g. 'And ladies and gents, *spoiler alert*, he's not about to start now'). Moreover, the parenthetical appears to be prosodically, semantically and syntactically independent from the utterance in which it is linearly integrated (see also Serrano-Losada 2020 on *end up* parentheticals).

As argued by Kaltenböck, Heine and Kuteva (2011: 879), frequent repetition of cooptation can lead to grammatical change. Thus, even though a coopted unit such as *spoiler alert* might first appear spontaneously, recurrent repetition probably led to the entrenchment and eventual grammaticalisation of the parenthetical expression. It goes without saying that cooptation and grammaticalisation are distinct processes. However, as argued by Heine (2013: 1223), cooptation could well be a prerequisite for the emergence of grammaticalised parentheticals expressions. Thus, once an element has been coopted as a thetical expression, it may then evolve from a spontaneous to a formulaic parenthetical.

## 7 Conclusion

The present chapter has explored the diachronic emergence and present-day uses of parenthetical *spoiler alert*. My findings reveal that, albeit its specialised origins in online film discussions, the expression has attained a surprisingly wide dispersion, appearing across all text genres in COCA. Its meaning, which originally invoked a warning, has acquired mirative nuances, as well as assumed evidential extensions via pragmatic extension in humorous or ironic contexts. Thus, in some contexts *spoiler alert* does not introduce newsworthy or surprising information. Rather, it may convey a humorous or an ironic twist: far from introducing revealing information, *spoiler alert* may be used to signal a predictable fact. In this sense, *spoiler alert* has an interactional and intersubjective function.

The actual development of parenthetical *spoiler alert* is remarkable insofar as it involves the generalisation of an expression emerged in the (underground) fandom subculture, i.e., as a domain-specific expression that eventually made it into the general language. This recently emerged parenthetical expression seems to be on the rise and is ubiquitous across genres, despite having a restricted use in its inception.

The corpus data indicate that, through a process of semantic generalisation and subjectification, this domain specific expression of warning acquired mirative nuances – when used outside of its original contexts to reveal new, surprising information – as well as assumed evidential meanings as a result of pragmatic enrichment – when used with a humorous or an ironic intent. Furthermore, the development of this parenthetical expression seems to be the result of a process of grammaticalisation via cooptation.

This chapter, however, does not suffice to fully account for the development of parenthetical *spoiler alert*. Further accounts should take into consideration related expressions, which in turn would allow us to explore the relationship between mirativity and assumed evidentiality further. The role of text genres in its development deserves a detailed analysis, as they may prove key to explore the diffusion and entrenchment of the parenthetical expression. Moreover, studying internet-related expressions like *spoiler alert* or *plot twist* is essential to further explore the possible role that internet communication might be playing in the diffusion of linguistic innovations.[8]

## Sources

COCA = *Corpus of Contemporary American English*, 2008-. Compiled by M. Davies. http://corpus.byu.edu/coca/.

NOW = *Corpus of News on the Web: 3+ billion words from 20 countries, updated every day*, 2010. Compiled by M. Davies. http://corpus.byu.edu/now/.

OED = *Oxford English Dictionary Online*. Oxford University Press. https://www.oed.com/.

8 See, for instance, the debate on the *Journal of Sociolinguistics* 18(2), as a response to Sayers (2014), in which the possible role of the influence of the media on language change is explored from different perspectives.

## References


Adelaar, W. F. H. (2013). 'A Quechuan Mirative?' In A. Storch and A. Y. Aikhenvald (eds), *Perception and Cognition in Language and Culture*, pp. 95–109. Leiden: Brill.

Aijmer, K. (2009). '*Seem* and Evidentiality', *Functions of Language*, 16(1), 63–88.

Aikhenvald, A. Y. (2003). *A Grammar of Tariana, from Northwest Amazonia*. Cambridge: Cambridge University Press.

Aikhenvald, A. Y. (2004). *Evidentiality*. Oxford: Oxford University Press.

Aikhenvald, A. Y. (2012). 'The Essence of Mirativity', *Linguistic Typology*, 16(3), 435–485.

Aikhenvald, A. Y. (2015). 'Evidentials: Their Links with other Grammatical Categories', *Linguistic Typology*, 19(2), 239–277.

Andersen, G. (2015). 'Relevance'. In K. Aijmer and C. Rühlemann (eds), *Corpus Pragmatics*, pp. 143–168. Cambridge: Cambridge University Press.

Beeching, K. (2016). *Pragmatic Markers in British English: Meaning in Social Interaction*. Cambridge: Cambridge University Press.

Blanco-Suárez, Z. and Serrano-Losada, M. (2017). 'The Rise and Development of Parenthetical *Needless to Say*: An Assumed Evidential Strategy', *Journal of Historical Linguistics*, 7(1/2), 134–159.

Brinton, L. J. (2008). *The Comment Clause in English: Syntactic Origins and Pragmatic Development*. Cambridge: Cambridge University Press.

Brinton, L. J. (2017). *The Evolution of Pragmatic Markers in English: Pathways of Change*. Cambridge: Cambridge University Press.

Burgers, C. F. (2010). *Verbal Irony: Use and Effects in Written Discourse*. Radboud University. Available at: <https://repository.ubn.ru.nl/handle/2066/81993> accessed 10 September 2020.

Celle, A. (2009). 'Hearsay Adverbs and Modality'. In R. Salkie, P. Busuttil, and J. van der Auwera (eds), *Modality in English*, pp. 269–294. Berlin: Mouton de Gruyter.

Dehé, N. (2014). *Parentheticals in Spoken English: The Syntax-Prosody Relation*. Cambridge: Cambridge University Press.

Dehé, N. and Kavalova, Y. (eds) (2007). *Parentheticals*. Amsterdam: John Benjamins Publishing Company.

DeLancey, S. (1997). 'Mirativity: The Grammatical Marking of Unexpected Information', *Linguistic Typology*, 1(1), 33–52.

DeLancey, S. (2001). 'The Mirative and Evidentiality', *Journal of Pragmatics*, 33(3), 369–382.

DeLancey, S. (2012). 'Still Mirative after All these Years', *Linguistic Typology*, 16(3), 529–564.

Faller, M. T. (2002). *Semantics and Pragmatics of Evidentials in Cuzco Quechua*. PhD dissertation. Stanford University. <http://personalpages.manchester.ac.uk/staff/martina.t.faller/documents/Thesis.pdf> accessed 10 September 2020.

Gentens, C. *et al.* (2016). 'Mirativity and Rhetorical Structure'. In G. Kaltenböck, E. Keizer, and A. Lohmann (eds), *Outside the clause: Form and function of extra-clausal constituents*, 125–156. Amsterdam: John Benjamins Publishing Company.

Heine, B. (2013). 'On Discourse Markers: Grammaticalization, Pragmaticalization, or Something Else?', *Linguistics*, 51(6), 1205–1247.

Heine, B. et al. (2013). 'An outline of Discourse Grammar'. In S. Bischoff and C. Jany (eds), *Functional Approaches to Language*, pp. 155–206. Berlin: De Gruyter Mouton.

Heine, B. et al. (2017). 'Cooptation as a Discourse Strategy', *Linguistics*, 55(4), 813–855.

Huddleston, R. D. and Pullum, G. K. (2002). *The Cambridge Grammar of the English Language*. Cambridge: Cambridge University Press.

Kaltenböck, G. (2007). 'Spoken Parenthetical Clauses in English: A Taxonomy'. In N. Dehé and Y. Kavalova (eds), *Parentheticals*, pp. 25–52. Amsterdam: John Benjamins Publishing Company.

Kaltenböck, G., Heine, B. and Kuteva, T. (2011). 'On Thetical Grammar', *Studies in Language*, 35(4), 852–897.

Kaltenböck, G., Keizer, E. and Lohmann, A. (eds) (2016). *Outside the Clause: Form and Function of Extra-clausal Constituents*. Amsterdam: John Benjamins Publishing Company.

Martin, K. C. (2018). *Spoiler Alert! New Words Notes for June 2018. Oxford English Dictionary*. <https://public.oed.com/blog/new-words-notes-june-2018/> accessed 28 March 2021.

Peterson, T. (2015). 'Grammatical Evidentiality and the Unprepared Mind', *Review of Cognitive Linguistics*, 13(2), 314–352.

Quirk, R. et al. (1985). *A Comprehensive Grammar of the English Language*. London: Longman.

Rozumko, A. (2019). 'Between Acknowledgement and Countering: Interpersonal Functions of English Reportative Adverbs', *Journal of Pragmatics*, 140, 1–11.

Serrano-Losada, M. (2017). 'On English *Turn Out* and Spanish *Resultar* Mirative Constructions: A Case of Ongoing Grammaticalization?', *Journal of Historical Linguistics*, 7(1/2), 160–189.

Serrano-Losada, M. (2020). 'Analogy-driven Change: The Emergence and Development of Mirative *End Up* Constructions in American English', *English Language & Linguistics*, 24(1), 97–121.

Traugott, E. C. (2003). 'From Subjectification to Intersubjectification'. In R. Hickey (ed.), *Motives for Language Change*, 124–140. Cambridge: Cambridge University Press.

Traugott, E. C. (2015). 'Investigating "Periphery" from a Functionalist Perspective', *Linguistics Vanguard*, 1(1), 119–130.

Traugott, E. C. and Dasher, R. B. (2002). *Regularity in Semantic Change*. Cambridge: Cambridge University Press.

Van linden, A. (2020). 'The Diachrony of Stance Constructions with *"No" Chance* and *"No" Wonder*', *Language Sciences*, 82, 1–14.

www.ingramcontent.com/pod-product-compliance
Ingram Content Group UK Ltd.
Pitfield, Milton Keynes, MK11 3LW, UK
UKHW021921120926
8556IPUK00042BA/1087